THE
2004 LSATs
DECONSTRUCTED

"*LSATs Deconstructed* was the perfect self-study guide. I took the practice tests, pinpointed my weaknesses, and found the best approaches to the different types of questions."

Whit Remer, Tallahassee, FL

POWERSCORE
TEST PREPARATION

First Edition published 2007

Published by
PowerScore Publishing, a division of PowerScore Incorporated
37V New Orleans Road
Hilton Head Island, SC 29928

Authors: David M. Killoran
                Jon M. Denning
                Steven G. Stein

Contributing Authors:

                Brook Miscoski
                Jason Crandall

Published in the United States
January 2007

ISBN: 978-0-9721296-4-0

Also Available...

PowerScore LSAT Logic Games Bible

The ultimate guide for attacking the analytical reasoning section of the LSAT. *The LSAT Logic Games Bible*™ features a detailed methodology for attacking the games section, extensive drills, and 21 real LSAT logic games with detailed analyses.

Available on the PowerScore website for $41.99.
Website: www.powerscore.com/pubs.htm

PowerScore LSAT Logical Reasoning Bible

One of the most highly anticipated publications in LSAT history, the *PowerScore LSAT Logical Reasoning Bible*™ is a comprehensive how-to manual for solving every type of Logical Reasoning question. Featuring over 100 real Logical Reasoning questions with detailed explanations, the Bible is the ultimate resource for improving your LSAT Logical Reasoning score.

Available on the PowerScore website for $49.99.
Website: www.powerscore.com/pubs.htm

PowerScore Logic Games Ultimate Setups Guide

The Ultimate Setups Guide features setups for every game in each released LSAT PrepTest from 1995 to 2002. Each setup includes a diagram of the rules and the variables, as well an identification of key inferences. A number of questions are explained, and additional game notes are included. *The Ultimate Setups Guide* also includes the setup for every single game in the *10 More Actual, Official LSAT PrepTests*.

Available on the PowerScore website for $29.99.
Website: www.powerscore.com/pubs.htm

PowerScore Silent Timer

The PowerScore standard silent timer is perfect for practice. Tested and preferred by PowerScore. Large display - 3/4 inch digits - Completely Silent! - Built in memory - Magnetic back clip and easel stand - AAA battery included!

Available on the PowerScore website only for $16.99.
Website: www.powerscore.com/pubs.htm

PowerScore LSAT Private and Telephone Tutoring

Tutoring is ideal for students unable to enroll in one of our preparation courses, or who need assistance with a specific area. Whether you need personalized lesson plans designed for you, or you just need to work on a few concepts, we can create a tutoring experience that will address all of your LSAT difficulties. Since both you and the instructor work off the same materials, describing the correct approach and appropriate diagramming is easy.

Our tutors are the same people that teach our classes, and every tutor has scored in the 99th percentile on a LSAC-administered LSAT. We offer in-person tutoring or telephone tutoring, with multiple price points and package rates. Please visit www.powerscore.com for more information.

PowerScore Law School Admissions Counseling

While your LSAT score and GPA will undeniably be major factors in admissions, you can separate yourself from the rest of the applicant pool by assembling the most powerful application folder possible. To do this you must have a perfect personal statement, top-notch letters of recommendation, and flawless overall presentation. PowerScore has gathered a team of admissions experts—including former law school admissions board members, top lawyers, and students from top-ten law schools—to address your admissions counseling and personal statement needs.

CONTENTS

CHAPTER ONE: INTRODUCTION

CHAPTER TWO: THE JUNE 2004 LSAT

CHAPTER THREE: THE JUNE 2004 LSAT DECONSTRUCTED

CHAPTER FOUR: THE OCTOBER 2004 LSAT

CHAPTER FIVE: THE OCTOBER 2004 LSAT DECONSTRUCTED

CHAPTER SIX: THE DECEMBER 2004 LSAT

I

CHAPTER SEVEN: THE DECEMBER 2004 LSAT DECONSTRUCTED

CHAPTER EIGHT: GLOSSARY

MORE INFORMATION

About PowerScore

PowerScore is one of the nation's fastest growing test preparation companies. Headquartered on Hilton Head Island in South Carolina, PowerScore offers LSAT, GMAT, GRE, and SAT preparation classes in over 75 locations in the U.S. and abroad. For more information, please visit our website at www.powerscore.com.

IV

CHAPTER ONE: INTRODUCTION

Introduction

Welcome to *The 2004 LSATs Deconstructed* by PowerScore. The purpose of this book is to help you better understand the methods and procedures of the test makers by deconstructing every question in three actual Law School Admission Tests (LSATs). We strongly believe that by studying the logic behind each question you will increase your ability to perform well on the LSAT.

The three tests contained in this book—the June 2004 LSAT, the October 2004 LSAT, and the December 2004 LSAT—are the three released LSAT PrepTests from the year 2004. The fourth test from that year—the February 2004 LSAT—has not been released yet and thus the text of that exam is not available.

The use of real questions while preparing is essential to your success on the LSAT, and no question in this book has been modified from its original form.

How to Use this Book

We strongly suggest that you take each of the tests in this book as a timed practice test. Accordingly, prior to each test we have provided a Timing Notes page that explains how to properly time yourself.

After you complete each test, we suggest that carefully read the explanation of each problem, including the explanation of the correct answer choice and the explanations of the incorrect answer choices. Closely examine each problem and determine which elements led to the correct answer, and then study the analyses provided in the book and check them against your own work. By doing so you will greatly increase your chances of recognizing the patterns present within the LSAT.

The remainder of this chapter provides a brief overview of the section of the LSAT, how the LSAT is scored, the uses of the LSAT in law school admissions, and how to approach each section of the test. The next chapters contain each LSAT followed by complete explanations. The final chapter provides a glossary of terms used in this books and a brief overview of the concepts that appear on the LSAT.

If you are looking to further improve your LSAT score, we recommend that you pick up a copy of the renowned *PowerScore LSAT Logic Games Bible* and *PowerScore LSAT Logical Reasoning Bible*. The *Logic Games Bible* contains our system for attacking the Analytical Reasoning section of the LSAT. The

Logical Reasoning Bible details the PowerScore approach to the Logical Reasoning sections of the LSAT. When the two are combined, they provide a formidable methodology for attacking the test. The *LSAT Bibles* are available through our website at www.powerscore.com and at fine retailers everywhere.

Because access to accurate and up-to-date information is critical, we have devoted a section of our website to *2004 Deconstructed* students. This free online resource area offers supplements to the book material, answers questions posed by students, and provides updates as needed. There is also an official book evaluation form that we strongly encourage you to use. The exclusive *2004 Deconstructed* online area can be accessed at:

www.powerscore.com/2004decon

If we can assist you in your LSAT preparation in any way, or if you have any questions or comments, please do not hesitate to contact us via email at lsat@powerscore.com. Additional contact information is provided at the end of this book. We look forward to hearing from you!

A Brief Overview of the LSAT

The Law School Admission Test is administered four times a year: in February, June, September/October, and December. This standardized test is required for admission to any American Bar Association-approved law school. According to Law Services, the producers of the test, the LSAT is designed "to measure skills that are considered essential for success in law school: the reading and comprehension of complete texts with accuracy and insight; the organization and management of information and the ability to draw reasonable inferences from it; the ability to reason critically; and the analysis and evaluation of the reasoning and argument of others." The LSAT consists of the following five sections:

- 2 Sections of Logical Reasoning (short arguments, 24-26 total questions)
- 1 Section of Reading Comprehension (3 long reading passages, 2 short comparative reading passages, 26-28 total questions)
- 1 Section of Analytical Reasoning (4 logic games, 22-24 total questions)
- 1 Experimental Section of one of the above three section types.

You are given 35 minutes to complete each section. The experimental section is unscored and is not returned to the test taker. A break of 10 to 15 minutes is given between the 3rd and 4th sections.

The five-section test is followed by a 35 minute writing sample.

The Logical Reasoning Section

Each Logical Reasoning Section is composed of approximately 24 to 26 short arguments. Every short argument is followed by a question such as: "Which one of the following weakens the argument?" "Which one of the following parallels the argument?" or "Which one of the following must be true according to the argument?" The key to this section is time management and an understanding of the reasoning types and question types that frequently appear.

Since there are two scored sections of Logical Reasoning on every LSAT, this section accounts for approximately 50% of your score.

The Analytical Reasoning Section

This section, also known as Logic Games, is probably the most difficult for students taking the LSAT for the first time. The section consists of four games or puzzles, each followed by a series of five to eight questions. The questions are designed to test your ability to evaluate a set of relationships and to make inferences about those relationships. To perform well on this section you must understand the major types of games that frequently appear and develop the ability to properly diagram the rules and make inferences.

When you take an actual LSAT, they take your thumbprint at the testing site. This is done in case of test security problems.

At the conclusion of the LSAT, and for five business days after the LSAT, you have the option to cancel your score. Unfortunately, there is no way to determine exactly what your score would be before cancelling.

The Reading Comprehension Section

This section is composed of three long reading passages, each approximately 450 words in length, and two shorter comparative reading passages. The passage topics are drawn from a variety of subjects, and each passage is followed by a series of five to eight questions that ask you to determine viewpoints in the passage, analyze organizational traits, evaluate specific sections of the passage, or compare facets of two different passages. The key to this section is to read quickly with understanding and to carefully analyze the passage structure.

The Experimental Section

Each LSAT contains one experimental section, which does not count towards your score. The experimental can be any of the three section types described above, and the purpose of the section is to test and evaluate questions that will be used on *future* LSATs. By pretesting questions before their use in a scored section, the experimental helps the makers of the test determine the test scale. To learn more about the experimental section, we suggest you visit the PowerScore website, where you can find an extensive discussion of the experimental section, including how to identify the section and how to approach the section.

The Writing Sample

A 35-minute Writing Sample is given at the conclusion of the LSAT. The Writing Sample is not scored, but a copy is sent to each of the law schools to which you apply.

The format of the Writing Sample is called the Decision Prompt: you are asked to consider two possible courses of action, decide which one is superior, and then write a short essay supporting your choice. Each course of action is described in a short paragraph and you are given two primary criteria to consider in making your decision. Typically the two courses of action each have different strengths and weaknesses, and there is no clearly correct decision.

You must attempt the Writing Sample! If you do not, Law Services reserves the right not to score your test.

Do not agonize over the Writing Sample; in law school admissions, the Writing Sample is usually not a determining element for three reasons: the admissions committee is aware that the essay is given after a grueling three hour test and is about a subject you have no personal interest in; they already have a better sample of your writing ability in the personal statement; and the committee has a limited amount of time to evaluate applications.

The LSAT Scoring Scale

Each administered LSAT contains approximately 101 questions, and your LSAT score is based on the total number of questions you answer correctly, a total known as the raw score. After the raw score is determined, a unique Score Conversion Chart is used for each LSAT to convert the raw score into a scaled LSAT score. Since June 1991, the LSAT has utilized a 120 to 180 scoring scale, with 120 being the lowest possible score and 180 being the highest possible score. Notably, this 120 to 180 scale is just a renumbered version of the 200 to 800 scale most test takers are familiar with from such tests as the SAT and GMAT. Just drop the "1" and add a "0" to the 120 and 180.

Although the number of questions per test has remained relatively constant over the last eight years, the overall logical difficulty of each test has varied. This is not surprising since the test is made by humans and there is no precise way to completely predetermine logical difficulty. To account for these variances in test "toughness," the test makers adjust the Scoring Conversion Chart for each LSAT in order to make similar LSAT scores from different tests mean the same thing. For example, the LSAT given in June may be logically more difficult than the LSAT given in December, but by making the June LSAT scale "looser" than the December scale, a 160 on each test would represent the same level of performance. This scale adjustment, known as equating, is extremely important to law school admissions offices around the country. Imagine the difficulties that would be posed by unequated tests: admissions officers would have to not only examine individual LSAT scores, but also take into account which LSAT each score came from. This would present an information nightmare.

The LSAT Percentile Table

It is important not to lose sight of what LSAT scaled scores actually represent. The 120 to 180 test scale contains 61 different possible scores. Each score places a student in a certain relative position compared to other test takers. These relative positions are represented through a percentile that correlates to each score. The percentile indicates where the test taker ranks in the overall pool of test takers. For example, a score of 165 represents the 93rd percentile, meaning a student with a score of 165 scored better than 93 percent of the people who have taken the test in the last three years. The percentile is critical since it is a true indicator of your positioning relative to other test takers, and thus law school applicants.

Charting out the entire percentage table yields a rough "bell curve." The number of test takers in the 120s and 170s is very low (only 1.9% of all test takers receive a score in the 170s), and most test takers are bunched in the middle, comprising the "top" of the bell. In fact, approximately 40% of all test takers score between 145 and 155 inclusive, and about 70% of all test takers score between 140 and 160 inclusive.

Since the LSAT has 61 possible scores, why didn't the test makers change the scale to 0 to 60? Probably for merciful reasons. How would you tell your friends that you scored a 3 on the LSAT? 123 sounds so much better.

There is no penalty for answering incorrectly on the LSAT. Therefore, you should guess on any questions you cannot complete.

The median score on the LSAT scale is approximately 151. The median, or middle, score is the score at which approximately 50% of test takers have a lower score and 50% of test takers have a higher score. Typically, to achieve a score of 151, you must answer between 56 and 61 questions correctly from a total of 101 questions. In other words, to achieve a score that is perfectly average, you can miss between 40 and 45 questions. Thus, it is important to remember that you do not have to answer every question correctly in order to receive an excellent LSAT score. There is room for error, and accordingly you should never let any single question occupy an inordinate amount of your time.

The Use of the LSAT

The use of the LSAT in law school admissions is not without controversy. Experts agree that your LSAT score is one of the most important determinants of the type of school you can attend. At many law schools an admissions index consisting of your LSAT score and your undergraduate grade point average is used to help determine the relative standing of applicants, and at some schools a sufficiently high admissions index guarantees your admission.

For all the importance of the LSAT, the exam is not without flaws. As a standardized test currently given in the paper-and-pencil format, there are a number of skills that the LSAT cannot measure, including listening skills, note-taking ability, perseverance, etc. Law Services is aware of these limitations and on an annual basis they warn all law school admission offices about overemphasizing LSAT results. Still, because the test ultimately returns a number for each student, the tendency to rank applicants is strong. Fortunately, once you get to law school the LSAT is forgotten. For the time being consider the test a temporary hurdle you must leap in order to reach the ultimate goal.

For more information on the LSAT, or to register for the test, contact Law Services at (215) 968-1001 or at their website at www.lsac.org.

The Logic Games Section

There are three parts to every Logic Game: the scenario, the rules, and the questions. The scenario describes the game—what players are involved in the game and what situation those players are involved in; the rules provide the parameters those players must act under. Always read the scenario and rules before you begin diagramming.

After reading the scenario and the rules, make a main diagram at the bottom of the page. Your diagram should include the following:

- A list the variables and their exact total number
- An identification of any variable that is random (that is, a variable that does not appear in any of the rules)
- A diagram of the variable sets
- A diagram of each rule
- A listing of each inference

Logic Games Question Types

Games questions are either Global or Local. Global questions ask about information derived only from the initial rules, such as "Who can finish first?" or "Which one of the following must be true?" Use your main diagram to answer global questions. Local questions occur when the question imposes a new condition in addition to the initial rules, such as "If Laura sits in the third chair, which one of the following must be true?" The additional conditions imposed by local questions apply to that question only and do not apply to any of the other questions. It is essential that you focus on the implications of the new conditions. Ask yourself how this condition affects the variables and the existing rules. For local questions, do your work next to the question; do not use your main diagram except as a reference.

Local questions almost always require you to produce a "mini-setup" next to the question.

Within the global/local designation all questions ultimately ask for one of four things: what must be true, what is not necessarily true, what could be true, and what cannot be true. All questions are a variation of one of these four basic ideas. At all times, you must be aware of the exact nature of the question you are being asked, especially when "except" questions appear. If you find that you are missing questions because you miss words such as "false" or "except" when reading, then take a moment at the beginning of the game to circle the key words in each question, words such as "must," "could," etc.

If you frequently misread games questions, circle the key part of each question before you begin the game. You will not forget about a word like "except" if you have it underlined!

Logic Games General Notes

The key to optimal performance on Logic Games is to be focused and organized. This involves a number of factors:

1. Play to your strengths and away from your weaknesses

You are not required to do the games in the order presented on the test, and you should not expect that the test makers will present the games in the best order for you. Students who expect to have difficulty on the games section should attack the games in order of their personal preferences and strengths and weaknesses.

2. Create a strong setup for the game

PowerScore offers a selection of silent timers on our website, powerscore.com.

The key to powerful games performance is often to create a good setup. At least 80% of the games on the LSAT are "setup games" wherein the quality of your setup dictates whether or not you are successful in answering the questions.

3. Look to make inferences

There are always inferences in a game, and the test makers expect you to make at least a few of them. Always check the rules and your setup with an eye towards finding inferences, and then always look to use your inferences when answering questions.

4. Be smart during the game

If necessary, skip over time consuming questions and return to them later. Remember that it is sometimes advisable to do the questions out of order. For example, if the first question in a game asks you for a complete and accurate list of the positions "C" could occupy, because of time considerations it would be advisable to skip that question and complete the remaining questions. Then you could return to the first question and use the knowledge you gained from the other questions to quickly and easily answer the first question.

5. Do not be intimidated by size

A lengthy game scenario and a large number of initial rules do not necessarily equal greater difficulty. Some of the longest games are easy because they contain so many restrictions and limitations.

6. Keep an awareness of time

As stated previously, you have approximately eight minutes and forty-five seconds to complete each game and bubble in your answers. Use a timer during the LSAT so you always know how much time remains, and do not let one game or question consume so much time that you suffer later in the section.

If you do only three games, you have 11 minutes and 40 seconds to complete each game. If you do just two games, you have 17 minutes and 30 seconds to complete each game.

7. Maintain a positive attitude and concentrate

Above all, you must attack each game with a positive and energetic attitude. The games themselves are often challenging yet fun, and students who actively involve themselves in the games generally perform better overall.

The Logical Reasoning Section

As outlined in the *Logical Reasoning Bible*, to attack Logical Reasoning questions we use a general approach that systematically breaks down the stimulus and the answer choices. This approach is organized in steps called the Primary Objectives™:

Primary Objective #1: Determine whether the stimulus contains an argument or if it is only a set of factual statements.

Primary Objective #2: If the stimulus contains an argument, identify the conclusion of the argument. If the stimulus contains a fact set, examine each fact.

Primary Objective #3: If the stimulus contains an argument, determine if the argument is strong or weak.

Primary Objective #4: Read closely and know precisely what the author said. Do not generalize!

Primary Objective #5: Carefully read and identify the question stem. Do not assume that certain words are automatically associated with certain question types.

Primary Objective #6: Prephrase: after reading the question stem, take a moment to mentally formulate your answer to the question stem.

Primary Objective #7: Always read each of the five answer choices.

Primary Objective #8: Separate the answer choices into Contenders and Losers. After you complete this process, review the Contenders and decide which answer is the correct one.

Primary Objective #9: If all five answer choices appear to be Losers, return to the stimulus and re-evaluate the argument.

By consistently applying the points above, you give yourself the best opportunity to succeed on each question.

The Thirteen Logical Reasoning Question Types

Each question stem that appears in the Logical Reasoning section of the LSAT can be classified into one of thirteen different types:

1. Must Be True/Most Supported
2. Main Point
3. Point at Issue
4. Assumption
5. Justify the Conclusion
6. Strengthen/Support
7. Resolve the Paradox
8. Weaken
9. Method of Reasoning
10. Flaw in the Reasoning
11. Parallel Reasoning
12. Evaluate the Argument
13. Cannot Be True

Occasionally, students ask if we refer to the question types by number or by name. We always refer to the questions by name as that is an easier and more efficient approach. Numerical question type classification systems force you to add two unnecessary levels of abstraction to your thinking process. For example, consider a question that asks you to "weaken" the argument. In a numerical question classification system, you must first recognize that the question asks you to weaken the argument, then you must classify that question into a numerical category (say, Type 10), and then you must translate Type 10 to mean "Weaken." Literally, numerical classification systems force you to perform an abstract, circular translation of the meaning of the question, and the translation process is both time-consuming and valueless.

In the following pages we will discuss each question type in brief. Later we will examine each question type in its own chapter.

1. Must Be True/Most Supported

   This category is simply known as "Must Be True." Must Be True questions ask you to identify the answer choice that is best proven by the information in the stimulus. Question stem examples:

   "If the statements above are true, which one of the following must also be true?"

   "Which one of the following can be properly inferred from the passage?"

2. Main Point

Main Point questions are a variant of Must Be True questions. As you might expect, a Main Point question asks you to find the primary conclusion made by the author. Question stem example:

"The main point of the argument is that"

3. Point at Issue

Point at Issue questions require you to identify a point of contention between two speakers, and thus these questions appear almost exclusively with two-speaker stimuli. Question stem example:

"Larew and Mendota disagree about whether"

4. Assumption

These questions ask you to identify an assumption of the author's argument. Question stem example:

"Which one of the following is an assumption required by the argument above?"

5. Justify the Conclusion

Justify the Conclusion questions ask you to supply a piece of information that, when added to the premises, proves the conclusion. Question stem example:

"Which one of the following, if assumed, allows the conclusion above to be properly drawn?"

6. Strengthen/Support

These questions ask you to select the answer choice that provides support for the author's argument or strengthens it in some way. Question stem examples:

"Which one of the following, if true, most strengthens the argument?"

"Which one of the following, if true, most strongly supports the statement above?"

7. Resolve the Paradox

Every Resolve the Paradox stimulus contains a discrepancy or seeming contradiction. You must find the answer choice that best resolves the situation. Question stem example:

"Which one of the following, if true, would most effectively resolve the apparent paradox above?"

8. Weaken

Weaken questions ask you to attack or undermine the author's argument. Question stem example:

"Which one of the following, if true, most seriously weakens the argument?"

9. Method of Reasoning

Method of Reasoning questions ask you to describe, in abstract terms, the way in which the author made his or her argument. Question stem example:

"Which one of the following describes the technique of reasoning used above?"

10. Flaw in the Reasoning

Flaw in the Reasoning questions ask you to describe, in abstract terms, the error of reasoning committed by the author. Question stem example:

"The reasoning in the astronomer's argument is flawed because this argument"

11. Parallel Reasoning

Parallel Reasoning questions ask you to identify the answer choice that contains reasoning most similar in structure to the reasoning presented in the stimulus. Question stem example:

"Which one of the following arguments is most similar in its pattern of reasoning to the argument above?"

12. Evaluate the Argument

   With Evaluate the Argument questions you must decide which answer choice will allow you to determine the logical validity of the argument. Question stem example:

   "The answer to which one of the following questions would contribute most to an evaluation of the argument?"

13. Cannot Be True

   Cannot Be True questions ask you to identify the answer choice that cannot be true or is most weakened based on the information in the stimulus. Question stem example:

   "If the statements above are true, which one of the following CANNOT be true?"

As you attack each problem, remember that each question stem falls into one of four Families that governs the flow of information within the problem:

- The First Family uses the stimulus to prove one of the answer choices must be true. No information outside the sphere of the stimulus is allowed in the correct answer choice. Example question types include Must Be True, Main Point, Point at Issue, Method of Reasoning, Flaw in the Reasoning, and Parallel Reasoning.

- The Second Family takes the answer choices as true and uses them to help the stimulus. Information outside the sphere of the stimulus is allowed in the correct answer choice. Example question types include Strengthen, Justify the Conclusion, Assumption, and Resolve the Paradox.

- The Third Family takes the answer choices as true and uses them to hurt the stimulus. Information outside the sphere of the stimulus is allowed in the correct answer choice. The primary question type is Weaken.

- The Fourth Family uses the stimulus to prove that one of the answer choices cannot occur. No information outside the sphere of the stimulus is allowed in the answer choices. The primary question type is Cannot Be True.

Within the stimulus, there are different types of reasoning used, such as conditional Reasoning and Causal Reasoning, and we will address these as they appear in each question.

The Reading Comprehension Section

As you begin the Reading Comprehension section, search for passages with interesting or appealing subject matter. If all else is equal, choose the passage with the greatest number of questions. Also keep in mind that on a number of occasions the last passage has been the easiest passage.

Be sure to read each passage at your normal reading speed. Reading too slowly will prevent you from having adequate time to answer all of the questions. Reading too quickly will cause you to miss much of the detailed information presented in the passage and will force you to reread most of the passage, something that will also prevent you from answering all the questions. Do not skim the paragraphs. Skimming will not effectively prepare you to answer all the questions.

Your primary goal while reading is to find the main point of the passage. Although in the majority of passages the main point is stated in the first paragraph, it is not always the case that the main point appears in the first or second sentence. The main point of many passages has appeared in the final sentence of the first paragraph or in the first sentence of the second paragraph. On average, about 30% of the questions deal directly with the main idea.

As you read, attempt to identify the underlying logical structure of the passage. This will help you quickly find information once you begin to answer the questions. For example, many passages open by stating the background of a thesis that will be challenged later in the passage. In the following paragraphs the author will present an alternative viewpoint to the thesis and perhaps specific counterexamples which provide support for the alternative view. Awareness of this general structure will allow you to reduce the time you spend searching for information when you need to refer back to the passage.

Keep in mind that it is neither possible nor necessary for you to know every detail of a passage. For many questions you should return to the passage to confirm what you remember from your first reading of the passage.

Once you have finished reading the passage, take a moment to focus on the main point and the arguments that support the main point. Many students get so caught up in absorbing the information presented in a passage that they fail to take the time to mentally organize that information. If you are having difficulty remembering the main point of the passage, take a moment after reading the passage to write down the main point in a short, simple sentence.

Refrain from heavily underlining or marking up the passage. This will waste entirely too much time. Limit what you write to noting where the author makes a major point or changes the course of his or her argument.

Pay attention to the language the author uses in the passage. The following basic word lists can help identify the direction the author is taking with his or her argument:

Continuing the same idea	Introducing a new idea
furthermore	however
moreover	but
additionally	still
similarly	yet
in fact	although
indeed	in contrast
for example	nevertheless

Your state of mind when approaching these passages is extremely important. Make sure that you take a positive, energetic attitude to the passages. Many passages in the Reading Comprehension section discuss conflicts between different viewpoints and this makes the reading inherently more interesting. Getting involved in the argument will make the passage more enjoyable for you and will also allow you to focus more clearly on the material.

Always remember what the author is trying to achieve. In almost every case, he or she is discussing a body of information and trying to draw new points about that information. Rarely will the writer simply restate known situations without bringing in a new view of the situation. As is the case with any person trying to sound perceptive, the author will often use intellectual and complex language. Don't be intimidated by this—although the terminology may be difficult, the main point seldom is.

Reading Comprehension Question Types

Over 70% of the questions in the Reading Comprehension section are exactly the same as Must Be True Logical Reasoning questions. Whether the question asks for the main point or for details from the passage, the answer must be true according to what you have read. The following question types appear within the Must Be True designation:

- Main Point/Primary Purpose (MP)

  As in the Logical Reasoning section, main point questions ask you to select the statement which best sums up the author's core ideas. Primary purpose questions ask you to describe why the author wrote the passage.

- Passage Organization (PO)

  These questions ask you to describe a characteristic of the overall structure of the passage.

For example, "The second paragraph serves primarily to...," and "Which one of the following best describes the organization of the passage." These questions are similar to the Method of Reasoning questions in the Logical Reasoning section, but they are generally broader.

- Author's Perspective and Tone (AP)

  Author's perspective questions ask you to select the answer choice that best reflects the author's views, such as "The author of the passage would most likely agree with which one of the following statements?" Tone questions ask you to identify the author's attitude toward a subject.

- Function (F)

  Function questions ask why the author referred to a particular word, phrase, or idea. This is essentially an extended Method of Reasoning question, requiring you to go beyond simply identifying the argument structure, and asking you the reasons behind the author's use of words or ideas.

- Specific Reference (SR)

  These questions provide you with a specific line reference or a reference to an easily found word or phrase within the passage. To attack these questions, refer to the reference in the question and then begin reading about 5 lines above the reference.

The following question types appear outside of the Must Be True designation:

- Strengthen and Weaken Questions

  These questions are the same in both the Logical Reasoning section and Reading Comprehension section.

- Parallel Reasoning Questions

  In Reading Comprehension, Parallel Reasoning questions are usually broader in scope, asking you to find the scenario most analogous to an action in the passage. There is less of a focus on identifying premises and conclusions than in the Logical Reasoning section

As always, if you have difficulty answering one of the questions in a passage, continue on and complete the other questions in the passage first. Many students have a tendency to stop when confronted with a difficult question and reread the answer choices over and over. If you cannot choose an answer within a reasonable amount of time, go on and return to the question later.

Reading Comprehension Passage Features

Reading Comprehension passages tend to possess many of the same general characteristics. The most common are:

- **Strong purpose or main point:** Always remember that your primary goal while reading is to find the main point. There will almost always be at least one question on this idea.

- **Difficult words, phrases, or concepts:** The test makers use these words and ideas to distract you. Try to look past the word or phrase; instead, focus on the underlying meaning in order to understand the big picture.

- **Enumerations/Lists:** If a decision was made in the passage and several reasons are given to explain that decision, expect to be questioned on your knowledge of those reasons. This is a very common question indicator!

- **Authoritative references:** When authorities are cited by the text, be prepared to be asked about the function and application of the citation. Sometimes different groups will be associated with conflicting ideas—be sure that you are careful not to confuse the groups being referenced.

- **Dates and Numbers:** These are useful because they help mark the chronology of the passage. If there are many dates, they can also be confusing, so make sure you are careful to match the dates given to the correct event.

- **Mixed References:** If a phrase or topic is mentioned in one area of the passage and then again in an entirely different area, be prepared for a specific reference question which will refer to only one of the two citings. Although you will be referred to a specific line in the passage, the relevant information for answering the question is usually found elsewhere in the passage where that same topic or phrase was discussed.

- **Competing perspectives:** If several alternative viewpoints are offered on a particular subject, make certain you know the details of each view as well as who is supporting each view. Several of the questions will probably test your knowledge of the different viewpoints.

  Further, when explaining arguments, many authors bring up counterpoints or drawbacks to that argument in an effort to show their awareness of other viewpoints. These counterpoints are often introduced by terms such as "however," "although," and "yet," and test takers are sometimes questioned on their understanding of these counterpoints, however brief they might have been.

- **Definitions:** If a definition is given during the course of a passage, make a notation and expect to be questioned on your understanding of that definition.

- **Initial Information:** Many questions are asked about information that is presented in the first five lines of a passage. The test makers have found that students often forget what was initially stated in the passage and instead concentrate on the information presented in the main body of the passage, so these questions could be hard to answer if you were not reading carefully from the very beginning.

As you read through each passage, you must keep track of each of these elements as they appear, as you are likely to be tested on each idea if it is present.

CHAPTER TWO: THE JUNE 2004 LSAT

Taking the June 2004 LSAT

This chapter contains the complete text of the June 2004 LSAT, including an answer key and scoring scale. For the closest possible re-creation of the conditions of the LSAT, take this exam as a timed exercise. The exam will take just less than three hours, and there is an answer sheet included so that you can record your answers. Per Law Services protocol, here are the directions for taking the test under timed conditions:

> Section 1 = allow yourself exactly 35 minutes
> Section 2 = allow yourself exactly 35 minutes
> Section 3 = allow yourself exactly 35 minutes
> Section 4 = allow yourself exactly 35 minutes
>
> Writing Sample = allow yourself exactly 30 minutes (Writing Samples prior to June 2005 were 30 minutes instead of 35 minutes)

The rules for the test are as follows:

> During the test you are allowed to work only on the section being timed. You cannot go back or forward to work on any other section of the test.
>
> Do not take a break between any of the sections (on the actual LSAT, an unscored experimental section will be included, and a 10-15 minute break will be given after section 3; because this test has no experimental section, you should not take a break between any of the sections).
>
> You may not use any scratch paper while working on the test; only the test pages themselves are available for your use.

After completing the test, refer to the answer key and the "Computing Your Score" section at the end of the test to find your LSAT score.

Your answer sheet is on the next page, and complete explanations are in the following chapter.

SECTION I
Time—35 minutes
28 Questions

Directions: Each passage in this section is followed by a group of questions to be answered on the basis of what is stated or implied in the passage. For some of the questions, more than one of the choices could conceivably answer the question. However, you are to choose the best answer; that is, the response that most accurately and completely answers the question, and blacken the corresponding space on your answer sheet.

The accumulation of scientific knowledge regarding the environmental impact of oil well drilling in North America has tended to lag behind the actual drilling of oil wells. Most attempts to
(5) regulate the industry have relied on hindsight: the need for regulation becomes apparent only after undesirable events occur. The problems associated with oil wells' potential contamination of groundwater—fresh water within the earth that
(10) supplies wells and springs—provide a case in point.

When commercial drilling for oil began in North America in the mid-nineteenth century, regulations reflected the industry's concern for the purity of the wells' oil. In 1893, for example, regulations were
(15) enacted specifying well construction requirements to protect oil and gas reserves from contamination by fresh water. Thousands of wells were drilled in such a way as to protect the oil, but no thought was given to the possibility that the groundwater itself might need
(20) protection until many drinking-water wells near the oil well sites began to produce unpotable, oil-contaminated water.

The reason for this contamination was that groundwater is usually found in porous and
(25) permeable geologic formations near the earth's surface, whereas petroleum and unpotable saline water reservoirs are generally found in similar formations but at greater depths. Drilling a well creates a conduit connecting all the formations that it
(30) has penetrated. Consequently, without appropriate safeguards, wells that penetrate both groundwater and oil or saline water formations inevitably contaminate the groundwater. Initial attempts to prevent this contamination consisted of sealing off the
(35) groundwater formations with some form of protective barrier to prevent the oil flowing up the well from entering or mixing with the natural groundwater reservoir. This method, which is still in use today, initially involved using hollow trees to seal off the
(40) groundwater formations; now, however, large metal pipe casings, set in place with cement, are used.

Regulations currently govern the kinds of casing and cement that can be used in these practices; however, the hazards of insufficient knowledge
(45) persist. For example, the long-term stability of this

way of protecting groundwater is unknown. The protective barrier may fail due to corrosion of the casing by certain fluids flowing up the well, or because of dissolution of the cement by these fluids.
(50) The effects of groundwater bacteria, traffic vibrations, and changing groundwater chemistry are likewise unassessed. Further, there is no guarantee that wells drilled in compliance with existing regulations will not expose a need for research in additional areas: on
(55) the west coast of North America, a major disaster recently occurred because a well's location was based on a poor understanding of the area's subsurface geology. Because the well was drilled in a channel accessing the ocean, not only was the area's
(60) groundwater completely contaminated, but widespread coastal contamination also occurred, prompting international concern over oil exploration and initiating further attempts to refine regulations.

1. Which one of the following most accurately states the main point of the passage?

(A) Although now recognized as undesirable, occasional groundwater contamination by oil and unpotable saline water is considered to be inevitable wherever drilling for oil occurs.

(B) Widespread coastal contamination caused by oil well drilling in North America has prompted international concern over oil exploration.

(C) Hindsight has been the only reliable means available to regulation writers responsible for devising adequate safeguard regulations to prevent environmental contamination associated with oil well drilling.

(D) The risk of environmental contamination associated with oil well drilling continues to exist because safeguard regulations are often based on hindsight and less-than-sufficient scientific information.

(E) Groundwater contamination associated with oil well drilling is due in part to regulations designed to protect the oil from contamination by groundwater and not the groundwater from contamination by oil.

GO ON TO THE NEXT PAGE.

2. The passage states which one of the following about underground oil reservoirs?

(A) They are usually located in areas whose subsurface geology is poorly understood.

(B) They are generally less common in coastal regions.

(C) They are usually located in geologic formations similar to those in which gas is found.

(D) They are often contaminated by fresh or saline water.

(E) They are generally found at greater depths than groundwater formations.

3. The author's attitude regarding oil well drilling regulations can most accurately be described as

(A) cynical that future regulatory reform will occur without international concern

(B) satisfied that existing regulations are adequate to prevent unwarranted tradeoffs between resource collection and environmental protection

(C) concerned that regulatory reform will not progress until significant undesirable events occur

(D) optimistic that current scientific research will spur regulatory reform

(E) confident that regulations will eventually be based on accurate geologic understandings

4. The author uses the phrase "the hazards of insufficient knowledge" (line 44) primarily in order to refer to the risks resulting from

(A) a lack of understanding regarding the dangers to human health posed by groundwater contamination

(B) a failure to comprehend the possible consequences of drilling in complex geologic systems

(C) poorly tested methods for verifying the safety of newly developed technologies

(D) an inadequate appreciation for the difficulties of enacting and enforcing environmental regulations

(E) a rudimentary understanding of the materials used in manufacturing metal pipe casings

5. Based on the information in the passage, if a prospective oil well drilled near a large city encounters a large groundwater formation and a small saline water formation, but no oil, which one of the following statements is most likely to be true?

(A) Groundwater contamination is unlikely because the well did not strike oil and hence will not be put in operation.

(B) Danger to human health due to groundwater contamination is unlikely because large cities generally have more than one source of drinking water.

(C) Groundwater contamination is likely unless the well is plugged and abandoned.

(D) Groundwater contamination is unlikely because the groundwater formation's large size will safely dilute any saline water that enters it.

(E) The risk of groundwater contamination can be reduced if casing is set properly and monitored routinely for breakdown.

GO ON TO THE NEXT PAGE.

In many bilingual communities of Puerto Rican Americans living in the mainland United States, people use both English and Spanish in a single conversation, alternating between them smoothly and
(5) frequently even within the same sentence. This practice—called code-switching—is common in bilingual populations. While there are some cases that cannot currently be explained, in the vast majority of cases subtle factors, either situational or rhetorical,
(10) explain the use of code-switching.

Linguists say that most code-switching among Puerto Rican Americans is sensitive to the social contexts, which researchers refer to as domains, in which conversations take place. The main
(15) conversational factors influencing the occurrence of code-switching are setting, participants, and topic. When these go together naturally they are said to be congruent; a set of three such congruent factors constitutes a conversational situation. Linguists
(20) studying the choice between Spanish and English among a group of Puerto Rican American high school students classified their conversational situations into five domains: family, friendship, religion, education, and employment. To test the effects of these domains
(25) on code-switching, researchers developed a list of hypothetical situations made up of two of the three congruent factors, or of two incongruent factors, approximating an interaction in one of the five domains. The researchers asked the students to
(30) determine the third factor and to choose which mix of language—on a continuum from all English to all Spanish—they would use in that situation. When given two congruent factors, the students easily supplied the third congruent factor and strongly
(35) agreed among themselves about which mix they would use. For instance, for the factors of participants "parent and child" and the topic "how to be a good son or daughter," the congruent setting chosen was "home" and the language mix chosen was Spanish
(40) only. In contrast, incongruent factors such as the participants "priest and parishioner" and the setting "beach" yielded less agreement on the third factor of topic and on language choice.

But situational factors do not account for all
(45) code-switching; it occurs even when the domain would lead one not to expect it. In these cases, one language tends to be the primary one, while the other is used only sparingly to achieve certain rhetorical effects. Often the switches are so subtle that the
(50) speakers themselves are not aware of them. This was the case with a study of a family of Puerto Rican Americans in another community. Family members believed they used only English at home, but their taped conversations occasionally contained some
(55) Spanish, with no change in situational factors. When asked what the presence of Spanish signified, they commented that it was used to express certain attitudes such as intimacy or humor more emphatically.

6. Which one of the following most accurately expresses the main point of the passage?

(A) The lives of Puerto Rican Americans are affected in various ways by code-switching.
(B) It is not always possible to explain why code-switching occurs in conversations among Puerto Rican Americans.
(C) Rhetorical factors can explain more instances of code-switching among Puerto Rican Americans than can situational factors.
(D) Studies of bilingual communities of Puerto Rican Americans have caused linguists to revise many of their beliefs about code-switching.
(E) Most code-switching among Puerto Rican Americans can be explained by subtle situational and rhetorical factors.

7. In lines 56-59, the author mentions the family members' explanation of their use of Spanish primarily in order to

(A) report evidence supporting the conclusion that the family's code-switching had a rhetorical basis
(B) show that reasons for code-switching differ from one community to another
(C) supply evidence that seems to conflict with the researchers' conclusions about why the family engaged in code-switching
(D) refute the argument that situational factors explain most code-switching
(E) explain how it could be that the family members failed to notice their use of Spanish

8. Which one of the following questions is NOT characterized by the passage as a question to which linguists sought answers in their code-switching studies involving high school students?

(A) Where do the students involved in the study think that a parent and child are likely to be when they are talking about how to be a good son or daughter?
(B) What language or mix of languages do the students involved in the study think that a parent and child would be likely to use when they are talking at home about how to be a good son or daughter?
(C) What language or mix of languages do the students involved in the study think that a priest and a parishioner would be likely to use if they were conversing on a beach?
(D) What topic do the students involved in the study think that a parent and child would be most likely to discuss when they are speaking Spanish?
(E) What topic do the students involved in the study think that a priest and parishioner would be likely to discuss on a beach?

GO ON TO THE NEXT PAGE.

9. The primary function of the third paragraph of the passage is to

(A) consider a general explanation for the phenomenon of code-switching that is different from the one discussed in the preceding paragraphs
(B) resolve an apparent conflict between two explanations for code-switching that were discussed in the preceding paragraphs
(C) show that there are instances of code-switching that are not explained by the factors discussed in the previous paragraph
(D) report some of the patterns of code-switching observed among a family of Puerto Rican Americans in another community
(E) show that some instances of code-switching are unconscious

10. Based on the passage, which one of the following is best explained as rhetorically determined code-switching?

(A) A speaker who does not know certain words in the primary language of a conversation occasionally has recourse to familiar words in another language.
(B) A person translating a text from one language into another leaves certain words in the original language because the author of the text invented those words.
(C) For the purpose of improved selling strategies, a businessperson who primarily uses one language sometimes conducts business in a second language that is preferred by some people in the community.
(D) A speaker who primarily uses one language switches to another language because it sounds more expressive.
(E) A speaker who primarily uses one language occasionally switches to another language in order to maintain fluency in the secondary language.

11. It can be inferred from the passage that the author would most likely agree with which one of the following statements?

(A) Research revealing that speakers are sometimes unaware of code-switching casts doubt on the results of a prior study involving high school students.
(B) Relevant research conducted prior to the linguists' work with high school students would lead one to expect different answers from those the students actually gave.
(C) Research conducted prior to the study of a family of Puerto Rican Americans was thought by most researchers to explain code-switching in all except the most unusual or nonstandard contexts.
(D) Research suggests that people engaged in code-switching are usually unaware of which situational factors might influence their choice of language or languages.
(E) Research suggests that the family of Puerto Rican Americans does not use code-switching in conversations held at home except for occasional rhetorical effect.

12. Which one of the following does the passage offer as evidence that code-switching cannot be entirely explained by situational factors?

(A) Linguists have observed that bilingual high school students do not agree among themselves as to what mix of languages they would use in the presence of incongruent situational factors.
(B) Code-switching sometimes occurs in conversations whose situational factors would be expected to involve the use of a single language.
(C) Bilingual people often switch smoothly between two languages even when there is no change in the situational context in which the conversation takes place.
(D) Puerto Rican Americans sometimes use Spanish only sparingly and for rhetorical effect in the presence of situational factors that would lead one to expect Spanish to be the primary language.
(E) Speakers who engage in code-switching are often unaware of the situational factors influencing their choices of which language or mix of languages to speak.

13. Which one of the following, if true, would most cast doubt on the author's interpretation of the study involving the family discussed in the third paragraph?

(A) In a previous twelve-month study involving the same family in their home, their conversations were entirely in English except when situational factors changed significantly.
(B) In a subsequent twelve-month study involving the same family, a particular set of situational factors occurred repeatedly without any accompanying instances of code-switching.
(C) In a subsequent twelve-month study involving the same family, it was noted that intimacy and humor were occasionally expressed through the use of English expressions.
(D) When asked about the significance of their use of Spanish, the family members replied in English rather than Spanish.
(E) Prior to their discussions with the researchers, the family members did not describe their occasional use of Spanish as serving to emphasize humor or intimacy.

GO ON TO THE NEXT PAGE.

Reader-response theory, a type of literary theory that arose in reaction to formalist literary criticism, has endeavored to shift the emphasis in the interpretation of literature from the text itself to the
(5) contributions of readers to the meaning of a text. According to literary critics who endorse reader-response theory, the literary text alone renders no meaning; it acquires meaning only whenencountered by individual readers, who always bring varying
(10) presuppositions and ways of reading to bear on the text, giving rise to the possibility—even probability—of varying interpretations. This brand of criticism has met opposition from the formalists, who study the text alone and argue that reader-response theory can
(15) encourage and even validate fragmented views of a work, rather than the unified view acquired by examining only the content of the text. However, since no theory has a monopoly on divining meaning from a text, the formalists' view appears
(20) unnecessarily narrow.

The proponents of formalism argue that their approach is firmly grounded in rational, objective principles, while reader-response theory lacks standards and verges on absolute subjectivity. After
(25) all, these, proponents argue, no author can create a work that is packed with countless meanings. The meaning of a work of literature, the formalists would argue, may be obscure and somewhat arcane; yet, however hidden it may be, the author's intended
(30) meaning is legible within the work, and it is the critic's responsibility to search closely for this meaning. However, while a literary work is indeed encoded in various signs and symbols that must be translated for the work to be understood and
(35) appreciated, it is not a map. Any complicated literary work will invariably raise more questions than it answers. What is needed is a method that enables the critic to discern and make use of the rich stock of meanings created in encounters between texts and
(40) readers.

Emphasizing the varied presuppositions and perceptions that readers bring to the interpretations of a text can uncover hitherto unnoticed dimensions of the text. In fact, many important works have received
(45) varying interpretations throughout their existence, suggesting that reader-based interpretations similar to those described by reader-response theory had been operating long before the theory's principles were articulated. And while in some cases critics' textual
(50) interpretations based on reader-response theory have unfairly burdened literature of the past with contemporary ideologies, legitimate additional insights and understandings continue to emerge years after an ostensibly definitive interpretation of a major
(55) work has been articulated. By regarding a reader's

personal interpretation of literary works as not only valid but also useful in understanding the works, reader-response theory legitimizes a wide range of perspectives on these works and thereby reinforces
(60) the notion of them as fluid and lively forms of discourse that can continue to support new interpretations long after their original composition.

14. Which one of the following most accurately describes the author's attitude toward formalism as expressed in the passage?

(A) scholarly neutrality
(B) grudging respect
(C) thoughtless disregard
(D) cautious ambivalence
(E) reasoned dismissal

15. Which one of the following persons displays an approach that most strongly suggests sympathy with the principles of reader-response theory?

(A) a translator who translates a poem from Spanish to English word for word so that its original meaning is not distorted
(B) a music critic who insists that early music can be truly appreciated only when it is played on original instruments of the period
(C) a reviewer who finds in the works of a novelist certain unifying themes that reveal the novelist's personal concerns and preoccupations
(D) a folk artist who uses conventional cultural symbols and motifs as a way of conveying commonly understood meanings
(E) a director who sets a play by Shakespeare in nineteenth-century Japan to give a new perspective on the work

16. With which one of the following statements would the author of the passage be most likely to agree?

(A) Any literary theory should be seen ultimately as limiting, since contradictory interpretations of texts are inevitable.
(B) A purpose of a literary theory is to broaden and enhance the understanding that can be gained from a work.
(C) A literary theory should provide valid and strictly objective methods for interpreting texts.
(D) The purpose of a literary theory is to make clear the intended meaning of the author of a work.
(E) Since no literary theory has a monopoly on meaning, a reader should avoid using theories to interpret literature.

GO ON TO THE NEXT PAGE.

17. The passage states that reader-response theory legitimizes which one of the following?

    (A) a wide range of perspectives on works of literature
    (B) contemporary ideology as a basis for criticism
    (C) encoding the meaning of a literary work in signs and symbols
    (D) finding the meaning of a work in its text alone
    (E) belief that an author's intended meaning in a work is discoverable

18. Which one of the following most accurately describes the author's purpose in referring to literature of the past as being "unfairly burdened" (line 51) in some cases?

    (A) to reinforce the notion that reader-based interpretations of texts invariably raise more questions than they can answer
    (B) to confirm the longevity of interpretations similar to reader-based interpretations of texts
    (C) to point out a fundamental flaw that the author believes makes reader-response theory untenable
    (D) to concede a minor weakness in reader-response theory that the author believes is outweighed by its benefits
    (E) to suggest that reader-response theory can occasionally encourage fragmented views of a work

19. Which one of the following, if true, most weakens the author's argument concerning reader-response theory?

    (A) Reader-response theory is reflected in interpretations that have been given throughout history and that bring additional insight to literary study.
    (B) Reader-response theory legitimizes conflicting interpretations that collectively diminish the understanding of a work.
    (C) Reader-response theory fails to provide a unified view of the meaning of a literary work.
    (D) Reader-response theory claims that a text cannot have meaning without a reader.
    (E) Reader-response theory recognizes meanings in a text that were never intended by the author.

20. The author's reference to "various signs and symbols" (line 33) functions primarily to

    (A) stress the intricacy and complexity of good literature
    (B) grant that a reader must be guided by the text to some degree
    (C) imply that no theory alone can fully explain a work of literature
    (D) illustrate how a literary work differs from a map
    (E) show that an inflexible standard of interpretation provides constant accuracy

21. Which one of the following can most reasonably be inferred from the information in the passage?

    (A) Formalists believe that responsible critics who focus on the text alone will tend to find the same or similar meanings in a literary work.
    (B) Critical approaches similar to those described by formalism had been used to interpret texts long before the theory was articulated as such.
    (C) Formalists would not find any meaning in a text whose author did not intend it to have anyone particular meaning.
    (D) A literary work from the past can rarely be read properly using reader-response theory when the subtleties of the work's social-historical context are not available.
    (E) Formalism is much older and has more adherents than reader-response theory.

GO ON TO THE NEXT PAGE.

Faculty researchers, particularly in scientific, engineering, and medical programs, often produce scientific discoveries and invent products or processes that have potential commercial value. Many
(5) institutions have invested heavily in the administrative infrastructure to develop and exploit these discoveries, and they expect to prosper both by an increased level of research support and by the royalties from licensing those discoveries having
(10) patentable commercial applications. However, although faculty themselves are unlikely to become entrepreneurs, an increasing number of highly valued researchers will be sought and sponsored by research corporations or have consulting contracts with
(15) commercial firms. One study of such entrepreneurship concluded that "if universities do not provide the flexibility needed to venture into business, faculty will be tempted to go to those institutions that are responsive to their commercialized desires." There is
(20) therefore a need to consider the different intellectual property policies that govern the commercial exploitation of faculty inventions in order to determine which would provide the appropriate level of flexibility.
(25) In a recent study of faculty rights, Patricia Chew has suggested a fourfold classification of institutional policies. A supramaximalist institution stakes out the broadest claim possible, asserting ownership not only of all intellectual property produced by faculty in the
(30) course of their employment while using university resources, but also for any inventions or patent rights from faculty activities, even those involving research sponsored by nonuniversity funders. A maximalist institution allows faculty ownership of inventions
(35) that do not arise either "in the course of the faculty's employment [or] from the faculty's use of university resources." This approach, although not as all-encompassing as that of the supramaximalist university, can affect virtually all of a faculty
(40) member's intellectual production. A resource-provider institution asserts a claim to faculty's intellectual product in those cases where "significant use" of university time and facilities is employed. Of course, what constitutes significant use of resources is a
(45) matter of institutional judgment.
As Chew notes, in these policies "faculty rights, including the sharing of royalties, are the result of university benevolence and generosity. [However, this] presumption is contrary to the common law,
(50) which provides that faculty own their inventions." Others have pointed to this anomaly and, indeed, to the uncertain legal and historical basis upon which the ownership of intellectual property rests. Although these issues remain unsettled, and though universities
(55) may be overreaching due to faculty's limited

knowledge of their rights, most major institutions behave in the ways that maximize university ownership and profit participation.
But there is a fourth way, one that seems to be
(60) free from these particular issues. Faculty-oriented institutions assume that researchers own their own intellectual products and the rights to exploit them commercially, except in the development of public health inventions or if there is previously specified
(65) "substantial university involvement." At these institutions industry practice is effectively reversed, with the university benefiting in far fewer circumstances.

22. Which one of the following most accurately summarizes the main point of the passage?

(A) While institutions expect to prosper from increased research support and royalties from patentable products resulting from faculty inventions, if they do not establish clear-cut policies governing ownership of these inventions, they run the risk of losing faculty to research corporations or commercial consulting contracts.

(B) The fourfold classification of institutional policies governing exploitation of faculty inventions is sufficient to categorize the variety of steps institutions are taking to ensure that faculty inventors will not be lured away by commercial firms or research corporations.

(C) To prevent the loss of faculty to commercial firms or research corporations, institutions will have to abandon their insistence on retaining maximum ownership of and profit from faculty inventions and adopt the common-law presumption that faculty alone own their inventions.

(D) While the policies of most institutions governing exploitation of faculty inventions seek to maximize university ownership of and profit from these inventions, another policy offers faculty greater flexibility to pursue their commercial interests by regarding faculty as the owners of their intellectual products.

(E) Most institutional policies governing exploitation of faculty inventions are indefensible because they run counter to common-law notions of ownership and copyright, but they usually go unchallenged because few faculty members are aware of what other options might be available to them.

GO ON TO THE NEXT PAGE.

23. Which one of the following most accurately characterizes the author's view regarding the institutional intellectual property policies of most universities?

(A) The policies are in keeping with the institution's financial interests.
(B) The policies are antithetical to the mission of a university.
(C) The policies do not have a significant impact on the research of faculty.
(D) The policies are invariably harmful to the motivation of faculty attempting to pursue research projects.
(E) The policies are illegal and possibly immoral.

24. Which one of the following institutions would NOT be covered by the fourfold classification proposed by Chew?

(A) an institution in which faculty own the right to some inventions they create outside the institution
(B) an institution in which faculty own all their inventions, regardless of any circumstances, but grant the institution the right to collect a portion of their royalties
(C) an institution in which all inventions developed by faculty with institutional resources become the property of the institution
(D) an institution in which all faculty inventions related to public health become the property of the institution
(E) an institution in which some faculty inventions created with institutional resources remain the property of the faculty member

25. The passage suggests that the type of institution in which employees are likely to have the most uncertainty about who owns their intellectual products is the

(A) commercial firm
(B) supramaximalist university
(C) maximalist university
(D) resource-provider university
(E) faculty-oriented university

26. According to the passage, what distinguishes a resource-provider institution from the other types of institutions identified by Chew is its

(A) vagueness on the issue of what constitutes university as opposed to nonuniversity resources
(B) insistence on reaping substantial financial benefit from faculty inventions while still providing faculty with unlimited flexibility
(C) inversion of the usual practices regarding exploitation of faculty inventions in order to give faculty greater flexibility
(D) insistence on ownership of faculty inventions developed outside the institution in order to maximize financial benefit to the university
(E) reliance on the extent of use of institutional resources as the sole criterion in determining ownership of faculty inventions

27. The author of the passage most likely quotes one study of entrepreneurship in lines 16-19 primarily in order to

(A) explain why institutions may wish to develop intellectual property policies that are responsive to certain faculty needs
(B) draw a contrast between the worlds of academia and business that will be explored in detail later in the passage
(C) defend the intellectual property rights of faculty inventors against encroachment by the institutions that employ them
(D) describe the previous research that led Chew to study institutional policies governing ownership of faculty inventions
(E) demonstrate that some faculty inventors would be better off working for commercial firms

28. The passage suggests each of the following EXCEPT:

(A) Supramaximalist institutions run the greatest risk of losing faculty to jobs in institutions more responsive to the inventor's financial interests.
(B) A faculty-oriented institution will make no claim of ownership to a faculty invention that is unrelated to public health and created without university involvement.
(C) Faculty at maximalist institutions rarely produce inventions outside the institution without using the institution's resources.
(D) There is little practical difference between the policies of supramaximalist and maximalist institutions.
(E) The degree of ownership claimed by a resource-provider institution of the work of its faculty will not vary from case to case.

S T O P

IF YOU FINISH BEFORE TIME IS CALLED, YOU MAY CHECK YOUR WORK ON THIS SECTION ONLY.
DO NOT WORK ON ANY OTHER SECTION IN THE TEST.

SECTION II
Time—35 minutes
25 Questions

<u>Directions:</u> The questions in this section are based on the reasoning contained in brief statements or passages. For some questions, more than one of the choices could conceivably answer the question. However, you are to choose the <u>best</u> answer; that is, the response that most accurately and completely answers the question. You should not make assumptions that are by commonsense standards implausible, superfluous, or incompatible with the passage. After you have chosen the best answer, blacken the corresponding space on your answer sheet.

1. Pettengill: Bebop jazz musicians showed their distaste for jazz classics by taking great liberties with them, as though the songs could be made interesting only through radical reshaping.

   Romney: Only compelling, versatile songs can stand such radical reshaping. Bebop musicians recognized this and their revolutionary approach to the jazz classics enabled them to discover previously unknown depths in the music.

   Pettengill and Romney disagree over whether

   (A) bebop jazz was radically different from the jazz music that preceded it
   (B) bebop jazz was an improvement on the jazz classics that preceded it
   (C) bebop musicians showed appreciation for jazz classics in radically reshaping them
   (D) jazz music requires musicians to adhere closely to the original version in order to be widely popular
   (E) bebop musicians were influenced by the more conservative styles of their predecessors

2. Essayist: Earth is a living organism, composed of other organisms much as animals are composed of cells, not merely a thing upon which creatures live. This hypothesis is supported by the fact that, like all organisms, Earth can be said to have a metabolism and to regulate its temperature, humidity, and other characteristics, divorced from the influences of its surroundings. Of course, Earth does not literally breathe, but neither do insects (they have no lungs), though they respire successfully.

   The assertion that insects do not literally breathe plays which one of the following roles in the essayist's argument?

   (A) a reason for not rejecting Earth's status as an organism on the basis of its not breathing
   (B) a reason for rejecting as false the belief that Earth is a living organism
   (C) an illustration of the general claim that to be an organism, a creature must have a metabolism
   (D) an example of a type of organism whose status, like Earth's, is unclear
   (E) an illustration of a type of organism out of which Earth is composed

3. Cognitive psychologist: In a recent survey, citizens of Country F were asked to state which one of the following two scenarios they would prefer: (1) Country F is the world economic leader, with a gross national product (GNP) of $100 billion, and Country G is second, with a GNP of $90 billion; or (2) Country G is the economic leader, with a GNP of $120 billion, and Country F is second, with a GNP of $110 billion. Despite the fact that, under scenario 2, Country F would have a higher GNP than under scenario 1, the majority of respondents stated that they preferred scenario 1.

   Which one of the following, if true, would most help to explain the survey results described by the cognitive psychologist?

   (A) Most citizens of Country F believe their country has a higher economic growth rate than Country G.
   (B) Most citizens of Country F want their country to have a GNP higher than $120 billion.
   (C) Most citizens of Country F believe that their personal welfare is unconnected to GNP.
   (D) Most citizens of Country F believe GNP is a poor measure of a nation's economic health.
   (E) Most citizens of Country F want their country to be more economically powerful than Country G.

GO ON TO THE NEXT PAGE.

4. A study claims that the average temperature on Earth has permanently increased, because the average temperature each year for the last five years has been higher than any previous yearly average on record. However, periods of up to ten years of average temperatures that have consistently been record highs are often merely part of the random fluctuations in temperature that are always occurring.

Which one of the following is most strongly supported by the information above?

(A) All large increases in average temperature on record have occurred in ten-year periods.
(B) Five successive years of increasing annual average temperature does not always signify a permanent increase in temperature.
(C) Record high temperatures can be expected on Earth for another five years.
(D) Random fluctuations in Earth's average temperature typically last less than ten years.
(E) The average temperature on Earth never increases except in cases of random temperature fluctuation.

5. Shipping Coordinator: If we send your shipment by air express, it will arrive tomorrow morning. If we send your shipment via ground carrier, it will arrive either tomorrow or the next day. Ground carrier is less expensive than air express, so which do you prefer?

Customer: If I don't choose air express, then I will not receive my shipment tomorrow, so I clearly have no choice but to spend the extra money and have it sent via air express.

The customer's response can best be explained on the assumption that she has misinterpreted the shipping coordinator to mean which one of the following?

(A) Ground carrier is as reliable a shipping method as air express.
(B) If the shipment is sent by air express, it will arrive tomorrow.
(C) Ground carrier is not more expensive than air express.
(D) Unless the shipment is sent by air express, it will not arrive tomorrow.
(E) The greater the shipping cost, the faster the shipment will arrive.

6. Therapists who treat violent criminals cannot both respect their clients' right to confidentiality and be sincerely concerned for the welfare of victims of future violent crimes. Reporting a client's unreported crimes violates the client's trust, but remaining silent leaves the dangerous client out of prison, free to commit more crimes.

Which one of the following, if true, most weakens the argument?

(A) Most therapists who treat violent criminals are assigned this task by a judicial body.
(B) Criminals are no more likely to receive therapy in prison than they are out of prison.
(C) Victims of future violent crimes also have a right to confidentiality should they need therapy.
(D) The right of victims of violent crimes to compensation is as important as the right of criminals in therapy to confidentiality.
(E) A therapist who has gained a violent criminal's trust can persuade that criminal not to commit repeat offenses.

GO ON TO THE NEXT PAGE.

7. Failure to rotate crops depletes the soil's nutrients gradually unless other preventive measures are taken. If the soil's nutrients are completely depleted, additional crops cannot be grown unless fertilizer is applied to the soil. All other things being equal, if vegetables are grown in soil that has had fertilizer applied rather than being grown in non-fertilized soil, they are more vulnerable to pests and, as a consequence, must be treated with larger amounts of pesticides. The more pesticides used on vegetables, the greater the health risks to humans from eating those vegetables.

Suppose there were some vegetables that were grown in soil to which fertilizer had never been applied. On the basis of the passage, which one of the following would have to be true regarding those vegetables?

(A) The soil in which the vegetables were grown may have been completely depleted of nutrients because of an earlier failure to rotate crops.

(B) It is not possible that the vegetables were grown in soil in which crops had been rotated.

(C) The vegetables were grown in soil that had not been completely depleted of nutrients but not necessarily soil in which crops had been rotated.

(D) Whatever the health risks to humans from eating the vegetables, these risks would not be attributable to the use of pesticides on them.

(E) The health risks to humans from eating the vegetables were no less than the health risks to humans from eating the same kinds of vegetables treated with pesticides.

8. Criminologist: Increasing the current prison term for robbery will result in no significant effect in discouraging people from committing robbery.

Each of the following, if true, supports the criminologist's claim EXCEPT:

(A) Many people who rob are motivated primarily by thrill-seeking and risk-taking.

(B) An increase in the prison term for embezzlement did not change the rate at which that crime was committed.

(C) Prison terms for robbery have generally decreased in length recently.

(D) Most people committing robbery believe that they will not get caught.

(E) Most people committing robbery have no idea what the average sentence for robbery is.

9. Activist: As electronic monitoring of employees grows more commonplace and invasive, we hear more and more attempted justifications of this practice by employers. Surveillance, they explain, keeps employees honest, efficient, and polite to customers. Such explanations are obviously self-serving, and so should not be taken to justify these unwarranted invasions of privacy.

A questionable technique used in the activist's argument is to

(A) attack an argument different from that actually offered by the employers

(B) presume that employees are never dishonest, inefficient, or rude

(C) insist that modern business practices meet moral standards far higher than those accepted in the past

(D) attack employers' motives instead of addressing their arguments

(E) make a generalization based on a sample that there is reason to believe is biased

10. When students receive negative criticism generated by computer programs, they are less likely to respond positively than when the critic is a human. Since the acceptance of criticism requires that one respond positively to it, students are more likely to learn from criticism by humans than from criticism by computers.

Which one of the following is an assumption on which the argument depends?

(A) Students are more likely to learn from criticism that they accept than from criticism they do not accept.

(B) Unlike human critics, computers are incapable of showing compassion.

(C) Students always know whether their critics are computers or humans.

(D) Criticism generated by computers is likely to be less favorable than that produced by human critics in response to the same work.

(E) Criticism generated by computers is likely to be no more or less favorable than that produced by human critics in response to the same work.

GO ON TO THE NEXT PAGE.

11. After examining the options, the budget committee discovered that QI's office-phone system would be inexpensive enough to be within the cost limit that had been set for the committee. However, Corelink's system must also be inexpensive enough to be within the limit, since it is even less expensive than QI's system.

The reasoning in the argument above is most closely paralleled by that in which one of the following?

(A) Marissa is just tall enough that she can touch the ceiling when she jumps as high as she can, and since Jeff is taller than Marissa, he too must be able to touch the ceiling when he jumps.

(B) By reducing the number of cigarettes she smoked per day, Kate was able to run five miles, and since Lana smokes fewer cigarettes per day than Kate now does, she too must be able to run five miles.

(C) John's blood-alcohol level was far above the legal limit for driving, so even if it turns out that Paul's blood-alcohol level was lower than John's, it too must have been above the legal limit.

(D) This chocolate is not quite dark enough for it to be the kind that Luis really likes, but that chocolate over there is darker, so it might be just right.

(E) Health Dairy's sharp cheddar cheese is low enough in fat to meet the labeling standard for "low fat" cheddar cheese, and since its mild cheddar cheese is even lower in fat, it too must meet the labeling standard.

12. Essayist: People once believed that Earth was at the center of the universe, and that, therefore, Earth and its inhabitants were important. We now know that Earth revolves around a star at the outskirts of a spiral arm of one of countless galaxies. Therefore, people's old belief that Earth and its inhabitants were important was false.

A flaw in the essayist's argument is that the argument

(A) presumes, without providing justification, that only true statements can have good reasons to be believed

(B) neglects to consider that a statement that was believed for questionable reasons may nevertheless have been true

(C) fails to consider that there can be no reason for disbelieving a true statement

(D) overlooks the fact that people's perception of their importance changed from century to century

(E) neglects the fact that people's perception of their importance varies from culture to culture

13. Davis: The only relevant factor in determining appropriate compensation for property damage or theft is the value the property loses due to damage or the value of the property stolen; the harm to the victim is directly proportional to the pertinent value.

Higuchi: I disagree. More than one factor must be considered: A victim who recovers the use of personal property after two years is owed more than a victim who recovers its use after only one year.

Davis's and Higuchi's statements most strongly support the view that they would disagree with each other about which one of the following?

(A) It is possible to consistently and reliably determine the amount of compensation owed to someone whose property was damaged or stolen.

(B) Some victims are owed increased compensation because of the greater dollar value of the damage done to their property.

(C) Victims who are deprived of their property are owed compensation in proportion to the harm they have suffered.

(D) Some victims are owed increased compensation because of the greater amount of time they are deprived of the use of their property.

(E) The compensation owed to victims should be determined on a case-by-case basis rather than by some general rule.

14. Resident: Residents of this locale should not consider their loss of farming as a way of life to be a tragedy. When this area was a rural area it was economically depressed, but it is now a growing bastion of high-tech industry with high-wage jobs, and supports over 20 times the number of jobs it did then.

Which one of the following, if true, does the most to justify the conclusion of the resident's argument?

(A) Farming is becoming increasingly efficient, with the result that fewer farms are required to produce the same amount of food.

(B) The development of high-tech industry is more valuable to national security than is farming.

(C) Residents of this locale do not value a rural way of life more than they value economic prosperity.

(D) Many residents of this locale have annual incomes that are twice what they were when the locale was primarily agricultural.

(E) The loss of a family farm is often perceived as tragic even when no financial hardship results.

GO ON TO THE NEXT PAGE.

15. Kendrick: Governments that try to prevent cigarettes from being advertised are justified in doing so, since such advertisements encourage people to engage in an unhealthy practice. But cigarette advertisements should remain legal since advertisements for fatty foods are legal, even though those advertisements also encourage people to engage in unhealthy practices.

Which one of the following, if true, most helps to resolve the apparent conflict between Kendrick's statements?

(A) Any advertisement that encourages people to engage in an unhealthy practice should be made illegal, even though the legality of some such advertisements is currently uncontroversial.

(B) The advertisement of fattening foods, unlike that of cigarettes, should not be prevented, because fattening foods, unlike cigarettes, are not addictive.

(C) Most advertisements should be legal, although advertisers are always morally responsible for ensuring that their advertisements do not encourage people to engage in unhealthy practices.

(D) Governments should try to prevent the advertisement of cigarettes by means of financial disincentives rather than by legal prohibition.

(E) Governments should place restrictions on cigarette advertisements so as to keep them from encouraging people to engage in unhealthy practices, but should not try to prevent such advertisements.

16. Environmentalist: Many people prefer to live in regions of natural beauty. Such regions often experience an influx of new residents, and a growing population encourages businesses to relocate to those regions. Thus, governmentally mandated environmental protection in regions of natural beauty can help those regions' economies overall, even if such protection harms some older local industries.

Which one of the following is an assumption on which the environmentalist's argument depends?

(A) Regions of natural beauty typically are beautiful enough to attract new residents only until governmentally mandated environmental protection that damages local industries is imposed.

(B) The economies of most regions of natural beauty are not based primarily on local industries that would be harmed by governmentally mandated environmental protection.

(C) If governmentally mandated environmental protection helps a region's economy, it does so primarily by encouraging people to move into that region.

(D) Voluntary environmental protection usually does not help a region's economy to the degree that governmentally mandated protection does.

(E) A factor harmful to some older local industries in a region need not discourage other businesses from relocating to that region.

GO ON TO THE NEXT PAGE.

17. No small countries and no countries in the southern hemisphere have permanent seats on the United Nations Security Council. Each of the five countries with a permanent seat on the Security Council is in favor of increased international peacekeeping efforts and a greater role for the United Nations in moderating regional disputes. However, some countries that are in favor of increased international peacekeeping efforts are firmly against increased spending on refugees by the United Nations.

If the statements above are true, which one of the following must also be true?

(A) Some small countries do not want the United Nations to increase its spending on refugees.

(B) Some countries in the southern hemisphere are not in favor of increased international peacekeeping efforts.

(C) Some countries that have permanent seats on the United Nations Security Council are against increased spending on refugees by the United Nations.

(D) Some small countries are in favor of a greater role for the United Nations in moderating regional disputes.

(E) Some countries that are in favor of a greater role for the United Nations in moderating regional disputes are not located in the southern hemisphere.

18. Editorial: It is clear that what is called "health education" is usually propaganda rather than education. Propaganda and education are never the same thing. The former is nothing but an attempt to influence behavior through the repetition of simplistic slogans, whereas the latter never involves such a method. Though education does attempt to influence behavior, it does so by offering information in all its complexity, leaving it up to the individual to decide how to act on that information. Sadly, however, propaganda is much more successful than education.

The conclusion drawn by the editorial follows logically if it is assumed that what is called "health education" usually

(A) does not leave it up to the individual to decide how to act on information

(B) does not offer information in all its complexity

(C) does not involve the repetition of simplistic slogans

(D) attempts to influence behavior solely by repeating simplistic slogans

(E) is very successful in influencing people's behavior

19. Marc: The fact that the people of our country look back on the past with a great deal of nostalgia demonstrates that they regret the recent revolution.

Robert: They are not nostalgic for the recent past, but for the distant past, which the prerevolutionary regime despised; this indicates that although they are troubled, they do not regret the revolution.

Their dialogue provides the most support for the claim that Marc and Robert agree that the people of their country

(A) tend to underrate past problems when the country faces troubling times

(B) are looking to the past for solutions to the country's current problems

(C) are likely to repeat former mistakes if they look to the country's past for solutions to current problems

(D) are concerned about the country's current situation and this is evidenced by their nostalgia

(E) tend to be most nostalgic for the things that are the farthest in their past

20. Social critic: One of the most important ways in which a society socializes children is by making them feel ashamed of their immoral behavior. But in many people this shame results in deep feelings of guilt and self-loathing that can be a severe hardship. Thus, moral socialization has had a net effect of increasing the total amount of suffering.

The social critic's argument is most vulnerable to criticism on the grounds that it

(A) overlooks the possibility that the purported source of a problem could be modified to avoid that problem without being eliminated altogether

(B) fails to address adequately the possibility that one phenomenon may causally contribute to the occurrence of another, even though the two phenomena do not always occur together

(C) presumes, without providing justification, that a phenomenon that supposedly increases the total amount of suffering in a society should therefore be changed or eliminated, regardless of its beneficial consequences

(D) takes for granted that a behavior that sometimes leads to a certain phenomenon cannot also significantly reduce the overall occurrence of that phenomenon

(E) presumes, without providing justification, that if many people have a negative psychological reaction to a phenomenon, then no one can have a positive reaction to that phenomenon

GO ON TO THE NEXT PAGE.

21. Curator: A magazine recently ran a very misleading story on the reaction of local residents to our controversial art exhibit. They quoted the responses of three residents, all of whom expressed a sense of moral outrage. These quotations were intended to suggest that most local residents oppose the exhibit; the story failed to mention, however, the fact that the three residents are all close friends.

Which one of the following principles most helps to justify the curator's argumentation?

(A) It is misleading to present the opinions of people with no special expertise on a subject as though they were experts.

(B) It is misleading to present the opinions of people on only one side of an issue when the population is likely to be evenly divided on that issue.

(C) It is misleading to present the opinions of a few people as evidence of what the majority thinks unless the opinions they express are widely held.

(D) It is misleading to present testimony from close friends and thereby imply that they must agree with each other.

(E) It is misleading to present the opinions of a potentially nonrepresentative sample of people as if they represent public opinion.

22. All parrots can learn to speak a few words and phrases. Not all parrots have equally pleasant dispositions, though some of those native to Australia can be counted on for a sweet temper. Almost any parrot, however, will show tremendous affection for an owner who raised the bird from a chick by hand-feeding it.

If the statements above are true, then which one of the following must be true?

(A) Some parrots that can learn to speak are sweet tempered.

(B) If a parrot is not native to Australia, then it will be sweet tempered only if it is hand-fed as a chick.

(C) The sweetest-tempered parrots are those native to Australia.

(D) Australia is the only place where one can find birds that can both learn to speak and be relied on for a sweet temper.

(E) All species of pet birds that are native to Australia can be counted on for a sweet temper.

23. Toxicologist: Recent research has shown that dioxin causes cancer in rats. Although similar research has never been done on humans, and probably never will be, the use of dioxin should be completely banned.

That dioxin causes cancer in rats figures in the argument in which one of the following ways?

(A) It is presented as the hazard that the researcher is concerned with preventing.

(B) It is presented as a benefit of not acting on the recommendation in the conclusion.

(C) It is presented as evidence for the claim that similar research will never be done on humans.

(D) It is presented as a finding that motivates the course of action advocated in the conclusion.

(E) It is presented as evidence for the claim that similar research has never been done on humans.

GO ON TO THE NEXT PAGE.

24. Politician: The law should not require people to wear seat belts in cars. People are allowed to ride motorcycles without seat belts, and riding a motorcycle even while wearing a seat belt would be more dangerous than riding in a car without wearing one.

Which one of the following arguments is most similar in its flawed reasoning to the politician's argument?

(A) Marielle and Pat should allow their children to have snacks between meals. They currently allow their children to have a large dessert after dinner, and allowing them to have snacks between meals instead would improve their nutrition.

(B) Any corporation should allow its employees to take time off when they are under too much stress to concentrate on their work. Some corporations allow any employee with a bad cold to take time off, and even a healthy employee under stress may be less productive than an unstressed employee with a bad cold.

(C) Amusement parks should allow people to stand while riding roller coasters. It is legal for people to stand at the edges of high cliffs, and even sitting at the edge of a high cliff is more likely to result in a fatal fall than standing while riding a roller coaster.

(D) It should be illegal for anyone to smoke in a public place, for it certainly should be illegal to pollute public drinking water, and smoking even in the privacy of one's home can be more harmful to the health of others than polluting their water would be.

(E) Vanessa should be allowed to let her dog run around in the park without a leash. She already lets the dog roam around her yard without a leash, and the park differs from her yard only in size.

25. Burying beetles do whatever they can to minimize the size of their competitors' broods without adversely affecting their own. This is why they routinely destroy each other's eggs when two or more beetles inhabit the same breeding location. Yet, after the eggs hatch, the adults treat all of the larvae equally, sharing in the care of the entire population.

Which one of the following, if true, most helps to explain burying beetles' apparently contradictory behavior?

(A) Burying beetles whose eggs hatch before their competitors' are more likely to have large broods than are burying beetles whose eggs hatch later.

(B) The cooperation among adult burying beetles ensures that the greatest possible number of larvae survive.

(C) Burying beetles are unable to discriminate between their own larvae and the larvae of other burying beetles.

(D) Many of the natural enemies of burying beetles can be repelled only if burying beetles cooperate in defending the breeding site.

(E) Most breeding sites for burying beetles can accommodate only a limited number of larvae.

S T O P

IF YOU FINISH BEFORE TIME IS CALLED, YOU MAY CHECK YOUR WORK ON THIS SECTION ONLY.
DO NOT WORK ON ANY OTHER SECTION IN THE TEST.

SECTION III
Time—35 minutes
26 Questions

Directions: The questions in this section are based on the reasoning contained in brief statements or passages. For some questions, more than one of the choices could conceivably answer the question. However, you are to choose the best answer; that is, the response that most accurately and completely answers the question. You should not make assumptions that are by commonsense standards implausible, superfluous, or incompatible with the passage. After you have chosen the best answer, blacken the corresponding space on your answer sheet.

1. The development of new inventions is promoted by the granting of patent rights, which restrict the right of anyone but the patent holders to profit from these inventions for a specified period. Without patent rights, anyone could simply copy another's invention; consequently, inventors would have no financial incentive for investing the time and energy required to develop new products. Thus, it is important to continue to grant patent rights, or else no one will engage in original development and consequently no new inventions will be forthcoming.

   Which one of the following is an assumption on which the argument depends?

   (A) Financial reward is the only incentive that will be effective in motivating people to develop new inventions.

   (B) When an inventor sells patent rights to a manufacturer, the manufacturer makes less total profit on the invention than the inventor does.

   (C) Any costs incurred by a typical inventor in applying for patent rights are insignificant in comparison to the financial benefit of holding the patent rights.

   (D) Patent rights should be granted only if an inventor's product is not similar to another invention already covered by patent rights.

   (E) The length of a patent right is usually proportional to the costs involved in inventing the product.

2. The Fenwicks returned home from a trip to find two broken bottles on their kitchen floor. There was no sign of forced entry and nothing in the house appeared to have been taken. Although the Fenwicks have a pet cat that had free run of the house while they were away, the Fenwicks hypothesized that they had left a back door unlocked and that neighborhood children had entered through it, attempted to raid the kitchen, and left after breaking the bottles.

   Each of the following, if true, helps to support the Fenwicks' hypothesis EXCEPT:

   (A) A neighbor thought he had seen the Fenwicks' back door closing while the Fenwicks were away.

   (B) When the Fenwicks returned home, they found children's footprints on the back porch that had not been there before their trip.

   (C) The two bottles that the Fenwicks found broken on their kitchen floor had been in the refrigerator when the Fenwicks left on vacation.

   (D) There have been several recent burglaries in the Fenwicks' neighborhood in which neighborhood children were suspected.

   (E) The Fenwicks returned home from their trip later than they had planned.

GO ON TO THE NEXT PAGE.

3. In an experiment, tennis players who were told that their performance would be used to assess only the quality of their rackets performed much better than an equally skilled group of tennis players who were told that their tennis-playing talent would be measured.

The situation described above most closely conforms to which one of the following propositions?

(A) People do less well on a task if they have been told that they will be closely watched while doing it.

(B) People execute a task more proficiently when they do not believe their abilities are being judged.

(C) People perform a task more proficiently when they have confidence in their abilities.

(D) People who assess their talents accurately generally perform near their actual level of proficiency.

(E) People who think that a superior performance will please those who are testing them generally try harder.

4. Sydonie: Parents differ in their beliefs about the rules to which their children should be subject. So any disciplinary structure in schools is bound to create resentment because it will contradict some parental approaches to raising children.

Stephanie: Your conclusion is incorrect; educational research shows that when parents list the things that they most want their children's schools to provide, good discipline is always high on the list.

Stephanie's argument is most vulnerable to criticism on the grounds that

(A) it focuses on educational research rather than educational practice

(B) it addresses a more general issue than that addressed in Sydonie's argument

(C) it does not counter Sydonie's suggestion that parents have diverse ideas of what constitutes good discipline

(D) the phrase "high on the list" is not specific enough to give useful information about what parents desire from a school

(E) it fails to discuss educators' attitudes toward discipline in schools

5. Art critic: The aesthetic value of a work of art lies in its ability to impart a stimulating character to the audience's experience of the work.

Which one of the following judgments most closely conforms with the principle cited above?

(A) This painting is aesthetically deficient because it is an exact copy of a painting done 30 years ago.

(B) This symphony is beautiful because, even though it does not excite the audience, it is competently performed.

(C) This sculpted four-inch cube is beautiful because it is carved from material which, although much like marble, is very rare.

(D) This painting is aesthetically valuable because it was painted by a highly controversial artist.

(E) This poem is aesthetically deficient because it has little impact on its audience.

6. Antonia: The stock market is the best place to invest your money these days; although it is often volatile, it provides the opportunity to make a large profit quickly.

Maria: I agree that the stock market provides the opportunity to make large profits quickly, but one is just as likely to take a huge loss. I think it is better to invest in savings bonds, which provide a constant, reliable income over many years.

Antonia's and Maria's statements provide the most support for holding that they disagree about whether

(A) the stock market is often volatile but provides the opportunity to make a large profit quickly

(B) savings bonds can provide a large return on one's investment

(C) the stock market provides the opportunity for an investor to make a constant, reliable income over many years

(D) it is safer to invest in savings bonds than to invest in the stock market

(E) it is preferable to pick an investment offering a reliable income over a riskier opportunity to make a large profit quickly

GO ON TO THE NEXT PAGE.

7. Very little is known about prehistoric hominid cave dwellers. However, a recent study of skeletons of these hominids has revealed an important clue about their daily activities: skeletal fractures present are most like the type and distribution of fractures sustained by rodeo riders. Therefore, it is likely that these cave dwellers engaged in activities similar to rodeo riders—chasing and tackling animals.

Which one of the following principles, if valid, most helps to justify the argumentation above?

(A) The primary source of clues about the lives of prehistoric hominids is their skeletal remains.
(B) The most important aspect of prehistoric life to be studied is how food was obtained.
(C) If direct evidence as to the cause of a phenomenon is available, then indirect evidence should not be sought.
(D) If there is a similarity between two effects, then there is probably a similarity between their causes.
(E) The frequency with which a hazardous activity is performed is proportional to the frequency of injuries resulting from that activity.

8. Studies suggest that, for the vast majority of people who have normal blood pressure, any amount of sodium greater than that required by the body is simply excreted and does not significantly raise blood pressure. So only persons who have high blood pressure and whose bodies are incapable of safely processing excess sodium need to restrict their sodium intake.

Which one of the following, if true, would most seriously weaken the argument?

(A) High blood pressure is more harmful than was previously believed.
(B) High blood pressure is sometimes exacerbated by intake of more sodium than the body requires.
(C) Excess sodium intake over time often destroys the body's ability to process excess sodium.
(D) Every human being has a physiological need for at least some sodium.
(E) Any sodium not used by the body will increase bloodpressure unless it is excreted.

9. Most lecturers who are effective teachers are eccentric, but some noneccentric lecturers are very effective teachers. In addition, every effective teacher is a good communicator.

Which one of the following statements follows logically from the statements above?

(A) Some good communicators are eccentric.
(B) All good communicators are effective teachers.
(C) Some lecturers who are not effective teachers are not eccentric.
(D) Most lecturers who are good communicators are eccentric.
(E) Some noneccentric lecturers are effective teachers but are not good communicators.

10. Recently, photons and neutrinos emitted by a distant supernova, an explosion of a star, reached Earth at virtually the same time. This finding supports Einstein's claim that gravity is a property of space itself, in the sense that a body exerts gravitational pull by curving the space around it. The simultaneous arrival of the photons and neutrinos is evidence that the space through which they traveled was curved.

Which one of the following, if true, would most strengthen the reasoning above?

(A) Einstein predicted that photons and neutrinos emitted by any one supernova would reach Earth simultaneously.
(B) If gravity is not a property of space itself, then photons and neutrinos emitted simultaneously by a distant event will reach Earth at different times.
(C) Photons and neutrinos emitted by distant events would be undetectable on Earth if Einstein's claim that gravity is a property of space itself were correct.
(D) Photons and neutrinos were the only kinds of particles that reached Earth from the supernova.
(E) Prior to the simultaneous arrival of photons and neutrinos from the supernova, there was no empirical evidence for Einstein's claim that gravity is a property of space itself.

GO ON TO THE NEXT PAGE.

11. Geneticist: Billions of dollars are spent each year on high-profile experiments that attempt to link particular human genes with particular personality traits. Though such experiments seem to promise a new understanding of human nature, they have few practical consequences. Meanwhile, more mundane and practical genetic projects—for example, those that look for natural ways to make edible plants hardier or more nutritious— are grossly underfunded. Thus, funding for human gene research should be reduced while funding for other genetic research should be increased.

Which one of the following principles, if valid, most helps to justify the geneticist's reasoning?

(A) Experiments that have the potential to help the whole human race are more worthwhile than those that help only a small number of people.

(B) Experiments that focus on the genetics of plants are more practical than those that focus on the genetics of human nature.

(C) Experiments that help prevent malnutrition are more worthwhile than those that help prevent merely undesirable personality traits.

(D) Experiments that have modest but practical goals are more worthwhile than those that have impressive goals but few practical consequences.

(E) Experiments that get little media attention and are not widely supported by the public are more valuable than are those that get much media coverage and have wide public support.

12. Some argue that because attaining governmental power in democracies requires building majority coalitions, it is a necessary evil that policymakers do not adhere rigorously to principle when dealing with important issues, but rather shift policies as they try to please different constituents at different times. But it is precisely this behavior that allows a democracy to adapt more easily to serve public interests, and thus it is more a benefit than an evil.

Which one of the following is an assumption required by the argument?

(A) Government policymakers cannot retain power if they ignore any of the various factions of their original winning coalition.

(B) Democracies are more likely than nondemocratic forms of government to have policymakers who understand the complexity of governmental issues.

(C) In the formulation of government policy, the advantage conferred by adaptability to diverse or fluctuating public interests outweighs the detriment associated with a lack of strict fidelity to principle.

(D) In dealing with an important issue, policymakers in a democracy appeal to a principle in dealing with an issue only when that principle has majority support.

(E) Democracies appear to be more flexible than nondemocratic forms of government, but are not actually so.

GO ON TO THE NEXT PAGE.

13. Up until about 2 billion years ago, the sun was 30 percent dimmer than it is now. If the sun were that dim now, our oceans would be completely frozen. According to fossil evidence, however, life and liquid water were both present as early as 3.8 billion years ago.

Which one of the following, if true, most helps to resolve the apparent discrepancy described above?

(A)   Our atmosphere currently holds in significantly less heat than it did 3.8 billion years ago.

(B)   The liquid water present 3.8 billion years ago later froze, only to melt again about 2 billion years ago.

(C)   A significant source of heat other than the sun contributed to the melting of ice sheets approximately 2 billion years ago.

(D)   Evidence suggests that certain regions of ocean remained frozen until much more recently than 2 billion years ago.

(E)   When large portions of the globe are ice-covered, more of the sun's heat is reflected and not absorbed by the earth than when only the poles are ice-covered.

14.   Social critic: The operas composed by Bizet and Verdi are nineteenth-century European creations, reflecting the attitudes and values in France and Italy at the end of that century. Several recent studies impugn these operas on the grounds that they reinforce in our society many stereotypes about women. But only a small minority of contemporary North Americans, namely opera lovers, have had any significant exposure to these works.

Which one of the following most accurately expresses the conclusion that the social critic's argument, as it is stated above, is structured to establish?

(A)   Bizet and Verdi constructed images of women that have significantly influenced contemporary stereotypes.

(B)   Nineteenth-century French and Italian images of women are quite different from contemporary North American images of women.

(C)   The operas of Bizet and Verdi have not significantly contributed to stereotypical images of women in contemporary North America.

(D)   Opera is not an important factor shaping social attitudes in contemporary North America.

(E)   People cannot be influenced by things they are not directly exposed to.

15. In 1975, a province reduced its personal income tax rate by 2 percent for most taxpayers. In 1976, the personal income tax rate for those taxpayers was again reduced by 2 percent. Despite the decreases in the personal income tax rate, the total amount of money collected from personal income taxes remained constant from 1974 to 1975 and rose substantially in 1976.

Each of the following, if true, could help to resolve the apparent discrepancy described above EXCEPT:

(A)   The years 1975 and 1976 were ones in which the province's economy was especially prosperous.

(B)   The definition of "personal income" used by the province was widened during 1975 to include income received from personal investments.

(C)   The personal income tax rate for the wealthiest individuals in the province rose during 1975 and 1976.

(D)   The province's total revenue from all taxes increased during both 1975 and 1976.

(E)   A large number of people from other provinces moved to the province during 1975 and 1976.

16. Everything that is commonplace and ordinary fails to catch our attention, so there are things that fail to catch our attention but that are miracles of nature.

The conclusion of the argument follows logically if which one of the following is assumed?

(A)   Only miracles of nature fail to be ordinary and commonplace.

(B)   Some things that are ordinary and commonplace are miracles of nature.

(C)   Some things that are commonplace and ordinary fail to catch our attention.

(D)   Everything that fails to catch our attention is commonplace and ordinary.

(E)   Only extraordinary or unusual things catch our attention.

GO ON TO THE NEXT PAGE.

17. If one of the effects of a genetic mutation makes a substantial contribution to the survival of the species, then, and only then, will that mutation be favored in natural selection. This process is subject to one proviso, namely that the traits that were not favored, yet were carried along by a trait that was favored, must not be so negative as to annul the benefits of having the new, favored trait.

If the statements above are true, each of the following could be true EXCEPT:

(A)   A species possesses a trait whose effects are all neutral for the survival of that species.
(B)   All the effects of some genetic mutations contribute substantially to the survival of a species.
(C)   A species possesses a trait that reduces the species' survival potential.
(D)   A genetic mutation that carries along several negative traits is favored in natural selection.
(E)   A genetic mutation whose effects are all neutral to a species is favored in natural selection.

18. In a highly publicized kidnapping case in Ontario, the judge barred all media and spectators from the courtroom. Her decision was based on the judgment that the public interest would not be served by allowing spectators. A local citizen argued, "They pleaded with the public to help find the victim; they pleaded with the public to provide tips; they aroused the public interest, then they claimed that allowing us to attend would not serve the public interest. These actions are inconsistent."

The reasoning in the local citizen's argument is flawed because this argument

(A)   generalizes from an atypical case
(B)   trades on an ambiguity with respect to the term "public interest"
(C)   overlooks the fact that the judge might not be the one who made the plea to the public for help
(D)   attempts to support its conclusion by making sensationalistic appeals
(E)   presumes that the public's right to know is obviously more important than the defendant's right to a fair trial

19. Today's farmers plant only a handful of different strains of a given crop. Crops lack the diversity that they had only a few generations ago. Hence, a disease that strikes only a few strains of crops, and that would have had only minor impact on the food supply in the past, would devastate it today.

Which one of the following, if true, would most weaken the argument?

(A)   In the past, crop diseases would often devastate food supplies throughout entire regions.
(B)   Affected crops can quickly be replaced from seed banks that store many strains of those crops.
(C)   Some of the less popular seed strains that were used in the past were more resistant to many diseases than are the strains popular today.
(D)   Humans today have more variety in their diets than in the past, but still rely heavily on cereal crops like rice and wheat.
(E)   Today's crops are much less vulnerable to damage from insects or encroachment by weeds than were crops of a few generations ago.

20.   Interviewer: A certain company released a model of computer whose microprocessor design was flawed, making that computer liable to process information incorrectly. How did this happen?

Industry spokesperson: Given the huge number of circuits in the microprocessor of any modern computer, not every circuit can be manually checked before a computer model that contains the microprocessor is released.

Interviewer: Then what guarantee do we have that new microprocessors will not be similarly flawed?

Industry spokesperson: There is no chance of further microprocessor design flaws, since all microprocessors are now entirely computer designed.

The industry spokesperson's argument is most vulnerable to criticism on the grounds that it

(A)   presumes, without providing justification, that the microprocessor quality-control procedures of the company mentioned are not representative of those followed throughout the industry
(B)   ignores the possibility that a microprocessor can have a flaw other than a design flaw
(C)   overlooks the possibility that a new computer model is liable to malfunction for reasons other than a microprocessor flaw
(D)   treats a single instance of a microprocessor design flaw as evidence that there will be many such flaws
(E)   takes for granted, despite evidence to the contrary, that some computers are not liable to error

GO ON TO THE NEXT PAGE.

21. Each of the many people who participated in the town's annual spring cleanup received a community recognition certificate. Because the spring cleanup took place at the same time as the downtown arts fair, we know that there are at least some spring cleanup participants who are not active in the town's artistic circles.

If the statements above are true, which one of the following must be true?

(A) Some of the persons who are active in the town's artistic circles received community recognition certificates.
(B) Not all of those who received community recognition certificates are active in the town's artistic circles.
(C) No participants in the downtown arts fair received community recognition certificates.
(D) No person who received a community recognition certificate has not participated in the spring cleanup.
(E) Persons who are active in the town's artistic circles are not concerned with the town's environment.

22. Taking advanced mathematics courses should increase a student's grade point average, for, as numerous studies have shown, students who have taken one or more advanced mathematics courses are far more likely to have high grade point averages than students who have not taken such courses.

The flawed pattern of reasoning in the argument above is most similar to that in which one of the following?

(A) Fur color is in large measure hereditary, for, as many studies have shown, black cats are more likely than others to have black kittens, and orange cats are more likely to have orange kittens.
(B) Water can cause intoxication. After all, imbibing scotch and water, whiskey and water, bourbon and water, gin and water, and vodka and water all cause intoxication.
(C) Eating a diet consisting primarily of fats and carbohydrates may cause weight gain in some people. Studies have shown that many overweight people eat such diets.
(D) Buying running shoes should increase the frequency with which a person exercises, since those who buy two or more pairs of running shoes each year tend to exercise more often than those who buy at most one pair.
(E) Reading to children at an early age should inspire them to read on their own later, since studies have shown that children who have not been read to are less likely to develop an interest in reading than children who have been read to.

23. Each of many different human hormones can by itself raise the concentration of glucose in the blood. The reason for this is probably a metabolic quirk of the brain. To see this, consider that although most human cells can produce energy from fats and proteins, brain cells can use only glucose. Thus, if blood glucose levels fall too low, brain cells will rapidly starve, leading to unconsciousness and death.

Which one of the following most accurately expresses the main conclusion of the argument above?

(A) Each of many different human hormones can by itself raise blood glucose levels.
(B) The reason that many different hormones can each independently raise blood glucose levels is probably a metabolic quirk of the brain.
(C) Although most human cells can produce energy from fats and proteins, brain cells can produce energy only from glucose.
(D) If blood glucose levels fall too low, then brain cells starve, resulting in loss of consciousness and death.
(E) The reason brain cells starve if deprived of glucose is that they can produce energy only from glucose.

24. Human resources director: While only some recent university graduates consider work environment an important factor in choosing a job, they all consider salary an important factor. Further, whereas the only workers who consider stress level an important factor in choosing a job are a few veteran employees, every recent university graduate considers vacation policy an important factor.

If all of the statements of the human resources director are true, then which one of the following must be true?

(A) All people who consider work environment an important factor in choosing a job also consider salary an important factor.
(B) At least some people who consider work environment an important factor in choosing a job consider vacation policy an important factor as well.
(C) At least some veteran employees do not consider work environment an important factor in choosing a job.
(D) All people who consider vacation policy an important factor in choosing a job also consider salary an important factor.
(E) No one for whom salary is an important factor in choosing a job also considers stress level an important factor.

GO ON TO THE NEXT PAGE.

25. Wealth is not a good thing, for good things cause no harm at all, yet wealth is often harmful to people.

Which one of the following arguments is most similar in its pattern of reasoning to the argument above?

(A) Alex loves to golf, and no one in the chess club loves to golf. It follows that Alex is not in the chess club.

(B) Isabella must be a contented baby. She smiles a great deal and hardly ever cries, like all happy people.

(C) Growth in industry is not a good thing for our town. Although the economy might improve, the pollution would be unbearable.

(D) Sarah's dog is not a dachshund, for he hunts very well, and most dachshunds hunt poorly.

(E) There is usually more traffic at this time of day, unless it is a holiday. But since today is not a holiday, it is surprising that there is so little traffic.

26. In the aftermath of the Cold War, international relations between Cold War allies became more difficult. Leaders of previously allied nations were required to conduct tactful economic negotiations in order not to arouse tensions that had previously been overlooked.

The situation described above conforms most closely to which one of the following propositions?

(A) International economic competition is a greater cause of tension than is international military competition.

(B) Bonds between allies are stronger when they derive from fear of a common enemy than when they derive from common economic goals.

(C) When there is a military commitment between countries, fundamental agreement between them on economic matters is more easily reached.

(D) Economic matters are considered unimportant during periods of actual or threatened war.

(E) A common enemy contributes to a strengthened bond between nations, enabling them to ignore economic tensions that would otherwise be problematic.

S T O P

IF YOU FINISH BEFORE TIME IS CALLED, YOU MAY CHECK YOUR WORK ON THIS SECTION ONLY.
DO NOT WORK ON ANY OTHER SECTION IN THE TEST.

Directions: Each group of questions in this section is based on a set of conditions. In answering some of the questions, it may be useful to draw a rough diagram. Choose the response that most accurately and completely answers each question and blacken the corresponding space on your answer sheet.

Questions 1–5

There are exactly six groups in this year's Civic Parade: firefighters, gymnasts, jugglers, musicians, puppeteers, and veterans. Each group marches as a unit; the groups are ordered from first, at the front of the parade, to sixth, at the back. The following conditions apply:

At least two groups march behind the puppeteers but ahead of the musicians.

Exactly one group marches behind the firefighters but ahead of the veterans.

The gymnasts are the first, third, or fifth group.

1. Which one of the following could be an accurate list of the groups in the Civic Parade in order from first to last?

    (A)   firefighters, puppeteers, veterans, musicians, gymnasts, jugglers
    (B)   gymnasts, puppeteers, jugglers, musicians, firefighters, veterans
    (C)   veterans, puppeteers, firefighters, gymnasts, jugglers, musicians
    (D)   jugglers, puppeteers, gymnasts, firefighters, musicians, veterans
    (E)   musicians, veterans, jugglers, firefighters, gymnasts, puppeteers

2. If the gymnasts march immediately ahead of the veterans, then which one of the following could be the fourth group?

    (A)   gymnasts
    (B)   jugglers
    (C)   musicians
    (D)   puppeteers
    (E)   veterans

3. If the veterans march immediately behind the puppeteers, then which one of the following could be the second group?

    (A)   firefighters
    (B)   gymnasts
    (C)   jugglers
    (D)   musicians
    (E)   veterans

4. If the jugglers are the fifth group, then which one of the following must be true?

    (A)   The puppeteers are the first group.
    (B)   The firefighters are the first group.
    (C)   The veterans are the second group.
    (D)   The gymnasts are the third group.
    (E)   The musicians are the sixth group.

5. Which one of the following groups CANNOT march immediately behind the gymnasts?

    (A)   firefighters
    (B)   jugglers
    (C)   musicians
    (D)   puppeteers
    (E)   veterans

GO ON TO THE NEXT PAGE.

Questions 6-12

A rowing team uses a boat with exactly six seats arranged in single file and numbered sequentially 1 through 6, from the front of the boat to the back. Six athletes—Lee, Miller, Ovitz, Singh, Valerio, and Zita—each row at exactly one of the seats, The following restrictions must apply:

Miller rows closer to the front than Singh.

Singh rows closer to the front than both Lee and Valerio.

Valerio and Zita each row closer to the front than Ovitz.

6. Which one of the following could be an accurate matching of athletes to seats?

(A) Miller: seat 1; Valerio: seat 5; Lee: seat 6
(B) Singh: seat 3; Valerio: seat 4; Zita: seat 5
(C) Miller: seat 1; Valerio: seat 3; Lee: seat 6
(D) Lee: seat 3; Valerio: seat 4; Ovitz: seat 5
(E) Zita: seat 2; Valerio: seat 3; Ovitz: seat 6

7. If Valerio rows at seat 5, then which one of the following must be true?

(A) Miller rows at seat 1.
(B) Singh rows at seat 2.
(C) Zita rows at seat 3.
(D) Lee rows at seat 4.
(E) Ovitz rows at seat 6.

8. If Lee rows at seat 3, then each of the following could be true EXCEPT:

(A) Zita rows immediately behind Valerio.
(B) Ovitz rows immediately behind Valerio.
(C) Ovitz rows immediately behind Zita.
(D) Valerio rows immediately behind Lee.
(E) Singh rows immediately behind Zita.

9. Which one of the following CANNOT be true?

(A) Ovitz rows closer to the front than Singh.
(B) Zita rows closer to the front than Miller.
(C) Lee rows closer to the front than Valerio.
(D) Singh rows closer to the front than Zita.
(E) Valerio rows closer to the front than Lee.

10. Exactly how many different seats could be the seat occupied by Zita?

(A) two
(B) three
(C) four
(D) five
(E) six

11. If Valerio rows closer to the front than Zita, then which one of the following must be true?

(A) Miller rows immediately in front of Singh.
(B) Lee rows immediately in front of Valerio.
(C) Zita rows immediately in front of Ovitz.
(D) Singh rows immediately in front of Lee.
(E) Singh rows immediately in front of Valerio.

12. Suppose the restriction that Miller rows closer to the front than Singh is replaced by the restriction that Singh rows closer to the front than Miller. If the other two restrictions remain in effect, then each of the following could be an accurate matching of athletes to seats EXCEPT:

(A) Singh: seat 1; Zita: seat 2; Miller: seat 6
(B) Singh: seat 1; Valerio: seat 3; Ovitz: seat 5
(C) Singh: seat 3; Lee: seat 4; Valerio: seat 5
(D) Valerio: seat 3; Miller: seat 4; Lee: seat 5
(E) Valerio: seat 4; Miller: seat 5; Ovitz: seat 6

GO ON TO THE NEXT PAGE.

Questions 13-17

Exactly six of an artist's paintings, entitled *Quarterion, Redemption, Sipapu, Tesseract, Vale,* and *Zelkova,* are sold at auction. Three of the paintings are sold to a museum, and three are sold to a private collector. Two of the paintings are from the artist's first (earliest) period, two are from her second period, and two are from her third (most recent) period. The private collector and the museum each buy one painting from each period. The following conditions hold:

Sipapu, which is sold to the private collector, is from an earlier period than *Zelkova,* which is sold to the museum.
Quarterion is not from an earlier period than *Tesseract.*
Vale is from the artist's second period.

13. Which one of the following could be an accurate list of the paintings bought by the museum and the private collector, listed in order of the paintings' periods, from first to third?

   (A)   museum: *Quarterion, Vale, Zelkova*
         private collector: *Redemption, Sipapu, Tesseract*
   (B)   museum: *Redemption, Zelkova, Quarterion*
         private collector: *Sipapu, Vale, Tesseract*
   (C)   museum: *Sipapu, Zelkova, Quarterion*
         private collector: *Tesseract, Vale, Redemption*
   (D)   museum: *Tesseract, Quarterion, Zelkova*
         private collector: *Sipapu, Redemption, Vale*
   (E)   museum: *Zelkova, Tesseract, Redemption*
         private collector: *Sipapu, Vale, Quarterion*

14. If *Sipapu* is from the artist's second period, which one of the following could be two of the three paintings bought by the private collector?

   (A)   *Quarterion* and *Zelkova*
   (B)   *Redemption* and *Tesseract*
   (C)   *Redemption* and *Vale*
   (D)   *Redemption* and *Zelkova*
   (E)   *Tesseract* and *Zelkova*

15. Which one of the following is a complete and accurate list of the paintings, any one of which could be the painting from the artist's first period that is sold to the private collector?

   (A)   *Quarterion, Redemption*
   (B)   *Redemption, Sipapu*
   (C)   *Quarterion, Sipapu, Tesseract*
   (D)   *Quarterion, Redemption, Sipapu, Tesseract*
   (E)   *Redemption, Sipapu, Tesseract, Zelkova*

16. If *Sipapu* is from the artist's second period, then which one of the following paintings could be from the period immediately preceding *Quarterion's* period and be sold to the same buyer as *Quarterion*?

   (A)   *Redemption*
   (B)   *Sipapu*
   (C)   *Tesseract*
   (D)   *Vale*
   (E)   *Zelkova*

17. If *Zelkova* is sold to the same buyer as *Tesseract* and is from the period immediately preceding *Tesseract's* period, then which one of the following must be true?

   (A)   *Quarterion* is sold to the museum.
   (B)   *Quarterion* is from the artist's third period.
   (C)   *Redemption* is sold to the private collector.
   (D)   *Redemption* is from the artist's third period.
   (E)   *Redemption* is sold to the same buyer as *Vale*.

GO ON TO THE NEXT PAGE.

Questions 18-22

Each of exactly six lunch trucks sells a different one of six kinds of food: falafel, hot dogs, ice cream, pitas, salad, or tacos. Each truck serves one or more of exactly three office buildings: X, Y, or Z. The following conditions apply:

The falafel truck, the hot dog truck, and exactly one other truck each serve Y.

The falafel truck serves exactly two of the office buildings.

The ice cream truck serves more of the office buildings than the salad truck.

The taco truck does not serve Y.

The falafel truck does not serve any office building that the pita truck serves.

The taco truck serves two office buildings that are also served by the ice cream truck.

18. Which one of the following could be a complete and accurate list of each of the office buildings that the falafel truck serves?

(A)   X
(B)   X, Z
(C)   X, Y, Z
(D)   Y, Z
(E)   Z

19. For which one of the following pairs of trucks must it be the case that at least one of the office buildings is served by both of the trucks?

(A)   the hot dog truck and the pita truck
(B)   the hot dog truck and the taco truck
(C)   the ice cream truck and the pita truck
(D)   the ice cream truck and the salad truck
(E)   the salad truck and the taco truck

20. If the ice cream truck serves fewer of the office buildings than the hot dog truck, then which one of the following is a pair of lunch trucks that must serve exactly the same buildings as each other?

(A)   the falafel truck and the hot dog truck
(B)   the falafel truck and the salad truck
(C)   the ice cream truck and the pita truck
(D)   the ice cream truck and the salad truck
(E)   the ice cream truck and the taco truck

21. Which one of the following could be a complete and accurate list of the lunch trucks, each of which serves all three of the office buildings?

(A)   the hot dog truck, the ice cream truck
(B)   the hot dog truck, the salad truck
(C)   the ice cream truck, the taco truck
(D)   the hot dog truck, the ice cream truck, the pita truck
(E)   the ice cream truck, the pita truck, the salad truck

22. Which one of the following lunch trucks CANNOT serve both X and Z?

(A)   the hot dog truck
(B)   the ice cream truck
(C)   the pita truck
(D)   the salad truck
(E)   the taco truck

S T O P

IF YOU FINISH BEFORE TIME IS CALLED, YOU MAY CHECK YOUR WORK ON THIS SECTION ONLY.
DO NOT WORK ON ANY OTHER SECTION IN THE TEST.

LSAT® Writing Sample Topic

Alma owns a small art gallery that is situated in the middle of a busy commercial district. She is considering two different approaches to adding to the inventory of pieces she offers for sale. Write an essay in which you argue for one plan over the other, keeping in mind the following goals:

• Alma would like to specialize in locally produced artwork.
• The new items should attract new customers.

In the first plan, Alma would introduce a line of metalwork sculptures, made available through a regional consortium of artists, to fill a gap in her inventory for small, affordable gift items. Initially, the items would bring in new business from existing foot traffic and from those browsing or shopping during the lunch hour. Should these pieces do well, she would then bring in additional small-scale artwork in the hopes of establishing herself more firmly in the market for smaller pieces. Although Alma would be able to cater to a wider customer base, she would have competition from several stores in the area that also offer small gift items, although none specializes in the original artwork of local artists.

In the second plan, Alma would take advantage of an opportunity to become the sole representative for the artwork in the estate of a deceased painter whose works are now being valued at ever increasing amounts. The painter lived most of his life in the area, but his later works, making up most of the paintings in the estate, were actually painted elsewhere. By becoming the sole representative for the painter's work, she would acquire a limited collection of paintings for which there is a well-established niche market. The art gallery presently has only a small number of very expensive pieces, but attracting this small, specialized clientele would give Alma an established audience for other high-end works she might acquire in the future.

Scratch Paper
Do not write your essay in this space.

Directions:

1. Use the Answer Key on the next page to check your answers.

2. Use the Scoring Worksheet below to compute your raw score.

3. Use the Score Conversion Chart to convert your raw score into the 120-180 scale.

Scoring Worksheet

1. Enter the number of questions you answered correctly in each section.

	Number Correct
SECTION I......................	_____
SECTION II....................	_____
SECTION III..................	_____
SECTION IV..................	_____

2. Enter the sum here: _____

   This is your Raw Score.

Conversion Chart:
For Converting Raw Score to the 120-180 LSAT Scaled Score
LSAT Form 5LSN67

Reported Score	Raw Score Lowest	Raw Score Highest
180	99	101
179	98	98
178	97	97
177	96	96
176	95	95
175	94	94
174	93	93
173	92	92
172	91	91
171	90	90
170	89	89
169	88	88
168	86	87
167	85	85
166	84	84
165	82	83
164	81	81
163	79	80
162	78	78
161	76	77
160	75	75
159	73	74
158	71	72
157	70	70
156	68	69
155	67	67
154	65	66
153	63	67
152	62	64
151	60	62
150	58	61
149	57	59
148	55	57
147	53	56
146	51	52
145	50	50
144	48	49
143	46	47
142	45	45
141	43	44
140	42	42
139	40	41
138	38	39
137	37	37
136	35	36
135	34	34
134	33	33
133	31	32
132	30	30
131	28	29
130	27	27
129	26	26
128	25	25
127	23	24
126	22	22
125	21	21
124	20	20
123	18	19
122	17	17
121	16	16
120	0	15

SECTION I

1.	D	8.	D	15.	E	22.	D
2.	E	9.	C	16.	B	23.	A
3.	C	10.	D	17.	A	24.	B
4.	B	11.	E	18.	D	25.	D
5.	E	12.	B	19.	B	26.	E
6.	E	13.	A	20.	B	27.	A
7.	A	14.	E	21.	A	28.	E

SECTION II

1.	C	8.	C	15.	D	22.	A
2.	A	9.	D	16.	E	23.	D
3.	E	10.	A	17.	E	24.	C
4.	B	11.	E	18.	D	25.	C
5.	D	12.	B	19.	D		
6.	E	13.	D	20.	D		
7.	C	14.	C	21.	E		

SECTION III

1.	A	8.	C	15.	D	22.	D
2.	E	9.	A	16.	B	23.	B
3.	B	10.	B	17.	E	24.	B
4.	C	11.	D	18.	B	25.	A
5.	E	12.	C	19.	B	26.	E
6.	E	13.	A	20.	E		
7.	D	14.	C	21.	B		

SECTION IV

1.	D	8.	E	15.	D	22.	C
2.	E	9.	A	16.	B		
3.	A	10.	D	17.	B		
4.	E	11.	A	18.	D		
5.	B	12.	C	19.	C		
6.	C	13.	B	20.	E		
7.	E	14.	B	21.	A		

CHAPTER THREE: THE JUNE 2004 LSAT DECONSTRUCTED

The explanations below are presented in the same order that the questions are given on the exam. Page headers are provided to help you identify which questions are explained on each page, and if you encounter any unknown terms, a glossary is provided at the end of the book. Also, please keep in mind that all explanations draw on methods discussed in *The PowerScore LSAT Logic Games Bible* and *The PowerScore LSAT Logical Reasoning Bible*. Please refer to those texts if you desire a more detailed discussion of a particular concept or approach.

JUNE 2004 SECTION 1: READING COMPREHENSION

This reading comprehension section is considered particularly difficult, in part because of its length. Reading comprehension sections with twenty-eight questions have become more common in recent testing administrations, but they are still somewhat rare.

The subject matter of this section is fairly representative of most LSAT Reading Comprehension sections. The first passage is a "hard" science passage about oil well exploration and includes a discussion of legal implications. It is pro-environment and pro-regulation. The next passage is a "soft" or "known" science passage focusing on an under-represented minority group. The author discusses several factors which may explain why Puerto Rican Americans often use both English and Spanish within a single conversation. The third passage is a humanities passage describing two conflicting theories of literary analysis. It is critical to note the author's perspective and to clearly distinguish between the two theories presented to perform well on this passage. The final passage discusses four possible institutional approaches to ownership of faculty research.

The questions in the section are evenly mixed between global and local questions. Each of the passages had at least one Analogy question where specific passage concepts must be applied to evaluate five hypothetical situations. Each of the passages also asks test takers to identify the Author's Perspective and three of the four passages have a Main Point question. There are also two Weaken questions and two Function questions.

Paragraph 1 Overview

This paragraph begins with a broad characterization of the impact of oil well exploration. The author notes a very specific temporal relationship here: first, an oil well is drilled. Then an undesirable event occurs which impacts the environment. The event is studied scientifically and the results of that study reveal the need for regulation (interestingly enough, this chain of events is also reflected in the passage structure and paragraph organization). The implications here are that the reasoned application of scientific evidence will lead to increased regulation, and that both are desirable. As a general rule, the test makers tend to advocate regulation as an effective solution for a broad range of problems, including the protection of natural resources. The final sentence here indicates that the remainder of the passage will deal with a specific undesirable result of oil drilling: the potential contamination of groundwater. Note the careful definition of groundwater – test takers are told what groundwater is, where it is found, and what purpose it serves. Be sure to make note of each of these elements.

Paragraph 2 Overview

Not surprisingly, the author begins the second paragraph by providing a historical context for assessing the problem of groundwater contamination discussed in paragraph one. Here, the author supports the notion that the knowledge necessary for successful regulation typically comes in retrospect. The author notes the creation of regulations in the late nineteenth century designed to protect oil from contamination by groundwater but no regulations to protect groundwater from contamination by oil. "Thousands of wells were drilled" (line 17) in this manner and, inevitably, undesirable events occurred. In this case, nearby drinking water became unpotable and oil-contaminated (lines 20- 22). Although the word "unpotable" is not explicitly defined, the sentence structure associates unpotable with oil-contaminated and contrasts it with drinking water. The test makers assume no prior knowledge and will always provide sufficient context for attentive readers to grasp the meaning of unfamiliar words. Developing the ability to quickly categorize unfamiliar concepts and to recognize their functional meaning is essential to performing well on the Reading Comprehension section.

Paragraph 3 Overview

This paragraph provides a scientific analysis of the undesirable environmental event. The author proceeds by describing the relative location of groundwater and oil reservoirs, indicating that the geologic formations are similarly porous and permeable, but that ground water is generally found closer to the surface than oil reserves. Thus, oil wells are often drilled directly through existing groundwater reservoirs. This process connects all of the penetrated formations and, in the absence of appropriate safeguards, will inevitably contaminate groundwater. The author also introduces saline water reservoirs, a new element which is found at the same depths as oil reservoirs and poses much the same threat to groundwater. Although the introduction of saline water may seem tangential or incidental to the main discussion, it provides an excellent opportunity for the test makers to catch inattentive test takers off-guard. Understanding the relationship between saline water and oil reserves and properly characterizing saline water as an additional potential contaminant for groundwater will help test takers avoid this potential pitfall. This paragraph concludes by describing early attempts to prevent the mixing of groundwater and oil, first by using hollow trees as a protective barrier and now by placing large metal pipe casings in cement. Both methods attempt to create a non-permeable barrier between the oil and the groundwater. Interestingly, this paragraph does not mention regulations at all; it is strictly concerned with the process of groundwater contamination and the methods of prevention that are used.

Paragraph 4 Overview

The final paragraph contains the expected return to a discussion of regulation. Readers are told that there are regulations governing the materials used to create the protective barriers and would expect the author to be pleased with this knowledge. However, the author's concern is not alleviated and he or she suggests that regulation alone is insufficient. For the author, it is the combination of scientific knowledge and effective regulation that is needed to address this problem. The author delineates several areas in which our current knowledge is inadequate. We do not know how long these barriers will last, what effect various subsurface fluids will have on the casing or on the cement, and what the environmental impact of groundwater bacteria, groundwater chemistry, and traffic vibrations may be. Finally, the author suggests that additional factors, such as access to the ocean, may prevent existing regulations from performing properly. Such lists provide excellent source material for test questions and test takers can fully expect to be tested on their understanding of this list. The major disaster, described beginning in line 55, occurred not necessarily because the oil company failed to follow regulations, but because it failed to properly evaluate the location. Properly using protective barriers as described in the third paragraph may have prevented oil from mixing with groundwater, but did not prevent ocean water from mixing with groundwater or oil from mixing with ocean water. This event prompted new research and has begun the cycle anew. Once again, the problem became evident only after the disaster occurred. It is obvious that the author believes this problem will continue until an accumulation of scientific knowledge – and the resulting regulatory efforts – "catches up" to the actual drilling of oil wells.

Passage Summary

There are numerous risks of environmental damage associated with oil well drilling, and until there is more sufficient scientific knowledge that can be used to better regulate drilling, these hazards will persist.

Passage Structure

Paragraph 1: Introduces oil drilling and the issues of hindsight-based regulation and groundwater contamination
Paragraph 2: Gives a history of lagging regulatory efforts and the contamination that occurred as a result
Paragraph 3: Discusses the process of contamination and provides specific examples of prevention methods
Paragraph 4: Emphasizes that a combination of scientific knowledge and effective regulation is needed to prevent future disasters

Question #1: Main Point. The correct answer choice is (D)

This question asks test takers to identify the main point of the passage. As discussed above, test takers can expect the correct answer choice to include these elements: there are harms/risks associated with oil well drilling and these risks will continue to exist until more appropriate regulations are put into effect based on a greater body of scientific knowledge (rather than on hindsight).

Answer choice (A): This answer choice suggests that hindsight is necessary primarily to realize that groundwater contamination is undesirable and inevitable. This inappropriate focus and the total absence of any discussion of scientific knowledge or regulation can be used to quickly classify this as a Loser.

Answer choice (B): In typical LSAT fashion, this answer choice highlights the tendency of many readers to overemphasize the importance of recent information. While the information is technically accurate and properly summarized, it is important not to confuse a specific example with the primary point.

Answer choice (C): This answer choice suggests that regulation writers are the primary focus of the passage when, in fact, this group is never mentioned at all. Although the passage makes numerous references to regulations, it does not ever refer to the people who write these regulations.

Answer choice (D): This is the correct answer choice. It clearly links the environmental risk of oil well drilling with hindsight and less-than-sufficient scientific information, and appropriately demonstrates that this is a continuing problem.

Answer choice (E): Much like answer choice (B), this answer choice asserts that a specific example offered in support of the conclusion is the conclusion itself. Remember that the correct answer to a main point question must contain all of the critical elements of a passage and their proper relationship to one another.

Question #2: Must Be True. The correct answer choice is (E)

The characteristics of underground oil reservoirs are primarily discussed in paragraph two and this is where test takers should look to find the answer to this question. In the second paragraph, the author states that underground oil reservoirs are found in porous, permeable formations similar to areas where groundwater is found, but generally at greater depths. Readers also learn that environments conducive to oil reservoirs also favor unpotable saline water reservoirs.

Answer choice (A): While the passage does mention at least one instance of an underground oil reservoir whose subsurface geology was poorly understood, it does not suggest that this is generally true. The passage's preoccupation with insufficient knowledge cannot be properly applied to this answer choice.

Answer choice (B): Again, we see the test makers return to the final example mentioned in the passage, but there is no indication as to how common coastal oil reservoirs may be.

Answer choice (C): This answer choice begins well ("geologic formations similar to those") but then plays a Shell Game by introducing a new element (gas) that was never discussed in the passage.

Answer choice (D): While the passage does state that the oil industry is concerned about this form of contamination, it cannot be known how often this may occur and whether such concerns are valid.

Answer choice (E): This is the correct answer choice. It is a direct paraphrase of the opening sentence of paragraph two (lines 27-28).

Question #3: Author's Perspective. The correct answer choice is (C)

The author clearly believes that more scientific knowledge is needed to better regulate oil well drilling and that, until more is known, the need for regulation will become apparent only after undesirable events occur (lines 5-7).

Answer choice (A): This answer choice is essentially a Mistaken Negation. The author clearly believes that international concern leads to regulatory reform, but does not believe that the lack of international concern will preclude such reform. Also, the word "cynical" is too extreme to describe the author's tone.

Answer choice (B): The passage does not suggest that the author is satisfied with current regulations or that the author is concerned about an appropriate balance between resource collection and environmental protection; in every example given, the author leans heavily toward environmental protection.

Answer choice (C): This is the correct answer choice. It correctly describes a pattern the author has noted in the past and reflects the author's apparent belief that the pattern may continue in the future. It also captures the somewhat negative tone of the passage.

Answer choice (D): Though the author believes in the power of science, he or she does not seem content with current research. Indeed, the author suggests various venues for future research rather than discussing how existing research will change existing regulations. "Optimistic" is too positive.

Answer choice (E): This answer choice expresses much the same idea as answer choice (D), only with the further limitation of scientific research as meaning "accurate geologic understanding." It fails for the same reasons.

Question #4: Specific Reference, Function. The correct answer choice is (B)

This question directs you to paragraph four. As discussed previously, this paragraph deals primarily with challenges and questions that remain in spite of existing regulation. The "hazards of insufficient knowledge" could be properly characterized as a topic sentence for this entire paragraph. Thus, the correct answer choice must account for all of the potential consequences of this lack of knowledge mentioned in this paragraph (potential flaws in the usage of metal pipe casings; effects of groundwater bacteria, traffic vibrations, and changing groundwater chemistry; complications that could result from a poor understanding of an area's subsurface geology).

Answer choice (A): A specific knowledge of how groundwater contamination affects human beings is not necessary to conclude that drinking water should remain pure. Though this lack of understanding may present some hazards itself, it is not among the areas which this paragraph suggests as requiring further research.

Answer choice (B): This is the correct answer choice. Among the concerns listed in this section of the passage are questions about the durability of the protective barriers, the presence of bacteria, the impact of traffic vibrations and groundwater chemistry, and the poor understanding of subsurface geology. These various concerns can be correctly categorized as possible consequences of drilling and all reflect the absence of full comprehension.

Answer choice (C): Though the author expresses concern about the safety of technologies such as the metal pipe casings, the methods for testing such technologies are not specifically questioned. According to the author, we need *more* research, not necessarily *better* research. This answer choice is incomplete.

Answer choice (D): This answer choice attempts to shift the focus away from the difficulty of creating effective environmental regulations to the difficulty of enforcing such regulations. In fact, the author clearly states that the hazards of insufficient knowledge remain even in cases where regulations have been enacted and enforced, such as the drilling on the west coast of North America (line 55).

Answer choice (E): This could be an appealing answer choice for many of the same reasons why some respondents chose answer choice (C). The author does talk about the potential hazards posed by materials used in metal pipe casings very shortly after the phrase indicated in the question stem. But the author's concern is about the interaction between these materials and the geologic environment, and not the properties of the materials themselves. Further, the author is concerned about the risks posed by an insufficient knowledge of numerous threats, not just the materials used in manufacturing pipe metal casings.

Question #5: Specific Reference, Parallel Reasoning. The correct answer choice is (E)

This question tests readers' ability to apply the principles of the passage to an analogous situation. It adds several elements to the discussion – the size of the city, the relative size of the groundwater formation and the saline formation, and the absence of oil – about which no specific information is given in the passage. Therefore, any inferences which are contingent upon those specific factors are unwarranted and cannot be the basis for the correct answer choice. What can be known is that drilling oil wells connects all formations that it penetrates (saline water, groundwater, and oil) and that the contamination is inevitable unless appropriate safeguards are implemented (lines 28-33). Since the passage lists saline water as a contaminant of groundwater (lines 30-33), the correct answer choice must take into account the possibility of contamination.

Answer choice (A): Answer choice (A) can be eliminated because it contradicts the information about the inevitability of contamination among all penetrated formations; whether the well actually operates or not is irrelevant since the conduit has already been created.

Answer choice (B): This answer choice asks test takers to make an unwarranted inference based upon their understanding of water supplies in large cities. Is it likely that a large city will have more than one water source? Of course. But this assumption does not follow from the information in the passage, nor does it affect the actual danger to human health from groundwater contamination. Groundwater contamination remains a danger to human health regardless of how many drinking water sources a city has.

Answer choice (C): This answer choice may be appealing if "plugging and abandoning a well" is equated to implementing appropriate safeguards. However, it cannot be assumed to be similar, nor can it be accepted as correct since it introduces an idea that does not appear in the passage.

Answer choice (D): No proper inference about the dilution of saline water in groundwater can be drawn from the information in this passage. The idea of groundwater contamination is treated as an absolute throughout the passage, and as a result, test takers should accept the idea that any amount of contamination is to be avoided.

Answer choice (E): This is the correct answer choice. Independent of considerations about the city's size or the absence of oil, the question specifically states that both formations were penetrated. From the passage, readers know contamination will occur unless appropriate safeguards are implemented. Setting the casings properly and monitoring them routinely certainly seem to be appropriate measures and can be logically said to reduce the risk of contamination (i.e. from 100% risk to something less than 100%). This is the only answer choice that does not make any unwarranted assumptions.

Passage #2: Code-Switching among Puerto Rican Americans (Questions 6 – 13)

Paragraph 1 Overview

This passage discusses the observation of an interesting phenomenon (code-switching) among an underrepresented minority group (Puerto Rican Americans). Readers can reasonably expect the tone of this passage to be either positive (likely) or completely neutral toward Puerto Rican Americans. The author introduces the phenomenon of code-switching and provides a clear definition (lines 3-7). This definition is worth noting, as the test makers frequently question readers' understanding of new or difficult words, and an awareness of central concepts such as this one is critical to performing well on this section. It is useful to develop a standard notation system, such as bracketing or underlining, which can be used to highlight every definition and other key idea encountered in Reading Comprehension passages.

The author then explains the main point of this passage: Most code-switching in these communities can be explained by subtle situational and rhetorical factors. As with any well-written thesis statement, this sentence also foreshadows the structure of the passage. One portion of the passage will discuss situational factors which influence code-switching and another portion will discuss rhetorical factors. Many readers are understandably curious about the instances which "cannot currently be explained" and the test makers likely expect that this will catch the attention of test takers. However, as will be seen shortly, the test makers do not include a discussion of these instances in the passage. Thus far, the tone is that of a dispassionate but interested observer; there is nothing here to indicate a bias.

Paragraph 2 Overview

As predicted, this paragraph addresses the situational factors that often lead to code-switching. The author defines several new concepts and describes the methodology of one study of this phenomenon. Here are the primary definitions:

domain: social context in which conversations take place; common examples include family, friendship, religion, education, and employment.

conversational factor: variables which influence the occurrence of code-switching; three primary factors are setting, topic, and participants.

congruence/incongruence: the degree to which conversational factors "naturally" go together; setting, topic, and participants that match each other are congruent, those that do not are incongruent.

conversational situation: a set of three congruent conversational factors.

When reading about the methodology of this study, test takers should be asking themselves basic questions. Who were the participants? What did they do? What was the study intended to demonstrate? What did it actually demonstrate? In very simple terms, this study was an exercise in filling-in-the-blanks. Two out of three factors were pre-determined and the students supplied the third factor as well as the appropriate language mix. Some of these factors were congruent and some were incongruent. When the pre-determined factors naturally matched each other, the students "filled in the blanks" consistently with one another. When the two given factors were incongruent, students responded less consistently. These findings suggest that knowledge about the domain of a conversation, particularly congruent domains, can be used with some success to predict the amount of code-switching.

Paragraph 3 Overview

The third paragraph discusses subtle rhetorical factors which influence code-switching. This code-switching occurs even when factors such as participants, setting, and topic remain the same. Here, researchers recorded the conversations of a Puerto Rican American family at home discussing various topics. Both the researchers and the family were apparently surprised to find various levels of code-switching. Researchers did not expect the amount of code-switching to vary without a change in situational factors and the family believed they spoke only English at home. The family members suggested that this code-switching was used for certain emphasis. In this paragraph, words such as "sparingly," "occasionally," and "subtle" indicate that rhetorical factors account for relatively few instances of code-switching.

Passage Summary

Although not perfectly predictable, the majority of code-switching can be explained by either situational factors such as domain congruence, or rhetorical factors where code-switching is used to better express certain attitudes.

Passage Structure

> Paragraph 1: Introduces code-switching and gives two factors – situational and rhetorical – that typically explain its occurrence
> Paragraph 2: Describes some specific situations where code-switching occurs and examines the predictability of code-switching resulting from varying factors
> Paragraph 3: Discusses rhetorical factors as being responsible for instances of code-switching not resultant from situational causes

Question #6: Main Point. The correct answer choice is (E)

The main point, as discussed previously, is something similar to "the vast majority of code-switching in bilingual communities of Puerto Rican Americans can be explained by subtle factors, either situational or rhetorical."

Answer choice (A): When considering answer choice (A), consider the following: "After reading this passage, can I describe the various ways in which the lives of Puerto Rican Americans are affected by code-switching?" Since the answer is clearly "No," this cannot be the correct answer choice.

Answer choice (B): Answer choice (B), though supported by line 7, does not accurately express the main point of the passage. As noted previously, the author does not discuss these inexplicable cases and focuses exclusively on the instances of code-switching which can be explained.

Answer choice (C): The passage asserts that "most code-switching among Puerto Rican Americans is sensitive to the social contexts…in which conversations take place" (lines 11-14). Since social contexts are given as an example of situational factors, and these factors can explain more than half the instances of code-switching, this answer choice cannot be correct. Further, it is too limited to express the main point of the entire passage.

Answer choice (D): Again, test takers must ask themselves if this answer choice accurately expresses what they have learned as a result of this passage. Can readers know what linguists believed about code-switching prior to these studies of Puerto Rican Americans? No. From the passage, any knowledge that test takers have regarding linguists' beliefs about code-switching is based entirely on these studies and cannot be used to say how those beliefs have been revised.

Answer choice (E): This is the correct answer choice. As is often the case in LSAT Reading Comprehension passages, the correct answer choice to a Main Point question is a paraphrase of the passage's topic sentence. Scanning the answers choices quickly for critical elements, such as situational and rhetorical factors, should quickly lead readers to the correct answer choice.

Question #7: Specific Reference, Function. The correct answer choice is (A)

The families in the last paragraph indicate that they switch from English to Spanish to express certain attitudes more emphatically. This is further proof that the code-switching is based on rhetorical factors.

Answer choice (A): This is the correct answer choice. Once again, the test makers draw readers' attention to the final section of the passage. In this case, the specific reference is used as a supporting premise in the author's discussion of rhetoric-based code-switching.

Answer choice (B): This answer choice attempts to catch readers who may make inappropriate comparisons between different groups. The author notes that this family was from a different community than the high-school students described in the preceding paragraph (line 52), but this is not significant. If both the family and the high school students had participated in the same study but produced different results, this answer choice would be more strongly supported.

Answer choice (C): This is an Opposite Answer. This evidence does not *conflict* with the researchers' conclusions; it *confirms* them. In fact, this evidence actually provides a basis for the conclusions.

Answer choice (D): Since the author has already observed that rhetorical code-switching constitutes only a small portion of all code-switching, the family's explanation does not confirm or refute any argument about what causes most code-switching.

Answer choice (E): The fact that Spanish phrases were mostly used to emphasize humor and intimacy does not explain why the family believed they spoke only English at home.

Question #8: Must Be True. The correct answer choice is (D)

This question is an excellent example of the benefits of personalizing LSAT Reading Comprehension passages. By knowing what the researchers were looking for and what the students were asked to do in the study described in the second paragraph, there is no need to refer back to the passage. Test takers can simply look for an answer choice that does not fit the pattern of the study.

Answer choice (A): In answer choice (A), the linguists provide participants and topic and are asking for setting. This fits the methodology of the study and is a restatement of the hypothetical example from lines 36 – 40.

Answer choice (B): This is merely the other "blank" for the scenario from answer choice (A). It fits the methodology and can be quickly eliminated.

Answer choice (C): This answer choice is drawn from the second hypothetical example in the passage (lines 40 – 43). Here, participant and setting are supplied and the student is asked to provide the missing language mix. Again, since this matches the study pattern it can be eliminated.

Answer choice (D): This is the correct answer choice. Here, the researchers supply participants and language mix. But in the study, students were asked to provide the language mix in every case. This answer choice is correct because it uniquely fails to fit the study methodology.

Answer choice (E): Like answer choice (A), this answer choice provides two of the three conversational factors and asks for the third. It is likewise an incorrect answer choice.

Question #9: Specific Reference, Function. The correct answer choice is (C)

Remember that the correct answer choice to a Function question must explain how the described section fits within the structure of the overall passage. In this case, test takers must properly explain the function of the third paragraph – providing an explanation for the rhetorical factors that sometimes cause code-switching – with respect to the first two.

Answer choice (A): This answer choice is cleverly written but two words cause it to be incorrect. First, the word "general" is incorrect because the rhetorical factors discussed in paragraph three are a specific explanation. Second, the word "paragraphs" is wrong, since rhetorical factors were discussed (albeit briefly) in only the first of the two preceding paragraphs.

Answer choice (B): This answer choice is incorrect because there is no apparent conflict between these two explanations. Each explanation is applied to different instances and both can be true without affecting the validity of the other.

Answer choice (C): This is the correct answer choice. This answer correctly describes the function of the third paragraph as explaining some instances of code-switching (rhetorical) that the second paragraph did not explain.

Answer choice (D): Although this is an adequate summary of the third paragraph, it does not explain what role that paragraph serves in the passage as a whole. This answer choice might be the correct answer for a Main Point question, but cannot be correct for a Function question.

Answer choice (E): This is a premise mentioned in the third paragraph, but it does not describe the function of the third paragraph as a whole. The third paragraph is designed to show that some instances of code-switching are done based on rhetorical factors.

Question #10: Specific Reference. The correct answer choice is (D)

Rhetorically determined code-switching is discussed in the third paragraph and is described as using a secondary language to better express a certain emotional attitude or feeling.

Answer choice (A): The third paragraph states that rhetorical code-switching is "used only sparingly to achieve certain rhetorical effects" (line 50). The example given here is not technically code-switching but rather a lack of fluency and is motivated by necessity rather than a desire to achieve certain rhetorical effects.

Answer choice (B): Although this method of translation may achieve a certain rhetorical effect, code-switching is the frequent and smooth alternation between two languages in a conversation and does not necessarily apply to written translations. Further, the code-switching in this example is done to preserve originality (the author invented the words), not achieve a certain rhetorical emphasis.

Answer choice (C): Here, the businessman is not alternating between languages within a conversation. The use of the second language is a conscious decision which reflects situational factors determined by the preference of an audience.

Answer choice (D): This is the correct answer choice. This answer choice correctly describes rhetorically determined code-switching as defined by the passage.

Answer choice (E): Again, the language switch described here is not code-switching and does not have a rhetorical motivation. It should now be obvious how developing a firm understanding of the key terms defined in this passage will help to maximize a test taker's score on this section of the test.

Question #11: Author's Perspective. The correct answer choice is (E)

Answer choice (A): This answer choice tests readers' understanding of the relationship between the two studies described in the passage. The results of the study involving high school students indicated that the conversational situation is linked to the amount of code-switching present. The researchers did not make any claim regarding speakers' awareness of code-switching. Code-switching does not have to be conscious for it to be linked to conversational factors. That is, the third paragraph is not given in an attempt to refute the second.

Answer choice (B): The passage refers to only two studies – the study of Puerto Rican American high school students in one community and the study of a Puerto Rican American family in another. The passage contains no dates and never indicates which of the two studies came first. Did linguists conduct relevant research prior to the study of the high school students? Perhaps, but that cannot be known for certain. Did this research lead the researchers to predict different results? Again, this cannot be known. The passage does contain enough information for test takers to reasonably infer that the author would agree with this statement.

Answer choice (C): Again, there is no information regarding what research was conducted when. Since the high school study is discussed earlier than the family study, readers are tempted to conclude that the high school study took place first, but this cannot be determined with any certainty. Further, the wording "all except the most unusual or nonstandard contexts" is too extreme. While researchers believe that most code-switching is explained by situational factors (line 11), rhetorical code-switching, such as that found among the family, cannot correctly be considered a "most unusual or nonstandard" context.

Answer choice (D): This contradicts the results of the high school study, which demonstrated a high awareness of which situational factors influence the choice of language. If the high school students were usually unaware of these factors, they would likely have been far less consistent in responding to congruent conversational situations. The author would not be likely to agree with this statement.

Answer choice (E): This is the correct answer choice. In the third paragraph, the author explains that rhetorical code-switching "tends to be…used only sparingly to achieve certain rhetorical effects" (lines 47-49). He or she then explicitly notes that "this was the case with a study of a family of Puerto Rican Americans" (line 52). Since this study is used as an explicit example to support the author's conclusion, answer choice (E) is the correct answer.

Question #12: Must Be True. The correct answer choice is (B)

Answer choice (A): This answer choice is drawn from lines 40-43, but is not offered as evidence that code-switching cannot be entirely explained by situational factors. Look at the results of the study a little more closely: If student A says that a conversation between a priest and a parishioner on the beach would take place entirely in Spanish and student B says that conversation would take place in half-Spanish and half-English, does that mean that the code-switching is unexplained by situational factors? No, because the students provided *both* the third situational factor and the language mix. When the third factor is unknown and the given factors are incongruent, it is not surprising that students fail to agree about the predicted effect of those situational factors. It may still be possible to explain code-switching here through situational factors even when the students are in disagreement.

Answer choice (B): This is the correct answer choice. Answer choice B is drawn from lines 45-46 of the passage. In this instance, all of the situational factors are known, but the actual mix of languages occurring is different from the predicted mix. Since our knowledge of the situation is complete and the prediction is wrong, it follows that situational factors cannot entirely explain code-switching. This is not analogous to answer choice (A), where we see multiple predictions based on incomplete knowledge.

Answer choice (C): Some sets of situational factors would lead us to expect bilingual people to switch smoothly between two languages within a single conversation. This answer choice does nothing more than describe what code-switching is and is not used by the passage in the manner indicated.

Answer choice (D): This is a Shell Game answer where the test makers have added incorrect elements to an otherwise correct answer choice. The test makers have created a situation very similar but not identical to the situation which is offered in the passage as evidence that not all code-switching can be explained by situational factors. Here is a version of this answer choice that would be correct: "Puerto Rican Americans sometimes use Spanish only sparingly and for rhetorical effect in the presence of situational factors that would lead on to expect *English* to be the *only* language."

Answer choice (E): This answer choice is not supported by the passage and seems to contradict the results of the high-school study. The passage does indicate that speakers are sometimes unaware of the code-switching itself (lines 49-50), but does not suggest that speakers are often unaware of the setting, topics, or participants.

Question #13: Weaken. The correct answer choice is (A)

The author's interpretation of the study involving the family is that not all of the code-switching in their conversations could be explained by situational factors. If another study showed that all of the family's code-switching *could* be explained by situational factors, it would cast doubt on the interpretation given in the passage. Demonstrating that the presumed cause (i.e. changes in situational factors) and the predicted effect (i.e. code-switching) have consistently occurred together in the past makes it more difficult to believe that the effect ever occurs without that cause.

Answer choice (A): This is the correct answer choice. This is the same scenario as the one described in the third paragraph, however in this instance the code-switching was situational and not rhetorical. This casts doubt on the rhetoric-based code-switching that the author proposes in lines 46-49.

Answer choice (B): Here, the presumed cause is shown to be present several times without the accompanying effect. Since the author believes that the presumed cause is not always linked to the effect, this study would not cast doubt on the author's interpretation.

Answer choice (C): This answer choice says that on some occasions, code-switching did not occur. But this does not help to evaluate whether or not all code-switching which *does* occur can be explained by situational factors. Therefore, it cannot cast doubt on the author's interpretation.

Answer choice (D): Discussing the results of the study in English does not constitute code-switching, even if the family was discussing Spanish. Therefore, this answer choice cannot help to evaluate the author's claim regarding the causes of code-switching.

Answer choice (E): The passage indicates that the family was not even aware of their occasional use of Spanish prior to their discussions with the researchers. When the family discovered this code-switching and how they interpreted it is not relevant to this question.

Passage #3: Reader-response theory, formalism, and divining meaning from a text (Questions 14-21)

Paragraph 1 Overview

This passage opens with a characterization of two contrasting literary theories: reader-response theory and formalist literary criticism. It is very common for LSAT passages to present multiple approaches to a given subject. In most cases, the author of the passage will endorse one of these approaches and provide justification for doing so. A test takers primary task when reading such passages is to identify the defining characteristics of each approach, along with the purported strengths and weaknesses. In the passage, the defining characteristics are immediately evident: formalism places "emphasis in the interpretation of literature [on] the text itself" and reader-response theory shifts that emphasis "to the contributions of readers to the meaning of a text" (lines 3-5). Note also that reader-response theory is a reaction to formalism, indicating that reader-response theory arose subsequent to formalism. The passage further informs readers that reader-response theory imbues literary texts with no meaning independent of individual readers and that this attribute increases the probability of varying interpretations. These varying interpretations are labeled "fragmented views" by formalists, who advocate a unified approach to literary texts. The final sentence of this paragraph gives readers their first indication of the author's perspective by labeling the formalists' view "unnecessarily narrow" (line 20).

Paragraph 2 Overview

The passage continues by contrasting the two referenced approaches with regard to the search for meaning within literary texts. Formalists characterize their approach as rational and objective while maintaining that reader-response theory lacks standards and is almost completely subjective. The second sentence of this paragraph bears further analysis: since authors cannot pack countless meanings into literary texts, countless interpretations of those texts must be meaningless. This seems to be the primary concern of formalists regarding reader-response theory – that the real meaning of the text will be lost amidst innumerable fragmented interpretations, and that this outcome can be avoided by responsible critics who search a literary text closely to find the author's intended meaning. The author agrees that texts must be closely searched (lines 32-35), but argues that this search need not lead to a singular destination. The final sentence provides a rebuttal of the formalists' premise that no author can create a work that is packed with countless meanings. The author of a literary text does not have to pack countless meanings into a text since many of these meanings are "created in encounters between text and readers" (lines 39-40). These additional meanings necessitate an approach that recognizes and uses them, an approach such as reader-response theory.

Paragraph 3 Overview

As noted in paragraph one, reader-response theory emphasizes the varying presuppositions and perceptions of readers. The author now adds that the emphasis "can uncover hitherto unnoticed dimensions of the text" (lines 43-44). The second sentence of this paragraph is rather lengthy and should be read carefully to avoid misinterpretation. Be careful not to conclude that this information changes the temporal relationship between formalism and reader-response theory. In lines 49-55, the author concedes a potential weakness of reader-response theory, but believes that this weakness is outweighed by "legitimate additional insights and understandings." Note that the author believes that burdening literature of the past with contemporary ideologies is sometimes unfair; the author does not necessarily believe that contemporary reinterpretations are always inappropriate. Again, be careful to avoid overstating or oversimplifying the arguments within any Reading Comprehension passage. The passage closes with a strong endorsement of reader-response theory.

Passage Summary

Written texts are fluid and lively forms of discourse and are subject to multiple interpretations as proposed by reader-response theory, a theory that provides more appropriate insight into a literary text than formalism.

Passage Structure

Paragraph 1: Describes two contrasting literary theories and argues that one is inferior (formalism)

Paragraph 2: Examines the tenets of both theories in greater detail and provides further support for the more recent theory (reader-response theory)

Paragraph 3: Argues that the potential benefits of the more recent theory greatly outweigh the possible harms, and concludes that this newer theory is the more preferable of the two

Question #14: Author's Perspective. The correct answer choice is (E)

The correct answer choice must describe the author's negative, albeit tempered, view of formalism.

Answer choice (A): Though the passage has a scholarly tone, even a causal reading indicates that the author was not neutral toward formalism.

Answer choice (B): The term "grudging" suggests that the author respects formalism in spite of him or herself. Although the author devotes nearly an entire paragraph to describing the views of formalism, there is no indication that the author admires or respects those views.

Answer choice (C): Whereas answer choice (A) suggests that the author had no stance toward formalism and answer choice (B) suggests that the author had a positive stance, this answer choice correctly indicates the author's negative stance toward formalism. However, it is difficult to characterize any aspect of this passage as "thoughtless." The author explores both approaches in relative depth and clearly indicates a rationale for rejecting formalism.

Answer choice (D): Because the author takes a definite stance on this issue, his attitude toward formalism cannot be described as "ambivalence."

Answer choice (E): This is the correct answer choice. Like answer choice (C), this answer choice correctly denotes the author's negative stance toward formalism. Unlike answer choice (C), however, this answer choice also credits the author with a rational approach. Among the author's reasons for dismissing formalism are his or her belief that formalism is "unnecessarily narrow" and the belief that formalism does not fully enable critics to discern and make use of the rich stock of meanings in a text.

Question #15: Must Be True, Analogy. The correct answer choice is (E)

Among the principles of reader-response theory is that varying interpretations of literary works are "not only valid but also useful" (lines 56-57). The correct answer choice to this question should provide an example of someone subjecting a text to a new or unique perspective.

Answer choice (A): An approach such as this one which seeks to limit the number of possible interpretations does not suggest sympathy with the principles of reader-response theory.

Answer choice (B): Perhaps this answer choice is drawn from the author's claim that it is sometimes unfair to burden literature of the past with contemporary ideology (although burdening music of the past with contemporary instrumentation is not completely analogous). Still, we cannot eliminate this answer choice solely because of differing subject matter (music versus literature). Instead, this answer choice is incorrect because it contradicts the "notion of [works] as fluid and lively forms of discourse that can continue to support new interpretations long after their original composition" (lines 60-62).

Answer choice (C): This answer choice quite closely describes a critic's search for the author's intended meaning within a work as discussed in paragraph two of the passage. Indeed, some literary theorists would likely applaud the reviewer's discovery of these unifying themes. Of course, this approach is clearly advocated by proponents of formalism and does not suggest sympathy toward reader-response theory.

Answer choice (D): The emphasis in this answer choice is on the creation of a literary work rather than the interpretation of it. The folk artist's approach most strongly approximates the creation of a map pointing toward a single meaning. Although reader-response theory is concerned with understanding cultural symbols and motifs, it does not suggest that those symbols should convey commonly understood meanings.

Answer choice (E): This is the correct answer choice. Setting a Shakespearean play in nineteenth-century Japan would certainly be different from Shakespeare's own interpretations of his work. However, reader-response theory "legitimizes a wide range of perspectives on [literary] works" (lines 59-60) and uses these perspectives to "uncover hitherto unnoticed dimensions" (line 43) of the work. The director's approach here strongly suggests sympathy with these principles.

Question #16: Author's Perspective. The correct answer choice is (B)

Remember, the author is a supporter of reader-response theory and would likely advocate that literary texts are subject to multiple interpretations and that literary theories can be used to "uncover hitherto unnoticed dimensions of the text" (lines 43-44).

Answer choice (A): The author writes that reader-response theory gives rise to the probability of varying interpretations. However, these interpretations are not necessarily contradictory, nor inevitable. The word "any" in this answer choice is also a red flag. Be very wary of choosing answer choices with absolute language unless the tone of the passage is similarly absolute.

Answer choice (B): This is the correct answer choice. In paragraph two, the author writes that a method is needed "to discern and make use of the rich stock of meanings created in encounters between texts and readers" (lines 38-40). The author also writes that reader-response theory can "uncover hitherto unnoticed dimensions of a text" (lines 43-44) and is "is useful in understanding the works" (line 57). Each of these claims provides evidence that the author believes a literary theory should broaden and enhance the understanding that can be gained from a work. This answer choice is further strengthened by saying "*A* purpose…" rather than "*The* purpose…," which is much more absolute.

Answer choice (C): This answer choice is only partially correct. The author of the passage would certainly agree that a literary theory should provide valid methods for interpreting texts. However, it is the proponents of formalism who argue for strictly objective methods and the author is certainly not a proponent of formalism.

Answer choice (D): Notice that this answer choice begins, "*The* purpose …" This construction dramatically increases the burden of proof necessary for choosing this answer choice. For this to be the correct answer choice, the author must be most likely to agree that this is the *only* purpose of a literary theory. Of course, making "clear the intended meaning of the author of a work" is an aim of formalists described in paragraph two and is not the author's conception of the purpose of a literary theory.

Answer choice (E): This answer choice is also only partially correct. The author would be likely to agree that no literary theory has a monopoly on meaning (line 18), but he or she would not be likely to agree that this is a reason for avoiding the use of literary theories altogether.

Question #17: Must Be True. The correct answer choice is (A)

Reader-response theory emphasizes varied perspectives when interpreting a literary work and the correct answer choice must reiterate this idea.

Answer choice (A): This is the correct answer choice. This is the easiest question in this section. Line 58 reads, "reader-response theory legitimizes a wide range of perspectives on these works," which is reproduced nearly verbatim in this answer choice. Most test takers can confidently prephrase this answer choice and move on to the next question.

Answer choice (B): The passage indicates that contemporary ideology is not always a fair basis for criticism. It may be appropriate in some instances but the passage does not legitimize that inference.

Answer choice (C): The authors writes that "a literary work is indeed encoded in various signs and symbols" (lines 32-34), but cites this as an example of a premise common to both reader-response theory and formalism. But this premise is presented as independent of either theory and is therefore incorrect.

Answer choice (D): This statement is given in the passage as a premise of formalism. According to the passage, reader-response theory legitimizes finding the meanings of a work in the encounters between the text and its readers.

Answer choice (E): Lines 29-30 state that "the author's intended meaning is legible within the work." However, like answer choice (D), this is described as a premise of formalism. It is unclear from the passage whether or not proponents of reader-response theory would agree with this statement.

Question #18: Specific Reference, Function. The correct answer choice is (D)

This reference is a negative aspect of reader-response theory however the author believes that it is far outweighed by the positive aspects of this theory.

Answer choice (A): This answer choice is drawn from several different portions of the passage, none of which is directly related to the phrase contained in the question stem. It is perhaps most closely linked to the author's claim that "any complicated literary work will invariably raise more questions than it answers" (lines 35-37). However, that claim is based on the complexity of the literary work rather than the application of reader-response theory and has nothing to do with the reference in line 51.

Answer choice (B): The best approach for specific reference questions is to find the reference indicated and begin reading the passage approximately five lines prior to that reference. This will allow for a more thorough understanding of the full context of the reference. The source for this answer choice is at least within five lines of the specific reference. However, the longevity of reader-based interpretations is a separate claim and has no direct link to the "unfairly burdened" literature of the past.

Answer choice (C): This is the best answer choice so far, but it is too extreme. The reference to literature of the past as being unfairly burdened is not cited as a fundamental flaw of reader-response theory but an occasional consequence. Furthermore, this reference is not intended to portray reader-response theory as untenable.

Answer choice (D): This is the correct answer choice. In the reference given, the author notes that reader-response theory may lead to negative consequences in some cases, but immediately points out that it has positive consequences as well. The author's strong endorsement of the theory in the concluding sentence of the passage reiterates the author's belief that the benefits of reader-response theory outweigh its potential weaknesses.

Answer choice (E): While the author writes that reader-response theory increases the probability of varying interpretations, he does not classify these interpretations as fragmented views of a work. That classification is attributed to formalists. More importantly, this idea is not supported by the reference contained in line 51.

Question #19: Weaken. The correct answer choice is (B)

The author states that reader-response theory provides numerous additional, beneficial insights into understanding a literary text. To weaken that conclusion, the correct answer choice should show that these insights are somehow harmful or detrimental to understanding a literary work.

Answer choice (A): In lines 44-45, the author writes that "many important works have received varying interpretations throughout their existence" in order to support the claim that these interpretations can help us better understand literature. Since this answer choice is a restatement of one of the author's premises, it does not weaken the author's argument.

Answer choice (B): This is the correct answer choice. This answer choice attacks one of the author's proposed advantages of reader-response theory. The author writes that reader-response theory provides "legitimate additional insights and understandings" (lines 52-53) which are "useful in understanding the works" (line 57). If these additional insights conflicted with or contradicted one another, or if they diminished the understanding of a literary work, they would be less useful in understanding the works and reader-response theory would be weakened.

Answer choice (C): Do not confuse criticisms of a theory with weaknesses in the author's argument. A Reading Comprehension author may defend a flawed theory very effectively or advocate a "flawless" theory very poorly. Also, the most effective authors account for the weaknesses of their theories in their argumentation. Test takers who are careful to distinguish between theory and argumentation will not be fooled by incorrect answer choices.

The fact that reader-response theory fails to provide a unified view of the meaning of a work is a legitimate criticism of the theory by formalists. However, it is not a weakness in the author's argument because the author does not claim that good theories should provide a unified view. Instead, he writes that an effective method "enables the critic to discern and make use of the rich stock of meanings created in encounters between texts and readers" (lines 37-40). According the author, the lack of unified meaning is virtue of reader-response theory, not a weakness.

Answer choice (D): The vast majority of test takers recognize this statement as one of the key characteristics of reader-response theory discussed in paragraph one. Confirming the author's description of reader-response theory does not weaken the author's argumentation.

Answer choice (E): Like answer choice (C), this a criticism advanced by the proponents of formalism. The author freely admits that many of the meanings are created "only when encountered by individual readers" (lines 6-7), but the author views the creation of additional meanings as a positive consequence of reader-response theory.

Question #20: Specific Reference. The correct answer choice is (B)

The "signs and symbols" referred to in paragraph two are given to illustrate that a literary text does contain some inherent indications of the author's intent. These signs must be interpreted with reliable literary theories in order to gain a more accurate understanding of the work.

Answer choice (A): This answer choice might be attractive to some test takers because the author mentions "complicated literary work" in the very next sentence (lines 35-37). But the author's point here is that complicated literature is confusing, not that good literature is complicated. Furthermore, the reference to "various signs and symbols" is not directly linked to the following sentence. It must serve a different function.

Answer choice (B): This is the correct answer choice. Reader-response theory leads to varying interpretations of literary works, but it does not legitimize interpretations that have no basis in the text. By pointing out that the "various signs and symbols must be translated for the work to be understood," the author "grants that a reader must be guided by the text to some degree."

Answer choice (C): This answer choice is also drawn from the immediate context of the specific reference. Since any complicated work will invariably raise more questions than it answers, some test takers may infer that no theory can fully explain such literature. But the specific reference given does not address the explanatory power of literary theories; instead, it describes a portion of the appropriate relationship between a reader and a text.

Answer choice (D): This was a commonly chosen incorrect answer. Test takers can easily identify the author's claim that a literary work is not a map and mistakenly assume that the rest of the sentence is a premise to support that claim. But the author actually refers to "signs and symbols" as a similarity between maps and literary texts. Maps and texts both use signs and symbols that must be translated in order for each to be understood and appreciated, but they lead to different destinations. This is a good example of an Attractive Distractor.

Answer choice (E): Test takers should immediately identify this answer choice with formalism and recognize that the author's purpose with this reference is not to advocate formalism. The author does not ask readers to apply an inflexible standard of interpretation in order to accurately arrive at the correct meaning of a text.

Question #21. Must Be True. The correct answer choice is (A)

The correct answer choice will likely contain information about either reader-response theory (the better theory; provides a more useful means to evaluate and understand a literary text by allowing readers to apply their personal interpretation to the work) or formalism (the less useful theory; implies that a literary work has an objective meaning and a proper evaluation of the content of the text will yield a unified view).

Answer choice (A): This is the correct answer choice. Formalists argue that an author's intended meaning is always legible within a work, no matter how obscured or hidden that meaning may be. Since it is a critic's duty to look for this meaning, responsible critics should tend to find it or something similar to it.

Answer choice (B): The passage states that interpretations similar to reader-response theory existed long before reader-response theory was articulated (lines 44-49) and that formalist literary criticism existed before reader-response theory (line 2). However, the author does not mention anything about the precursors to formalism and so readers cannot infer that formalist approaches existed long before the theory itself existed.

Answer choice (C): This is an intriguing question: if formalists are always looking for the author's intended meaning, what will they find if there is no intended meaning? Unfortunately, the passage does not provide enough information to answer this question. It may be that formalists would find no meaning or many different meanings. In any case, formalists would likely argue that this issue is irrelevant since every author must have at least one particular intended meaning.

Answer choice (D): This answer choice is essentially a Mistaken Negation of the author's claim in lines 49-52. While the passage does suggest that reader-response theory may result in interpretations that are unfairly contemporary, it does not argue that reader-response theory must use historical context to be valid.

Answer choice (E): Most test takers can eliminate this answer choice as an exaggeration and an unwarranted assumption. The passage does note that formalism is older than reader-response theory, but it cannot be known if formalism is a day older, a week older, or a decade older. Also, at no point does the passage discuss which theory has more adherents or that the older theory is more popular.

Passage #4: Approaches to institutional ownership of faculty inventions (Questions 22-28)

Paragraph 1 Overview

At many research-oriented institutions, most faculty discoveries, particularly those with commercial value, are owned by the institution. Institutions benefit from this ownership in at least two different ways. First, valuable discoveries may encourage donors to sponsor additional research. Second, any discoveries which can be licensed or patented may generate royalties for the institution. When reading this passage, test takers should be wondering how the faculty react to this institutional policy. The passage suggests that faculty are unlikely to start their own businesses but may be recruited by existing research companies. A study warns that institutions which are not flexible enough to allow faculty some freedom for business ventures may lose those faculty altogether. This leads to the main point of the passage: institutions must consider various policies toward ownership of faculty research in order to meet their own needs and the desires of faculty.

Paragraph 2 Overview

Here, the passage suggests implementing a fourfold classification of institutional policies. For each of the four policies, readers should carefully note the established criteria for institutional ownership and how these criteria differ from policy to policy. This can be very challenging for some test takers and provides a wealth of possible questions for the test makers. Expect several of the questions to include aspects of the four policies among the answer choices, as well as a fifth concept that may not be directly supported by the passage. Readers who are unable to distinguish the four policies from one another (and possibly from a fifth, unmentioned element) will not do well on this passage.

The three policies discussed in this paragraph are supramaximalist, maximalist, and resource-provider. They are presented in order from the broadest ownership claim to the narrowest. Supramaximalist institutions claim ownership of research that meets any of three criteria: if it is produced during the course of employment at a university, if it is produced through university resources, or if it is the result of any other faculty activity, regardless of the sponsor. Maximalist institutions use the first two criteria, and resource-provider institutions depend solely on the "significant use" of university resources to determine ownership. Note that all three policies can be applied to give institutions ownership of nearly all faculty research.

<u>Paragraph 3 Overview</u>

The third paragraph notes that these three policies have an "uncertain legal and historical basis" (line 52). These uncertainties do not deter most universities and may encourage them to continue to use such policies, since the extent of faculty's rights cannot be clearly determined. Under common law, faculty should own their inventions, but these institutions presume the opposite. Some institutions may grant faculty rights such as royalty sharing, but "most major institutions behave in the ways that maximize university ownership and profit participation" (lines 56-58).

<u>Paragraph 4 Overview</u>

Finally, the passage discusses a fourth approach which does not suffer from the issues mentioned in the third paragraph. This approach is faculty-oriented and presumes that intellectual property belongs fundamentally to the faculty. Except in cases of public health developments and "substantial university involvement" (line 65), faculty are free to exploit their own discoveries. This approach is not contrary to common law and legitimizes a far lesser degree of university ownership and profit participation than the other three approaches mentioned previously. Readers should note that this is the only approach which distinguishes by the type of product rather than just the manner of research. Readers should also be aware that the author does not explicitly advocate this approach for all institutions.

<u>Passage Summary</u>

In order to meet their own needs and the desires of faculty, institutions must consider various policies toward ownership of faculty research. Specifically, most institutions should seek to become faculty-oriented institutions, as this allows for researchers to own their own intellectual products without universities infringing upon the legal rights of the faculty members (as is often the case with the three other classifications of institutional policies).

<u>Passage Structure</u>

> Paragraph 1: Introduces the need to consider the different intellectual property policies that govern universities' ownership rights to faculty inventions
> Paragraph 2: Describes three institutional policies that give universities the majority that are frequently used and that give universities the majority of ownership rights
> Paragraph 3: Discusses the uncertain legal and historical status of the three policies examined in the previous paragraph
> Paragraph 4: Presents a fourth policy that gives ownership rights to the faculty, and that is free of the issues mentioned in paragraph three

Question #22: Main Point. The correct answer choice is (D)

The correct answer choice will likely include the following: (1) institutions seek to profit from the inventions of their faculty, (2) the majority of institutional policies seem to give universities the rights to faculty inventions, (3) these policies are questionable based upon their uncertain legal basis, and (4) there is another policy that seems preferable and that grants faculty members ownership rights.

Answer choice (A): This seems like a very good description of the main point at first. Lines 7-10 discuss the expectations of universities to profit from faculty research and lines 16-19 discuss the risk of losing faculty to other commercial interests. However, the phrase "establish clear-cut policies" should be a red-flag. A very clear-cut policy which does not provide appropriate flexibility to faculty will do nothing to curtail the risk of losing faculty to research corporations or commercial consulting contracts.

Answer choice (B): This answer choice discusses the fourfold classification system mentioned in paragraph two, but emphasizes that this system "is sufficient to categorize the variety of steps institutions are taking" to prevent the loss of faculty. The comprehensiveness of Patricia Chew's system is irrelevant to the passage's main focus on the need for institutions to choose an appropriate policy.

Answer choice (C): According to the passage, only faculty-oriented institutions "adopt the common law presumption that faculty alone own their inventions." But this approach does not guarantee that faculty will not leave for commercial firms or research corporations. Furthermore, the passage does not assert that all institutions should adopt the faculty-oriented approach. It only states that they must "provide the appropriate level of flexibility" so that faculty will not be tempted to leave (lines 23-24). This answer choice is too extreme and too narrow.

Answer choice (D): This is the correct answer choice. Answer choice (D) is a good paraphrase of the transition between the third and fourth paragraphs. For this reason, some test takers may deem this answer choice too narrow to describe the main point of the passage, but the test makers have included all of the necessary elements in this sentence. It addresses all four policies, along with the respective motivations of universities and researchers regarding the exploitation of faculty inventions.

Answer choice (E): Although the third paragraph claims that the policies discussed in the preceding paragraph are based upon a presumption that is contrary to common law, it does conclude that these policies are indefensible. The third paragraph also suggests that these policies may take advantage of "faculty's limited knowledge of their rights" (lines 55-56), but does not claim that these policies go unchallenged. This answer choice also fails to address the faculty-oriented institutional policy.

Question #23: Author's Perspective. The correct answer choice is (A)

The author believes that the intellectual property policies of most institutions are intended to "maximize university ownership and profit participation" (lines 57-58).

Answer choice (A): This is the correct answer choice. Again, the author believes that the intellectual property policies of the majority of institutions are designed to "maximize university ownership and profit participation" (lines 57-58). Such goals clearly represent financial interests of the institution and answer choice (A) is therefore correct. Most test takers answered this question correctly.

Answer choice (B): Remember that most Reading Comprehension questions are a variation of Must Be True questions and must be supported by specific information from the passage. This passage talks about the expectations and policies of a university but never mentions its mission. Therefore, one cannot conclude that the author feels these policies are antithetical to the university's mission.

Answer choice (C): The passage does not explicitly describe what impact, if any, the various policies will have on faculty research. Does this mean that readers can assume there is no significant impact? No, and they cannot assume that the author believes this, either. Absence of evidence does not constitute evidence of absence.

Answer choice (D): Again, there is no evidence of what impact these policies have on faculty research. Where the last answer choice asked test takers to assume there was no impact, this answer choice asks them to assume there is always a harmful impact. Both conclusions are equally unfounded.

Answer choice (E): Although paragraph three notes that the ownership of intellectual property has as an "uncertain legal and historical basis" (line 52), the author never claims that these policies are illegal. Being uncertain or unsettled is certainly not equivalent to being "illegal and possibly immoral."

Question #24: Cannot Be True. The correct answer choice is (B)

This question tests readers' ability to identify the distinguishing characteristics of each institutional policy. Some institutions may fit several classifications, but one institution will fit none of them. In each answer choice, try to identify a policy that fits the institution described and then quickly move on to the next answer choice.

Answer choice (A): A faculty-oriented institution would allow faculty to own the right to some inventions created outside the institution if those inventions were not related to public health. A resource-provider institution would allow faculty the same right if there was no significant use of university resources, as would a maximalist institution, provided the invention also occurred outside the course of university employment.

Answer choice (B): This is the correct answer choice. None of the four policies described in the passage allow faculty to own all their inventions, regardless of any circumstances. Even faculty-oriented institutions, which exercise the narrowest ownership claim, will claim ownership of faculty inventions under certain circumstances. This institution would not be covered by Chew's fourfold classification system.

Answer choice (C): The institution described here claims ownership of all inventions produced with institutional resources. Both supramaximalist and maximalist institutions exercise such broad claims and fit within the fourfold classification system.

Answer choice (D): This institution could be a faculty-oriented institution since the passage states that faculty-oriented institutions maintain a claim to all faculty inventions related to public health.

Answer choice (E): Some inventions produced with institutional resources at resource-provider institutions and at faculty-oriented institutions may remain the property of the faculty member. Such an institution could fall into either category of Chew's classification system.

Question #25: Must Be True. The correct answer choice is (D)

The most ambiguous of the four policies is the resource-provider policy (from lines 43-45).

Answer choice (A): After reading this passage, one cannot determine who owns intellectual products at commercial firms. But the question asks which institution's ownership policy is most unclear to its employees. Just because the ownership is uncertain to us does not mean that it is uncertain to the employees. This answer choice cannot be supported by the passage.

Answer choice (B): Employees at a supramaximalist institution should have no uncertainty about who owns their intellectual products. Supramaximalist universities claim ownership of all intellectual products from their faculty activity, whether or not that activity involved university resources.

Answer choice (C): Faculty members at a maximalist university can determine quite clearly who owns their intellectual products. If they were produced during the course of university employment or using university resources, they belong to the university. If neither of those conditions occurred, the property belongs to the faculty.

Answer choice (D): This is the correct answer choice. In order to determine ownership of intellectual property at a resource-provider university, faculty must ask themselves if the property was developed through the use of university time or facilities. If the answer is no, then the property belongs to the faculty. However, if the answer is yes, the ownership remains uncertain. The faculty may retain ownership in some cases, but the university will claim ownership if it determines that the use of university resources was "significant." This answer choice is correct because of the ambiguity in determining "significant use."

Answer choice (E): Faculty at faculty-oriented universities must answer two questions to determine ownership of their intellectual products. First, is the product a public health development? If the answer is yes, then it belongs to the university. If the answer is no, then they must ask if there was "previously specified 'substantial university involvement.'" Again, if the answer is yes, the product belongs to the university, but if the answer is no, then the product belongs to the faculty.

Question #26: Must Be True. The correct answer choice is (E)

A resource-provider institution is characterized by its use of university "time and facilities" (line 43) to determine ownership of faculty inventions.

Answer choice (A): Resource-provider institutions may be somewhat vague about what constitutes "significant use" of university resources, but there is no indication that this vagueness extends to the definition of university resources.

Answer choice (B): This answer choice is only partially correct. Resource-provider institutions are grouped among the three institutions which attempt to maximize university profit participation, but none of the institutions provides faculty with unlimited flexibility. Each of the four policies, including faculty-oriented policy, has some restraints regarding faculty freedom.

Answer choice (C): The inversion of industry practice for exploiting faculty inventions is a distinguishing characteristic of faculty-oriented institutions. Resource-provider institutions follow the standard practice, but impose fewer restrictions than maximalist or supramaximalist institutions. Test takers should have no difficulty identifying this answer choice as incorrect.

Answer choice (D): All four institutions could claim ownership of faculty inventions developed outside of the institution under certain circumstances. Supramaximalist universities would claim ownership if any faculty activity was involved, and maximalist universities would claim ownership if the invention was developed in the course of the faculty's employment. Resource-provider universities would claim the invention if it involved significant use of university time, and faculty-oriented institutions would claim it if it were related to public health.

Answer choice (E): This is the correct answer choice. Although faculty-oriented institutions have some provision for the extent of use of institutional resources, only resource-provider institutions rely upon this criterion alone for determining ownership of faculty inventions. The other three institutions all rely upon at least two criteria and neither supramaximalist nor maximalist institutions are concerned with the extent of use of institutional resources.

Question #27: Specific Reference, Function. The correct answer choice is (A)

The study of entrepreneurship mentioned is given as a warning to universities that do not develop more flexible, faculty-driven policies for determining ownership rights to faculty inventions.

Answer choice (A): This is the correct answer choice. The study quoted in lines 16-19 warns that faculty who are not provided with adequate flexibility will be tempted to leave universities for business ventures. The author uses this finding to justify the claim that universities must develop appropriate intellectual property policies as described in this answer choice.

Answer choice (B): The passage does not explore a contrast between the worlds of academia and business in any detail beyond this reference. In fact, the passage does not mention the business world again after this sentence.

Answer choice (C): This study does not address the intellectual property rights of inventors, nor does it claim that those rights are being encroached. The study only mentions the commercialized desires of faculty inventors. Faculty rights are first discussed in the following paragraph.

Answer choice (D): It is unclear from the passage whether this study preceded Chew's study of faculty rights. Furthermore, the passage does not indicate whether Chew was influenced by or even aware of the study quoted here. Answer choice (D) is clearly incorrect.

Answer choice (E): One could argue that this study proves that some faculty inventors would be better off working for commercial firms. After all, why else would they be tempted to leave universities? But the question does not ask test takers to identify any possible implication of the study; it asks test takers to identify how the author uses this study. Obviously, the author is not trying to prove that faculty members should work for commercial firms, so this answer choice is incorrect.

Question #28: Must Be True Except. The correct answer choice is (E)

The four incorrect answer choices for this question will all be supported by information from the passage; the correct answer choice will either be unmentioned by the author or will contradict information given.

Answer choice (A): This answer choice can be confirmed by the first two paragraphs. The passage identifies supramaximalist institutions as having the broadest ownership claims on faculty inventions. The broader these claims are, the less flexibility faculty has in pursuing commercialized interests and the more tempted they will be to pursue jobs in institutions which are more responsive to their needs.

Answer choice (B): To confirm this answer choice, readers should immediately return to the fourth paragraph. Beginning in line 60, the passage states "faculty-oriented institutions assume that researchers own their own intellectual products…except in the development of public health inventions or if there is previously specified 'substantial university involvement'" (lines 60-65). Thus, faculty-oriented institutions will not claim any product which does not satisfy at least one of these requirements.

Answer choice (C): The second paragraph states that maximalist institutions claim ownership of inventions that "arise either 'in the course of the faculty's employment [or] from the faculty's use of university resources'" (lines 35-37). All other inventions belong to the faculty. However, the passage further notes that "this [maximalist] approach…can affect virtually all of a faculty member's intellectual production" (lines 37-40). If this is true, then most faculty inventions at maximalist institutions must be produced inside the institution or using the institution's resources.

Answer choice (D): After confirming answer choice (C), it is quite easy to show that there is little practical difference between maximalist and supramaximalist policies. Supramaximalist policies assert ownership "of all intellectual property produced by faculty" (line 29) and "for any inventions or patent rights from faculty activities" (lines 31-32). Maximalist policy "can affect virtually all of a faculty member's intellectual production" (line 40). In practice, then, both policies have nearly the same effect on intellectual property ownership.

Answer choice (E): This is the correct answer choice. Rather than using any objective standard for determining property ownership, resource-provider institutions rely strictly on the subjective definition of "significant use" of university resources to assert claims on faculty discoveries. Since "what constitutes significant use of resources is a matter of institutional judgment" (lines 44-45), the passage does not suggest that this standard will be constant in all cases.

Overview: Overall, this section is considered to be somewhat easier than the second Logical Reasoning section on this test. As is typically the case, the first several questions in the section are generally easier than the questions appearing later in the section (although questions #22 and 23 are among the easiest questions in the section and question #10 is one of the more difficult questions). The first Logical Reasoning section contains three Assumption questions, with both Supporter and Defender assumption models represented. Questions #1 and #13 are both Point at Issue questions, while question #19 is a Must be True question that is sometimes mistaken for Point at Issue. Some test takers had difficulty with questions #7, #17, and #22, which each had significant formal logic features. The explanations provided for these questions are very thorough and should provide a greater understanding of the most effective approaches to formal logic questions. The section has three Strengthen questions (questions #8, #14, and #21) but only one Weaken question (question #6). Question #15 is a very difficult Resolve the Paradox question and question #21 is indicative of the test makers' attitude toward surveys and public opinion polls.

Question #1: Point at Issue. The correct answer choice is (C)

This Point at Issue question contrasts two viewpoints about bebop jazz musicians. Both Pettengill and Romney agree that bebop musicians "radically reshaped" jazz classics, but disagree about the musicians' motivation for doing so. Pettengill argues that bebop musicians found jazz classics distasteful and uninteresting, while Romney contends that these artists appreciated the compelling, versatile nature of jazz classics and sought to discover deeper levels in the original music. Answer choice (C) correctly expresses this disagreement.

Answer choice (A): Pettengill and Romney both use the term "radical reshaping" to describe bebop musicians' reinterpretation of jazz classics. Since both authors agree with this statement, it cannot be the correct answer choice.

Answer choice (B): This answer choice is the most attractive of the incorrect answers. Romney claims that bebop musicians "discover[ed] previously unknown depths in the music" they reshaped. So Romney would likely agree with this statement. What about Pettengill? While Pettengill certainly seems negatively inclined toward bebop musicians, Pettengill never makes a value judgment about bebop music itself. It is possible (though perhaps unlikely) that Pettengill believes that jazz classics can "be made interesting only through radical reshaping." Since Pettengill's position regarding the final state of the reshaped music is uncertain, answer choice (B) is incorrect.

Answer choice (C): This is the correct answer choice. The correct answer choice to any Point at Issue question must pass the Agree/Disagree Test: Romney agrees that "bebop musicians showed appreciation for jazz classics" by recognizing them as "compelling, versatile" songs. Pettengill argues that bebop musicians showed "distaste for jazz classics" and therefore disagrees with this statement.

Answer choice (D): The stimulus does not provide enough information to determine how either Pettengill or Romney would respond to this statement. Neither speaker addresses widespread popularity, so this cannot be the correct answer choice.

Answer choice (E): Both Pettengill and Romney would agree that bebop musicians were influenced by their predecessors and that alone is sufficient to eliminate this answer choice. Further, it is unclear whether either or both speakers necessarily consider earlier styles to be more conservative than the style of bebop musicians. It is possible that the radical reshaping both speakers attribute to bebop musicians was simply from one liberal style of jazz to another.

Question #2: Method of Reasoning—Argument Part. The correct answer choice is (A)

In any LSAT logic reasoning question which contains a conclusion, it is essential to correctly identify and isolate that conclusion. This stimulus is structured as follows:

Conclusion: Earth is a living organism, composed of other organisms much as animals are composed of cells, not merely a thing upon which creatures live.

Premise: This hypothesis is supported by the fact that, like all organisms, Earth can be said to have a metabolism and to regulate its temperature, humidity, and other characteristics, divorced from the influences of its surroundings.

Premise: Of course, Earth does not literally breathe, but neither do insects (they have no lungs), though they respire successfully.

The second premise regarding insects breathing is unusual and most test takers are immediately drawn to it because, unlike the first premise, this sentence is not offered as direct evidence to support the essayist's claim. Instead, this sentence is a response to a potential objection against the essayist's conclusion. For instance, someone reading this essay might say to themselves, "Well, maybe the Earth can be said to have a metabolism and regulate itself, but it does not breathe and every living organism has to breathe, right? Therefore, the Earth must not be a living organism." In anticipation of this objection, the essayist concedes that Earth does not literally breathe but offers an example of something else which does not breathe and must be considered a living organism. Therefore, some things that do not literally breathe, such as Earth and insects, are nonetheless living organisms. This premise could be classified as a Defender premise, as it defends the conclusion against a possible criticism.

Answer choice (A): This is the correct answer choice. As was discussed in the analysis of the stimulus, some readers might seek to reject the essayist's hypothesis on the basis of Earth's not breathing. The assertion that insects also do not literally breathe provides a reason for not rejecting the claim on this basis alone. Whether the conclusion is actually valid or not is irrelevant and remains to be proven (for example, one might point out that the essayist has failed to prove that, like insects, the Earth respires successfully).

Answer choice (B): This is a fairly obvious Opposite Answer. Even the most balanced and objective LSAT author will never attempt to explicitly disprove his or her own conclusion. In any case where a conclusion is present, the author of the stimulus is completely committed to that conclusion. Since this stimulus presents only one viewpoint, any evidence that the author presents within the stimulus will be given in an attempt to support that viewpoint (although authors will sometimes mistakenly undermine their own conclusion by presenting conflicting information – this type of flaw is often referred to as an Internal Contradiction – it is never the author's intention to do so).

Answer choice (C): The essayist does posit that all organisms, including Earth, "can be said to have a metabolism." However, the example of insects in the third sentence is not given in order to support this claim. Rather, both premises are used to support the primary conclusion that "Earth is a living organism."

Answer choice (D): The essayist does not feel that Earth or insects are a type of organism whose status is unclear. In fact, the essayist presumes that the status of insects as living organisms is unquestionably clear. If the author had any question about the status of insects as living organisms, they would not be given as support for the conclusion that some things which do not literally breathe can be considered living organisms.

Answer choice (E): Though it can be reasonably inferred that insects are a type of organism out of which Earth is composed, this inference does not explain why the essayist points out that insect do not literally breathe. The correct answer choice must do so, as was seen in answer choice (A).

Question #3: Resolve the Paradox. The correct answer choice is (E)

Two features of this stimulus help identify it as a Resolve the Paradox question: First, there is no conclusion given. The stimulus describes a survey and reports the findings, but does not offer any interpretation. Second, the results are contrary to normal expectations. One would expect that most citizens of country F would prefer a higher GNP over a lower one. Indeed, it would be quite surprising if a survey reported that the majority of citizens said, "I would prefer country F to be worth less rather than more." But this survey did not ask citizens to consider GNP on an absolute basis alone, but rather to compare the GNP of country F to the GNP of country G. The majority of respondents preferred a scenario in which country F's absolute GNP was lower, but its production relative to country G was higher. This suggests that the majority of citizens of country F believe that some aspect of outperforming country G is more desirable than actually having a higher GNP. Answer choice (E) most nearly expresses this idea.

Answer choice (A): Knowing that the citizens of country F believe that their economic growth rate is higher than that of country G does not help to explain why the majority of country F's citizens prefer a scenario where their country has a lower total GNP. The correct answer choice must explain why the majority of country F's citizens are willing to sacrifice some of their GNP in order to have a higher GNP than country G.

Answer choice (B): While it may in fact be true that most citizens of country F want a GNP higher than $120 billion, neither of the survey scenarios included this possibility (both scenarios presented GNPs lower than $120 billion). Therefore, this knowledge cannot help explain the survey results.

Answer choice (C): This answer choice does not explain why the majority of respondents chose scenario 1; citizens who believe that their personal welfare is unconnected to the GNP might just as reasonably have preferred scenario 2. Further, this answer choice does not provide a reason for the majority of respondents' willingness to forego $10 billion in GNP simply to be the world economic leader.

Answer choice (D): This answer choice can be eliminated on much the same grounds as answer choice (C): if true, it provides no logical impetus for selecting scenario 1 over scenario 2.

Answer choice (E): This is the correct answer choice. In contrast to answer choices (C) and (D), this answer choice does provide a logical impetus for preferring scenario 1. If most citizens of country F want their country to be more economically powerful than country G, this consideration may be sufficient to outweigh the lower overall GNP of scenario 1. Remember that the inhabitants of the LSAT world believe their behavior is logical and consistent; if they make a choice, there must be some internal rationale behind that choice. No matter how faulty their reasoning may be, LSAT world inhabitants are never capricious or arbitrary.

Question #4: Must Be True. The correct answer choice is (B)

This question tests your ability to draw proper inferences from two opposing explanations of an observed phenomenon. The stimulus begins with the words "A study claims", which is a very common way for the test makers to introduce contrasting viewpoints in a Logical Reasoning question. Both the study and the author of the stimulus agree that the "average temperature each year for the last five years has been higher than any previous yearly average on record." The study uses this evidence as a premise in support of the claim that "the average temperature on Earth has permanently increased," while the author points out that even ten years of average temperatures which are record highs may be merely random and would not be sufficient to conclude that the increase has become permanent. Answer choice (B) correctly expresses this conclusion.

Answer choice (A): This answer choice is an exaggeration and over-generalization. The stimulus does not address all increases in average temperature on record, nor does it preclude the possibility that a large increase in average temperature has at sometime occurred from one year to the next. Remember, in a Must be True question the correct answer choice will present information that is addressed in the stimulus, and cannot provide details that the stimulus does not mention.

Answer choice (B): This is the correct answer choice. Answer choice (B) is most strongly supported by the information above, as it states that five years of higher than average temperatures does not necessarily mean that those higher temperatures are permanent.

Answer choice (C): This answer choice attempts to trick the reader into viewing the author's premise as a prediction of future circumstances. Just because random fluctuations in temperature can account for up to ten consecutive years of record high temperature does not necessarily mean that any five such years will be followed by five more. Attentive readers should have no difficulty dismissing this answer choice.

On a related note, be particularly wary of any attempt by the test makers to make a definitive prediction about the future. These predictive efforts are almost always flawed and should be viewed accordingly.

Answer choice (D): Answer choice (D) is the most attractive of the incorrect answer choices, but it is inaccurate and incomplete. The author notes that random fluctuations in temperature are always occurring, and that periods of higher than average temperatures can still be considered random, but the stimulus does not indicate how long these random fluctuations "typically" last.

Answer choice (E): Like answer choice (A), this answer choice goes too far. The stimulus makes no mention of whether the average temperature of the Earth could ever increase due to something other than random fluctuation. Further, the tentative word choice in the author's explanation ("up to ten years", "are often...part of") is sufficient to indicate that the correct answer choice will likely also be tentative. The absolute phrasing of this answer choice is enough to quickly eliminate it from further consideration.

Question #5: Assumption—SN. The correct answer choice is (D)

This is very straightforward assumption question. In this type of question, you are given a statement and an illogical response to that statement. Remember, however, that LSAT individuals are never intentionally illogical; that is, their reasoning always seems sound to them, so there must be some presumed condition or statement which would have logically led to the customer's response. The task here is to determine which of the answer choices best describes that misunderstood statement.

In this scenario, the shipping coordinator presents the customer with two options for shipment: air express or ground carrier. The following conditions are expressed:

A (Air express) $\longrightarrow$ T (arrives tomorrow)

G (Ground carrier) $\longrightarrow$ T or $\cancel{T}$ (does not arrive tomorrow)

The customer mistakenly interprets the first condition as:

T $\longrightarrow$ A

That is, if the shipment is to arrive tomorrow, then it must be shipped by air express. This is commonly referred to as a Mistaken Reversal, where the relationship between the Sufficient condition and the Necessary condition is reversed. Answer choice (D) correctly expresses this misinterpretation. For this question, the expense of each option is irrelevant.

Answer choice (A): Reliability is not an issue, as the customer mistakenly assumes that the only way that the shipment can arrive tomorrow is to ship it with Air Express.

Answer choice (B): This is a correct interpretation of the shipping coordinator's first statement (essentially a restatement) and does not explain the customer's response. Again, the customer mistakenly reverses the relationship between shipping via Air Express and receiving the package the following day.

Answer choice (C): This is a correct interpretation of the shipping coordinator's third statement, and the latter half of the customer's response clearly indicates that she understands this point.

Answer choice (D): This is the correct answer choice. Answer choice D is a very close paraphrase of the customer's expressed rationale. This answer choice can be diagrammed as:

T $\longrightarrow$ A

Answer choice (E): This is the most attractive incorrect answer choice (although still chosen quite infrequently by test takers). Though the customer is clearly aware of the increased cost of the air express, this is not the critical factor in her response. The critical factor is her belief that air express is the only way to get the package tomorrow.

Question #6: Weaken. The correct answer choice is (E)

This question describes a legitimate occupational dilemma for therapists: What do you do when a client tells you about an unreported crime? Do you report it and violate the client's trust or do you choose not to report it and thereby jeopardize the public? According to the stimulus, it is impossible for a therapist to keep a client's information private while at the same time making efforts to ensure the public's wellbeing. In order to weaken this argument, you must provide a position that allows a therapist "to both respect their clients' right to confidentiality and be sincerely concerned for the welfare of victims of future violent crimes." In other words, the correct answer choice must provide a way for therapists to somehow reduce the risk of future violent crimes without violating their clients' right to confidentiality. Answer choice (E) best expresses this idea.

Answer choice (A): Whether the therapist voluntarily sought out violent criminals or was assigned to work with them has no impact on the moral dilemma expressed here. Court-appointed therapists would be under the same obligations as any other therapists and this information does not make the two obligations presented in the stimulus any less difficult to meet.

Answer choice (B): The likelihood of a criminal receiving therapy, or the physical location of the criminal when he or she receives therapy, does nothing to weaken this conclusion, as it does not provide a way for therapists to protect the public while still maintaining their clients' right to confidentiality.

Answer choice (C): Remember that the argument is about the dilemma that faces therapists who treat violent criminals. In order to weaken that argument, the correct answer choice must allow for the two obligations of a therapist to coexist. Proving that victims and criminals are entitled to the same rights of confidentiality does not do so.

Answer choice (D): Although it is perfectly acceptable for Weaken answer choices to introduce new information, the idea of compensation for victims of violent crimes in this answer choice has no effect on the argument.

Answer choice (E): This is the correct answer choice. Besides answer choice (A), this is the only other answer choice which actually addresses therapists. Identifying this feature will help you accelerate through the incorrect answer choices to the most likely correct answer choices. In this case, a therapist who has gained a violent criminal's trust (presumably enough so that the criminal confesses an unreported crime) can convince that criminal not to commit future crimes. Thus, it is possible for therapists to simultaneously fulfill their obligations to both the criminal and the public, and the stimulus's conclusion is thereby weakened.

Question #7: Must Be True—SN. The correct answer choice is (C)

For most test takers, this is the hardest question in the section so far. The stimulus contains multiple conditional statements, each of which is also qualified or limited in some way. Much of the difficulty here lies in appropriately diagramming these statements and drawing proper inferences from each one. To best attack this question, consider each sentence individually and attempt to make inferences by combining the sentences based on their common terms (the conditional indicators are italicized).

1. "Failure to rotate crops depletes the soil's nutrients gradually *unless* other preventive measures are taken."

To diagram this sentence, ask yourself, "How can I know for sure that this soil's nutrients have been gradually depleted?" The only way to ensure that nutrient depletion has occurred is to verify that the crops have not been rotated and no other preventive measures were taken. Diagrammatically:

RC = rotate crops
D = soil's nutrients depleted
PM = other preventive measures taken

$$\begin{array}{c} \cancel{RC} \\ \text{and} \\ \cancel{PM} \end{array} \longrightarrow D$$

The contrapositive thus becomes:

$$\cancel{D} \longrightarrow \begin{array}{c} RC \\ \text{or} \\ PM \end{array}$$

That is, if the soil's nutrients are not depleted, than either the crops were rotated or other preventive measures were taken.

2. "If the soil's nutrients are completely depleted, additional crops cannot be grown unless fertilizer is applied to the soil."

This sentence can be diagrammed similarly to the first sentence:

D = soil's nutrients depleted
AC = additional crops grown
F = fertilizer applied

$$\begin{array}{c} D \\ \text{and} \\ \cancel{F} \end{array} \longrightarrow \cancel{AC}$$

The contrapositive is:

$$AC \longrightarrow \begin{array}{c} \cancel{D} \\ \text{or} \\ F \end{array}$$

That is, if additional crops are grown, the soil is either not completely depleted or fertilizer was applied. This inference can be linked to the contrapositive of sentence one through identifying the common term $\cancel{D}$, creating an additive inference and removing the common term. This yields the inference that if additional crops are grown then the crops were rotated, other preventive measures were taken, or fertilizer was applied.

The final two sentences should be evaluated, but need not be diagrammed. Taken together, these sentences indicate that, "all other things being equal," vegetables grown in fertilized soil are more vulnerable to insects, need more pesticide, and pose a greater risk to human health than vegetables grown in non-fertilized soil.

Finally, the question stem indicates that vegetables were grown without fertilizer. Using the contrapositive of sentence two, one can immediately conclude that the soil in which these vegetables grew was not completely depleted of nutrients (crops require either fertilizer or non-depleted soil; these vegetables did not have fertilizer, so the soil could not have been completely depleted of nutrients). And from the contrapositive of the first sentence, if the soil's nutrients are not completely depleted, then either the crops were rotated or other preventative measures were taken (at least one of these two conditions must occur). So what must be true is that the soil's nutrients are not completely depleted, and that either the crops were rotated or other preventative measures were taken.

Answer choice (A): One can know that the soil's nutrients are not completely depleted, because if the soil was completely depleted of nutrients, and the vegetables were not given fertilizer, the vegetables could not grow (from the contrapositive of sentence two). Since the vegetables grew without fertilizer, the soil could not have been completely depleted of nutrients.

Answer choice (B): Answer choice (B) is not correct because it is very much possible that these vegetables grew in soil in which crops had been rotated. Remember, either the crops were rotated or other preventative measures were taken.

Answer choice (C): This is the correct answer choice. This answer choice begins well – "The vegetables were grown in soil that had not been completely depleted of nutrients" – but then becomes somewhat more confusing when it states, "but not necessarily soil in which crops had been rotated." Is crop rotation the only explanation for why the soil had not been completed depleted of nutrients? No. From the contrapositive of the first sentence, when soil's nutrients are not completely depleted, then either the crops were rotated or other preventative measures were taken. So the crops do not have to be rotated (it is not necessary) as long as other preventative measures were taken.

Answer choice (D): This answer choice is incorrect because it cannot be clearly known whether pesticides are the actual cause of health risks to humans who eat the vegetables (although answer choice (D) does seem to contradict the last sentence: the stimulus states that the more pesticides used on vegetables, the greater the health risks to humans, which goes against this answer choice).

Answer choice (E): Much like answer choice (D), answer choice (E) contradicts the last sentence of the stimulus, which states that the more pesticides used on vegetables, the greater the health risks to humans. Thus vegetables treated with pesticides would pose a greater risk than vegetables that were not treated with pesticides.

Question #8: Strengthen Except—CE. The correct answer choice is (C)

This is a StrengthenX question, which indicates that the four incorrect answer choices will all strengthen the argument and the correct answer choice will either have no effect or will weaken the argument. The criminologist claims that the proposed action (increasing the current prison term) will not have the desired effect (discouraging people from committing robbery). Thus, any answer choice that weakens this causal relationship will support the criminologist. Answer choices (A), (B), (D), and (E) all weaken the causal link between the length of a person's prison term and his or her desire to commit robbery. Only answer choice (C) does not weaken this causal relationship and is therefore the correct answer choice.

Answer choice (A): Increasing the current prison term for robbery logically increases the risk to criminals considering robbery. But if many people who rob are motivated by risk-taking, then increasing the prison term would provide increased motivation and would not discourage people from committing robbery.

Answer choice (B): This analogous situation describes an instance in which the same proposed action failed to have the desired effect. If this observation is true for embezzlement, the likelihood that it will prove true for robbery is increased. This strengthens the argument that increasing the prison term for robbery will not discourage people from committing robbery.

Answer choice (C): This is the correct answer choice. Answer choice (C) describes a situation in which the opposite of the proposed action occurs. But since no information is given about what effect this alternate cause has, one cannot draw any conclusions from it. By itself, this information neither supports nor refutes the criminologist's claim. To strengthen the argument, decreasing the prison term length would have to be causally linked to an increase in the number of people committing robberies, however since no further information is given, this is the correct answer.

In StrengthenX or WeakenX questions, one can typically expect the correct answer choice to have no effect on the argument. This is because the test makers want to limit the variance between the correct answer choice and all of the incorrect answer choices. An answer choice that weakens an argument will be significantly different from four answer choices than strengthen that argument and may be easier to isolate than one that has no effect. That said, do not expect the correct answer choice to be utterly irrelevant, either, as that, too, would be relatively easy to identify.

Answer choice (D): This answer choice supports the criminologist's claim by providing additional evidence that there is not a strong link between the crime and the punishment. If most people committing robbery believe they will not get caught, then they will not be deterred by the knowledge that people who do get caught must spend more time in prison.

Answer choice (E): Like the group of people described in answer choice (D), this group of people will also not be deterred by the proposed action. If most criminals were unaware of the length of the prison term for convicted robbers, then a longer prison term would not discourage them from committing a robbery.

Question #9: Flaw in the Reasoning. The correct answer choice is (D)

This is a fairly straightforward example of a Flaw in the Reasoning question. The activist describes the increasingly common practice of electronically monitoring employees and an attempted justification of this practice by employers. The given justification is that electronic monitoring "keeps employees honest, efficient, and polite." The activist concludes that these justifications should not be accepted because they "are obviously self-serving." The activist fails to respond to the justification itself. By questioning the employers' motivation rather than addressing the reasoning that employers use in making their argument, the activist uses the questionable technique described in answer choice (D).

Answer choice (A): Flaw in the Reasoning questions can be valuable study tools because the incorrect answer choices often describe strategies that are employed elsewhere on the LSAT. Answer choice (A) describes a common argumentation technique – known as a Straw Man argument – in which one person misconstrues the opposing position and responds to this distorted version. In this stimulus, the activist is not really attacking any argument at all – just the source of the argument.

Answer choice (B): An implication of the employers' justification for electronic surveillance is that employees are sometimes dishonest, inefficient, or rude; otherwise, why would employers have to keep them honest, efficient, and polite? Presuming this inference to be false without providing adequate justification would certainly be a questionable argumentative technique, but it is not the one used by the activist.

Answer choice (C): This issue is neither addressed by the activist nor necessarily a questionable technique. Introducing moral considerations into an argument is not inherently questionable.

Answer choice (D): This is the correct answer choice. This questionable technique is referred as an ad hominem (against the person) attack (or a Source Argument) and is frequently employed by children and politicians on the LSAT.

Answer choice (E): The activist does not criticize a sample group as being unrepresentative or biased, but rather attacks the employers on a personal level.

This incorrect answer choice has appeared numerous times with very similar wording on the LSAT. Hence, it is very worthwhile to understand what a biased sample is when preparing for the LSAT. A brief discussion of this flaw—as well as each of the other flaws discussed here—can be found in chapter 13 of the PowerScore Logical Reasoning Bible.

Question #10: Assumption. The correct answer choice is (A)

This is a standard example of a Supporter Assumption question. In this type of question, the pieces of an argument are not fully connected and additional information must be provided to link the pieces together. This most often occurs when the test-makers introduce a new, essential element or term in the conclusion that is not addressed elsewhere in the stimulus (thus the author assumes the conclusion with the new information is true, despite the fact that it cannot be properly concluded without providing additional information). The correct answer choice to these questions will generally link the premises to the conclusion via this new term/phrase.

This argument contains two premises and a conclusion:

Premise: Students are less likely to respond positively to negative criticism from computer programs than to negative criticism from humans.

Premise: One must respond positively to criticism in order to accept it.

Conclusion: Students are more likely to learn from criticism by humans than from criticism by computers.

Does this argument seem logical? Perhaps, but the idea of students learning from criticism in this conclusion does not logically follow from anything in the premises. For the conclusion to be logical, one must connect the new information that it contains (students learning) to the premises. Thus the correct answer choice to this question should describe the appropriate relationship between accepting criticism and learning from criticism.

Answer choice (A): This is the correct answer choice. Many test takers intuitively close the gap in this argument as they are reading the stimulus. Answer choice (A) is an assumption on which the argument depends because it explicitly states the link between the second premise and the conclusion.

Answer choice (B): This answer choice is not required by the argument. Even if computers were compassionate, students still might be less likely to respond to criticism from computers than criticism from humans. Therefore, the argument does not depend on assuming that computers are uncompassionate.

Answer choice (C): Whether the less positive response to computer generated criticism was a conscious rejection or an unconscious reaction (i.e. the result of knowing that the criticism was computer generated), the author still concludes that students are more likely to learn from criticism by humans and the correct answer choice must address this new information.

Answer choice (D): One way to determine if an answer choice is a necessary assumption is to negate it and consider the resulting effect on the argument. When a necessary assumption is negated, the argument becomes completely invalid. If the argument remains valid in spite of the negated answer choice, that answer choice is not a necessary assumption and cannot be correct. This is called the Assumption Negation Technique and is extremely useful when attempting Assumption questions.

In this case, would the argument be destroyed if humans were more critical of a given work than computers? No. The argument only compares the students' reaction to negative criticism from both sources. The relative frequency, or the severity, of negative criticism from either source is therefore irrelevant and not an assumption upon which the argument depends.

Answer choice (E): This answer choice can be eliminated by using the same reasoning as was used to eliminate answer choice (D). Whether computers are more critical than humans, just as critical as humans, or less critical than humans, the argument itself is unaffected.

Question #11: Parallel Reasoning. The correct answer choice is (E)

This question is quite easy but provides a good opportunity to discuss some of the basics in approaching Parallel Reasoning questions. In this question, there are four key characteristics of the stimulus that must be paralleled in the correct answer choice. First, there must be an established threshold and two items given (in the stimulus, the threshold is the cost limit and the two phone-systems are the items). Second, the threshold and both items must be defined by the same characteristic (all three are defined with regard to expense). Third, with regards to this characteristic, the items must have the same relationship to each other as one of the items has to the threshold (QI is less expensive than the cost limit and Corelink is less expensive than OI). Fourth, the conclusion must validly prove that each item has the same relationship to the threshold (therefore, Corelink's system must also be inexpensive enough to be within the limit). Only answer choice (E) matches the stimulus in each of these four aspects and is therefore correct.

Answer choice (A): This answer choice has a threshold (being able to touch the ceiling) and two items (Marissa and Jeff). However, Marissa's relationship to the threshold (able to touch the ceiling when she jumps as high as she can) is not defined by the same characteristic as Marissa's relationship to Jeff (Jeff is taller than Marissa). Since jumping ability and height are different and independent characteristics, this answer choice does not parallel the stimulus.

Answer choice (B): This answer choice commits the same fallacy as answer choice (A), though in a more obvious fashion. The threshold is "able to run five miles," which Kate is able to do. The relationship between Kate and Lana is "Lana smokes fewer cigarettes per day than Kate now does." This is clearly not the same as establishing that Lana is able to run further than Kate, which would parallel the reasoning in the stimulus.

Answer choice (C): This is the first answer choice that defines both items and the threshold by the same characteristic (i.e. blood-alcohol level). But it is wrong for two reasons. First, the relationship between John's blood-alcohol level and Paul's blood-alcohol level is unknown. This does not match the stimulus. Second, whereas the conclusion in the stimulus is logically valid, the conclusion in answer choice (C) is not logically valid since Paul's blood-alcohol level could be significantly lower than John's and thus be below the threshold. Note that the conclusion of the correct answer choice in a parallel reasoning question will always have the same validity as the conclusion in the stimulus (known as the Validity Test).

Some test takers will ask if this answer choice can be eliminated because both items here are above this threshold while both items in the stimulus are below the threshold there. The answer is no. Logically, it does not matter in which direction the two items vary from the threshold; it is only important that they vary in the same way. In other words, if this answer choice said that Paul's blood-alcohol level must be above the legal limit since his blood-alcohol level was higher than John's, it would logically parallel the stimulus and could be correct.

Answer choice (D): The threshold here is "dark enough…to be the kind that Luis really likes." "This chocolate" is "not quite dark enough" and fails to meet the threshold. Is this characteristic sufficient to eliminate this answer choice? No. It could still be correct if the second item had the same relationship to the first as the first item has to the threshold. If "that chocolate over there" were lighter than "this chocolate," one could logically conclude that "that chocolate over there" is also not dark enough to be the kind that Luis really likes. However, since that is not the case in this answer choice, it does parallel the stimulus and is incorrect.

Answer choice (E): This is the correct answer choice. Most test takers who read all five answer choices correctly selected this answer choice. Health Dairy's sharp cheddar cheese is lower in fat than the threshold for the "low-fat" labeling standard. Health Dairy's mild cheddar cheese is lower in fat than its sharp cheddar cheese and is therefore lower in fat than the threshold. This answer choice parallels the stimulus in all of its critical logical elements.

Question #12: Flaw in the Reasoning. The correct answer choice is (B)

This stimulus addresses the geocentric view once maintained by Orthodox Christianity. One premise of this view was that "Earth was at the center of the universe" and one of its conclusions was that "Earth and its inhabitants were important." The essayist's premise that Earth is "at the outskirts of a spiral arm of one of countless galaxies" refutes the geocentric premise. Thus, reasons the essayist, the geocentrists' conclusion must also be refuted. The flaw in this argument is obvious: just because one reason for believing something is shown to be false does not necessarily prove that the belief itself is false. Whether or not Earth and its inhabitants are important depends far more on the definition of important than on the location of Earth. Answer choice (B) correctly expresses this idea.

Answer choice (A): This is the most commonly chosen incorrect answer. The essayist's argument is essentially that if the reason for believing something is bad, then the belief itself is false. This answer choice says that if the reason for believing something is good, then the belief is true. Answer choice (A) is actually a Mistaken Negation of the essayist's argument and is not a flaw in the argument.

Answer choice (B): This is the correct answer choice. Believing something for the wrong reason does not mean that the belief itself is incorrect. If I believe that the sky is blue because outer space is that color, my rationale is clearly incorrect. According to the essayist, however, my belief that the sky is blue would also be false. Since the essayist fails to consider the possibility that Earth and its inhabitants may still be important even if Earth is not at the center of the universe, this answer choice is correct.

Answer choice (C): This is a confusing answer choice due to the negative wording. For this to be a flaw in the argument, it must be true that resolving it would strengthen the argument (any time a flaw in an argument is corrected that argument is strengthened). Would the essayist's argument be strengthened if the essayist considered that there can be no reason for disbelieving true statements? No, since the essayist has already given a reason to disbelieve that the Earth is important (because it is not the center of the universe), the argument would be unaffected by including the idea that he or she does not need a reason to hold that belief.

Answer choice (D): The essayist writes, "People once believed…" and "people's old belief…" This construction indicates that the argument is dealing with a specific belief that was held during a specific time. It is not necessary to show that people had different beliefs at different times if the author deals with beliefs from a specific time.

Answer choice (E): Answer choice (E) is very similar to answer choice (D) and is incorrect for similar reasons. The essayist has limited the scope of his argument to people who believed Earth and inhabitants were important because of Earth's position at the center of the universe. These people may be from one or several cultures, but the essayist has no obligation to discuss people from cultures which do not fit the scope of his argument. Limiting the scope of an argument to a specific group or specific time is not a flaw as long as the argument does not make conclusions about other groups or other times.

Question #13: Point at Issue. The correct answer choice is (D)

In any Point at Issue question, it is important to understand each viewpoint and how they differ from one another. Davis's viewpoint has several features. Davis suggests that it is appropriate to compensate the victims of property damage, and that the value of the damage or loss is the only factor that should be considered in determining compensation. Higuchi disagrees with Davis's conclusion but does not dispute any of Davis's premises: both individuals agree that the amount of damage or loss should be considered, while Higuchi also believes that the amount of time involved in recovering the use of personal property should be considered. Answer choice (D) is the only answer choice which correctly characterizes this key distinction between Davis's and Higuchi's arguments.

Answer choice (A): Davis believes that only the value of the lost property is relevant to determining compensation while Higuchi believes that the lost value and time are both relevant. However, neither specifically discusses how consistently or reliably these factors can be applied. Thus it is impossible to know how either Davis or Higuchi would respond to answer choice (A).

Answer choice (B): Davis certainly agrees with this statement – it is the premise of his argument. For this answer choice to be correct, it must then be shown that Higuchi disagrees with it according to the Agree/Disagree Test. However, it is quite probable that Higuchi also agrees with this statement since Higuchi does not openly refute any of Davis's premises. Therefore, answer choice (B) cannot be correct.

Answer choice (C): This answer choice, like answer choice (B), is a premise of Davis's argument and, therefore, Davis must agree with it. Higuchi also believes that victims are owed compensation in proportion to the harm they have suffered. Although Davis and Higuchi would disagree about the appropriate method for determining how much harm the victims have suffered, both would agree that amount of harm should determine the amount of compensation.

Answer choice (D): This is the correct answer choice. Higuchi argues that the amount of time a victim is deprived of the use of their property should be one of the factors in determining the amount of compensation, and thus compensation is not strictly based upon the value of the property (some victims are entitled to greater compensation if they are deprived of the use of their property for a longer period of time). Davis argues that monetary loss or damage is the only relevant factor (and thus the time involved is not a factor). Since Higuchi would agree with the statement in answer choice (D) and Davis would not, answer choice (D) is the correct answer choice.

Answer choice (E): This is the most commonly chosen incorrect answer choice. The amount of monetary loss and the amount of time property is missing can vary infinitely from case to case. Since Davis and Higuchi argue that these variable factors should determine the amount of compensation, both would agree that the compensation owed to victims should be determined on a case-by-case basis rather than by some general rule. Like answer choice (C), this statement cannot be the point of disagreement if both speakers agree with it.

Question #14: Strengthen. The correct answer choice is (C)

In Strengthen questions, the correct answer choice will provide additional support for the conclusion. The conclusion of this argument is, "Residents of this locale should not consider their loss of farming as a way of life to be a tragedy." Why? Because when the residents of this locale had farming as a way of life, the area was economically depressed. Now that farming is no longer a way of life in this area, the area is prospering economically. Of course, this change could still be considered a tragedy if the value lost (rural, farming-based way of life) is greater than the value gained (economic prosperity). In order to strengthen the resident's conclusion, it must be shown that the residents of this locale gained at least as much or more than they lost and answer choice (C), if true, does just that.

Answer choice (A): The increased efficiency of farming may help to explain why the locale could not continue to maintain a rural, farming-based economy (increased efficiency means that fewer farms would be needed), however this answer choice does not strengthen the conclusion that the loss of farms in this locale is not tragic. Regardless of how efficient farms become, this answer choice does nothing to show why residents should prefer economic success to their former, rural lifestyle.

Answer choice (B): This answer choice suggests that the residents of the locale gained more valuable contributions to national security through the development of high-tech industry. But there is no basis given for concluding that this gain is worth more to the residents than the loss of farming as a way of life. If residents consider farming as a way of life to be more valuable than contributions to national security, then their loss could still be considered a tragedy.

Answer choice (C): This is the correct answer choice. This is only answer choice that provides a basis for comparing what was lost to what was gained. The stimulus states that although the area was once rural and economically depressed, it is now industrializing and economically prospering. Since, according to answer choice (C), the residents feel that the loss of a rural way of life was no greater than the gain of economic prosperity, they should not consider this loss a tragedy.

Answer choice (D): The knowledge that many residents now make more money than they did before does not determine how they should feel about the loss of farming as a way of life and whether that loss is tragic. The non-monetary benefits of farming may outweigh the increased income for these residents.

Answer choice (E): This answer choice weakens the conclusion. It suggests that farms are worth more than their simple monetary value. If that were the case, than the loss of farming as a way of life would likely be a tragedy regardless of how much the area is now prospering.

Question #15: Resolve the Paradox. The correct answer choice is (D)

This question is perhaps the most difficult question in this section, and it is certainly the hardest Resolve the Paradox question on the test. Kendrick's first statement is that governments should try to prevent cigarettes from being advertised because cigarettes are unhealthy. After reading the statement, many test takers will infer that Kendrick advocates a legal ban of cigarette advertising. But Kendrick's second statement is that cigarette advertising should remain legal, because advertisements for other unhealthy products are legal. The test makers have now created a paradox: should the government try to prevent cigarette advertisements or permit them to remain legal? According to Kendrick, the government should do both. In reality, trying to prevent cigarette advertisements is not the opposite of permitting them to remain legal, as a legal ban is not the only way for a government to try to prevent cigarettes from being advertised. Answer choice (D) suggests a method that would satisfy both of Kendrick's statements and thus successfully resolves the paradox.

Answer choice (A): The correct answer choice in a Resolve the Paradox question must support both of the apparently conflicting positions and suggest a way for them to coexist. Since making advertisements that encourage people to engage in an unhealthy practice illegal is one way that a government could try to prevent them, this answer choice supports Kendrick's initial statement. But this answer choice directly contradicts Kendrick's second statement that advertisements for cigarettes should remain legal and is therefore incorrect.

Answer choice (B): Kendrick uses fatty foods as an example of an advertisement that is legal, despite encouraging people to engage in unhealthy practices. This answer choice offers a rationale for not preventing the advertisement of fatty foods, but explicitly states that this rationale does not apply to cigarettes. But it is already known that Kendrick feels that the advertisement of cigarettes should be prevented. Restating that cigarette advertisements should be prevented does not explain how to prevent them while still keeping them legal.

Answer choice (C): This answer choice states that most advertisements should remain legal, but it places the responsibility for ensuring that people do not engage in unhealthy practices on the advertisers. But if most advertisements should be legal and advertisers bear the burden of discouraging people from engaging in unhealthy practices, why would Kendrick feel that governments are justified in trying to prevent the advertisement of cigarettes? Remember, the correct answer will provide a way for the government to prevent cigarette advertisements without making them illegal.

Answer choice (D): This is the correct answer choice. According to answer choice (D), governments would be justified in financially "punishing" cigarette companies in an effort to prevent the advertisement of cigarettes. In this way governments could try to prevent cigarette advertisements without making them illegal, and the paradox from the stimulus is resolved.

Answer choice (E): Answer choice (E) seems quite attractive initially since placing restrictions on cigarette advertisements would apparently prevent them without making them illegal. However, this answer choice then says the government "should not try to prevent such advertisements," directly contradicting Kendrick's first statement that governments are justified in trying to prevent such advertisements. Because answer choice (E) contradicts one of the premises in the stimulus, it is incorrect.

Question #16: Assumption. The correct answer choice is (E)

This is a Defender Assumption question, where the correct answer choice will protect or defend the conclusion from potentially harmful information. First, analyze the logical structure of the stimulus:

Premise: People want to live in areas of natural beauty.

Premise: As people move into those areas, businesses will be encouraged to relocate to those areas, presumably boosting local economies.

Conclusion: Governmental protection of the local environment (preserving the region's beauty) can help the economy, even if there is some harm to older local industries.

For the conclusion to be possible, the harm to older local industries cannot discourage or adversely affect other businesses interested in relocating to that region, as there would likely be no overall economic benefit. This assumption is best expressed by answer choice (E).

Answer choice (A): Most test takers will be able to dismiss this answer choice quickly. The conditional structure of this sentence can be expressed as follows:

NB = regions of natural beauty which are beautiful enough to attract new residents
EP = environmental protection that damages local industries

$$EP \longrightarrow \cancel{NB}$$

This means that if environmental protection that damages local industries is imposed in regions of natural beauty, those regions will no longer be beautiful enough to attract new residents. If this is the true, the harm to local industries would be compounded by the lack of new residents and the regions' overall economy would be doubly harmed. This is a Weaken answer choice.

Answer choice (B): This answer choice is considerably more appealing than answer choice (A) and is focused on a critical aspect of the stimulus: harm to local industries. In fact, this was the most popular answer choice among test takers attempting this exam. However, as was discussed in the evaluation of the stimulus, the determining factor in this argument is the relationship between the economic harm done to older industries vs. the economic benefit of relocating businesses when governmental protection occurs. As long as the benefit is greater than the harm, the argument remains valid (a region's overall economy would benefit). This answer choice states that local economies are not based primarily on local industries that would be harmed by mandated environmental protection. Is this statement necessary for the conclusion to remain plausible? To determine the necessity of answer choice (B), negate it and evaluate the effects according to the Assumption Negation Technique: the economies of most regions of natural beauty *are* based primarily on local industries that would be harmed. Does this undermine the conclusion that overall the economy can benefit? Possibly, but not necessarily. Even if local industries are the primary economic source in a region, and these local industries are harmed, it is still entirely possible that the benefit of the new businesses that move to that region would outweigh the harm done to the local industries. If that were the case, the overall economy would still be helped and the conclusion would remain unharmed. Since negating answer choice (B) does not invalidate the conclusion, answer choice (B) is not an assumption of the argument.

Answer choice (C): The conclusion of this argument is that government protections can help the economy overall. Does the argument depend on encouraging people to move in to an area as the primary economic benefit of these protections? No. There could be several other ways in which protection benefits the local economy and determining which of the effects of protection is of primary benefit to the economy does not affect the conclusion's validity.

Answer choice (D): This answer choice presents an alternative method for helping a region's economy and concludes that this method is not as effective as the method given in the stimulus. Proving that governmentally mandated environmental protections are more effective than other options would be important if the argument implied that these protections were the best way to help a region's economy. However, since the conclusion makes no such claim, this comparison is unnecessary and this answer choice is incorrect.

Answer choice (E): This is the correct answer choice. Answer choice (E) can be dentified as a contender because it focuses on the important relationship between older local industries and relocating businesses. As with any Assumption question, and as was seen with answer choice (B), the correct answer choice can be confirmed with the Assumption Negation Technique. If this is the correct answer choice, then negating it will render the conclusion invalid. The logical negation of this answer choice is, "A factor harmful to some older local industries in a region will discourage other businesses from relocating to that region." If governmentally mandated environmental protection were a factor that both harmed some older local industries and discouraged other businesses from relocating to that region, then local economies would not have an overall benefit and the conclusion could not be true. Because negating answer choice (E) invalidates the conclusion, answer choice (E) is an assumption necessary for the argument.

Question #17: Must Be True—Formal Logic. The correct answer choice is (E)

Formal logic questions can be very intimidating for some test takers. However, by diagramming carefully and drawing appropriate inferences, most formal logic mistakes can be easily avoided. Consider each statement individually and then jointly to determine any additive inferences.

First statement:

SC = small country
SH = southern hemisphere
PS = permanent seat on the United Nations Security council

$$\begin{matrix} SC \\ or \\ SH \end{matrix} \longrightarrow \cancel{PS}$$

The contrapositive of this statement is:

$$PS \longrightarrow \begin{matrix} \cancel{SC} \\ and \\ \cancel{SH} \end{matrix}$$

Second statement:

IP = increased international peacekeeping
MR = greater role in moderating regional disputes

$$PS \longrightarrow \begin{matrix} IP \\ and \\ MR \end{matrix}$$

Third statement:

ISR = increased spending on refugees

$$IP \longleftrightarrow^{s} \cancel{ISR}$$

The next step is to find common terms in multiple statements and combine the statements to draw additional inferences. IP is common to both the second and third statements, but the "some" condition of the third statement prevents us from linking it to the second statement. The third statement cannot be used to conclude anything about the permanent members of the UN Security Council
(PS $\longrightarrow$ IP $\longleftrightarrow^{s}$ $\cancel{ISR}$ does not yield any inferences). This is an important inference and will be tested in answer choice (C).

PS is common to the second statement and the contrapositive of the first statement. Combining these two statements produces:

$$\begin{array}{ccc} \cancel{SC} & & IP \\ and & \longleftrightarrow^{s} & and \\ \cancel{SH} & & MR \end{array}$$

This inference can be stated in a number of ways, including, "Some countries that are in favor of a greater role for the United Nations in moderating regional disputes are not located in the southern hemisphere." Thus, answer choice (E) is correct.

Answer choice (A): All that is known about small countries is that they do not have permanent seats on the United Nations Security Council. This information about small countries cannot be linked to any conclusion about their position on refugee spending.

Answer choice (B): Again, one can only know that no country in the southern hemisphere is permanently on the Security Council. It cannot be known whether any of these countries are in favor of or against increased international peacekeeping efforts. This answer choice could be confusing if it were read as, "Some countries in favor of increased international peacekeeping efforts are not in the southern hemisphere," as that is proven true by the stimulus, but that is not what this answer choice states.

Answer choice (C): It has already been shown that any attempt to draw a conclusion about countries with a permanent seat on the UN Security Council based on the facts of the third statement is invalid. All five countries with permanent seats on Security Council are in favor of increased international peacekeeping efforts and may also be in favor of increased spending on refugees.

Answer choice (D): This answer choice is incorrect for the same reasons that answer choices (A) and (B) are incorrect. The information provided about small countries does not support any inferences about their positions on any of the other topics mentioned in the stimulus.

Answer choice (E): This is the correct answer choice. From the stimulus, one can correctly infer that there are at least five countries (i.e. all the members of the Security Council with permanent seats) that are both in favor of a greater role for the United Nations in moderating regional disputes and are not located in the southern hemisphere.

Question #18: Justify the Conclusion. The correct answer choice is (D)

The conclusion drawn by the editorial is, "It is clear that what is called 'health education' is usually propaganda rather than education." Ironically, this conclusion is not at all clear from the remainder of the editorial, since "health education" is not mentioned again. The stimulus states that education and propaganda are mutually exclusive, as propaganda influences behavior through the repetition of simplistic slogans, and education never involves this method of influence via slogan repetition. Because this is a Justify the Conclusion question, the correct answer choice, when combined with the remainder of the stimulus, must prove that the conclusion is true (the Justify Formula). Thus, the correct answer choice must prove that health education is indeed propaganda and not education. Since propaganda always attempts to influence behavior by repeating simplistic slogans and education never uses this method, and the conclusion states that health education is propaganda, the correct answer choice must show that health education attempts to influence behavior by repeating simplistic slogans.

Answer choice (A): If health education usually "does not leave it up to the individual to decide how to act on information," then it is clearly unlike education. However, this does not conclusively prove that health education is propaganda, since it is entirely possible that health education could be neither education nor propaganda.

Answer choice (B): As discussed previously, proving that health education is unlike education is not sufficient for the conclusion to be logically drawn. The answer choice does not prove that health education must be propaganda.

Answer choice (C): This is an Opposite Answer. If health education does not involve the repetition of simplistic slogans, then it is clearly not propaganda. It may be education or it may be something else altogether.

Answer choice (D): This is the correct answer choice. If health education attempts to influence behavior solely by repeating simplistic slogans, then the conclusion that health education is propaganda can be logically drawn.

Answer choice (E): This answer choice could be appealing since it seems to agree with one of the premises in the stimulus ("propaganda is much more successful than education"). However, just because propaganda is much more successful than education, it cannot be logically concluded that propaganda is very successful. Do not confuse relative and absolute statements. Further, this answer choice does nothing to prove that health education is propaganda, which is the ultimate goal in a Justify the Conclusion question.

Question #19: Must Be True. The correct answer choice is (D)

This Must be True question is somewhat unusual because the question stem asks what Marc and Robert agree about rather than what is proven true by their statements. However, the same principles that apply to other Must be True questions apply here: the correct answer choice will come directly from the information provided in the stimulus and no new information can be introduced. The only additional consideration is that the correct answer must be agreed upon by both Marc and Robert.

Marc says that the people of his country are nostalgic because they regret the recent revolution. Robert agrees that the people are nostalgic but not because of the recent revolution. He implies that the people may prefer the current situation to the pre-revolutionary regime, but do not prefer it to the situation before that regime. Both Marc and Robert agree that there was a revolution, but this is unlikely to be the correct answer choice. They also agree that the people of their country are not completely satisfied with the current situation and feel nostalgia for the past. This agreement is best expressed by answer choice (D).

Answer choice (A): Neither Marc nor Robert suggests that the people of their country should not be nostalgic or that the people have mistaken impressions of the past.

Answer choice (B): Being nostalgic does not necessarily mean looking to past for solutions; it could simply be a way to find comfort. Marc and Robert are discussing the cause of the nostalgia, not the purpose of it. One cannot infer that they would both agree with this statement.

Answer choice (C): This answer choice goes one step further than answer choice (B). It suggests a possible negative consequence of being nostalgic to find solutions for current problems. The stimulus provides even less support for this answer choice than for the previous answer choice, as neither Marc nor Robert indicates that the people are likely to repeat former mistakes.

Answer choice (D): This is the correct answer choice. Marc says that the people "regret the revolution" and Robert says "they are troubled." Both phrases indicate the people's dissatisfaction with the current situation and this dissatisfaction is manifested in their nostalgia.

Answer choice (E): Marc believes that the nostalgia of his country's people is for the period before the recent revolution and Robert believe that this feeling is directed at the more distant past. Neither of these beliefs implies a correlation between the amount of nostalgia and the amount of time past. There is no mention of the degree of nostalgia in the stimulus so this answer choice cannot be correct.

Question #20: Flaw in the Reasoning. The correct answer choice is (D)

The stimulus states that moral socialization is a way in which society socializes children by making them feel ashamed of their immoral behavior. This seems like an appropriate action since immoral behavior is likely harmful to society, however the social critic concludes that moral socialization actually results in guilt and self-loathing for many people and thereby increases the net amount of suffering in society. In personalizing this argument, hopefully the flaw is clear: just because an action affects some people negatively does not mean that the overall effect of that action – the net effect – is negative. In this case, the amount of suffering that some people feel as a result of moral socialization could be far less than the suffering prevented by moral socialization, and the net effect would ultimately be a reduced amount of suffering (even though not everyone would experience that effect). Also, be careful to note here that, although the social critic does not recommend altering or eliminating moral socialization in the stimulus, nor is an alternative suggestion proposed, this omission is not necessarily a flaw; this will help to eliminate incorrect answer choices.

Answer choice (A): The social critic's argument is vulnerable to criticism only in so far as it fails to prove its conclusion (greater net suffering). Any other considerations are beyond the scope of the argument. The critic does not propose that social moralization be eliminated and so cannot be criticized for failing to consider alternatives to that elimination.

Answer choice (B): It may be true that moral socialization sometimes occurs without causing guilt and self-loathing or that guilt and self-loathing may occur without moral socialization, but the critic already believes that moral socialization causally contributes to feelings of guilt and self-loathing. Suggesting that cases where one phenomenon occurs without the other can be dismissed does not describe the flaw in the social critic's argument.

Answer choice (C): Remember, the correct answer choice in a Flaw in the Reasoning question must come directly from the stimulus (similar to Must be True), hence any answer choice that introduces new information not discussed in the stimulus can be immediately eliminated. The social critic's argument is that moral socialization results in more harm than good, however there is never any mention in the stimulus of changing or eliminating moral socialization, so answer choice (C) is incorrect.

Answer choice (D): This is the correct answer choice. The social critic proposes that moral socialization leads to guilt and self-loathing which increase the net amount of suffering in society. However, the critic fails to consider that moral socialization may also decrease the amount of suffering in society by limiting the amount of immoral behavior. The argument is flawed because it is possible that more suffering is prevented by the decrease in immoral behavior than is caused by the increase in feelings of guilt, and thus there is no net increase in the total amount of suffering.

Answer choice (E): The critic does not presume that everyone will respond negatively to moral socialization; he or she only presumes that some number of people respond negatively enough to increase the net amount of suffering in society. This answer choice is not a valid description of the flaw in the social critic's argument.

Question #21: Strengthen—Principle. The correct answer choice is (E)

In general, the test makers believe that surveys and opinion polls can be useful indicators of public sentiment, but only if conducted correctly. Hence they will occasionally formulate questions that are based upon the principles of appropriate sampling. A truly representative sample must be significant, random, and unbiased. A sample is significant if it is large enough for its characteristics to reflect the characteristics of the entire population. A sample is random if any member of the population had an equal chance of being included in the sample. A sample is unbiased if there is no evidence of collusion among the sample members or persuasion/incentive given by those conducting the survey. Because a representative survey requires the correct execution of so many elements, more often than not when an argument on the LSAT is based upon public opinion or a survey, that argument will be flawed.

The curator argues that this sample used by the magazine story is misleading. In order to strengthen this conclusion, one must show that the sample was insignificant, not random, or biased. Is it possible for three residents to comprise a significant sample? That depends on the size and attributes of the entire population, which is not known. Were these three residents randomly chosen? We do not know what methodology the magazine used, but it may have been random. Are these three residents likely to be unbiased? Here is the curator's complaint with the magazine story. Since all three residents are close friends, they are likely to have similar opinions and may have even discussed their opinions regarding the exhibit with each other. Thus the fact that three residents all had the same opinion about the exhibit cannot be used to claim that most residents had the same opinion as well.

Answer choice (A): The three residents quoted in the story are never credited as experts, so the curator does not feel the story is misleading for quoting people who were unqualified to express their reactions. The curator is angry because the three people quoted are not representative of the group (most people) that they are intended to represent.

Answer choice (B): This consideration is only applicable if the local residents of the town are likely to be evenly divided on their reaction to the art exhibit. Since the stimulus does not provide enough evidence for this conclusion, this answer choice cannot be used to strengthen the curator's argument.

Answer choice (C): The curator certainly believes that it is misleading for the magazine story to present the opinions of these three residents as evidence of what the majority thinks. But the stimulus does not tell us whether the sense of moral outrage expressed by these residents was widely held. Since it is possible that their opinions were widely held, the magazine story is not necessarily misleading and this answer choice would not strengthen the curator's conclusion.

Answer choice (D): The story does not imply that the three close friends must agree with each other; it demonstrates that these friends did agree with each other and thereby implies that most other local residents did as well.

Answer choice (E): This is the correct answer choice. As noted in the discussion of the stimulus, a sample must be unbiased to be representative. The opinions of the three close friends are not necessarily biased, but there is certainly substantial evidence to believe that they are. Therefore, it is misleading for the magazine to present the friend's opinions as if they represent public opinion. This statement greatly strengthens the curator's argument.

Question #22: Must Be True—Formal Logic. The correct answer choice is (A)

This is another formal logic problem like question #17. Begin by diagramming each of the statements in the stimulus and combining them via any common terms.

The first statement is very straightforward:

P = parrots
LS = learn to speak a few words and phrases

$$P \longrightarrow LS$$

The contrapositive of this statement is probably not useful, since the entire stimulus is about "parrots" rather than "not parrots."

The second sentence, "Not all parrots have equally pleasant dispositions," can be diagrammed as:

EPD = equally pleasant dispositions

$$P \overset{s}{\longleftrightarrow} \cancel{EPD}$$

"Some" statements do not yield contrapositives, but may lead to other inferences. Because the first and second sentences have a common term, P, they can be combined:

$$LS \longleftrightarrow P \xleftrightarrow{\;S\;} \cancel{EPD}$$

Since "some" statements are reversible (they can be read from left to right or right to left), the inference from these two sentences is that some parrots that can learn to speak a few words or phrases do not have equally pleasant dispositions. Diagrammatically:

$$LS \xleftrightarrow{\;S\;} \cancel{EPD}$$

The statement "Some of those native to Australia can be counted on for a sweet temper" should be diagrammed thus:

P_A = parrots native to Australia
ST = can be counted on for a sweet temper

$$P_A \xleftrightarrow{\;S\;} ST$$

Since all parrots (native to Australia or elsewhere) can also learn to speak a few words and phrases (from the first sentence), combining this statement with the above "some" statement yields the following:

$$LS \longleftrightarrow P_A \xleftrightarrow{\;S\;} ST$$

So it can be concluded:

$$LS \xleftrightarrow{\;S\;} ST$$

That is, some parrots that can learn to speak a few words and phrases can be counted on for a sweet temper (and vice versa). This is the strongest inference made thus far. Some test takers will recognize this inference and immediately scan the answer choices to find it, and by doing so can find the correct answer without working through the rest of the stimulus. Recognizing powerful inferences like this one can help to save valuable time in Logical Reasoning.

The third statement says, "Almost any parrot will show tremendous affection for an owner who raised the bird from a chick by hand-feeding it." This statement is a little bit more difficult to diagram than the others. "Almost any" is logically equivalent to "most" and "show tremendous affection for an owner" is easy to represent. Keep in mind the group of parrots to which this statement applies. It is only valid for parrots that were raised from a chick by hand-feeding, so this must be represented this in the diagram.

This is an effective representation:

P_{HF} = parrots that were raised by hand-feeding
AO = show tremendous affection for owner

$$P_{HF} \xrightarrow{\;M\;} AO$$

Remember that "most" also implies "some," meaning that "Some parrots which show tremendous affection for an owner were raised from a chick by hand-feeding." Since this is true, the following can be concluded:

$$LS \xleftrightarrow{\ \ s\ \ } AO$$

Please note that "affection for an owner," "sweet temper," and "pleasant disposition" are closely related, but are not similar enough to allow for inferences to be made (that is, they cannot be considered common terms).

Answer choice (A): This is the correct answer choice. From the above discussion it should now be clear that some parrots that can learn to speak can also be counted on for a sweet temper. This is the inference made from combining the first sentence and the second half of the second sentence.

Answer choice (B): This statement means that all sweet tempered parrots are either native to Australia or hand-fed as chicks. It also means that if a parrot is sweet tempered and not native to Australia, it must have been hand-fed as a chick. Any of these statements will be a variation of this diagram:

$$\begin{array}{l} ST \\ and \\ \cancel{P}_A \end{array} \longrightarrow P_{HF}$$

There are several problems with this answer choice. Even if "sweet-tempered" is assumed to be equivalent to "shows affection for owner," this conclusion would still contain a Mistaken Reversal. Furthermore, all that can be known about parrots not native to Australia is that all of them can learn to speak and not all of them have an equally pleasant disposition. Thus this answer choice cannot be inferred from the statements in the stimulus.

Answer choice (C): Most test takers have little difficulty eliminating answer choice (C). Nothing in the stimulus implies that the sweetest tempered parrots are those native to Australia. The author states that some parrots that are native to Australia have a sweet temper, but it is never made clear how sweet these parrots are.

Answer choice (D): This answer choice says that if a bird can learn to speak and be relied on for a sweet temper, it must be from Australia. Here is a diagram:

$$\begin{array}{l} LS \\ and \\ ST \end{array} \longrightarrow A$$

From the stimulus, the author states that all Australian parrots can learn to speak and some are sweet-tempered. But having these two characteristics does not absolutely guarantee that a given parrot is from Australia, let alone any other bird.

Answer choice (E): Again, very few test takers selected this answer choice. The stimulus deals exclusively with different groups of parrots and one cannot use information about parrots in Australia to make claims about all species of pet birds in Australia.

Question #23: Method of Reasoning—Argument Part. The correct answer choice is (D)

The test makers will often reward test takers who have good time-management skills with a relatively easy question at the end of a section. Hence test takers who are simply marking random answer choices for the last several questions may forfeit some easy points.

In this stimulus, the toxicologist notes that dioxin causes cancer in rats. Because of this the toxicologist recommends that the use of dioxin should be banned. Even though dioxin has not been proven harmful to humans, the fact that it causes cancer in rats is used to justify a complete ban on dioxin. This is best expressed by answer choice (D).

Answer choice (A): The toxicologist is concerned with preventing cancer in general (particularly in humans), and that is why he or she advocates a dioxin ban. If the toxicologist were only concerned with preventing cancer in rats, then the conclusion would simply state, "Because dioxin causes cancer in rats, rats should not be exposed to dioxin." But by advocating a complete ban on dioxin in the conclusion, it is clear that the toxicologist is concerned with more than preventing cancer in rats.

Answer choice (B): This is similar to an Opposite Answer. The toxicologist presents the recent research on rats exposed to dioxin to illustrate a potential harm of not acting on the conclusion, not to show a benefit.

Answer choice (C): The fact that dioxin causes cancer in rats may very explain why similar research will never be done on humans, but the argument does not use that fact in this manner. The toxicologist is not trying to prove anything about human research; the toxicologist is trying to prove that the use of dioxin should be completely banned.

Answer choice (D): This is the correct answer choice. The course of action advocated in the conclusion is to completely ban the use of dioxin. The toxicologist advocates this ban because dioxin causes cancer in rats. The inference, of course, is that it may also cause cancer in or be similarly harmful to humans or other species.

Answer choice (E): Again, the toxicologist is not trying to prove any claims about human research. In fact, this question type (Method of Reasoning) instructs test takers to accept the claim that similar research has never been done on humans without having to provide any evidence to that effect. It is true simply because the toxicologist states that it is true.

Question #24: Parallel Reasoning. The correct answer choice is (C)

The Politician concludes that people should not be legally required to wear seat belts because seat belts are not required in another type of vehicle (or situation) that is even more dangerous even when seat belts are worn. In drawing this conclusion, the Politician makes a comparison to a situation that is somewhat similar, but not similar enough to provide valid support for the conclusion. The premises have two notable features that must be paralleled in the correct answer choice:

1. A comparison that is not reasonably similar enough to be valid.
2. The situation being compared is even more dangerous even though the activity/restriction in question ("seat belts" in the stimulus) is performed.

Interestingly, none of the answer choices matches the wording of the conclusion exactly, but the intent of the wording in the conclusion is matched ("does not require" in this context is the same as "should allow") in several of the answers.

Answer choice (A): This answer does not contain a comparison, so it is automatically incorrect.

Answer choice (B): The comparison in this answer is not the same because illness and stress are similar enough to be valid, and there is also no implied danger in the activities mentioned in the stimulus.

Answer choice (C): This is the correct answer choice. This answer contains the same flaw as the argument. In this case, standing on a roller coaster is compared to standing on the edge of the cliff, and this comparison is not close enough to be valid. Also, the comparative danger feature is addressed perfectly: sitting on the edge of a cliff (the implied appropriate way to ride a roller coaster) is more dangerous than standing on a roller coaster.

Answer choice (D): There are multiple points of concern with this answer. First, the intent of the conclusion differs from that in the stimulus, because the stimulus concludes that something should be allowed (no seat belts), while this answer choice concludes that something should be disallowed (smoking in a public place). Second, the situation being discussed in this answer choice shifts from a public place to a private place. Third, the situation being compared ("drinking water) is not found to be more harmful than the situation in the conclusion.

Answer choice (E): This answer does not contain a discussion of comparative danger, and therefore this answer can also be eliminated quickly.

Question #25: Resolve the Paradox. The correct answer choice is (C)

Once again, the correct answer for a Resolve the Paradox question must help explain both conditions – in this case two behaviors – that are described in the stimulus. Many of the incorrect answer choices will provide support for one of the behaviors without addressing the other, or will even attempt to discredit or disprove one condition. In this stimulus, the contradictory behaviors are that burying beetles (1) try to minimize the size of their competitor's broods, going so far as to destroy the eggs of other beetles when possible, and yet (2) treat all of the larvae equally after they have hatched. The first behavior seems motivated by a concern only for one's own offspring, while the second seems motivated by a concern for the entire community.

The correct answer must reconcile these two behaviors by providing a possible cause for the discrepancy. To resolve the paradox, one could show that burying beetle destroying each other's eggs is just as "generous" as raising each other's larvae, or that raising each other's larvae is just as "selfish" as destroying each other's eggs. Answer choice (C) shows how the second behavior/condition – helping to raise each other's larvae – could be motivated solely by a concern for one's own offspring. If burying beetles only care about their own offspring but cannot distinguish their own larvae from others' larvae, they must protect all of the larvae to ensure that their own survive.

Answer choice (A): This reinforces the idea that there is competition among burying beetles. Each burying beetle would want to lay its eggs first, destroy its competitor's eggs, and have the largest possible brood. But this answer choice does not explain why burying beetles cooperate with each other in raising larvae.

Answer choice (B): This answer choice provides a plausible explanation for the second behavior. It suggests that burying beetles cooperate in raising larvae to ensure that the greatest possible number of larvae survive. But if this is their primary motivation, then why would they try to minimize each others' broods before the eggs hatch? This answer choice does not explain the first behavior.

Answer choice (C): This is the correct answer choice. The stimulus states that burying beetles "destroy each other's eggs." This means that the beetles must be able to distinguish their own broods from their competitors (i.e. their own eggs from those of their competitors). But if they are unable to discriminate between their own larvae and the larvae of other burying beetles, they would be unable to destroy each other's larvae without potentially destroying some of their own larvae. Thus, the instinct of burying beetles to preserve their own offspring explains both behaviors.

Answer choice (D): While the thought of burying beetles banding together to fend off predators may seem reasonable, it does not explain either behavior from the stimulus. The need to fend off predators would not require burying beetles to treat all larvae equally and it certainly would not explain why the beetles "routinely destroy each other's eggs."

Answer choice (E): Competition for limited resources or space at breeding sites would certainly help explain the first behavior. Burying beetles would kill each other's eggs to prevent overcrowding. But this does not explain why burying beetles treat all larvae equally after they have hatched. If this answer choice were true, one would still expect burying beetles to prefer their own larvae to the larvae of other beetles.

Overview: Most test takers found this section somewhat more difficult than the first Logical Reasoning Section. The section has two Parallel Reasoning questions near the end (#22 and #25), of which question #25 is particularly useful to study (and also particularly difficult). Question #13 is an excellent example of a Resolve the Paradox and has been added to the PowerScore Weekend LSAT course. There are also a large number of Strengthen questions in this section. As is typically the case, the questions increase in difficulty as the section progresses, although, unlike the questions in most Logical Reasoning sections, the final few questions do not seem to get slightly easier. Questions #18-20 are difficult for many test takers, in part, perhaps, because the wording of these questions can seem ambiguous or confusing. Finally, question #15 is a good example of a Numbers and Percentages problem and contains a useful discussion of comparing percentage change to the change in overall amount.

Question #1: Assumption—CE. The correct answer choice is (A)

Proponents of intellectual property rights, such as the right to patent new inventions, argue that the best way to ensure continued innovation is to maximize the property holders' (patent holders') right to benefit financially from their developments. The stimulus takes this argument one step further and makes the extreme claim that original development will cease altogether if there is no financial incentive for inventing new products. For this conclusion to be possible, it must be assumed that nothing other than financial incentive could motivate original development and invention. Answer choice (A) is correct because it shows that financial incentive is singularly necessary.

Answer choice (A): This is the correct answer choice. As with any correct answer choice to an Assumption question, this answer choice must pass the Assumption Negation Test. Once negated, the correct answer choice will invalidate the argument. For answer choice (A), if the stimulus is negated it states that financial reward is not the only effective incentive in motivating people to develop new inventions, and the conclusion of the stimulus is no longer correct. That is, some people will continue to engage in original development even if patent rights are not granted because these people will not need a financial incentive to produce new inventions. Because answer choice (A) shows the absolute necessity of financial incentive, it is the correct answer.

Answer choice (B): Some proponents of intellectual property rights are concerned about the relationship between inventors and manufacturers. But the argument in the stimulus is not contingent upon the nature of that relationship. The conclusion is that without patent rights and the financial incentives that they provide no new inventions will be developed. Thus, the conclusion does not depend upon the assumption that inventors make more total profit than manufacturers.

Answer choice (C): This answer choice suggests that the economic benefit to an inventor of obtaining patent rights must be significantly greater than the associated cost. Presumably, this is necessary to justify the investment of time and energy in obtaining a patent. But the conclusion is drawn from the complete absence of financial incentive. Knowledge about the cost of applying for patent rights does not allow for an evaluation of whether the lack of financial incentive would cause original development to cease.

Answer choice (D): The stimulus is not dependent upon the restriction of patent rights to those products which are sufficiently unique. Very similar products may provide enough financial incentive to promote continued innovation and the stimulus only predicts what will occur if there is no financial incentive present.

Answer choice (E): The duration of patent rights and the development cost of new inventions are not directly linked to the financial incentive mentioned in the stimulus. Therefore, the relationship between these two factors need not be known in order to successfully draw the conclusion. Furthermore, if this answer choice is negated and the length of patent rights for inventions that were inexpensive to develop was longer than the length of patent rights for expensive inventions, the conclusion would be unaffected.

Question #2: Strengthen Except. The correct answer choice is (E)

A key to success on the LSAT Logical Reasoning section is to read aggressively and to personalize each argument. Test takers who perform best on this section are those who become actively immersed in each stimulus. For this stimulus, try to picture the scene at the Fenwicks' home. There are two possible culprits for the broken bottles: the Fenwicks' pet cat and neighborhood children. The Fenwicks suspect the neighborhood children, and thus one must sort through the five answer choices to find the one piece of evidence that does not strengthen their suspicion; that is, the one answer choice that does not make it seem more likely that the neighborhood children broke the two bottles.

Of course, the test makers have several different options for the correct answer choice to this question. They could include information that refutes the children's involvement in the incident, implies the cat's involvement, or has no effect on the hypothesis. As predicted, the credited response here, answer choice (E), neither supports nor undermines the Fenwicks' hypothesis.

Answer choice (A): According to the stimulus, there was no sign of forced entry, and according to the neighbor, the back door may have been open while the Fenwicks were away. If this is true, it helps support the Fenwicks' hypothesis that they left the back door unlocked and that someone could have entered through it. One cannot know how the door closed; it may have been the neighborhood children, the Fenwicks' cat, or just the wind. But the mere fact that the back door may have been open and was not forced suggests that it was probably unlocked, and this lend some credibility to the possibility that the neighborhood kids could have entered the Fenwicks' home and broken the bottles.

Answer choice (B): The presence of children's footprints on the back porch certainly lends credence to the hypothesis that children entered the Fenwicks' home through the back door. Thus answer choice (B) strengthens the conclusion and is incorrect.

Answer choice (C): This answer choice supports the Fenwicks' hypothesis by attacking an alternative explanation. The Fenwicks believe neighborhood children broke the bottles, and that the Fenwicks' cat was not responsible. It is unlikely that the Fenwicks left their refrigerator door open while they were away and more unlikely still that their cat could open the door. Therefore, if the bottles had been in the refrigerator when the Fenwicks left on vacation, then the cat was probably not responsible for breaking them. Reducing the probability of an alternate cause lends strength to the other possible causes; in this case, the possibility that neighborhood children are responsible.

Answer choice (D): If neighborhood children were suspected of several recent, nearby burglaries, then it seems more likely that they may also be involved in this incident. Although they have not been proven guilty of other burglaries, the implication that they have been involved in other burglaries makes it more probable that they were involved in breaking the two bottles in the Fenwicks' home. Like answer choice (B), this evidence directly supports the Fenwicks' hypothesis that neighborhood children entered their home and broke the bottles.

Answer choice (E): This is the correct answer choice. The two explanations most consistent with the evidence presented in the stimulus are that neighborhood children broke the bottles – the Fenwicks' stated hypothesis – or that the Fenwicks' pet cat broke the bottles. What effect would the length of the Fenwicks' vacation have on the relative probability of each explanation? None. Each additional day of vacation is one more day during which either the children or the cat could have broken the bottles. Since this answer choice does not make either explanation more or less likely to be correct, it does nothing to support the Fenwicks' hypothesis.

Question #3: Strengthen—Principle. The correct answer choice is (B)

Many people become self-conscious or anxious when they are being observed. If someone was watching test takers attempting the LSAT, those test takers might be understandably uncomfortable and their performance would likely suffer. However, if the test takers were assured that they were only being observed to determine how well their pencils worked, they would probably feel less pressure and, quite possibly, would exhibit a stronger performance.

Similarly, the group of tennis players who believed their talent was being measured performed worse than the group of players who believed their rackets were being assessed. All five answer choices seem to be reasonable assertions, but only answer choice (B) explains how the differing beliefs of each group may have influenced their performances.

Answer choice (A): This answer choice could account for the different performance of the two groups only if the second group had been told they would be closely watched and the first group had not been told this. Otherwise, this answer choice offers no explanation or support for the observed phenomenon in the stimulus, as it cannot be known whether either group was told that they would be closely watched.

Answer choice (B): This is the correct answer choice. This answer choice helps to explain why the first group, who believed that their abilities were not being evaluated, would outperform the second group, who believed that their abilities were being judged.

Also, notice that this statement does not mention tennis. This is because a principle is a generalized conclusion which should be broadly applicable. Such a conclusion could apply equally to tennis players or LSAT takers.

Answer choice (C): Common sense and real world experience would suggest that this answer choice is true, but that does not mean that it is correct. Since the stimulus gives no indication about the relative confidence of either group of tennis players, it cannot be concluded that the situation conforms to this proposition.

Answer choice (D): The stimulus gives no indication as to whether the tennis players judged their own talents, therefore the stimulus cannot conform to any statement about people who assess their talents accurately.

Answer choice (E): Once again, there is no evidence that either group thought a superior performance would please those who were testing them. Also, trying harder cannot logically be equated with performing better. For both reasons, answer choice (E) cannot be correct.

Question #4: Flaw in the Reasoning. The correct answer choice is (C)

This is a Flaw in the Reasoning question with multiple viewpoints. According the question stem, the correct answer choice will be the one that best describes the flaw in Stephanie's viewpoint. Since Stephanie's viewpoint is a response to Sydonie's argument, it makes sense to begin by examining Sydonie's argument.

Here is Sydonie's argument:

Premise: Parents differ in their beliefs about the rules to which their children should be subject.

Premise: [Any disciplinary structure] will contradict some parental approaches to raising children.

Conclusion: Any disciplinary structure in schools is bound to create some parental resentment.

Stephanie's argument attempts to disprove Sydonie's conclusion. In doing so, Stephanie's argument must either prove that Sydonie's premises are incorrect or that Sydonie's conclusion does not follow from those premises. However, proving that parents want their children's schools to provide good discipline does neither. Stephanie's response does not prove that parents have similar ideas about good discipline or that a given disciplinary structure will not cause resentment. Answer choice (C) best describes this flaw in Stephanie's argument.

Answer choice (A): Stephanie's argument does, in fact, focus on educational research rather than educational practice. However, this is not the flaw that her argument exhibits in attempting to refute Sydonie's conclusion. Stephanie's use of educational research is acceptable; it is the conclusion that she draws from this research – parents' desire for good discipline proves that there will be no resentment – that is flawed.

Answer choice (B): This is not true. Both arguments address the issue of parental attitudes toward discipline at their children's schools. If anything, Sydonie's argument is the more general of the two, since it based on a broad characterization rather than a specific finding.

Answer choice (C): This is the correct answer choice. Stephanie disagrees with Sydonie's conclusion, insisting that parents widely desire their children's schools to provide good discipline. Therefore, reasons Stephanie, parents would not resent any disciplinary structure in their children's schools. Of course, Stephanie fails to account for Sydonie's premises, which suggest that parental definitions of good discipline may vary widely. If this is true, then even a universal desire among parents for good discipline in school would not prevent resentment of any particular approach. Thus, answer choice (C) accurately describes the flaw in Stephanie's response.

Answer choice (D): The real problem with Stephanie's argument is the subjectivity of the research, not the specificity. Stephanie's mistake is that, despite parents' desire for good discipline, and regardless of how high that desire ranks among their list of desirable things, parents still differ in their definition of "good discipline" and thus there would likely still be some resentment. Stephanie's argument does not adequately refute Sydonie's conclusion.

Answer choice (E): Stephanie's argument should only be criticized for failing to accomplish its purported purpose. The purpose of her argument is to refute Sydonie's conclusion. Since Sydonie's conclusion does not address the attitude of educators toward good discipline, Stephanie's argument need not do so, either. This is not a valid criticism of Stephanie's argument.

Question #5: Must Be True—Principle. The correct answer choice is (E)

The art critic offers a sole criterion for evaluating the aesthetic value of a work of art. Any work of art which stimulates the audience has aesthetic value, and any work which fails to do so has no aesthetic value. Such a clear demarcation makes the answer choices relatively easy to evaluate. Only answer choices (B) and (E) discuss the relationship between a work of art and an audience, and (B) contradicts the critic's principle. Therefore, (E) is the correct answer.

Answer choice (A): According to the critic, a work of art need not be original to have aesthetic value. If the painting done 30 years ago and this exact copy both stimulate their audiences, then both paintings would be aesthetically valuable.

Answer choice (B): Any work of art which does not excite the audience, no matter how well performed, will not have aesthetic value by this criterion. Furthermore, possessing aesthetic value does not necessarily render a work of art beautiful. This evaluation of the symphony does not conform to the principle cited above.

Answer choice (C): Like answer choice (B), this answer choice makes the dubious substitution of beautiful for aesthetically valuable. Also, the scarcity of the material from which this cube was sculpted is irrelevant in establishing its aesthetic value.

Answer choice (D): This answer choice may be somewhat appealing because it equates aesthetic value with controversy, which may be considered a form of stimulation. However, it is incorrect for at least two reasons. First, the term controversy describes the impact upon society, which may or may not reflect the impact upon a given audience. Second, the source of controversy is the artist, not the painting. The painting itself may not be stimulating to anyone. If so, this painting has no aesthetic value.

Answer choice (E): This is the correct answer choice. This answer choice appropriately demonstrates the described relationship between aesthetic value and ability to impact an audience. Since the poem does not impart a stimulating character to the audience's experience, it is aesthetically deficient.

Question #6: Point at Issue. The correct answer choice is (E)

Antonia advocates investing in the volatile stock market because it provides the opportunity to make a large profit quickly. Maria recommends savings bonds instead because a reliable income is better than a volatile opportunity. The question stem asks test takers to identify what issue Maria and Antonia are most likely to disagree about. As always, be careful to avoid answer choices about which both speakers would have the same position or either speaker's position is unclear. Using this rule, known as the Agree/ Disagree Test, answer choice (E) can be easily identified as the correct response.

Answer choice (A): Test takers should have no trouble eliminating this answer choice. Antonia quotes this sentence nearly verbatim and Maria also agrees with it. Since both speakers believe this answer is true, it cannot be the correct choice.

Answer choice (B): While Maria advocates investment in savings bonds, she does not necessarily believe that savings bonds can provide a large return. Antonia does not refer to saving bonds at all and since neither speaker's position can be clearly determined, this answer choice is incorrect.

Answer choice (C): Again, this is a clear Loser. Neither speaker believes the stock market to be a constant or reliable investment.

Answer choice (D): Maria certainly would agree with this position, based on her contention that savings bonds provide a reliable income. However, Antonia's position regarding this statement is unclear, as she does not mention savings bonds in her argument. Regardless, it cannot be known that the speakers disagree with each other over this point.

Answer choice (E): This is the correct answer choice. Maria would agree that a reliable investment is better than a volatile one, while Antonia feels that the best investment is a risky opportunity to make a large profit quickly. This is the only answer the passes the Agree/Disagree Test.

Question #7: Strengthen—CE. The correct answer choice is (D)

As always, it is extremely important to identify the conclusion in any stimulus where an argument is present. In this case, the author concludes that cave dwellers probably chased and tackled animals much like rodeo riders today, due to the fact that the skeletons of cave dwellers display injuries similar to those suffered by rodeo riders. Since the injuries are similar, the author believes these injuries were caused by similar activities. Answer choice (D) expresses this principle accurately and helps to strengthen the author's claim.

Answer choice (A): Although the author's conclusion is drawn from a study of skeletal remains, this principle does not help to justify the author's argument. Establishing the primary source of evidence is irrelevant. Whether the evidence came from skeletal remains, tools, or cave art, the argument depends upon strengthening the causal link between archaeological evidence and modern observation.

Answer choice (B): There are several problems with this answer. First, the author makes no claim about the relative importance of studying a particular aspect of prehistoric life. There is no justification for determining that food-gathering is the most important aspect. Second, chasing and tackling animals may have nothing to do with food-gathering. Perhaps these activities were sport for prehistoric cave dwellers. This principle does not help justify the argumentation in any way.

Answer choice (C): If an answer choice is going to strengthen an argument, the argument should appear more believable when that answer is considered alongside the other premises. For example, imagine if the stimulus read: "skeletal fractures present are most like the type and distribution of fractures sustained by rodeo riders. If direct evidence as to the cause of a phenomenon is available, then indirect evidence should not be sought. Therefore, it is likely that these cave dwellers engaged in activities similar to rodeo riders – chasing and tackling animals." Does this answer choice provide additional support for the conclusion? No. It might support the claim that researchers should ignore certain kinds of evidence, but that is not the author's argumentation. To strengthen the conclusion there must be further support for the causal relationship that the author proposes.

Answer choice (D): This is the correct answer choice. As with answer choice (C), try adding this principle into the stimulus immediately preceding the conclusion. Notice how well this principle leads from the author's premise to the conclusion – it even matches the word "probably" with the word "likely" in the conclusion. "If there is a similarity between two effects, then there is probably a similarity between their causes. [S]keletal fractures present [in cave dwellers] are most like the type and distribution of fractures sustained by rodeo riders. Therefore, it is likely that these cave dwellers engaged in activities similar to rodeo riders – chasing and tackling animals." The author's reasoning now seems more solid and the conclusion is thereby strengthened.

Answer choice (E): There is no information presented in the stimulus about how frequently prehistoric hominids participated in hazardous activities or how often the hominids were injured, so the correlation between these activities is irrelevant to the author's argument.

Question #8: Weaken. The correct answer choice is (C)

The inference of this conclusion is that people with normal blood pressure who can process excess sodium do not need to restrict their sodium intake. The clearest way to weaken this argument is to demonstrate that that there is some compelling reason for these people (i.e. the vast majority who have normal blood pressure) to also avoid excess sodium intake. Neither (A) nor (B) would provide these people with incentive to limit their sodium intake. Answer choice (D) suggests that everyone must consume some sodium and answer choice (E) would only concern those people whose bodies do not simply excrete any amount of unused or unneeded sodium. Answer choice (C), if true, asserts that excess sodium intake over time can be detrimental to anyone, including those people with normal blood pressure, and would therefore seriously weaken the argument.

Answer choice (A): This answer would certainly help motivate persons with high blood pressure to correct that problem. However, the vast majority of people would be unmoved by this argument, since their blood pressure is normal and excess sodium intake does not significantly raise their blood pressure.

Answer choice (B): Remember that the goal is to prove that it is also necessary for people with normal blood pressure to restrict their sodium intake. This answer choice only demonstrates that excess sodium intake may worsen an existing high blood pressure condition. Therefore, people without this condition would not be motivated to restrict their sodium intake and the author's conclusion would be unaffected.

Answer choice (C): This is the correct answer choice. If it is true that excess sodium intake impairs the body's ability to process excess sodium, then even people who have normal blood pressure need to restrict their sodium intake. Thus, the author's claim that only certain groups of people need to restrict their sodium intake is weakened by this answer choice.

Answer choice (D): The conclusion argues that certain groups of people need to *restrict* their sodium intake, not eliminate it altogether. So stating that everyone needs some sodium does not weaken that conclusion.

Answer choice (E): Since people with normal blood pressure do excrete any amount of sodium not used by the body, this answer does not weaken the author's conclusion.

Question #9: Must Be True—Formal Logic. The correct answer choice is (A)

This is the first formal logic problem of this section. Since the stimulus has no conclusion, one can reasonably expect that the correct answer choice will be an additive inference drawn from these premises. Examining each premise individually will allow for a determination of which inferences can correctly be drawn. For a complete discussion of formal logic principles, please see Chapter 11 of the Logical Reasoning Bible.

1. "Most lecturers who are effective teachers are eccentric."

> ET = lecturers who are effective teachers
> ECC = eccentric

$$ET \xleftarrow{\quad M \quad} ECC$$

Because "most" statements are not universal, they do not have a valid contrapositive. However, this premise does yield the inherent inference that some people who are eccentric are effective teachers (and vice versa), or

$$ECC \xleftarrow{\quad S \quad} ET$$

2. "Some noneccentric lecturers are very effective teachers."

> E̶C̶C̶ = noneccentric

$$\cancel{ECC} \xleftarrow{\quad S \quad} ET$$

Like "most" statements, "some" statements have no logical contrapositive. Also, "some" statements can only be combined with universal relationships to create additive inferences. Thus, there are no additive inferences between the first and second premises of this argument.

3. "Every effective teacher is a good communicator."

> GC = good communicator

$$ET \xrightarrow{\quad\quad} GC$$

This final premise yields a contrapositive ("Those who are not good communicators are not effective teachers") and can be combined with our existing premises to form additive inferences. For example, one can now conclude that some noneccentric lecturers are good communicators by combining the second and third premises:

$$\cancel{ECC} \xleftarrow{\quad S \quad} ET \xrightarrow{\quad\quad} GC, \text{ therefore: } \cancel{ECC} \xleftarrow{\quad S \quad} GC$$

Also, the inherent inference from the first premise can be combined with the third premise in the following manner:

$$\text{ECC} \xleftrightarrow{\text{ s }} \text{ET} \longrightarrow \text{GC, therefore: ECC} \xleftrightarrow{\text{ s }} \text{GC}$$

Since all "some" relationships are inherently reversible, this inference is identical to answer choice (A).

Answer choice (A): This is the correct answer choice. As demonstrated above, the first premise contains an inherent "some" inference ("Some lecturers who are eccentric are effective teachers"). This "some" inference, together with the third premise, leads to the additive inference that "Some lecturers who are eccentric are good communicators." Reversing this relationship yields "Some good communicators are eccentric."

Answer choice (B): This is simply a Mistaken Reversal of the third premise. Some good communicators may not be effective teachers, so this answer is incorrect.

Answer choice (C): From the third premise, one can infer that those who are not good communicators will not be effective teachers. However, this inference cannot be combined with any other premise or inference to determine whether or not such people will be eccentric. Thus, this answer is unsupported by the stimulus.

This is a very common incorrect answer choice in "some"-based formal logic questions, as test takers often mistakenly presume that "Some are XYZ" implies that "Some are not XYZ." In other words, just because it can be determined that some noneccentric lecturers *are* effective teachers (from the second premise; reversed: some lectures who *are* effective teachers are not eccentric) does not mean that some noneccentric lecturers *are not* effective teachers (or vice versa; that some lectures who *are not* effective teachers are not eccentric).

Answer choice (D): The terms "effective teacher" and "good communicator" are not logically equivalent. Being a good communicator does not necessarily ensure that one will also be an effective teacher. Thus, the latter term (good communicator) cannot correctly be substituted for the former (effective teacher) in the first premise.

Answer choice (E): According to the third premise, it is not possible for someone to be an effective teacher without being a good communicator. Since this answer choice contradicts one of the premises, this inference cannot be correct.

Question #10: Strengthen. The correct answer choice is (B)

Although the physics behind this phenomenon may be quite complex, the author's argument is very simple. If photons and neutrinos from a distant explosion arrived at Earth at the same time, there is evidence that they traveled through curved space. If the space through which they travel is curved, then Einstein's claim that gravity is a property of space itself is supported. The author's conclusion that Einstein is correct – that gravity is a property of space itself – must be strengthened by the correct answer choice.

Answer choice (A): This answer choice may lend Einstein some credibility, but keep in mind that the correct answer choice should not simply supply additional information to help validate Einstein's claims, but rather should strengthen the main conclusion of the argument (that gravity is a property of space itself). While it may be true that Einstein's prediction in answer choice (A) has been found to be correct, that does not mean that the rest of his theory is correct (alternative explanations could still exist for why the photons and neutrinos arrived simultaneously).

Answer choice (B): This is the correct answer choice. This answer choice directly strengthens the reasoning in the stimulus. It states that the only way in which photons and neutrinos emitted simultaneously by a distant event will reach Earth at the same time is if gravity is a property of space itself. Since the photons and neutrinos did arrive at virtually the same time, Einstein's claim (and the author's conclusion) must be correct.

Diagrammatically, this answer choice clearly supports the author's conclusion:

GPS = gravity is a property of space
PNST = photons and neutrinos reach Earth at the same time

Answer choice (B) states: GPS ⟶ PNST

Contrapositive: PNST ⟶ GPS

The contrapositive of answer choice (B) shows that, because photons and neutrinos did reach Earth simultaneously, the conclusion that gravity is a property of space is correct. It is rare that a Strengthen question will have an answer choice that essentially proves the conclusion to be correct, but test takers should be aware that this possibility exists and that the correct answer choice will be the one that *most* strengthens the argument in the stimulus.

Answer choice (C): If this answer were true, then the mere fact that observers could tell that photons and neutrinos had arrive at Earth would prove Einstein's claim incorrect. This is an Opposite answer which actually weakens the reasoning above and most test takers can quickly classify it as a Loser.

Answer choice (D): Without knowing the predicted impact of Einstein's claim on subatomic particles besides photons and neutrinos, this answer choice cannot be used to evaluate the reasoning in the stimulus. It neither strengthens nor weakens the author's conclusion.

Answer choice (E): Lack of previous empirical evidence of Einstein's claim does not strengthen the argument above. Since there could be several explanations for the lack of evidence besides a flaw in Einstein's theory (such as technological limitations), this answer also does not suggest that the author's conclusion is wrong. Answer choice (E) neither strengthens nor weakens the conclusion.

Question #11: Strengthen—Principle. The correct answer choice is (D)

The first step in solving this problem is to identify and isolate the geneticist's conclusion. Most test takers have little difficulty recognizing the final sentence as the conclusion of this sentence. Simply put, the geneticist feels that less money should be spent on human gene research and more should be spent on other types of more practical genetic research. The correct answer choice will provide a principle that, if true, will strengthen this reasoning.

In each of the answer choices, the first portion of the answer choice is advocated over the second portion. Obviously, the geneticist advocates the "plant" research projects over the "human" projects. Therefore, the best answer choice will be one in which the first portion correctly characterizes "plant" research (mundane but practical) and the second characterizes "human" research (high-profile but impractical). Also, the correct answer choice must lead to the conclusion that more money should be spent on the former than on the latter. Answer choices (A), (C) and (E) all incorrectly characterize at least one of these types of research. Answer choice (B) provides no justification for the action recommended by the stimulus, since proving that one type of research is more practical than the other does not justify the funding change. Only answer choice (D) meets both of these criteria.

Answer choice (A): While the stimulus suggests that research into modifying edible plants has practical application, it does not suggest that these experiments have the potential to help the whole human race. Furthermore, the current lack of practical results from human genetic research does not indicate that these experiments will help only a small number of people.

Answer choice (B): The task is not to prove the practicality of experiments that focus on the genetics of plants; the correct answer choice should help to justify the proposed change in funding. This answer choice is essentially a restatement of the third sentence in the stimulus and does not provide additional justification for the argument.

Answer choice (C): This answer choice characterizes the cited "plant" research as experiments that help prevent malnutrition, which seems fairly reasonable, but it mischaracterizes human genetic research. High-profile experiments that attempt to link particular human genes with particular personality traits will not necessarily prevent undesirable personality traits.

Answer choice (D): This is the correct answer choice. The geneticist describes "plant" research as "more mundane and practical" than human genetic research. Although human genetic experiments "seem to promise a new understanding of human nature," they "have few practical consequences." Because this answer choice correctly characterizes both types of research and shows that the former is more worthwhile than the latter, it strengthens the geneticist's conclusion.

Answer choice (E): Human genetic experiments are described as high-profile in the stimulus, but that does not indicate wide public support. Also, the fact that research into making edible plants hardier and more nutritious is grossly underfunded does not mean that these experiments get little media attention or lack public support. This answer choice cannot be used to support the geneticist's conclusion.

Question #12: Assumption. The correct answer choice is (C)

This stimulus begins with a common argumentative technique where the author states the viewpoint of a group that he or she will ultimately argue against. This is seen frequently on the LSAT, and can be recognized by common phrasings such as, "Some people argue…," "A group of scientists has hypothesized…," "There are those who believe…," etcetera. When an author begins his or her argument by introducing the beliefs of another group, the main point of the author's argument will almost always be the exact opposite of the opinion held by the other group that the author references. This is extremely consistent on the LSAT and useful for quickly determining an author's position.

The stimulus begins by stating that some people recognize the necessity of shifting alliances and policies to maintain governmental power, but see this as a drawback of democratic governments since it prevents policymakers from strictly adhering to fixed principles. Predictably, the conclusion of this argument is the opposite of that view, as the author believes that the flexibility of government policymakers is actually beneficial. The author argues that this flexibility grants governments the adaptability they need to respond to public interests. Implicit in the author's conclusion is a direct comparison of the value of each approach. If responding to public needs is more worthy than strictly adhering to principle, then this flexibility is more a benefit than an evil. If not, the author's conclusion is illogical.

Answer choice (A): There is a distinction between attaining power and retaining power. In attaining governmental power, policymakers must build a majority coalition. Once in power, however, the policymakers are not bound to the factions of their original winning coalition. As the stimulus indicates, policymakers "shift policies as they try to please different constituents at different times." Policymakers can constantly realign coalitions and retain power as long as they enjoy majority support.

Answer choice (B): The stimulus does not discuss nondemocratic forms of government and does not depend on a comparison between democratic policymakers and nondemocratic policymakers. Such a comparison has no impact on the validity of the author's conclusion.

Answer choice (C): This is the correct answer choice. Note that the author does not say that lack of strict fidelity to principle (adaptability) is entirely positive. Indeed, the assertion that governmental flexibility is "more a benefit than an evil" suggests that there may well be some negative aspect to this behavior. But, in making his or her conclusion, the author assumes that the benefits of adaptability outweigh any associated detriments. If this were not true, the conclusion would be invalid. Since the conclusion depends on the veracity of this assumption, this answer choice is correct.

Answer choice (D): If a principle has majority support, policymakers may adhere rigorously to principle and still please different constituents. But the conclusion does not rest upon the assumption that policymakers can sometimes behave consistently with both of these positions. This assumption is not required by the argument.

Answer choice (E): Like answer choice (B), this answer discusses nondemocratic forms of government. Since the stimulus does not address these forms of government, it is not necessary to assume that they are actually more flexible than democratic forms of government.

Question #13: Resolve the Paradox. The correct answer choice is (A)

Many LSAT questions contain multiple viewpoints or time periods. Whenever one of these questions occurs, it is absolutely critical to keep track of which characteristics belong to which viewpoint or time period. It is important to organize the information contained in this stimulus into clear and manageable segments. One approach is to treat 2 billion years ago as the demarcation point between the modern and ancient eras. It may seem counterintuitive to call 2 billion years ago the "modern era," but the name is used only to indicate a meaningful distinction between present conditions and earlier conditions. Readers are told that at any time prior to 2 billion years ago, the sun was 30 percent dimmer than it is now and any time since then, the sun has not been that much dimmer. One common feature of both eras is that life and liquid water were present.

What, then, is the apparent discrepancy? The stimulus states that if the sun were as dim during the modern era as it had been during the ancient era, there would not be liquid water today. So, in order for liquid water to have been present during the ancient era, there must be some other factor which counteracted the diminished heat from the sun during that era.

When scanning the answer choices, aggressively search for this factor. Also note that the discrepancy in the stimulus is between conditions now and conditions 3.8 billion years ago. Therefore, the correct answer choice is likely to include these two time periods. Only answer choices (A) and (B) describe two different time periods. Both (C) and (D) are about one time period only and (E) discusses a principle which is unrelated to any specific time period.

Answer choice (A): This is the correct answer choice. After reading the stimulus, many test takers will prephase an answer that involves heat. They understand that the critical factor in explaining this discrepancy is explaining how the earth could have been hot enough for presence of liquid water as early as 3.8 billion years ago, despite the diminished sunlight. In this case, that factor is the amount of heat retained by the atmosphere. In the modern era, a brighter sun allows liquid water to exist, despite lower heat retention in the atmosphere. In the ancient era, higher atmospheric heat retention allowed liquid water to exist, despite a dimmer sun.

Answer choice (B): This is the most frequently chosen incorrect answer choice. In this scenario, liquid water that was present 3.8 billion years ago later froze, and then melted about 2 billion years ago. However, the stimulus notes that the sun was 30 percent dimmer than it is now up until 2 billion years ago. This mean that throughout the entire ancient era, including 3.8 billion years ago, the sun was not generating as much heat as is now necessary for the presence of liquid water. Merely reaffirming that there was liquid water at some point in the ancient era does not help resolve this apparent discrepancy. Remember, to resolve the paradox the correct answer choice must present an explanation for how both sides of the paradox could occur. Answer choice (B) does not give any explanation for how liquid water could have existed 3.8 billion years ago, so it cannot be correct.

Answer choice (C): This answer choice seems promising because it addresses a source of heat other than the sun. However, test takers should be wary of this answer choice because it only addresses one time period. Specifically, it talks about ice sheets melting 2 billion years ago. An additional source of heat at that time would explain how liquid water has been present throughout the modern era, but does not account for the presence of liquid water during the ancient era (3.8 billion years ago).

Answer choice (D): This answer suggests that even after the sun became less than 30 percent dimmer than it is now, the earth was still cold enough that certain regions remained frozen. Of course, this does not explain how liquid water could have been present at all 3.8 billion years ago, when the sun was at least 30 percent dimmer than it is now.

Answer choice (E): If this answer is true, the apparent discrepancy would become even worse. A dimmer sun would generate less heat which would lead to lower temperatures. Lower temperatures would probably increase the portion of the globe that is ice-covered. The ice would reflect more of the sun's heat, cooling the planet even further. This cycle would make it even more difficult to explain the presence of liquid water 3.8 billion years ago under conditions which would preclude liquid water today.

Question #14: Main Point. The correct answer choice is (C)

Despite the unusual wording of the question stem, this is nothing more than a Main Point question, where test takers must identify the social critic's conclusion. The first sentence of this stimulus is merely a statement of fact regarding the origins and historical context of operas composed by Bizet and Verdi. No details about the argument structure or the author's point of view are evident from this sentence. The second sentence begins with the phrase, "Several recent studies." As mentioned previously, in LSAT logical reasoning questions such phrases are typically used to introduce viewpoints with which the author disagrees. These studies criticize the operas of Bizet and Verdi for reinforcing societal stereotypes about women. But the author argues that very few North Americans have really been exposed to these works. How, then, can the author's conclusion be prephased? If the exposure of these operas has been significantly limited, one can infer that their influence is equally limited. Therefore, the author would likely conclude that the operas of Bizet and Verdi have had little, if any, impact on reinforcing societal stereotypes about women.

Answer choice (A): This is an Opposite answer. As discussed above, several recent studies have found that Bizet and Verdi's images of women have reinforced modern stereotypes. However, the author's conclusion is that these images have not significantly influenced society because only opera lovers are even aware of Bizet and Verdi's interpretations of women.

Answer choice (B): Based on the stimulus, one cannot know what either nineteenth-century images of women or contemporary images actually are. If the author's argument was structured to establish this conclusion, one of the author's premises would likely focus on significant differences between the two interpretations of women. Instead, the author focuses on the limited exposure of Bizet's and Verdi's operas.

Answer choice (C): This is the correct answer choice. By including a conclusion indicator and adding this answer choice to the stimulus one can see how it follows smoothly and logically from the existing premises.

Answer choice (D): This answer choice is similar in form to the correct answer choice, but much too broad in scope. The stimulus is focused on the operas of Bizet and Verdi, rather than all opera, and societal stereotypes about women, rather than social attitudes in general.

Answer choice (E): While this is not the correct answer choice, it is nonetheless instructive to examine. By including the conclusion from answer (C), this stimulus could easily be rewritten as an assumption question. Answer choice (E) would then be an excellent description of one assumption upon which such a stimulus would depend. If people could be influenced by things they are not directly exposed to, then the author's premise would not refute the results of the studies. Always take the time to study both correct and incorrect answer choices, as the test makers are fairly consistent with the way that they construct questions and an awareness of these patterns is extremely useful for quickly eliminating incorrect answers that could otherwise seem tempting.

Question #15: Resolve Except—#%. The correct answer choice is (D)

LSAT test makers have long written questions to test test takers' understanding of proportionality. Previous tests have sometimes included as many as three questions of this type, but the frequency of this question type has decreased as test takers have become better prepared to answer them. Question #15 is the only question of this type on the June 2004 test. To perform well on proportionality questions, test takers must understand the difference between ratio (percentage) and amount. Changes in the percentage of a proportion do not necessarily lead to the same type of change in the actual amount, and vice versa.

In this instance, the ratio of the income tax rate for most taxpayers in consecutive years decreases from 1974 to 1975 and again from 1975 to 1976. From the stimulus, one can determine that income tax rate in 1975 is 98% of the initial rate in 1974 and the rate in 1976 is slightly more than 96% of the rate in 1974. But the amount of money collected at the 1975 rate for most taxpayers was the same as the amount collected in 1974 at the original rate for those taxpayers, and the amount of money collected in 1976 was much higher than both preceding years. Most test takers will quickly think of several potential explanations for this result and the test makers have provided four possibilities among the answer choices. Of course, the correct answer choice will be the one that does not help to resolve the apparent discrepancy.

Answer choice (A): Although a prosperous economy is not necessarily linked to higher incomes, it is reasonable to assume that the income of some taxpayers will increase during especially prosperous times. If the average income of the taxpayers in question rose about 2% between 1974 and 1975 (to offset the reduced tax rate), and rose substantially more than that between 1975 and 1976, the discrepancy would be resolved.

Answer choice (B): Besides an increase in the actual amount of income earned, a broader definition of taxable income would help explain why tax revenue did not decrease despite a reduction in tax rates. Assuming the amount of income received by most taxpayers from personal investments in 1975 was equal to 2% of their income in 1974, this would explain how the province collected the same amount of personal income tax in each of those years. This new definition cannot independently explain the increase in personal income tax collected during 1976, but it would resolve the paradox if the income earned from personal investments increased significantly in that year.

Answer choice (C): Some test takers may feel that this answer choice cannot help resolve the discrepancy because it may contradict the stimulus. After all, the stimulus states that the province decreased tax rates during 1975 and 1976. Of course, astute test takers will notice immediately that the tax cuts mentioned in the stimulus only apply to *most* taxpayers within the province. If the wealthiest taxpayers were asked to pay a higher rate while everyone else's rate declined, this could explain the amounts of personal income tax collected in 1975 and 1976.

On a more general note, it is important not to waste time fighting the answer choices. When the question stem says, "Each of the following, *if true*…," one should assume that the test makers understand this test and have written five potentially true answer choices. The correct answer choice to such questions will not be something which is blatantly false or inconsistent with the conditions of the stimulus. Instead, it will be a feasible statement that test takers should evaluate based upon its impact on the stimulus.

Answer choice (D): This is the correct answer choice. It is entirely feasible that the province's total revenue from all taxes increased during this time period. But does that help to explain why a decrease in the personal income tax rate did not result in a similar decline in the amount of personal income tax collected? Of course not. This information leaves the paradox unresolved and is therefore the correct answer choice.

It is no coincidence that this is a Resolve Except question. Through PowerScore's techniques and other test preparation methods, proportional questions have lost much of their predictive ability. Even poor test takers with only minimal preparation can often prephrase a solution to these questions. This question remains useful through the question stem, which may induce careless test takers to simply select the answer choice which best matches their prephrased solution. Do not be fooled into making this mistake. Always understand the question stem before evaluating the answer choices.

Answer choice (E): Many test takers may have prephrased this solution after reading the stimulus. Any increase in the pool of taxable income will counteract a decrease in the income tax rate. Higher average personal incomes, more taxable assets, or a greater number of liable personal incomes would all help explain the results observed in the stimulus.

Question #16: Justify the Conclusion. The correct answer choice is (B)

When reading this stimulus, one notices a rather jarring gap between the premise and the conclusion. The premise may be diagrammed as:

CO = things that are commonplace and ordinary
COA = catch our attention

$$CO \longrightarrow \cancel{COA}$$

Here is the conclusion:

MN = miracles of nature

$$\cancel{COA} \xleftrightarrow{\ s\ } MN$$

This statement introduces a third variable (miracles of nature) and determines its relationship to one of the previous variables. But how did the stimulus get from "everything that is commonplace and ordinary" to "miracles of nature"? In order to prove this conclusion, the proper relationship between miracles of nature and things that are commonplace and ordinary must be established. Only answer choices (A) and (B) contain the needed elements (a quick scan for the new term "miracles of nature" immediately eliminates answer choices (C), (D), and (E)), so they are the only possible Contenders for this question.

Answer choice (A): This can be diagrammed as follows:

$$\cancel{CO} \longrightarrow MN$$

Combining this answer choice with the contrapositive of the premise gives:

$$\text{COA} \longrightarrow \cancel{\text{CO}} \longrightarrow \text{MN, therefore: COA} \longrightarrow \text{MN}$$

In other words, if something catches our attention then it is a miracle of nature. This is not the same inference as the conclusion given in the stimulus (there are things that fail to catch our attention but that are miracles of nature) and, since this answer choice does not logically lead to the conclusion, answer choice (A) is incorrect.

Answer choice (B): This is the correct answer choice. Answer choice (B) can be diagrammed as follows:

$$\text{CO} \xleftarrow{\ \ s\ \ }\!\!\!\longrightarrow \text{MN}$$

Since "some" statements are reversible, this statement can be reordered and combined with the premise from the stimulus thus:

$$\text{MN} \xleftarrow{\ \ s\ \ }\!\!\!\longrightarrow \text{CO} \longrightarrow \cancel{\text{CO}}\text{A}$$

When combining relationships of different strengths, the relationship is reduced to the strength of the weakest element. In this case, the relationship becomes "Some miracles of nature will fail to catch our attention," which is logically equivalent to the conclusion. Therefore this answer choice leads to the correct conclusion and is proven correct.

Of course, this problem can also be solved without diagramming it. Assuming this answer choice is true, any ordinary or commonplace miracles must fail to catch our attention. This assumption completes the proper relationship between all the elements of the stimulus and is therefore correct.

Answer choice (C): If all things that are commonplace and ordinary fail to catch our attention, it is inherently true that some ordinary and commonplace things will likewise fail to catch our attention. This is simply an inherent inference of the argument's premise and does not lead to the conclusion. Further, this answer choice does not provide an explanation for the new term introduced in the conclusion and cannot be correct.

Answer choice (D): Here is the diagram of this statement:

$$\cancel{\text{CO}}\text{A} \longrightarrow \text{CO}$$

This is clearly a Mistaken Reversal of the first premise. Although it is useful practice to identify this answer choice as a Mistaken Reversal, the answer is not incorrect simply because it does not logically follow from the premise. Rather, it is incorrect because it does not explain anything about "miracles of nature." Even when this inference is added to the stimulus, it does not lead to the conclusion.

Answer choice (E): Like answer choice (D), this answer is also an invalid inference. Since "extraordinary or unusual things" are not commonplace or ordinary, this statement can be diagrammed thus:

$$\cancel{CO} \longrightarrow COA$$

Once again, however, demonstrating that this answer is a Mistaken Negation is not sufficient to prove that it is incorrect. Only by proving that this statement does not bridge the gap between the premise and the conclusion can it be safely eliminated from consideration. Since this statement does not clarify the relationship between miracles of nature and things which fail to catch our attention, it is not the correct answer.

Question #17: Cannot Be True—SN. The correct answer choice is (E)

This stimulus is a simplified description of the process of natural selection. That is, any traits, and only those traits, that convey a significant advantage to a species will be favored in natural selection. To evaluate this stimulus, it is critical to note that any given genetic mutation may have numerous effects. Some of these may help a species survive, some may harm the species, and others may have no effect at all. A species may have any number of genetic mutations, but only those whose cumulative effect is beneficial to the species will be favored in natural selection.

For example, suppose that a genetic mutation led to the birth of the first rhinoceros with a horn. Some effects of this mutation – such as the rhinoceros' unusual appearance – would probably be neutral to the animal's survival. Other effects, such as increased weight and drag of the horn, may have made this rhinoceros somewhat slower and easier to catch than other rhinoceroses. This is obviously negative. Of course, this rhino's ability to maim and gouge predators with its horn would make a substantial contribution to its survival. As long as the advantage of being able to wound predators outweighed the disadvantage of running slower, then the trait of possessing a horn would be favored in natural selection (unless the horn made the rhinoceros so odd or undesirable that it was unable to attract a mate).

The stimulus also contains an interesting feature, in that it uses the phrase "then, and only then" to relate the ideas of a trait making a substantial contribution to the survival of a species and the favorability of that trait. "Then, and only then" yields the following diagram in this instance:

SC = substantial contribution to the survival of a species
MF = mutation favored in natural selection

$$SC \longleftrightarrow MF$$

The double-arrow is due to the fact that "then, and only then" indicates that the idea of a genetic mutation making a substantial contribution to the survival of a species is both a sufficient and a necessary condition with respect to that mutation being favored in natural selection. This is a crucial inference and will be tested in the correct answer.

A quick scan of the answer choices reveals that only (D) and (E) address natural selection, which is clearly a critical aspect of the stimulus. Although each answer choice will be discussed sequentially below, test takers will save time and increase accuracy during the test by accelerating to the most likely answer choices as quickly as possible.

Answer choice (A): The stimulus places no restrictions upon the kinds of traits which a species may already possess. Having two tails would probably be completely neutral for the survival of a rhinoceros, but it could be possible. Such a trait could certainly exist, however, if the stimulus is true, such a trait could not be favored in natural selection (but could be, as the stimulus mentions, a trait that was carried along by a trait favored in natural selection).

Answer choice (B): It is certainly possible that all the effects of some genetic mutations contribute substantially to the survival of a species. Furthermore, such mutations, if present, would almost certainly be favored in natural selection.

Answer choice (C): The stimulus does not preclude the existence of traits which reduce the survival potential of a species. It only states that such traits will not be favored in natural selection. Therefore, this answer is possible and is not the correct choice.

Answer choice (D): So long as the associated benefit of the mutation in question is greater than all of the negative traits that it carries, that mutation would still be favored in natural selection. Thus, answer choice (D) could also be true.

Answer choice (E): This is the correct answer choice. According to the stimulus, for a mutation to be favored in natural selection it must make a substantial contribution to the survival of the species (remember the "then, and only then" diagram: SC $\longleftrightarrow$ MF). So it cannot be true that a mutation who effects are neutral (not substantially positive) is favored in natural selection. Therefore, the scenario in answer choice (E) could not be true.

Question #18: Flaw in the Reasoning. The correct answer choice is (B)

The flaw in the stimulus is a fairly common flaw presented in this type of Logical Reasoning question: Uncertain Use of a Term or Concept. The key to quickly identifying this flaw is to recognize that the term "public interest" shifts in meaning in the local citizen's argument. When the citizen says, "they aroused the public interest," this term indicates that the public became aware of or even fascinated by the case as citizens helped to find the victim and provided tips. In the next clause, however, "public interest" means something more akin to that which is best for the public (the public's best interests). By allowing this term to have a somewhat ambiguous meaning the local citizen makes the judge's actions *seem* inconsistent (the conclusion of the citizen's argument), despite the fact that the actions taken by the judge may not be inconsistent at all. This leads to the credited answer choice (B), which states that the argument is flawed because it "trades on an ambiguity with respect to the term 'public interest.'"

Answer choice (A): Generalization is a common logical fallacy, but is not one of the flaws in the citizen's argument. There is also no evidence to suggest that this case is atypical.

Answer choice (B): This is the correct answer choice. By using the term "public interest" imprecisely in the argument, the local citizen attempted to prove that the actions in this case should have been more harmonious with one another. If "public interest" has different meanings in each of the stated contexts, then the citizen's argument becomes much harder to defend.

A key to recognizing this type of flaw is to look for the repetitive use of a word or phrase by an author in an attempt to support a conclusion. This type of flaw is also a common incorrect answer choice in other Logical Reasoning scenarios that can be somewhat tempting if not fully understood.

Answer choice (C): Although this answer choice is incorrect, it is still a weakness in the argument. The citizen's argument depends on a broad definition of the term "they," which includes the judge as well as those who aroused the public interest. But the more broadly that "they" is defined, the less meaningful the term "inconsistent" becomes (if the judge did not specifically plead with the public for help, then her actions in barring the public would seem less inconsistent). Nonetheless, answer choice (B) remains the stronger answer choice.

Answer choice (D): Sensationalism involves grossly overstating the potential consequences of a given course of action. Since the citizen does not describe any possible consequence of these actions, this argument cannot be described as sensationalistic.

Answer choice (E): Although it is possible that the citizen's argument is motivated by a concern for the public's right to know, the stimulus does not provide any evidence to confirm this supposition. Furthermore, any belief that one principle is more important than another cannot rightly be called a flaw, since such a belief is strictly a matter of personal judgment.

Question #19: Weaken—CE. The correct answer choice is (B)

Many test takers enjoy Weaken questions because these questions necessitate the use of skills often required in real-world situations. Test takers are quite accustomed to finding inconsistencies, loopholes, flaws, and shortcomings in other people's arguments and these abilities can prove to be quite useful on the LSAT. Such test takers may think of several different ways to attack this argument. Remember, however, that the test makers will almost never attack the premises in a Weaken question. It is very unlikely that the correct answer choice will say, "Today's farmers actually plant many different strains of a given crop," or, "No known disease exists which would strike only a few strains of crops." Rather than questioning the author's evidence, the correct answer will attack the author's use of that evidence in drawing a conclusion.

Here, the author uses the evidence to make two claims. First, a disease that strikes only a few strains of crops would have had only minor impact on the food supply in the past. Second, such a disease would devastate the food supply today. It should be obvious that the latter claim is the author's main argument. So the primary objective is to find an answer choice which proves that this disease would not devastate the food supply.

Answer choice (A): This statement would only contradict the author's secondary claim (and not the conclusion) if the crop diseases mentioned here struck only a few strains of crops. It is possible that the devastating crop diseases mentioned in answer choice (A) are different than the disease(s) that strikes only a few strains of crops mentioned in the stimulus. Hence, this answer choice does not attack the author's conclusion.

Answer choice (B): This is the correct answer choice. This answer choice requires a number of assumptions. First, "quickly" must mean that the replacement crops can be used before the food supply becomes devastated, otherwise the conclusion could still be correct. Also, some of the strains among the many strains stored in the seed banks must not be affected by the disease. Finally, replacing the affected crops must not itself be devastating to the food supply. If all these things are true, then the author's argument would be weakened. While not the most clear Weaken answer choice on the test, this is the strongest answer choice available.

Answer choice (C): If this is true, it probably strengthens the author's argument by adding evidence that popular seed strains used today are less resistant than some of the less popular strains used previously.

Answer choice (D): The increased variety of human diets, and a heavy reliance on rice and wheat, does not suggest that the food supply would not be devastated by a crop disease. In fact, an argument could be made that this choice potentially strengthens the conclusion, as a heavy reliance on specific crops could theoretically result in the devastation of the food supply if those specific crops (rice and wheat in this example) were wiped out by disease. Because there is nothing to suggest that wheat and rice are particularly invulnerable to disease, or that they would likely not be devastated in the event of a disease outbreak, this answer choice certainly does not weaken the conclusion.

Answer choice (E): While it may be comforting to know that today's crops are more pest- and weed-resistant than they once were, this knowledge does not weaken the author's argument. Remember, the author is only concerned with the devastating impact of *disease* upon today's overly homogenous crop strains, and crops' resistance to other threats does nothing to offset their susceptibility to disease.

Thus, answer choice (B) is the only remaining Contender. It may not be perfect, but it is the only answer choice which could plausibly weaken the author's claim.

Question #20: Flaw in the Reasoning. The correct answer choice is (E)

This is an unusual stimulus because it contains four statements between the interviewer and the industry spokesperson. Most Logical Reasoning questions with multiple speakers are limited to two or possibly three statements. The interviewer first asks how computers could be released with flawed microprocessors. According to the spokesperson, the mistake occurred because it is impossible to manually check every circuit on a microprocessor before releasing the computer. The interviewer then asks how similar flaws will be prevented in the future and the spokesperson answers that such design flaws cannot occur again since the microprocessors are designed entirely by computer.

It seems somewhat ironic, if not foolish, that the industry would rely upon computers – some of which have recently been found to process information incorrectly – to prevent other computers from being flawed. That is, if a computer with a flawed microprocessor happens to be constructed to design other microprocessors it seems that any newly-designed microprocessors would likely be flawed as well. Further, to correctly conclude that there is "no chance" of future design flaws is virtually impossible and extremely vulnerable to attack, as could be expected of any conclusion that is limited to such an extreme degree.

Answer choice (A): Actually, the industry spokesperson makes no distinction whatsoever between the company mentioned and the rest of the industry. The spokesperson's comments imply that no companies can manually check all circuits and that all companies currently use computers to design microprocessors. Based on the stimulus, one must conclude that the quality control processes *are* representative of those followed throughout the industry.

Answer choice (B): The interviewer asks what guarantee there is that new microprocessors will not be similarly flawed. Since "similarly flawed" clearly refers to the types of flaws just mentioned, this question must be about preventing microprocessor design flaws. Therefore, the industry spokesperson is not required to account for the possibility that a microprocessor can have a flaw other than a design flaw. Although the statement in answer choice (B) is certainly not a valid criticism of the spokesperson's argument, this is nonetheless the most frequently chosen incorrect answer choice.

Answer choice (C): Since the industry spokesperson's argument is in response to a question about microprocessor flaws, there is no need for this argument to address the possibility of other computer malfunctions.

Answer choice (D): The industry spokesperson does not commit the common logical fallacy of overgeneralization. Instead, the spokesperson explains a single instance of a microprocessor design flaw and offers evidence that there will be no such flaws in the future.

Answer choice (E): This is the correct answer choice. The stimulus contains evidence that some computers are liable to error and the industry spokesperson then takes for granted that certain computers will not make mistakes in microprocessor design.

Question #21: Must Be True—Formal Logic. The correct answer choice is (B)

This question clearly demonstrates the importance of understanding the correct flow of information between the stimulus and the answer choices. On a Must Be True question, like this one, all of the information in the stimulus is presumed true and used to prove one of the answer choices. Any answer choice or prephrased solution which cannot be proven solely by evidence from the stimulus must be incorrect, no matter how well it seems to fit.

The language in the stimulus – "each," "at least some," "some…are not" – indicates that this is a Formal Logic question. As with most Formal Logic questions, consider diagramming the stimulus and examining the resultant inferences, as this is often the key to quickly locating the correct answer. The first sentence can be diagrammed as:

SC = participated in the town's annual spring cleanup
CRC = received a community recognition certificate

SC $\longrightarrow$ CRC

The second sentence would appear as:

TAC = active in the town's artistic circles

SC $\overset{s}{\longleftrightarrow}$ T̶A̶C̶

Because these two sentences share the common term, SC, they can be combined:

T̶A̶C̶ $\overset{s}{\longleftrightarrow}$ SC $\longrightarrow$ CRC, therefore: CRC $\overset{s}{\longleftrightarrow}$ T̶A̶C̶

The inference that can be drawn is that some people who received a community recognition certificate are not active in the town's artistic community. This is the exact idea presented in answer choice (B).

Answer choice (A): Does answer choice (A) have to be true based upon the stimulus? No. The inference in the stimulus is that some people who received a community recognition certificate *are not* active in the town's artistic community, but this does not imply that some people who received a community recognition certificate *are* active in the town's artistic community. This is a common incorrect answer choice when dealing with "some" statements.

Answer choice (B): This is the correct answer choice. To many test takers, this answer seems almost too obvious to be correct. The stimulus states that everyone at the spring cleanup received a certificate and that some people at the spring cleanup are not active in the artistic circles, then it is evident that some people who received certificates are not active in the town's artistic circles. Remember, though, that this is a Must Be True question – the answer is *supposed* to be evident. This is the correct answer, even though it contributes nothing to test takers' understanding of the stimulus.

Answer choice (C): The stimulus does not infer that only spring cleanup participants received community recognition certificates. Perhaps the arts fair participants received certificates, as well. Furthermore, it is possible that some people participated in both events (even though they were at the same time, it is possible that some people could have left one event early to attend the other).

Answer choice (D): This answer choice can be diagrammed as "CRC ⟶ SC," which is a Mistaken Reversal of the first sentence. Remember the difference between "Every A is a B" and "Only an A is a B" – specifying that all spring cleanup participants received certificates (the first sentence) is not equivalent to proving that they were the only ones who received such certificates (answer choice (D)).

Answer choice (E): Answer choice (E) is simply beyond the scope of the stimulus. It is entirely possible that every member of this community, including those who are active in the town's artistic circles, is concerned with the town's environment. It is equally possibly that everyone in town, including those who participated in the spring cleanup, is only concerned with collecting community recognition certificates.

Question #22: Parallel Reasoning—CE. The correct answer choice is (D)

Test takers who can quickly and appropriately identify common methods of reasoning will tend to do very well on Parallel Reasoning questions. The first step in classifying any argument is to identify the conclusion. Here, the conclusion is, "Taking advanced mathematics courses should increase a student's grade point average." The basis for this conclusion is the observation that students who take advanced math classes tend to have higher grade point averages than students who do not take such courses. Of course, the correlation between advanced mathematics courses and high grade point averages does not necessarily mean that taking such courses will increase a student's grade point average; this is a mistaken attribution of causality. Being intelligent may cause some students to take advanced math courses *and* have a high grade point average. That is, intelligence could be the cause for both the courses taken by a student and the student's grade point average (thus advanced courses and GPA would be unrelated from a causal standpoint, as they would both be effects of a common cause). Less intelligent students who take advanced mathematics courses would likely even decrease their grade point averages.

So, how can this stimulus be used to prephrase characteristics of the correct answer choice? First, the conclusion of the stimulus must be paralleled by the conclusion of the correct answer choice. The correct conclusion should be a prediction, rather than a statement of fact. It should indicate that taking some action *should* yield a certain result. Furthermore, this action must be based on evidence that it (the action) is positively correlated to the result. Finally, the correct answer choice must be flawed in the same manner as the stimulus. So any valid argument is automatically incorrect, as is any argument not based on a mistaken attribution of causality.

Answer choice (A): The conclusion of this argument is a statement of fact and does not parallel the conclusion of the stimulus. Additionally, this argument is not logically flawed, since the stated evidence does suggest that fur color is in large measure hereditary. Since neither the conclusion nor the validity of this argument matches the stimulus, answer choice (A) is incorrect.

Answer choice (B): The claim that water can cause intoxication is certainly a mistaken attribution of causality. However, there is no prediction (e.g. "Drinking more water should lead to increased intoxication"). Also, the conclusion is not based on evidence that the amount of water consumed is positively linked to the degree of intoxication. It is simply based on the fact that water is present in several solutions of alcoholic beverages.

Answer choice (C): Here, the conclusion is a less of a prediction ("something is likely to happen") than a mere possibility ("these two things may be related"). Further, is the attribution of causality mistaken? Probably not. This argument seems reasonably well supported, unlike that of the stimulus, which is clearly invalid. Also, the evidence here is structured differently than the evidence in the stimulus. This evidence focuses solely on overweight people who eat diets consisting primarily of fats and carbohydrates, rather than comparing those who eat such diets with those who do not. The correct answer must match the stimulus much more closely.

Answer choice (D): This is the correct answer choice. This answer contains a prediction and incorrect causality. There is a positive correlation (given as a prediction) between the number of shoes a person owns and the frequency with which they exercise. Also, the causality here is most likely reversed, as it is rather more likely that exercising frequently causes a person to buy new shoes more frequently than it is that owning two or more pairs of running shoes causes a person to start exercising more often. So this answer matches the stimulus in its conclusion, its logical validity, and its use of evidence.

Answer choice (E): Test takers should quickly determine that this answer has the correct type of conclusion (the word "should" appears in the conclusion of the stimulus and the conclusion of this answer choice). The type of evidence used here is also quite similar to that used in the stimulus. However, like answer choices (A) and (C), this reasoning seems valid. Whether or not the conclusion of this argument is in fact true, it is at least a logical interpretation of the evidence. Thus, answer choice (E) can also be eliminated.

Question #23: Main Point. The correct answer choice is (B)

This Main Point question is considered to be very difficult by most test takers because it features multiple conclusions – a main conclusion and a subsidiary conclusion. Since the test makers are aware that test takers use common indicators to identify conclusions, many subsidiary conclusions are prefaced by words like "thus" or "therefore." Also, the test makers often seek to draw attention away from the main conclusion by deliberately placing the subsidiary conclusion at the end of the stimulus.

For this stimulus, the first sentence is clearly a premise. The second statement is a conclusion which explains the first observation. The third statement begins with the words, "To see this," indicating that this portion of the argument will provide additional clarification of the conclusion that was just presented. The final sentence is a secondary (or subsidiary) conclusion, indicated by the word "thus." This conclusion is based on the previous sentence and explains the consequence of low blood glucose levels.

To correctly identify the main conclusion, consider the primary purpose of the argument. Is the argument primarily structured to prove that low blood glucose levels can lead to unconsciousness and death? If so, would the stimulus need to mention that several hormones can independently raise blood glucose levels? This premise would be superfluous if the stimulus was primarily intended to demonstrate the effects of low blood glucose levels. Do not be fooled by the conclusion indicator and order of presentation – the main conclusion of this stimulus is the second sentence.

As proof of this interpretation, test takers may wish to recompose the stimulus. Here is a possible paraphrase of the stimulus which emphasizes the correct conclusion: "Since brain cells can only use glucose to produce energy, low blood glucose levels can lead to unconsciousness or death. This metabolic quirk of the brain is probably the reason why each of many different human hormones can by itself raise the concentration of glucose in the blood."

Answer choice (A): As previously discussed, answer choice (A) is a premise of the stimulus given in support of the second sentence.

Answer choice (B): This is the correct answer choice. Each of the other statements in the stimulus is intended to support this conclusion. Note that the pronoun "this" in the second sentence has been replaced here with its antecedent (the information in the first sentence).

Answer choice (C): Like answer choice (A), this is another premise in the stimulus (the third sentence). It leads to the subsidiary conclusion.

Answer choice (D): This secondary conclusion is based on the evidence provided in answer choice (C). Based on this conclusion, the evolutionary advantage of having several different ways to raise blood glucose levels becomes clear.

Answer choice (E): Do not eliminate this answer choice simply because it does not appear in the stimulus. Some questions require test takers to provide a conclusion that is not explicitly contained within the stimulus. This answer choice closely resembles the correct answer choice in form. However, the content of this answer is incomplete. Rather than explaining the entire argument, this statement only refers to the relationship between the second premise and the subsidiary conclusion (the third and fourth sentences).

Question #24: Must Be True—Formal Logic. The correct answer choice is (B)

Like question #21, the language in the stimulus – "some," "all," "only," "every" – indicates that this is a Formal Logic problem and, like most Formal Logic problems, question #24 can be represented diagrammatically.

The first premise (the initial part of the first sentence) can be diagrammed as:

RUG = recent university graduates
WEI = consider work environment an important factor in choosing a job

$$WEI \xleftrightarrow{\ s\ } RUG$$

The second premise (the final part of sentence one) can be diagrammed thus:

SALI = consider salary an important factor in choosing a job

$$RUG \longrightarrow SALI$$

Because these premises share a common term, RUG, they can be combined:

$$WEI \xleftrightarrow{\ s\ } RUG \longrightarrow SALI, \text{ therefore: } WEI \xleftrightarrow{\ s\ } SALI$$

The inference is that some people who consider work environment to be an important factor in choosing a job also consider salary to be an important factor in choosing a job.

The second sentence introduces two new premises (the third and fourth premises of the stimulus). The third premise is:

SLI = consider stress level an important factor in choosing a job
VE = veteran employees

$$SLI \longrightarrow VE$$

This premise does have any shared terms with anything presented thus far, so all that can be inferred is the contrapositive: $\cancel{VE} \longrightarrow \cancel{SLI}$

The final part of the second sentence (premise four) can be represented as:

VPI = consider vacation policy an important factor in choosing a job

$$RUG \longrightarrow VPI$$

This fourth premise can be combined with the information from the first sentence:

$$\text{WEI} \xleftrightarrow{\;s\;} \text{RUG} \longrightarrow \genfrac{}{}{0pt}{}{\text{SALI}}{\text{and}} \atop \text{VPI}$$

There are three inferences that result from this combination:

1. WEI $\xleftrightarrow{\;s\;}$ SALI (there are some people who consider work environment to be an important factor in choosing a job who also consider salary to be an important factor in choosing a job; this inference was already discussed above)

2. WEI $\xleftrightarrow{\;s\;}$ VPI (there are some people who consider work environment to be an important factor in choosing a job who also consider vacation policy to be an important factor in choosing a job; this is answer choice (B))

3. SALI $\xleftrightarrow{\;s\;}$ VPI (there are some people who consider salary to be an important factor in choosing a job who also consider vacation policy to be an important factor in choosing a job; this inference is the most difficult but is not presented as an answer choice)

At this point, three strong "some" inferences have been made and one of these will be the correct answer choice.

Answer choice (A): The very first answer choice illustrates the importance of correctly interpreting each clause in the stimulus. Referring back to the first inference made (the combination of the first and second premises in sentence one): there are some people who consider work environment to be an important factor in choosing a job who also consider salary to be an important factor in choosing a job. However, the correct interpretation of that clause means there could be workers who consider work environment important but do not consider salary important (or vice versa).

Answer choice (B): This is the correct answer choice. Diagrammatically this answer choice would be represented as WEI $\xleftrightarrow{\;s\;}$ VPI (the second of the three inferences above). Notice that this answer choice combines the first clause with the final clause. It is quite common for the test makers to separate key pieces of information as much as possible within the stimulus.

Answer choice (C): The stimulus does not restrict the range of workers who consider work environment an important factor to just a few recent university graduates. That is, it is possible that all veteran employees consider work environment to be an important factor in choosing a job. In fact, the stimulus does not provide enough information to infer anything about veteran employees except what is explicitly stated – veteran employees are the only employees who consider stress level an important factor in choosing a job (SLI $\longrightarrow$ VE).

Answer choice (D): It is true that some people who consider vacation policy an important factor also consider salary an important factor (SALI $\xleftrightarrow{\;s\;}$ VPI; the third inference above). However, the stimulus does not eliminate the possibility that some veteran workers consider vacation policy important and do not consider salary important (or vice versa).

Answer choice (E): This answer choice is probably drawn from the fact that all recent university graduates consider salary important and none of them consider stress level important (only veteran employees consider stress level important). However, the veteran employees who do consider stress level an important factor may also consider salary an important factor. Nothing in the stimulus implies that these considerations are mutually exclusive.

Question #25: Parallel Reasoning. The correct answer choice is (A)

This problem combines formal logic with parallel reasoning and can be quite challenging for unprepared test takers. Learning to identify the salient features of these problems is critical to quickly and accurately identifying the correct answer choice.

First, recognize that this stimulus consists of a conclusion and two premises. The order of presentation is logically irrelevant, but the method of reasoning is critical. The correct answer choice must also have two premises and a conclusion. Also, because the stimulus is logically valid (if the stimulus contains flawed reasoning the question stem will indicate that there is a flaw), the correct answer choice must be logically valid. This can be demonstrated as follows:

Premise: Good things cause no harm at all

> GT = good things
> H = causes any harm at all

$$ GT \longrightarrow \cancel{H} $$

Therefore, things which cause any harm at all are not good things (the contrapositive).

$$ H \longrightarrow \cancel{GT} $$

Premise: Wealth is often harmful to people

> W = wealth

$$ W \longrightarrow H $$

Some test takers may question this representation, arguing that it implies that wealth always causes harm. However, the most accurate interpretation of this statement is that wealth is among those things which cause any harm at all. This formulation is logically valid and can be appropriately manipulated to reach the correct conclusion.

Combining this premise with the contrapositive of the first premise yields:

$$ W \longrightarrow H \longrightarrow \cancel{GT} $$

That is, wealth, since it causes harm, cannot be a good thing. This conclusion is an additive inference, correctly derived from the premises. The correct answer choice must exhibit the same pattern of reasoning.

Answer choice (A): This is the correct answer choice. A quick glance reveals that this answer choice also consists of a conclusion and two premises (although the order of presentation is reversed from the stimulus). Here is the diagram:

Premise: Alex loves to golf

> A = Alex
> LG = loves to golf
>
> $$A \longrightarrow LG$$

Premise: No one in the chess club love to golf

> CC = chess club
>
> $$CC \longrightarrow \cancel{LG}$$

Conversely:

> $$LG \longrightarrow \cancel{CC}$$

Therefore:

> $$A \longrightarrow LG \longrightarrow \cancel{CC}$$

In other words, Alex, who loves to golf, must not be in the chess club. Since this conclusion is an additive inference correctly drawn from both of the premises, answer choice (A) correctly parallels the reasoning in the stimulus.

Answer choice (B): It should be immediately clear that the premises in this answer choice are quite different from those in the stimulus. Closer examination also reveals that the reasoning in this answer choice is not logically valid. The argument may be represented as follows:

Premise: Isabella smiles a great deal and hardly ever cries.

> I = Isabella
> SGD and HEC = smiles a great deal and hardly ever cries
>
> $$I \longrightarrow SGD \text{ and } HEC$$

Premise: Happy people do the same.

> HP = Happy people
>
> $$HP \longrightarrow SGD \text{ and } HEC$$

Of course, smiling a great deal and hardly ever crying does not prove that Isabelle is a happy person, anymore than having four wheels and two doors proves that a pickup truck is a Ferrari. Shared necessary conditions do not lead to additive inferences. Therefore, this answer choice is incorrect.

Answer choice (C): This answer choice is interesting because it could use the stimulus as a principle for justifying its conclusion. If pollution causes harm, then growth in industry would not be a good thing for this town. Nevertheless, having a superficially similar rationale for its conclusion does not mean that this is the correct answer choice. This conclusion is based on a cost-benefit analysis rather than an additive inference from logical premises.

Answer choice (D): This was by far the most commonly chosen incorrect answer choice. The conclusion is clearly an additive inference and there are two logical premises. Some test takers may even argue that "most dachshunds hunt poorly" is very similar to "wealth is often harmful to people," since neither premise is universal.

However, these premises are vastly different in implication. "Most dachshunds hunt poorly" allows for the possibility that "Some dachshunds do not hunt poorly," which means that is it possible that for some dachshunds to hunt very well. Therefore, the fact that Sarah's dog hunts very well does not preclude the possibility that Sarah's dog is a dachshund. Here, the possibility of an exception invalidates the conclusion.

On the other hand, in the stimulus, the certainty of an exception actually proves the conclusion. The statement, "wealth is often harmful" guarantees that wealth will cause harm in at least one instance. Even a single such instance proves that wealth is not a good thing since good things cannot *ever* cause harm. Since this answer choice is logically invalid, it cannot be correct.

Answer choice (E): It should be quite easy to eliminate this answer choice. The second sentence is essentially a restatement of the first sentence: If it is not a holiday, there should be more traffic. It is not a holiday today, so there should be more traffic. Very few test takers selected this answer choice.

Question #26: Strengthen—Principle. The correct answer choice is (E)

This is a very well-written question, since the correct answer choice is difficult to prephrase precisely and each of the incorrect answer choices are wrong in very precise ways. During the Cold War, many countries were united by the significance of their common military and ideological interests, despite their varying economic interests. In the aftermath of the Cold War, formerly allied nations found that they were no longer bound by a common enemy, and were thus forced to interact delicately to maintain their allegiance in the face of the varying economic goals that still existed. Note that these economic tensions may have been overlooked during the Cold War, but they were not completely absent. The tensions were merely overshadowed by more pressing issues that required international cooperation. Such distinctions, minor as they may appear, are often the key to eliminating incorrect answer choices.

Answer choice (A): The stimulus describes the increased economic strain on international relations between previously allied nations. Since allied nations cooperated militarily with each other during the Cold War, there is no comparison between nations that once competed militarily and are now competing economically. Therefore, the stimulus does not conform to the proposition that international economic competition cause greater tension than international military competition.

Answer choice (B): This answer choice begins well by mentioning the strength of bonds derived from fear a common enemy, which certainly describes the state of international relations during the Cold War. However, the stimulus does not state that these countries shared common economic goals. Rather, it implies the opposite since certain economic tensions were no longer as easy to overlook as they once were. Without evidence of bonds between allies derived from common economic goals, this proposition cannot be said to conform to the stimulus.

Answer choice (C): Like answer choice (B), this answer choice begins well. The Cold War was a period of military commitment between countries. However, the fact that allied nations were once more willing to overlook economic tensions does not mean they ever reached a fundamental agreement about economic matters. Be careful not to assume more than the stimulus permits – overlooking economic concerns is clearly not the same as agreeing about them. Also, the ease with which countries are able to reach economic agreement is never discussed in the stimulus, so this answer choice cannot be correct.

Answer choice (D): This answer choice is an overstatement of the information presented in the stimulus. While the stimulus suggests that certain economic matters among allied nations are now considered more important than they were during the Cold War (or that international economic competition was overshadowed by the need for international military cooperation), it does not follow that such matters were ever considered unimportant.

Answer choice (E): This is the correct answer choice. This answer choice is measured and precise, without exaggeration or unwarranted comparisons. Like answer choice (B), this answer choice mentions the impact of a common enemy upon the strength of bond between nations. Unlike (B), however, this answer choice also correctly describes the impact of that bond upon economic tensions between those nations. This proposition effectively explains the situation described in the stimulus.

Overall, this section ranks as one of the easier LSAT games sections in history. The first three games in particular are quite straightforward, and test takers receive an additional benefit in that the section only contains 22 questions. Of course, the relative ease of this section is offset by the fact that the scale for this test is tight. Each game is dissected in detail below.

June 2004 Game #1: Questions 1-5

This is a basic linear game featuring six groups placed in six spaces, with exactly one group per space (a Defined, Balanced game). Games of this nature—ordered with the exact number of variables for the given spaces—are considered the easiest type of Logic Game, and this is a perfect way to start a Logic Games section. The only drawback is that there are just five questions in this game; it would be preferable to see a greater number of questions attached to such a simple game scenario.

Considering just the game scenario and the rules, you should make the following basic setup for this game:

F G J M P V ^{6}

$*$

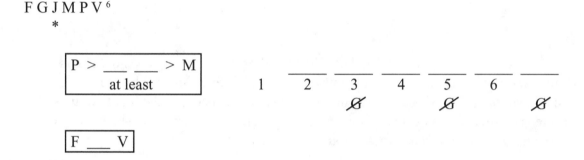

Note that the third rule, which involves G, is represented by Not Laws on groups 2, 4, and 6, and this representation indicates that G can only be in groups 1, 3, or 5.

Although the diagram above captures the basic meaning of each rule, it does not capture the inferences created by the first and second rules (such as Not Laws, etc.). In fact, you have an interesting choice at this juncture of the game: you can either show all the Not Laws that result from the two blocks or you can show templates based on the placement of the blocks. Either approach will work, although the templates approach tends to be faster. Regardless, let's show how each diagramming approach would unfold.

Approach 1: Diagram the Not Laws

Using the diagram above as a base, we can add Not Laws drawn from each of the first two rules.

Rule #1. This rule creates a large, flexible split-block involving P and M. Because there must be at least two groups between P and M, this block takes up a minimum of four spaces (leaving three options if the block is compressed as tightly as possible: groups 1-4, 2-5, or 3-6). Consequently, we can deduce that M can never appear in groups 1, 2, or 3, and we can deduce that P can never appear in groups 4, 5, or 6. Adding these Not Laws to the diagram, we arrive at:

1	2	3	4	5	6
	Ø̶		Ø̶		Ø̶
M̶	M̶	M̶	P̶	P̶	P̶

Rule #2. This rule creates a fixed split block involving F and V. Because V is always two groups behind F, V can never appear in groups 1 or 2; because F is always two groups ahead of V, F can never appear in groups 5 or 6. Adding these Not Laws to the prior diagram, we arrive at:

1	2	3	4	5	6
	Ø̶		Ø̶		Ø̶
M̶	M̶	M̶	P̶	P̶	P̶
V̶	V̶			F̶	F̶

What becomes immediately apparent from these Not Laws is that groups 2 and 6 are the most restricted, and each has only three options:

1	F/J/P	3	4	5	J/M/V
	2				6

At this point in the game, you have diagrammed and considered all of the rules, so you should head towards the questions. And, since the meaning of the third rule is completely captured by the Not Laws in the diagram, you will simply need to focus on the first two rules (as an aside, of the first two rules of the game, the first rule is more problematic because it contains a degree of uncertainty—how many other groups are between P and M—that you *must* track throughout the game).

Approach 2: Diagram the Templates

The alternative approach is to diagram the game based on templates created by the blocks. Your first choice is which block to use as the basis for the templates. In this case, the choice should be easy: use the FV block created by the second rule. This block is the better choice because it is fixed, with exactly one group between F and V. Although the PM block is larger and takes up more space, it is an inferior choice because it is flexible, and the number of groups between P and M is not fixed; this flexibility creates more options, and ultimately, more templates.

Using the FV block, we can place the block in four positions: groups 1-3, 2-4, 3-5, and 4-6. The following diagram shows each scenario:

	1	2	3	4	5	6
Template #4:				F		V
Template #3:			F		V	
Template #2:		F		V		
Template #1:	F		V			

Of course, the other rules can also be applied to derive more information about each template. Let's start with the third rule since it is more concrete than the first rule (thereafter, we will consider the first rule).

Rule #3. Since G must always be placed in group 1, 3, or 5, in Template #1 G must be placed in group 5 (groups 1 and 3 are already occupied by F and V). Likewise, in Template #3 G must be placed in group 1 (groups 3 and 5 are already occupied by F and V). Applying these two inferences, we can add G to Templates #1 and #3:

Template #4:	___	___	___	F	___	V
Template #3:	G	___	F	___	V	___
Template #2:	___	F	___	V	___	___
Template #1:	F	___	V	___	G	___
	1	2	3	4	5	6

Rule #1. Because the block created by this rule is so large, it has somewhat limited placement options around F and V, especially in the Templates #1 and #3, which are more restricted now that G has been placed in each. Let's examine the effect of the first rule on each template:

Template #1: Because P and M must be separated by at least two groups, in this template P must be placed in group 2 and M must be placed in group 6. The only remaining group is group 4, which must be filled by J, the random. Thus, this template has only one solution:

F	P	V	J	G	M
1	2	3	4	5	6

Template #2: The PM block has several options within Template #2. It can be placed in groups 1-5, 1-6, or 3-6. Consequently, this template will not fill in as completely as Template #1. Aside from the general position of P (group 1 or 3) and M (group 5 or 6), we can deduce that group 6 will be filled by J or M (from the initial Not Laws, group 6 cannot be filled by F, G, or P, and, in this template, group 6 cannot be filled by V, leaving only J or M). Adding all the information together, this template is still only partially complete:

P/	F	/P	V	M/	J/M
1	2	3	4	5	6

Note that if G marches in group 1 or 3, that will create a chain reaction forcing P into the remainder of group 1 or 3. If P is forced into group 3, then M must be in group 6 (and J must be in group 5).

Template #3: As in Template #1, the placement of the PM block is limited in this template. Because P and M must be separated by at least two groups, in this template P must be placed in group 2 and M must be placed in group 6. The only remaining group is group 4, which must be filled by J, the random. Thus, this template has only one solution:

G	P	F	J	V	M
1	2	3	4	5	6

Template #4: At first glance it may appear that not much can be done with this template. However, the size of the PM block again leads to a useful inference. The PM block can only be placed in groups 1-5 or 2-5. Consequently, we can infer that M must always march in group 5 in Template #4, that P can only march in group 1 or 2, and that either G or J must march in group 5:

P/	/P	G/J	F	M	V
1	2	3	4	5	6

Note that if P or G marches in group 1, that will create a chain reaction that, depending on which group is in group 1, either forces P into group 2 or forces G into group 3 (G, from the third rule, can only march in group 1, 3, or 5).

Compiling all four templates, we arrive at the following setup:

Template #4:	P/	/P	G/J	F	M	V
Template #3:	G	P	F	J	V	M
Template #2:	P/	F	/P	V	M/	J/M
Template #1:	F	P	V	J	G	M
	1	2	3	4	5	6

After applying all the rules, we have two very complete and powerful templates, and two other templates that contain a fair amount of information. We are now ready to attack the questions, and we will use the templates as they are more efficient that the Not Law setup.

Question #1: Global, List. The correct answer choice is (D)

As with any List question, simply apply the rules to the answer choices. Remember to apply the rules in order of the easiest to "see" within the answers. In this game, that order would be rule #3, rule #2, and then rule #1.

Answer choice (A): This answer is eliminated by the first rule. In this instance, there is only one group separating P and M.

Answer choice (B): This answer choice is eliminated by the third rule. In this answer there is no group between F and V.

Answer choice (C): This answer is eliminated by the third rule because G marches in group 4.

Answer choice (D): This is the correct answer choice.

Answer choice (E): This answer violates both the first and second rules. Interestingly, if you misdiagram the first two rules by reversing the order of the variables (for example, "V __ F"), this answer would appear correct.

One of the great benefits of this question is that we are given a free hypothetical solution to the game, in this case J-P-G-F-M-V. This could be useful in a later question.

Question #2: Local, Could Be True. The correct answer choice is (E)

This question imposes a local condition that you must address before moving to the answer choices. In this instance, the question stipulates that G and V form a block, and combining this condition with the second rule, we can form a FGV super-block where F, G, and V must appear in consecutive order. Applying our templates, the only place an FGV block can occur is in Template #2, where F is in group 2 and V is in group 4:

Template #2:	P/	F	/P	V	M/	J/M
	1	2	3	4	5	6

Accordingly, G must march in group 3, which forces P to march in group 1. The only remaining uncertainty is the placement of J and M:

Question #2:	P	F	G	V	M/J	J/M
	1	2	3	4	5	6

With the information above, we can quickly determine that (E) is the correct answer choice.

Answer choice (A): Under the condition in this question, G must march in group 3.

Answer choice (B): Under the condition in this question, J must march in group 5 or 6.

Answer choice (C): Under the condition in this question, M must march in group 5 or 6.

Answer choice (D): Under the condition in this question, P must march in group 1.

Answer choice (E): This is the correct answer choice.

Question #3: Local, Could Be True. The correct answer choice is (A)

If V marches immediately behind P, then, by adding the first rule we arrive at the following block:

$$\boxed{P\ V} > \underline{\quad} > M$$
$$\text{at least}$$

And, after adding the second rule, we arrive at the following super-block:

$$\boxed{F\ P\ V} > \underline{\quad} > M$$
$$\text{at least}$$

The question asks for which could be the second group, and a quick glance at the templates shows that Template #1 conforms to the block above. However, the group that marches second in Template #1—P—is not one of the answer choices. Hence, we must look at one of the other templates for the answer. Because Templates #3 and #4 cannot conform to the super-block above, the only possible source of the correct answer is Template #2. Because Template #2 features F as the second group, the correct answer to this problem must be F, and answer choice (A) must be correct. However, let's take a moment to examine this further.

In Template #2, F and V are in groups 2 and 4, respectively. Applying the super-block, we can create the following diagram:

Question #3:

	F	P	V		M
1	2	3	4	5	6

At this juncture, the only remaining uncertainty is the placement of G and J, which can be placed in group 1 or 5:

Question #3:

G/J	F	P	V	J/G	M
1	2	3	4	5	6

As this hypothetical meets the rules of the game and the condition imposed in question #3, it shows that F can be in the second group.

Answer choice (A): This is the correct answer choice.

Answer choice (B): Under the condition in this question, G must march in group 1 or 5.

Answer choice (C): Under the condition in this question, J must march in group 1 or 5.

Answer choice (D): Under the condition in this question, M must march in group 6.

Answer choice (E): Under the condition in this question, V must march in group 4.

Question #4: Local, Must Be True. The correct answer choice is (E).

Within the templates, the only time J can be the fifth group is under Template #2:

Template #2:

P/	F	/P	V	M/	J/M
1	2	3	4	5	6

If J is in group 5, them M must be in group 6:

Question #4:

P/	F	/P	V	J	M
1	2	3	4	5	6

The only remaining uncertainty is the placement of G and P, which can rotate between the first and third groups:

Question #4:

G/P	F	P/G	V	J	M
1	2	3	4	5	6

Because this is Must be true question, you can use the hypothetical above to quickly accelerate through the questions. In this instance, answer choice (E) is quickly proven correct.

Answer choice (A): Although P could be in the first group, P could also be in the third group, and so this answer choice does not have to be true. Note how the test makers immediately attack you on the uncertainty within this question.

Answer choice (B): F must be in the second group, not the first group.

Answer choice (C): V must be in the fourth group, not the second group.

Answer choice (D): Although G could be in the third group, G could also be in the first group, and so this answer choice does not have to be true.

Answer choice (E): This is the correct answer choice.

Question #5: Global, Cannot Be True. The correct answer choice is (B)

This question asks you to identify the group that cannot march immediately behind G. There are two ways to work out the correct answer to this question: either eliminate those variables that *can* march behind G, or find the variable that cannot march behind G. Given the considerable amount of information we have amassed in the templates, and in the hypotheticals in the answer choices, the second approach is likely to be the fastest (unless, of course, you have already deduced which variable cannot march behind G).

First, consider the templates: in Template #1, M marches immediately behind G, and thus we can eliminate M from the answer choices. In Template #3, P marches immediately behind G, and thus we can eliminate P from the answer choices.

Second, and especially important if you did not use the template approach, do not forget to consider the hypotheticals created while you answered the questions. Let's review each hypothetical:

Question #1: In this question we were given the solution J-P-G-F-M-V. This solution eliminates F from the answer choices.

Question #2: In this question we arrived at the solution P-F-G-V-M/J-J/M. This hypothetical eliminates V from the answer choices.

Question #3: In this question we arrived at the solution G/J-F-P-V-J/G-M. If G marched first, this hypothetical eliminates F from the answer choices; if G marched fifth, this hypothetical eliminates M from the answer choices.

Adding all the information together (some of it redundant), we have eliminated F, M, P, V from marching immediately behind G. Thus, only J can march immediately behind G, and therefore answer choice (B) is correct.

Answer choice (A): F can march behind G, as proven by the solution to questions #1 and #3.

Answer choice (B): This is the correct answer choice. If J marches immediately behind G, then there is not enough room to place the other blocks without violating one of the rules (try it: the GJ block would have to be placed in groups 1-2, 3-4, or 5-6; in each instance the MP block can be placed successfully, but doing so leaves no room for the FV block).

Answer choice (C): M can march behind G, as proven by Template #1 and the solution to question #3.

Answer choice (D): P can march behind G, as proven by Template #3.

Answer choice (E): V can march behind G, as proven by the solution to question #2.

Note that a question of this nature reveals that you do not have to have every piece of information about a game in order to successfully complete the game. Students often miss inferences during the setup, only to discover them during the game without negative repercussion. In this case, having the templates makes the game manageable even if you miss an inference or two.

This is a linear game controlled by pure sequencing rules, and because the sequential rules are so dominant, we classify this as a Pure Sequencing game. The key to this game is to make a usable sequence from the three rules, and then to understand the possibilities within that sequence.

From the game scenario, we know the following:

L M O S V Z [6]

Each of the rules can be diagrammed individually, but as you diagram, you should combine the rules in a super-sequence. First we will show the diagram for each rule:

Rule #1:

$$M > S$$

Rule #2:

```
            L
    S > - - - - - -
            V
```

Rule #3:

```
    V
- - - - - - > O
    Z
```

Now, combine the rules.

Rule #1 and #2 combined:

```
                L
    M > S > - - - - - -
                V
```

The addition of the third rule is more problematic, and requires careful consideration. First, from the third rule we know that V > O:

```
                L
    M > S > - - - - - - - - -
                V > O
```

This leaves Z to be added to the diagram, a potential stumbling block because Z > O, but, unlike V, Z is not necessarily farther from the front than S. Use an arrow to show the relationship of O and Z:

Rule #1, #2, and #3 combined:

```
                          L
        M > S > - - - - - - - - - -
                        V > O
                              ┐
                        Z ←┘
```

Z is a very unrestricted variable in this game: Z could be as far forward as seat 1, or as far back as seat 5.

At this juncture we could choose to diagram all the Not Laws, but this would not be a wise choice since we already have the very powerful super-sequence to use to attack the questions. The one thing worth noting is which variables can be first or last. In this case, either M or Z must be first, and either L or O must be last:

```
   M/Z  ____  ____  ____  ____  L/O
    1     2     3     4     5     6
```

Question #6: Global, List. The correct answer choice is (C)

This is a harder-than-average List question. Our analysis of who is first and last only eliminates answer choice (D)—either L or O must be last, yet (D) features L in seat 3 and O in seat 5.

Answer choice (A): If V is in seat 5, then O must be in seat 6 since V > O. However, this answer features V in seat 5 and L in seat 6, and so it is incorrect.

Answer choice (B): There are two different ways this answer can be eliminated:

1. If S rows in seat 3, then M and Z must occupy seats 1 and 2 in some order. However, this answer features Z in seat 5, and that assignment does not leave enough athletes for seats 1 and 2.

2. According to the rules L must row behind S, and O must row behind V and Z. With S, V, and Z rowing at seats 3, 4, and 5, only seat 6 available for both L and O, a violation of the rules.

Answer choice (C): This is the correct answer choice.

Answer choice (D): This answer choice is incorrect because either L or O must be in seat 6, and neither can be under this scenario.

Answer choice (E): According to the rules, M and S must row ahead of V. When Z and V row at seats 2 and 3, only seat 1 is available for both M and S, a violation of the rules.

Question #7: Local, Must Be True. The correct answer choice is (E)

If V rows at seat 5, then according to the third rule O must row in seat 6. Consequently, answer (E) must be correct.

Answer choices (A), (B), (C), and (D): Each of these answer choices could be true, but none of them have to be true and therefore each is incorrect.

Answer choice (E): This is the correct answer choice.

Question #8: Local, Could Be True, Except. The correct answer choice is (E)

If L rows at seat 3, then according to our sequence, M must row at seat 1 and S must row at seat 2:

$$\frac{M}{1} \quad \frac{S}{2} \quad \frac{L}{3} \quad \frac{}{4} \quad \frac{}{5} \quad \frac{}{6}$$

Because either L or O must row last, and L is already assigned to seat 3, we can also deduce that O must row at seat 6:

$$\frac{M}{1} \quad \frac{S}{2} \quad \frac{L}{3} \quad \frac{}{4} \quad \frac{}{5} \quad \frac{O}{6}$$

The only remaining choice is the positioning of V and Z, and since the two do not have a direct relationship, either can row at seat 4 or 5:

$$\frac{M}{1} \quad \frac{S}{2} \quad \frac{L}{3} \quad \frac{V/Z}{4} \quad \frac{Z/V}{5} \quad \frac{O}{6}$$

Answer choices (A), (B), (C), and (D): Each of these answer choices could be true and therefore each is incorrect.

Answer choice (E): This is the correct answer choice. As proven by the diagram above, since S rows at seat 2, S can never row immediately behind Z, which must row at seat 4 or 5.

Question #9: Global, Cannot Be True. The correct answer choice is (A)

A Global question requires you to examine your diagram for the information needed to evaluate each answer choice. In this instance, our diagram primarily consists of the super-sequence, so use that to attack each answer choice.

Answer choice (A): This is the correct answer choice. As shown in the diagram, O must always row somewhere behind V, which rows somewhere behind S. Thus, O can never row ahead of S.

Answer choice (B): Because the only rule involving Z states that Z must row closer to the front than O, it is possible for Z to row closer to the front than M. Therefore, this answer choice could be true and it is incorrect.

Answer choice (C): The second rule states that L and V row somewhere behind S. However, this rule does not indicate that L rows ahead of V, or that V rows ahead of L. Consequently, it is possible for L to row closer to the front than V, and this answer choice is incorrect. The hypothetical produced in question #8 also helps show that this scenario could occur.

Answer choice (D): Although Z could be as far forward as seat 1, Z could also be as far back as seat 5. Hence, it is possible for S to row closer to the front than Z, and this answer choice is incorrect. As with answer choice (C), the hypothetical produced in question #8 helps show that this scenario is possible.

Answer choice (E): This answer choice can be eliminated by the similar reasoning used to eliminate answer choice (C). Just as we were able to show that L could row closer to the front than V, it is possible that V can row closer to the front than L.

Question #10: Global, Maximum. The correct answer choice is (D)

In our discussion of diagramming the sequence, we discussed the possibilities for Z: Z could row as far forward as seat 1, or as far back as seat 5. Consequently, Z could occupy any of five different seats, and answer choice (D) is correct.

Answer choices (A), (B), and (C): Because the question stem asks for how many different seats Z can occupy, these answer choices are insufficient since they each supply a number that is less than the maximum number of seats that Z can occupy.

Answer choice (D): This is the correct answer choice.

Answer choice (E): From the third rule we know that V must always row closer to the front than O. Consequently, V can never row at seat 6, and therefore V cannot row in all six different seats. This answer is therefore incorrect.

Question #11: Local, Must Be True. The correct answer choice is (A)

The question stem adds a condition that modifies the original sequence established by the rules. In this instance, the question stem stipulates that V > Z, and thus the original diagram can be re-diagrammed as follows:

$$
\begin{array}{c}
\qquad\qquad\qquad L \\
M > S > \text{-----------} \\
\qquad\qquad V > Z > O
\end{array}
$$

Accordingly, we know that M must row at seat 1, and S must row at seat 2. V, Z, and O are in a sequence, but L can float freely among seats 3, 4, 5, and 6.

Answer choice (A): This is the correct answer choice. Answer choice (A) is shown to be true by the discussion of the placement of M and S.

Answer choices (B), (C), (D), and (E): Each of these answer choices could be true, but none of them have to be true and therefore each is incorrect.

Question #12: Local, Suspension. The correct answer choice is (C)

This is a suspension question, that is, a question that suspends one of the original rules of the game. This type of question requires the original sequence to be re-diagrammed before you attack the questions. And, in this case, because an additional condition is added to the mix, that must also be accounted for in the new diagram. Suspension questions are generally very time-consuming, and you should avoid them if you have difficulty completing the games section.

Because the first rule has been removed, only the combination of the second and third rules remains:

$$
\begin{array}{c}
L \\
S > - - - - - - - - - \\
V > O \\
Z \leftarrow \rfloor
\end{array}
$$

The question stem reverses the first rule, which by itself would be diagrammed as:

$$S > M$$

Adding this new condition to the diagram of the second and third rules, we arrive at the following diagram for question #12:

$$
\begin{array}{c}
M \\
- - - - - - - - \\
S > \quad L \\
- - - - - - - - \\
V > O \\
Z \leftarrow \rfloor
\end{array}
$$

Although S may appear to row at seat 1, Z is still a virtual wild card in this question, and Z could also row at seat 1. However, the latest that S can row is at seat 2.

Answer choices (A), (B), (D), and (E): Each of these answer choices could be true, but because the question asks for an answer choice that cannot be true, each of these answers is incorrect.

Answer choice (C): This is the correct answer choice. As discussed above, the latest that S can row is at seat 2, and because this answer attempts to place S in seat 3, it cannot be true and is therefore correct.

This Advanced Linear game is about equal in difficulty to the previous two games. Like the previous two games, this game has only six variables and three rules, and so creating the diagram is not an especially lengthy process.

From the game scenario, we know that there are two purchasers: a private collector and a museum. There are three different periods (periods 1, 2, and 3, from earliest to latest) and that suggests a linear setup with two stacks, one for the private collector and one for the museum:

$$Q\ R\ S\ T\ V\ Z^6$$
$$*$$

Private: ____   ____   ____

Museum: ____   ____   ____
            1   2   3

The first rule can be diagrammed as :

$$S_P > Z_M$$

This rule indicates that Z cannot be from the first period (and thus must be from the second or third period), and that S cannot be from the third period (and thus must be from the first or second period). The rule also indicates that S cannot be sold to the museum and that Z cannot be sold to the private collector:

Private: S/   /S   ____   ~Z

Museum: ____   Z/   /Z   ~S
              1   2   3
             ~Z   ~S

Because there are only three periods, if S is from the second period, then Z must be from the third period. Conversely, if Z is from the second period, then S must be from the first period:

$$S_2 \longrightarrow Z_3$$

$$Z_2 \longrightarrow S_1$$

The second rule can be a bit tricky to diagram. The rule states that Q is *not from an earlier period* than T. Many students interpret this rule to mean that T must be from an *earlier* period than Q; that is not correct. Although Q cannot be from an earlier period than T, Q could be from the *same* period as T (remember, always read the rules closely!). Consequently, this rule is best diagrammed as:

$$T \geq Q$$

Because T and Q could be from the same period, no Not Laws can be drawn from this rule. However, if T is from the third period, then Q must also be from the third period, and if Q is from the first period, T must also be from the first period.

The third rule indicates that V is from the second period, and that consequently V cannot be from the first or third periods:

Private: _____ $\underline{V/}$ _____

Museum: $\underline{}$ $\underline{/V}$ $\underline{}$
　　　　　1　　　　2　　　　3
　　　　　X　　　　　　　X

The actions of V clearly impact the first rule. If V is sold to the private collector, then S must be from the first period; if V is sold to the museum, then Z must be from the third period:

$$V_{2P} \longrightarrow S_1$$

$$V_{2M} \longrightarrow Z_3$$

Combining all the rules and inferences together, we arrive at the following diagram for the game:

Q R S T V Z [6]
　*

$S_P > Z_M$ 　　　　Private: $\underline{S/}$ 　$\underline{V/S/}$ 　_____ 　$\cancel{Z}$

$T \geq Q$ 　　　　Museum: $\underline{}$ 　$\underline{Z/V/}$ 　$\underline{/Z}$ 　$\cancel{S}$
　　　　　　　　　　　　　　1　　　2　　　3
　　　　　　　　　　　　　$\cancel{Z}$ 　　　　$\cancel{S}$
$Z = 2$ 　　　　　　　　 $\cancel{X}$ 　　　　$\cancel{X}$

$$S_2 \longrightarrow Z_3$$

$$Z_2 \longrightarrow S_1$$

$$V_{2P} \longrightarrow S_1$$

$$V_{2M} \longrightarrow Z_3$$

Given the amount of information in the diagram, some students ask if it would be wise to make four templates based on the position of S, V, and Z (when V is sold to the private collector, S must be from the first period and Z can be from the second or third period; when V is sold to the museum, Z must be from the third period and S can be from the first or second period). Although at first glance this may seem like a powerful strategy, it only places S, V, and Z in four arrangements, and none of those arrangements definitively place Q, R, or T. Hence, the templates provide little additional insight into the placement of the variables, and it is better to attack the game with a straightforward setup.

Question #13: Global, List. The correct answer choice is (B)

As usual, use the rules to attack a List question. The best order to apply the rules is to apply the third rule, then the first rule, and finally the second rule.

Note that the physical formatting of this question is a good example of how Law Services can make things harder for test takers by neglecting to present the information clearly. If this question was formatted so the paintings in each answer choice were indented to the same point to the right of the private collector and museum, it would be much easier to compare the order of the paintings. Instead, test takers are forced to waste valuable time examining which paintings are from which period.

Answer choice (A): This answer choice violates the second rule because Q is from an earlier period than T. Therefore this answer is incorrect.

Answer choice (B): This is the correct answer choice.

Answer choice (C): This answer is incorrect because it violates the first rule by selling S to the museum.

Answer choice (D): V must always be from the artist's second period, but in this answer V is from the artist's third period. Thus, this answer choice is incorrect.

Answer choice (E): According to the first rule S is from an earlier period than Z. Thus, this answer choice is incorrect because it places S and Z in the same period.

Question #14: Local, Could Be True. The correct answer choice is (B)

This is an unusually easy question. The first rule of the game establishes that Z must be purchased by the museum. Thus, any answer choice in this question featuring Z must be incorrect. Using that logic, we can eliminate answer choices (A), (D), and (E).

The question stem places S in the artist's second period, which, from our initial discussion of the rules, forces Z into the artist's third period. V, which must also be from the artist's second period, has to be purchased by the museum:

Private:	___	_S_	___
Museum:	___	_V_	_Z_
	1	2	3

At this point, we have established that V must be purchased by the museum, and consequently answer choice (C) can be eliminated.

Answer choice (B): This is the correct answer choice.

Question #15: Global, List. The correct answer choice is (D)

Through the Not Laws we have established that neither V nor Z can be paintings from the artist's first period that are sold to the private collector. Consequently, most students correctly surmise that the remaining four paintings could be the first period paintings sold to the private collector. However, let's systematically prove that assertion.

First, any answer choice containing V or Z can be eliminated. This process removes answer choice (E) from consideration. Second, from question #13, we know that S can be a first period painting sold to the private collector, and since answer choice (A) does not contain S, we can eliminate (A). Third, using the base diagram created in question #14, we can deduce that any of Q, R, and T can be a first period painting sold to the private collector, and thus the correct answer choice must contain those paintings as well.

Answer choice (D): This is the correct answer choice. The deduction above eliminates every answer choice except answer choice (D).

Question #16: Local, Could Be True. The correct answer choice is (B)

From question #14, we know the following diagram is produced when S is from the artist's second period:

```
Private:    _____        S        _____

Museum:     _____        V          Z
              1          2          3
```

The wording of the question stem also provides a clue into the placement of Q: by referencing the period "immediately preceding Q's period," it is clear that Q will not be first in this scenario (there is no period that precedes the first period). Consequently, because the second period is already occupied, Q must be from the third period in this question, and since the museum's third period painting is already occupied by Z, Q must be the third period painting of the private collector (and R and T rotate in the first period):

```
Private:     R/T         S          Q

Museum:      T/R         V          Z
              1          2          3
```

Answer choices (A), (C), and (E): None of these answer choices contain a painting that can be from a period immediately preceding Q's period. Thus, each of these answer choices is incorrect.

Answer choice (B): This is the correct answer choice. From the diagram, we can determine that S can be the painting from the same buyer in the period immediately preceding Q.

Answer choice (D): Although V can be a painting from the period immediately preceding Q's period, V is sold to a different buyer than Q, and thus this answer choice is incorrect.

Question #17: Local, Must Be True. The correct answer choice is (B)

The conditions in the question stem establish a horizontal ZT block:

Z T

Because we have already established that Z can only be sold to the museum as either the second or third period piece, the block *must* be placed so that Z is from the second period and T is from the third period:

Private: _____   _____   _____

Museum: _____   Z   T
               1   2   3

At this point, we can apply the first rule and third rules, which serve to establish that S is from the first period and that V is sold to the private collector:

Private: S   V   _____

Museum: _____   Z   T
               1   2   3

The only remaining variables yet to be placed are Q and R. From the second rule we know that $T \geq Q$, and thus Q must be from the third period (otherwise it would violate the second rule). Consequently, Q must be sold to the private collector, and R, the random, occupies the museum's first period:

Private: S   V   Q

Museum: R   Z   T
               1   2   3

Using this analysis, the problem is easy.

Answer choices (A), (C), (D), and (E): Each of these answer choices cannot occur, and therefore each is incorrect.

Answer choice (B): This is the correct answer choice.

This game was widely considered the most difficult of the June 2004 exam. After three linear-based games, the test makers saved a partially defined Grouping game for last, but test takers do get a break because this game has only five questions.

At first, this game appears to be a straight defined Grouping game: six lunch trucks serve three office buildings. However, the game scenario does not specify that each truck serves only one building, and in fact the second rule explicitly indicates that a truck can serve more than one building (by itself, this fact opens up the game to many more possible solutions). If each lunch truck served only one building, the game would be considerably easier because the assignment of a truck to a building would eliminate that truck from further consideration. Thus, one reason test takers felt this game was more difficult was because there is much more to consider within the setup of this game compared to the prior three games (there are also twice as many rules in this game as in any of the other games on this test).

The first decision in this game is what variable set to choose as the base. Either the lunch trucks or the buildings could serve as the base, but we will use the buildings since there are fewer buildings and each of the rules references the trucks going to the buildings. There is also an intuitive element here as it is easier to see the trucks going to the buildings; if the buildings were assigned to the trucks it would be counter to how things work in the real world (trucks move, buildings don't).

With that in mind, we can create the following basic representation of the variable sets:

F H I P S T [6]

$$\underline{} \qquad \underline{} \qquad \underline{}$$
$$\quad X \qquad\qquad Y \qquad\qquad Z$$

Now, let's examine each rule.

Rule #1. The first rule establishes that Y is served by exactly three lunch trucks, two of which are F and H:

$$\begin{array}{ccc} & 3 & \\ & \overline{} & \\ & H & \\ & \overline{F} & \\ \underline{} & \underline{Y} & \underline{} \\ X & Y & Z \end{array}$$

Rule #2. This rule indicates that F serves two buildings, one of which is Y, and the other is X or Z:

$$\begin{array}{ccc} & 3 & \\ & \overline{} & \\ & H & \\ \overline{F/} & \overline{F} & \overline{/F} \\ X & Y & Z \end{array}$$

Rule #3. Like the first two rules, this rule addresses a numerical relationship within the game. Given the open-ended nature of the truck assignments in the game scenario, you *must* look for rules that establish exact numbers, and, hopefully, a complete Numerical Distribution of trucks to buildings. More on this point later.

According to this rule, I must serve more buildings than S:

$$\#I > \#S$$

So, at this point, I must serve either two or three buildings, and S must serve either one or two buildings (note that it *is* possible for I and S to serve the same building). This rule is worth tracking since other rules can (and will) impact these possibilities.

Rule #4. This rule, which states that T does not serve Y, can be added as a Not Law to our setup:

3

F/	H	/F
	F	
X	Y	Z
	T̶	

Rule #5. This is a powerful rule, and one whose implications can be easily overlooked. First, the diagram for this rule is as follows:

$$\boxed{\frac{F}{P}}\!\!\!\diagup$$

If F and P do not serve the same building, the obvious deduction is that P does not serve building Y. However, we already know from the second rule that F serves exactly two buildings. Since P cannot serve those two buildings and there are only three buildings, we can infer that P can serve only one building and that it must be the building *not* served by F. Thus, for example, if F is assigned to building X, then P would have to be assigned to building Z. There are several variations on this rule, but the gist in each case is the same: when one of F or P is assigned to building X, the other is assigned to building Z, when one of F or P is assigned to building Z, the other is assigned to building X. We can represent this with a dual F/P option on buildings X and Z:

3

F/P	H	P/F
	F	
X	Y	Z
	T̶	
	P̶	

Thus, numerically we have now established that P can serve only one building, and from the second rule we know that F serves exactly two buildings.

With this rule we have also eliminated several lunch trucks from serving building Y. With two trucks assigned to Y (trucks F and H), and two trucks eliminated from serving Y (trucks T and P), only two trucks remain to fill the third space at Y: truck I or S. This can also be diagrammed with a dual-option:

$$3$$

F/P	I/S	P/F
	H	
	F	
X	Y	Z

~~T~~
~~P~~

Rule #6. This rule can be diagrammed as:

$$I \longleftrightarrow S$$
$$2$$

The first part of this rule indicates that T serves two buildings. Since from rule #4 we know that T cannot serve building Y, we can infer that T serves buildings X and Z. The second part of this rule indicates that T and I serve two of the same buildings, and this means that I must also serve buildings X and Z. I could also serve building Y, but does not have to. With the information above, the diagram is:

$$3$$

F/P	I/S	P/F
I	H	I
T	F	T
X	Y	Z

~~T~~
~~P~~

Note that I can still serve the remaining building, building Y. This rule only specifies that T serves two buildings also served by I; I could serve all three buildings without violating this rule (or any other).

The setup above is the final setup for the game, but given all of the numerical rules in this game, you must examine the numerical possibilities for each variable before proceeding to the questions (remember, always examine rules about numbers!). Let's examine the options for each lunch truck:

F: As specified in the second rule, F serves exactly two buildings, one of which is Y.

H: H is somewhat of a wild card in this game. H must serve at least building Y, but there is no other rule limiting how many buildings H must serve. Consequently, H could serve one, two, or three buildings.

I: I must serve at least two buildings (X and Z), and possibly all three buildings.

P: Because of the interaction of the second and fifth rules, P can only serve one building (X or Z).

S: From the third rule we know that S is limited to serving either one or two buildings, but which buildings those are is undetermined.

T: From the third and sixth rules we know that T serves exactly two buildings, and those buildings are X and Z.

This distribution is critical, and having command of the numerical possibilities will allow you to easily solve several of the questions.

Reviewing the game, there are three elements of uncertainty that must be tracked throughout the questions:

1. The F/P dual-option.
2. How many buildings H serves.
3. The relationship between I and S.

Question #18: Global, List. The correct answer choice is (D)

This is one of the easiest LSAT games questions ever (proving that even if you miss the setup completely, you can still answer some questions correctly in a game just by applying the rules). From the first rule we know that F must serve building Y. Since answer choices (A), (B), and (E) fail to include Y, they are incorrect. From the second rule we know that F must serve exactly two buildings. Since answer choice (C) contains three buildings, it is incorrect.

Answer choice (D): This is the correct answer choice.

Question #19: Global, Must Be True. The correct answer choice is (C)

This question asks you to identify two trucks that must serve the same building (although they could serve other buildings as well). There are several pairs that should immediately jump to mind—including F and H, and I and T—but none of the obvious pairs is listed as a possible answer. Consequently, you should consider each answer choice on its own merits.

Answer choice (A): Although H and P could serve the same building, they do not *have* to serve the same building. For example, H could serve just building Y, and P could serve just building Z. Thus, this answer choice is incorrect.

Answer choice (B): Although T must serve both buildings X and Z, it is possible that H serves only building Y. Thus, H and T do not have to serve the same building and this answer choice is incorrect.

Answer choice (C): This is the correct answer choice. I must serve both buildings X and Z. From our discussion of the F/P dual-option, we know that P must serve either building X or Z, and thus there must be one building that both I and P serve together.

Answer choice (D): This answer choice is incorrect because it is possible for I to serve just buildings X and Z, and for S to serve just building Y. Thus, I and S do not have to serve the same building.

Answer choice (E): Although T must serve both buildings X and Z, it is possible that S serves only building Y. Thus, S and T do not have to serve the same building and this answer choice is incorrect.

Question #20: Local, Must Be True. The correct answer choice is (E)

The condition in the question stem affects the Numerical Distribution discussed in the setup analysis. From the discussion of the distribution we know that I serves either two or three buildings. If, as stipulated in this question, I is to serve fewer office buildings than H, then I cannot serve all three office buildings and we can deduce that I serves exactly two office buildings. This also allows us to deduce that H must serve all three buildings. In addition, from the third rule, we know that I serves more office buildings than S, so S must serve exactly one building.

With the above numerical information, we know that I serves only buildings X and Z, and that therefore S must serve building Y:

3

F/P		P/F
H	S	H
I	H	I
T	F	T
X	Y	Z

From this diagram it is apparent that I and T serve exactly the same buildings, and therefore answer choice (E) is correct.

Answer choice (A): Because F always serves two buildings and H serves three buildings in this question, this answer choice cannot be correct.

Answer choice (B): In this question S serves only one building but F always serves two buildings. Thus, this answer choice is incorrect.

Answer choice (C): Because P always serves one buildings and I serves two buildings in this question, this answer choice cannot be correct.

Answer choice (D): From the third rule we know that I always serves more buildings than S, so the two trucks could never serve exactly the same buildings, and this answer choice must be wrong.

Answer choice (E): This is the correct answer choice.

Question #21: Global, List. The correct answer choice is (A)

This question also trades on the Numerical Distribution established by the rules, so let's take a moment to revisit that Numerical Distribution:

F: F serves exactly two buildings.
H: H could serve one, two, or three buildings.
I: I must serve at least two buildings, and possibly all three buildings.
P: P can only serve one building.
S: S is limited to serving either one or two buildings.
T: T serves exactly two buildings.

The distribution proves that only H and I can serve all three buildings, and thus answer choice (A) is correct.

Answer choice (A): This is the correct answer choice.

Answer choice (B): Because S can serve only one or two buildings, this answer choice is incorrect.

Answer choice (C): Because T serves exactly two buildings, this answer choice is incorrect.

Answer choice (D): Because P serves exactly one building, this answer choice is incorrect.

Answer choice (E): Because P serves exactly one building, and S can serve only one or two buildings, this answer choice is incorrect.

Question #22: Global, Cannot Be True. The correct answer choice is (C)

Again, we can use the distribution to quickly and easily destroy this question.

As we have previously established, lunch truck P can serve only one building. Hence, P could never serve both buildings X and Z, and therefore (C) is the correct answer choice.

Answer choice (A): Because H could serve all three buildings, H could serve both X and Z. Therefore, this answer choice could be true and it is incorrect.

Answer choice (B): As established in the setup of this game, I serves both X and Z. Therefore, this answer choice must be true and it is incorrect.

Answer choice (C): This is the correct answer choice.

Answer choice (D): If I served all three buildings, then S could serve buildings X and Z. Hence, this answer choice could be true and it is incorrect.

Answer choice (E): As established in the setup of this game, T serves both X and Z. Therefore, this answer choice must be true and it is incorrect.

Chapter Four: The October 2004 LSAT

This chapter contains the complete text of the October 2004 LSAT, including an answer key and scoring scale. For the closest possible re-creation of the conditions of the LSAT, take this exam as a timed exercise. The exam will take just less than three hours, and there is an answer sheet included so that you can record your answers. Per Law Services protocol, here are the directions for taking the test under timed conditions:

> Section 1 = allow yourself exactly 35 minutes
> Section 2 = allow yourself exactly 35 minutes
> Section 3 = allow yourself exactly 35 minutes
> Section 4 = allow yourself exactly 35 minutes
>
> Writing Sample = allow yourself exactly 30 minutes (Writing Samples prior to June 2005 were 30 minutes instead of 35 minutes)

The rules for the test are as follows:

> During the test you are allowed to work only on the section being timed. You cannot go back or forward to work on any other section of the test.
>
> Do not take a break between any of the sections (on the actual LSAT, an unscored experimental section will be included, and a 10-15 minute break will be given after section 3; because this test has no experimental section, you should not take a break between any of the sections).
>
> You may not use any scratch paper while working on the test; only the test pages themselves are available for your use.

After completing the test, refer to the answer key and the "Computing Your Score" section at the end of the test to find your LSAT score.

Your answer sheet is on the next page, and complete explanations are in the following chapter.

SECTION I
Time-35 minutes
27 Questions

Directions: Each passage in this section is followed by a group of questions to be answered on the basis of what is stated or implied in the passage. For some of the questions, more than one of the choices could conceivably answer the question. However, you are to choose the best answer; that is, the response that most accurately and completely answers the question, and blacken the corresponding space on your answer sheet.

The Canadian Auto Workers' (CAW) Legal Services Plan, designed to give active and retired autoworkers and their families access to totally prepaid or partially reimbursed legal services, has
(5) been in operation since late 1985. Plan members have the option of using either the plan's staff lawyers, whose services are fully covered by the cost of membership in the plan, or an outside lawyer. Outside lawyers, in turn, can either sign up with the plan as a
(10) "cooperating lawyer" and accept the CAW's fee schedule as payment in full, or they can charge a higher fee and collect the balance from the client. Autoworkers appear to have embraced the notion of prepaid legal services: 45 percent of eligible union
(15) members were enrolled in the plan by 1988. Moreover, the idea of prepaid legal services has been spreading in Canada. A department store is even offering a plan to holders of its credit card.
        While many plan members seem to be happy to
(20) get reduced-cost legal help, many lawyers are concerned about the plan's effect on their profession, especially its impact on prices for legal services. Some point out that even though most lawyers have not joined the plan as cooperating lawyers, legal fees
(25) in the cities in which the CAW plan operates have been depressed, in some cases to an unprofitable level. The directors of the plan, however, claim that both clients and lawyers benefit from their arrangement. For while the clients get ready access to
(30) reduced-price services, lawyers get professional contact with people who would not otherwise be using legal services, which helps generate even more business for their firms. Experience shows, the directors say, that if people are referred to a firm and
(35) receive excellent service, the firm will get three to four other referrals who are not plan subscribers and who would therefore pay the firm's standard rate.
        But it is unlikely that increased use of such plans will result in long-term client satisfaction or in a
(40) substantial increase in profits for law firms. Since lawyers with established reputations and client bases can benefit little, if at all, from participation, the plans function largely as marketing devices for lawyers who have yet to establish themselves. While
(45) many of these lawyers are no doubt very able and conscientious, they will tend to have less expertise and to provide less satisfaction to clients. At the same time, the downward pressure on fees will mean that the full-fee referrals that proponents say will come
(50) through plan participation may not make up for a

firm's investment in providing services at low plan rates. And since lowered fees provide little incentive for lawyers to devote more than minimal effort to cases, a "volume discount" approach toward the
(55) practice of law will mean less time devoted to complex cases and a general lowering of quality for clients.

1. Which one of the following most accurately expresses the main point of the passage?

(A) In the short term, prepaid legal plans such as the CAW Legal Services Plan appear to be beneficial to both lawyers and clients, but in the long run lawyers will profit at the expense of clients.

(B) The CAW Legal Services Plan and other similar plans represent a controversial, but probably effective, way of bringing down the cost of legal services to clients and increasing lawyers' clientele.

(C) The use of prepaid legal plans such as that of the CAW should be rejected in favor of a more equitable means of making legal services more generally affordable.

(D) In spite of widespread consumer support for legal plans such as that offered by the CAW, lawyers generally criticize such plans, mainly because of their potential financial impact on the legal profession.

(E) Although they have so far attracted many subscribers, it is doubtful whether the CAW Legal Services Plan and other similar prepaid plans will benefit lawyers and clients in the long run.

2. The primary purpose of the passage is to

(A) compare and contrast legal plans with the traditional way of paying for legal services
(B) explain the growing popularity of legal plans
(C) trace the effect of legal plans on prices of legal services
(D) caution that increased use of legal plans is potentially harmful to the legal profession and to clients
(E) advocate reforms to legal plans as presently constituted

GO ON TO THE NEXT PAGE.

3. Which one of the following does the author predict will be a consequence of increased use of legal plans?

(A) results that are largely at odds with those predicted by lawyers who criticize the plans

(B) a lowering of the rates such plans charge their members

(C) forced participation of lawyers who can benefit little from association with the plans

(D) an eventual increase in profits for lawyers from client usage of the plans

(E) a reduction in the time lawyers devote to complex cases

4. Which one of the following sequences most accurately and completely corresponds to the presentation of the material in the passage?

(A) a description of a recently implemented set of procedures and policies; a summary of the results of that implementation; a proposal of refinements in those policies and procedures

(B) an evaluation of a recent phenomenon; a comparison of that phenomenon with related past phenomena; an expression of the author's approval of that phenomenon

(C) a presentation of a proposal; a discussion of the prospects for implementing that proposal; a recommendation by the author that the proposal be rejected

(D) a description of an innovation; a report of reasoning against and reasoning favoring that innovation; argumentation by the author concerning that innovation

(E) an explanation of a recent occurrence; an evaluation of the practical value of that occurrence; a presentation of further data regarding that occurrence

5. The passage most strongly suggests that, according to proponents of prepaid legal plans, cooperating lawyers benefit from taking clients at lower fees in which one of the following ways?

(A) Lawyers can expect to gain expertise in a wide variety of legal services by availing themselves of the access to diverse clientele that plan participation affords.

(B) Experienced cooperating lawyers are likely to enjoy the higher profits of long-term, complex cases, for which new lawyers are not suited.

(C) Lower rates of profit will be offset by a higher volume of clients and new business through word-of-mouth recommendations.

(D) Lower fees tend to attract clients away from established, nonparticipating law firms.

(E) With all legal fees moving downward to match the plans' schedules, the profession will respond to market forces.

6. According to the passage, which one of the following is true of CAW Legal Services Plan members?

(A) They can enjoy benefits beyond the use of the services of the plan's staff lawyers.

(B) So far, they generally believe the quality of services they receive from the plan's staff lawyers is as high as that provided by other lawyers.

(C) Most of them consult lawyers only for relatively simple and routine matters.

(D) They must pay a fee above the cost of membership for the services of an outside lawyer.

(E) They do not include only active and retired autoworkers and their families.

7. Which one of the following most accurately represents the primary function of the author's mention of marketing devices (line 43)?

(A) It points to an aspect of legal plans that the author believes will be detrimental to the quality of legal services.

(B) It is identified by the author as one of the primary ways in which plan administrators believe themselves to be contributing materially to the legal profession in return for lawyers' participation.

(C) It identifies what the author considers to be one of the few unequivocal benefits that legal plans can provide.

(D) It is reported as part of several arguments that the author attributes to established lawyers who oppose plan participation.

(E) It describes one of the chief burdens of lawyers who have yet to establish themselves and offers an explanation of their advocacy of legal plans.

GO ON TO THE NEXT PAGE.

In the field of historiography—the writing of history based on a critical examination of authentic primary information sources—one area that has recently attracted attention focuses on the responses (5) of explorers and settlers to new landscapes in order to provide insights into the transformations the landscape itself has undergone as a result of settlement. In this endeavor historiographers examining the history of the Pacific Coast of the (10) United States have traditionally depended on the records left by European American explorers of the nineteenth century who, as commissioned agents of the U.S. government, were instructed to report thoroughly their findings in writing.

(15) But in furthering this investigation some historiographers have recently recognized the need to expand their definition of what a source is. They maintain that the sources traditionally accepted as documenting the history of the Pacific Coast have too (20) often omitted the response of Asian settlers to this territory. In pan this is due to the dearth of written records left by Asian settlers; in contrast to the commissioned agents, most of the people who first came to western North America from Asia during this (25) same period did not focus on developing a self-conscious written record of their involvement with the landscape. But because a full study of a culture's historical relationship to its land cannot confine itself to a narrow record of experience, these (30) historiographers have begun to recognize the value of other kinds of evidence, such as the actions of Asian settlers.

As a case in point, the role of Chinese settlers in expanding agriculture throughout the Pacific Coast (35) territory is integral to the history of the region. Without access to the better Sand, Chinese settlers looked for agricultural potential in this generally arid region where other settlers did not. For example, where settlers of European descent looked at willows (40) and saw only useless, untillable swamp, Chinese settlers saw fresh water, fertile soil, and the potential for bringing water to more arid areas via irrigation. Where other settlers who looked at certain weeds, such as wild mustard, generally saw a nuisance, (45) Chinese settlers saw abundant raw material for valuable spices from a plant naturally suited to the local soil and climate.

Given their role in the labor force shaping this territory in the nineteenth century, the Chinese settlers (50) offered more than just a new view of the land. Their vision was reinforced by specialized skills involving swamp reclamation and irrigation systems, which helped lay the foundation for the now well-known and prosperous agribusiness of the region. That (55) 80 percent of the area's cropland is now irrigated and that the region is currently the top producer of many specialty crops cannot be fully understood by historiographers without attention to the input of Chinese settlers as reconstructed from their interactions with that landscape.

8. Which one of the following most accurately states the main point of the passage?

(A) The history of settlement along the Pacific Coast of the U.S., as understood by most historiographers, is confirmed by evidence reconstructed from the actions of Asian settlers.
(B) Asian settlers on the Pacific Coast of the U.S. left a record of their experiences that traditional historiographers believed to be irrelevant.
(C) To understand Asian settlers' impact on the history of the Pacific Coast of the U.S., historiographers have had to recognize the value of nontraditional kinds of historiographic evidence.
(D) Spurred by new findings regarding Asian settlement on the Pacific Coast of the U.S. historiographers have begun to debate the methodological foundations of historiography.
(E) By examining only written information, historiography as it is traditionally practiced has produced inaccurate historical accounts.

9. Which one of the following most accurately describes the author's primary purpose in discussing Chinese settlers in the third paragraph?

(A) to suggest that Chinese settlers followed typical settlement patterns in this region during the nineteenth century
(B) to argue that little written evidence of Chinese settlers' practices survives
(C) to provide examples illustrating the unique view Asian settlers had of the land
(D) to demonstrate that the history of settlement in the region has become a point of contention among historiographers
(E) to claim that the historical record provided by the actions of Asian settlers is inconsistent with history as derived from traditional sources

10. The passage states that the primary traditional historiographic sources of information about the history of the Pacific Coast of the U.S. have which one of the following characteristics?

(A) They were written both before and after Asian settlers arrived in the area.
(B) They include accounts by Native Americans in the area.
(C) They are primarily concerned with potential agricultural uses of the land.
(D) They focus primarily on the presence of water sources in the region.
(E) They are accounts left by European American explorers.

GO ON TO THE NEXT PAGE.

11. The author would most likely disagree with which one of the following statements?

   (A)   Examining the actions not only of Asian settlers but of other cultural groups of the Pacific Coast of the U.S. is necessary to a full understanding of the impact of settlement on the landscape there.

   (B)   The significance of certain actions to the writing of history may be recognized by one group of historiographers but not another.

   (C)   Recognizing the actions of Asian settlers adds to but does not complete the writing of the history of the Pacific Coast of the U.S.

   (D)   By recognizing as evidence the actions of people, historiographers expand the definition of what a source is.

   (E)   The expanded definition of a source will probably not be relevant to studies of regions that have no significant immigration of non-Europeans.

12. According to the passage, each of the following was an aspect of Chinese settlers' initial interactions with the landscape of the Pacific Coast of the U.S. EXCEPT:

   (A)   new ideas for utilizing local plants
   (B)   a new view of the land
   (C)   specialized agricultural skills
   (D)   knowledge of agribusiness practices
   (E)   knowledge of irrigation systems

13. Which one of the following can most reasonably be inferred from the passage?

   (A)   Most Chinese settlers came to the Pacific Coast of the U.S. because the climate was similar to that with which they were familiar.

   (B)   Chinese agricultural methods in the nineteenth century included knowledge of swamp reclamation.

   (C)   Settlers of European descent used wild mustard seed as a spice.

   (D)   Because of the abundance of written sources available, it is not worthwhile to examine the actions of European settlers.

   (E)   What written records were left by Asian settlers were neglected and consequently lost to scholarly research.

14. Which one of the following, if true, would most help to strengthen the author's main claim in the last sentence of the passage?

   (A)   Market research of agribusinesses owned by descendants of Chinese settlers shows that the market for the region's specialty crops has grown substantially faster than the market for any other crops in the last decade.

   (B)   Nineteenth-century surveying records indicate that the lands now cultivated by specialty crop businesses owned by descendants of Chinese settlers were formerly swamp lands.

   (C)   Research by university agricultural science departments proves that the formerly arid lands now cultivated by large agribusinesses contain extremely fertile soil when they are sufficiently irrigated.

   (D)   A technological history tracing the development of irrigation systems in the region reveals that their efficiency has increased steadily since the nineteenth century.

   (E)   Weather records compiled over the previous century demonstrate that the weather patterns in the region are well-suited to growing certain specialty crops as long as they are irrigated.

GO ON TO THE NEXT PAGE.

The survival of nerve cells, as well as their performance of some specialized functions, is regulated by chemicals known as neurotrophic factors, which are produced in the bodies of animals,
(5) including humans. Rita Levi-Montalcini's discovery in the 1950s of the first of these agents, a hormonelike substance now known as NGF, was a crucial development in the history of biochemistry, which led to Levi-Montalcini sharing the Nobel Prize
(10) for medicine in 1986.

In the mid-1940s, Levi-Montalcini had begun by hypothesizing that many of the immature nerve cells produced in the development of an organism are normally programmed to die. In order to confirm this
(15) theory, she conducted research that in 1949 found that, when embryos are in the process of forming their nervous systems, they produce many more nerve cells than are finally required, the number that survives eventually adjusting itself to the volume of
(20) tissue to be supplied with nerves. A further phase of the experimentation, which led to Levi-Montalcini's identification of the substance that controls this process, began with her observation that the development of nerves in chick embryos could be
(25) stimulated by implanting a certain variety of mouse tumor in the embryos. She theorized that a chemical produced by the tumors was responsible for the observed nerve growth. To investigate this hypothesis, she used the then new technique of tissue culture, by
(30) which specific types of body cells can be made to grow outside the organism from which they are derived. Within twenty-four hours, her tissue cultures of chick embryo extracts developed dense halos of nerve tissue near the places in the culture where she
(35) had added the mouse tumor. Further research identified a specific substance contributed by the mouse tumors that was responsible for the effects Levi-Montalcini had observed: a protein that she named "nerve growth factor" (NGF).
(40) NGF was the first of many cell-growth factors to be found in the bodies of animals. Through Levi-Montalcini's work and other subsequent research, it has been determined that this substance is present in many tissues and biological fluids, and that it is
(45) especially concentrated in some organs. In developing organisms, nerve cells apparently receive this growth factor locally from the cells of muscles or other organs to which they will form connections for transmission of nerve impulses, and sometimes from
(50) supporting cells intermingled with the nerve tissue. NGF seems to play two roles, serving initially to direct the developing nerve processes toward the correct, specific "target" cells with which they must connect, and later being necessary for the continued
(55) survival of those nerve cells. During some periods of their development, the types of nerve cells that are affected by NGF—primarily cells outside the brain and spinal cord—die if the factor is not present or if they encounter anti-NGF antibodies.

15. Which one of the following most accurately expresses the main point of the passage?

(A) Levi-Montalcini's discovery of neurotrophic factors as a result of research carried out in the 1940s was a major contribution to our understanding of the role of naturally occurring chemicals, especially NGF, in the development of chick embryos.

(B) Levi-Montalcini's discovery of NGF, a neurotrophic factor that stimulates the development of some types of nerve tissue and whose presence or absence in surrounding cells helps determine whether particular nerve cells will survive, was a pivotal development in biochemistry.

(C) NGF, which is necessary for the survival and proper functioning of nerve cells, was discovered by Levi-Montalcini in a series of experiments using the technique of tissue culture, which she devised in the 1940s.

(D) Partly as a result of Levi-Montalcini's research, it has been found that NGF and other neurotrophic factors are produced only by tissues to which nerves are already connected and that the presence of these factors is necessary for the health and proper functioning of nervous systems.

(E) NGF, a chemical that was discovered by Levi-Montalcini, directs the growth of nerve cells toward the cells with which they must connect and ensures the survival of those nerve cells throughout the life of the organism except when the organism produces anti-NGF antibodies.

16. Based on the passage, the author would be most likely to believe that Levi-Montalcini's discovery of NGF is noteworthy primarily because it

(A) paved the way for more specific knowledge of the processes governing the development of the nervous system

(B) demonstrated that a then new laboratory technique could yield important and unanticipated experimental results

(C) confirmed the hypothesis that many of a developing organism's immature nerve cells are normally programmed to die

(D) indicated that this substance stimulates observable biochemical reactions in the tissues of different species

(E) identified a specific substance, produced by mouse tumors, that can be used to stimulate nerve cell growth

17. The primary function of the third paragraph of the passage in relation to the second paragraph is to

(A) indicate that conclusions referred to in the second paragraph, though essentially correct, require further verification

(B) indicate that conclusions referred to in the second paragraph have been undermined by subsequently obtained evidence

(C) indicate ways in which conclusions referred to in the second paragraph have been further corroborated and refined

(D) describe subsequent discoveries of substances analogous to the substance discussed in the second paragraph

(E) indicate that experimental procedures discussed in the second paragraph have been supplanted by more precise techniques described in the third paragraph

18. Information in the passage most strongly supports which one of the following?

(A) Nerve cells in excess of those that are needed by the organism in which they develop eventually produce anti-NGF antibodies to suppress the effects of NGF.

(B) Nerve cells that grow in the absence of NGF are less numerous than, but qualitatively identical to, those that grow in the presence of NGF.

(C) Few of the nerve cells that connect with target cells toward which NGF directs them are needed by the organism in which they develop.

(D) Some of the nerve cells that grow in the presence of NGF are eventually converted to other types of living tissue by neurotrophic factors.

(E) Some of the nerve cells that grow in an embryo do not connect with any particular target cells.

19. The passage describes a specific experiment that tested which one of the following hypotheses?

(A) A certain kind of mouse tumor produces a chemical that stimulates the growth of nerve cells.

(B) Developing embryos initially grow many more nerve cells than they will eventually require.

(C) In addition to NGF, there are several other important neurotrophic factors regulating cell survival and function.

(D) Certain organs contain NGF in concentrations much higher than in the surrounding tissue.

(E) Certain nerve cells are supplied with NGF by the muscle cells to which they are connected.

20. Which one of the following is most strongly supported by the information in the passage?

(A) Some of the effects that the author describes as occurring in Levi-Montalcini's culture of chick embryo extract were due to neurotrophic factors other than NGF.

(B) Although NGF was the first neurotrophic factor to be identified, some other such factors are now more thoroughly understood.

(C) In her research in the 1940s and 1950s, Levi-Montalcini identified other neurotrophic factors in addition to NGF.

(D) Some neurotrophic factors other than NGF perform functions that are not specifically identified in the passage.

(E) The effects of NGF that Levi-Montalcini noted in her chick embryo experiment are also caused by other neurotrophic factors not discussed in the passage.

GO ON TO THE NEXT PAGE.

The proponents of the Modern Movement in architecture considered that, compared with the historical styles that it replaced, Modernist architecture more accurately reflected the functional
(5) spirit of twentieth-century technology and was better suited to the newest building methods. It is ironic, then, that the Movement fostered an ideology of design that proved to be at odds with the way buildings were really built.
(10) The tenacious adherence of Modernist architects and critics to this ideology was in part responsible for the Movement's decline. Originating in the 1920s as a marginal, almost bohemian art movement, the Modern Movement was never very popular with the public,
(15) but this very lack of popular support produced in Modernist architects a high-minded sense of mission—not content merely to interpret the needs of the client, these architects now sought to persuade, to educate, and, if necessary, to dictate. By 1945 the
(20) tenets of the Movement had come to dominate mainstream architecture, and by the early 1950s, to dominate architectural criticism—architects whose work seemed not to advance the evolution of the Modern Movement tended to be dismissed by
(25) proponents of Modernism. On the other hand, when architects were identified as innovators—as was the case with Otto Wagner, or the young Frank Lloyd Wright—attention was drawn to only those features of their work that were "Modern"; other aspects were
(30) conveniently ignored.
The decline of the Modern Movement later in the twentieth century occurred partly as a result of Modernist architects' ignorance of building methods, and partly because Modernist architects were
(35) reluctant to admit that their concerns were chiefly aesthetic. Moreover, the building industry was evolving in a direction Modernists had not anticipated: it was more specialized and the process of construction was much more fragmented than in
(40) the past. Up until the twentieth century, construction had been carried out by a relatively small number of tradespeople, but as the building industry evolved, buildings came to be built by many specialized subcontractors working independently. The architect's
(45) design not only had to accommodate a sequence of independent operations, but now had to reflect the allowable degree of inaccuracy of the different trades. However, one of the chief construction ideals of the Modern Movement was to "honestly" expose
(50) structural materials such as steel and concrete. To do this and still produce a visually acceptable interior called for an unrealistically high level of craftmanship. Exposure of a building's internal structural elements, if it could be achieved at all,
(55) could only be accomplished at considerable cost—

hence the well-founded reputation of Modern architecture as prohibitively expensive.
As Postmodern architects recognized, the need to expose structural elements imposed unnecessary
(60) limitations on building design. The unwillingness of architects of the Modern Movement to abandon their ideals contributed to the decline of interest in the Modern Movement.

21. Which one of the following most accurately summarizes the main idea of the passage?

   (A) The Modern Movement declined because its proponents were overly ideological and did not take into account the facts of building construction.
   (B) Rationality was the theoretical basis for the development of the Modern Movement in architecture.
   (C) Changes in architectural design introduced by the Modern Movement inspired the development of modern construction methods.
   (D) The theoretical bases of the Modern Movement in architecture originated in changes in building construction methods.
   (E) Proponents of the Modern Movement in architecture rejected earlier architectural styles because such styles were not functional.

22. Which one of the following is most similar to the relationship described in the passage between the new methods of the building industry and pre-twentieth-century construction?

   (A) Clothing produced on an assembly line is less precisely tailored than clothing produced by a single garment maker.
   (B) Handwoven fabric is more beautiful than fabric produced by machine.
   (C) Lenses ground on a machine are less useful than lenses ground by hand.
   (D) Form letters produced by a word processor elicit fewer responses than letters typed individually on a typewriter.
   (E) Furniture produced in a factory is less fashionable than handcrafted furniture.

23. With respect to the proponents of the Modern Movement, the author of the passage can best be described as

   (A) forbearing
   (B) defensive
   (C) unimpressed
   (D) exasperated
   (E) indifferent

GO ON TO THE NEXT PAGE.

24. It can be inferred that the author of the passage believes which one of the following about Modern Movement architects' ideal of exposing structural materials?

(A) The repudiation of the ideal by some of these architects undermined its validity.
(B) The ideal was rarely achieved because of its lack of popular appeal.
(C) The ideal was unrealistic because most builders were unwilling to attempt it.
(D) The ideal originated in the work of Otto Wagner and Frank Lloyd Wright.
(E) The ideal arose from aesthetic rather than practical concerns.

25. Which one of the following, in its context in the passage, most clearly reveals the attitude of the author toward the proponents of the Modern Movement?

(A) "functional spirit" (lines 4-5)
(B) "tended" (line 24)
(C) "innovators" (line 26)
(D) "conveniently" (line 30)
(E) "degree of inaccuracy" (line 47)

26. The author of the passage mentions Otto Wagner and the young Frank Lloyd Wright (lines 27-28) primarily as examples of

(A) innovative architects whose work was not immediately appreciated by the public
(B) architects whom proponents of the Modern Movement claimed represented the movement
(C) architects whose work helped to popularize the Modern Movement
(D) architects who generally attempted to interpret the needs of their clients, rather than dictating to them
(E) architects whose early work seemed to architects of the Modern Movement to be at odds with the principles of Modernism

27. The author of the passage is primarily concerned with

(A) analyzing the failure of a movement
(B) predicting the future course of a movement
(C) correcting a misunderstanding about a movement
(D) anticipating possible criticism of a movement
(E) contrasting incompatible viewpoints about a movement

S T O P

IF YOU FINISH BEFORE TIME IS CALLED, YOU MAY CHECK YOUR WORK ON THIS SECTION ONLY.
DO NOT WORK ON ANY OTHER SECTION IN THE TEST.

SECTION II
Time-35 minutes
25 Questions

Directions:　The questions in this section are based on the reasoning contained in brief statements or passages. For some questions, more than one of the choices could conceivably answer the question. However, you are to choose the best answer; that is, the response that most accurately and completely answers the question. You should not make assumptions that are by commonsense standards implausible, superfluous, or incompatible with the passage. After you have chosen the best answer, blacken the corresponding space on your answer sheet.

1.　The tidal range at a particular location is the difference in height between high tide and low tide. Tidal studies have shown that one of the greatest tidal ranges in the world is found in the Bay of Fundy and reaches more than seventeen meters. Since the only forces involved in inducing the tides are the sun's and moon's gravity, the magnitudes of tidal ranges also must be explained entirely by gravitational forces.

Which one of the following most accurately describes a flaw in the reasoning above?

(A)　It gives only one example of a tidal range.
(B)　It fails to consider that the size of a tidal range could be affected by the conditions in which gravitational forces act.
(C)　It does not consider the possibility that low tides are measured in a different way than are high tides.
(D)　It presumes, without providing warrant, that most activity within the world's oceans is a result of an interplay of gravitational forces.
(E)　It does not differentiate between the tidal effect of the sun and the tidal effect of the moon.

2.　Cardiologist:　Coronary bypass surgery is commonly performed on patients suffering from coronary artery disease when certain other therapies would be as effective. Besides being relatively inexpensive, these other therapies pose less risk to the patient since they are less intrusive. Bypass surgery is especially debatable for single-vessel disease.

The cardiologist's statements, if true, most strongly support which one of the following?

(A)　Bypass surgery is riskier than all alternative therapies.
(B)　Needless bypass surgery is more common today than previously.
(C)　Bypass surgery should be performed when more than one vessel is diseased.
(D)　Bypass surgery is an especially expensive therapy when used to treat single-vessel disease.
(E)　Sometimes there are equally effective alternatives to bypass surgery that involve less risk.

3.　In the past, combining children of different ages in one classroom was usually a failure; it resulted in confused younger children, who were given inadequate attention and instruction, and bored older ones, who had to sit through previously learned lessons. Recently, however, the practice has been revived with excellent results. Mixed-age classrooms today are stimulating to older children and enable younger children to learn much more efficiently than in standard classrooms.

Which one of the following, if true, most helps to resolve the apparent discrepancy in the passage?

(A)　On average, mixed-age classrooms today are somewhat larger in enrollment than were the ones of the past.
(B)　Mixed-age classrooms of the past were better equipped than are those of today.
(C)　Today's mixed-age classrooms, unlike those of the past, emphasize group projects that are engaging to students of different ages.
(D)　Today's mixed-age classrooms have students of a greater range of ages than did those of the past.
(E)　Few of the teachers who are reviving mixed-age classrooms today were students in mixed-age classrooms when they were young.

GO ON TO THE NEXT PAGE.

4. The top 50 centimeters of soil on Tiliga Island contain bones from the native birds eaten by the islanders since the first human immigration to the island 3,000 years ago. A comparison of this top layer with the underlying 150 centimeters of soil—accumulated over 80,000 years—reveals that before humans arrived on Tiliga, a much larger and more diverse population of birds lived there. Thus, the arrival of humans dramatically decreased the population and diversity of birds on Tiliga.

Which one of the following statements, if true, most seriously weakens the argument?

(A) The bird species known to have been eaten by the islanders had few natural predators on Tiliga.

(B) Many of the bird species that disappeared from Tiliga did not disappear from other, similar, uninhabited islands until much later.

(C) The arrival of a species of microbe, carried by some birds but deadly to many others, immediately preceded the first human immigration to Tiliga.

(D) Bones from bird species known to have been eaten by the islanders were found in the underlying 150 centimeters of soil.

(E) The birds that lived on Tiliga prior to the first human immigration generally did not fly well.

5. The corpus callosum—the thick band of nerve fibers connecting the brain's two hemispheres—of a musician is on average larger than that of a nonmusician. The differences in the size of corpora callosa are particularly striking when adult musicians who began training around the age of seven are compared to adult nonmusicians. Therefore, musical training, particularly when it begins at a young age, causes certain anatomic brain changes.

Which one of the following is an assumption on which the argument depends?

(A) The corpora callosa of musicians, before they started training, do not tend to be larger than those of nonmusicians of the same age.

(B) Musical training late in life does not cause anatomic changes to the brain.

(C) For any two musicians whose training began around the age of seven, their corpora callosa are approximately the same size.

(D) All musicians have larger corpora callosa than do any nonmusicians.

(E) Adult nonmusicians did not participate in activities when they were children that would have stimulated any growth of the corpus callosum.

6. Chai: The use of the word "tree" to denote both deciduous and coniferous plant forms, while acceptable as a lay term, is scientifically inadequate; it masks the fact that the two plant types have utterly different lineages.

Dodd: But the common name highlights the crucial fact that both are composed of the same material and have very similar structures; so it is acceptable as a scientific term.

The conversation provides the strongest grounds for holding that Chai and Dodd disagree over whether

(A) it is advisable to use ordinary terms as names for biological forms in scientific discourse

(B) using the same term for two biological forms with different lineages can be scientifically acceptable

(C) both deciduous and coniferous plant forms evolved from simpler biological forms

(D) it is important that the lay terms for plant forms reflect the current scientific theories about them

(E) biological forms with similar structures can have different lineages

7. Increases in the occurrence of hearing loss among teenagers are due in part to their listening to loud music through stereo headphones. So a group of concerned parents is recommending that headphone manufacturers include in their product lines stereo headphones that automatically turn off when a dangerous level of loudness is reached. It is clear that adoption of this recommendation would not significantly reduce the occurrence of hearing loss in teenagers, however, since almost all stereo headphones that teenagers use are bought by the teenagers themselves.

Which one of the following, if true, provides the most support for the argument?

(A) Loud music is most dangerous to hearing when it is played through stereo headphones.

(B) No other cause of hearing loss in teenagers is as damaging as their listening to loud music through stereo headphones.

(C) Parents of teenagers generally do not themselves listen to loud music through stereo headphones.

(D) Teenagers who now listen to music at dangerously loud levels choose to do so despite their awareness of the risks involved.

(E) A few headphone manufacturers already plan to market stereo headphones that automatically turn off when a dangerous level of loudness is reached.

GO ON TO THE NEXT PAGE.

8. Most plants have developed chemical defenses against parasites. The average plant contains about 40 natural pesticides-chemical compounds toxic to bacteria, fungi, and other parasites. Humans ingest these natural pesticides without harm every day. Therefore, the additional threat posed by synthetic pesticides sprayed on crop plants by humans is minimal.

Each of the following, if true, weakens the argument EXCEPT:

(A)   Humans have been consuming natural plant pesticides for millennia and have had time to adapt to them.
(B)   The concentrations of natural pesticides in plants are typically much lower than the concentrations of synthetic pesticides in sprayed crop plants.
(C)   Natural plant pesticides are typically less potent than synthetic pesticides, whose toxicity is highly concentrated.
(D)   Natural plant pesticides generally serve only as defenses against specific parasites, whereas synthetic pesticides are often harmful to a wide variety of organisms.
(E)   The synthetic pesticides sprayed on crop plants by humans usually have chemical structures similar to those of the natural pesticides produced by the plants.

9. In addition to the labor and materials used to make wine, the reputation of the vineyard where the grapes originate plays a role in determining the price of the finished wine. Therefore, an expensive wine is not always a good wine.

Which one of the following is an assumption on which the argument depends?

(A)   The price of a bottle of wine should be a reflection of the wine's quality.
(B)   Price is never an accurate indication of the quality of a bottle of wine.
(C)   The reputation of a vineyard does not always indicate the quality of its wines.
(D)   The reputation of a vineyard generally plays a greater role than the quality of its grapes in determining its wines' prices.
(E)   Wines produced by lesser-known vineyards generally are priced to reflect accurately the wines' quality.

10. Before their larvae hatch, each parental pair of *Nicrophorus* beetles buries the carcass of a small vertebrate nearby. For several days after the larvae hatch, both beetles feed their voracious larvae from the carcass, which is entirely consumed within a week. Since both parents help with feeding, larvae should benefit from both parents' presence; however, removing one parent before the hatching results in larvae that grow both larger and heavier than they otherwise would be.

Which one of the following, if true, best helps to explain why removing one parent resulted in larger, heavier larvae?

(A)   Two beetles can find and bury a larger carcass than can a single beetle.
(B)   Both parents use the carcass as their own food supply for as long as they stay with the larvae.
(C)   Beetle parents usually take turns feeding their larvae, so that there is always one provider available and one at rest.
(D)   After a week, the larvae are capable of finding other sources of food and feeding themselves.
(E)   Two parents can defend the carcass from attack by other insects better than a single parent can.

11. For many centuries it was believed that only classical Euclidean geometry could provide a correct way of mathematically representing the universe. Nevertheless, scientists have come to believe that a representation of the universe employing non-Euclidean geometry is much more useful in developing certain areas of scientific theory. In fact, such a representation underlies the cosmological theory that is now most widely accepted by scientists as accurate.

Which one of the following is most strongly supported by the statements above?

(A)   Scientists who use Euclidean geometry are likely to believe that progress in mathematical theory results in progress in natural science.
(B)   Scientists generally do not now believe that classical Euclidean geometry is uniquely capable of giving a correct mathematical representation of the universe.
(C)   Non-Euclidean geometry is a more complete way of representing the universe than is Euclidean geometry.
(D)   An accurate scientific theory cannot be developed without the discovery of a uniquely correct way of mathematically representing the universe.
(E)   The usefulness of a mathematical theory is now considered by scientists to be more important than its mathematical correctness.

GO ON TO THE NEXT PAGE.

12. Experts hired to testify in court need to know how to make convincing presentations. Such experts are evaluated by juries in terms of their ability to present the steps by which they arrived at their conclusions clearly and confidently. As a result, some less expert authorities who are skilled at producing convincing testimony are asked to testify rather than highly knowledgeable but less persuasive experts.

Which one of the following most closely conforms to the principle illustrated by the passage above?

(A) Successful politicians are not always the ones who best understand how to help their country. Some lack insight into important political issues but are highly skilled at conducting an election campaign.

(B) Trial lawyers often use the techniques employed by actors to influence the emotions of jurors. Many lawyers have studied drama expressly for the purpose of improving their courtroom skills.

(C) The opera singer with the best voice is the appropriate choice even for minor roles, despite the fact that an audience may be more affected by a singer with greater dramatic ability but a lesser voice.

(D) It is often best to try to train children with gentle reinforcement of desired behavior, rather than by simply telling them what to do and what not to do. This results in children who behave because they want to, not because they feel compelled.

(E) Job applicants are usually hired because their skills and training best meet a recognized set of qualifications. Only rarely is a prospective employer convinced to tailor a position to suit the skills of a particular applicant.

13. The solution to any environmental problem that is not the result of government mismanagement can only lie in major changes in consumer habits. But major changes in consumer habits will occur only if such changes are economically enticing. As a result, few serious ecological problems will be solved unless the solutions are made economically enticing.

The conclusion drawn in the argument above follows logically if which one of the following is assumed?

(A) Few serious ecological problems are the result of government mismanagement.

(B) No environmental problems that stem from government mismanagement have solutions that are economically feasible.

(C) Major changes in consumer habits can be made economically enticing.

(D) Most environmental problems that are not the result of government mismanagement are major ecological problems.

(E) Few serious ecological problems can be solved by major changes in consumer habits.

14. The economy is doing badly. First, the real estate slump has been with us for some time. Second, car sales are at their lowest in years. Of course, had either one or the other phenomenon failed to occur, this would be consistent with the economy as a whole being healthy. But, their occurrence together makes it quite probable that my conclusion is correct.

Which one of the following inferences is most strongly supported by the information above?

(A) If car sales are at their lowest in years, then it is likely that the economy is doing badly.

(B) If the economy is doing badly, then either the real estate market or the car sales market is not healthy.

(C) If the real estate market is healthy, then it is likely that the economy as a whole is healthy.

(D) If the economy is in a healthy state, then it is unlikely that the real estate and car sales markets are both in a slump.

(E) The bad condition of the economy implies that both the real estate and the car sales markets are doing badly.

GO ON TO THE NEXT PAGE.

15. According to current geological theory, the melting of ice at the end of the Ice Age significantly reduced the weight pressing on parts of the earth's crust. As a result, lasting cracks in the earth's crust appeared in some of those parts under the stress of pressure from below. At the end of the Ice Age Sweden was racked by severe earthquakes. Therefore, it is likely that the melting of the ice contributed to these earthquakes.

Which one of the following, if true, most strengthens the argument above?

(A) The earth's crust tends to crack whenever there is a sudden change in the pressures affecting it.

(B) There are various areas in Northern Europe that show cracks in the earth's crust.

(C) Evidence of severe earthquakes around the time of the end of the Ice Age can be found in parts of northern Canada.

(D) Severe earthquakes are generally caused by cracking of the earth's crust near the earthquake site.

(E) Asteroid impacts, which did occur at the end of the Ice Age, generally cause severe earthquakes.

16. Sociologist: Some economists hold that unregulated markets should accompany democratic sovereignty because they let people vote with their money. But this view ignores the crucial distinction between the private consumer and the public citizen. In the marketplace the question is, "What do I want?" At the voting booth the question is always, "What do we want?" Hence, supporters of political democracy can also support marketplace regulation.

Which one of the following most accurately expresses the conclusion drawn by the sociologist?

(A) Voters think of themselves as members of a community, rather than as isolated individuals.

(B) Unregulated markets are incompatible with democratic sovereignty.

(C) Where there is democratic sovereignty there should be unregulated markets.

(D) Private consumers are primarily concerned with their own self-interest.

(E) Opposition to unregulated markets is consistent with support for democracy.

17. The tiny hummingbird weighs little, but its egg is 15 percent of the adult hummingbird's weight. The volume and weight of an adult goose are much greater than those of a hummingbird, but a goose's egg is only about 4 percent of its own weight. An adult ostrich, much larger and heavier than a goose, lays an egg that is only 1.6 percent of its own weight.

Which one of the following propositions is best illustrated by the statements above?

(A) The eggs of different bird species vary widely in their ratio of volume to weight.

(B) The smaller and lighter the average adult members of a bird species are, the larger and heavier the eggs of that species are.

(C) The ratio of egg weight of a species to body weight of an adult member of that species is smaller for larger birds than for smaller ones.

(D) The size of birds' eggs varies greatly from species to species but has little effect on the volume and weight of the adult bird.

(E) Bird species vary more in egg size than they do in average body size and weight.

18. Bram Stoker's 1897 novel *Dracula* portrayed vampires—the "undead" who roam at night to suck the blood of living people—as able to turn into bats. As a result of the pervasive influence of this novel, many people now assume that a vampire's being able to turn into a bat is an essential part of vampire myths. However, this assumption is false, for vampire myths existed in Europe long before Stoker's book.

Which one of the following is an assumption on which the argument depends?

(A) At least one of the European vampire myths that predated Stoker's book did not portray vampires as strictly nocturnal.

(B) Vampire myths in Central and South America, where real vampire bats are found, portray vampires as able to turn into bats.

(C) Vampire myths did not exist outside Europe before the publication of Stoker's *Dracula*.

(D) At least one of the European vampire myths that predated Stoker's book did not portray vampires as able to turn into bats.

(E) At the time he wrote *Dracula*, Stoker was familiar with earlier European vampire myths.

GO ON TO THE NEXT PAGE.

19. It is unlikely that the world will ever be free of disease. Most diseases are caused by very prolific microorganisms whose response to the pressures medicines exert on them is predictable: they quickly evolve immunities to those medicines while maintaining their power to infect and even kill humans.

Which one of the following most accurately describes the role played in the argument by the claim that it is unlikely that the world will ever be free of disease?

(A) It is a conclusion that is claimed to follow from the premise that microorganisms are too numerous for medicines to eliminate entirely.

(B) It is a conclusion for which a description of the responses of microorganisms to the medicines designed to cure the diseases they cause is offered as support.

(C) It is a premise offered in support of the claim that most disease-causing microorganisms are able to evolve immunities to medicines while retaining their ability to infect humans.

(D) It is a generalization used to predict the response of microorganisms to the medicines humans use to kill them.

(E) It is a conclusion that is claimed to follow from the premise that most microorganisms are immune to medicines designed to kill them.

20. Scientist: My research indicates that children who engage in impulsive behavior similar to adult thrill-seeking behavior are twice as likely as other children to have a gene variant that increases sensitivity to dopamine. From this, I conclude that there is a causal relationship between this gene variant and an inclination toward thrill-seeking behavior.

Which one of the following, if true, most calls into question the scientist's argument?

(A) Many impulsive adults are not unusually sensitive to dopamine.

(B) It is not possible to reliably distinguish impulsive behavior from other behavior.

(C) Children are often described by adults as engaging in thrill-seeking behavior simply because they act impulsively.

(D) Many people exhibit behavioral tendencies as adults that they did not exhibit as children.

(E) The gene variant studied by the scientist is correlated with other types of behavior in addition to thrill-seeking behavior.

21. It is highly likely that Claudette is a classical pianist. Like most classical pianists, Claudette recognizes many of Clara Schumann's works. The vast majority of people who are not classical pianists do not. In fact, many people who are not classical pianists have not even heard of Clara Schumann.

The reasoning in the argument above is flawed in that it

(A) ignores the possibility that Claudette is more familiar with the works of other composers of music for piano

(B) presumes, without providing justification, that people who have not heard of Clara Schumann do not recognize her works

(C) presumes, without providing justification, that classical pianists cannot also play other musical instruments

(D) relies for its plausibility on the vagueness of the term "classical"

(E) ignores the possibility that the majority of people who recognize many of Clara Schumann's works are not classical pianists

GO ON TO THE NEXT PAGE.

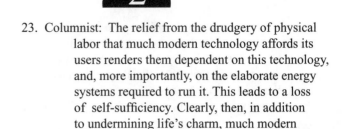

22. All the evidence so far gathered fits both Dr. Grippen's theory and Professor Heissmann's. However, the predictions that these theories make about the result of the planned experiment cannot both be true. Therefore, the result of this experiment will confirm one of these theories at the expense of the other.

The argument above exhibits an erroneous pattern of reasoning most similar to that exhibited by which one of the following?

(A) David and Jane both think they know how to distinguish beech trees from elms, but when they look at trees together they often disagree. Therefore, at least one of them must have an erroneous method.

(B) Although David thinks the tree they saw was a beech, Jane thinks it was an elm. Jane's description of the tree's features is consistent with her opinion, so this description must be inconsistent with David's view.

(C) David and Jane have been equally good at identifying trees so far. But David says this one is an elm, whereas Jane is unsure. Therefore, if this tree turns out to be an elm, we'll know David is better.

(D) David thinks that there are more beeches than elms in this forest. Jane thinks he is wrong. The section of forest we examined was small, but examination of the whole forest would either confirm David's view or disprove it.

(E) David thinks this tree is a beech. Jane thinks it is an elm. Maria, unlike David or Jane, is expert at tree identification, so when Maria gives her opinion it will verify either David's or Jane's opinion.

23. Columnist: The relief from the drudgery of physical labor that much modern technology affords its users renders them dependent on this technology, and, more importantly, on the elaborate energy systems required to run it. This leads to a loss of self-sufficiency. Clearly, then, in addition to undermining life's charm, much modern technology diminishes the overall well-being of its users.

Which one of the following is an assumption required by the columnist's argument?

(A) Physical labor is essential to a fulfilling life.
(B) Self-sufficiency contributes to a person's well-being.
(C) People are not free if they must depend on anything other than their own capacities.
(D) Anything causing a loss in life's charm is unjustifiable unless this loss is compensated by some gain.
(E) Technology inherently limits the well-being of its users.

GO ON TO THE NEXT PAGE.

24. Psychologist: Some psychologists mistakenly argue that because dreams result from electrical discharges in the brain, they must be understood purely in terms of their physiological function. They conclude, against Freud, that dreams reveal nothing about the character of the dreamer. But since dream content varies enormously, then even if electrical discharges provide the terms of the physiological explanation of dreams, they cannot completely explain the phenomenon of dreaming.

The claim that dream content varies enormously plays which one of the following roles in the argument?

(A) It is used to support the anti-Freudian conclusion that some psychologists draw concerning dreams.

(B) It is used to support the explicitly stated conclusion that a fully satisfactory account of dreams must allow for the possibility of their revealing significant information about the dreamer.

(C) It is used lo suggest that neither Freud's theory nor the theory of anti-Freudian psychologists can completely explain the phenomenon of dreaming.

(D) It is used to illustrate the difficulty of providing a complete explanation of the phenomenon of dreaming.

(E) It is used to undermine a claim that some psychologists use to argue against a view of Freud's.

25. The first bicycle, the Draisienne, was invented in 1817. A brief fad ensued, after which bicycles practically disappeared until the 1860s. Why was this? New technology is accepted only when it coheres with the values of a society. Hence some change in values must have occurred between 1817 and the 1860s.

The reasoning in the argument is flawed because the argument

(A) presumes, without giving justification, that fads are never indicative of genuine acceptance

(B) fails to recognize that the reappearance of bicycles in the 1860s may have indicated genuine acceptance of them

(C) offers no support for the claim that the Draisienne was the first true bicycle

(D) poses a question that has little relevance to the argument's conclusion

(E) ignores, without giving justification, alternative possible explanations of the initial failure of bicycles

S T O P

IF YOU FINISH BEFORE TIME IS CALLED, YOU MAY CHECK YOUR WORK ON THIS SECTION ONLY.
DO NOT WORK ON ANY OTHER SECTION IN THE TEST.

SECTION III
Time-35 minutes
22 Questions

<u>Directions</u>: Each group of questions in this section is based on a set of conditions. In answering some of the questions, it may be useful to draw a rough diagram. Choose the response that most accurately and completely answers each question and blacken the corresponding space on your answer sheet.

<u>Questions 1-6</u>

In the course of one month Garibaldi has exactly seven different meetings. Each of her meetings is with exactly one of five foreign dignitaries: Fuentes, Matsuba, Rhee, Soleimani, or Tbahi. The following constraints govern Garibaldi's meetings:

    She has exactly three meetings with Fuentes, and exactly one with each of the other dignitaries.
    She does not have any meetings in a row with Fuentes.
    Her meeting with Soleimani is the very next one after her meeting with Tbahi.
    Neither the first nor last of her meetings is with Matsuba.

1. Which one of the following could be the sequence of the meetings Garibaldi has with the dignitaries?

   (A)   Fuentes, Rhee, Tbahi, Soleimani, Fuentes, Matsuba, Rhee
   (B)   Fuentes, Tbahi, Soleimani, Matsuba, Fuentes, Fuentes, Rhee
   (C)   Fuentes, Rhee, Fuentes, Matsuba, Fuentes, Tbahi, Soleimani
   (D)   Fuentes, Tbahi, Matsuba, Fuentes, Soleimani, Rhee, Fuentes
   (E)   Fuentes, Tbahi, Soleimani, Fuentes, Rhee, Fuentes, Matsuba

2. If Garibaldi's last meeting is with Rhee, then which one of the following could be true?

   (A)   Garibaldi's second meeting is with Soleimani.
   (B)   Garibaldi's third meeting is with Matsuba.
   (C)   Garibaldi's fourth meeting is with Soleimani.
   (D)   Garibaldi's fifth meeting is with Matsuba.
   (E)   Garibaldi's sixth meeting is with Soleimani.

3. If Garibaldi's second meeting is with Fuentes, then which one of the following is a complete and accurate list of the dignitaries with any one of whom Garibaldi's fourth meeting could be?

   (A)   Fuentes, Soleimani, Rhee
   (B)   Matsuba, Rhee, Tbahi
   (C)   Matsuba, Soleimani
   (D)   Rhee, Tbahi
   (E)   Fuentes, Soleimani

4. If Garibaldi's meeting with Rhee is the very next one after Garibaldi's meeting with Soleimani, then which one of the following must be true?

   (A)   Garibaldi's third meeting is with Fuentes.
   (B)   Garibaldi's fourth meeting is with Rhee.
   (C)   Garibaldi's fifth meeting is with Fuentes.
   (D)   Garibaldi's sixth meeting is with Rhee.
   (E)   Garibaldi's seventh meeting is with Fuentes.

5. If Garibaldi's first meeting is with Tbahi, then Garibaldi's meeting with Rhee could be the

   (A)   second meeting
   (B)   third meeting
   (C)   fifth meeting
   (D)   sixth meeting
   (E)   seventh meeting

6. If Garibaldi's meeting with Matsuba is the very next meeting after Garibaldi's meeting with Rhee, then with which one of the following dignitaries must Garibaldi's fourth meeting be?

   (A)   Fuentes
   (B)   Matsuba
   (C)   Rhee
   (D)   Soleimani
   (E)   Tbahi

GO ON TO THE NEXT PAGE.

Questions 7-12

During a certain week, an animal shelter places exactly six dogs—a greyhound, a husky, a keeshond, a Labrador retriever, a poodle, and a schnauzer—with new owners. Two are placed on Monday, two on Tuesday, and the remaining two on Wednesday, consistent with the following conditions:

The Labrador retriever is placed on the same day as the poodle.

The greyhound is not placed on the same day as the husky.

If the keeshond is placed on Monday, the greyhound is placed on Tuesday.

If the schnauzer is placed on Wednesday, the husky is placed on Tuesday.

7. Which one of the following could be a complete and accurate matching of dogs to the days on which they are placed?

(A)   Monday: greyhound, Labrador retriever
        Tuesday: husky, poodle
        Wednesday: keeshond, schnauzer
(B)   Monday: greyhound, keeshond
        Tuesday: Labrador retriever, poodle
        Wednesday: husky, schnauzer
(C)   Monday: keeshond, schnauzer
        Tuesday: greyhound, husky
        Wednesday: Labrador retriever, poodle
(D)   Monday: Labrador retriever, poodle
        Tuesday: greyhound, keeshond
        Wednesday: husky, schnauzer
(E)   Monday: Labrador retriever, poodle
        Tuesday: husky, keeshond
        Wednesday: greyhound, schnauzer

8. Which one of the following must be true?

(A)   The keeshond is not placed on the same day as the greyhound.
(B)   The keeshond is not placed on the same day as the schnauzer.
(C)   The schnauzer is not placed on the same day as the husky.
(D)   The greyhound is placed on the same day as the schnauzer.
(E)   The husky is placed on the same day as the keeshond.

9. If the poodle is placed on Tuesday, then which one of the following could be true?

(A)   The greyhound is placed on Monday.
(B)   The keeshond is placed on Monday.
(C)   The Labrador retriever is placed on Monday.
(D)   The husky is placed on Tuesday.
(E)   The schnauzer is placed on Wednesday.

10. If the greyhound is placed on the same day as the keeshond, then which one of the following must be true?

(A)   The husky is placed on Monday.
(B)   The Labrador retriever is placed on Monday.
(C)   The keeshond is placed on Tuesday.
(D)   The poodle is not placed on Wednesday.
(E)   The schnauzer is not placed on Wednesday.

11. If the husky is placed the day before the schnauzer, then which one of the following CANNOT be true?

(A)   The husky is placed on Monday.
(B)   The keeshond is placed on Monday.
(C)   The greyhound is placed on Tuesday.
(D)   The poodle is placed on Tuesday.
(E)   The poodle is placed on Wednesday.

12. If the greyhound is placed the day before the poodle, then which one of the following CANNOT be placed on Tuesday?

(A)   the husky
(B)   the keeshond
(C)   the Labrador retriever
(D)   the poodle
(E)   the schnauzer

GO ON TO THE NEXT PAGE.

Questions 13-17

A tour group plans to visit exactly five archaeological sites. Each site was discovered by exactly one of the following archaeologists—Ferrara, Gallagher, Oliphant—and each dates from the eighth, ninth, or tenth century (A.D.). The tour must satisfy the following conditions:

The site visited second dates from the ninth century.

Neither the site visited fourth nor the site visited fifth was discovered by Oliphant.

Exactly one of the sites was discovered by Gallagher, and it dates from the tenth century.

If a site dates from the eighth century, it was discovered by Oliphant.

The site visited third dates from a more recent century than does either the site visited first or that visited fourth.

13. Which one of the following could be an accurate list of the discoverers of the five sites, listed in the order in which the sites are visited?

(A) Oliphant, Oliphant, Gallagher, Oliphant, Ferrara
(B) Gallagher, Oliphant, Ferrara, Ferrara, Ferrara
(C) Oliphant, Gallagher, Oliphant, Ferrara, Ferrara
(D) Oliphant, Oliphant, Gallagher, Ferrara, Gallagher
(E) Ferrara, Oliphant, Gallagher, Ferrara, Ferrara

14. If exactly one of the five sites the tour group visits dates from the tenth century, then which one of the following CANNOT be a site that was discovered by Ferrara?

(A) the site visited first
(B) the site visited second
(C) the site visited third
(D) the site visited fourth
(E) the site visited fifth

15. Which one of the following could be a site that dates from the eighth century?

(A) the site visited first
(B) the site visited second
(C) the site visited third
(D) the site visited fourth
(E) the site visited fifth

16. Which one of the following is a complete and accurate list of the sites each of which CANNOT be the site discovered by Gallagher?

(A) third, fourth, fifth
(B) second, third, fourth
(C) first, fourth, fifth
(D) first, second, fifth
(E) first, second, fourth

17. The tour group could visit at most how many sites that were discovered by Ferrara?

(A) one
(B) two
(C) three
(D) four
(E) five

GO ON TO THE NEXT PAGE.

Questions 18-22

Each day of a five-day workweek (Monday through Friday), Anastasia parks for the entire day in exactly one of three downtown parking lots—X, Y, and Z. One of the lots costs $10 for the day, another costs $12, and the other costs $15. Anastasia parks in each of the three lots at least once during her workweek. The following conditions must apply:

On Thursday, Anastasia parks in the $15 lot.
Lot X costs more than lot Z.
The lot Anastasia parks in on Wednesday costs more than the one she parks in on Friday.
Anastasia parks in lot Z on more days of the workweek than she parks in lot X.

18. Which one of the following could be a complete and accurate list of which lot Anastasia parks in each day, listed in order from Monday through Friday?

   (A)   Y, Z, X, Y, Z
   (B)   Y, Z, Z, Y, X
   (C)   Z, Z, X, X, Y
   (D)   Z, Z, X, X, Z
   (E)   Z, Z, X, Z, Y

19. Anastasia CANNOT park in the $15 lot on which one of the following days?

   (A)   Monday
   (B)   Tuesday
   (C)   Wednesday
   (D)   Thursday
   (E)   Friday

20. If lot Z is the $12 lot, then on which one of the following days must Anastasia park in lot Y?

   (A)   Monday
   (B)   Tuesday
   (C)   Wednesday
   (D)   Thursday
   (E)   Friday

21. Anastasia CANNOT park in lot Z on which one of the following days?

   (A)   Monday
   (B)   Tuesday
   (C)   Wednesday
   (D)   Thursday
   (E)   Friday

22. Which one of the following could be a complete and accurate list of the days on which Anastasia parks in the $10 lot?

   (A)   Monday
   (B)   Tuesday
   (C)   Monday, Tuesday
   (D)   Monday, Wednesday
   (E)   Monday, Thursday

S T O P

IF YOU FINISH BEFORE TIME IS CALLED, YOU MAY CHECK YOUR WORK ON THIS SECTION ONLY.
DO NOT WORK ON ANY OTHER SECTION IN THE TEST.

SECTION IV
Time-35 minutes
26 Questions

Directions: The questions in this section are based on the reasoning contained in brief statements or passages. For some questions, more than one of the choices could conceivably answer the question. However, you are to choose the <u>best</u> answer; that is, the response that most accurately and completely answers the question. You should not make assumptions that are by commonsense standards implausible, superfluous, or incompatible with the passage. After you have chosen the best answer, blacken the corresponding space on your answer sheet.

1. Jones fell unconscious on the job and it was suspected that he had swallowed a certain chemical, so he was rushed to the local hospital's emergency room. In making her diagnosis, the emergency-room physician knew that if Jones had swallowed the chemical, a deficiency in the content of a mineral in his blood would result. She also knew that deficiency in the mineral causes inflammation of the skin. Since Jones's skin was not inflamed when he was admitted to the emergency room, the physician concluded that Jones had not swallowed the chemical.

   Which one of the following, if true, would undermine the physician's conclusion?

   (A) Jones did not know that the chemical was dangerous.
   (B) Jones had suffered inflammation of the skin in the past.
   (C) It takes 48 hours for the chemical to bring about deficiency of the mineral in the blood.
   (D) Jones often worked with the chemical.
   (E) Deficiency in minerals other than the mineral in question can cause inflammation of the skin.

2. Pacifist: It is immoral to do anything that causes harm to another person. But, since using force causes harm to another person, it is also immoral to threaten to use force, even when such a threat is made in self-defense.

   Which one of the following principles, if valid, would most help to justify the pacifist's reasoning?

   (A) Given the potential harm caused by the use of force, the line between use of force in self-defense and the aggressive use of force is always vague.
   (B) It is immoral to threaten to do what it is immoral to do.
   (C) It is immoral to do anything that causes more harm than good.
   (D) Whether a threat made in self-defense is immoral depends on the circumstances.
   (E) It is immoral to carry out a threat if making the threat is itself immoral.

3. Beginning in the 1950s, popular music was revolutionized by the electrification of musical instruments, which has enabled musicians to play with increased volume. Because individual musicians can play with increased volume, the average number of musicians per band has decreased. Nevertheless, electrification has increased rather than decreased the overall number of musicians who play popular music professionally.

   Which one of the following is most strongly supported by the statements above, if those statements are true?

   (A) The number of amateur musicians who play popular music has decreased.
   (B) Most professional musicians are able to play both electric and nonelectric instruments.
   (C) The number of professional musicians in some bands has increased.
   (D) The total number of professional bands has increased as a result of electrification.
   (E) Many professional musicians play in more than one band.

4. Statistics indicating a sudden increase in the incidence of a problem often merely reflect a heightened awareness of the problem or a greater ability to record its occurrence. Hence we should be wary of proposals for radical solutions to problems when those proposals are a reaction to new statistical data.

   The argumentation conforms most closely to which one of the following principles?

   (A) A better cognizance of a problem does not warrant the undertaking of a radical solution to the problem.
   (B) Attempts to stop the occurrence of a problem should be preceded by a determination that the problem actually exists.
   (C) Proposals for radical solutions to problems should be based on statistical data alone.
   (D) Statistical data should not be manipulated to make a radical solution to a problem seem more justified than it actually is.
   (E) Radical solutions to problems can cause other problems and end up doing more harm than good.

GO ON TO THE NEXT PAGE.

5. Barr: The National Tea Association cites tea's recent visibility in advertising and magazine articles as evidence of tea's increasing popularity. However, a neutral polling company, the Survey Group, has tracked tea sales at numerous stores for the last 20 years and has found no change in the amount of tea sold. We can thus conclude that tea is no more popular now than it ever was.

Which one of the following, if true, most seriously weakens Barr's argument?

(A)   The National Tea Association has announced that it plans to carry out its own retail survey in the next year.
(B)   A survey by an unrelated polling organization shows that the public is generally receptive to the idea of trying new types of tea.
(C)   The Survey Group is funded by a consortium of consumer advocacy groups.
(D)   The stores from which the Survey Group collected information about tea sales are all located in the same small region of the country.
(E)   Tea has been the subject of an expensive and efficient advertising campaign funded, in part, by the National Tea Association.

6. Doctors urge people to reduce their cholesterol levels through dietary changes. But moderate dietary changes often do not work to lower cholesterol levels. One may need, therefore, to make more dramatic changes, such as switching to a vegetarian diet.

The statement that moderate dietary changes often do not work to lower cholesterol levels plays which one of the following roles in the argument?

(A)   It is presented to counter doctors' suggestions that cholesterol levels can be reduced through dietary changes.
(B)   It is a premise offered in support of the claim that vegetarian diets are more healthful than any diets containing meat.
(C)   It is a premise offered in support of the claim that reducing cholesterol levels may require greater than moderate dietary changes.
(D)   It is offered as an explanation of the success of vegetarian diets in reducing cholesterol levels.
(E)   It is a conclusion for which the claim that dramatic changes in one's diet are sometimes required to reduce cholesterol levels is offered as support.

7. Since empathy is essential for people to be willing to follow moral codes that sometimes require them to ignore their own welfare to help others, civilized society could not exist without empathy.

Which one of the following is an assumption required by the argument?

(A)   Civilized society can exist only if there are people who are willing to at least sometimes ignore their own welfare to help others.
(B)   Failure to empathize with other people usually leads to actions detrimental to civilized society.
(C)   If everyone in a society is sometimes willing to ignore his or her own welfare to help others, that society will be civilized.
(D)   Moral codes that include the requirement that people disregard their own welfare in order to help others have arisen within some civilized societies.
(E)   People who feel empathy tend to ignore their own welfare for the sake of others.

8. Insurgent political parties that are profoundly dissatisfied with the dominant party's reign and justificatory ideology always produce factions whose views and aims differ as greatly from each other's as they do from the dominant party's. Although these factions ignore their own disagreements for the sake of defeating the dominant party, their disagreements inevitably come forward upon victory. Therefore, _____.

Which one of the following is the most logical completion of the argument?

(A)   no victorious insurgent party ever manages to stay in power for as long as the party it displaces did
(B)   a victorious insurgent party must address the disagreements between its factions if it is to stay in power
(C)   the heretofore insurgent party will not always promulgate a new ideology to justify its own policies, once it is victorious
(D)   a victorious insurgent party always faces opposition from the party it recently ousted
(E)   it is impossible for the different factions of a victorious insurgent party to effect the compromises necessary to keep the new party in power

GO ON TO THE NEXT PAGE.

9. Manager: When Sullivan was passed over for promotion, people said that the deciding factor was his being much older than the competition. But this is clearly not the case. Several recent promotions have been given to people older than Sullivan.

The manager's argument is most vulnerable to criticism because it fails to consider the possibility that

(A) Sullivan was well qualified for the promotion
(B) age is only one of a number of factors that kept Sullivan from being promoted
(C) people often associate age with experience and good judgment
(D) the people older than Sullivan who were promoted had no younger competitors
(E) Sullivan's employer tries to keep deliberations involving promotion decisions confidential

10. Council member P: Alarmists are those who see an instance of pollution and exaggerate its significance into a major character fault of society. Such alarmists fail to distinguish the incident and the behavior that caused it from the disposition of people not to pollute.

Council member Q: To think that there is a lot of pollution based on the discovery of a serious single instance of pollution is simply an application of the widely accepted principle that actions tend to follow the path of least resistance, and it is surely easier to pollute than not to pollute.

Council members P and Q disagree over whether

(A) pollution should be considered a problem
(B) actions tend to follow the path of least resistance
(C) people are responsible for pollution
(D) people can change their behavior and not pollute
(E) people are inclined to pollute

11. It is easy to see that the board of directors of the construction company is full of corruption and should be replaced. There are many instances of bribery by various persons on the staff of board member Wagston that are a matter of public record. These bribes perniciously influenced the awarding of government contracts.

The argument's reasoning is most vulnerable to criticism on the grounds that

(A) the argument fails to show that corruption is not limited to Wagston's staff
(B) the argument fails to show that Wagston's staff engaged in any bribery other than bribery of government officials
(C) the argument fails to specify the relation between bribery and corruption
(D) the argument presumes without giving justification that all of Wagston's staff have engaged in corruption
(E) the argument attempts to deflect attention away from substantive issues by attacking the character of the board

12. Coffee and tea contain methylxanthines, which cause temporary increases in the natural production of vasopressin, a hormone produced by the pituitary gland. Vasopressin causes clumping of blood cells, and the clumping is more pronounced in women than in men. This is probably the explanation of the fact that women face as much as a tenfold higher risk than men do of complications following angioplasty, a technique used to clear clogged arteries.

Which one of the following statements is most strongly supported by the information above?

(A) Men, but not women, should be given methylxanthines prior to undergoing angioplasty.
(B) In spite of the risks, angioplasty is the only effective treatment for clogged arteries.
(C) Women probably drink more coffee and tea, on average, than do men.
(D) Prior to undergoing angioplasty, women should avoid coffee and tea.
(E) Angioplasty should not be used to treat clogged arteries.

GO ON TO THE NEXT PAGE.

13. Whether a machine performs its intended function is plain for all to see, but recognition of excellence in art requires a rare subtlety of perception. So whereas engineers usually maintain their composure when their work is being evaluated, artists tend to become anxious under such circumstances.

The reasoning above conforms most closely to which one of the following propositions?

(A) People who have an interest in working as artists are no more likely to have especially anxious personalities than are people who have an interest in working as engineers.

(B) The value of a machine is independent of the feelings of those who create it, while the value of an artwork is not.

(C) Evaluation of the work of engineers should be based on a different set of standards than is evaluation of the work of artists.

(D) People who create things whose success can be easily ascertained worry less about others' opinions of their work than do people who create things whose value cannot be easily ascertained.

(E) Someone who creates a work that cannot be easily evaluated tends to be less confident about its value than are those who evaluate it.

14. Scientists hypothesize that a particular type of fat known as "P-fat" is required for the development of eyesight. Researchers were led to this hypothesis by observing that babies who are fed formulas low in P-fat tend to have worse eyesight than babies fed mother's milk, which is high in P-fat. It has also been shown that babies that are five to six weeks premature tend to have worse eyesight than babies carried to term.

Which one of the following, if true, most supports the scientists' hypothesis?

(A) Adults whose diets lack P-fat tend to have worse eyesight than those whose diets are high in P-fat.

(B) A fetus typically receives high levels of P-fat from the mother during only the last four weeks of pregnancy.

(C) Babies whose mothers have poor eyesight do not tend to have poor eyesight themselves.

(D) Babies generally prefer mother's milk to formulas low in P-fat.

(E) The eyesight of a fetus develops during the last trimester of pregnancy.

15. Artists have different ways of producing contours and hatching, and analysis of these stylistic features can help to distinguish works by a famous artist both from forgeries and from works genuinely by other artists. Indeed, this analysis has shown that many of the drawings formerly attributed to Michelangelo are actually by the artist Giulio Clovio, Michelangelo's contemporary.

If the statements above are true, then which one of the following must also be true?

(A) Contours and hatching are the main features that distinguish the drawing styles of different artists.

(B) Many of the drawings formerly attributed to Michelangelo are actually forgeries.

(C) No forgery can perfectly duplicate the contour and hatching styles of a famous artist.

(D) The contour and hatching styles used to identify the drawings of Clovio cited can be shown to be features of all Clovio's works.

(E) There is an analyzable difference between Clovio's contour and hatching styles and those of Michelangelo.

16. Moralist: Immoral actions are those that harm other people. But since such actions eventually harm those who perform them, those who act immorally do so only through ignorance of some of their actions' consequences rather than through a character defect.

Which one of the following is an assumption required by the moralist's argument?

(A) People ignorant of their actions' consequences cannot be held morally responsible for those consequences.

(B) An action harms those who perform it only if it also eventually harms others.

(C) Only someone with a character defect would knowingly perform actions that eventually harm others.

(D) Those who, in acting immorally, eventually harm themselves do not intend that harm.

(E) None of those who knowingly harm themselves lack character defects.

GO ON TO THE NEXT PAGE.

17. Climatologists believe they know why Earth has undergone a regular sequence of ice ages beginning around 800,000 years ago. Calculations show that Earth's orbit around the Sun has fluctuations that coincide with the ice-age cycles. The climatologists hypothesize that when the fluctuations occur, Earth passes through clouds of cosmic dust that enters the atmosphere; the cosmic dust thereby dims the Sun, resulting in an ice age. They concede, however, that though cosmic dust clouds are common, the clouds would have to be particularly dense in order to have this effect.

Each of the following, if true, would lend support to the climatologists' hypothesis EXCEPT:

(A) Earth did not pass through clouds of cosmic dust earlier than 800,000 years ago.

(B) Two large asteroids collided 800,000 years ago, producing a tremendous amount of dense cosmic dust that continues to orbit the Sun.

(C) Earth's average temperature drops slightly shortly after volcanic eruptions spew large amounts of dust into Earth's atmosphere.

(D) Large bits of cosmic rock periodically enter Earth's atmosphere, raising large amounts of dust from Earth's surface.

(E) Rare trace elements known to be prevalent in cosmic debris have been discovered in layers of sediment whose ages correspond very closely to the occurrence of ice ages.

18. Philosopher: The rational pursuit of happiness is quite different from always doing what one most strongly desires to do. This is because the rational pursuit of happiness must include consideration of long-term consequences, whereas our desires are usually focused on the short term. Moreover, desires are sometimes compulsions, and while ordinary desires result in at least momentary happiness when their goals are attained, compulsions strongly drive a person to pursue goals that offer no happiness even when reached.

If all of the philosopher's statements are true, each of the following could be true EXCEPT:

(A) The majority of people do not have compulsions.

(B) Attaining the goal of any desire results in momentary happiness.

(C) Most people do not pursue happiness rationally.

(D) Most people want more than their own personal happiness.

(E) All actions have long-term consequences.

19. Political scientist: All governments worthy of respect allow their citizens to dissent from governmental policies. No government worthy of respect leaves minorities unprotected. Thus any government that protects minorities permits criticism of its policies.

The flawed pattern of reasoning in which one of the following most closely parallels that in the political scientist's argument?

(A) Politicians are admirable if they put the interests of those they serve above their own interests. So politicians who sometimes ignore the interests of their own constituents in favor of the nation as a whole deserve admiration, for they are putting the interests of those they serve above their own.

(B) All jazz musicians are capable of improvising and no jazz musician is incapable of reading music. Therefore all musicians who can read music can improvise.

(C) Ecosystems with cool, dry climates are populated by large mammals. No ecosystems populated by large mammals have abundant and varied plant life. Thus ecosystems that do not have cool, dry climates have abundant and varied plant life.

(D) Some intellectuals are not socially active, and no intellectual is a professional athlete. Therefore any professional athlete is socially active.

(E) First-person narratives reveal the thoughts of the narrator but conceal those of the other characters. Some third-person narratives reveal the motives of every character. Thus books that rely on making all characters' motives apparent should be written in the third person.

GO ON TO THE NEXT PAGE.

20. Advertisement: Each of the Economic Merit Prize winners from the past 25 years is covered by the Acme retirement plan. Since the winners of the nation's most prestigious award for economists have thus clearly recognized that the Acme plan offers them a financially secure future, it is probably a good plan for anyone with retirement needs similar to theirs.

The advertisement's argumentation is most vulnerable to criticism on which one of the following grounds?

(A) It ignores the possibility that the majority of Economic Merit Prize winners from previous years used a retirement plan other than the Acme plan.

(B) It fails to address adequately the possibility that any of several retirement plans would be good enough for, and offer a financially secure future to, Economic Merit Prize winners.

(C) It appeals to the fact that supposed experts have endorsed the argument's main conclusion, rather than appealing to direct evidence for that conclusion.

(D) It takes for granted that some winners of the Economic Merit Prize have deliberately selected the Acme retirement plan, rather than having had it chosen for them by their employers.

(E) It presumes, without providing justification, that each of the Economic Merit Prize winners has retirement plan needs that are identical to the advertisement's intended audience's retirement plan needs.

21. A small car offers less protection in an accident than a large car does, but since a smaller car is more maneuverable, it is better to drive a small car because then accidents will be less likely.

Which one of the following arguments employs reasoning most similar to that employed by the argument above?

(A) An artist's best work is generally that done in the time before the artist becomes very well known. When artists grow famous and are diverted from artistic creation by demands for public appearances, their artistic work suffers. So artists' achieving great fame can diminish their artistic reputations.

(B) It is best to insist that a child spend at least some time every day reading indoors. Even though it may cause the child some unhappiness to have to stay indoors when others are outside playing, the child can benefit from the time by learning to enjoy books and becoming prepared for lifelong learning.

(C) For this work, vehicles built of lightweight materials are more practical than vehicles built of heavy materials. This is so because while lighter vehicles do not last as long as heavier vehicles, they are cheaper to replace.

(D) Although it is important to limit the amount of sugar and fat in one's diet, it would be a mistake to try to follow a diet totally lacking in sugar and fat. It is better to consume sugar and fat in moderation, for then the cravings that lead to uncontrolled binges will be prevented.

(E) A person who exercises vigorously every day has less body fat than an average person to draw upon in the event of a wasting illness. But one should still endeavor to exercise vigorously every day, because doing so significantly decreases the chances of contracting a wasting illness.

GO ON TO THE NEXT PAGE.

22. Trainer: Research shows that when dogs are neutered in early puppyhood, their leg bones usually do not develop properly. Improper bone development leads in turn to problems with arthritis as dogs grow older. Thus, if you want to protect your dog from arthritis you should not neuter your dog until it is full-grown.

Of the following, which one is a criticism to which the reasoning in the trainer's argument is most vulnerable?

(A) It fails to state exactly what percentage of dogs neutered in early puppyhood experience improper bone development.

(B) It fails to explain the connection between improper bone development and arthritis.

(C) It fails to address the effects of neutering in middle or late puppyhood.

(D) It fails to consider the possibility that the benefits of neutering a dog early might outweigh the risk of arthritis.

(E) It fails to consider the possibility that dogs with properly developed bones can develop arthritis.

23. Political scientist: One of the most interesting dilemmas in contemporary democratic politics concerns the regulation of political campaign spending. People certainly should be free, within broad limits, to spend their money as they choose. On the other hand, candidates who can vastly outspend all rivals have an unfair advantage in publicizing their platforms. Democratic governments have a strong obligation to ensure that all voices have an equal chance to be heard, but governments should not subsidize expensive campaigns for each candidate. The resolution of the dilemma, therefore, is clear: _____.

Which one of the following most logically completes the political scientist's argument?

(A) only candidates with significant campaign resources should be permitted to run for public office

(B) an upper limit on the political campaign spending of each candidate is warranted

(C) government subsidization of all political campaigns at a low percentage of their total cost is warranted

(D) all wealthy persons should be prohibited from spending their own money on political campaigns

(E) each candidate should be allowed to spend as much money on a political campaign as any other candidate chooses to spend

24. Some people have maintained that private ownership of the means of production ultimately destroys any society that sanctions it. This may be true of a less technologically advanced society that must share its economic resources to survive. But since only private ownership of the means of production permits individuals to test new technologies without the majority's consent, a technologically advanced society will actually endanger its survival if the means of production become public property.

The proposition that private ownership of the means of production ultimately destroys any society that sanctions it plays which one of the following roles in the argument above?

(A) It is a generalization that the argument suggests is no more applicable to less technologically advanced societies than to more technologically advanced societies.

(B) It is a hypothesis for whose widespread acceptance the argument offers an explanation.

(C) It is a general hypothesis that the argument suggests is inapplicable to societies more dependent for survival upon the introduction of new technologies than upon the sharing of resources.

(D) It is a contention about the consequences of an economic arrangement that the argument claims is incompatible with the needs of any society.

(E) It is a generalization about societies that according to the argument is true for any society in which the majority of its citizens does not impede the introduction of new technologies.

GO ON TO THE NEXT PAGE.

25. A certain medication that is frequently prescribed to lower a patient's cholesterol level is generally effective. A recent study of 1,000 subjects ranging widely in age indicates, however, that the cholesterol level of someone taking the medication is typically 12 to 15 percent higher than the average for that person's age group.

Which one of the following, if true, most helps to explain how both of the claims made above could be true?

(A) A recently developed cholesterol-lowering medication is more effective than the medication described above.

(B) Another medication is prescribed to treat high cholesterol just as often as the medication described above is.

(C) In most cases, people with high cholesterol levels are not treated with drug therapy but are put on restrictive low-cholesterol diets.

(D) The medication described above is usually prescribed only for people whose cholesterol level is at least 30 percent above the average for their age group.

(E) Within the population as a whole, approximately the same number of people have relatively high cholesterol levels as have relatively low cholesterol levels.

26. Political theorist: For all of its members to be strong in foreign policy, an alliance of countries must respond aggressively to problems. An alliance will do so only if every member of the alliance perceives the problems as grave. But the European Union countries will not all perceive a problem as grave unless they all agree that it threatens their alliance's economy. Thus, not all of the member countries of the European Union will be strong in foreign policy.

The conclusion drawn above follows logically if which one of the following is assumed?

(A) Countries that refuse to join alliances generally respond more aggressively to problems than do countries that do join alliances.

(B) Countries become less aggressive in foreign policy if greater wealth leads them to think that they have more to lose by responding to problems aggressively.

(C) Problems that appear to some member countries of the European Union to threaten the alliance's economy will not appear so to others.

(D) European Union member countries that fail to perceive the economic relevance of problems are generally weak in foreign policy.

(E) Alliances that are economically beneficial for a given country are not necessarily beneficial with regard to foreign policy.

S T O P

IF YOU FINISH BEFORE TIME IS CALLED, YOU MAY CHECK YOUR WORK ON THIS SECTION ONLY.
DO NOT WORK ON ANY OTHER SECTION IN THE TEST.

LSAT® Writing Sample Topic

The program manager of a public television station intends to purchase a documentary program on diabetes and has narrowed the choice down to two programs. Write an argument for purchasing one program over the other, taking into account the following:

- The program manager wants to increase youth awareness of diabetes by engaging a younger audience.
- The program manager wants to air a well-researched and accurate depiction of the challenges of living with diabetes.

"What's Up, Doc?" tells the story of 19-year-old Carlene, a popular rap artist. A physician who worked with Carlene is interviewed, but the documentary focuses primarily on Carlene, her family, and the musicians who work with her. The discussion centers on how Carlene has dealt with her diabetes since it was diagnosed at the age of 14. Carlene explains the innovative and interesting ways she found to integrate the daily monitoring and control of the disease into her very demanding schedule. The program touches on risk factors, warning signs, complications, and self-care skills for managing diabetes. Carlene ends the program by directing a plea to teenagers to learn about the symptoms of diabetes and become more aware of the disease.

"Living with Diabetes" is an investigation of teenagers with diabetes in four different high schools across the country narrated by Andre Smith, a well-known, prizewinning health reporter. Smith interviews a number of students with the disease, along with school administrators and teachers, about the effect of diabetes on the students' lives. He visits local hospitals and counseling centers to interview doctors and psychologists, who outline the various physical and psychological effects of diabetes. The camera also takes viewers to the Diabetes Research Institute's information outreach program, where visitors meet researchers and learn what they are doing to find a cure for the disease. Included in the program are detailed descriptions of treatment options available and their costs, as well as advice about prevention and testing.

Scratch Paper
Do not write your essay in this space.

Directions:

1. Use the Answer Key on the next page to check your answers.

2. Use the Scoring Worksheet below to compute your raw score.

3. Use the Score Conversion Chart to convert your raw score into the 120-180 scale.

```
┌─────────────────────────────────────────────┐
│           Scoring Worksheet                   │
│                                               │
│ 1. Enter the number of questions you answered │
│    correctly in each section.                 │
│                                               │
│                          Number               │
│                          Correct              │
│      SECTION I.....................  _____   │
│      SECTION II....................  _____   │
│      SECTION III...................  _____   │
│      SECTION IV....................  _____   │
│                                               │
│                                               │
│ 2. Enter the sum here:        _____          │
│                  This is your Raw Score.      │
└─────────────────────────────────────────────┘
```

Conversion Chart:
For Converting Raw Score to the 120-180 LSAT Scaled Score
LSAT Form G-4LSN61

Reported Score	Raw Score Lowest	Raw Score Highest
180	98	100
179	—*	—*
178	97	97
177	96	96
176	95	95
175	—*	—*
174	94	94
173	93	93
172	92	92
171	91	91
170	90	90
169	89	89
168	88	88
167	87	87
166	85	86
165	84	84
164	82	83
163	81	81
162	80	80
161	78	79
160	76	77
159	75	75
158	73	74
157	72	72
156	70	71
155	68	69
154	67	67
153	65	66
152	63	64
151	61	62
150	60	60
149	58	59
148	56	57
147	54	55
146	53	53
145	51	52
144	49	50
143	47	48
142	46	46
141	44	45
140	42	43
139	41	41
138	39	40
137	37	38
136	36	36
135	34	35
134	32	33
133	31	31
132	29	30
131	28	28
130	26	27
129	25	25
128	23	24
127	22	22
126	20	21
125	19	19
124	27	18
123	16	16
122	15	15
121	14	14
120	0	13

*There is no raw score that will produce this scaled score for this form.

SECTION I

1.	E	8.	C	15.	B	22.	A
2.	D	9.	C	16.	A	23.	C
3.	E	10.	E	17.	C	24.	E
4.	D	11.	E	18.	E	25.	D
5.	C	12.	D	19.	A	26.	B
6.	A	13.	B	20.	D	27.	A
7.	A	14.	B	21.	A		

SECTION II

1.	B	8.	E	15.	D	22.	E
2.	E	9.	C	16.	E	23.	B
3.	C	10.	B	17.	C	24.	E
4.	C	11.	B	18.	D	25.	E
5.	A	12.	A	19.	B		
6.	B	13.	A	20.	B		
7.	D	14.	D	21.	E		

SECTION III

1.	C	8.	B	15.	A	22.	C
2.	D	9.	A	16.	E		
3.	E	10.	E	17.	D		
4.	E	11.	D	18.	A		
5.	D	12.	A	19.	E		
6.	A	13.	E	20.	E		
7.	E	14.	C	21.	D		

SECTION IV

1.	C	8.	B	15.	E	22.	C
2.	B	9.	D	16.	D	23.	B
3.	D	10.	E	17.	D	24.	C
4.	A	11.	A	18.	B	25.	D
5.	D	12.	D	19.	B	26.	C
6.	C	13.	D	20.	D		
7.	A	14.	B	21.	E		

CHAPTER FIVE: THE OCTOBER 2004 LSAT DECONSTRUCTED

The explanations below are presented in the same order that the questions are given on the exam. Page headers are provided to help you identify which questions are explained on each page, and if you encounter any unknown terms, a glossary is provided at the end of the book. Also, please keep in mind that all explanations draw on methods discussed in *The PowerScore LSAT Logic Games Bible* and *The PowerScore LSAT Logical Reasoning Bible*. Please refer to those texts if you desire a more detailed discussion of a particular concept or approach.

OCTOBER 2004 SECTION 1: READING COMPREHENSION

The first passage, which offers an evaluation of a legal services plan, is not overly complicated, although the last two questions on this passage did give test takers difficulty. The second passage deals with historiography, and the actions of early Chinese settlers as a valuable source of evidence for this field of study. Given the author's recurrent focus on this central theme, test takers found the set of questions that follow this passage to be the least challenging in the section. The third passage deals with the discovery of Nerve Growth Factor and its importance. Many found this to be the most challenging passage in the section. The last passage deals with the Modern Movement in architecture, and how the Modernists' lack of practicality led to the Movement's decline. The passage itself is not difficult to read, as the author deals with one theme throughout, but several of the questions require careful consideration.

Passage 1: Legal Services Plans

In this passage, the author introduces the concept of the legal services plan, discusses perspectives from both sides of the issue, and assesses the plan as unlikely to be beneficial to any of the parties involved.

Paragraph 1 Overview

In the first paragraph of this stimulus, the author introduces the concept of the pre-paid legal service plan, and the example of the plan used by The Canadian Auto Workers (CAW). There are several important elements that define the plan:

1. Members receive pre-paid or partially reimbursed legal services.
2. Plan staff lawyers are fully covered by the plan.
3. Members can use outside lawyers, who may or may not charge an additional fee.

The plan has operated since 1985, and as of 1988 included 45 percent of eligible CAW members, so it seems there has been a good response to the plan in the short term.

Paragraph 2 Overview

The second paragraph provides various arguments for and against the CAW plan, without taking a position on either side of the argument. The first half of the paragraph is devoted to lawyers' arguments against the plan, and the second half to the directors' arguments for the plan. We should be sure to note these *opposing viewpoints*, a very common theme among LSAT passages.
The lawyers are concerned that the plan tends to depress legal fees; although most lawyers in CAW

cities have not joined the plan, legal fees in those cities have dropped, in some cases to an unprofitable level. The plan's directors argue that clients benefit from reduced prices, and that lawyers benefit from increased business. The directors claim that if lawyers give excellent service, clients refer others who will pay the standard rate.

We might notice that the lawyers' arguments are based on evidence, while the directors' arguments are based on claims which are a bit more speculative.

Paragraph 3 Overview

The third paragraph begins with the author's evaluation, that pre-paid legal service plans in general will probably fail to benefit both lawyers and clients. We should note that this first sentence provides a strong statement of the author's main idea. The author lists the following arguments against these plans:
1. Established lawyers generally have plenty of clients, so this sort of plan would likely become a marketing device for less established lawyers, who tend to have less expertise and offer less client satisfaction.
2. Although lawyers can potentially get full-fee referrals, it is not clear that those referrals make up for providing plan services at the lower rates.
3. The lower fees brought in by Plan cases are likely to lead to less time spent on them by assigned lawyers, and lower quality overall.

Passage Summary

The author's *main point* is that pre-paid legal service plans, in the long-term, will probably fail to benefit both lawyers and clients. The author's *attitude*, therefore, is negative with respect to predictions for the long-term ramifications of adopting these plans.

The structure of the passage is as follows:

> Paragraph 1: Introduce one example of a pre-paid legal service plan
> Paragraph 2: Present arguments for and against this type of plan
> Paragraph 3: Assess these plans as unlikely to be beneficial, listing several
> specific reasons for this assertion.

Question #1: Main Point. The correct answer choice is (E)

The first question asks us to identify the main point of the passage, which makes the answer particularly conducive to prephrasing. On a main point question, it is always worthwhile to try to prephrase the main point of a passage before even looking at the answer choices. In this case, it seems that the author wrote this passage to introduce the reader to the concept of these legal plans, discuss perspectives on both sides of the issue, and, in the end, argue that the plans are unlikely to be of long term benefit to either law firms or clients.

Answer choice (A): This answer choice is wrong, because the author concludes in lines 38-40 that the plan will benefit neither clients nor lawyers. This choice incorrectly asserts that the plan will benefit lawyers in the long run.

Answer choice (B): This response is incorrect, because the author concludes that the plan is probably a bad idea. This choice makes the false claim that the plan will likely benefit both lawyers and clients.

Answer choice (C): This response may seem attractive, because it claims that pre-paid legal plans such as CAW's ought to be rejected. However, this choice claims that we should find "a more equitable plan." Since the author never discusses another plan, this claim is unsupported. Furthermore, the phrase "more equitable" implies that the author believes the plans discussed to be unfair to either lawyers or clients. Actually, the author argues that the plans would eventually hurt both lawyers and clients, so the author doesn't think that equitability, or fairness, is the problem.

Answer choice (D): This response merely reports the position of the lawyers, without including the author's evaluation. We should keep in mind that the correct answer to a main point question will likely cover the passage as a whole.

Answer choice (E): This is the correct answer choice, as it accurately sums up the main point of the passage, as well as our prephrase. The author's point is stated in lines 38-40, and this choice is little more than a paraphrase of those lines. Furthermore, by mentioning that the plans currently seem popular, this choice brings in the discussion from the first two paragraphs, and thus covers the entire passage.

Question #2: Main Point. The correct answer choice is (D)

A primary purpose question is much like a main point question, conducive to the same sort of prephrasing, prior to reading the answer choices. Again, the purpose of writing this passage seems to have been to introduce the reader to the concept of legal services, discuss points of view from both sides of the issue, and come out against these plans.

Answer choice (A): Since the passage does not discuss traditional methods of paying for legal services, this response is wrong.

Answer choice (B): The passage does discuss the growing popularity of pre-paid legal plans, but that is not the *primary* purpose of the passage, so this response is incorrect. Like many attractive wrong answers for this type of question, this response provides a topic that was discussed, but which does not represent the main purpose of the passage.

Answer choice (C): The author does not *trace* the effect of pre-paid plans on legal fees; the discussion of these potential effects is more speculative. Further, since this topic is covered only as part of a larger discussion, this does not represent the primary purpose.

Answer choice (D): This is the correct answer choice. Since the author discusses whether pre-paid legal plans will be beneficial in the long run, and decides that they probably will not be, this passage appears to have a cautionary purpose.

Answer choice (E): Since the passage never mentions any potential remedies to the author's concerns, this choice is incorrect.

Question #3: Must Be True. The correct answer choice is (E)

The author's predictions are found toward the end of the passage; we should note then that this question refers to the final paragraph. The correct response should reflect one of the reasons the author listed as a potential consequence of increased use of these legal plans.

Answer choice (A): Actually, the author believes that the pre-paid plans may have negative effects, and so do the lawyers who are critical of the plan, as discussed in the second paragraph.

Answer choice (B): The passage says that plan members would have access to reduced-cost legal services, not that the plans would then reduce the fees they charge.

Answer choice (C): The author states that lawyers who cannot benefit from the plan will refuse to become involved. This answer choice contradicts the author, so it is incorrect.

Answer choice (D): The author believes that the outcome will probably be negative for both lawyers and clients.

Answer choice (E): This is the correct answer choice. In lines 52-57, the author specifically states that lawyers will spend less time on complex cases.

Question #4: Passage Organization. The correct answer is (D)

This is a question about the organization of the passage, and these types of questions are often conducive to prephrasing. Since taking note of the organization is one of our primary tasks when reading a passage, we should again be aware that in this case, the author defines a concept, presents conflicting viewpoints, and then offers evaluation in favor of one side of the argument.

Answer choice (A): The passage doesn't really discuss *results*; most of the discussion is more theoretical, dealing with what *is likely to happen*. Also, although the author does not see these plans as beneficial, no proposals are offered to improve them.

Answer choice (B): This answer choice is incorrect on two counts. First, the author never compares past and present phenomena. Second, the author does not approve of the pre-paid legal plans.

Answer choice (C): This answer choice might be very attractive, but it is incorrect. The author does not discuss a proposal, but rather a course of action that has already been implemented. Further, the author does not make any recommendations, but rather speculates about the lack of long term benefits likely to be associated with implementation of this course of action (the use of legal services plans like the CAW).

Answer choice (D): This is the correct answer choice, as it accurately and completely corresponds to the presentation of material in the passage. This answer choice underscores the value of a strong prephrase as well.

Answer choice (E): This answer choice is incorrect, most notably based on its final assertion; the passage does not end with a presentation of further data, but rather will argumentation about the lack of benefits likely to be associated with legal plans like the CAW. Further, what the second part of this answer choice calls "evaluation of the practical value" is more a presentation of both sides of the issue than an evaluation.

Question #5: Must Be True. The correct answer choice is (C)

This question asks how proponents of the CAW plan believe cooperating lawyers will benefit. Once again it pays to be familiar with the Passage Organization, since the proponents' arguments can all be found in the second paragraph. Further, since the author discusses conflicting viewpoints, we should focus on the second half of the paragraph, which contains arguments in support of the plan.

Answer choice (A): While it does seem likely that there might be a more diverse clientele, and this answer choice provides an apparently reasonable assertion, the passage never suggests anything about participating lawyers' gaining expertise.

Answer choice (B): This answer choice involves issues brought up in the third paragraph, but it does not reflect what the proponents of the plan perceive as beneficial about adopting such plans. Again, although this seems a reasonable assertion, it is not "strongly suggested" in the passage, so this response is incorrect.

Answer choice (C): This is the correct answer choice, as it reflects the argument found in lines 33-37.

Answer choice (D): Since the passage suggests the possibility that lower fees will attract customers away from other firms, this response is incorrect. In fact, this response is somewhat contrary to lines 29-32 of the passage, which deal with the claim that these plans will attract customers who wouldn't otherwise use legal services.

Answer choice (E): This answer choice actually provides an argument *against* the legal plans, rather than one offered by proponents of the plan, so this choice is wrong.

Question #6: Must Be True. The correct answer choice is (A)

This question asks what *must be true* about members of the CAW plan. This answer must come from the first paragraph, which defines the plan. The second and third paragraphs are argumentative, not descriptive, and discuss what might be true, rather than what is certain.

Answer choice (A): This is the correct answer choice. In the first paragraph the author describes the CAW plan, and points out that members can use outside lawyers.

Answer choice (B): The author never discusses what the CAW plan members believe about the relative quality of legal services. While subscriptions to this service appear to be growing in number, this may be attributable to purely economic factors. We cannot assume anything about members' perceptions of quality.

Answer choice (C): The passage does not specifically state what kinds of legal services the plan members will require, so this response is incorrect.

Answer choice (D): The author states in lines 8-12 that outside lawyers can charge an additional fee, not that they always will. While it seems reasonable to assume that extra fees might be commonplace, we cannot assume that in *every* case members must pay an additional fee for outside services.

Answer choice (E): The author points out that the CAW plan was designed to benefit active and retired auto workers and their families. This answer choice, which asserts that membership is not limited to this group, cannot be justifiably concluded. There may be other members who are allowed to benefit from this plan, but the passage offers no information about any other members.

Question #7: Specific Reference, Function. The correct answer choice is (A)

This question refers to line 43, so it is advisable to begin reading for context a few lines earlier. The third paragraph begins with a pessimistic prediction about the long-term ramifications of these plans, and the author goes on to assert that the plans' main role will probably be to serve as marketing devices for unestablished attorneys. Since the passage goes on to say that this class of attorney is likely to offer less expertise and less customer satisfaction, it appears that the author does not believe that such use, as marketing devices, will be beneficial.

Answer choice (A): This is the correct answer choice. The author believes that the use of these plans as marketing devices is likely to bring more clients to lawyers with less expertise, thus reducing client satisfaction. It would therefore seem the author focuses on this aspect of the plan in order to point out its potential detriment.

Answer choice (B): Since the author does not discuss what plan administrators believe, this answer choice is incorrect. While it seems reasonable to believe that administrators might perceive their role in this way, the author never makes this point.

Answer choice (C): The author doesn't seem to believe the plans offer any long-term benefits to lawyers and clients, and specifically discusses how the aspect of marketing can be harmful. This response states that marketing is an "unequivocal" benefit, an assertion which is contrary to the passage.

Answer choice (D): The last paragraph consists of the author's own opinions, and does not attribute any ideas to established opponents of the plan.

Answer choice (E): Even though the discussion of marketing might explain why lawyers who are not yet established are willing to sign on to the plan, the passage does not define marketing as a "chief burden."

Passage 2: Historiography's New Source

Here, the author introduces the field of historiography, and one source of evidence that has recently been recognized as valuable in this field of study; on the Pacific coast, consideration of the actions of the early Chinese settlers can provide valuable insights into the developmental history of the region.

Paragraph 1 Overview

This passage begins with a definition of *historiography*, the writing of history based on certain authentic sources. The author points to an area that has recently attracted attention: The focus on response of explorers and settlers to their new landscapes to provide insight into the land's transformations. Previously, settlers' accounts have been used as the primary source of information about the settling of the United States Pacific Coast. European American explorers have been the traditional sources of such accounts, as they were commissioned by the U.S. government to keep detailed written records of their findings.

Paragraph 2 Overview

In the second paragraph, the author discusses historiographers' recent recognition of the need to expand their definition of a *source*. Historical accounts have often omitted the perspectives of Chinese settlers, in part because these people were less focused on documentation of such matters and therefore left less written records. Ignoring their influence would leave a cultural study incomplete, however, which is why historiographers have come to rely on other sources of historical data, including the actions of the Pacific Coast's Chinese settlers.

Paragraph 3 Overview

The third paragraph offers examples of the actions of the early Chinese settlers, showing how such evidence is relevant to the creation of a more complete cultural history of the area. With less access to more fertile soil, the Chinese found potential where the Europeans had not, using irrigation and taking advantage of some of the area's natural harvests, such as wild mustard, which had generally been seen only as a nuisance.

Paragraph 4 Overview

In the last paragraph, the author again emphasizes the importance of the Chinese settlers in shaping this territory, given their vision and expertise in irrigation and swamp reclamation. In the final sentence, the author argues that historiographers should pay attention to the Chinese influence on this region's settlement, considering its modern day irrigated farmlands and various specialty crops.

Summary

This passage was written to introduce the concept of historiography, and to point out the importance non-traditional information sources, especially with respect to the actions of the Chinese settlers, in understanding the development of the Pacific Northwest landscape. The *author's attitude* appears positive with respect to the settlers, and supportive of the appropriate addition of relevant sources to the field of historiography.

The structure of the passage is as follows:

Paragraph 1:   Introduce historiography, and its traditional sources of evidence
Paragraph 2:   Discuss the recent recognition of the need to expand on sources used, to include consideration of the actions of Chinese settlers
Paragraph 3:   List specific influences of the Chinese settlers
Paragraph 4:   Restate the importance of considering the input of these settlers on the landscape that developed

Question #8: Main Point. The correct answer choice is (C)

Since this is a Main Point question, we should attempt to form a prephrase before beginning to assess the answer choices. The main point of this passage, roughly, is to introduce historiography and discuss the need to include early settlers' actions as a source of historical information.

Answer choice (A): Part of the point of this passage is that historiographers need to expand their definition of a source if they are to have a complete understanding of the development of the landscape. If historiographers *need* to pay attention to non-written evidence made by Chinese settlers, it must be that this new evidence would offer some insight, so it seems highly unlikely that such new sources might simply confirm what historians already knew.

Answer choice (B): The passage suggested that the attention to the influence of Chinese settlers is recent, but that doesn't mean that historiographers have traditionally assumed that such evidence is irrelevant. They might simply have failed to see the existence of such evidence.

Answer choice (C): This is the correct answer choice, as it sums up the author's main point in writing this passage. The author states in lines 15-17 that historiographers have recognized a need to expand their definition a source, and in lines 54-60 the author states that historiographers cannot understand the development of the U.S. Pacific Coast without considering the actions of Chinese settlers.

Answer choice (D): Since the passage never suggests that Pacific Coast historiographers are divided over whether to pay attention to new types of evidence, this answer choice is unfounded. Furthermore, since historiographers recognize the need for new types of evidence, there appears to be some consensus. Finally, adding a new type of evidence is not the same as challenging a methodological foundation.

Answer choice (E): The author's point is not that until recently accounts have been *inaccurate*, but rather *incomplete*. Further, since the author explicitly confines the discussion to the historiography of the US Pacific Coast, we cannot justifiably select a response that refers to the whole of historiography.

Question #9: Specific Reference, Function. The correct answer choice is (C)

Since this question specifically refers to the third paragraph, it is once again advantageous to have an understanding of the structure of the passage. The third paragraph provides examples of the integral role of the Chinese settlers on the landscape, which is what we should prephrase, before moving on to the answer choices.

Answer choice (A): The examples in the third paragraph illustrate that Chinese settlers were atypical, and the author doesn't examine their settlement patterns.

Answer choice (B): It seems true that there is little written evidence of the practices of the Chinese settlers. But this is not because such records didn't survive, but because the Chinese settlers simply didn't leave "a self-conscious written record" (lines 21-27).
Further, since the question is about the function of the *third* paragraph, we can confidently eliminate this incorrect answer choice.

Answer choice (C): This is the correct answer choice. The author argues that considering the Chinese perspective on the landscape is critical to understanding the transformation of the US Pacific Coast. The third paragraph develops that argument by showing how the Chinese perspective was distinctive from the European perspective.

Answer choice (D): This answer choice is incorrect, since no debate among the historiographers is even alluded to in the passage. On the contrary, there appears to be a consensus among historiographers that new sources must be considered to have a more complete perspective on the development of the region.

Answer choice (E): The author's claim is not that the new source of evidence is *inconsistent* with traditional accounts, but rather that information about the actions of the Chinese settlers would *complement* the sources already considered. The new sources, when considered along with the traditional, would offer a more complete historiography.

Question #10: Must Be True. The correct answer choice is (E)

Since this question concerns the traditional sources of information for historiographers, the relevant reference point, considering the organization of the passage, would be the first paragraph.

Answer choice (A): Since the passage offers no information as to the timing of the Chinese settlement relative to the writing of the traditional sources of historiography, this answer choice is incorrect.

Answer choice (B): No mention is made in the passage concerning Native American accounts, so we cannot confidently confirm or deny this assertion. Since this is never stated in the passage, this answer choice is incorrect.

Answer choice (C): While it does seem likely that traditional sources are concerned with potential agricultural uses of the land, the author never specifies this, and certainly does not assert that this was a *primary* concern.

Answer choice (D): Once again, the author does not indicate precisely an American-European explorer's focus. The passage explicitly states that the Chinese were concerned with water sources, which should not be confused with American-European concern. Furthermore, once again there is no evidence as to the *primary* concern of any of the parties in the passage.

Answer choice (E): This is the correct answer choice, as it references the author's explicit statements in lines 8-14. Since historiographers have traditionally *depended* on the written records of European-American explorers, it makes sense that, traditionally, the *primary sources* have been the accounts of those explorers.

Question #11: Author's Perspective. The correct answer choice is (E)

Since this question asks for the response that the author would most likely disagree with, we should look for the answer choice that cannot be true based on the information provided in the stimulus.

Answer choice (A): Since the author acknowledges that a specific new source is likely to be valuable to the formation of a complete cultural perspective, this answer choice provides an assertion with which the author would likely agree.

Answer choice (B): Since there has been a change in what historiographers of the US Pacific Coast view as a source, some time might lapse before every historiographer knows of these new sources to be considered, so the author might agree with this assertion. In any case, there is no reason to assume that the author would disagree, so this answer choice is incorrect.

Answer choice (C): The author asserts that the historiography was incomplete without consideration of the acts of early Chinese settlers, so the same might be said for other sources not previously considered. Since the author would be likely to agree with this statement, this answer choice is incorrect.

Answer choice (D): Since this answer basically paraphrases the claims found in lines 15-17, this assertion is not one with which the author would *disagree*, so this answer is wrong.

Answer choice (E): This is the correct answer choice. The author's arguments relay the idea that, wherever written evidence neglects an important, contributing population, historiographers should investigate this new source of information. This assertion is based not on the fact that the settlers were *non-European*, but rather that they made *important contributions*. Thus the author would disagree with this answer choice, which asserts non-European participation is required to expand the definition of a source.

Question #12: Must be True, Except. The correct answer choice is (D)

This is another example of a question which becomes much easier when one considers passage organization. Since this question concerns early Chinese settler's interactions with the landscape, it seems that the relevant reference point would be the third paragraph, which deals almost exclusively with Chinese influences on the initial development of the region.

Answer choice (A): The new utilizations of local plants are discussed in lines 43-47, which describe the Chinese use of the wild mustard plant. Because this is an Except question, this answer choice, which accurately reflects information in the passage, should be eliminated.

Answer choice (B): The author specifically discusses the Chinese view of the land in lines 36-42, so this response provides an aspect discussed in the passage, and is therefore incorrect.

Answer choice (C): The discussion of Chinese ability to find unexpected agricultural potential in new areas and new plants, and use irrigation, as described in the third paragraph, is evidence that the Chinese had specialized agricultural skills. Since this is discussed in the passage, this answer choice is incorrect.

Answer choice (D): This is the correct answer choice, because the author makes no mention of initial

Chinese knowledge of agribusiness practices. The Chinese settlers helped lay the *foundations* for what is *now* the well-known, prosperous agribusiness of the region (lines 50-54). Since the question asked about the *settlers' initial interactions*, and the passage discusses the agribusiness of a later era, this choice is the only answer that is unsupported, and it is therefore the correct response to this EXCEPT question.

Answer choice (E): Since the passage explicitly states in lines 48-54 that the Chinese settlers had knowledge of irrigation systems, this choice is supported, and incorrect.

Question #13: Must be True. The correct answer choice is (B)

This question asks for the response that can be most reasonably inferred from the passage, so we must find the answer choice that is consistent with the author's reasoning. Often the most efficient approach to this sort of question is to review the choices and quickly eliminate any that are inconsistent with the passage, and then examine the remaining responses more closely.

Answer choice (A): While the early Chinese settlers did have important, transferable skills, there is no reason to presume that these were the result of having come from similar climates, and the passage offers no insight into whether the climate was the reason for their migration.

Answer choice (B): This is the correct answer choice, based on the fact that Chinese settlers brought these swamp reclamation skills to the Pacific Coast (lines 50-54). As for the fact that these methods were used in the 19th century, this is confirmed by the fact that the historiographers of the US Pacific Coast region have, as explicitly stated, traditionally used nineteenth-century European-American accounts (lines 8-14), and the Chinese settlers discussed fall in the same period (lines 21-27).

Answer choice (C): According to the passage, it was the Chinese settlers who used the wild mustard seeds, while the European settlers generally viewed the plants as weeds (lines 43-47).

Answer choice (D): It is valuable to study the actions of the Chinese settlers because there was little recorded by them. The actions of the *European* settlers have presumably already been considered by the historiographers, and this is *because* of the abundance of written sources available.

Answer choice (E): Since the author explicitly states in lines 21-22 that written records never existed in many cases, this choice, which suggests that such written records did exist at one time, is unsupported.

Question #14: Strengthen, Specific Reference. The correct answer choice is (B)

This question asks which answer choice most effectively strengthens the author's claim in the last sentence, which basically states the main point of the passage: a complete historiography requires consideration of the actions of the early Chinese settlers.

Answer choice (A): Since this response implies nothing directly about Chinese involvement in transforming the landscape, this answer is incorrect. Things change with time, and knowing what occurred during the past decade does not prove what occurred over a century ago. Further, the speed of the growth of the specialty crops relative to that of other crops has no clear relevance.

Answer choice (B): This is the correct answer choice, as this response would lend credibility to the claim that it was Chinese ancestors who converted the swamplands to grow the specialty crops currently cultivated by their Chinese descendants.

Answer choice (C): While this answer choice does provide evidence that irrigation is beneficial to agribusiness, it does nothing to provide support for the assertion that this benefit is attributable to early Chinese influence. Since this answer does not strengthen the claim from the last sentence in the passage, this choice is incorrect.

Answer choice (D): A steady increase in the efficiency of irrigations systems does not offer insight into their original source in the region. While this answer choice does appear to support the claim that irrigations improvements began in the nineteenth century, it does little to strengthen the claim that the early *Chinese* influence must be considered to form a more complete historiography.

Answer choice (E): Since we already know, given the passage, that agribusiness in the US Pacific Coast region is thriving, it does not strengthen the author's argument to add reasons to believe that things can grow well in that area. Although this response might make it more likely that irrigation is a good idea, it has nothing to do with whether such irrigation is attributable to early Chinese influence.

Passage #3: NGF

In this passage, the author discusses some of the specific research that led to Rita Levi-Montalcini's Nobel Prize winning discovery of NGF, or "Nerve Growth Factor," and the broad ramifications of this and subsequent discoveries regarding neurotrophic factors.

Paragraph 1 Overview

The author begins this passage with an introduction to the concept of neurotrophic factors: Chemicals which regulate the survival of nerve cells in animals. The first of these agents, known as NGF, was discovered in the 1950's by Rita Levi-Montalcini, who in 1986 shared the Nobel Prize for this discovery.

Paragraph 2 Overview

In the second paragraph, the author takes us back in time, to the mid-1940's, at which point Levi-Montalcini had hypothesized that many of a developing organism's immature nerve cells are normally programmed to die. She did research to confirm this study, and in 1949 found that embryos produce many more nerve cells than are needed, and that the number of cells adjusts downward to suit the tissue's necessity.
A later phase of the research dealt with chick embryos, whose nerve development could be stimulated with tumor implantation. Rita's hypothesis was that this stimulation is caused by a chemical produced by the tumors. The technique of tissue culture, which grows cells outside an organism, was used to investigate and then prove her hypothesis. Further research identified the tumor substance responsible for the observed effects, and Levi-Montalcini called it NGF, which stands for "nerve growth factor."

Paragraph 3 Overview

The author begins the third paragraph by pointing out that NGF was the first of many cell-growth factors found in animals. Levi-Montalcini's work, supplemented by later research, led to the determination that NGF is present in many tissues and fluids, and in heavy concentrations in some organs. This growth factor appears to be supplied by muscle cells, by organs over which nerve impulses will be transmitted, or sometimes by cells that are interspersed with the nerve tissues. The cells affected by NGF, generally those outside the brain and spinal cord, die if NGF is absent, or if anti-NGF antibodies are present.

Passage Summary

Paragraph One: Introduce the chemical NGF, its function, and its Nobel Prize winning discoverer.
Paragraph Two: Provide specific background on the hypotheses and research that lead to the discovery of NGF.
Paragraph Three: Provide further information about subsequent research which shed light on sources of NGF within an organism.

Question #15: Main Point. The correct answer choice is (B)

Again, with Main Point questions we should always try to prephrase an answer before looking at the choices provided. In this case, the main point of this passage is to introduce the reader to the important scientific discovery of NGF, as well as the steps taken by the scientist in confirming early hypotheses, and further details about NGF uncovered through subsequent research

Answer choice (A): The first half of this answer choice looks good, but the importance of the scientist's discovery was not to simply increase our understanding of chick embryos. Since the ramifications of Rita's discovery were further-reaching, this choice is wrong.

Answer choice (B): This is the correct answer choice. Most importantly, this response concludes that the discovery of NGF was pivotal to biochemistry, a fact reflected in the first paragraph.

Answer choice (C): This answer choice is relevant only to the second paragraph. Since the question asks for the main point of the passage, this answer should be eliminated. Furthermore, the passage states that Levi-Montalcini used the tissue-culture technique, not that she *devised* it.

Answer choice (D): This response confines its observations to the last paragraph, and does not reflect the main point of the passage. Furthermore, the passage actually stated that NGF is produced by tissues *to which the nerve cells will connect*, and this choice contrarily claims that NGF is produced only when nerve cells have already connected.

Answer choice (E): Once again, this response should be immediately eliminated simply because it is relevant only to the last paragraph. Furthermore, this choice is false given the passage, because it leaves out the possibility that nerve cells die if NGF is simply removed.

Question #16: Author's Perspective. The correct answer choice is (A)

This question asks why the discovery of NGF is important, from the perspective of the author. Since the author referenced the Nobel Prize and the importance this discovery to biochemistry in general, and because an entire paragraph is dedicated to the discoveries that Rita's findings made possible, we should look for an answer that underscores the significance of this contribution.

Answer choice (A): This is the correct answer choice. The last paragraph describes the more specific understanding that subsequent research led to, and the first paragraph describes the contribution to biochemistry as "crucial," and indicates that the contribution led to Rita's eventually winning the Nobel Prize.

Answer choice (B): Since Rita actually expected many of the results that she eventually observed, there is no support for the idea that the author believes anything about "unanticipated" results.

Answer choice (C): It seems that the discoveries in the last paragraph have been the most important from the author's perspective, rather than this particular confirmation. The author refers to the development as "crucial" to biochemistry, and it is advisable to look for a choice that explains the crucial nature of the development.

Answer choice (D): Levi-Montalcini's experiments did show observable reactions in the tissues of different species; however, the ultimate significance in these experiments lies in the fact that they led to the expansion of knowledge of how the nervous system develops and functions.

Answer choice (E): The experiments did identify a substance, produced by mouse tumors, that stimulates nerve growth. However, that was not the ultimate finding of this important scientific discovery, so this choice is wrong.

Question #17: Passage Organization, Function. The correct answer choice is (C)

This question exemplifies the value of understanding Passage Organization. Again, the second paragraph describes the experiments, and the third paragraph describes subsequent developments, so the correct response should reflect such a relationship. In reviewing the answer choices, it is advisable to eliminate any response that is not aligned with this description, and compare the remaining ones to the information in the passage.

Answer choice (A): The third paragraph offers no indication that Rita's conclusions required further confirmation. In fact, the third paragraph deals with some of the findings that are built on discoveries dealt with in the second paragraph.

Answer choice (B): In the third paragraph, the author discusses how science has built upon Levi-Montalcini's conclusions, which is rather contrary to the idea that science has undermined those conclusions.

Answer choice (C): This is the correct answer choice, as the third paragraph deals with further scientific developments based on discoveries discussed in the second paragraph.

Answer choice (D): In the third paragraph the author does not introduce any new, analogous substances, so this answer is incorrect.

Answer choice (E): Since the third paragraph discusses no experimental techniques, this response cannot be a description of the its function.

Question #18: Must Be True. The correct answer choice is (E)

In approaching this Must Be True question, we need to eliminate responses that are contrary to the facts and inferences within the passage.

Answer choice (A): This answer choice states that nerve cells produce anti-NGF, and is therefore unsupported by the passage, which never indicates precisely where anti-NGF is produced.

Answer choice (B): This choice asserts that cells not affected by NGF are less numerous than those affected by NGF, and that the different cells have the same qualities. While the passage does support the idea that there are different types of cells, not all of which are affected by NGF, but no further detail is offered as to similarities or quantitative comparisons.

Answer choice (C): The passage does suggest that a significant number of nerve cells probably die off in the process of an organism's development. However, since the passage never offers any information about the relative number of surviving cells, the conclusion that "few" cells are needed is unsupported.

Answer choice (D): Nothing in the passage indicates that some nerve cells have the capacity to change into other types of living tissue, so this answer choice is incorrect.

Answer choice (E): This is the correct answer choice, as it is supported by the discussion in the second paragraph. The passage states that an embryo initially produces more nerve cells than needed, and that the extra cells die off, which already supports the idea that the embryo produces nerve cells that do not end up connecting to anything. Furthermore, the second paragraph indicates that NGF governs the process by which some nerve cells develop and others die off (lines 14-26), and the third paragraph explains, in detail, that NGF is the causal factor that helps direct nerve cells toward target cells. It is reasonable to conclude that since some nerve cells will die off, they do not receive NGF, and do not connect with target cells.

Question #19: Must Be True. The correct answer choice is (A)

There is only one specifically described experiment, and that is the one that tests Rita's hypothesis that a chemical produced by mouse tumors stimulated nerve growth.

Answer choice (A): This is the correct answer choice. Lines 20-28 deal with Rita's hypothesis that a mouse tumor produces a chemical that stimulates nerve growth, and lines 28-39 provide a description the experiment.

Answer choice (B): This choice contains true information; in lines 14-20, the passage informs us that Rita actually did test the hypothesis that many nerve cells are pre-programmed to die. However, the passage does not *describe* that experiment, offering no details about the *process* of the experiment.

Answer choice (C): The author indicates in the first paragraph that NGF is not the only neurotrophic factor, and mentions anti-NGF antibodies in the last paragraph; however, the author never provides the particulars of experiments that tested any such hypothesis or produced these results.

Answer choice (D): The information in this answer choice may be true, given the fact that NGF is "especially concentrated in some organs." However, the passage does not deal with organs' concentration relative to that of surrounding tissue. Further, this is not the hypothesis that the passage described the *testing experiment* for, so this answer choice is incorrect.

Answer choice (E): While this is apparently the case, given the information in the third paragraph, the passage never deals with any specific experiment that confirmed this hypothesis.

Question #20: Must Be True. The correct answer choice is (D)

Once again, for Must Be True questions, we should seek to eliminate all answer choices that are clearly contrary to the information within the passage.

Answer choice (A): Since the author never discusses neurotrophic factors other than NGF, this response is unsupported.

Answer choice (B): This answer choice is only partially accurate, and therefore incorrect. It is true that NGF was the first neurotrophic factor to be identified, and that other such substances have since been found. However, the passage never offers any information about the relative degree to which these various factors are currently understood, so this answer is incorrect.

Answer choice (C): The passage only deals with the scientist's discovery of NGF. While there is discussion of other such factors, there is no reference to her having discovered them. This answer choice is thus unsupported and incorrect.

Answer choice (D): This is the correct answer choice. In the first paragraph, the author describes NGF as the *first* such agent discovered, and that neurotrophic factors regulate nerve cell survival as well as "some specialized functions." Since these further functions are not specified within the passage, and the role of NGF as discussed seems to be relevant only to growth and survival, the assertion in this answer choice seems quite likely.

Answer choice (E): Since the experiments discussed in the passage only concern NGF with respect to nerve growth, there is no reason to assume that the observed effect were caused by other neurotrophic factors. Other factors certainly *might have* come into play, but we cannot assume that this was the case.

Passage Four: Architecture's Modern Movement

In this passage, the author deals with the Modern Movement in architecture, whose aesthetic ideals made construction prohibitively expensive, helping to lead to the Movement's decline.

Paragraph 1 Overview

The author begins this passage by introducing the perspective of proponents of the Modern Movement in architecture: they believed that Modernist architecture better reflected technological advances of the time, and was better suited to modern building methods, than the older styles of architecture. As is the case with many LSAT passages, however, the author provides this perspective only to then refute it, with the observation that Modernist architecture fostered designs that were actually not very well-suited to building methods of the time.

Paragraph 2 Overview

The author begins this paragraph with the assertion that it was the strict adherence of the Modernist architects and critics to their ideology that probably led to the decline of the Movement (lines 10-12). The author then provides a timeline of the growth of the Movement's popularity, from its counter-culture beginnings in the 1920's, to its dominance of mainstream architecture in the 1940's. By the 1950's, according to the passage, only those architects who advanced the Movement received favorable architectural critiques. These positive critiques tended to ignore all else to focus exclusively on the "Modern" features of the works of various architects, including Otto Wagner and Frank Lloyd Wright (since the author provides these two as examples of architects who received favorable treatment from the Modernist critics, their names will likely be worth noting).

Paragraph 3 Overview

In the third paragraph the author expands on the Movement's decline, attributable in part to the Modernists' ignorance of building methods, and to their reluctance to admit that their concerns were chiefly aesthetic. Further, specialization within the construction industry fragmented a process that had previously involved only a small group of tradesmen. Thus architectural design had to allow for a greater degree of error from the group effort of various trades. One chief Modernist ideal, to expose structural materials, required extremely high levels of craftsmanship, making this style prohibitively expensive.

Paragraph 4 Overview

In the final paragraph, the author points out that, as Postmodernist architects recognized, the exposure of structural elements limited Modernist building design. Since Modernist architects would not abandon their ideals, this impractical design contributed to the Movement's decline in popularity.

Passage Summary

The Modern Movement in architecture, in spite of enjoying popularity during the early to mid-twentieth century, eventually declined, resulting in part from Modernist architects' unwillingness to abandon impractical ideals.

The *structure* of the passage is as follows:

Paragraph 1: Introduce Modernists's claims about their architecture and refute them
Paragraph 2: Provide timeline of the Movement's rise in popularity and critical reception
Paragraph 3: Expand on why the Movement was impractical and prohibitively expensive
Paragraph 4: Conclude, restating some of the reasons for the Movement's decline

Question #21: Main Point. The correct answer choice is (A)

Again we see a Main Point question as the first to follow the passage, so we should prephrase an answer and look for the answer choice that most closely aligns with our prephrase.

Answer choice (A): This is the correct answer choice. The author's statements suggest that the Modernists were too devoted to their ideology, and did not tend to incorporate practical considerations into their designs.

Answer choice (B): The author suggests that the Modernist architects were not entirely rational with respect to practical design, so this choice is incorrect.

Answer choice (C): In fact, Modernist architecture appears to have been highly incompatible with modern construction methods of the time, so this response is contrary to the passage.

Answer choice (D): Since Modernist architecture was so inconsistent with modern construction methods, it would not make sense to conclude that Modernist architecture came from those methods.

Answer choice (E): The passage offers a critique of the Modern Movement, but does not seek to explain what proponents believed.

Question #22: Must Be True. The correct answer choice is (A)

This question asks us to choose a situation that is similar to the problems with construction industry changes described in the passage, which brought a more fragmented process and less accuracy as a result.

Answer choice (A): This is the correct answer choice. Lines 40-44 relate a movement from a craft carried out by a relatively few tradespeople to an industry involving many specialized workers, which is similar to the movement from garment maker to assembly line. The effect described in lines 44-47 was that design had to account for a new process and greater inaccuracy at each stage, which is similar to the scenario of an assembly line that would produce less precisely tailored clothing.

Answer choice (B): Since lines 40-47 discuss accuracy, not beauty, this answer choice does not provide a proper analogy. While accuracy can be readily measured, beauty is subjective.

Answer choice (C): Since the relevant lines in the stimulus do not refer to usefulness, but only to accuracy, this response is incorrect.

Answer choice (D): While the inaccuracy described in the passage was a part of the process of initial production, the reaction of people who receive a letter is not part of the process of composing the letter, so this is not a proper analogy.

Answer choice (E): Lines 40-47 deal with accuracy, but not with what is fashionable, (another subjective measure), so this response is incorrect.

Question #23: Author's Perspective. The correct answer choice is (C)

This question asks for the best description of the author's attitude toward the proponents of the Modern Movement. We should look for an answer that reflects the author's perspective that they prioritized aesthetics over practicality, which led to the Movement's decline.

Answer choice (A): "Forbearing" indicates that the author held back. Since the author is actually highly critical and very direct, this choice is not accurately descriptive of the attitude reflected in the passage.

Answer choice (B): The author neither defends the proponents nor takes a defensive stance towards them.

Answer choice (C): This is the correct answer choice. The author is definitely unimpressed by the proponents' lack of practicality with respect to construction.

Answer choice (D): This is an attractive answer choice, because the author's discussion might be seen as reflecting frustration at the Movement's failure to consider realistic construction costs. However, "exasperation" suggests an emotional response that goes beyond what is reflected in the stimulus. The author is not exactly at wit's end concerning how to deal with the now defunct Modern Movement, so this is not the appropriate response.

Answer choice (E): If the author were completely indifferent to the Movement, this passage would probably not have been written. This author clearly has an opinion, so this choice is incorrect.

Question #24: Author's Perspective. The correct answer choice is (E)

This question concerns the author's attitude about the Modernist ideal of exposing structural elements, so we can always refer to the third paragraph if we are unsure. As noted previously, the author believes that this ideal ignored the realities of construction and contributed to the decline of Modernist architecture.

Answer choice (A): This ideal was not "repudiated" by its architects; it was these architects' unwillingness to abandon this idea that led to the decline of the Movement. Furthermore, the actions of architects themselves did not undermine the ideal; the practical realities of the construction industry did.

Answer choice (B): Since the passage did not relate popular appeal to the frequency of production of Modernist architecture, this response is incorrect. If anything, the passage implies that the expense of Modernist architecture may have contributed to some rarity. In any case, the passage does not explicitly claim that this ideal of Modernist architecture was rarely achieved.

Answer choice (C): The passage states that the ideal was unrealistic because the requirements of construction made it prohibitively expensive. The author never discusses whether builders were willing to attempt these projects, so this choice is incorrect.

Answer choice (D): The author mentions Frank Lloyd Wright and Otto Wagner as examples of somewhat Modernist architects whom the modernists championed as wholly Modernist architects. The claim that those two originated the ideal of exposing structural elements, however, is unsupported.

Answer choice (E): This is the correct answer choice. The theme of the third paragraph is that Modernist architects did not understand the practicalities of construction, and were actually interested primarily in aesthetics (lines 34-36). The fact that the Modernists insisted on exposing structural elements despite the problems, described in lines 48-57, illustrates that they were impractical with regard to this issue.

Question #25: Author's Perspective, Specific Reference. The correct answer choice is (D)

This question asks which words, in context, best reveal the author's attitude toward the Modernists. With this kind of question it is always advisable to read the material surrounding the reference in each choice. The appropriate response must involve the author's evaluation of the proponents; anything else should be immediately eliminated. If left with more than one response, we should seek the one that most closely reflects the author's general opinion of the proponents: their ideology committed them to ignore some of the practical realities of construction.

Answer choice (A): The author does not agree that Modernist architecture reflects a truly functional spirit, as is evidenced by his criticism that the Modernist architects do not seem to consider functional concerns, so this response is incorrect.

Answer choice (B): "Tended," in context, references an observation about how the proponents of Modernist architecture treated non-modernist architects. Since this offers little insight into the author's attitude about the proponents themselves, this answer choice is incorrect.

Answer choice (C): The author has a generally negative view of Modernist proponents and probably does not view them as innovators. Furthermore, "innovators" is used to describe two architects that the author implies were not fully Modernist. The author would not use the term "innovators" to describe the proponents of the Modern Movement.

Answer choice (D): This is the correct answer choice, as this selection specifically describes the actions of the proponents from the author's perspective. "Conveniently" describes the fact that the proponents acknowledged only the evidence that appeared to support the Movement. That is consistent with the author's view that the proponents' beliefs were impractical.

Answer choice (E): "Degree of inaccuracy" describes the realities of the construction industry that the Modernist architects did not allow for, and not the position of the proponents from the author's perspective.

Question #26: Specific Reference, Function. The correct answer choice is (B)

The author referred to Wright and Wagner as examples of architects who were touted by Modernists as innovators within the Movement. Although their works were not exclusively Modernist, proponents conveniently focused on Modern aspects of the work.

Answer choice (A): This response might be attractive, because it seems to coincide with the idea that the Modern Movement eventually grew somewhat unpopular. However, we cannot conclude that Frank Lloyd Wright and Otto Wagner were initially unpopular simply because the Modern Movement later declined.

Answer choice (B): This is the correct answer choice. Proponents did claim that these architects represented the Movement, and chose to emphasize aspects of their work which supported this claim.

Answer choice (C): The passage never suggests that Wagner and Wright helped to popularize the movement, only that they were referred to as innovators by some within the Movement.

Answer choice (D): The passage does not offer much insight into what inspired the work of Wagner and Wright, other than to refer to some Modernist aspects. Since we have no way of knowing how clients' needs came into play, this answer choice is incorrect.

Answer choice (E): Since proponents of Modernist architecture treated Frank Lloyd Wright and Otto Wagner as young, Modernist innovators, there is no reason to conclude that they were perceived to be "at odds with the principles of Modernism."

Question 27: Main Point. The correct answer choice is (A)

The correct response to a primary purpose question should always align with the main point of the passage, which in this case is that the ideology of the Modernists led to the decline of their movement.

Answer choice (A): This is the correct answer choice. The author describes some major factors that contributed to the decline of the Modern Movement in architecture, and this response reflects the author's strong statements of point.

Answer choice (B): This passage references only past events, with no predictions for the future, so this response is incorrect.

Answer choice (C): This choice may appear attractive, since the author does attack the Modernist proponent's viewpoint. Since the Movement appears to have already declined, however, the author's purpose is not to correct misunderstandings amongst Modernist proponents, but rather to explain likely reasons for the decline.

Answer choice (D): The author does not anticipate a possible criticism of the Modernist Movement, but rather presents one, so this choice is incorrect.

Answer choice (E): This choice might appear attractive, because it mentions incompatible viewpoints, and the author's viewpoint is definitely incompatible with that of the Movement's proponents. However, this response mentions "contrasting," which does not necessarily imply evaluation. Since the author stands clearly on one side of this discussion, and believes the proponents had a flawed position. Generally, this sort of response would describe a passage in which the author contrasted *other peoples' viewpoints*.

Overview: Most test takers found this section to be the more challenging of the two logical reasoning sections on this LSAT. Both sections present the most difficult questions toward the end of the section, as is often the case with the LSAT, but this section begins with a challenging Flaw in the Reasoning question, and includes many different question types among the most difficult. Question #20 is a very hard Weaken question, #22 provides a challenging Parallel Reasoning problem, and many test takers had particular difficulty with questions #24 (Method of Reasoning, Argument Part) and #16 (Main Point). This section contains four Must Be True questions, and four Assumption questions, three of which are Supporter Assumption questions (#9, #18, and #23) and only one of which is a Defender Assumption question (#5). The section contains three Weaken questions, one of which is also an Except question, and three Flaw in the Reasoning questions.

Question #1: Flaw in the Reasoning—CE. The correct answer choice is (B)

This stimulus provides a definition of the term "tidal range," followed by information about one particularly large one. The author then makes the following causal argument:

> Premise: The only forces involved in causing *tides* are gravitational in nature.

> Conclusion: Thus the *magnitude* of tidal ranges must be entirely caused by those same gravitational forces.

Note that the argument jumps from a premise that deals with the cause of *tides* to a conclusion about the cause of *the magnitude of tidal ranges*. That leap is unjustified; although tides are induced by gravity, tidal range size may be affected by other factors. Since the question asks us to identify the flaw, we should look for a response that discusses this leap (or any answer choice that points out the failure to consider alternative causes of a tidal range's magnitude).

Answer choice (A): The use of only one example is not a flaw in the reasoning; the example was used to illustrate how big tidal ranges can get, so more examples wouldn't be necessarily required in this context.

Answer choice (B): This is the correct answer choice, as it points out the author's failure to consider other conditions (alternative causes) that might affect the size of a tidal range.

Answer choice (C): The author discusses what causes the actual magnitude of tidal ranges, not their measurement. This choice does not describe a flaw, so it is incorrect.

Answer choice (D): The author does not discuss *most* activity in the world's oceans, only tides and tidal ranges, so this choice is wrong.

Answer choice (E): Since the argument concludes only that gravitational forces account for the magnitude of tidal ranges, it is not important to differentiate between the tidal effects of the moon's gravity and those of the sun's.

Question #2: Must Be True. The correct answer choice is (E)

In this stimulus, the cardiologist makes several observations about whether bypass surgery is always the best remedy for coronary artery disease:

> 1. Coronary bypass surgery is commonly performed when certain less expensive and less risky procedures would be as effective.
> 2. Bypass surgery is especially debatable for single-vessel disease.

Answer choice (A): The operative term in this choice is "all." The stimulus does not support the idea that coronary bypass surgery is riskier than *all* other therapies.

Answer choice (B): We cannot infer from the use of "commonly" that there has been any increase in frequency over time, especially since the stimulus does not concern different time periods. Furthermore, it is wrong to infer that bypass surgery is "needless," just because alternative (or even superior) remedies exist.

Answer choice (C): The cardiologist says that bypass surgery is *especially* debatable when only one vessel is involved, which does not necessarily mean that such surgery is desirable when more than one vessel is involved.

Answer choice (D): While bypass surgery is especially debatable for single-vessel disease, the cardiologist does not say that it especially expensive.

Answer choice (E): This is the correct answer choice. The stimulus states that bypass surgery is commonly performed when other equally effective, less risky remedies are available.

Question #3: Resolve the Paradox. The correct answer choice is (C)

This stimulus presents the following paradox:

> Premise: In the past, combining different age groups caused confusion and boredom.

> Premise: Now, mixed-age classrooms are turning out to be stimulating and beneficial.

In Resolve the Paradox questions, we must look for the answer choice which is compatible with the two apparently contradictory premises in the stimulus. Sometimes we can prephrase the resolution of this paradox. For example, the shift from "confusion and boredom" to "more efficient learning and stimulation" suggests a possible change in teaching style, materials, etc. It is also possible that certain subjects are better suited to combined age groups.

Answer choice (A): It is unclear that a larger classroom could resolve the "confusion and boredom." Even if we felt that the "larger enrollment" was indicative of the current, better situation, that increase would not resolve the apparent discrepancy.

Answer choice (B): The present classes are the good ones, but this response says that the past classes were better equipped. This Opposite answer would serve to broaden the apparent discrepancy.

Answer choice (C): This is the correct choice, as it offers an explanation for the improvement that come with the shift from old classrooms and the new ones: A new emphasis on group projects. This idea is consistent with both premises in the stimulus and explains why modern mixed-age classrooms enjoy greater success.

Answer choice (D): A greater range of ages would seem likely to result in more confusion and boredom. This choice appears to broaden the paradox and is therefore incorrect.

Answer choice (E): This choice might help to explain why the learning environment has changed, without other information there would be no reason to assume this would cause an improved learning environment.

Question #4: Weaken—CE. The correct answer choice is (B)

In this stimulus, the author considers two variables which are correlated, and jumps to the conclusion that there is a causal relationship:

> Premise: Human arrival on Tiliga Island coincided with decrease in population and diversity of bird species on the island.

> Conclusion: Therefore humans must have *caused* this decrease.

This is a Cause/Effect stimulus with a weaken question, and as we know, there are several specific ways to weaken a Cause/Effect argument. Since we know the supposed effect in this case (diminishing bird population and diversity), we might want to keep alternative causes in mind as we consider the answer choices.

Answer choice (A): This answer choice actually strengthens the argument in the stimulus. If there were no other natural predators of this species, it seems more likely that the decrease was attributable to the human presence on the island.

Answer choice (B): This choice strengthens the causal argument, by pointing out that when humans were not present, species apparently did not disappear as quickly.

Answer choice (C): This is the correct answer choice. A deadly microbe could serve as an alternate cause for the bird extinctions, thus weakening the causal argument in the stimulus.

Answer choice (D): The birds that the islanders ate likely lived on the island before the islanders' arrival, so evidence of the birds' earlier existence has no effect on the causal argument. This response does not weaken the author's argument.

Answer choice (E): The inability to fly would likely make these birds an easier target for their new human predators, so this answer choice would seem to strengthen the argument in the stimulus. This choice certainly does not weaken the argument and is therefore incorrect.

Question #5: Assumption—CE. The correct answer choice is (A)

In this stimulus, the author discusses the correlation of two variables and incorrectly concludes that a causal relationship exists:

> Premise: Musician adults trained from childhood have, on average, larger corpus callosa than adult non-musicians.

> Conclusion: Therefore musical training must *cause* these differences in the brain.

This argument is flawed, because the author attempts to draw a causal conclusion (that musical training increases corpus callosum size), where only a correlation between the two variables has been shown. Since this is a Cause/Effect question, we should consider other possibilities. Perhaps there is some other variable at work, causing both an enlarged corpus and a predisposition to music. Or perhaps cause and effect have been reversed, and in reality having a larger corpus callosum *predisposes* one to take up music.

Since this is an assumption question, we can apply the Assumption Negation technique by seeking a response which, when negated, weakens the causal argument.

Answer choice (A): This is the correct answer choice. Negating this choice, if the corpus callosa of musicians were naturally larger, the argument would fail. Thus the argument must assume that the corpus collasa are initially similarly sized.

Answer choice (B): The argument concludes that musical training *in general* causes changes in the brain, and that the effect is *particularly pronounced* when training begins at an early age. This response states that music training at older ages cannot cause anatomic brain changes, which is somewhat contrary to the author's argument. Therefore this cannot be an assumption required by the argument.

Answer choice (C): The argument compares musicians to non-musicians, so it does not matter whether two similarly trained musicians have roughly equal corpus callosa, only whether those musicians in general have larger callosa than non-musicians.

Answer choice (D): The argument specifically stated that, *on average*, the corpus callosum of a musician is larger than that of a non-musician, so the argument would not make the needless assumption that *all* musicians have larger corpus callosa. Applying the Assumption Negation Technique, we would see that the argument is unaffected by the assertion that "*not* all musicians have larger corpus collosa than any non-musicians."

Answer choice (E): By logically negating this answer choice, we get, "adult non-musicians *did* participate in stimulating activities when they were children." This negated version does nothing to weaken the author's argument, so we know this choice does not reflect an assumption required by the argument.

Question #6: Point at Issue. The correct answer choice is (B)

The dialogue presented in this stimulus reflects Chai's belief that the term "tree" is *scientifically inadequate*, because this one term is used to describe plants with different lineages. Dodd responds that use of the term "tree" does highlight some important structural similarities between the two, making the term *scientifically acceptable*.

With a dialogue stimulus, we can often glean more about the point at issue from the words of the second speaker, who is more likely to spell out the point of contention between the two. In this case the pair is arguing about the scientific adequacy of the term "tree."

Answer choice (A): The dialogue does not reflect either speaker's opinion on the general advisability of using ordinary terms; the discussion surrounds the acceptability of a term for a specific context.

Answer choice (B): This is the correct answer choice. Chai claims that because of the different lineages, "tree" is unacceptable. Dodd argues that "tree" is acceptable, so the two disagree on this issue.

Answer choice (C): We are not given enough information in the stimulus to assess either speaker's perspective on this issue, so this choice is incorrect.

Answer choice (D): Neither Chai nor Dodd is concerned about lay terminology; they are interested in whether certain terms are scientifically adequate.

Answer choice (E): Both Chai and Dodd would agree with this statement, given that Chai accepts Dodd's definition. Even if Chai did not accept that coniferous and deciduous plants were similar in structure, he might still agree with this general assertion.

Question #7: Strengthen. The correct answer choice is (D)

This stimulus concerns plans for a controlled volume headphone, recommended to reduce hearing loss among teenagers. The author concludes that the plan will not work, based on the premise that teenagers are the ones who purchase the headphones. The apparent assumption in this case is that teenagers prefer not to have the volume of their music controlled in this way, despite the risks involved.

Answer choice (A): Even if stereo headphones pose the greatest threat, that does not strengthen the case that teenagers will refuse to buy the safer headphones.

Answer choice (B): Even if no other cause is as damaging as loud music through stereo headphones, this does not help to demonstrate that teenagers will continue to buy the unsafe headphones. This choice is irrelevant to the argument and therefore incorrect.

Answer choice (C): The fact that parents do not tend to listen to loud music through headphones does not strengthen the argument that teenagers would avoid volume control, so this choice is incorrect.

Answer choice (D): This is the correct answer choice. If teenagers choose the louder levels despite the risk, they would not be likely to purchase the new, volume-controlled headphones.

Answer choice (E): This choice offers a different type of headphone than the one already being planned. This is irrelevant to the argument in the stimulus.

Question #8: Weaken Except. The correct answer choice is (E)

The argument in this stimulus is fairly straightforward, though clearly flawed:

> Premise: Natural pesticides aren't harmful.

> Conclusion: Thus the additional threat from *synthetic* pesticides is minimal.

This reasoning is weak, because it neglects the potential dissimilarities between natural and synthetic pesticides. Since this is an Except question, we should eliminate the four choices that *do* weaken the argument, in search of the single answer choice that *does not weaken* the argument.

Answer choice (A): This response weakens the argument; by pointing out that humans have had a long time to get used to natural pesticides, the author strengthens the contrast between natural and synthetic pesticides.

Answer choice (B): This response points out that spraying with synthetic pesticides leads to higher relative concentrations, which makes it more likely that spraying with synthetics could be dangerous. This response weakens the argument, and is incorrect.

Answer choice (C): If synthetic pesticides have a more highly concentrated toxicity, they might be more dangerous, so this is another response which weakens the argument.

Answer choice (D): If synthetic pesticides affect a wider variety of species, this would increase the likelihood that humans might be affected, so this choice weakens the author's argument.

Answer choice (E): This is the correct answer choice. If the synthetic pesticides are similar in chemical structure to the natural pesticides, that would strengthen the claim that we might expect the same degree of harmlessness in synthetic pesticides as in their natural counterparts. This response does not weaken the argument and is therefore correct.

Question #9: Assumption. The correct answer choice is (C)

The conclusion in this case is presented in the last sentence of the stimulus: "an expensive wine is not always a good wine." In other words, an expensive wine is sometimes not a good wine. This conclusion is based on the premise that vineyard reputation is a factor in wine pricing:

> Premise: High Price $\longrightarrow$ Based on good reputation

> Conclusion: High Price $\overset{s}{\longleftrightarrow}$ Good wine

When we diagram these two conditional statements, the variable present in both is "High Price." For the conclusion above to be properly drawn, there must be some other premise that is not explicitly stated; this is our supporter assumption, which fills in the gap between the premise and the conclusion.

We should thus seek the answer choice that somehow links the remaining two variables: "Based on reputation" and "Good wine."

Answer choice (A): The author concludes that price is not always a good indicator of a wine's quality, not that some breach of justice has occurred because of that discrepancy. What *should* occur is irrelevant, so this choice is wrong.

Answer choice (B): The author concludes that expense is *not always* a good indicator of quality, so the claim that price is *never* a good indicator is not an assumption required by the argument. Furthermore, referring back to our prephrase, since this answer choice makes no reference to reputation, we know that it cannot be correct.

Answer choice (C): This is the correct answer choice. This answer choice links the two variables as discussed above. If we add this premise to those provided in the stimulus, we can see that the conclusion can then be properly drawn:

> Premise: High Price $\longrightarrow$ Based on good reputation
> Assumption: Good reputation $\xleftarrow{s}\rightarrow$ Good wine

> Thus, we can link the two statements:
> High Price $\longrightarrow$ Based on good reputation $\xleftarrow{s}\rightarrow$ Good wine

> This allows us to properly draw the inference which is the author's conclusion:
> High Price $\xleftarrow{s}\rightarrow$ Good wine

Answer choice (D): This answer choice does not link the variables discussed above, and instead introduces the new variable, grape quality. Since this choice does not involve the quality of the *wine*, it cannot be the supporter assumption required by the argument.

Answer choice (E): We cannot glean anything about the pricing methods of reputed wines based on the pricing of lesser-known vineyards. Logically, this choice has no effect on the argument, so it is incorrect.

Question #10: Resolve the Paradox. The correct answer choice is (B).

The paradox in this case involves nicrophorus beetle parents, who remain in pairs to feed their larvae, leading to the expectation that the larvae benefit from the presence of both parents. Surprisingly, however, the larvae grow larger when one parent is removed.

Since we've been presented with a potential discrepancy, and the question asks us to explain the situation, we should consider why the larvae might fare better with only one parent. If we can prephrase an answer, we should do so. Otherwise we should look for the answer choice that is consistent with the apparently contrary premises in the stimulus.

Answer choice (A): This answer choice actually broadens the paradox, making it more difficult to explain why the larvae would grow larger with only one parent present.

Answer choice (B): This is the correct answer choice. If both parent beetles would normally consume the family food supply, the absence of one would mean more food for the larvae.

Answer choice (C): This is another answer choice which broadens the paradox. If there is a parent resting while the other one is providing, there would be more reason to expect that the larvae with two parents might be better off.

Answer choice (D): Since the stimulus concerns the first week, and this response concerns occurrences from after this period, this choice cannot help to resolve the discrepancy and is therefore incorrect.

Answer choice (E): If this is the case, we might expect greater results from the pair. This broadens the paradox, rather than explaining it.

Question #11: Must Be True. The correct answer choice is (B)

This stimulus consists of several observations and no conclusion, so a Must Be True question is likely to follow. A few facts are introduced:

> 1. Scientists once thought classical Euclidean geometry was *essential* to mathematically representing the universe.
> 2. Scientists came to feel *non*-Euclidean geometries were more useful in developing certain areas of scientific theory.
> 3. One most widely accepted theory is based on non-Euclidean geometry.

The suggestion is that most scientists believe that Euclidean geometry may be inessential to the formation of a correct mathematical representation of the universe, because other geometries might provide better bases for certain theories. If a non-Euclidean geometry is *sufficient*, then Euclidean geometry is *not necessary*.

Answer choice (A): There is no suggestion about scientists' beliefs concerning the progression of science relative to that of math.

Answer choice (B): This is the correct answer choice. The author suggests that most scientists do not believe that Euclidean geometry is essential to creating a correct mathematical representation of the universe.

Answer choice (C): The stimulus concerns *accurate, useful*, theories, and never discusses *completeness*. This choice is unsupported by the stimulus, and therefore incorrect.

Answer choice (D): This choice discusses "uniquely correct" methods, which is not a concept presented in the stimulus. Furthermore, the stimulus never argues that *all* accurate scientific theories *require* mathematical bases, just that *certain* scientific theories find some mathematical bases *useful*.

Answer choice (E): The stimulus does not establish that Euclidean geometry was the only mathematically correct means of representing the universe. The inference that scientists currently prefer useful theories to correct theories is thus unsupported.

Question #12: Must Be True—Principle. The correct answer choice is (A)

In this stimulus, we are told that lawyers will sometimes employ authorities with less expertise, simply because these people sound more convincing in court. Since we are asked to choose a scenario that most closely conforms to the reflected principle, we can apply the *test of abstraction*. We might abstract as follows: "In some cases, persuasiveness can be more important than knowledge as a criterion for selection."

Answer choice (A): This is the correct answer choice. Some politicians win on the basis of public perception; they can run a persuasive campaign, without necessarily having particular expertise with regard to political issues. This is a case in which persuasiveness is more important than knowledge.

Answer choice (B): This response might appear slightly attractive, because it involves persuasiveness. It is not perfectly analogous, however because it doesn't involve a contrast to any other criterion.

Answer choice (C): This choice is an Opposite answer, because it involves selection on the basis of the merit of a singer's voice, and recommends that public perception be ignored. This principle is contrary to the one reflected in the stimulus.

Answer choice (D): The stimulus does not concern coercion, with or without reinforcement, nor does the stimulus prescribe any particular course of action, so this choice is incorrect.

Answer choice (E): This answer choice provides that companies generally try to fit the person to the job rather than vice versa. This is different from the principle reflected in the stimulus, which is more focused on selection criteria.

Question #13: Justify the Conclusion. The correct answer choice is (A)

In this stimulus, we are given several conditional statements:

1) The solution to any *non-government-caused* serious environmental problem can *only* lay in major consumer habit changes (MC). This can be diagrammed as follows:

   $$S_{\cancel{\varnothing}} \longrightarrow MC$$

2) These major changes will *only* occur with economic enticement (EE):

   $$MC \longrightarrow EE$$

3) Therefore (i.e., in *conclusion*), few problems of any kind will be solved without enticement. In other words, if there is no enticement, not many problems will be solved:

   $$\cancel{EE} \longrightarrow \text{many problems solved. (contrapositive: many problems solved} \longrightarrow EE)$$

The leap between the premises is subtle, but important: The argument begins with the premise that economic enticement is needed to bring about consumer changes necessary to solve *non-government-caused problems*. The author then jumps to the conclusion that without these economic enticements, few environmental *problems* will be solved (whether or not government-caused). When we notice a leap like this one and are asked to justify the conclusion, we should seek the answer choice which fills in this gap and allows for the conclusion to be properly drawn.

Answer choice (A): This is the correct answer choice. The premises in the stimulus only offer information about non-government-caused problems. If we assume, as this answer choice provides, that most problems fall into this category (of non-government-caused problems), then the premises in the stimulus justify the author's conclusion.

This answer choice can be diagrammed as follows:

        Major problem —— ^{M} —→ Not Due to Government

If we add this to the premises from the stimulus, we arrive at the following logic chain:

        Major problem —— ^{M} —→ Not Due to Government ————→ S̸ ————→ MC ————→ EE

In other words, we can now properly conclude that most major problems will indeed require economic enticement, which is another way to phrase the conclusion in the stimulus.

Answer choice (B): This answer choice concerns environmental problems that *are* the result of government mismanagement, and the feasibility of their solutions. The stimulus deals with environmental problems that are *not* the result of government mismanagement. Since these are entirely different sets of problems, this choice is incorrect.

Answer choice (C): This choice concerns the feasibility of offering economic enticements, but the stimulus only concerns whether it is *necessary* to make enticements. Note: A necessary condition *can be impossible*; this would not prove that the condition was not necessary, it would merely prove that the sufficient condition could not occur. This choice does not address the gap in the stimulus and is therefore incorrect.

Answer choice (D): This choice is not a supporter assumption; it addresses the proportion of non-government-caused environmental problems that are major. This is not relevant to the discussion, and it does not provide any required link between the variables in the stimulus.

Answer choice (E): The argument in the stimulus does not concern whether changes in consumer habits are *sufficient* to solve the most serious problems, but rather whether major changes are *necessary* to solve those problems, so this answer choice does not reflect an assumption required by the argument. Furthermore, this choice does not address the leap in the stimulus from non-government-induced problems to serious problems in general.

Question #14: Must Be True—SN. The correct answer choice is (D)

This stimulus provides some conditional reasoning, with the conclusion presented in the first sentence: The economy is doing badly. This is based on the premise that two indicators (real estate and car sales) are performing poorly.

And the contrapositive:

R.E.Slump
   and   ————→ Bad Economy likely   Bad E̸conomy————→
Low Car Sales

R.E.S̸lump
   or
Low C̸ar Sales

(Note that the author's logic requires that *both* indicators perform poorly in order to draw the conclusion that the economy is probably doing badly).

Answer choice (A): This choice is incorrect, because it suggests that low car sales *alone* are sufficient to indicate a bad economy. The stimulus suggests that either low car sales or a real estate slump alone is consistent with a good economy, which means a slump in either variable alone would be insufficient to establish the likelihood of a bad economy.

Answer choice (B): This answer choice characterizes the Bad Economy as the sufficient variable, but claims that success in the real estate or car sales market is *consistent* with a good economy, not that success in those markets *guarantee* a good economy. This choice is a Mistaken Reversal of the author's assertion that poor performance in real estate and car sales is likely to indicate a poor economy.

Answer choice (C): Poorly performing real estate or car sales performance is *consistent* with a good economy. This does not mean that a healthy economy is *likely,* only that it is possible, so this answer choice is incorrect.

Answer choice (D): This is the correct answer choice, as it reflects the logic from the contrapositive diagrammed above: A healthy economy ("Bad Economy" from the diagram) means that *at least one* of the two variables (real estate & car sales) is *not* faltering, which rules out at the possibility that *both* indicators are performing poorly.

Answer choice (E): This answer choice provides another example of a Mistaken Reversal. The stimulus tells us that poor performance in both real estate and car sales is sufficient to conclude that a bad economy is likely, which is much different from claiming that these factors are the necessary variables if we actually know that the economy is doing badly.

Question #15: Strengthen—CE. The correct answer choice is (D)

This Cause/Effect stimulus is much like many others on the LSAT; a causal relationship is presumed to exist where only a correlation has been shown. The stimulus explains that at the end of the Ice Age, the melting of ice depressurized the Earth's crust, causing it to crack. The author then concludes that the melting of ice likely helped to *cause* the earthquakes that took place in Sweden at the end of the Ice Age. As we know, there are several ways to weaken a Cause/Effect argument. Since we are asked to strengthen the argument, however, we should seek to better establish this causal connection.

Answer choice (A): Since this cracking would not necessarily cause any kind of large earthquakes, this choice would not help explain the earthquakes discussed in the stimulus.

Answer choice (B): The cracks in Northern Europe do not help establish the connection between the cracks and earthquakes, so this choice is incorrect.

Answer choice (C): Since we cannot assume that Northern Canada was significantly affected by melt-off from the Ice Age, and cannot assume that the crust in Canada cracked, this choice does not help establish a relationship between the cracks and earthquakes.

Answer choice (D): This is the correct answer choice. If cracks generally cause severe earthquakes in the immediate area, it seems more likely that they had something to do with the earthquakes in Sweden. Since this answer provides a causal connection between the cracks and the earthquakes, it is the correct choice.

Answer choice (E): By offering an alternative cause of earthquakes, this answer choice actually weakens the causal argument.

Question #16: Main Point. The correct answer choice is (E)

In this stimulus, the sociologist concludes that the supporters of political democracy can also support marketplace regulation. This conclusion, which comes at the end of the stimulus and is introduced with the word "hence," is based on the premise that there is a crucial distinction between the private consumer and the public citizen: Private consumers choose based on self-interest, argues the author, but the public citizen decides on the basis of beliefs about what is best for society.

In this case the question asks for the conclusion, which we should prephrase: supporters of political democracy can also support marketplace regulation.

Answer choice (A): This is perhaps an implication found in the stimulus, but it is not the conclusion, so this choice is incorrect.

Answer choice (B): The author's conclusion is that *regulated* markets are *compatible* with democratic sovereignty, not that *unregulated* markets are *incompatible*. This answer choice is basically a Mistaken Negation and is therefore incorrect.

Answer choice (C): This answer choice specifically reflects the belief of "some economists," as described in the stimulus, which is a position the author attacks. This choice is thus incorrect.

Answer choice (D): This is a premise used to support the conclusion, it is not the conclusion itself, so this answer choice is incorrect.

Answer choice (E): This is the correct answer choice. It is basically a rephrasing of the conclusion, found at the end of the stimulus.

Question #17: Must Be True. The correct answer choice is (C)

This stimulus consists of information with no explicit conclusion, but the numbers presented indicate a trend. It seems, at least anecdotally, that as the weight of a bird increases, the weight of its egg, relative to the size of the bird, decreases. This trend will likely be relevant, since we are asked which proposition is illustrated by the statements in the stimulus.

Answer choice (A): This choice might seem attractive, because the stimulus does discuss wide variation, but no volume-to-weight ratios are addressed.

Answer choice (B): The stimulus supports the idea that the ratio of egg-weight to body-weight increases as the bird gets smaller, but that does not mean the eggs themselves are larger in any absolute sense.

Answer choice (C): This is the correct answer choice, as it reflects a proposition illustrated by the stimulus. As the size of the adult bird increases, the ratio of egg-weight to body-weight decreases.

Answer choice (D): The stimulus itself does not allow us to make conclusions about the absolute sizes of the eggs, so we cannot make this comparison.

Answer choice (E): Since the stimulus never offered specific numbers to allow for comparison of bird size, we cannot conclude from the stimulus whether bird size or egg size has greater variation.

Question #18: Assumption. The correct answer choice is (C)

The argument concludes that, since vampire myths existed long before Bram Stoker's *Dracula*, the ability to become a bat is not an essential part of vampire myths.

The argument assumes some older vampire myths did not include bats as essential. Without this assumption, the observation that vampire myths existed before Bram Stoker's *Dracula* does not establish the conclusion. Since we are asked for a necessary assumption, we must address this gap, otherwise known as a *supporter assumption*.

Answer choice (A): This choice might be attractive, but we must not confuse "strictly nocturnal" with "turning into bats."

Answer choice (B): The corroboration of other sources on bats certainly does not lend credibility to the argument that bats are not essential parts of vampire myths, so this choice is wrong. Logically, this choice is meaningless, as it does not necessarily help establish anything about the European mythology, because the Central and South American myths could have arisen later.

Answer choice (C): The argument would not assume that vampire myths did not exist elsewhere, because it is possible that the existence of different vampire myths could help prove that bats are inessential.

Answer choice (D): This is the correct answer choice. At least one of the earlier myths must not portray vampires as able to turn into bats, if the advent of Bram Stoker's *Dracula* is to mean anything about whether bats are essential to the vampire myth. If all of the previous myths contained vampires with this ability, it would seem more likely that this ability actually is essential.

Answer choice (E): This fact might be helpful in determining where Stoker got his ideas, but it establishes nothing without knowing whether bats were used before him.

Question #19: Method of Reasoning—Argument Part. The correct answer choice is (B)

The conclusion in this case is presented in the first sentence of the stimulus: It is unlikely that the world will ever be free of disease. This conclusion is based on the premise that most diseases are caused by microorganisms that quickly adapt to new medicines, while maintaining the ability to infect and kill humans.

The question asks us to identify the role of the first sentence, which is the conclusion of the argument.

Answer choice (A): Even though the first sentence is the conclusion, it is not supported by any premises about numerous microorganisms. "Prolific" means "productive," and in this context it simply refers to the ability of the microorganisms to adapt, survive, and continue infecting and killing humans. This choice is wrong.

Answer choice (B): This is the correct answer choice, because the first sentence is the conclusion, and it is supported by the premise that disease-causing microorganisms adapt well to medicines.

Answer choice (C): The claim in question is not a premise, so this choice is incorrect.

Answer choice (D): The first sentence in the stimulus is not a "generalization used to predict," so this choice is incorrect.

Answer choice (E): The claim in question is the conclusion, but the argument is only that disease-causing microorganisms *adapt well* to medicines, not that they are *immune*.

Question #20: Weaken—CE. The correct answer choice is (B)

The scientist's conclusion (which happens to follow the words "I conclude") is that there is a causal connection between the gene variant and thrill-seeking behavior. This is based on the premise that children who engage in impulsive behavior similar to adult thrill-seeking behavior tend to have the gene variant.

The scientist's argument is flawed for many reasons. First, there is no established causal link between the dopamine response (essentially the variant) and impulsive behavior. Second, it is not shown that impulsive behavior would have the same cause as thrill-seeking behavior.

Answer choice (A): The scientist makes the leap from impulsive children to thrill-seeking adults, so, oddly enough, impulsive adults are irrelevant to the argument.

Answer choice (B): This is the correct answer choice, as it weakens the argument with an attack on the data. If it is not possible to distinguish impulsive behavior from other types of behavior, then what sample are we studying? If this is the case, then the scientist's argument really has no basis.

Answer choice (C): There is no claim in the stimulus that the children were engaging in thrill-seeking behavior, so implying that children are misrepresented as thrill-seeking will not weaken the argument.

Answer choice (D): In the stimulus the author alludes to one possible cause of certain tendencies in children and of similar tendencies in adults. The fact that behavioral changes take place in "many" people between childhood and adulthood does not serve to weaken the argument.

Answer choice (E): It does not matter whether thrill-seeking correlates with other behaviors; this choice fails to attack the causal argument.

Question #21: Flaw in the Reasoning. The correct answer choice is (E)

The flawed reasoning in this stimulus can be broken down as follows:

> Premise: Most people who are not classical pianists don't recognize Schumann.
>
> Premise: Most classical pianists do recognize Schumann's work.
>
> Premise: Claudette does recognize Schumann's work.
>
> Conclusion: Claudette is "highly likely" to be a classical pianist.

The discussion concerns one test case (Claudette), and her placement in one of two groups, classical pianists or non classical pianists. Since we know nothing of the absolute or even relative sizes of these two groups, we have no way to assess the likelihood of Claudette's proper placement into one group or the other.

In order to determine the likelihood that Claudette is classical pianist, we would need to consider the population of people who recognize Schumann. Within this group are there more classical pianists or non-pianists? This would tell us more about the likelihood that Claudette is a classical pianist. The assumption in the stimulus appears to be that within this Schumann recognition group, there are more classical pianists than non-classical-pianists.

Answer choice (A): It is not a flaw to ignore this possibility. Familiarity with other works would not prove that Claudette is not a classical pianist, so this choice is incorrect.

Answer choice (B): Ignoring the possibility that people could recognize works without knowing of the composer has no effect on the argument, because the author never stated that Claudette knew the composer's name, only that she recognized the works.

Answer choice (C): The stimulus contains no assertions, implicit or explicit, about classical musicians' abilities with other musical instruments.

Answer choice (D): The term "classical" when describing a pianist is not vague.

Answer choice (E): This is the correct answer choice. In arriving at the conclusion that Claudette is highly likely to be a classical pianist, the author must assume that most who recognize Schumann are classical pianists, thus ignoring the possibility that most Schumann recognizers are actually not classical-pianists.

Question #22: Parallel Reasoning. The correct answer choice is (E)

Based on the premise that Dr. Grippen's and Dr. Heissmann's theories predict mutually exclusive outcomes, the author concludes that the planned experiment will confirm one theory at the expense of the other.

The reasoning is flawed, because it ignores the possibility that the experiment might disprove both theories. There is no reason to presume that one of the theories must be confirmed. Since we are asked to parallel the flaw, we must find a choice that similarly neglects the possibility of two negative evaluations.

Answer choice (A): This reasoning is fairly sound. If David and Jane often disagree, *at least one* of their methods is probably flawed. This choice does not parallel the reasoning in the stimulus, because *at least one* in this case means *either one or both*.

Answer choice (B): The reasoning in this choice is bad, but only because it neglects the possibility that both David and Jane agree on the description of the tree, but simply disagree over its name, which is not a similar flaw.

Answer choice (C): This choice is wrong, because it ignores that even if David is one tree better, a difference of one tree is really not enough to decide who is better at identifying trees. However, the two flaws are not analogous, so this choice is wrong.

Answer choice (D): The reasoning in this choice is sound. Examining the whole forest would establish whether David is correct to believe there are more beeches than elms in the forest, so this response contains no logical flaw and is incorrect.

Answer choice (E): This is the correct answer choice. Both David and Jane could be wrong, so Maria does not have to confirm either of these judgments, but the choice ignores that possibility. That is exactly the flaw in the stimulus. In this case, David and Jane are the scientists, and Maria is the experiment.

Question #23: Assumption. The correct answer choice is (B)

The conclusion in this case is presented at the end of the stimulus: Modern technology reduces the well-being of its users. This is based on the premise that the relief modern technology provides renders its users dependent on it, thus reducing self-sufficiency.

Since the columnist leaps from self-sufficiency to well-being, an implicit premise (or *assumption*) is that well-being and self-sufficiency are somehow related. Since we are asked to identify an essential assumption, we should seek this Supporter Assumption, which will fill a gap in the argument by linking these two variables.

Answer choice (A): This choice is neither supported nor required by the stimulus. The columnist argues that it is the lack of self-sufficiency that reduces well-being, not the lack of physical labor. Furthermore, the author argues that there is a *reduction* in *well-being*, which is not equivalent to saying that something is *essential* to a fulfilling life.

Answer choice (B): This is the correct answer choice. The argument assumes that self-sufficiency and well-being are related, and this answer choice reflects that relationship. Applying the Assumption Negation technique, if self-sufficiency did not contribute to well-being, then we wouldn't be able to conclude that modern technology reduces the well-being of its users.

Answer choice (C): Since the argument in the stimulus does not concern freedom, this answer choice can be confidently eliminated. Although "freedom" is aligned with the concept of "self-sufficiency," this choice does not provide the necessary link to well-being. This is not the supporter assumption we are seeking.

Answer choice (D): Since the columnist does not consider whether anything discussed is *justifiable*, but rather discusses only outcome, this choice is off-topic and incorrect.

Answer choice (E): This choice does not reflect an assumption required by the argument. The author claims that *modern* technology, not technology *in general*, reduces the well-being of its users. Applying the Assumption Negation technique, we can negate this answer choice to arrive at the following: "Technology doesn't necessarily inherently limit the well-being of its users." This negated version does not weaken the argument in the stimulus, so we know that this choice cannot be an assumption on which the author's argument relies.

Question #24: Method of Reasoning—Argument Part. The correct answer choice is (E)

In this stimulus, the psychologist concludes that since dream content varies widely, dreams cannot be entirely explained as simply physiological phenomena. The psychologist makes this argument to counter the claim that dreams, as purely physical processes, reveal nothing about character or psychology.

The question asks us to identify the role of the claim that dream content varies enormously. This claim is a premise offered by the psychologist to support the conclusion. It is also worth noting that this claim attacks the other psychologists' conclusions.

Answer choice (A): The claim is not used to support any anti-Freudian conclusion. In fact, the author appears to be defending Freud, disputing those with anti-Freudian views.

Answer choice (B): This choice might be attractive, but it is wrong, because "explicit" means "definitively stated." The speaker implies that a fully satisfactory, or complete, explanation of dreams might allow for psychological considerations; the psychologist never explicitly states this conclusion, however, so this answer choice is incorrect.

Answer choice (C): The psychologist does not make the claim that neither line of reasoning offers a complete explanation, only that dreams cannot be completely understood in terms of physiological function.

Answer choice (D): The stimulus is not meant to illustrate the general difficulties of *completely* explaining dreaming, but rather to argue that dreams cannot be completely understood in terms of physiological function.

Answer choice (E): This is the correct answer choice. The claim is a premise which supports the psychologist's conclusion, and serves to undermine an opposing claim.

Question #25: Flaw in the Reasoning—CE. The correct answer choice is (E)

This stimulus seeks to explain why, after a brief stint in 1817, bicycles virtually disappeared until 1860. The premise offered is that the acceptance of a technology *requires* coherence with society's values, and based on this the author concludes that a change in values must have been the *cause* of the 43 year disappearance.

When we recognize this to be a Cause/Effect question we should immediately consider the various ways to weaken such an argument (in this case we know the supposed effect, and we are asked to identify a flaw, so we might start by considering possible alternative causes).

Answer choice (A): The argument does not presume that fads are *never* indicative of genuine acceptance, but instead points out that *this particular* fad was not initially indicative of genuine acceptance.

Answer choice (B): The argument does not fail to recognize that the reappearance of bicycles indicated a genuine acceptance; in fact, the author implies in the conclusion that there *has* been general acceptance.

Answer choice (C): Failure to provide support for one of the premises is not a flaw.

Answer choice (D): The question posed has direct relevance to the conclusion. It is a request for an explanation, which is provided by the conclusion (even though the underlying reasoning is flawed).

Answer choice (E): This is the correct answer choice, as it articulates the flaw in many causal arguments: The failure to consider possible alternative causes.

Overview: This section is more challenging than the June 2004 LSAT games section. The mix of games is more varied, and there is a greater reliance on conditional rules, which most students find difficult. That said, with only 22 questions, this section does not rank high on the difficulty scale. Of course, the relative ease of this section was offset by the fact that the scale for this test was tight. Each game is dissected in detail below.

October 2004 Game #1: Questions 1-6

This is a basic linear game featuring five dignitaries placed in seven meetings. Because there are only five dignitaries, this game is underfunded, but the very first rule establishes that F must meet with Garibaldi three times, and so the composition of the group of dignitaries is precisely defined and balanced.

After reviewing the game scenario and the rules, you should make the following basic setup for this game:

F F F M R S T[7]

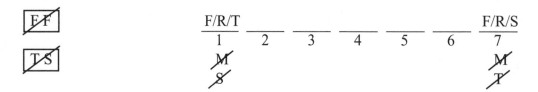

Note that the fourth rule involving M is represented by Not Laws on meetings 1 and 7. Let's take a moment to discuss the second and third rules.

Rule #2. This rule establishes that none of the three meetings with F can be consecutive. At a minimum, then, the three meetings with F require five spaces (meaning that among other things that if the TS block created by rule #3 is placed at the beginning or end of the meeting schedule then the placement of the three F's will automatically be determined). Given the open-ended nature of this rule, and the fact that it addresses three of the seven meetings, this rule will play a major role in the game.

Rule #3. This rule creates a fixed block involving T and S. Because S is always the next meeting after T, S can never be Garibaldi's first meeting; because T is always the meeting before S, T can never be Garibaldi's last meeting. These two inferences are shown as Not Laws on the diagram above.

This game does not present a large amount of information in the scenario and rules, and you should expect to see a fair number of Local questions, which will supply the additional information needed to place some of the variables. Given the dearth of information generated in the setup, we have elected to show the triple-options present for the first and last meetings. Since there are only five dignitaries, and the Not Laws eliminate two of those dignitaries from attending the first or last meeting, only three possible dignitaries could attend either meeting.

One other point of note is that R is a random in this game, and R can attend the first or last meeting.

Question #1: Global, List. The correct answer choice is (C)

As with any List question, simply apply the rules to the answer choices. Remember to apply the rules in order of the easiest to "see" within the answers. In this game, that order would be rule #4, rule #3, rule #2, and then rule #1 (rule #2 and rule #3 are equally easy to see, but we chose to apply rule #3 first since that allows rules #2 and #1—both of which involve F— to be applied together).

Answer choice (A): This answer is eliminated by the first rule. In this instance, there are only two meetings with F, instead of three.

Answer choice (B): This answer choice is incorrect because two of the meetings with F are consecutive, a violation of the second rule.

Answer choice (C): This is the correct answer choice.

Answer choice (D): Because T and S are not a block, this answer choice violates the third rule, and is therefore incorrect.

Answer choice (E): Because M is last, this answer choice violates the fourth rule and is incorrect.

Question #2: Local, Could Be True. The correct answer choice is (D)

This question is best attacked with hypotheticals. The question stem establishes that R is Garibaldi's seventh meeting:

$$\underset{1}{\underline{\hspace{2em}}} \quad \underset{2}{\underline{\hspace{2em}}} \quad \underset{3}{\underline{\hspace{2em}}} \quad \underset{4}{\underline{\hspace{2em}}} \quad \underset{5}{\underline{\hspace{2em}}} \quad \underset{6}{\underline{\hspace{2em}}} \quad \underset{7}{\overset{R}{\underline{\hspace{2em}}}}$$

From our discussion of the first and last meetings, we know that either F or T must now be Garibaldi's first meeting. However, the placement of R has limited the options for F, and if T is placed first then from the third rule S must be the second meeting, and there would not be sufficient room to separate the three meetings with F (meetings 1, 2, and 7 would be occupied, leaving only meetings 3-6 for the three F's). Consequently, we can infer that F must be Garibaldi's first meeting:

$$\underset{1}{\overset{F}{\underline{\hspace{2em}}}} \quad \underset{\underset{\cancel{F}}{2}}{\underline{\hspace{2em}}} \quad \underset{3}{\underline{\hspace{2em}}} \quad \underset{4}{\underline{\hspace{2em}}} \quad \underset{5}{\underline{\hspace{2em}}} \quad \underset{6}{\underline{\hspace{2em}}} \quad \underset{7}{\overset{R}{\underline{\hspace{2em}}}}$$

At this point, the placement of the TS block and the two remaining F's must be considered. The TS block cannot occupy meetings #3-4 or #5-6 because that would force two of the three F's to be consecutive (if this does not appear logical, try placing the TS block in either of those positions and observe the results). Consequently, there are only two possible scenarios:

1. TS occupies the second and third meetings and the remaining two F's occupy the meetings fourth and sixth meetings. M is then forced into the fifth meeting.

2. TS occupies the fourth and fifth meetings and the remaining two F's occupy the third and sixth meetings. M is then forced into the second meeting.

The two scenarios can be diagrammed as follows:

Scenario #2:	F	M	F	T	S	F	R

Scenario #1:	F	T	S	F	M	F	R
	1	2	3	4	5	6	7

Answer choices (A), (C), and (E): According to the two solutions to this question, Garibaldi's meets with S in either the third or fifth meetings. Consequently, each of these answer choices is incorrect.

Answer choice (B): As shown by the two diagrams, Garibaldi's third meeting must either be with F or S, and thus this answer choice is incorrect.

Answer choice (D): This is the correct answer choice.

Question #3: Local, List. The correct answer choice is (E)

The assignment of F to the second meeting has an immediate impact on the choices for the *first* meeting. We know that only F, R or T could be Garibaldi's first meeting. With F as the second meeting, the first meeting cannot be with F as that would violate the second rule. The first meeting also cannot be with T as there is no room to place S immediately after T. Consequently, when F is Garibaldi's second meeting, R *must* be Garibaldi's first meeting:

R	F					
1	2	3	4	5	6	7

~~M~~
~~S~~
~~F~~
~~T~~

This powerful deduction immediately eliminates answer choices (A), (C), and D), each of which contain R. A very insightful test maker might realize at this point which variables could be Garibaldi's fourth meeting, but let's continue analyzing this problem as if we did not have that insight.

Comparing the remaining two answer choices, (B) and (E), both contain S, so the comparison should focus on M and F, the unique variables in each of the remaining answer choices.

Answer choice (B): A quick test of this answer would be to create a hypothetical that places M into the fourth meeting:

R	F		M			
1	2	3	4	5	6	7

Placing M fourth immediately forces the two remaining F's into the fifth and seventh meetings:

R	F		M	F		F
1	2	3	4	5	6	7

At this point there is no room for the TS block, and so we can eliminate this answer choice since placing M fourth does not allow us to create a viable solution.

Answer choice (E): This is the correct answer choice. The following hypothetical proves that F can be Garibaldi's fourth meeting:

R	F	M	F	T	S	F
1	2	3	4	5	6	7

Question #4: Local, Must Be True. The correct answer choice is (E)

The condition in the question stem creates an SR block. Adding this to the third rule, we arrive at the following super-block:

$$\boxed{\text{T S R}}$$

The size of this block presents immediate problems for the three F's, and you must consider the placement options of the block prior to attacking the answer choices. First, the block cannot be placed at the beginning or the end of the series of meetings because that would not leave sufficient room to separate the three meetings with F (if meetings 1-3 are occupied by the block, then only meetings 4-7 are available for the three F's; if meetings 5-7 are occupied by the block, then only meetings 1-4 are available for the three F's). Consequently, the TSR block must be placed in either meetings 2-4, 3-5, or 4-6. We can also deduce that F must be Garibaldi's first meeting because only F, R, or T could be Garibaldi's first meeting, and with T and R involved in the block neither can be first. With this fact in hand, you should quickly create hypotheticals reflecting each placement option:

Option #1: TSR as the second, third, and fourth meetings

When the TSR block is placed as the second, third, and fourth meetings, the remaining two F's must be placed as the fifth and seventh meetings, leaving M as the sixth meeting.

F	T	S	R	F	M	F
1	2	3	4	5	6	7

Option #2: TSR as the third, fourth, and fifth meetings

Hopefully you realized that this placement option would be unworkable prior to drawing out the diagram. When the TSR block is placed as the third, fourth, and fifth meetings, there is no way to place the other two F's so that they do not violate the second rule. Consequently, TSR cannot be placed in this position and a viable hypothetical cannot be created.

F		T	S	R		
1	2	3	4	5	6	7
	F̷					

Option #3: TSR as the fourth, fifth, and sixth meetings

When the TSR block is placed as the fourth, fifth, and sixth meetings, the remaining two F's must be placed as the third and seventh meetings, leaving M as the second meeting.

F	M	F	T	S	R	F
1	2	3	4	5	6	7

Thus, the condition in the question stem only allows for two solutions to the question:

TSR in 4-5-6:

F	M	F	T	S	R	F

TSR in 2-3-4:

F	T	S	R	F	M	F
1	2	3	4	5	6	7

Answer choices (A), (B), (C), and (D): Each of these answer choices could be true. However, this is a Must be true question, and thus each of these answers is incorrect.

Answer choice (E): This is the correct answer choice. As proven by the two solutions above, F is always the last meeting.

Question #5: Local, Could Be True. The correct answer choice is (D)

This is one of the easier questions in the game. If Garibaldi's first meeting is with T, then according to the third rule, Garibaldi's second meeting must be with S:

T	S					
1	2	3	4	5	6	7

At this juncture, the three F's must be placed in such a way that they are not consecutive. There is only one way that this can occur, by placing F in the third, fifth, and seventh meetings :

T	S	F		F		F
1	2	3	4	5	6	7

The remaining two variables—M and R—form a dual-option in the fourth and sixth meetings:

T	S	F	M/R	F	R/M	F
1	2	3	4	5	6	7

Consequently, Garibaldi's meeting with R could be either the fourth or sixth meeting, and answer choice (D) is correct.

Answer choices (A), (B), (C), and (E): Each of these answer choices is proven incorrect by the diagram above.

Answer choice (D): This is the correct answer choice.

Question #6: Local, Must Be True. The correct answer choice is (A)

The condition in this question stem creates an RM block. Initially, it may seem as though this block has a wide number of placement options, but take a moment to consider the five variable groups created by this rule:

The interaction of the RM block, the TS block, and the second rule limits the placement options of each variable (creating a classic Separation Principle scenario). For example, because the F's cannot be consecutive, they must be separated by the two blocks. Consider this for a moment—if you have to separate the three F's with just two blocks, where must the F's be placed? One of the blocks has to separate the first two F's, and the other block has to separate the last two F's, like so:

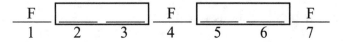

If the two blocks are not placed as they are above, at least two of the F's will be consecutive, violating the second rule. Consequently, the F's are forced into the first, fourth, and seventh meetings. The two blocks are interchangeable, and either TS or RM could be in either position 2-3 or 5-6.

Answer choice (A): This is the correct answer choice. If you are still uncertain about this answer choice, try placing a variable other than F into the fourth meeting. You will quickly see that any variable other than F in the fourth meeting will not allow for a workable solution.

Answer choices (B), (C), (D), and (E): Each of these answer choices is incorrect because they would not yield a viable solution for the question.

This game has a Linear structure paired with four Grouping rules. Because there are two dogs placed each day, our diagram will feature the days as the base, with two spaces per day:

G H K L P S [6]

The first two rules include one block and one not-block:

Since these two rules address four of the six dogs in the game, what is the relationship between the two dogs—S and K—not included in these two rules? To determine this relationship, first analyze what happens when the blocks are placed (in this analysis, disregard the linear aspect of the game and just consider the groups).

1. L and P must occupy one entire day:

2. G and H cannot be placed on the same day, and since there are only two days open, G and H must form a dual-option that occupies one space on each day:

L	___	___
P	G/H	H/G
Day	Day	Day

3. By Hurdling the Uncertainty, we can infer that the two remaining variables, K and S, can never be placed on the same day:

$\underline{\text{L}}$	$\underline{\text{K/S}}$	$\underline{\text{S/K}}$
$\underline{\text{P}}$	$\underline{\text{G/H}}$	$\underline{\text{H/G}}$
Day	Day	Day

Consequently, we can infer that S and K form a not-block:

This inference is directly tested in question #8.

There are also two powerful conditional rules in the game:

The third rule: $K_M \longrightarrow G_T$

The fourth rule: $S_W \longrightarrow H_T$

Because these rules involve two separate days and they both involve the second rule, they ultimately result in a single solution to the game:

The third rule. When K is placed on Monday, then G must be placed on Tuesday. The LP block must then be placed on Wednesday. Consequently, because G is on Tuesday, H must be placed on Monday. The last remaining dog, S, must then be placed on Tuesday. Thus, when K is placed on Monday, there is only one solution to the game:

$\underline{\text{H}}$	$\underline{\text{S}}$	$\underline{\text{L}}$
$\underline{\text{K}}$	$\underline{\text{G}}$	$\underline{\text{P}}$
M	T	W

The fourth rule. When S is placed on Wednesday, then H must be placed on Tuesday. The LP block must then be placed on Monday. Consequently, because H is on Tuesday, G must be placed on Wednesday. The last remaining dog, K, must then be placed on Tuesday. Thus, when S is placed on Wednesday, there is only one solution to the game:

$\underline{\text{L}}$	$\underline{\text{K}}$	$\underline{\text{G}}$
$\underline{\text{P}}$	$\underline{\text{H}}$	$\underline{\text{S}}$
M	T	W

The information above provides more than sufficient information to attack the questions, but a savvy test taker might suspect that given the powerful rules in this game, and the fact that there are no randoms, that there might be a limited number of solutions to this game. In fact, there are only eight solutions to the game, and these eight solutions can be captured using five templates. One option for attacking this game would be to show the templates, and in the interests of absolute clarity we will discuss how to make each template.

The basis for the templates is the placement of the LP block. Since the LP block can go on any of the three days, there are three basic avenues that lead to the templates:

LP on Monday:

When the LP block is placed on Monday, H and G must be split between Tuesday and Wednesday. However, the placement of S and K has an impact on G and H because of the action of the fourth rule. This ultimately creates two templates:

Template #1:
LP on Monday
S on Tuesday, K on Wednesday

L	G/H	H/G

P	S	K
M	T	W

Template #2:
LP on Monday
S on Tuesday, K on Wednesday

L	H	G

P	K	S
M	T	W

Template #1 contains two solutions; template #2 contains only one solution.

LP on Tuesday:

When the LP block is placed on Tuesday, both the third and fourth rules are affected: K cannot be placed on Monday, and S cannot be placed on Wednesday. Consequently, K must be placed on Wednesday and S must be placed on Monday. G and H form a dual-option that rotates between Monday and Wednesday:

Template #3:
LP on Monday

G/H	L	H/G

S	P	K
M	T	W

This template contains two solutions.

LP on Wednesday:

When the LP block is placed on Wednesday, H and G must be split between Monday and Tuesday. However, the placement of S and K has an impact on G and H because of the action of the third rule. This ultimately creates two templates:

Template #4:
LP on Wednesday
S on Monday, K on Tuesday

Template #5:
LP on Wednesday
S on Tuesday, K on Monday

G/H	H/G	L
S	K	P
M	T	W

H	G	L
K	S	P
M	T	W

Template #4 contains two solutions; template #5 contains only one solution.

Either a regular setup or the template approach will effectively solve this game. In our explanations of the questions we will use the regular setup because more people attack the game using that method, and the template method still leaves several possible solutions undefined.

Question #7: Global, List. The correct answer choice is (E)

As with any List question, simply apply the rules to the answer choices. In this game, the best order to apply the rules is: rule #1, rule #2, rule #3, and then rule #4.

Answer choice (A): This answer choice violates the first rule and is therefore incorrect.

Answer choice (B): This answer choice violates the third rule and is therefore incorrect.

Answer choice (C): This answer choice violates the second rule and is therefore incorrect.

Answer choice (D): This answer choice violates the fourth rule and is therefore incorrect.

Answer choice (E): This is the correct answer choice.

Question #8: Global, Must Be True. The correct answer choice is (B)

As discussed in the setup to this game, because of the interaction of the first two rules, we can deduce that K and S can never be placed on the same day. Consequently, answer choice (B) is correct.

Answer choices (A), (C), (D), and (E): Each of these answer choices could be true, but none of them must be true, and therefore each is incorrect.

Answer choice (B): This is the correct answer choice.

Question #9: Local, Could Be True. The correct answer choice is (A)

When the L is placed on Tuesday, then from the first rule we know that P is also placed on Tuesday. With Tuesday occupied, both the third and fourth rules are affected: K cannot be placed on Monday (because G cannot be placed on Tuesday), and S cannot be placed on Wednesday (because H cannot be placed on Tuesday). Consequently, K must be placed on Wednesday and S must be placed on Monday. G and H form a dual-option that rotates between Monday and Wednesday:

$$\frac{\text{G/H}}{\quad} \qquad \frac{\text{L}}{\quad} \qquad \frac{\text{H/G}}{\quad}$$

$$\frac{\text{S}}{\text{M}} \qquad \frac{\text{P}}{\text{T}} \qquad \frac{\text{K}}{\text{W}}$$

Answer choice (A): This is the correct answer choice.

Answer choice (B): This answer choice violates the third rule. K cannot be placed on Monday because there is no space for G to be placed on Tuesday.

Answer choice (C): The question stem stipulates that P must be placed on Tuesday, and from the first rule L must also be placed on Tuesday. Therefore, this answer choice cannot occur and it is incorrect.

Answer choice (D): Since L and P occupy the two spaces on Tuesday, no other dog can be placed on Tuesday, and thus this answer choice is incorrect.

Answer choice (E): This answer choice violates the fourth rule. S cannot be placed on Wednesday because there is no space for H to be placed on Tuesday.

Question #10: Local, Must Be True. The correct answer choice is (E)

The question stem places G and K in a block:

Since L and P are also aligned in a block, two of three days must be completely filled by those two blocks:

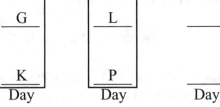

Thus, because the only two remaining spaces are on the same day, the two remaining dogs—H and S—must also be in a block, and the key to this question is to determine the days on which each block can be placed. Let's examine each block in closer detail:

The GK block: The only rule applicable to this block is the third rule, which states that if K is placed on Monday then G must be placed on Tuesday. Consequently, we can infer that the GK block cannot be placed on Monday since that placement would violate this rule.

The LP block: The LP block could be placed on any one of the three days.

The HS block: The only rule applicable to this block is the fourth rule, which states that if S is placed on Wednesday then H must be placed on Tuesday. Consequently, we can infer that the HS block cannot be placed on Wednesday since that placement would violate this rule.

With the information above, we are ready to attack the answer choices.

Answer choice (A): Although H could be placed on Monday, H does not have to be placed on Monday and so this answer choice is incorrect.

Answer choice (B): Although L could be placed on Monday, L does not have to be placed on Monday and so this answer choice is incorrect.

Answer choice (C): Although K could be placed on Tuesday, K does not have to be placed on Tuesday and so this answer choice is incorrect.

Answer choice (D): This answer choice, like answer choice (E), slips a "not" into the middle of the answer (remember, read carefully!). Because P could be placed on Wednesday, this answer choice is incorrect.

Answer choice (E): This is the correct answer choice. As discussed above, the HS block cannot be placed on Wednesday because doing so would violate the fourth rule.

Question #11: Local, Cannot Be True. The correct answer choice is (D)

The question stem creates a horizontal HS block:

$$\boxed{H \ S}$$

This block must be placed on either Monday and Tuesday, or Tuesday and Wednesday. Consequently, the LP vertical block must be placed on Monday or Wednesday. This deduction is sufficient to show that P cannot be placed on Tuesday, and so answer choice (D) is correct. However, in the interests of fully understanding the relationships at work in this question, let's continue our analysis. So far we have two blocks, and since HS is a horizontal block, we will show the other spaces with H and S:

The remaining two variables are G and K. Because the second rule specifies that G and H cannot be placed on the same day, we can infer that G must placed with S. K must then be placed with H:

<u>K</u> <u>G</u> <u>H</u> <u>S</u>	<u>L</u> <u>P</u>

Because of the fortuitous arrangement of the variables, the blocks can be placed in any order. Answer choices (A), (B), (C) and (E): Each of these answer choices could be true, as proven by the following hypothetical:

$$\frac{K}{} \qquad \frac{G}{} \qquad \frac{L}{}$$

$$\frac{H}{M} \qquad \frac{S}{T} \qquad \frac{P}{W}$$

Answer choice (D): This is the correct answer choice. As discussed above, the LP vertical block must be placed on either Monday or Wednesday.

Question #12: Local, Cannot Be True. The correct answer choice is (A)

One approach to attacking this question is to use the hypotheticals from the previous three questions. Each contains scenarios that match the condition in this question stem, and collectively that information can be used to eliminate every incorrect answer choice. If you do not choose that approach, this question can still be done easily by making hypotheticals.

The condition in the question stem, in combination with the first rule, creates a powerful GLP block:

<u>   </u> <u>L</u> <u>G</u> <u>P</u>

This block can only be placed on Monday-Tuesday or Tuesday-Wednesday:

Hypothetical #1:
GLP on Monday-Tuesday

Hypothetical #2:
GLP on Tuesday-Wednesday

$$\frac{}{} \quad \frac{L}{} \quad \frac{}{} \qquad\qquad \frac{}{} \quad \frac{}{} \quad \frac{L}{}$$

$$\frac{G}{M} \quad \frac{P}{T} \quad \frac{H}{W} \qquad\qquad \frac{H}{M} \quad \frac{G}{T} \quad \frac{P}{W}$$

Of course, due to the second rule, H cannot be placed on the same day as G, so H must be placed on

Wednesday in the first hypothetical and on Monday in the second hypothetical.

In addition, because of the fourth rule, in the first hypothetical S must be placed on Monday (otherwise, if it were placed on Wednesday H could not be placed on Monday), and therefore K is placed on Monday in the first hypothetical. In the second hypothetical K and S form a dual option:

Hypothetical #1:
GLP on Monday-Tuesday

S	L	K
G	P	H
M	T	W

Hypothetical #2:
GLP on Tuesday-Wednesday

S/K	K/S	L
H	G	P
M	T	W

Answer choice (A): This is the correct answer choice.

Answer choices (B), (C), (D), and (E): As shown in the two hypotheticals, G, K, L, P, and S could be placed on Tuesday. Thus, each of these answer choices is incorrect.

The setup to this Advanced Linear game is more challenging than the setup of the first two games of this section, primarily because although this game appears to have only a few initial inferences, the relationship of the rules is such that most of the diagram can be filled in. With the proper diagram, the questions are relatively easy.

From the game scenario, we know that there are three variable sets: the five archaeological sites, the three archaeologists, and the three centuries. The five archaeological sites and the three centuries each have numerical order, but the archaeological sites are the better choice for the base since each site has a single archaeologist and a single date. This choice creates a linear setup with two stacks, one for the archaeologists and one for the centuries (remember to leave ample vertical space between the two stacks since each row will likely have its own Not Laws):

Centuries: 8 9 10 ^{3}
Archaeologists: F G O ^{3}
                        *

Cent: ____ ____ ____ ____ ____

Arch: ____ ____ ____ ____ ____
                   1   2   3   4   5

Because the rules have so many consequences, let's examine each rule individually.

Rule #1. This rule is the most straightforward rule of the game, and it can be represented by placing a "9" in second site space of the Century row:

Cent: ____ 9 ____ ____ ____

Arch: ____ ____ ____ ____ ____
                   1   2   3   4   5

Rule #2. If neither the fourth or fifth site was discovered by O, we can place O Not Laws on each space. And, because there are only three archaeologists, with O eliminated from discovering the fourth and fifth sites we can infer that either F or G discovered those sites. This fact can be represented by individual F/G dual-options on each site:

Cent: ____   9   ____   ____   ____

Arch: ____   ____   ____   F/G   F/G
              1   2   3   4   5
                                   Ø̸   Ø̸

Rule #3. While the first two rules can be represented directly on the diagram, this rule must be diagrammed separately. The rule is a bit challenging to represent because it contains two separate pieces of information. The first piece of information is that G discovered exactly one site, and the second piece of information is that the site discovered by G dates from the 10th century. There are different ways to represent this rule, but we will use the following diagram:

$$G_{Once} \longrightarrow 10$$

From the contrapositive of this rule we can infer that any site that dates from the 8th or 9th century was not discovered by G, and must therefore have been discovered by F or O. Also, be careful not to make a Mistaken Reversal and assume that any site that dates from the 10th century was discovered by G; that is not necessarily the case.

Using the information above, we can infer that since the second site dates from the 9th century it was not discovered by G, and must therefore have been discovered by F or O:

Cent: ____   9   ____   ____   ____

Arch: ____   F/O   ____   F/G   F/G
              1   2   3   4   5
                     G̸   Ø̸   Ø̸

Rule #4. This is another important conditional rule, which can be diagrammed as follows:

$$8 \longrightarrow O$$

Operationally, this rule indicates that every time a site dates from the 8th century, it must have been discovered by O. The contrapositive of this rule reveals that if a site was not discovered by O, then it cannot date from the 8th century and must instead date from the 9th or 10th century. Thus, the fourth and fifth sites, which were not discovered by O, cannot date from the 8th century, and they must date from the 9th or 10th century. We can add this to our diagram with dual-options:

Cent: ____   9   ____   9/10   9/10
                                 ~~8~~   ~~8~~

Arch: ____   F/O   ____   F/G   F/G
          1   2   3   4   5
                 ~~G~~   ~~G~~   ~~G~~

Rule #5. Although we have already gained a fair amount of information from the first four rules, the final rule will allow us to fill in most of the remaining spaces in the diagram.

The last rule states that the third site dates from a *more recent* century than either the first or fourth site. Thus, the third site cannot date from the 8th century, and the first and fourth sites cannot date from the 10th century. By itself, this information only seems to result in a series of dual-options for the dates of these sites. However, because we have already concluded that the fourth site must date from the 9th or 10th century (this inference was produced by combining the second and fourth rules), and this rule indicates that the fourth site cannot date from the 10th century, we can conclude that the fourth site dates from the 9th century. And, because the fourth site must date from the 9th century, we can use this rule to determine that the third site must date from the 10th century. Consequently, we can fill in the entire century row with either the exact site dates or with dual-options:

Cent: 8/9   9   10   9   9/10
          1   2   3   4   5
         ~~10~~   ~~8~~   ~~8~~
                            ~~10~~

Further, because the fourth site cannot date from the 10th century, from the third rule we can infer G cannot discover the fourth site, and so the fourth site must be discovered by F. We can also use the third rule to determine that the first site was not discovered by G, and must have been discovered by F or O. These inferences allow us to arrive at our final diagram:

Cent: 8/9   9   10   9   9/10
         ~~10~~   ~~8~~   ~~8~~
                        ~~10~~

Arch: F/O   F/O   ____   F   F/G
          1   2   3   4   5
         ~~G~~   ~~G~~   ~~G~~ ~~G~~
                             ~~G~~

Note that all of the dual-options are not independent. For example, if the first site dates from the 8th century, then according to the fourth rule it must have been discovered by O. The third rule is also active, and during the game you must keep track of the placement of G. Regardless, you now have a powerful setup with which to attack the game.

Question #13: Global, List. The correct answer choice is (E)

In this List question, if you use just the given rules, only rules #2 and #3 provide useful information. Thus, the easiest approach is to use the archaeologist row from the diagram to attack the answer choices.

Answer choice (A): According to the second rule, O cannot have discovered the fourth site, and thus this answer choice is incorrect.

Answer choice (B): From our discussion of the setup to this game, we know that G cannot discover the first site, and hence this answer choice is incorrect.

Answer choice (C): From the combination of the first and third rules of the game, we know that G cannot have discovered the second site, and so this answer choice is incorrect.

Answer choice (D): The second rule stipulates that G discovered exactly one of the sites. Because this answer choice shows G discovering two of the sites, it is incorrect.

Answer choice (E): This is the correct answer choice.

Question #14: Local, Cannot Be True. The correct answer choice is (C)

The question stem asserts that only one of the five sites dates from the 10th century, and because we have already established that the third site dates from the 10th century, we know that the third site is the only site from the 10th century. In addition, from the third rule we know that G must discover a site from the 10th century, and so we can conclude that G must discover the third site. In this Cannot be true question, then, F cannot discover the third site and answer choice (C) is correct.

Note that although other deductions could be made (such as that the fifth site dates from the 9th century), and an entire diagram could be drawn out for this question, there is no point in doing so since our initial diagram already determined that the third site was from the 10th century and that provides the starting point for a fast and clear path to the correct answer.

Answer choices (A), (B), (D), and (E): Because F could discover any of the sites listed in these answer choices, each of these choices is incorrect.

Answer choice (C): This is the correct answer choice.

Question #15: Global, Could Be True. The correct answer choice is (A)

Although creating the setup to this game takes a fair amount of time, Global questions such as this one allow us to make up time. Our setup indicates that only one site—the first—could date from the 8th century, and thus answer choice (A) is correct.

Answer choice (A): This is the correct answer choice.

Answer choices (B), (C), (D), and (E): Each of these sites must be from either the 9th or 10th century.

Question #16: Global, List. The correct answer choice is (E)

Again, our initial setup easily answers this question. The setup indicates that G cannot discover the first, second, and fourth sites. The only answer choice that contains these three sites is answer choice (E).

Answer choices (A), (B), (C), and (D): Because G could have discovered the third or fifth site, any answer choice that contains the third or fifth site is incorrect.

Answer choice (E): This is the correct answer choice.

Question #17: Global, Maximum. The correct answer choice is (D)

From the diagram, we know that F discovered the fourth site, and the dual-options and Not Laws indicate that F could have discovered each of the other sites as well. Thus, it might appear that F could have discovered all five sites. However, this would be an incorrect conclusion because the third rule states that G must have discovered exactly one site. Thus, F cannot have discovered all five sites and answer choice (E) can be eliminated from contention.

As F is a random in this game, four appears to be a very likely correct answer. Before simply choosing four as the correct answer, however, the rules regarding O should be examined to ensure that O does not have to discover one or more of the sites. A quick review of the rules and the diagram indicates that O does not have to discover any of the sites, and thus answer choice (D) is correct.

Answer choices (A), (B), and (C): Because the question stem asks for the *maximum* number of sites discovered by F, and each one of these answer choices is less than the maximum, these answers are incorrect.

Answer choice (D): This is the correct answer choice.

Answer choice (E): Because G must have discovered exactly one site, F cannot discover all five sites and this answer choice is incorrect.

Like the third game, this is an Advanced Linear game. While there are three variable sets presented in the game scenario, the days of the week should be chosen as the base. Remember, when days of the week appear in a game, they should almost always be used as the base of the game.

With the days of the week as the base, two stacks can be created—one for the parking lots and one for the prices (again, leave ample vertical space between the two stacks for individual Not Laws):

Lots: X Y Z [3]
Cost: 10 12 15 [3]

Cost: ____ ____ ____ ____ ____

Lot: ____ ____ ____ ____ ____
       M   T   W   Th   F

Unlike the third game, the setup for this game will not conclude with most of the spaces occupied. However, the rules still yield a fair amount of information, and several of the rules in particular require more than a surface analysis.

Rule #1. This simple rule results in a "15" being placed on Thursday in the Cost stack.

Rule #2. To capture the literal meaning of this rule, diagram it as follows:

$$\$X > \$Z$$

If X costs more than Z, then we can conclude that X cannot cost \$10 and that Z cannot cost \$15. Hence, X must cost \$12 or \$15, and Z must cost \$10 or \$12:

$$X \longrightarrow 12/15$$

$$Z \longrightarrow 10/12$$

The connection between X and Z is such that if X is \$12, then Z must be \$10, and if Z is \$12, then X must be \$15:

$$X_{12} \longrightarrow Z_{10}$$

$$Z_{12} \longrightarrow X_{15}$$

At this point, since the first rule has already established that the Thursday lot costs $15, we can infer that Anastasia cannot park in lot Z on Thursday, and that she must park in lot X or Y. That inference can be shown with a dual-option on Thursday:

Cost: ____ ____ ____   15   ____

Lot: ____ ____ ____   X/Y   ____
               M   T   W   Th   F
                                  Z̶

Rule #3. This rule establishes a connection between the cost of the Wednesday and Friday lots, namely that the Wednesday lot must cost more than the Friday lot. The literal meaning of this rule can be diagrammed as:

$W > $F

Functionally, we can conclude that the Wednesday lot cannot cost $10 and that the Friday lot cannot cost $15. Hence, the Wednesday lot must cost $12 or $15, and the Friday lot must cost $10 or $12:

Wednesday ⟶ 12/15

Friday ⟶ 10/12

These inferences can be shown with by dual-options in the Cost row on Wednesday and Friday:

Cost: ____ ____ 12/15   15   10/12
                            1̶0̶   1̶5̶

Lot: ____ ____ ____   X/Y   ____
               M   T   W   Th   F
                                  Z̶

The connection between Wednesday and Friday is such that if the Wednesday lot is $12, then the Friday lot must be $10, and if the Friday lot is $12, then the Wednesday lot must be $15:

Wednesday$_{12}$ ⟶ Friday$_{10}$

Friday$_{12}$ ⟶ Wednesday$_{15}$

Rule #4. This rule establishes a numerical distribution for the lots. Like the prior two rules there is a simple diagram for this rule, but the relationships that follow from the rule prove more useful than the diagram of the rule itself. The rule can be diagrammed as:

$$\#Z > \#X$$

Numerically, then, there must be more than one day on which Anastasia parks in lot Z. And, because the game scenario establishes that Anastasia parks in each lot at least once, we can infer that she cannot park in Z more than three times (parking in X and Y one time each leaves a maximum of three days to park in Z). Thus, Anastasia must park in lot Z either two or three times, leading to the following two distributions:

If Anastasia parks in lot Z three times, then she must park in lot X once and in lot Y once, creating the following fixed 3-1-1 distribution (Anastasia cannot park in lot X twice because then there would not be a day for her to park in lot Y):

ZZZ X Y

If Anastasia parks in lot Z two times, then she can only park in lot X once, and the remaining two times she must park in lot Y, creating the following fixed 2-1-2 distribution:

ZZ X YY

The two scenarios above are the only two possible distributions of the parking lots to the five days. Note that regardless of the scenario, Anastasia can only park in lot X a single time.

Because the fourth rule establishes fixed numerical distribution but does not allow us to place any of the variables within the diagram, the linear diagram created during the discussion of rule #3 is the final diagram for the game (excluding the diagramming of each of the rules, of course). In reviewing this diagram, you should note that Monday and Tuesday are completely open, and thus, when attacking the questions you should not initially look to Monday or Tuesday to solve a question. Wednesday, Thursday, and Friday are much better starting points for your analysis. And, although the linear diagram of the five days has a number of open spaces, the second, third, and fourth rules provide a wealth of information with which to attack the questions.

Question #18: Global, List. The correct answer choice is (A)

Because this List question includes only the parking lots and not the costs, at first you may not think you have enough information to eliminate each of the four incorrect answer choices. However, two of the answer choices can be eliminated by the numerical distribution, and the other two answer choices can be eliminated by combining the rules.

Answer choice (A): This is the correct answer choice.

Answer choice (B): This is probably the most difficult answer choice to eliminate, and it relies on an inference that is very difficult to make during the setup.

In this answer choice, lot Z is listed on Wednesday. According to our analysis of Wednesday costs, this lot must cost either $12 or $15. In this same answer, lot X is listed on Friday, and from our analysis of Friday costs, this lot must cost either $10 or $12. This combination presents a problem because the second rule indicates that lot X must cost more than lot Z. If the most that lot X can cost is $12, and the least that lot Z can cost is $12, then there is no way to conform to the second rule, and this answer choice must be incorrect.

This relationship reveals the inference that Z cannot be the Wednesday lot and X cannot be the Friday lot *in the same solution* (Z could be the Wednesday lot if X is not the Friday lot, and X could be the Friday lot if Z is not the Wednesday lot).

Answer choice (C): Because this answer choice has an equal number of X and Z lots, it violates the last rule and is therefore incorrect.

Answer choice (D): The game scenario stipulates that Anastasia parks in each of three lots at least once during the week. This answer choice does not include lot Y, and therefore it is incorrect. Note that, whenever you have a distribution in a game, there is often a List question answer choice that will attempt to drop one of the variables that must be present.

Answer choice (E): As discussed in the setup, the combination of the first two rules yields the inference that Anastasia must park in lot X or Y on Thursday. Because this answer specifies that she parks in lot Z on Thursday, this answer is incorrect.

Question #19: Global, Cannot Be True. The correct answer choice is (E)

This is the second easiest question of the entire section (#21 is the easiest). As detailed in the setup, the third rule states that the Wednesday lot must cost more than the Friday lot, and that consequently the Wednesday lot cannot cost $10 and that the Friday lot cannot cost $15. Hence, answer choice (E) is correct in this Cannot be true question.

Answer choices (A), (B), (C), and (D): Any of the days listed in these answer choices could be the $15 lot, and hence each one of these answers is incorrect.

Answer choice (E): This is the correct answer choice.

Question #20: Local, Must Be True. The correct answer choice is (E)

This is an extremely challenging question if you do not understand the distribution of lots in this game. Remember, Anastasia can only park in lot X a single time.

If lot Z is the $12 lot, then from the second rule we can infer that lot X is the $15 lot. With the cost of X and Z established, we can infer that lot Y must be the $10 lot.

Because X is the $15 lot, Anastasia must park in lot X on Thursday. And, because Anastasia can only park in lot X a single time, she cannot park in X on any of the other days. This fact has a direct impact on Wednesday and Friday. Wednesday's lot, which must cost either $12 or $15, cannot cost $15 because that would mean X was Wednesday's lot. Consequently, Anastasia must park in lot Z on Wednesday.

And, since according to the third rule the Wednesday lot costs more than the Friday lot, we can conclude that Anastasia must park in lot Y, the $10 lot, on Friday. Hence, answer choice (E) must be correct.

Answer choices (A) and (B): Neither of the days listed in these answer choices must be a day on which Anastasia parks in lot Y, and hence both of these answers are incorrect.

Answer choices (C) and (D): Neither of these answers could be a day on which Anastasia parks in lot Y, and hence both of these answers are incorrect.

Answer choice (E): This is the correct answer choice.

Question #21: Global, Cannot Be True. The correct answer choice is (D)

This is the easiest question of the entire section. As detailed in the setup, the combination of the first two rules yields the inference that Anastasia cannot park in lot Z on Thursday because doing so would lead to a violation of the second rule. Hence, answer choice (D) is correct.

Answer choices (A), (B), (C), and (E): Any of the days listed in these answer choices could days on which Anastasia parks in lot Z, and hence each one of these answers is incorrect.

Answer choice (D): This is the correct answer choice.

Question #22: Global, List. The correct answer choice is (C)

Please note that this question asks for the list of days on which Anastasia could park in the $10 lot in a *single solution* to the game, not the complete list of *all possible* days on which Anastasia could park in the $10 lot. Thus, the correct answer choice must be part of a single workable solution.

From our initial diagram we know that neither Wednesday nor Thursday can be a day on which Anastasia parks in the $10 lot. This information eliminates answer choices (D) and (E) from contention.

The remaining three answer choices involve Monday or Tuesday or both, and as discussed in the setup, there are no rules regarding Monday or Tuesday. Thus, at first it may appear that any of the three remaining answer choices could be the correct answer. At this point, if you were running out of time you should guess (C) because it is "different" than the other two answers in that it contains two days whereas the other two answers only contain one day. Answer choice (C) does turn out to be correct, but obviously it is better to select that answer based on facts as opposed to an educated guess. With that in mind, let's use answer choice (A) to show why both answer choices (A) and (B) are incorrect.

Answer choice (A): If Monday is the *only* day on which Anastasia parks in the $10 lot, then from the numerical distribution, the $10 lot cannot be Z and it must be X or Y (lot Z must appear more than once in the five days). But, of course, from the second rule we know that lot X costs more than lot Z, and thus the $10 lot cannot be X, and therefore the lot that Anastasia parks in on Monday must be lot Y.

We can also infer that Friday will be a $12 lot (remember, there can be only one $10 lot, and Friday must be $10 or $12), and that therefore Wednesday will be a $15 lot (because the third rule stipulates that Wednesday's lot costs more than Friday's lot).

Further, because we have inferred that lot Y is the $10 lot, we know that Thursday's $15 lot, which could only have been lot X or Y, must in fact be lot X. This deduction leads to the further deduction that lot Z is the $12 lot. This establishes the following relationship of lots to cost:

Lot X = $15
Lot Y = $10
Lot Z = $12

These deductions lead to the following setup:

Cost:	10	12/15		15	15	12

Lot:	Y	Z/X	X	X	Z	
	M	T	W	Th	F	

However, astute test takers may have already noticed a problem—lot X has appeared twice in our setup and we have already established that X can only appear once in this game. Thus, assigning Monday as the only $10 lot does not allow for a viable solution to the game.

Answer choice (B): The reasoning used to eliminate answer choice (A) also applies to (B); simply shift the $10 lot to Tuesday and proceed with the same logic.

Answer choice (C): This is the correct answer choice.

Answer choice (D): Because Wednesday cannot be a $10 lot, this answer choice can be eliminated.

Answer choice (E): Because Thursday must be a $15 lot, this answer choice can be eliminated.

Overview: Test takers found this section to be somewhat easier than the first Logical Reasoning section, with no truly difficult questions among the first ten. Again, the most challenging questions are presented toward the end of the section. Test takers found the two Flaw in the Reasoning questions, #20 and #22, and the two Parallel Reasoning questions, #19 and #21, among the most difficult. This section contains five Strengthen questions, the most difficult of which is probably the Strengthen/Except question, #17. There are three Must be True questions, three Weaken questions, and three Flaw in the Reasoning questions. The section also contains two Assumption questions, #7 and #16, both of which deal with Supporter Assumptions, and two Method of Reasoning/Argument Part questions, #6 and #24, with only one Point at Issue question (#10), one very difficult Cannot be True question (#18), one Resolve the Paradox question (#25) and one challenging Justify the Conclusion question (#26).

Question #1: Weaken. The correct answer choice is (C)

The reasoning in this stimulus is fairly straightforward, though not completely sound:

> Premise: If Jones were to swallow a particular chemical, a blood deficiency would result, causing inflammation to his skin.

> Premise: Jones' skin was not inflamed when he was admitted to the ER.

> Conclusion: Therefore Jones must not have swallowed the chemical.

The physician ignores the fact that it may take time to develop a mineral deficiency and possibly more time to exhibit signs of inflammation. This leap in logic will likely be important, especially considering that we are asked to weaken the argument.

Answer choice (A): Even if Jones did not know the chemical was dangerous, he would not necessarily seek to consume it; most would avoid ingesting random unlabeled chemicals.

Answer choice (B): Jones' having suffered inflammation in the past makes it no more or less likely that he consumed the chemical in this instance.

Answer choice (C): This is the correct answer choice. If it takes 48 hours for the deficiency to occur, it may take even longer for the rash to appear. Jones was *rushed* to the emergency room after falling unconscious, so the absence of other symptoms proves nothing about whether he consumed the chemical in question. This represents an effective attack on the doctor's flawed reasoning.

Answer choice (D): It is impossible to determine the exact effect of Jones' having worked with the chemical. Jones could have become careless around the chemical, or, knowing the dangers involved, become more careful. Perhaps Jones was suicidal. In any case, this response has nothing to do with the causal association of the chemical and the symptoms, so this choice is incorrect.

Answer choice (E): Since Jones showed no signs of inflammation, it is completely irrelevant that there are other possible causes of inflammation.

Question #2: Strengthen—Principle: The correct answer choice is (B)

The pacifist in the stimulus presents a couple of premises, and then takes a broad leap to the conclusion:

> Premise: It is immoral to do anything that causes harm to another person.

> Premise: Using force causes harm to another person.

> Conclusion: Therefore the *threat* of force (even in self-defense) is immoral.

From the first two premises, we can conclude that using force to cause harm to another is immoral, but it is a big jump in logic to conclude that even the *threat* of force is immoral.
Since we are asked to justify his reasoning, we must select a response that links threats with actions.

Answer choice (A): This choice does not address the pacifist's leap, so it is incorrect. One of the argument's premises is that harm is always immoral, so the ability to draw a clear line between self-defense and aggression is not relevant. Either way, according to the author, the described behavior is immoral, so this answer choice is incorrect.

Answer choice (B): This is the correct answer choice, because if this is true, we can draw conclusions about threats based on what we know about actions. This answer choice provides the required link between actions and threats.

Answer choice (C): This response introduces a new consideration (that of good versus harm) but does not address the leap in the author's logic.

Answer choice (D): This answer choice is contrary to the conclusion in the stimulus, so it cannot possibly help to justify the pacifist's reasoning.

Answer choice (E): The stimulus concerns the morality of making a threat, not that of carrying out a threat, so this response is off-topic and incorrect.

Question #3: Must be True. The correct answer choice is (D)

In this stimulus, the author discusses the electrification of instruments in popular music, which has led to fewer musicians *per band*. Electrification has, nevertheless, increased the *total number* of musicians who play popular music professionally.

When we consider these facts, it seems that if there are fewer musicians *per band*, yet a *greater number* of professional popular musicians, these musicians' play must then be accommodated by a *greater number of professional bands overall*. Since the stimulus provides something of a paradox, and the question asks what is most strongly supported, we should watch for an answer choice that provides such a resolution.

Answer choice (A): The stimulus provides no information about the number of amateur musicians who play popular music, so this response is not necessarily true.

Answer choice (B): The stimulus provides no information about the proportion of professional musicians able to play electric instruments. This answer is not supported by the statements in the stimulus, and is therefore incorrect.

Answer choice (C): This answer choice is not necessarily true. There could simply be many new professional bands, so the number of professional musicians would not necessarily increase in any single band.

Answer choice (D): This is the correct answer choice, as it resolves the paradox presented in the stimulus (which made this answer quite conducive to prephrasing). If the total number of professional bands has increased due to electrification, then it makes sense that the number of professional musicians has increased despite a lower number of musicians per band.

Answer choice (E): If many professionals each play in more than one band, it becomes more difficult to explain an increase in the number of professional musicians.

Question #4: Strengthen—Principle. The correct answer choice is (A)

The argument claims that when new statistics indicate that a problem occurs more often, this is often the result of people's taking more note of it, rather than the result of an increase in occurrence. The argument then concludes that we should be wary of radical solutions as responses to new statistics.

The argument is based on the reasoning that a greater degree of awareness isn't sufficient to warrant radical solutions, and that radical solutions may be unnecessary. Since we are asked to identify the principle to which the argument conforms, the correct choice should reflect this concept.

Answer choice (A): This is the correct answer choice. "Better cognizance" basically means "better awareness," and, according to the reasoning in the stimulus, better awareness doesn't warrant radical solutions. This is the reasoning underlying the author's argument.

Answer choice (B): The discussion in the stimulus does not concern determination of the existence of a problem, but rather what to do when new statistics reflect an increase in the occurrence of a problem.

Answer choice (C): This Opposite answer choice states that statistical data alone should be used, while the author maintains that we should guard against overreacting to new statistical data.

Answer choice (D): Since the stimulus never suggests manipulation of the statistics to justify radical solutions, this choice is incorrect. When the author warns against overestimating the value of newer statistics, it is for fear of the result of heightened public awareness, as opposed to deliberate manipulation.

Answer choice (E): The stimulus contains no discussion of why radical solutions might be undesirable, so this response does not conform to the argument in the stimulus.

Question #5: Weaken. The correct answer choice is (D)

Barr's argument, as presented in the stimulus, is as follows: Based on the premise that Survey Group has tracked tea sales at numerous stores over the last 20 years and observed no increase in tea sales, it can be concluded that tea's popularity has not actually increased (in spite of the recent increase in visibility).

Often an LSAT argument will rest on evidence provided by a survey, but we should be wary of conclusions drawn from polls which are potentially unreliable. In this case, Barr's argument is weak, because Survey Group might be using a non-representative sample. "Numerous" is vague, and does not guarantee that Survey Group has polled a number sufficient to produce a good sample, so the survey results may be unreliable. Since we are asked to weaken Barr's argument, we should watch for an answer choice which reflects this flaw.

Answer choice (A): This choice provides no actual evidence, only amorphous plans for a future survey to be conducted by a special interest group. Since this answer has no effect on the strength of the argument in the stimulus, it certainly doesn't weaken the conclusion and is thus incorrect.

Answer choice (B): This choice does not weaken the argument that tea's popularity has not actually increased. It might establish only that amongst people who drink tea, there is receptiveness to variety.

Answer choice (C): This choice concerns only the source of the evidence discussed, but information about funding does not provide evidence of a particular survey's validity. In any case, it is not possible to know whether "consumer advocacy groups" would make the study more accurate, less accurate, or have any effect at all.

Answer choice (D): This is the correct answer choice. If the stores are all located in the same small region, there is a good chance that the sample is not representative, and that tea-sales could have vastly increased in other, unstudied, areas of the country. This response effectively attacks the statistical flaw in Barr's argument.

Answer choice (E): Even if a campaign is expensive and efficient, this does not prove it successful, so this response does not weaken the argument.

Question #6: Method of Reasoning—Argument Part. The correct answer choice is (C)

The argument in this stimulus breaks down as follows:

> Premise: Doctors urge patients to lower cholesterol levels with moderate dietary changes.

> Premise: Moderate changes are often not effective in reduction of cholesterol.

> Conclusion: One may need to make more dramatic changes, like becoming vegetarian, in order to comply with their doctors' recommendations.

Since we are asked to identify the role that the second sentence plays in the argument, we should be aware that it is a premise which supports the author's conclusion.

Answer choice (A): This choice is incorrect. The premise suggests that one may have to engage in drastic dietary changes, which does not counter the doctors' suggestion in any way. Furthermore, the stimulus states that "often," moderate changes are insufficient, which leaves open the possibility that moderate changes are sometimes sufficient.

Answer choice (B): The argument presents a vegetarian diet as an example of a dramatic dietary change, not as a diet superior to any that contains meat. Since the argument does not make the claim that vegetarian diets are always superior, this choice is incorrect.

Answer choice (C): This is the correct answer choice. The author's conclusion is that more than a moderate dietary change might be necessary to reduce cholesterol levels, and the premise in the second sentence provides support for that conclusion.

Answer choice (D): The claim in question was not made to explain the success of vegetarian diets, but rather to point out the common necessity of making drastic dietary changes.

Answer choice (E): This choice reflects the value of breaking down each stimulus to its logical components. After isolating the conclusion and the premises of this argument, it is very clear that the second sentence is not a conclusion, so this answer choice is incorrect.

Question #7: Assumption—SN. The correct answer choice is (A)

This stimulus provides the following conditional argument:

> Premise: Empathy is essential to the following of moral codes, which sometimes require people to put the interests of others above self-interest.

> Conclusion: Therefore civilized society could not exist without empathy.

We can diagram the conditional reasoning in the premise and the conclusion as follows:

> Premise: MC ──────→ E (that is, if moral codes are to be followed, empathy is required)

> Conclusion: CS ──────→ E (that is, if civilized society is to exist, empathy is required)

When we examine the two conditional statements above, we can see that empathy is the overlapping theme, the necessary variable in both the premise and the conclusion. In order to justify that this conclusion be drawn from this premise, the argument requires a supporter assumption: A premise which, although not stated explicitly in the stimulus, bridges the gap between the two conditional statements. Since we are asked to find the choice that provides the required assumption, we should look for the answer that ties together the loose ends of this argument: Moral codes and civilized society.

Answer choice (A): This is the correct answer choice, as it supplies the needed link between moral codes and civilized society. We know from the stimulus that the following of moral codes requires at least some who will put others interests over their own, so without such people, moral codes could not be followed. If *civilized society* also depends on the existence of these sometimes selfless people, as this answer choice provides, then we can conclude that without such people, moral codes could not be followed, and civilized society could not exist.

Answer choice (B): This choice is causal rather than conditional, so it should be eliminated. Conditional reasoning requires conditional assumptions. Furthermore, since the stimulus specifies that empathy is only *sometimes* required, this leaves open the possibility that, most of the time, civilized society is fine without such empathy. Thus we need not assume that lack of empathy is usually detrimental.

Answer choice (C): This choice is the Mistaken Reversal of the required assumption, so we should eliminate it. Also, the stimulus sought to establish a *necessity*, whereas this choice concerns a *sufficiency*. That is, the stimulus says that civilized society requires some degree of selflessness, whereas this answer choice presents the assumption that this selflessness *guarantees* that a society will be civilized.

Answer choice (D): The fact that certain moral codes have arisen in some civilized societies does not establish a *conditional* link between civilized society and moral codes. It is therefore irrelevant to the conditional argumentative strategy in the stimulus.

Answer choice (E): A description of the results of empathy does not establish a link between moral codes and civilized society, so this choice is incorrect.

Question #8: Main Point. The correct answer choice is (B)

The stimulus consists of claims leading to an unstated conclusion, meant to fill in the blank. First, the argument claims that dissatisfied insurgent (non-dominant) parties always produce factions that are as much at odds with each other, in terms of views and aims, as they are with the dominant party. Second, the argument claims that, although differences are set aside temporarily, they emerge after the insurgent party claims victory.

We are asked in this case to choose the most logical completion of the argument. Since the victorious party has factions that disagree with each other as much as they disagreed with the previously dominant party, we have reason to believe that the newly victorious party might have to deal with the prospect of continued insurgence.

Answer choice (A): This conclusion, that the newly victorious party's tenure will not last as long as that of the previously dominant party, is unwarranted, so this choice is wrong. The stimulus offers no information concerning how long a fractured party would stay in power, and there is no reason to rule out the possibility that the new dominant party might resolve its conflicts.

Answer choice (B): This is the correct answer choice. Since some factions disagree with each other as much as the previously dominant party, these disagreements would likely need to be addressed to guard against continued insurgence.

Answer choice (C): The stimulus is based on the premise that factions will unite on a common, actual cause, not the claim that those factions would form their own justificatory ideology.

Answer choice (D): It may be true that the defeated party often resists, but the author never discusses, or even alludes to, what would happen to the previously dominant party. This answer cannot logically complete the argument in the stimulus.

Answer choice (E): While it may be true that the newly victorious party has some work to do, it is unwarranted to conclude that such compromise is impossible, so this choice is incorrect.

Question #9: Weaken—CE. The correct answer choice is (D)

The conclusion in the stimulus is as follows: It is incorrect to conclude that Sullivan's advanced age was the deciding factor when passed over for promotion. This conclusion is based on the premise that recent promotions have been given to employees older than Sullivan.

We know that Sullivan was older than his competition; however, we know little else about the other recent promotions within the company. Without more complete information, this argument is fairly weak. We are asked what the manager failed to consider, so we should focus on the fact that potentially relevant information, concerning the recent promotions of other older employees, might be lacking.

Answer choice (A): The author chooses to takes issue with what *kept* Sullivan from being promoted, rather than discussing the points in Sullivan's favor. The author doesn't fail to consider Sullivan's qualifications, but rather claims that Sullivan was passed over for some reason other than his advanced age, so this answer is incorrect.

Answer choice (B): The idea that other factors might have contributed is consistent with the author's conclusion that age was not the *deciding* factor. Thus the manager's argument is not vulnerable to this criticism, and this answer is incorrect.

Answer choice (C): The possibility that people associate age with wisdom likely strengthens the argument, making it less likely that ageism was a cause in passing over Sullivan.

Answer choice (D): This is the correct answer choice. If the older employees who were promoted had no younger competition, then their promotion really proves nothing about the company's attitude concerning older employees, or about the factors likely to have lead to Sullivan's non-promotion.

Answer choice (E): The argument does not fail to consider the possibility of confidentiality; the argument is based on the results of those deliberations, rather than on the deliberations themselves.

Question #10: Point at Issue. The correct answer choice is (E)

In this dialogue, council member P asserts that some who see an instance of pollution are alarmists, exaggerating its significance, since one incident should be distinguished from behavior reflecting the general inclination not to pollute.

Council member Q implies that those people are not alarmists, arguing that they are simply applying the general principle that people do what is easiest to do, and it is easier to pollute than to not pollute.

When asked to identify the point at issue, we should look for the basis of the fundamental disagreement. Council member P says the complainers *are* alarmists, and that there is a general inclination *not to* pollute. Council member Q argues that the people *aren't* alarmists, and that there is a general inclination *to* pollute. The correct answer choice will identify an issue with which one speaker would agree, and the other would disagree.

Answer choice (A): This answer may at first appear relevant to the discussion of whether or not people are "alarmist." However, both politicians might agree that pollution should be considered a problem without agreeing about the full extent of the problem or the appropriate response to its incidence, so this choice is incorrect.

Answer choice (B): Council member P does not have to disagree with this statement, because council member P could accept that people follow the easiest path, but argue that it is easier to not pollute.

Answer choice (C): Both council members might accept that people are responsible for pollution, so this choice is incorrect.

Answer choice (D): The stimulus offers no insight into the beliefs of the council members concerning people's ability to change their behavior.

Answer choice (E): This is the correct answer choice. It reflects the crux of the council members' disagreement. The council members' differing conclusions are based on different beliefs about people's inclination to pollute.

Question #11: Flaw in the Reasoning. The correct answer choice is (A)

The argument presented in this stimulus is as follows: Since there are many instances of bribery among members of the Wagston staff, and Wagston is a member of the board, the entire board must be corrupt and should therefore be replaced.

The argument is flawed, because it does not establish that Wagston is corrupt based on the fact that some members of his staff are, and does not logically establish that the problems in Wagston's staff extend to the entire board.

Answer choice (A): This is the correct answer choice. The argument inappropriately attributes the actions of some members of Wagston's staff, to the entire board, without giving any logical justification for this leap.

Answer choice (B): Since the possibility that Wagston's staff bribed more people is not harmful to the argument, this choice cannot represent a flaw.

Answer choice (C): There is no need to specify the relationship between two concepts that are related by definition. Bribery is always a form of corruption, so this choice is wrong.

Answer choice (D): The argument does overgeneralize; however, it does not do so to the point of arguing that every single staff member is corrupt. Furthermore, the argumentative strategy is to generalize from Wagston's staff to the entire board, not just within Wagston's staff.

Answer choice (E): Since board's alleged corruption is in fact a substantive issue in the argument, it is not a flaw to focus on that aspect of character. Furthermore, a character attack involves the use of "bad character" as an avoidance strategy in which the author sidesteps the actual point, issue, or argument. In this instance, that is not the case.

Question #12: Must Be True. The correct answer choice is (D)

The stimulus consists of information rather than any real argument, so a Must Be True question will often follow. The stimulus offers us the following three facts:

1. Methylxanthines found in Coffee and Tea increase the clumping of blood cells.
2. Clumping is in general more pronounced in women than in men.
3. Clumping is probably the cause of women's higher risk following angioplasty.

We are asked to find which answer choice is most supported by the information provided in the stimulus.

Answer choice (A): Since methylxanthines increase clumping, which increases the risk of complications after angioplasty, it makes no sense to give men these chemicals before such surgery.

Answer choice (B): The stimulus only concerns what factors might increase risk in angioplasty, never ruling out any other surgical procedures, so this choice is unsupported and incorrect.

Answer choice (C): We cannot, based on the information in the stimulus, conclude anything about men's versus women's consumption of coffee and tea. The fact that women have a higher risk following a particular procedure does not necessarily tell us anything about their consumption of coffee and tea.

Answer choice (D): This is the correct answer choice. Since women are already more prone to clumping after angioplasty, they should certainly avoid coffee and tea, because drinking coffee or tea makes the problem worse.

Answer choice (E): The stimulus is an observation of certain risks involved in angioplasty, not a general recommendation against the surgery.

Question #13: Strengthen—Principle. The correct answer choice is (D)

In this stimulus, the author points out that it is easy to recognize the merits of a machine, but the ability to recognize artistic excellence is rare. For this reason engineers tend to be relaxed about evaluation, whereas artists tend to get more anxious.

The principle suggested by this stimulus is that people are more anxious about having their work evaluated when the work's excellence is less easily recognizable.

Answer choice (A): The stimulus offers no insight into the personalities of artists relative to those of engineers. That is, one group's anxious response to evaluation does not translate into a generally anxious personality, so this choice is incorrect.

Answer choice (B): The stimulus does not concern empirical value, but rather subjective evaluation and anxiety.

Answer choice (C): Even if we believe that artwork and engineering should be evaluated differently, this does not address the anxiety of artists. Additionally, the stimulus is more factual, and doesn't address what "should be."

Answer choice (D): This is the correct answer choice. The principle which explains the stimulus is that when more people can easily recognize the success of a work, the creator is less anxious about its evaluation.

Answer choice (E): This comparison, between the relative confidence of different evaluators, is never made in the stimulus. The relevant comparison is between those who produce machines and those who produce art, and their reactions to evaluation.

Question #14: Strengthen—CE. The correct answer choice is (D)

The conclusion of this stimulus is presented in the first sentence: Scientists hypothesize that P-fat is necessary for eyesight development. This conclusion is based on the fact that babies that are fed milk formulas that contain less P-fat have worse eyesight than those that are fed mother's milk with high P-fat content.

The scientists' hypothesis is questionable, since other differences between formula and mother's milk might conceivably account for differences in eyesight development. Furthermore, the information could be consistent with P-fat as a beneficial but unnecessary factor.

The inclusion of information about premature versus full-term babies can be confusing, because it does not play an immediate role in the argument. In fact, this detail might make one wonder whether there is simply a correlation between babies that are born prematurely and those likely to be fed formula, which could mean that premature birth, rather than P-fat, is the cause.

Since we are asked to support the hypothesis, we should look for the choice which, if true, would make it more likely that P-fat is indeed a necessity.

Answer choice (A): Since the stimulus concerns the *development* of eyesight, it is unclear how levels of P-fat in *adults* is relevant.

Answer choice (B): This is the correct answer choice. If premature birth directly deprives the baby of P-fat, it seems more likely that P-fat is the cause, rather than some other factor associated with premature birth. This answer choice improves the *argument*, even if it doesn't completely justify the *conclusion*.

Answer choice (C): This incorrect choice might be initially attractive, as it appears to eliminate genetics as an alternate explanation, strengthening the *conclusion*. The argument in the stimulus, however, is that P-fat is *required*, and ruling out other potential causes of poor eyesight would not affect the claim that P-fat is necessary to eyesight development.

Answer choice (D): This answer choice is relevant only if we add the presumption that babies always prefer substances that are more supportive of their eyesight development.

Answer choice (E): This answer choice does nothing to strengthen the scientists' hypothesis that P-fat is required for eyesight development. It may help to strengthen the link between premature birth to poor eyesight, but that is not what we are looking for in response to this question.

Question #15: Must Be True. The correct answer choice is (E)

This stimulus consists primarily of information, with no strong argument or conclusion:

> 1. Artists' different ways of producing contours and hatching can help distinguish one artists' forgery or work from those of another artist.

> 2. Such analysis has shown that many originally attributed to Michelangelo were in fact painted by Giulio Clovio.

Before moving on to the question, we should pause and consider the facts. If contour and hatching analysis has allowed Michelangelo's work to be distinguished from Giulio Clovio's, what does this tell us? It seems clear that the two artists must have had differing methods with respect to contour and hatching, which would allow distinction between the two artists based on such analysis. This inference will likely be helpful as we move on to the question, which, not surprisingly, is a Must Be True, the question type that will often follow a factual stimulus with no real argumentation.

Answer choice (A): Contours and hatching are the discussed features, but that does not mean that they are the main distinguishing features among artists' works, so this choice is unwarranted and incorrect.

Answer choice (B): Although we know from the stimulus that many of the works formerly attributed to Michelangelo had been misattributed, but we cannot conclude based on this premise that Giulio was a forger, because the works could simply have been confused, or Giulio's passed off as Michelangelo's by some third party.

Answer choice (C): The argument merely stated that analysis of contours and hatching *can help*, and that artists use *different methods*, so we can not justifiably conclude that *no* forgery can be a perfect duplicate.

Answer choice (D): We cannot be sure that every single work by Clovio contains the same hatching and contour as his drawings. The argument concerns what can be helpful, not what is certain. Furthermore, it is quite possible that an artist's methods can differ from one medium to another (such as drawing versus painting) while still being unique in comparison to those of other artists.

Answer choice (E): This is the correct answer choice, as it ties together the factual statements in the stimulus. There must be such an analyzable difference between the two artists' contour and hatching styles if such analysis allows one to distinguish between Michelangelo's work and Giulio's.

Question #16: Assumption—CE. The correct answer choice is (D)

The moralist in this stimulus begins by defining immoral actions, and then presents the following conditional argument:

> Premise: Immoral actions eventually harm those who perform them:
> IA ——————→ HA   (immoral actions ——————→ harm actor)

> Conclusion: Those who act immorally do so out of ignorance:
> IA ——————→ I   (immoral actors ——————→ act out of ignorance)

The overlapping variable in the two statements is the IA, or Immoral Action. In order to properly draw the above conclusion from the premise provided, we might look to tie together the remaining two variables: Harm to the Actor, and Ignorance of the consequence.

Since we are asked to find the assumption required by the argument, we should look for the *Supporter Assumption* that ties up the loose ends of the argument, as discussed above.

Answer choice (A): Since the argument concerns causes of immorality rather than responsibility, this choice is off-topic and incorrect.

Answer choice (B): The argument requires a link between harming one's own self and ignorance of such consequence, not a discussion of whether moral acts could be harmful to their originators.

Answer choice (C): The argument in the stimulus assumes that harming one's own self and ignorance are linked, not character and harming others. This choice gives the assumption that would support a contrary argument.

Answer choice (D): This is the correct choice, as it links the two variables as needed to justify the conclusion in the stimulus: Harm to the Actor, and Ignorance of consequence (lack of intent). That is,

> HA ——————→ I

If we link this conditional statement to those in the stimulus, we get the following:

> IA ——————→ HA ——————→ I

This allows the conclusion in the stimulus to be properly drawn: IA ——————→ I

Answer choice (E): A correct reading of this choice yields the assumption: *all* who knowingly harm themselves have character defects. The argument in the stimulus, however, was that intent was essential, not that it was sufficient, so this choice is incorrect.

Question #17: Strengthen Except—CE. The correct answer choice is (D)

This stimulus tells us that the Earth has experienced a regular sequence of ice ages over the past 800,000 years, and that climatologists believe they have an explanation. They note that when Earth's orbit experiences certain fluctuations, an ice age tends to coincide, and they hypothesize a causal relationship to explain this correlation. The climatologists believe that the fluctuations take Earth through a dust cloud which enters the atmosphere and dims the Sun, thereby causing an ice age, noting that a particularly dense cloud is required for the effect.

The argument as stated is weak. Although there has been a correlation between ice ages and orbital fluctuations, one cannot logically conclude that a causal relationship even exists. Just because a dust cloud might be sufficient to cause an ice age does not mean that an ice age indicates a dust cloud-that presumption would be a Mistaken Reversal.

Test takers found this to be one of the most difficult in the section, probably because the "except" is often missed. We are asked to eliminate the supporting choices, and select the response which *fails to strengthen* the argument.

Answer choice (A): This response supports the climatologists' hypothesis by establishing that no dust clouds were passed through before the Earth's first ice-age. If there had been such dust clouds appearing without causing ice ages, the causal argument would be weakened, so ruling out this possibility lends some strength to the hypothesis. This answer choice is therefore incorrect.

Answer choice (B): This answer choice establishes that dense dust clouds (like those hypothesized by the scientists) do exist, and that the formation of one such dust cloud coincided with the Earth's first ice age. While this evidence is, of course, not conclusive, it does lend some credibility to the conclusion. Since this would strengthen the argument, this is not the correct answer.

Answer choice (C): If dust from volcanic eruptions decreases Earth's temperature slightly, that makes it more likely that dust in Earth's atmosphere, in sufficient concentrations, could cause an ice age.

Answer choice (D): This is the correct answer choice, because it offers no support for the hypothesis. The climatologists' hypothesis concern a dust cloud which *enters* the Earth's atmosphere, not a dust cloud created *within* the Earth's atmosphere.

Answer choice (E): This response suggests that cosmic trace elements are found in sedimentary layers that correspond with ice ages. That makes it more likely that a cosmic dust cloud was indeed involved.

Question #18: Cannot Be True. The correct answer choice is (B)

In this stimulus, the philosopher concludes that the rational pursuit of happiness does not amount to simply following one's strongest desires. This conclusion is based on the following two premises:

> Premise: The rational pursuit of happiness must include consideration of long-term consequences.

> Premise: Desires are usually focused on the short-term, and are sometimes compulsions, whose achievement offers no happiness.

We are asked to assume that the philosopher's statements are true, and to determine which answer choice cannot be true based on these statements.

Answer choice (A): We cannot infer anything about whether the majority of people experience compulsions. If something is uncertain, we cannot rule it out as a possibility, so this choice is incorrect.

Answer choice (B): This is the correct answer choice. The philosopher specifically states that desires are sometimes compulsions, but attaining the goal of compulsions never leads to any happiness. That means that attaining the goals of some desires (namely, the compulsions) does not lead to any happiness. This disproves the claim that attaining the goal of any desire leads to momentary happiness.

Answer choice (C): The stimulus only discusses the rational pursuit of happiness, not the portion of people who engage in it. Thus we have no insight into whether or not this represents a majority, so this response could be true.

Answer choice (D): There is no way to glean from the stimulus whether people want more than personal happiness, so this response could be true.

Answer choice (E): The philosopher's argument is entirely consistent with all actions' having some long-term consequences, so this response could be true.

Question #19: Parallel Reasoning—SN. The correct answer choice is (B)

In this stimulus, the political scientist provides the following conditional premises:

> Premise: All governments worthy of respect allow dissent from policies:
> GWR ———→ AD

> Premise: No government worthy of respect leaves minorities unprotected (so, if one does not protect minorities, one is not a government worthy of respect, and on the other side of the coin, if a government is worthy of respect, it will protect its minorities):
> GWR ———→ PM

The political scientist then jumps to the following unwarranted conclusion:

Conclusion: Any government that protects minorities permits criticism of its policies (that is, any government that protects minorities allows some dissent)

PM ⟶ AD

If we revisit the three statements as diagrammed, the political scientist's misstep in logic becomes clear:

GWR ⟶ AD
GWR ⟶ PM

The scientist's conclusion is that PM ⟶ AD, but the flaw is clear. What we really know based on the above premises is that any government worthy of respect (GWR) exhibits both of the other discussed attributes: that is, they allow dissent (AD), and they protect minorities (PM). The speaker cannot *logically* conclude that any government that protects minorities will also allow dissent from government policies, so the argument is flawed.

We are asked to find the answer that most closely parallels the argument in the stimulus, so we should look for the choice that employs a similar brand of flawed reasoning.

Answer choice (A): Although the reasoning in this answer is flawed, the mistake is of a different sort; here, the stimulus defines politicians as admirable if they put the interests of those they serve above *their own*. The author attempts to draw from this the conclusion that politicians are admirable for putting the nation's interests above those of *their constituents*. This leap is unjustified, but not in the same way as the conditional reasoning in the stimulus, so this answer is incorrect.

Answer choice (B): This is the correct answer choice, as it employs the same type of flawed reasoning:

All jazz musicians are capable of improvising: JM ⟶ I
No jazz musician is incapable of reading music
(which means every one is capable of reading music):   JM ⟶ RM

Conclusion: All who can read music can improvise: RM ⟶ I

In this example we can see the exact same pattern of flawed reasoning. The author has taken the two necessary variables from the premises and has attempted to tie them together in a sufficient/necessary relationship.

Answer choice (C): This answer choice also represents a mistake in logic, but the reasoning here does not parallel that found in the stimulus. Rather, this choice represents a mistaken negation, as follows:

Cool, dry ecosystems are populated by large mammals: CDE ⟶ LM
No such systems have abundant and varied plant life: LM ⟶ A̶V̶PL
If we link these two premises, we get the following: CDE ⟶ LM ⟶ A̶V̶PL
From the above statement this inference can be drawn: *CDE ⟶ A̶V̶PL*
But the *mistaken negation* is drawn instead: C̶D̶E ⟶ AVPL

Answer choice (D): The fact that the conditional variable in this case introduces "some" into the equation tells us that it will not logically parallel the method of argumentation used in the stimulus.

Answer choice (E): This answer also contains a "some," so we can safely conclude that it will not follow the same overall logical flow, and is incorrect.

Question #20: Flaw in the Reasoning. The correct answer choice is (D)

The advertisement presented here inappropriately presumes that, because each winner of the Economic Merit Prize for the past 25 years has been covered by the Acme retirement plan, these winners believe that the plan offers them an economically secure future. The author concludes that the Acme plan is good for those with similar needs.

In moving from the initial premise about coverage to the intermediate conclusion about security, the advertisement makes the unwarranted assumptions that the winners of the Economic Merit Prize had some control over the choice of their retirement plans, and that this choice was based in large part on their needs (and not, for example, on sponsorship).

Answer choice (A): The stimulus provides information on the retirement plans of the winners over the past 25 years. Information about plans from longer than 25 years ago is most likely irrelevant, and to ignore it is not a flaw.

Answer choice (B): The advertisement argues that the Acme retirement plan is *a* good plan, not that it is the *only* good plan, so this choice seems to misinterpret the argument as presented and is incorrect. When a stimulus concludes that something is *a solution*, it is not vulnerable to the criticism that there exist other solutions.

Answer choice (C): Since the winners of the Economic Merit Prize are never said to believe that the Acme plan is good for all those similar to themselves, those economists are not portrayed as endorsing the argument's main conclusion.

Answer choice (D): This is the correct answer choice. If the winners of the Economic Merit Prize did not select the Acme retirement plan themselves, the intermediate conclusion that they believe the plan is good does not follow from the argument, and the argument falls apart. Who selected the plan was never addressed, and this represents a flaw.

Answer choice (E): The argument in the stimulus makes no such assumption, so this choice is incorrect. The advertisement was geared to those with "similar" needs, not those with "identical" needs.

Question #21: Parallel Reasoning—CE. The correct answer choice is (E)

The argument presented here is that it is better to drive a small car because, although it offers less protection, a smaller car is more maneuverable, making accidents less likely.

The argument makes the questionable assumption that the gain from decreasing the likelihood of an accident outweighs the loss associated with driving a car less protected.

Since the question asks us to parallel the reasoning, it is valuable to realize the flaw. However, we should also take a moment to consider the general reasoning. The argument proceeds by weighing opposing considerations, and arrives at the determination that the pros outweigh the cons.

Answer choice (A): Since this answer does not involve the weighing of considerations to make a decision, this choice does not reflect the reasoning in the argument.

Answer choice (B): In the stimulus, the opposing considerations both speak to safety. In this choice, the opposing considerations do not speak to the same end goal.

Answer choice (C): This choice might seem attractive because it has an immediate similarity. However, the reasoning is geared towards which option is more costly, but concerns which option is more practical, and that constitutes a questionable leap from costliness to practicality. Furthermore, since this choice does not involve any sort of risk assessment, it does not parallel the reasoning in the stimulus.

Answer choice (D): This is an argument for finding a happy medium, but the stimulus did not advocate purchasing a mid-sized car, so this choice is wrong.

Answer choice (E): This is the correct answer choice. Exercising vigorously makes one more vulnerable if one catches a wasting illness, but exercising vigorously decreases the risk of contracting such illness, so the argument concludes that one should exercise vigorously. This represents exactly the same type of risk assessment as that found in the stimulus.

Question #22: Flaw in the Reasoning. The correct answer choice is (C)

The conclusion presented in the stimulus is that owners who wish to protect their dogs from arthritis should not neuter them until they are full-grown. This conclusion is based on the premise that neutering dogs early in puppyhood usually inhibits bone development, which leads to arthritis.

In this argument, the author makes the unjustified leap from "early in puppyhood" to "full grown." The more proper conclusion would be that, to protect their dogs from arthritis, owners should not neuter their dogs in early puppyhood. This does not necessarily mean waiting until full adulthood. The argument also assumes that neutering dogs early in puppyhood does not bring some detriment (with respect to arthritis) that may outweigh the associated benefits.

Answer choice (A): "Usually" is enough to determine whether a probability is in one's favor, so the failure to state exact percentages is irrelevant, and this choice does not describe a flaw. The exact percentages could establish exactly how imperative an action is, but would not change the general observation that the action should be taken.

Answer choice (B): The author does not need to explain why improper bone development leads to arthritis, so this choice is wrong. This choice incorrectly requires a premise that does not need to be established.

Answer choice (C): This is the correct answer choice. The argument leaps from a premise about "early puppyhood" to arrive at a conclusion about "full-grown," dogs, and never considered whether neutering sometime between early puppyhood and adulthood was acceptable.

Answer choice (D): This is a very popular answer choice among test takers, because the possibility discussed might lead one to argue for early neutering. By dealing with the totality of benefits, this answer choice goes beyond the scope of the argument, which only deals with arthritic concerns. The author's argument does not address overall health, so to ignore overall health is not a flaw.

Answer choice (E): Since the argument only concerns the avoidance of risk incurred by impeding bone development, the continued existence of some lesser risk would have no effect on the strength of the argument. Ignoring this possibility is not a flaw.

Question #23: Main Point. The correct answer choice is (B)

In this stimulus, a political scientist presents a democratic dilemma: While people should be free to spend their money as they wish, there is unfair advantage that comes with the ability to vastly outspend one's opponents. Democratic governments are obligated to ensure that all voices have equal chance of being heard, but should not have to subsidize every candidate. We are asked to supply the resolution, which would have to strike a balance between allowing for spending freedom and supporting candidates' equal access to the public.

Answer choice (A): Preventing the poorly funded from campaigning does not offer a resolution, but instead runs contrary to the principle that democracies are obligated to ensure an equal voice to all.

Answer choice (B): This is the correct answer choice. Placing an upper limit on campaign spending helps to minimize the advantage of those with greater resources, without requiring government subsidies for every candidate.

Answer choice (C): This choice would not help equalize spending. If the government finances each campaign at a low percentage of total cost, that defrays more cost for the wealthier campaigns, and does little for the underfunded campaigns.

Answer choice (D): To prevent the wealthy from campaigning with their own money is to violate the principle that a democracy should allow its citizens to spend their money, "within broad limits," so this choice is incorrect.

Answer choice (E): Allowing a candidate to spend as much as any other candidate chooses to spend does nothing to resolve the democratic dilemma presented in the stimulus. Since this rule is really no rule at all, this answer choice is incorrect.

Question #24: Method of Reasoning—Argument Part. The correct answer choice is (C)

The argument presented in this stimulus is as follows: Some people may be right that private ownership of the means of production destroys less advanced societies (which need to share to survive). Technologically advanced societies, however, require innovation that comes only from private ownership. Therefore, the author concludes, people who argue against private ownership are wrong with respect to advanced societies.

Since we are asked only to identify the role of the first sentence, we should seek the answer which reflects that the first sentence represents a position that the author counters.

Answer choice (A): This choice is incorrect, because the proposition is cast as more relevant to more primitive than to advanced societies.

Answer choice (B): The argument is set partially against the hypothesis, and cannot be said to explain its wide acceptance.

Answer choice (C): This is the correct answer choice. The argument in the stimulus suggests that the hypothesis is inapplicable to high tech societies, but makes sense if the society is more dependent upon sharing resources than upon its advanced technology.

Answer choice (D): This choice is incorrect, because, according to the reasoning in the stimulus, the contention referenced may be applicable to less technologically advanced societies.

Answer choice (E): The argument in the stimulus contends that the generalization is always untrue for technologically advanced societies. This choice says the generalization can be true for any society, so this choice contradicts the stimulus and is incorrect. Further, the stimulus concerns the *development*, not the *introduction*, of new technologies.

Question #25: Resolve the Paradox. The correct answer choice is (D)

The stimulus presents what purports to be a discrepancy, and asks us to explain how both of the following claims could be true:

1. A certain medication effectively lowers cholesterol.
2. Those using the medication have higher cholesterol levels than average.

It must be the case that those who are on this medication had their cholesterol reduced, while as a group maintaining a level higher on average than that of the overall population.

Answer choice (A): The relative effectiveness of another medication is completely irrelevant to the specific effects of this medication.

Answer choice (B): The effects of other medications do not explain the effects of this medication, so this choice is incorrect.

Answer choice (C): What happens to people who do not take the drug offers no insight into what happens to people who take the drug.

Answer choice (D): This is the correct answer choice, as it explains why those on the medication could have derived benefits but stayed at a higher level than that of the overall population.

Answer choice (E): The average distribution of cholesterol in the population does not help to explain why people receiving a cholesterol-lowering drug, nevertheless, have high cholesterol.

Question #26: Justify the Conclusion—Formal Logic. The correct answer choice is (C)

In this stimulus, the political theorist presents a series of conditional statements, which can be diagrammed as follows:

For an alliance to be strong, it must respond aggressively to problems:

AS ⟶ RA

An alliance will respond aggressively only if every member perceived gravity:

RA ⟶ PG

But the EU countries will not perceive a problem to be grave unless they all agree that it threatens their alliance's economy:

PG ⟶ ATAE

What we then have is the following chain of logic:

AS ⟶ RA ⟶ PG ⟶ ATAE

We can also draw from these statements the following contrapositive chain:

A̶T̶A̶E̶ ⟶ P̶G̶ ⟶ R̶A̶ ⟶ A̶S̶

The theorist concludes that, with respect to the European Union, *not all members* of the will *be strong* in foreign policy (this is the condition 'A̶S̶' diagrammed above). We are then asked to justify this conclusion. This means that from the answer choices we should select the one which, when added to the premises in the stimulus, allows for this conclusion (A̶S̶) to be properly drawn.

Answer choice (A): This answer choice concerns an irrelevant group—those countries which refuse to join an alliance. Since this information does not affect the conditional reasoning in the stimulus, this answer choice is incorrect.

Answer choice (B): This choice supplies another condition, and relates to the aggression level of individual countries rather than the responses of alliances.

Answer choice (C): This is the correct answer choice. If problems that appear economically threatening to some countries do not appear so to others, then at least some countries do not perceive the gravity of the threat, meaning P̶G̶ (that is, not all countries in the alliance perceive the threat), and if we know this then we know P̶G̶ ⟶ R̶A̶ ⟶ A̶S̶. In other words, from this information we can logically conclude A̶S̶.

Answer choice (D): It does not matter which countries are weak, and this choice does not prove that any countries do fail to perceive economic relevance, so this choice does not trigger any of the conditions in the stimulus needed to justify the conclusion.

Answer choice (E): The benefits derived by individual countries from alliance membership are irrelevant to the conclusion we seek to justify.

CHAPTER SIX: THE DECEMBER 2004 LSAT

Taking the December 2004 LSAT

This chapter contains the complete text of the December 2004 LSAT, including an answer key and scoring scale. For the closest possible re-creation of the conditions of the LSAT, take this exam as a timed exercise. The exam will take just less than three hours, and there is an answer sheet included so that you can record your answers. Per Law Services protocol, here are the directions for taking the test under timed conditions:

> Section 1 = allow yourself exactly 35 minutes
> Section 2 = allow yourself exactly 35 minutes
> Section 3 = allow yourself exactly 35 minutes
> Section 4 = allow yourself exactly 35 minutes
>
> Writing Sample = allow yourself exactly 30 minutes (Writing Samples prior to June 2005 were 30 minutes instead of 35 minutes)

The rules for the test are as follows:

> During the test you are allowed to work only on the section being timed. You cannot go back or forward to work on any other section of the test.
>
> Do not take a break between any of the sections (on the actual LSAT, an unscored experimental section will be included, and a 10-15 minute break will be given after section 3; because this test has no experimental section, you should not take a break between any of the sections).
>
> You may not use any scratch paper while working on the test; only the test pages themselves are available for your use.

After completing the test, refer to the answer key and the "Computing Your Score" section at the end of the test to find your LSAT score.

Your answer sheet is on the next page, and complete explanations are in the following chapter.

SECTION I
Time—35 minutes
26 Questions

Directions: The questions in this section are based on the reasoning contained in brief statements or passages. For some questions, more than one of the choices could conceivably answer the question. However, you are to choose the <u>best</u> answer; that is, the response that most accurately and completely answers the question. You should not make assumptions that are by commonsense standards implausible, superfluous, or incompatible with the passage. After you have chosen the best answer, blacken the corresponding space on your answer sheet.

1. The obsession of economists with consumption as a measure of economic well-being has prevented us from understanding the true nature of economic well-being. We get very little satisfaction out of the fact that our clothing wears out, our automobiles depreciate, and the gasoline in our tanks burns up and must be replaced.

    The author is arguing that

    (A) economic well-being cannot be defined solely in terms of consumption
    (B) satisfaction is possible without consumption
    (C) valid measures of consumption cannot be devised
    (D) modern products are designed for early obsolescence
    (E) satisfaction can provide an adequate quantitative measure of economic well-being

2. Commentator: Many people argue that the release of chlorofluorocarbons into the atmosphere is harming humans by damaging the ozone layer, thus allowing increased amounts of ultraviolet radiation to reach Earth. But 300,000 years ago a supernova greatly damaged the ozone layer, with no significant effect on our earliest ancestors. Because the supernova's disruption was much greater than the estimated effect of chlorofluorocarbons today, there is no reason to think that these chemicals in the atmosphere harm humans in this way.

    Which one of the following, if true, would most seriously weaken the commentator's argument?

    (A) Extraterrestrial influences on the ozone layer tend to occur less often than terrestrial ones.
    (B) Natural events, such as the eruption of volcanoes, continue to damage the ozone layer today.
    (C) Our earliest ancestors possessed genetic characteristics making them more resistant than we are to the harmful effects of ultraviolet radiation.
    (D) The ozone layer regenerates at a slow rate, barring counteractive processes.
    (E) Scientists have discovered that genetic changes occurred in our ancestors during the period in which the supernova affected Earth.

3. A reason Larson cannot do the assignment is that she has an unavoidable scheduling conflict. On the other hand, a reason Franks cannot do the assignment is that he does not quite have the assertiveness the task requires. So, the task must be assigned to Parker, the only supervisor in the shipping department other than Larson and Franks.

    The argument depends on assuming which one of the following?

    (A) Larson has the assertiveness the task requires.
    (B) The task cannot be assigned to anyone other than a supervisor in the shipping department.
    (C) Franks would be assigned the task if Franks had the assertiveness the task requires.
    (D) The task cannot be assigned to anyone who has any kind of scheduling conflict.
    (E) No one who is not a supervisor in the shipping department has the assertiveness this task requires.

GO ON TO THE NEXT PAGE.

4. Columnist: Analysts argue that as baby boomers reach the age of 50, they will begin seriously planning for retirement. This will lead them to switch from being primarily consumers to being savers. Thus, these analysts conclude, more money will flow into the stock market, resulting in continued gains in stock prices. Analysts would stand to gain if this were true, but they are being overly optimistic. As consumption decreases, so will corporate earnings; therefore high stock prices will not be justified, and thus boomers' money will more likely flow into investments other than stocks.

The columnist's argument does which one of the following?

(A) attempts to undermine the analysts' argument by questioning the truth of its premises
(B) attempts to undermine the analysts' argument by suggesting that the analysts present it for self-serving reasons
(C) attempts to undermine the analysts' argument by drawing an alternative conclusion from the analysts' premises
(D) argues that the analysts' conclusion is basically right, but suggests that it is somewhat too optimistic
(E) argues in favor of the analysts' conclusion, but does so on the basis of a different body of evidence

5. Item removed from scoring.

6. Maria: Popular music is bad art because it greatly exaggerates the role love plays in everyday life and thereby fails to represent reality accurately.

Theo: Popular music is not supposed to reflect reality; it performs other artistic functions, such as providing consoling fantasies and helping people create some romance in their often difficult lives. You should understand popular music before you condemn it.

The dialogue provides the most support for the claim that Maria and Theo disagree over whether

(A) most good art creates consoling illusions
(B) some bad art exaggerates the role love plays in everyday life
(C) art should always represent reality as it could be, not as it is
(D) art need not represent reality accurately to be good art
(E) popular music should not be considered to be an art form

7. An artificial hormone has recently been developed that increases milk production in cows. Its development has prompted some lawmakers to propose that milk labels should be required to provide information to consumers about what artificial substances were used in milk production. This proposal should not be implemented: just imagine trying to list every synthetic fertilizer used to grow the grass and grain the cows ate, or every fungicide used to keep the grain from spoiling!

The argument proceeds by

(A) proposing an alternative course of action for achieving the objectives of the proposal being argued against
(B) raising considerations in order to show that the proposal being argued against, if strictly implemented, would lead to absurd consequences
(C) using specific examples in order to show that an alternative to the proposal being argued against would better achieve the ends to which the original proposal was directed
(D) introducing a case analogous to the one under consideration to show that a general implementation of the proposal being argued against would be impossible
(E) questioning the motivation of those who made the proposal being argued against

GO ON TO THE NEXT PAGE.

8. Trust, which cannot be sustained in the absence of mutual respect, is essential to any long-lasting relationship, personal or professional. However, personal relationships, such as marriage or friendship, additionally require natural affinity. If a personal relationship is to endure, it must be supported by the twin pillars of mutual respect and affinity.

If the statements above are true, then which one of the following must also be true?

(A) A friendship supported solely by trust and mutual respect will not be long-lasting.

(B) In the context of any professional relationship, mutual respect presupposes trust.

(C) If a personal relationship is supported by mutual respect and affinity, it will last a long time.

(D) Personal relationships, such as marriage or friendship, are longer-lasting than professional relationships.

(E) Basing a marriage on a natural affinity will ensure that it will endure.

9. The use of phrases like "as so-and-so said" or "as the saying goes" suggests that the quote that follows has just been illustrated. Such phrases are inappropriately used when an apparent counterexample has just been given.

Which one of the following contains an inappropriate usage of a phrase, according to the principle stated above?

(A) Fatima was a mathematician who often thought about unsolved problems of mathematics, although it was unpleasant to be reminded that most would probably remain unsolved in her lifetime. As the saying goes, "Strange how much you've got to know before you know how little you know."

(B) Harold's friends were surprised when he revealed that he had left his wallet at home and asked that someone lend him money. But he had done the same thing many times before. As Halliard said, "The force of selfishness is as inevitable and as calculable as the force of gravitation."

(C) The best model of vacuum cleaner was the most expensive on the market, but it would have made Roger unhappy to purchase it. For although he never wanted anything but the best, he was also quite frugal, and would never have forgiven himself for spending the money. As the saying goes, "A penny saved is a penny earned."

(D) Sharon loved cats, but her husband was allergic to them. Still, he was occasionally willing to accompany her to cat shows. As the saying goes, "Shared lives mean shared loves."

(E) Raoul spent a year planning and preparing for a fantastic ski trip. He enjoyed his ski trip greatly until he broke his leg and had to spend two weeks in the hospital. As the saying goes, "All's well that ends well."

GO ON TO THE NEXT PAGE.

10. Rachel: Though contemporary artists are pleased to be free of the constraints that bound their predecessors, this freedom has caused a decline in the quality of art. Great art can be produced only when artists struggle to express themselves within externally imposed boundaries.

James: People have always been critical of the art of their own time. They forget all but the greatest art from past eras. Since inferior contemporary artworks have not yet been forgotten, people today mistakenly think that contemporary art is generally inferior to earlier art.

On the basis of their statements, Rachel and James are committed to disagreeing with each other about whether

(A) contemporary art is of lower quality than earlier art
(B) contemporary artists are bound by the same constraints as their predecessors
(C) great art is produced only when an artist struggles against limitations
(D) inferior art from past eras is generally forgotten
(E) one can correctly assess the quality of art only if it was produced in past eras

11. The average cost of groceries will rise again next month. Consequently, butter and eggs can be expected to cost more next month.

The flawed reasoning in the argument above most closely parallels the reasoning in which one of the following?

(A) The price of gasoline has been rising each month for the past year. Therefore, we can expect to pay more for gasoline next month.
(B) Either the government will reduce taxes or the economy will fall into a recession. The government is unlikely to reduce taxes Therefore, the economy will fall into a recession.
(C) The average amount of time spent by people younger than 20 in watching television has recently risen rapidly. Therefore, the amount of time fourth graders spend watching television must have risen recently.
(D) Since sugar is a major ingredient in ice cream, the price of ice cream increases whenever the price of sugar increases. The price of sugar is expected to increase next month. Therefore, the price of ice cream can be expected to increase next month.
(E) Real estate prices go down when the population of those from 20 to 30 years old declines, and the number in that age group will decrease over the next decade. Therefore, real estate prices will go down over that period.

12. Biologists have noted reproductive abnormalities in fish that are immediately downstream of paper mills. One possible cause is dioxin, which paper mills release daily and which can alter the concentration of hormones in fish. However, dioxin is unlikely to be the cause, since the fish recover normal hormone concentrations relatively quickly during occasional mill shutdowns and dioxin decomposes very slowly in the environment.

Which one of the following statements, if true, most seriously weakens the argument?

(A) Some of the studies that show that fish recover quickly during shutdowns were funded by paper manufacturers.
(B) The rate at which dioxin decomposes varies depending on the conditions to which it is exposed.
(C) Normal river currents carry the dioxin present in the river far downstream in a few hours.
(D) Some of the fish did not recover rapidly from the physiological changes that were induced by the changes in hormone concentrations.
(E) The connection between hormone concentrations and reproductive abnormalities is not thoroughly understood.

13. If the play were successful, it would be adapted as a movie or revived at the Decade Festival. But it is not successful. We must, regrettably, conclude that it will neither become a movie nor be revived at the Decade Festival.

The argument's reasoning is flawed because the argument

(A) fails to draw the conclusion that the play will not both be adapted as a movie and be revived at the Decade Festival, rather than that it will do neither
(B) fails to explain in exactly what way the play is unsuccessful
(C) equates the play's aesthetic worth with its commercial success
(D) presumes, without providing justification, that there are no further avenues for the play other than adaptation as a movie or revival at the Decade Festival
(E) fails to recognize that the play's not satisfying one sufficient condition does not preclude its satisfying a different sufficient condition for adaptation as a movie or revival at the Decade Festival

GO ON TO THE NEXT PAGE.

14. Physician: In order to investigate diseases caused by hormonal imbalances, a certain researcher wants to study, among others, 200 children whose pituitary glands fail to produce typical amounts of Human Growth Hormone (HGH). The study would involve administering a synthetic version of HGH to the children over a two-year period. But medical research should be permitted only if it is likely to reveal important information about a medical condition and is known to pose only a minimal risk to the subjects. The researcher's proposed study should be prohibited.

Which one of the following, if true, would most help to justify the physician's argumentation?

(A) The resources expended on the HGH study could be spent instead on research likely to lead to treatments for medical conditions more serious than diseases stemming from hormonal imbalances.

(B) About 10,000 children have already been given synthetic HGH without obvious side effects.

(C) Obtaining informed consent from children is impossible, because they are not yet mature enough to understand complex medical issues.

(D) Although hormonal imbalances can cause disease, the imbalances themselves do not constitute a medical condition.

(E) The long-term effects of synthetic HGH have never been tested and are unknown.

15. At the request of Grove Park residents, speed bumps were installed on all streets in their neighborhood. However, although through traffic does cause noise and congestion in Grove Park, this remedy is blatantly unfair. The neighborhood is not a private community, and its streets were built with public funds, and thus all drivers have the right to use them whenever they please.

The reasoning in the argument is most vulnerable to criticism on the grounds that it

(A) ignores the possibility that speed bumps may not reduce the speeds at which drivers drive through the neighborhood

(B) neglects the possibility that drivers frequently drive through the neighborhood at high speeds

(C) provides no evidence that drivers have complained about the new speed bumps in the neighborhood

(D) contains the tacit assumption that residents of neighborhoods should have the right to restrict traffic through their communities

(E) presumes, without providing justification, that speed bumps do prevent drivers from using the roads on which the bumps are found

16. Literary critic: Often the heirs of a successful writer decide to publish the manuscripts and the letters the dead writer left behind, regardless of the merit of the work. However, many writers have manuscripts that they judge to be unworthy of publication and with which they would not like to be publicly associated even after they die. Hence a successful writer who decides not to publish a recently completed manuscript should destroy it immediately.

Which one of the following statements, if true, most calls into question the soundness of the literary critic's advice?

(A) Some writers whose work becomes both popular and respected after they die received no literary recognition during their lifetimes.

(B) Writers who achieve a certain degree of fame can expect that some of their personal correspondence will become publicly available after they die.

(C) Most successful writers' judgments of their recently completed work is unnecessarily harsh and is often later revised.

(D) Many posthumously published books would have been published by the author had the author lived.

(E) Some heirs of successful writers do not consider themselves qualified to judge the merits of a literary work.

17. In practice the government will have the last word on what an individual's rights are, because its police will do what its officials and courts say. But that does not mean that the government's view is necessarily the correct view; anyone who thinks it is must believe that persons have only such moral rights as the government chooses to grant, which means that they have no moral rights at all.

Which one of the following most accurately expresses the conclusion of the argument?

(A) Individuals have no rights at all unless the government says that they do.

(B) What government officials and courts say an individual's rights are may not be correct.

(C) Individuals have rights unless the government says that they do not.

(D) The police always agree with government officials and the courts about what an individual's rights are.

(E) One should always try to uphold one's individual rights against the government's view of what those rights are.

GO ON TO THE NEXT PAGE.

18. There is evidence to suggest that our cave-dwelling ancestors polished many of their flints to a degree far surpassing what was necessary for hunting purposes. It seems, therefore, that early humans possessed an aesthetic sense.

Which one of the following statements, if true, most seriously weakens the argument?

(A)   Most flints used by our cave-dwelling ancestors were not highly polished.

(B)   The caves in which the highly polished flints were found are unadorned by cave paintings.

(C)   There is evidence that these highly polished flints were used for display in religious ceremonies.

(D)   Flints were often used by early humans for everyday chores other than hunting.

(E)   Any benefits that an aesthetic sense would have given to cave-dwelling humans are poorly understood.

19. Columnist: Much of North America and western Europe is more heavily forested and has less acid rain and better air quality now than five decades ago. Though this may be due largely to policies advocated by environmentalists, it nonetheless lends credibility to the claims of people who reject predictions of imminent ecological doom and argue that environmental policies that excessively restrict the use of natural resources may diminish the wealth necessary to adopt and sustain the policies that brought about these improvements.

Which one of the following, if true, most strengthens the columnist's reasoning?

(A)   Nations sustain their wealth largely through industrial use of the natural resources found within their boundaries.

(B)   The more advanced the technology used in a nation's industries, the greater is that nation's ability to devote a portion of its resources to social programs.

(C)   A majority of ecological disasters arise from causes that are beyond human control.

(D)   If a compromise between the proponents of economic growth and the environmentalists had been enacted rather than the current policies, the environment would have seen significantly less improvement.

(E)   The concern demonstrated by a nation for the health and integrity of its natural ecosystems leads to an increase in that nation's wealth.

20. Reviewer: Many historians claim, in their own treatment of subject matter, to be as little affected as any natural scientist by moral or aesthetic preconceptions. But we clearly cannot accept these proclamations of objectivity, for it is easy to find instances of false historical explanations embodying the ideological and other prejudices of their authors.

The reviewer's reasoning is most vulnerable to criticism on the grounds that it

(A)   takes for granted that the model of objectivity offered by the natural sciences should apply in other fields

(B)   offers evidence that undermines rather than supports the conclusion it reaches

(C)   fails to recognize that many historians employ methodologies that are intended to uncover and compensate for prejudices

(D)   takes for granted that some historical work that embodies prejudices is written by historians who purport to be objective

(E)   fails to recognize that not all historical explanations embodying ideologies are false

21. Although the geological record contains some hints of major meteor impacts preceding mass extinctions, there were many extinctions that did not follow any known major meteor impacts. Likewise, there are many records of major meteor impacts that do not seem to have been followed by mass extinctions. Thus the geological record suggests that there is no consistent causal link between major meteor impacts and mass extinctions.

Which one of the following assumptions enables the argument's conclusion to be properly inferred?

(A)   If there were a consistent causal link between major meteor impacts and mass extinctions, then all major meteor impacts would be followed by mass extinctions.

(B)   Major meteor impacts and mass extinctions cannot be consistently causally linked unless many mass extinctions have followed major meteor impacts.

(C)   Of the mass extinctions that did not follow any known major meteor impacts, few if any followed major meteor impacts of which the geological record contains no hints.

(D)   If there is no consistent causal link between major meteor impacts and mass extinctions, then not all mass extinctions could have followed major meteor impacts.

(E)   There could be a consistent causal link between major meteor impacts and mass extinctions even if not every major meteor impact has been followed by a mass extinction.

GO ON TO THE NEXT PAGE.

22. When uncontrollable factors such as lack of rain cause farmers' wheat crops to fail, fertilizer and seed dealers, as well as truckers and mechanics, lose business, and fuel suppliers are unable to sell enough diesel fuel to make a profit.

Which one of the following claims follows logically from the information above?

(A) If several of the businesses that sell to farmers do not prosper, it is because farming itself is not prospering.

(B) If rainfall is below average, those businesses that profit from farmers' purchases tend to lose money.

(C) Farmers are not responsible for the consequences of a wheat crop's failing if wheat growth has been affected by lack of rain.

(D) A country's dependence on agriculture can lead to major economic crises.

(E) The consequences of a drought are not restricted to the drought's impact on farm productivity.

23. For each action we perform, we can know only some of its consequences. Thus the view that in no situation can we know what action is morally right would be true if an action's being morally right were the same as the action's having the best consequences.

The conclusion follows logically if which one of the following is assumed?

(A) On some occasions we can come to learn that it is morally wrong to perform a certain action.

(B) On some occasions we can know what action is morally right.

(C) Knowing that an action has the best consequences requires knowing all the consequences of that action.

(D) Only the immediate consequences of our actions are relevant in determining whether they are morally right.

(E) An action may be morally right for one particular person without being morally right for all people.

24. In criminal proceedings, defense attorneys occasionally attempt to establish that a suspect was not present at the commission of a crime by comparing the suspect's DNA to the DNA of blood or hair samples taken from the scene of the crime. Although every person's DNA is unique, DNA tests often fail to distinguish among DNA samples taken from distinct individuals. Hence, it is a mistake to exonerate a suspect simply because that person's DNA did not match the DNA samples taken from the scene of the crime.

Which one of the following is an error in the reasoning above?

(A) It assumes without warrant that the use of physical evidence in identifying suspects is never mistaken.

(B) It confuses a test that incorrectly identifies DNA samples as coming from the same person with a test that incorrectly shows as coming from different persons samples that come from a single person.

(C) It generalizes about the reliability of all methods used to identify those involved in the commission of a crime on the basis of results that pertain to only a few such methods.

(D) It relies on experimental data derived from DNA testing that have not been shown to hold under non experimental conditions.

(E) It fails to demonstrate that physical evidence taken from the scene of a crime is the only sort of evidence that should be admitted in criminal court proceedings.

GO ON TO THE NEXT PAGE.

25. Some visitors to the park engage in practices that seriously harm the animals. Surely, no one who knew that these practices seriously harm the animals would engage in them. So it must be concluded that some of the visitors do not know that these practices seriously harm the animals.

The pattern of reasoning exhibited by which one of the following arguments is most similar to that exhibited by the argument above?

(A) Some of the people who worked on the failed project will be fired. Everyone in this department played an important part in that project. Therefore some people in this department will be fired.

(B) Some of the people who signed the petition were among the mayor's supporters. Yet the mayor denounced everyone who signed the petition. Hence the mayor denounced some of her own supporters.

(C) Some of the people polled live outside the city limits. However, no one who can vote in city elections lives outside the city. Therefore some of the people polled cannot vote in the upcoming city election.

(D) All of the five original planners are responsible for this problem. Yet none of the original planners will admit responsibility for the problem. Thus some of the people responsible for the problem will not admit responsibility.

(E) Some members of the Liberal Party are in favor of the proposed ordinance. But all members of the city council are opposed to the proposed ordinance. Hence some members of the city council are not Liberals.

26. Rapid population growth can be disastrous for a small city. Ideally there should be at least one municipal employee for every hundred residents; when too many people move in at once, city services responsible for utilities and permits are quickly overloaded. Most city budgets do not allow for the immediate hiring of new staff.

Which one of the following, if true, most strengthens the argument?

(A) During budget shortages, small cities tend to place a high priority on basic municipal services while cutting back on less essential services.

(B) New residents of any city bring with them new ideas about how a city should be run.

(C) Some large cities can absorb rapid population growth more readily than many small cities can.

(D) A low unemployment rate is one of the main reasons that new residents move to a city.

(E) New residents of most small cities do not start paying city taxes for at least a year.

S T O P

IF YOU FINISH BEFORE TIME IS CALLED, YOU MAY CHECK YOUR WORK ON THIS SECTION ONLY.
DO NOT WORK ON ANY OTHER SECTION IN THE TEST.

SECTION II
Time—35 minutes
27 Questions

Directions: Each passage in this section is followed by a group of questions to be answered on the basis of what is <u>stated</u> or <u>implied</u> in the passage. For some of the questions, more than one of the choices could conceivably answer the question. However, you are to choose the <u>best</u> answer; that is, the response that most accurately and completely answers the question, and blacken the corresponding space on your answer sheet.

A number of natural disasters in recent years— such as earthquakes, major storms, and floods—that have affected large populations of people have forced relief agencies, communities, and entire nations to
(5) reevaluate the ways in which they respond in the aftermaths of such disasters. They believe that traditional ways of dealing with disasters have proved ineffective on several occasions and, in some cases, have been destructive rather than helpful to the
(10) communities hit by these sudden and unexpected crises. Traditionally, relief has been based on the premise that aid in post disaster situations is most effective if given in the immediate aftermath of an event. A high priority also has been placed on the
(15) quantity of aid materials, programs, and personnel, in the belief that the negative impact of a disaster can be counteracted by a large and rapid infusion of aid.

Critics claim that such an approach often creates a new set of difficulties for already hard-hit
(20) communities. Teams of uninvited experts and personnel—all of whom need food and shelter—as well as uncoordinated shipments of goods and the establishment of programs inappropriate to local needs can quickly lead to a secondary "disaster" as
(25) already strained local infrastructures break down under the pressure of this large influx of resources. In some instances, tons of food have disappeared into local markets for resale, and, with inadequate accounting procedures, billions of dollars in aid
(30) money have gone unaccounted for.

To develop a more effective approach, experts recommend shifting the focus to the long term. A response that produces lasting benefit, these experts claim, requires that community members define the
(35) form and method of aid that are most appropriate to their needs. Grassroots dialogue designed to facilitate preparedness should be encouraged in disaster-prone communities long before the onset of a crisis, so that in a disaster's immediate aftermath, relief agencies
(40) can rely on members of affected communities to take the lead. The practical effect of this approach is that aid takes the form of a response to the stated desires of those affected rather than an immediate, though less informed, action on their behalf.
(45) Though this proposal appears sound, its success depends on how an important constituency, namely donors, will respond. Historically, donors—individuals, corporations, foundations, and governmental bodies—have been most likely to
(50) respond only in the immediate aftermath of a crisis.

However, communities affected by disasters typically have several long-term needs such as the rebuilding of houses and roads, and thus the months and years after a disaster are also crucial. Donors that
(55) incorporate dialogue with members of affected communities into their relief plans could foster strategies that more efficiently utilize immediate aid as well as provide for the difficulties facing communities in the years after a disaster.

1.   Which one of the following most accurately expresses the main point of the passage?

(A)   The most useful response to a natural disaster is one in which relief agencies allow victims to dictate the type of aid they receive, which will most likely result in the allocation of long-term rather than immediate aid.

(B)   The quantity of aid given after a natural disaster reflects the desires of donors more than the needs of recipients, and in some cases great quantities of aid are destructive rather than helpful.

(C)   Aid that focuses on long-term needs is difficult to organize because, by its very definition, it requires that relief agencies focus on constructing an adequate dialogue among recipients, providers, and donors.

(D)   Disaster relief efforts have been marked by inefficiencies that attest to the need for donors and relief agencies to communicate with affected communities concerning how best to meet not only their short-term but also their long-term needs.

(E)   Though the years after a disaster are crucial for communities affected by disasters, the days and weeks immediately after a disaster are what capture the attention of donors, thus forcing relief agencies into the role of mediators between the two extremes.

GO ON TO THE NEXT PAGE.

2. Which one of the following examples best illustrates the type of disaster response recommended by the experts mentioned in the third paragraph?

   (A) After a flood, local officials reject three more expensive proposals before finally accepting a contractor's plan to control a local river with a dam.
   (B) Following a plan developed several years ago by a relief agency in consultation with donors and community members, the relief agency provides temporary shelter immediately after a flood and later helps rebuild houses destroyed by the flood.
   (C) Immediately after a flood, several different relief agencies, each acting independently, send large shipments of goods to the affected community along with teams of highly motivated but untrained volunteers to coordinate the distribution of these goods.
   (D) At the request of its donors, a private relief agency delays providing any assistance to victims of a flood until after the agency conducts a thorough study of the types of aid most likely to help the affected community in the long run.
   (E) After a flood, government officials persuade local companies to increase their corporate giving levels and to direct more aid to the surrounding community.

3. The author of the passage would be most likely to agree with which one of the following statements?

   (A) Disaster relief plans are appropriate only for disaster-prone communities.
   (B) When communities affected by disasters have articulated their long-term needs, donors typically have been responsive to those needs.
   (C) Donors would likely provide more disaster relief aid if they had confidence that it would be used more effectively than aid currently is.
   (D) It is not the amount of aid but rather the way this aid is managed that is the source of current problems in disaster relief.
   (E) Few communities affected by disasters experience a crucial need for short-term aid.

4. The author discusses donors in the final paragraph primarily in order to

   (A) point to an influential group of people who have resisted changes to traditional disaster response efforts
   (B) demonstrate that the needs of donors and aid recipients contrast profoundly on the issue of disaster response
   (C) show that implementing an effective disaster relief program requires a new approach on the part of donors as well as relief agencies
   (D) illustrate that relief agencies and donors share similar views on the goals of disaster response but disagree on the proper response methods
   (E) concede that the reformation of disaster relief programs, while necessary, is unlikely to take place because of the disagreements among donors

5. It can be inferred from the passage that the author would be most likely to view a shift toward a more long-term perspective in disaster relief efforts as which one of the following?

   (A) a development that would benefit affected communities as well as aid providers who have a shared interest in relief efforts that are effective and well managed
   (B) a change that would help communities meet their future needs more effectively but would inevitably result in a detrimental reduction of short-term aid like food and medicine
   (C) an approach that would enable aid recipients to meet their long-term needs but which would not address the mismanagement that hampers short-term relief efforts
   (D) a movement that, while well intentioned, will likely be undermined by the unwillingness of donors to accept new methods of delivering aid
   (E) the beginning of a trend in which aid recipients play a major role after a disaster and donors play a minor role, reversing the structure of traditional aid programs

6. Which one of the following inferences about natural disasters and relief efforts is most strongly supported by the passage?

   (A) Although inefficiencies have long been present in international disaster relief programs, they have been aggravated in recent years by increased demands on relief agencies' limited resources.
   (B) Local communities had expressed little interest in taking responsibility for their own preparedness prior to the most recent years, thus leaving donors and relief agencies unaware of potential problems.
   (C) Numerous relief efforts in the years prior to the most recent provided such vast quantities of aid that most needs were met despite evidence of inefficiency and mismanagement, and few recipient communities questioned traditional disaster response methods.
   (D) Members of communities affected by disasters have long argued that they should set the agenda for relief efforts, but relief agencies have only recently come to recognize the validity of their arguments.
   (E) A number of wasteful relief efforts in the most recent years provided dramatic illustrations of aid programs that were implemented by donors and agencies with little accountability to populations affected by disasters.

GO ON TO THE NEXT PAGE.

The moral precepts embodied in the Hippocratic oath, which physicians standardly affirm upon beginning medical practice, have long been considered the immutable bedrock of medical ethics,
(5) binding physicians in a moral community that reaches across temporal, cultural, and national barriers. Until very recently the promises expressed in that oath—for example to act primarily for the benefit and not the harm of patients and to conform to various standards
(10) of professional conduct including the preservation of patients' confidences—even seemed impervious to the powerful scientific and societal forces challenging it. Critics argue that the oath is outdated; its fixed moral rules, they say, are incompatible with more flexible
(15) modern ideas about ethics. It also encourages doctors to adopt an authoritarian stance that depreciates the privacy and autonomy of the patient. Furthermore, its emphasis on the individual patient without regard for the wider social context frustrates the physician's
(20) emerging role as gatekeeper in managed care plans and impedes competitive market forces, which, some critics believe, should determine the quality, price, and distribution of health care as they do those of other commodities. The oath is also faulted for its
(25) omissions: its failure to mention such vital contemporary issues as human experimentation and the relationships of physicians to other health professionals. Some respected opponents even cite historical doubts about the oath's origin and
(30) authorship, presenting evidence that it was formulated by a small group of reformist physicians in ancient Greece and that for centuries it was not uniformly accepted by medical practitioners.
    This historical issue may be dismissed at the
(35) outset as irrelevant to the oath's current appropriateness. Regardless of the specific origin of its text—which, admittedly, is at best uncertain—those in each generation who critically appraise its content and judge it to express valid
(40) principles of medical ethics become, in a more meaningful sense, its authors. More importantly, even the more substantive, morally based arguments concerning contemporary values and newly relevant issues cannot negate the patients' need for assurance
(45) that physicians will pursue appropriate goals in treatment in accordance with generally acceptable standards of professionalism. To fulfill that need, the core value of beneficence—which does not actually conflict with most reformers' purposes—should be
(50) retained, with adaptations at the oath's periphery by some combination of revision, supplementation, and modern interpretation. In fact, there is already a tradition of peripheral reinterpretation of traditional wording; for example, the oath's vaguely and
(55) archaically worded proscription against "cutting for the stone" may once have served to forbid surgery, but with today's safer and more effective surgical techniques it is understood to function as a promise to practice within the confines of one's expertise,
(60) which remains a necessary safeguard for patients' safety and well-being.

7. Which one of the following most accurately states the main point of the passage?

(A) The Hippocratic oath ought to be reevaluated carefully, with special regard to the role of the physician, to make certain that its fundamental moral rules still apply today.

(B) Despite recent criticisms of the Hippocratic oath, some version of it that will continue to assure patients of physicians' professionalism and beneficent treatment ought to be retained.

(C) Codes of ethics developed for one society at a particular point in history may lose some specific application in later societies but can retain a useful fundamental moral purpose.

(D) Even the criticisms of the Hippocratic oath based on contemporary values and newly relevant medical issues cannot negate patients' need for assurance.

(E) Modern ideas about ethics, especially medical ethics, obviate the need for and appropriateness of a single code of medical ethics like the Hippocratic oath.

8. Which one of the following most accurately describes the organization of the material presented in the passage?

(A) A general principle is described, criticisms of the principle are made, and modifications of the principle are made in light of these criticisms.

(B) A set of criticisms is put forward, and possible replies to those criticisms are considered and dismissed.

(C) The history of a certain code of conduct is discussed, criticisms of the code are mentioned and partially endorsed, and the code is modified as a response.

(D) A general principle is formulated, a partial defense of that principle is presented, and criticisms of the principle are discussed and rejected.

(E) The tradition surrounding a certain code of conduct is discussed, criticisms of that code are mentioned, and a general defense of the code is presented.

GO ON TO THE NEXT PAGE.

9. The passage cites which one of the following as a value at the heart of the Hippocratic oath that should present no difficulty to most reformers?

   (A) creation of a community of physicians from all eras, nations, and cultures
   (B) constant improvement and advancement of medical science
   (C) provision of medical care to all individuals regardless of ability to pay
   (D) physician action for the benefit of patients
   (E) observance of established moral rules even in the face of challenging societal forces

10. The author's primary purpose in the passage is to

   (A) affirm society's continuing need for a code embodying certain principles
   (B) chastise critics within the medical community who support reinterpretation of a code embodying certain principles
   (C) argue that historical doubts about the origin of a certain code are irrelevant to its interpretation
   (D) outline the pros and cons of revising a code embodying certain principles
   (E) propose a revision of a code embodying certain principles that will increase the code's applicability to modern times

11. Based on information in the passage, it can be inferred that which one of the following sentences could most logically be added to the passage as a concluding sentence?

   (A) The fact that such reinterpretations are so easy, however, suggests that our rejection of the historical issue was perhaps premature.
   (B) Yet, where such piecemeal reinterpretation is not possible, revisions to even the core value of the oath may be necessary.
   (C) It is thus simply a failure of the imagination, and not any changes in the medical profession or society in general, that has motivated critics of the Hippocratic oath.
   (D) Because of this tradition of reinterpretation of the Hippocratic oath, therefore, modern ideas about medical ethics must be much more flexible than they have been in the past.
   (E) Despite many new challenges facing the medical profession, therefore, there is no real need for wholesale revision of the Hippocratic oath.

12. Each of the following is mentioned in the passage as a criticism of the Hippocratic oath EXCEPT:

   (A) The oath encourages authoritarianism on the part of physicians.
   (B) The version of the oath in use today is not identical to the oath formulated in ancient Greece.
   (C) The oath fails to address modern medical dilemmas that could not have been foreseen in ancient Greece.
   (D) The oath's absolutism is incompatible with contemporary views of morality.
   (E) The oath's emphasis on the individual patient is often not compatible with a market-driven medical industry.

13. Which one of the following can most accurately be used to describe the author's attitude toward critics of the Hippocratic oath?

   (A) enthusiastic support
   (B) bemused dismissal
   (C) reasoned disagreement
   (D) strict neutrality
   (E) guarded agreement

14. Which one of the following would be most suitable as a title for this passage if it were to appear as an editorial piece?

   (A) "The Ancients versus the Moderns: Conflicting Ideas About Medical Ethics"
   (B) "Hypocritical Oafs: Why 'Managed Care' Proponents are Seeking to Repeal an Ancient Code"
   (C) "Genetic Fallacy in the Age of Gene-Splicing: Why the Origins of the Hippocratic Oath Don't Matter"
   (D) "The Dead Hand of Hippocrates: Breaking the Hold of Ancient Ideas on Modern Medicine"
   (E) "Prescription for the Hippocratic Oath: Facelift or Major Surgery?"

GO ON TO THE NEXT PAGE.

A lichen consists of a fungus living in symbiosis (i.e., a mutually beneficial relationship) with an alga. Although most branches of the complex evolutionary family tree of fungi have been well established, the

(5)   evolutionary origins of lichen-forming fungi have been a mystery. But a new DNA study has revealed the relationship of lichen-forming fungi to several previously known branches of the fungus family tree. The study reveals that, far from being oddities,

(10)   lichen-forming fungi are close relatives of such common fungi as brewer's yeast, morel mushrooms, and the fungus that causes Dutch elm disease. This accounts for the visible similarity of certain lichens to more recognizable fungi such as mushrooms.

(15)   In general, fungi present complications for the researcher. Fungi are usually parasitic or symbiotic, and researchers are often unsure whether they are examining fungal DNA or that of the associated organism. But lichen-forming fungi are especially

(20)   difficult to study. They have few distinguishing characteristics of shape or structure, and they are unusually difficult to isolate from their partner algae, with which they have a particularly delicate symbiosis. In some cases the alga is wedged between

(25)   layers of fungal tissue; in others, the fungus grows through the alga's cell walls in order to take nourishment, and the tissues of the two organisms are entirely enmeshed and inseparable. As a result, lichen-forming fungi have long been difficult to

(30)   classify definitively within the fungus family. By default they were thus considered a separate grouping of fungi with an unknown evolutionary origin. But, using new analytical tools that allow them to isolate the DNA of fungi in parasitic or symbiotic

(35)   relationships, researchers were able to establish the DNA sequence in a certain gene found in 75 species of fungi, including 10 species of lichen-forming fungi. Based on these analyses, the researchers found 5 branches on the fungus family tree to which

(40)   varieties of lichen-forming fungi belong. Furthermore, the researchers stress that it is likely that as more types of lichen-forming fungi are analyzed, they will be found to belong to still more branches of the fungus family tree.

(45)   One implication of the new research is that it provides evidence to help overturn the long-standing evolutionary assumption that parasitic interactions inevitably evolve over time to a greater benignity and eventually to symbiosis so that the parasites will not

(50)   destroy their hosts. The addition of lichen-forming fungi to positions along branches of the fungus family tree indicates that this assumption does not hold for fungi. Fungi both harmful and benign can now be found both early and late in fungus

(55)   evolutionary history. Given the new layout of the fungus family tree resulting from the lichen study, it appears that fungi can evolve toward mutualism and then just as easily turn back again toward parasitism.

15. Which one of the following most accurately states the main point of the passage?

(A)   New research suggests that fungi are not only parasitic but also symbiotic organisms.

(B)   New research has revealed that lichen-forming fungi constitute a distinct species of fungus.

(C)   New research into the evolutionary origins of lichen-forming fungi reveals them to be closely related to various species of algae.

(D)   New research has isolated the DNA of lichen-forming fungi and uncovered their relationship to the fungus family tree.

(E)   New research into the fungal component of lichens explains the visible similarities between lichens and fungi by means of their common evolutionary origins.

16. Which one of the following most accurately describes the author's purpose in the last paragraph of the passage?

(A)   to suggest that new research overturns the assumption that lichen-forming fungi are primarily symbiotic, rather than parasitic, organisms

(B)   to show that findings based on new research regarding fungus classification have implications that affect a long-standing assumption of evolutionary science

(C)   to explain the fundamental purposes of fungus classification in order to position this classification within the broader field of evolutionary science

(D)   to demonstrate that a fundamental assumption of evolutionary science is verified by new research regarding fungus classification

(E)   to explain how symbiotic relationships can evolve into purely parasitic ones

GO ON TO THE NEXT PAGE.

17. Which one of the following most accurately describes the organization of the passage?

   (A)   explanation of the difficulty of classifying lichens; description of the DNA sequence of lichen-forming fungi; summary of the implications of this description

   (B)   definition of lichens; discussion of new discoveries concerning lichens' evolutionary history; application of these findings in support of an evolutionary theory

   (C)   definition of lichens; discussion of the difficulty in classifying their fungal components; resolution of this difficulty and implications of the resulting research

   (D)   discussion of the symbiotic relationship that constitutes lichens; discussion of how new research can distinguish parasitic from symbiotic fungi; implications of this research

   (E)   explanation of the symbiotic nature of lichens; discussion of the problems this poses for genetic researchers; delineation of the implications these problems have for evolutionary theory

18. According to the passage, the elimination of which one of the following obstacles enabled scientists to identify the evolutionary origins of lichen-forming fungi?

   (A)   The DNA of lichen-forming fungi was not easy to separate from that of their associated algae.

   (B)   Lichen-forming fungi are difficult to distinguish from several common fungi with which they are closely related.

   (C)   Lichen-forming fungi were grouped separately from other fungi on the fungus family tree.

   (D)   Lichen-forming fungi are far less common than more recognizable fungi such as mushrooms.

   (E)   The DNA of lichen-forming fungi is significantly more complex than that of other fungi.

19. Which one of the following, if true, most weakens the author's criticism of the assumption that parasitic interactions generally evolve toward symbiosis?

   (A)   Evolutionary theorists now postulate that symbiotic interactions generally evolve toward greater parasitism, rather than vice versa.

   (B)   The evolutionary tree of fungi is somewhat more complex than that of similarly parasitic or symbiotic organisms.

   (C)   The DNA of fungi involved in symbiotic interactions is far more difficult to isolate than that of fungi involved in parasitic interactions.

   (D)   The placement of lichen-forming fungi as a separate group on the fungus family tree masked the fact that parasitic fungi sometimes evolved much later than symbiotic ones.

   (E)   Branches of the fungus family tree that have evolved from symbiosis to parasitism usually die out shortly thereafter.

GO ON TO THE NEXT PAGE.

The following passage was written in the late 1980s.

The struggle to obtain legal recognition of aboriginal rights is a difficult one, and even if a right is written into the law there is no guarantee that the future will not bring changes to the law that
(5) undermine the right. For this reason, the federal government of Canada in 1982 extended constitutional protection to those aboriginal rights already recognized under the law. This protection was extended to the Indian, Inuit, and Métis peoples, the
(10) three groups generally thought to comprise the aboriginal population in Canada. But this decision has placed on provincial courts the enormous burden of interpreting and translating the necessarily general constitutional language into specific rulings. The
(15) result has been inconsistent recognition and establishment of aboriginal rights, despite the continued efforts of aboriginal peoples to raise issues concerning their rights.

Aboriginal rights in Canada are defined by the
(20) constitution as aboriginal peoples' rights to ownership of land and its resources, the inherent right of aboriginal societies to self-government, and the right to legal recognition of indigenous customs. But difficulties arise in applying these broadly conceived
(25) rights. For example, while it might appear straightforward to affirm legal recognition of indigenous customs, the exact legal meaning of "indigenous" is extremely difficult to interpret. The intent of the constitutional protection is to recognize
(30) only long-standing traditional customs, not those of recent origin; provincial courts therefore require aboriginal peoples to provide legal documentation that any customs they seek to protect were practiced sufficiently long ago—a criterion defined in practice
(35) to mean prior to the establishment of British sovereignty over the specific territory. However, this requirement makes it difficult for aboriginal societies, which often relied on oral tradition rather than written records, to support their claims.
(40) Furthermore, even if aboriginal peoples are successful in convincing the courts that specific rights should be recognized, it is frequently difficult to determine exactly what these rights amount to. Consider aboriginal land claims. Even when
(45) aboriginal ownership of specific lands is fully established, there remains the problem of interpreting the meaning of that "ownership." In a 1984 case in Ontario, an aboriginal group claimed that its property rights should be interpreted as full ownership in the
(50) contemporary sense of private property, which allows for the sale of the land or its resources. But the provincial court instead ruled that the law had previously recognized only the aboriginal right to use the land and therefore granted property rights so
(55) minimal as to allow only the bare survival of the

community. Here, the provincial court's ruling was excessively conservative in its assessment of the current law. Regrettably, it appears that this group will not be successful unless it is able to move its
(60) case from the provincial courts into the Supreme Court of Canada, which will be, one hopes, more insistent upon a satisfactory application of the constitutional reforms.

20. Which one of the following most accurately states the main point of the passage?

(A) The overly conservative rulings of Canada's provincial courts have been a barrier to constitutional reforms intended to protect aboriginal rights.

(B) The overwhelming burden placed on provincial courts of interpreting constitutional language in Canada has halted efforts by aboriginal peoples to gain full ownership of land.

(C) Constitutional language aimed at protecting aboriginal rights in Canada has so far left the protection of these rights uncertain due to the difficult task of interpreting this language.

(D) Constitutional reforms meant to protect aboriginal rights in Canada have in fact been used by some provincial courts to limit these rights.

(E) Efforts by aboriginal rights advocates to uphold constitutional reforms in Canada may be more successful if heard by the Supreme Court rather than by the provincial courts.

21. Which one of the following most accurately describes the author's main purpose in lines 11-14 of the passage?

(A) to demonstrate that the decisions of the provincial courts rarely conform to the goals of the constitutional reforms

(B) to locate the source of a systemic problem in protecting aboriginal rights in Canada

(C) to identify the specific source of problems in enacting constitutional reforms in Canada

(D) to describe one aspect of the process by which constitutional reforms are enacted in Canada

(E) to criticize the use of general language in the Canadian constitution

GO ON TO THE NEXT PAGE.

22. The passage explicitly states that which one of the following was intended as a consequence of the constitutional protection of aboriginal rights?

    (A) definition of the type of property rights that apply to aboriginal societies
    (B) establishment of the Supreme Court of Canada as the arbiter of aboriginal rights
    (C) recognition of traditional customs but not those of recent origin
    (D) clarification of which groups comprise the aboriginal population in Canada
    (E) creation of local governments for aboriginal communities

23. The passage provides the most evidence for the claim that the author has a negative attitude toward which one of the following?

    (A) the 1982 constitutional reforms' burdening the provincial courts with the task of interpretation
    (B) the difficulties in interpreting such terms as "indigenous" and "ownership"
    (C) the criterion used to determine which customs are too recent to merit constitutional protection
    (D) the requirement that aboriginal peoples provide documentation for traditional customs
    (E) the definition of ownership imposed by the provincial court in 1984

24. The passage provides evidence to suggest that the author would be most likely to assent to which one of the following proposals?

    (A) Aboriginal peoples in Canada should not be answerable to the federal laws of Canada.
    (8) Oral tradition should sometimes be considered legal documentation of certain indigenous customs.
    (C) Aboriginal communities should be granted full protection of all of their customs.
    (D) Provincial courts should be given no authority to decide cases involving questions of aboriginal rights.
    (E) The language of the Canadian constitution should more carefully delineate the instances to which reforms apply.

25. Which one of the following, if true, would lend the most credence to the author's statement in lines 56-58?

    (A) Other Ontario courts had previously interpreted "use" to include sale of the land or its resources.
    (B) The ruling created thousands of jobs by opening the land in question to logging by a timber corporation.
    (C) Previous court decisions in Ontario have distinguished the right to use land from the right to sell it.
    (D) The ruling prompted aboriginal groups in other provinces to pursue land claims in those courts.
    (E) Prior to the decision in question, the provincial court had not heard a case concerning the constitutional reforms.

26. Based on the information in the passage, the author would be most likely to agree with which one of the following statements about the 1984 case in Ontario?

    (A) The court's ruling directly contravened the language of the constitutional reforms protecting aboriginal land ownership rights in the full modem sense.
    (B) The Supreme Court remains the best hope for the recognition of full aboriginal property rights because provincial courts are not authorized to rule on the definition of property rights.
    (C) If there had been clear documentary evidence that the group had occupied the land before the establishment of British sovereignty, the court would probably have upheld the aboriginal claims.
    (D) The unsatisfactory ruling in the case was the result of pressure from conservative politicians and other conservative interests.
    (E) The court correctly understood the intent of the constitutional reforms, but it failed to apply them correctly because it misconstrued their relation to existing law.

27. The passage as a whole can most accurately be described as

    (A) an argument stressing the need for advocates of certain rights to adopt certain strategies
    (B) a comprehensive study of efforts to guarantee the protection of certain rights
    (C) an examination of problems associated with efforts to protect certain rights
    (D) an argument favoring the need for revising the definition of certain rights
    (E) an attempt to correct misunderstandings regarding the protection of certain rights

S T O P

IF YOU FINISH BEFORE TIME IS CALLED, YOU MAY CHECK YOUR WORK ON THIS SECTION ONLY.
DO NOT WORK ON ANY OTHER SECTION IN THE TEST.

SECTION III
Time—35 minutes
22 Questions

Directions: Each group of questions in this section is based on a set of conditions. In answering some of the questions, it may be useful to draw a rough diagram. Choose the response that most accurately and completely answers each question and blacken the corresponding space on your answer sheet.

Questions 1-6

On one afternoon, Patterson meets individually with each of exactly five clients—Reilly, Sanchez, Tang, Upton, and Yansky—and also goes to the gym by herself for a workout. Patterson's workout and her five meetings each start at either 1:00, 2:00, 3:00, 4:00, 5:00, or 6:00. The following conditions must apply:
  Patterson meets with Sanchez at some time before her workout.
  Patterson meets with Tang at some time after her workout. Patterson meets with Yansky either immediately before or immediately after her workout.
  Patterson meets with Upton at some time before she meets with Reilly.

1. Which one of the following could be an acceptable schedule of Patterson's workout and meetings, in order from 1:00 to 6:00?

 (A) Yansky, workout, Upton, Reilly, Sanchez, Tang
 (B) Upton, Tang, Sanchez, Yansky, workout, Reilly
 (C) Upton, Reilly, Sanchez, workout, Tang, Yansky
 (D) Sanchez, Yansky, workout, Reilly, Tang, Upton
 (E) Sanchez, Upton, workout, Yansky, Tang, Reilly

2. How many of the clients are there, anyone of whom could meet with Patterson at 1:00?

 (A) one
 (B) two
 (C) three
 (D) four
 (E) five

3. Patterson CANNOT meet with Upton at which one of the following times?

 (A) 1:00
 (B) 2:00
 (C) 3:00
 (D) 4:00
 (E) 5:00

4. If Patterson meets with Sanchez the hour before she meets with Yansky, then each of the following could be true EXCEPT:

 (A) Patterson meets with Reilly at 2:00.
 (B) Patterson meets with Yansky at 3:00.
 (C) Patterson meets with Tang at 4:00.
 (D) Patterson meets with Yansky at 5:00.
 (E) Patterson meets with Tang at 6:00.

5. If Patterson meets with Tang at 4:00, then which one of the following must be true?

 (A) Patterson meets with Reilly at 5:00.
 (B) Patterson meets with Upton at 5:00.
 (C) Patterson meets with Yansky at 2:00.
 (D) Patterson meets with Yansky at 3:00.
 (E) Patterson's workout is at 2:00.

6. Which one of the following could be the order of Patterson's meetings, from earliest to latest?

 (A) Upton, Yansky, Sanchez, Reilly, Tang
 (B) Upton, Reilly, Sanchez, Tang, Yansky
 (C) Sanchez, Yansky, Reilly, Tang, Upton
 (D) Sanchez, Upton, Tang, Yansky, Reilly
 (E) Sanchez, Upton, Reilly, Yansky, Tang

GO ON TO THE NEXT PAGE.

Questions 7-12

Exactly six people—Lulu, Nam, Ofelia, Pachai, Santiago, and Tyrone—are the only contestants in a chess tournament. The tournament consists of four games, played one after the other. Exactly two people play in each game, and each person plays in at least one game. The following conditions must apply:

Tyrone does not play in the first or third game.
Lulu plays in the last game.
Nam plays in only one game and it is not against Pachai.
Santiago plays in exactly two games, one just before and one just after the only game that Ofelia plays in.

7. Which one of the following could be an accurate list of the contestants who play in each of the four games?

(A) first game: Pachai, Santiago; second game: Ofelia, Tyrone; third game: Pachai, Santiago; fourth game: Lulu, Nam

(B) first game: Lulu, Nam; second game: Pachai, Santiago; third game: Ofelia, Tyrone; fourth game: Lulu, Santiago

(C) first game: Pachai, Santiago; second game: Lulu, Tyrone; third game: Nam, Ofelia; fourth game: Lulu, Nam

(D) first game: Nam, Santiago; second game: Nam, Ofelia; third game: Pachai, Santiago; fourth game: Lulu, Tyrone

(E) first game: Lulu, Nam; second game: Santiago, Tyrone; third game: Lulu, Ofelia; fourth game: Pachai, Santiago

8. Which one of the following contestants could play in two consecutive games?

(A) Lulu
(B) Nam
(C) Ofelia
(D) Santiago
(E) Tyrone

9. If Tyrone plays in the fourth game, then which one of the following could be true?

(A) Nam plays in the second game.
(B) Ofelia plays in the third game.
(C) Santiago plays in the second game.
(D) Nam plays a game against Lulu.
(E) Pachai plays a game against Lulu.

10. Which one of the following could be true?

(A) Pachai plays against Lulu in the first game.
(B) Pachai plays against Nam in the second game.
(C) Santiago plays against Ofelia in the second game.
(D) Pachai plays against Lulu in the third game.
(E) Nam plays against Santiago in the fourth game.

11. Which one of the following is a complete and accurate list of the contestants who CANNOT play against Tyrone in any game?

(A) Lulu, Pachai
(B) Nam, Ofelia
(C) Nam, Pachai
(D) Nam, Santiago
(E) Ofelia, Pachai

12. If Ofelia plays in the third game, which one of the following must be true?

(A) Lulu plays in the third game.
(B) Nam plays in the third game.
(C) Pachai plays in the first game.
(D) Pachai plays in the third game.
(E) Tyrone plays in the second game.

GO ON TO THE NEXT PAGE.

Questions 13-17

An album contains photographs picturing seven friends: Raimundo, Selma, Ty, Umiko, Wendy, Yakira, Zack. The friends appear either alone or in groups with one another, in accordance with the following:

Wendy appears in every photograph that Selma appears in.
Selma appears in every photograph that Umiko appears in.
Raimundo appears in every photograph that Yakira does not appear in.
Neither Ty nor Raimundo appears in any photograph that Wendy appears in.

13. Which one of the following could be a complete and accurate list of the friends who appear together in a photograph?

(A)   Raimundo, Selma, Ty, Wendy
(B)   Raimundo, Ty, Yakira, Zack
(C)   Raimundo, Wendy, Yakira, Zack
(D)   Selma, Ty, Umiko, Yakira
(E)   Selma, Ty, Umiko, Zack

14. If Ty and Zack appear together in a photograph, then which one of the following must be true?

(A)   Selma also appears in the photograph.
(B)   Yakira also appears in the photograph.
(C)   Wendy also appears in the photograph.
(D)   Raimundo does not appear in the photograph.
(E)   Umiko does not appear in the photograph.

15. What is the maximum number of friends who could appear in a photograph that Yakira does not appear in?

(A)   six
(B)   five
(C)   four
(D)   three
(E)   two

16. If Umiko and Zack appear together in a photograph, then exactly how many of the other friends must also appear in that photograph?

(A)   four
(B)   three
(C)   two
(D)   one
(E)   zero

17. If exactly three friends appear together in a photograph, then each of the following could be true EXCEPT:

(A)   Selma and Zack both appear in the photograph.
(B)   Ty and Yakira both appear in the photograph.
(C)   Wendy and Selma both appear in the photograph.
(D)   Yakira and Zack both appear in the photograph.
(E)   Zack and Raimundo both appear in the photograph.

GO ON TO THE NEXT PAGE.

Questions 18-22

The Export Alliance consists of exactly three nations: Nation X, Nation Y, and Nation Z. Each nation in the Alliance exports exactly two of the following five crops: oranges, rice, soybeans, tea, and wheat. Each of these crops is exported by at least one of the nations in the Alliance. The following conditions hold:

None of the nations exports both wheat and oranges.
Nation X exports soybeans if, but only if, Nation Y does also.
If Nation Y exports rice, then Nations X and Z both export tea.
Nation Y does not export any crop that Nation Z exports.

18. Which one of the following could be an accurate list, for each of the nations, of the crops it exports?

(A) Nation X: oranges, rice; Nation Y: oranges, tea; Nation Z: soybeans, wheat
(B) Nation X: oranges, tea; Nation Y: oranges, rice; Nation Z: soybeans, wheat
(C) Nation X: oranges, wheat; Nation Y: oranges, tea; Nation Z: rice, soybeans
(D) Nation X: rice, wheat; Nation Y: oranges, tea; Nation Z: oranges, soybeans
(E) Nation X: soybeans, rice; Nation Y: oranges, tea; Nation Z: soybeans, wheat

19. If Nation X exports soybeans and tea, then which one of the following could be true?

(A) Nation Y exports oranges.
(B) Nation Y exports rice.
(C) Nation Y exports tea.
(D) Nation Z exports soybeans.
(E) Nation Z exports tea.

20. If Nation Z exports tea and wheat, then which one of the following must be true?

(A) Nation X exports oranges.
(B) Nation X exports tea.
(C) Nation X exports wheat.
(D) Nation Y exports rice.
(E) Nation Y exports soybeans.

21. It CANNOT be the case that both Nation X and Nation Z export which one of the following crops?

(A) oranges
(B) rice
(C) soybeans
(D) tea
(E) wheat

22. Which one of the following pairs CANNOT be the two crops that Nation Y exports?

(A) oranges and rice
(B) oranges and soybeans
(C) rice and tea
(D) rice and wheat
(E) soybeans and wheat

S T O P

IF YOU FINISH BEFORE TIME IS CALLED, YOU MAY CHECK YOUR WORK ON THIS SECTION ONLY.
DO NOT WORK ON ANY OTHER SECTION IN THE TEST.

SECTION IV
Time—35 minutes
25 Questions

<u>Directions:</u>   The questions in this section are based on the reasoning contained in brief statements or passages. For some questions, more than one of the choices could conceivably answer the question. However, you are to choose the <u>best</u> answer; that is, the response that most accurately and completely answers the question. You should not make assumptions that are by commonsense standards implausible, superfluous, or incompatible with the passage. After you have chosen the best answer, blacken the corresponding space on your answer sheet.

1. Mayor McKinney's policies have often been criticized on the grounds that they benefit only wealthy city residents, but that is not a fair evaluation. Some of McKinney's policies have clearly benefited the city's less affluent residents. McKinney actively supported last year's proposal to lower the city's high property taxes. Because of this tax decrease, more development is taking place in the city, helping to end the housing shortage and stabilize the rents in the city.

    Which one of the following most accurately expresses the main conclusion of the argument?

    (A)   It is impossible to tell whether McKinney is more committed to the interests of the wealthy than to those of the poor.
    (B)   McKinney's policies have often been criticized for benefiting only wealthy city residents.
    (C)   The decrease in property taxes that McKinney supported caused more development to take place in the city.
    (D)   The criticism that McKinney's policies benefit only the wealthy is unjustified.
    (E)   McKinney's efforts helped end the housing shortage and stabilize the rents in the city.

2. A factory spokesperson argued that the factory should not be required to clean up the water in the nearby wetlands, maintaining that although wastewater from the factory polluted the wetlands over the past several years, the factory is not to blame for this, since the disposal of the factory's wastewater is handled entirely by an independent contractor.

    Which one of the following arguments most closely conforms to the principle underlying the reasoning in the spokesperson's argument?

    (A)   A recent survey revealed that over two-thirds of the teachers in the district are permitted to teach classes on subjects in which they have received no formal training. Thus parents of students in the district should check the qualifications of their children's teachers.
    (B)   I object to the policy of making parents responsible for the offenses of their older adolescent children. After all, these adolescents have minds of their own and freely choose to act as they do, often in ways that do not reflect the wishes of their parents.
    (C)   The students are justified in their objection to the reading assignment. Many of the topics concern material that is not covered in class, and students should not be required to do such reading in order to do well in the course.
    (D)   The most recent appointee to the prize committee should not be permitted to participate in the selection of this year's winner. Unlike each of the other committee members, the appointee has a relative in the contest.
    (E)   Despite all the publicity, I am skeptical of the politician's claims of having just returned from the remote village. Just two days ago a reporter spoke with the villagers and said that not a single one reported seeing the politician in the past several months.

GO ON TO THE NEXT PAGE.

3. Nylon industry spokesperson: Even though cotton and nylon are used for similar purposes, some people have the mistaken notion that cotton is natural but nylon is not. However, nylon's main components come from petroleum and from the nitrogen in the atmosphere. Clearly the atmosphere is natural. And petroleum comes from oil, which in turn comes from ancient plants—a natural source.

Which one of the following principles, if valid, most helps to justify the nylon industry spokesperson's reasoning?

(A) A substance is unnatural only if the function it serves is unnatural.
(B) A substance is no less natural than the processes used in its production.
(C) A substance is no more natural than its least natural component.
(D) One substance can be more natural than another if only one is wholly derived from natural substances.
(E) A substance is natural if the origins of its main cornponents are natural.

4. Computer manufacturers and retailers tell us that the complexity involved in connecting the various components of personal computers is not a widespread obstacle to their use, but this is wrong. Customers who install accessories to their personal computers have to take full responsibility for the setting of jumpers and switches to satisfy mysterious specifications. Many accessories require extra software that can cause other accessories to stop working; adding a modem, for instance, may disable a printer.

Which one of the following, if true, most seriously weakens the argument?

(A) Personal computer instruction manuals usually explain the purposes of the jumpers and switches.
(B) Software for accessories can often be obtained for free.
(C) Installing an accessory will become extremely easy in the foreseeable future.
(D) A personal computer is usually sold as part of a package that includes accessories and free installation.
(E) Computer manufacturers rarely take into account ease of installation when they are designing programs or accessones.

5. Rats fed high doses of the artificial sweetener saccharin develop silicate crystals that are toxic to cells lining the bladder. When the cells regenerate, some are cancerous and form tumors. Unlike rats, mice fed high doses of saccharin do not get bladder cancer.

Which one of the following, if true, does the most to resolve the apparent discrepancy in the information above?

(A) Urine proteins that react with saccharin to form silicate crystals are found in rats but not in mice.
(B) Cells in the bladder regenerate more quickly in mice than they do in rats.
(C) High doses of saccharin are much more likely to produce silicate crystals than lower doses are.
(D) The silicate crystals are toxic only to the cells lining the bladder and not to other bladder cells.
(E) High doses of other artificial sweeteners have. been. shown to produce silicate crystals in mice but not in rats.

6. Although we could replace the beautiful—but dilapidated—old bridge across Black River with a concrete skyway, we should instead replace it with a cable bridge even though this would be more expensive than building a concrete skyway. The extra cost is clearly justified by the importance of maintaining the beauty of our river crossing.

Which one of the following is an assumption on which the argument depends?

(A) It is no more costly to maintain a cable bridge than a concrete skyway.
(B) A concrete skyway would not have any practical advantages over a cable bridge.
(C) The beauty of the river crossing must be preserved.
(D) If the new cable bridge is built, most people who see it will think the extra money well spent.
(E) Building a cable bridge across Black River would produce a more aesthetically pleasing result than building a concrete skyway.

GO ON TO THE NEXT PAGE.

7. A typical gasoline-powered lawn mower emits about as much air-polluting material per hour of use as does an automobile. Collectively, such mowers contribute significantly to summer air pollution. Since electric mowers emit no air pollutants, people can help reduce air pollution by choosing electric mowers over gasoline ones whenever feasible.

Which one of the following, if true, provides the most support for the argument?

(A) Lawns help to clean the air, replacing pollutants with oxygen.

(B) Electric lawn mowers are more expensive to purchase and maintain than are gasoline mowers.

(C) Producing the power to run an electric mower for an hour causes less air pollution than does running an automobile for an hour.

(D) Most manufacturers of gasoline lawn mowers are trying to redesign their mowers to reduce the emission of air pollutants.

(E) Lawn mowers are used for fewer hours per year than are automobiles.

8. Ariel: Government art subsidies never benefit art, for art's role is to challenge society's values. A society's values, however, are expressed by its government, and artists cannot challenge the very institution upon which they depend.

Sasha: I agree that art should challenge society's values. However, by its very nature, a democratic government respects dissent and encourages challenges to its own values. Therefore, in a democratic society, government art subsidies ensure that artists can be fully committed to their work while expressing themselves freely.

The dialogue most supports the claim that Ariel and Sasha disagree with each other about whether

(A) art's role is to challenge society's values

(B) a society's values are expressed by its government

(C) artists can express themselves freely in a nondemocratic society

(D) art subsidies provided by a democratic government benefit art

(E) only governments that respect dissent ensure that art subsidies are fairly distributed

9. Public health expert: Until recently people believed that applications of biochemical research would eventually achieve complete victory over the microorganisms that cause human disease. However, current medical research shows that those microorganisms reproduce so rapidly that medicines developed for killing one variety will only spur the evolution of other varieties that are immune to those medicines. The most rational public health strategy, therefore, would place much more emphasis than at present on fully informing people about the transmission of diseases caused by microorganisms, with a view to minimizing the incidence of such diseases.

Of the following, which one most accurately expresses the conclusion drawn by the public health expert?

(A) A medicine that kills one variety of disease-causing microorganism can cause the evolution of a drug-resistant variety.

(B) A patient who contracts a disease caused by microorganisms cannot be effectively cured by present methods.

(C) There is good reason to make a particular change to public health policy.

(D) No one who is fully informed about the diseases caused by microorganisms will ever fall victim to those diseases.

(E) Some previous approaches to public health policy ignored the fact that disease-causing microorganisms reproduce at a rapid rate.

10. The enthusiastic acceptance of ascetic lifestyles evidenced in the surviving writings of monastic authors indicates that medieval societies were much less concerned with monetary gain than are contemporary Western cultures.

The reasoning in the argument is most vulnerable to criticism on the grounds that the argument

(A) employs the imprecise term "ascetic"

(B) generalizes from a sample that is likely to be unrepresentative

(C) applies contemporary standards inappropriately to medieval societies

(D) inserts personal opinions into what purports to be a factual debate

(E) advances premises that are inconsistent

GO ON TO THE NEXT PAGE.

11. Between 1976 and 1985, chemical wastes were dumped into Cod Bay. Today, 3 percent of the bay's bluefin cod population have deformed fins, and wary consumers have stopped buying the fish. In seeking financial reparations from companies that dumped the chemicals, representatives of Cod Bay's fishing industry have claimed that since the chemicals are known to cause genetic mutations, the deformity in the bluefin cod must have been caused by the presence of those chemicals in Cod Bay.

The answer to each of the following questions would be helpful in evaluating the representatives' claim EXCEPT:

(A)   What is the incidence of deformed fins in bluefin cod that are not exposed to chemicals such as those dumped into Cod Bay?

(B)   What was the incidence of deformed fins in bluefin cod in Cod Bay before the chemical dumping began?

(C)   Has the consumption of the bluefin cod from Cod Bay that have deformed fins caused any health problems in the people who ate them?

(D)   Are bluefin cod prone to any naturally occurring diseases that can cause fin deformities of the same kind as those displayed by the bluefin cod of Cod Bay?

(E)   Are there gene-altering pollutants present in Cod Bay other than the chemical wastes that were dumped by the companies?

12. Columnist: If you received an unsigned letter, you would likely have some doubts about the truth of its contents. But news stories often include statements from anonymous sources, and these are usually quoted with the utmost respect. It makes sense to be skeptical of these sources, for, as in the case of the writer of an unsigned letter, their anonymity makes it possible for them to plant inaccurate or slanted statements without ever having to answer for them.

The columnist's argument proceeds by

(A)   pointing out that a certain attitude would presumably be adopted in one situation, in order to support the claim that a similar attitude would be justified in an analogous situation

(B)   drawing an analogy between an attitude commonly adopted in one situation and a different attitude commonly adopted in another situation, and establishing that the latter attitude is better justified than the former

(C)   inferring that an attitude would be justified in all situations of a given type on the grounds that this attitude is justified in a hypothetical situation of that type

(D)   calling into question a certain type of evidence by drawing an analogy between that evidence and other evidence that the argument shows is usually false

(E)   calling into question the motives of those presenting certain information, and concluding for this reason that the information is likely to be false

13. Art theft from museums is on the rise. Most stolen art is sold to wealthy private collectors. Consequently, since thieves steal what their customers are most interested in buying, museums ought to focus more of their security on their most valuable pieces.

The argument depends on assuming which one of the following?

(A)   Art thieves steal both valuable and not-so-valuable art.

(B)   Art pieces that are not very valuable are not very much in demand by wealthy private collectors.

(C)   Art thieves steal primarily from museums that are poorly secured.

(D)   Most museums provide the same amount of security for valuable and not-so-valuable art.

(E)   Wealthy private collectors sometimes sell their stolen art to other wealthy private collectors.

GO ON TO THE NEXT PAGE.

14. Insufficient rain can cause crops to falter and agricultural prices to rise. Records indicate that during a certain nation's recent crisis, faltering crops and rising agricultural prices prompted the government to take over food distribution in an effort to prevent starvation. Thus, the weather must have played an important role in bringing about the crisis.

The argument's reasoning is most vulnerable to criticism on the grounds that the argument

(A) concludes, merely from the fact that the period of insufficient rain occurred before the nation's crisis, that insufficient rain caused the nation's crisis

(B) fails to take into account the possibility that the scarcity was not severe enough to justify the government's taking over food distribution

(C) uses the term "crisis" equivocally in the reasoning, referring to both a political crisis and an economic crisis

(D) infers, merely from the fact that one event could have caused a second event, that the first event in fact caused the second

(E) takes for granted that any condition that is necessary for an increase in agricultural prices is also sufficient for such an increase

15. The cost of a semester's tuition at a certain university is based on the number of courses in which a student enrolls that semester. Although the cost per course at that university has not risen in four years, many of its students who could afford the tuition when they first enrolled now claim they can no longer afford it.

Each of the following, if true, helps to resolve the apparent discrepancy above EXCEPT:

(A) Faculty salaries at the university have risen slightly over the past four years.

(B) The number of courses per semester for which full-time students are required to enroll is higher this year than any time in the past.

(C) The cost of living in the vicinity of the university has risen over the last two years.

(D) The university awards new students a large number of scholarships that are renewed each year for the students who maintain high grade averages.

(E) The university has turned many of its part-time office jobs, for which students had generally been hired, into full-time, nonstudent positions.

16. People are not happy unless they feel that they are needed by others. Most people in modern society, however, can achieve a feeling of indispensability only within the sphere of family and friendship, because almost everyone knows that his or her job could be done by anyone of thousands of others.

The statements above most strongly support which one of the following?

(A) People who realize that others could fill their occupational roles as ably as they do themselves cannot achieve any happiness in their lives.

(B) The nature of modern society actually undermines the importance of family life to an individual's happiness.

(C) Most people in modern society are happy in their private lives even if they are not happy in their jobs.

(D) A majority of people in modern society do not appreciate having the jobs that they do have.

(E) Fewer than a majority of people in modern society can find happiness outside the sphere of private interpersonal relationships.

17. Art critic: Criticism focuses on two issues: first, whether the value of an artwork is intrinsic to the work; and second, whether judgments about an artwork's quality are objective rather than merely matters of taste. These issues are related, for if an artwork's value is not intrinsic, then it must be extrinsic, and thus judgments about the quality of the work can only be a matter of taste.

The art critic's reasoning is most vulnerable to the criticism that it takes for granted that

(A) judgments about the quality of an artwork are always a matter of taste

(B) people sometimes agree about judgments that are only matters of taste

(C) judgments about extrinsic value cannot be objective

(D) judgments about intrinsic value are always objective

(E) an artwork's value is sometimes intrinsic to it

GO ON TO THE NEXT PAGE.

18. Decentralization enables divisions of a large institution to function autonomously. This always permits more realistic planning and strongly encourages innovation, since the people responsible for decision making are directly involved in implementing the policies they design. Decentralization also permits the central administration to focus on institution-wide issues without being overwhelmed by the details of daily operations.

The statements above most strongly support which one of the following?

(A) In large institutions whose divisions do not function autonomously, planning is not maximally realistic.
(B) Innovation is not always encouraged in large centralized institutions.
(C) For large institutions the advantages of decentralization outweigh its disadvantages.
(D) The central administrations of large institutions are usually partially responsible for most of the details of daily operations.
(E) The people directly involved in implementing, policies are always able to make innovative and realistic policy decisions.

19. According to some astronomers, Earth is struck by a meteorite large enough to cause an ice age on an average of once every 100 million years. The last such incident occurred nearly 100 million years ago, so we can expect that Earth will be struck by such a meteorite in the near future. This clearly warrants funding to determine whether there is a means to protect our planet from such meteorite strikes.

The reasoning in the argument is most subject to criticism on the grounds that the argument

(A) makes a bold prescription on the basis of evidence that establishes only a high probability for a disastrous event
(B) presumes, without providing justification, that the probability of a chance event's occurring is not affected by whether the event has occurred during a period in which it would be expected to occur
(C) moves from evidence about the average frequency of an event to a specific prediction about when the next such event will occur
(D) fails to specify the likelihood that, if such a meteorite should strike Earth, the meteorite would indeed cause an ice age
(E) presumes, without providing justification, that some feasible means can be found to deter large meteorite strikes

20. Polling data reveal that an overwhelming majority of nine-year-olds can correctly identify the logos of major cigarette brands. However, of those nine-year-olds who recognize such logos, less than 1 percent smoke. Therefore, there is little or no connection between recognition of cigarette brand logos and smoking.

Which one of the following uses flawed reasoning most similar to the flawed reasoning above?

(A) The concern about the long-term effect on dolphins of small quantities of mercury in the ocean is unfounded. During a three-month observation period, 1,000 dolphins were exposed to small quantities of mercury in seawater, with no effect on the animals.
(B) Many ten-year-olds dream of becoming actors. Yet it is not likely they will seriously consider becoming actors, because most parents discourage their children from pursuing such a highly competitive career.
(C) Most dentists recommend using fluoride to reduce the incidence of cavities, but few recommend giving up candy entirely; so, using fluoride is probably more effective in preventing cavities than is avoiding sweets.
(D) A large percentage of men exercise moderately throughout their lives, but the average life span of those who do so is not significantly greater than of those who get little or no exercise. So there is little or no correlation between moderate exercise and good health.
(E) Most people cannot name their legislative representatives. Nonetheless, this is insignificant, for when queried, most of them displayed an adequate command of current political issues.

GO ON TO THE NEXT PAGE.

21. Etiquette firmly opposes both obscene and malicious talk, but this does not imply that speech needs to be restricted by law. Etiquette does not necessarily even oppose the expression of offensive ideas. Rather, it dictates that there are situations in which the expression of potentially offensive, disturbing, or controversial ideas is inappropriate and that, where appropriate, the expression and discussion of such ideas is to be done in a civil manner.

Which one of the following judgments most closely corresponds to the principles of etiquette stated above?

(A) Neighbors should not be gruff or unfriendly to one another when they meet on the street.
(B) When prosecutors elicit testimony from a cooperative witness they should do so without intensive questioning.
(C) There should be restrictions on speech only if a large majority of the population finds the speech offensive and hateful.
(D) The journalists at a news conference should not ask a politician potentially embarrassing questions about a controversial policy issue.
(E) The moderator of a panel discussion of a divisive moral issue should not allow participants to engage in name-calling.

22. The only preexisting recordings that are transferred onto compact disc are those that record companies believe will sell well enough on compact disc to be profitable. So, most classic jazz recordings will not be transferred onto compact disc, because few classic jazz recordings are played on the radio.

The conclusion above follows logically if which one of the following is assumed?

(A) Few of the preexisting recordings that record companies believe can be profitably transferred to compact disc are classic jazz recordings.
(B) Few compact discs featuring classic jazz recordings are played on the radio.
(C) The only recordings that are played on the radio are ones that record companies believe can be profitably sold as compact discs.
(D) Most record companies are less interested in preserving classic jazz recordings than in making a profit.
(E) No recording that is not played on the radio is one that record companies believe would be profitable if transferred to compact disc.

23. Agricultural economist: Over the past several years, increases in worldwide grain production have virtually ceased. Further increases will be extremely difficult; most usable farmland is already being farmed with near-maximal efficiency. But worldwide demand for grain has been increasing steadily, due largely to continuing population growth. Hence, a severe worldwide grain shortage is likely.

Which one of the following most accurately describes the role played in the agricultural economist's argument by the claim that further increases in worldwide grain production will be extremely difficult?

(A) It is one of the two conclusions drawn by the agricultural economist, neither of which is used to provide support for the other.
(B) It is a description of a phenomenon, a causal explanation of which is the main conclusion of the argument.
(C) It is the only premise offered in support of the argument's main conclusion.
(D) It is a prediction for which the agricultural economist's first claim is offered as the primary justification.
(E) It is an intermediate conclusion that is presented as evidence for the argument's main conclusion.

GO ON TO THE NEXT PAGE.

24. Bardis: Extensive research shows that television advertisements affect the buying habits of consumers. Some people conclude from this that violent television imagery sometimes causes violent behavior. But the effectiveness of television advertisements could be a result of those televised images being specifically designed to alter buying habits, whereas television violence is not designed to cause violent behavior. Hence we can safely conclude that violent television imagery does not cause violence.

The reasoning in Bardis's argument is flawed because that argument

(A) relies on an illegitimate inference from the fact that advertisements can change behavior to the claim that advertisements can cause violent behavior

(B) fails to distinguish a type of behavior from a type of stimulus that may or may not affect behavior

(C) undermines its own position by questioning the persuasive power of television advertising

(D) concludes that a claim is false on the basis of one purported fault in an argument in favor of that claim

(E) fails to consider the possibility that the argument it disputes is intended to address a separate issue

25. Sarah: Our regulations for staff review are vague and thus difficult to interpret. For instance, the regulations state that a staff member who is performing unsatisfactorily will face dismissal, but they fail to define unsatisfactory performance. Thus, some staff may be dismissed merely because their personal views conflict with those of their supervisors.

Which one of the following generalizations, if applicable to Sarah's company, most helps to justify her reasoning?

(A) Performance that falls only somewhat below expectations results in disciplinary measures short of dismissal.

(B) Interpreting regulations is a prerogative that belongs solely to supervisors.

(C) A vague regulation can be used to make those subject to it answer for their performance.

(D) A vague regulation can be used to keep those subject to it in subordinate positions.

(E) Employees usually consider specific regulations to be fairer than vague regulations.

S T O P

IF YOU FINISH BEFORE TIME IS CALLED, YOU MAY CHECK YOUR WORK ON THIS SECTION ONLY.
DO NOT WORK ON ANY OTHER SECTION IN THE TEST.

LSAT® Writing Sample Topic

An architectural firm is growing dramatically and needs additional space. The firm is deciding whether to expand and remodel its present building near the center of the city or to build a new building on the city's outskirts. Write an argument in favor of choosing one option over the other, based on the following considerations:

- The firm needs to economically provide functional, convenient, and comfortable workspace for its growing staff.
- The firm wants to create an architecturally noteworthy showplace building to make a statement to prospective clients and enhance its image and reputation.

The firm is presently housed in an architecturally important historic building that has become associated with the firm's image. The building is in a popular, historic neighborhood of the city near the business district and public transportation. However, parking is difficult and quite costly. Expansion and remodeling would have to meet the stringent restrictions of the historic district, limiting the design options and adding to the complexity of the construction. The project would spotlight two of the firm's strengths: designing building additions that aesthetically complement existing structures, and creating modern working spaces in older buildings. The firm has a strong reputation for such work and dominates that type of business in the city, which has a large stock of older buildings.

Alternatively, the firm can build a new building on the outskirts of the city in its own distinctive architectural style, which integrates a building with its landscape and surroundings. A new building would require purchasing land, but it would provide more space than the alternative, and the lack of architectural constraints would allow for more design freedom and greater efficiency in creating working space. However, the city's outskirts are not well served by public transportation and many employees who drive to work would face longer commutes as well. There would, however, be plenty of room for on-site parking. The firm believes that the majority of the future architectural work in the area will be new buildings outside the city.

Scratch Paper
Do not write your essay in this space.

Directions:

1. Use the Answer Key on the next page to check your answers.

2. Use the Scoring Worksheet below to compute your raw score.

3. Use the Score Conversion Chart to convert your raw score into the 120-180 scale.

Scoring Worksheet

1. Enter the number of questions you answered correctly in each section.

	Number Correct
SECTION I.....................	_____
SECTION II....................	_____
SECTION III...................	_____
SECTION IV...................	_____

2. Enter the sum here: _____
   This is your Raw Score.

Conversion Chart:
For Converting Raw Score to the 120-180 LSAT Scaled Score
LSAT Form 5LSN64

Reported Score	Raw Score Lowest	Raw Score Highest
180	97	99
179	96	96
178	95	95
177	94	94
176	93	93
175	92	92
174	91	91
173	90	90
172	89	89
171	88	88
170	87	87
169	86	86
168	85	85
167	83	84
166	82	82
165	81	81
164	79	80
163	78	78
162	76	77
161	75	75
160	73	74
159	71	72
158	70	70
157	68	69
156	66	67
155	65	65
154	63	64
153	61	62
152	59	60
151	58	58
150	56	57
149	54	55
148	53	53
147	51	52
146	49	50
145	48	48
144	46	47
143	44	45
142	43	43
141	41	42
140	40	40
139	38	39
138	37	37
137	35	36
136	34	34
135	32	33
134	31	31
133	29	30
132	28	28
131	27	27
130	25	26
129	24	24
128	23	23
127	21	22
126	20	20
125	19	19
124	17	18
123	16	16
122	14	15
121	__*	__*
120	0	13

*There is no raw score that will produce this scaled score for this form.

SECTION I

1.	A	8.	A	15.	E	22.	E
2.	C	9.	E	16.	C	23.	C
3.	B	10.	A	17.	B	24.	B
4.	C	11.	C	18.	D	25.	C
5.	*	12.	C	19.	A	26.	E
6.	D	13.	E	20.	D		
7.	B	14.	E	21.	A		

SECTION II

1.	D	8.	E	15.	D	22.	C
2.	B	9.	D	16.	B	23.	E
3.	D	10.	A	17.	C	24.	B
4.	C	11.	E	18.	A	25.	A
5.	A	12.	B	19.	E	26.	E
6.	E	13.	C	20.	C	27.	C
7.	B	14.	E	21.	B		

SECTION III

1.	E	8.	A	15.	D	22.	C
2.	B	9.	A	16.	B		
3.	C	10.	A	17.	A		
4.	D	11.	C	18.	A		
5.	B	12.	E	19.	A		
6.	E	13.	B	20.	E		
7.	A	14.	E	21.	C		

SECTION IV

1.	D	8.	D	15.	A	22.	E
2.	B	9.	C	16.	E	23.	E
3.	E	10.	B	17.	C	24.	D
4.	D	11.	C	18.	A	25.	B
5.	A	12.	A	19.	C		
6.	E	13.	B	20.	A		
7.	C	14.	D	21.	E		

*Item removed from scoring.

CHAPTER SEVEN: THE DECEMBER 2004 LSAT DECONSTRUCTED

The explanations below are presented in the same order that the questions are given on the exam. Page headers are provided to help you identify which questions are explained on each page, and if you encounter any unknown terms, a glossary is provided at the end of the book. Also, please keep in mind that all explanations draw on methods discussed in *The PowerScore LSAT Logic Games Bible* and *The PowerScore LSAT Logical Reasoning Bible*. Please refer to those texts if you desire a more detailed discussion of a particular concept or approach.

DECEMBER 2004 SECTION 1: LOGICAL REASONING

Many students feel this is the harder of the two Logical Reasoning sections (the other Logical Reasoning section has four extremely easy questions in the first seven and so that section always starts well for most students). Overall, the mix of question types in this section is quite even, and no particular type of question is emphasized over the others. There are a number of easy questions, but also several quite challenging problems, plus a number of attractive wrong answer choices. A good test taker should score well on this section, but a test taker who is distracted or not strong with the concepts will miss more questions than expected. In short, this is a slightly harder than average Logical Reasoning section.

On a question-by-question level, the first ten questions are not overly challenging, and only question #8 seems to provide the average student with any real difficulty. The section does feature an extremely hard question in #12, and that question throws many test takers of their game for a bit. The last ten questions are a mix of mid-difficulty questions, but several of those problems feature very attractive wrong answer choices that can be quite tempting. There is also a lengthy Parallel Reasoning—FL question placed just before the last question that is both difficult and time-consuming for the typical test taker.

Question #1: Main Point. The correct answer choice is (A)

The first sentence of the stimulus presents an intellectual-sounding conclusion about economists and consumption. In the author's opinion, economists focus too much on consumption as a measure of economic well-being, and this obsession has prevented an understanding of the true nature of economic-well being. In other words, by overemphasizing the meaning of consumption, economists have misunderstood what economic well-being actually is.

The second sentence of the stimulus is a premise that provides real world examples to support the conclusion in the first sentence, and these examples are intended to show that just consuming certain goods does not necessarily make us economically well off. On a deeper logical level, the author uses the second sentence to imply that satisfaction is (or ought to be) a necessary measure of economic well-being. That is, when considering economic well-being we cannot just examine consumption; we must also examine satisfaction as a measure of whether economic well-being has been fully achieved.

The question stem asks you to identify the main point, so you should select a response that reflects the author's assertion that economic well-being cannot be measured by consumption alone.

Answer choice (A): This is the correct answer choice. The conclusion of the argument is that too great a focus on consumption prevents a true understanding of economic well-being, meaning that economic well-being cannot be defined solely by consumption.

Answer choice (B): In any Main Point question, you must ask yourself whether the choice under consideration is supported by the information in the passage. Although the passage states that we get very little satisfaction from certain aspects of consumption (namely, the wearing out and replacement of products), the passage does not suggest that consumption is not necessary to satisfaction.

Answer choice (C): The stimulus indicates that *one* current measure does not explain *economic well-being* completely. The author does not discuss measures of *consumption* and the author certainly does not suggest that valid measures cannot be devised for consumption (or for economic well-being, for that matter).

Answer choice (D): This is not the main point of the stimulus. The products cited were used to help explain that aspects of economic well-being are not captured by measuring consumption. Furthermore, you cannot infer from the examples of clothing, vehicles, and gasoline that modern products are designed for early obsolescence, because the stimulus does not discuss how quickly those three examples wear out, and the longevity of three product types has little to do with overall obsolescence rates in the entire market.

Answer choice (E): If you identified the first sentence as the conclusion, you could eliminate this answer choice immediately because it references the premise rather than the conclusion. Regardless, you cannot infer from the stimulus that satisfaction is an adequate, or sufficient, measure of economic well-being (while you could infer from the stimulus that satisfaction ought to be a necessary measure of economic well-being, you cannot be certain that satisfaction is a sufficient measure; that is, you cannot be sure that it alone is good enough). Even if you could infer that satisfaction is an adequate measure of economic well-being, that inference would still not be the main point of the stimulus.

Question #2: Weaken. The correct answer choice is (C)

The commentator's argument uses the familiar construction where a view is presented ("Many people argue that…") and then the author presents contrary information that leads to the main point that the view is incorrect. Remember, by knowing some of the common argument forms that appear on the LSAT, you can more quickly grasp the gist of the author's argument, and thereby complete questions more quickly.

In the last sentence of the stimulus, the commentator concludes that there is no reason to believe that chlorofluorocarbons harm humans by damaging the ozone layer enough to allow increased ultraviolet radiation to reach Earth. The commentator reaches this conclusion by using the premise that a supernova 300,000 years ago disrupted the ozone layer in a more significant manner than the estimated effect of chlorofluorocarbons today, but that disruption occurred without significantly affecting our earliest ancestors.

The conclusion drawn by the commentator is questionable. Most importantly, remember that in questions involving a lengthy time period, the author almost always makes the assumption that all things remain the same. In this case, the commentator has assumed that a comparison to ancestors from

300,000 years ago is meaningful because those ancestors are fundamentally similar to humans today. Of course, this assumption is flawed because those ancestors may have been different from us in ways that protected them from increased ultraviolet radiation. Or perhaps they did not live all that long and that fact prevented them from experiencing the long-term effects of increased ultraviolet radiation exposure. In any case, the "continuity of history" assumption is an important one for you to recognize when it appears in an LSAT question (and when it does appear, always look for an answer that addresses that assumption).

There are other issues with the commentator's conclusion, such as whether an effect must be significant to be harmful, and whether the estimations are completely accurate. Regardless, it should be clear that the commentator is using a very limited amount of evidence to draw a conclusion that is extremely questionable. Since you are asked to weaken the argument, you should search for a response that provides evidence that questions the commentator's conclusion.

Answer choice (A): This choice has to do with the *frequency* of categories of events, but the commentator made a comparison between the *impact* of two specific events. The commentator never attempted to generalize from these two events to a conclusion about whether terrestrial or extraterrestrial influences were overall more frequent (or important), so this choice does not weaken the argument.

Answer choice (B): This answer choice does nothing to the argument, because we cannot be sure whether the estimation of the effect of chlorofluorocarbons took into account natural processes such as volcanoes. If it did not, this choice might actually strengthen the conclusion by making the chlorofluorocarbons even less important.

Answer choice (C): This is the correct answer choice. Remember that one of the assumptions of the argument was that humans today are comparable to human ancestors who lived 300,000 years ago. This response shows that they are not the same with respect to a critical feature. Specifically, the answer choice establishes that our earliest ancestors were more resistant to the harmful effects of ultraviolet radiation than we are today. If the humans of 300,000 years ago were more resistant than humans today, then it may very well be that the chemicals in the atmosphere today could have a harmful effect. Consequently, this answer choice weakens the commentator's argument.

Answer choice (D): You may have chosen this response by concluding that recovery from a supernova would occur more quickly than recovery from chlorofluorocarbon damage because chemicals persist in the atmosphere. However, even if that is true, the commentator was discussing the current harm to humans, and not how harmful chlorofluorocarbons might become, or might prove to be over the long run. This answer choice is off-topic and incorrect.

Answer choice (E): This is the most frequently selected incorrect answer. This answer choice does not weaken the author's argument because it does not establish the nature of the genetic changes. You should not assume that the changes were the result of the increased ultraviolet radiation, that the changes had a harmful effect, or that the changes resulted in decreased genetic protection for today's humans. Because this answer offers no concrete information, this answer choice cannot weaken the argument.

Question #3: Assumption. The correct answer choice is (B)

The argument presents two premises followed by a sentence that contains both a conclusion and another premise:

> Premise 1:   Larson cannot do the assignment because of an unavoidable scheduling conflict.
>
> Premise 2:   Franks cannot do the assignment because he is not assertive enough for the task.
>
> Premise 3:   Parker is the only supervisor in the shipping department other than Larson and Franks.
>
> Conclusion: Parker must be assigned to the task.

When considering an argument, you should always be on the lookout for new terms that appear in only one premise or only in the conclusion. In this stimulus, the phrase "supervisor in the shipping department" appears in the last sentence. The use of this phrase is significant since it limits the group under discussion and indicates that the author is only considering shipping department supervisors for the position. This detail, of course, is reflected in the correct answer choice.

From another angle, the argument concludes that it is necessary to assign Parker to the task (the use of the term "must" indicates that the author believes that Parker is the only solution). Generally, such conclusions are vulnerable to attack by offering alternate solutions, and you should proceed to the question after making that analysis. If this were a Weaken question, you would look for answer that indicated that someone other than Parker could be assigned to the task. However, this is an Assumption question, so you should look for a choice that helps establish that alternate solutions do not exist, and that indeed Parker must be assigned to the task.

Answer choice (A): This answer choice tests to see whether you will assume that a mere possibility is an absolute certainty. The premise about Larson states that "a" reason Larson cannot be assigned to the task is the unavoidable scheduling conflict, and the use of "a" leaves open the possibility that other reasons also establish that Larson cannot do the assignment (the use of "the" would have been limiting, but the use of "a" is not). So, it is possible that there were other reasons that Larson could not do the assignment, but it is also possible there were no other reasons. Consequently, although Larson may have the assertiveness the task requires, the author has not assumed that she does, and this answer choice is incorrect.

Answer choice (B): This is the correct answer choice. This answer addresses the use of the phrase *supervisor in the shipping department* in the stimulus, and reflects the assumption made by the author that only supervisors from the shipping department can be assigned to the task. Remember, the author stated that there were only three supervisors in the shipping department, and since two of the supervisors could not be assigned to the task that therefore the third supervisor must be assigned to the task. This is a logical conclusion only if the author believes that a shipping department supervisor must be the person assigned to the task.

To double-check the validity of this answer choice, use the Assumption Negation Technique. Using the Technique, the negated answer becomes, "The task *can* be assigned to someone other than a supervisor in the shipping department." If the task can be assigned to non-supervisors, or to people who are not in the shipping department, the conclusion in the argument is severely weakened. Because the negated answer would clearly undermine the conclusion, this answer is confirmed as correct.

Answer choice (C): Although we know that Franks cannot be used for the task because he lacks assertiveness, we do not know that if he had the required assertiveness that he would be assigned the task. Similar to the reasoning used to discount answer choice (A), the premise about Franks states that "a" reason Franks cannot be assigned to the task is that he is not quite assertive enough. Thus, it is possible that there were other reasons that Franks could not do the assignment. Consequently, even if Franks had the assertiveness the task requires, the author has not assumed that he would be used for the task.

Answer choice (D): This choice is too broad because it addresses "any" conflict. The reason Larson could not do the assignment was that she had an *unavoidable* scheduling conflict, and so the author has not assumed that *any* scheduling conflict is problematic, just an *unavoidable* one (for example, perhaps Parker has a scheduling conflict, but it can be resolved prior to the start of the task). Since the author has not assumed that all scheduling conflicts preclude the assignment of the task, this answer choice is incorrect.

Answer choice (E): This answer choice contains the following conditional relationship:

Assertive enough $\longrightarrow$ Supervisor in shipping department

Has the author assumed that everyone who is assertive enough for the task is a supervisor in the shipping department? No, because the author has limited the candidates to the shipping department there could be other people who are assertive enough for the task, but they would not be qualified since they are not supervisors in the shipping department.

Question #4: Method of Reasoning. The correct answer choice is (C)

As you read through a stimulus, always keep in mind the structure of the argument being presented by the author. Knowing the structure will assist you in answering every type of question, and in the case of Method and Flaw questions, the structure of the argument *is* the answer. In this instance, the columnist considers the argument made by the analysts, accepts the initial premises used to draw the conclusion in the argument, but then uses those premises to draw a different conclusion than the conclusion drawn by the analysts.

Let us look at the details of the stimulus. The analysts claim that as baby boomers reach 50 they will begin to plan for retirement, and this will cause them to begin saving more. As a consequence, more money will be invested in the stock market, and stock prices will continue to rise. The columnist responds that the analysts are being overly optimistic about the stock price gains. This is based on the fact that the reduction in spending (consumption) will negatively affect corporate earnings, which will in turn affect stock valuation, which will in turn lead boomers to invest in investments other than stocks. Note that the columnist grants that as baby boomers reach 50 years of age, they will be inclined to save instead of spend; the columnist simply disagrees about how they will invest that savings.

Remember, in method of reasoning question answer choices, you should be on the lookout for short words or phrases (such as *premise* or *conclusion*) that represent an entire sentence or two of the stimulus. The test makers often try to throw off students by reducing a lengthy or complicated portion of the stimulus to one or two words.

Answer choice (A): Since the columnist grants the analysts' initial premises, and only argues against the conclusion based on those premises, this choice does not reflect the reasoning in the stimulus and is incorrect. In a method of reasoning question where the author has attacked one part of the argument, always expect one of the wrong answer choices to state that the author attacked a different part of the argument (as is the case here).

Answer choice (B): This choice is very attractive because the columnist does imply that the analysts might be self-serving in their conclusion ("Analysts would stand to gain…"). However, the argument against the analysts is not based on this observation. Instead, the columnist proceeds to consider the analysts' premises and offer a different interpretation to counter the analysts' conclusion. Thus, this answer choice focuses on an unessential element of the columnist's argument.

Answer choice (C): This is the correct answer choice. The columnist accepts the initial premises used by the analysts, but offers an alternative conclusion based upon consideration of other implications of those premises.

Answer choice (D): The columnist does state that the analysts' conclusion is too optimistic, but would not agree that the analysts' conclusion is "basically right." As the columnist states in the argument, "high stock prices will not be justified, and thus boomers' money will more likely flow into investments other than stocks." Since this assertion is contrary to the conclusion drawn by the analysts, there is no basis for the statement that the columnist believes the analysts' conclusion is basically right.

Answer choice (E): This choice is a classic Reverse answer. The columnist argues from the same body of information, not a different one, and argues for a different conclusion, not the same one.

Question #5: Removed from scoring

This question was removed after the test was administered but prior to the release of the exam results. Examinee responses to this question were not included in final score calculations (although, of course, any time spent by on an examinee on this question during the test was lost).

Question #6: Point at Issue. The correct answer choice is (D)

Maria's argument can be analyzed as follows:

Premise:	Popular music greatly exaggerates the role love plays in everyday life.
Premise/Conclusion:	Popular music fails to represent reality accurately.
Main Conclusion:	Popular music is bad art.

Maria claims that popular music is bad art because it does not accurately represent reality. Her conclusion commits her to the idea that it is *necessary* for art to represent reality accurately if it is to avoid being classified as "bad art.".

Theo argues that popular music is not supposed to reflect reality, as it performs other functions. He concludes that Maria should try to understand (the purpose of) popular music before claiming it is bad art. Because Theo proposes other *artistic functions* for art, and defends popular music, he is committed to the idea that representing reality accurately is *unnecessary* for art that is not bad.

The question stem asks you to identify the point of disagreement, so keep in mind that you can use the Agree/Disagree Test to determine the correct answer. Also, there are several points of contention in this exchange, including that Theo and Maria clearly disagree over the necessity of representing reality accurately and whether popular music is bad art, so you have several possible prephrases to consider while attacking the answer choices.

Answer choice (A): There are two ways to eliminate this answer choice. The first centers on the reference to "good art." Although Maria addresses "bad art" in her argument, she does not specifically address "good art" (remember, not all art is good or bad; some art can simply be neutral). Thus, we do not have specific grounds to state Maria's position (or Theo's, for that matter) on "good art."

Second, even if you make the assumption that all art is either good or bad, this answer choice still cannot be justified. Maria would disagree with this statement, because her reasoning commits her to the belief that no good art offers consoling illusions, to the extent that illusions get in the way of representing reality. However, you cannot be sure that Theo agrees with the word "most" in this response. Even though Theo defends popular music, or *some* art, on the grounds in this statement, you do not know that Theo believes that *most* good art offers consoling illusions.

Answer choice (B): Maria is committed to agreeing with this statement because of how she uses the premise of exaggerating the role of love to reach her judgment against popular music. However, you cannot be certain that Theo would disagree with this statement, because he does not address what constitutes bad art (remember, art is more than just popular music, and Theo has not discussed love in relation to other forms of art).

Answer choice (C): This is the most popular incorrect answer but one red flag is the word "always," which makes this an extreme answer. Remember, read very closely when you are attacking answer choices because the test makers will often slip in one or two words that change the strength of the answer choice.

Looking at the answer, Maria would probably disagree with this statement because it suggests that art should never consider immediate reality. However, although Theo believes that there are times when art should go beyond reality as it is, you cannot be sure that Theo would believe that art should *always* focus on what could be, rather than what is.

Answer choice (D): This is the correct answer choice. As discussed in the analysis of the stimulus, Maria and Theo disagree over whether it is necessary to accurately represent reality if art is to have a chance at being good.

Answer choice (E): Maria must reject this statement, because she has argued that popular music *is bad art*. Theo would also disagree with this statement because he has stated that popular music performs "other artistic functions." By making this statement, Theo indicates that he believes that popular music is art. Since both speakers disagree with the statement, the answer fails the Agree/Disagree Test and the choice is incorrect.

Question #7: Method of Reasoning. The correct answer choice is (B)

The argument notes that lawmakers are considering a proposal requiring milk labels to provide information about what artificial substances were used in the production of the milk. The conclusion of the argument is that "the proposal should not be implemented," because it would be unimaginably difficult to list every artificial substance that went into the process of producing milk.

Since you are asked to identify the method of reasoning, remember to avoid responses that do not pass the Fact Test (that is, responses that describe an event that did *not* occur in the stimulus).

Answer choice (A): The author proposes no "alternative course of action," so this response is incorrect.

Answer choice (B): This is the correct answer choice. The author does argue against the proposal, and the proposal does lead to absurd consequences because identifying all the substances involved could be tremendously difficult and listing the known substances would probably be impossible to fit onto a milk label.

Answer choice (C): The author does not offer any alternatives to the proposal.

Answer choice (D): This was the most popular incorrect answer. The key to eliminating this response is to rigorously examine each part of the answer. Many students accept the portion that refers to the analogous case because they believe that the references to fertilizer and fungicide qualify as analogous cases. But, examine those cases closely—they are not analogous cases but rather implications of the proposal regarding milk production (a qualifying analogy would likely have involved discussing a different animal or a different product than the ones the proposal covered.). Because the author did not make an analogous case, this choice is wrong.

Answer choice (E): This answer attempts to state that the author makes a source argument. The author never questions the motives of those making the proposal, only the ultimate logical and practical implications of the proposal.

Question #8: Must be True—SN. The correct answer choice is (A)

This is the first challenging question of the section, with all previous questions answered correctly by 80% or more of those who took the test.

This stimulus consists of a series of conditional statements, and you should diagram them in order to arrive be certain of the correct inference:

The first sentence contains several separate conditional relationships:

1. From the "Trust, which cannot be sustained in the absence of mutual respect" section:

    Trust ⟶ Mutual respect

2. From the "Trust…is essential to any long-lasting relationship, personal or professional" section, two relationships follow:

    Long-lasting personal relationship ⟶ Trust

    and

    Long-lasting professional relationship ⟶ Trust

The second sentence contains another conditional relationship:

    Personal relationship ⟶ Natural affinity

This relationship is a bit confusing since it somewhat overlaps one of the relationships in the first sentence (the difference being the "long-lasting" portion).

The third sentence contains another conditional relationship:

    Personal relationship endures ⟶ Mutual respect
    and
    Affinity

Note that the sufficient condition in the third sentence is functionally the same as the sufficient condition in the first sentence, and so the statements can be combined:

    Long-lasting personal relationship ⟶ Trust
    and
    Mutual respect
    and
    Affinity

The question asks what must be true, so you should look for a choice that expresses a condition or inference accurately, and especially be on the lookout for an answer that exploits the chain relationship between the first and third sentences.

Answer choice (A): This is the correct answer choice. If mutual respect and trust are the sole components of a friendship, and affinity is missing, then the personal relationship will not be long-lasting.

To confirm this idea, consider the contrapositive of the last sentence:

$$\begin{array}{c} \cancel{\text{Trust}} \\ \text{or} \\ \cancel{\text{Mutual respect}} \\ \text{or} \\ \cancel{\text{Affinity}} \end{array} \longrightarrow \text{Long-lasting pe\cancel{r}sonal relationship}$$

As indicated by the diagram, if affinity is not present, there will not be a long-lasting personal relationship.

Answer choice (B): This answer choice is incorrect for two independent reasons. First, the answer choice addresses *any* professional relationships, and the stimulus only provides information regarding *long-lasting* professional relationships. Because we have not been provided any information about other types of professional relationships, this answer choice fails the Fact Test and is incorrect.

Second, the answer choice contains a Mistaken Reversal. According to the relationship in the first sentence:

$$\text{Trust} \longrightarrow \text{Mutual respect}$$

The diagram above indicates that trust requires mutual respect, not the other way around.

Answer choice (C): This is the most popular incorrect answer. Although at first glance this answer appears identical to the last sentence of the stimulus, the wording is different. Whereas the stimulus indicated that mutual respect and affinity where necessary conditions, the wording in this answer indicates that mutual respect and affinity are sufficient conditions. Hence, this answer choice is a Mistaken Reversal and is incorrect.

In addition, even if you misinterpret the relationship in this answer choice, there is no mention of trust, and the first sentence indicates that trust is also a necessary component of a long-lasting personal relationship.

Answer choice (D): The stimulus does not discuss the relative longevity of personal and professional relationships, so this choice is unsupported and incorrect. In addition, though this response could be true, the stimulus puts an extra necessary condition on personal relationships (in that they require affinity), and that extra condition might make personal relationships *less likely* to last than professional relationships (by giving them more chances to go wrong).

Answer choice (E): The word "ensure" is a sufficient condition indicator, but affinity was stated to be a necessary element for personal relationships such as marriage. Consequently, this is a Mistaken Reversal.

Question #9: Must be True—Principle. The correct answer choice is (E)

The stimulus in this problem is fairly easy to understand: certain phrases are used to suggest that what follows the phrase has just been demonstrated. However, such a phrase is misused when it follows an apparent counterexample.

The question stem asks you to identify the answer that best fits the principle given in the last sentence of the stimulus. The principle is that a cliché like "as the saying goes" will follow a situation where the saying is not proven or is inappropriately described. Thus, you should select the response in which the scenario and the cliché appear contrary to one another.

Answer choice (A): Fatima is quite aware of the fact that much is unknown, and thus the scenario and saying do not contradict each other. The section that indicates that Fatima dislikes being reminded how much will go unsolved in her lifetime does not affect the cliché.

Answer choice (B): In one possible interpretation, the scenario might agree with the cliché in this problem. At worst, the scenario cannot be said to contradict the maxim, because there is no particular reason to suppose that Harold is *not* selfish. Either way, this choice is wrong.

Answer choice (C): The cliché actually reflects Roger's behavior, so this choice is incorrect.

Answer choice (D): The saying makes the unwarranted conclusion that Sharon's husband loves cat shows or cats, but it is at least true that Sharon's husband seems to pretend to share a love (or at least make a sacrifice that reflects regard), so this cliché follows fairly well, and this choice is incorrect.

Answer choice (E): This is the correct answer choice. Ending up with a broken leg and a partially ruined ski trip is unquestionably contradictory to everything ending well. This answer choice perfectly fits the principle in question.

Question #10: Point at Issue—CE. The correct answer choice is (A)

Rachel argues that the lack of constraints on contemporary art has led to a decline in the quality of art, because great art requires that artists struggle within boundaries, as did contemporary artists' predecessors. Rachel's conclusion is that freedom from constraints "has caused a decline in the quality of art."

James argues that people mistakenly conclude that contemporary art is inferior to the art of past eras, because while people have forgotten the poor artwork of past eras, they still remember the poor artwork of today. James' conclusion is that "people today mistakenly think that contemporary art is generally inferior to earlier art."

The causal aspect of the stimulus is that Rachel discusses why she thinks the quality of art has declined, and James discusses why he thinks the quality has not declined, and why people believe it has.

Since you are asked for James' and Rachel's point of disagreement, and their conclusions contain opposing ideas about quality of art, you should prephrase and search for a response that discusses whether there has been a decline in the quality of art.

Answer choice (A): This is the correct answer choice. Rachel states that contemporary art has declined, and James states that contemporary art is not inferior to past art, so James and Rachel disagree over whether there has been a decline in contemporary art relative to other periods. Remember, use the Agree/Disagree Test to confirm that this is the correct answer. In this instance, Rachel would agree with the statement and James would disagree.

Answer choice (B): Since James does not discuss constraints, we are uncertain of his opinion on this statement. Hence, this answer follows the classic "one view unknown" form, and we must eliminate this choice.

Answer choice (C): This is another answer choice that follows the "one view unknown" form. Since James does not discuss limits, you must eliminate this choice. You cannot be certain of James' opinion about something he does not discuss, and you should not assume that James opposes all of Rachel's beliefs.

Answer choice (D): James unquestionably agrees with this statement, but you do not know Rachel's opinion about whether the inferior art of past generations is forgotten. Thus, because one speaker's perspective is unknown, this answer choice cannot be correct.

Note that although James may have implied that Rachel herself has forgotten the inferior art of the past ("They all forget…"), that does not commit Rachel to disagreeing with James on the point about whether inferior art is *generally* forgotten.

Answer choice (E): Both Rachel and James in some way disagree with this choice, so in that respect they agree with each other, and this choice is wrong.

Rachel's discussion is centered on the presumption that one can accurately compare art from different periods to that of the contemporary era, so she would disagree with this statement. James' argument indicates that the quality of contemporary art can be compared to the quality of art from past eras ("people today mistakenly think that contemporary art is generally inferior to earlier art"), so he also disagrees with this statement.

Question #11: Parallel Flaw—#%. The correct answer choice is (C)

The stimulus argues that since the *average* price of groceries will rise next month, the price of two specific goods—butter and eggs—will rise next month. This is a classic error of division where a characteristic of the whole is presumed to apply to all of its parts. Specifically, in this problem the conclusion is unwarranted because the increase in the average price of groceries could be attributed to many items other than butter or eggs. In fact, the price of butter and eggs could have decreased because the overall qualities of a group are not necessarily shared by each part of the group.

Note that the correct answer must contain a flaw similar to the one in the stimulus. Any answer choice featuring valid reasoning or a different type of flaw should be eliminated.

Answer choice (A): This answer is incorrect on two counts. First, the choice projects a past trend into the future, whereas the argument in the stimulus involves the future but not the past. Second, this choice does not use a general average and apply it to specific items. Instead, a single item is addressed throughout the answer.

Answer choice (B): This choice states that only two outcomes are possible, and then concludes that a since one of the options is unlikely to occur that the other option must occur. Although the reasoning is flawed, it is not analogous to that found in the stimulus.

Answer choice (C): This is the correct answer choice. The answer addresses a characteristic (amount of time spent watching television) of a general group (people younger than 20) and indicates that the average characteristic is increasing. The answer then concludes that the characteristic of a part (fourth graders) of the general group must also have risen. Similar to the argument in the stimulus, this argument ignores the fact that an average increase does not mean that every part of the group has increased.

Answer choice (D): This choice contains valid conditional reasoning. If the price of ice cream rises whenever the price of sugar rises, and next month the price of sugar is expected to rise, then it follows that next month the price of ice cream is expected to rise. Conditionally speaking, one of the premises contains the following relationship:

Price of sugar rises $\longrightarrow$ Price of ice cream rises

Another premise indicates that next month the sufficient condition is expected to occur, and thus one can conclude that next month the necessary condition is likely to occur.

Note that although this argument contains a part to whole relationship, there is not the same flawed use of an average and its component parts.

Answer choice (E): This choice also contains conditional reasoning. The first sentence contains both a conditional relationship and the statement that the sufficient condition will occur over the next decade:

Conditional Relationship: Population 20-30 declines $\longrightarrow$ Real estate prices fall

Sufficient condition met: Population 20-30 declines *over next decade*

Consequently, we can conclude that the necessary condition will also occur over that period, and that real estate prices fall over the next decade.

Note also that there is no part to whole relationship within this answer, so this answer is incorrect on that count as well.

Question #12: Weaken—CE. The correct answer choice is (C)

This was one of the two hardest Logical Reasoning questions on this test (the other is question #20 of section 4). The argument can be reduced as follows:

Premise:	Biologists have noted reproductive abnormalities in fish that are immediately downstream of paper mills.
Premise:	One possible cause is dioxin, which paper mills release daily and which can alter the concentration of hormones in fish.
Premise:	However...since the fish recover normal hormone concentrations relatively quickly during occasional mill shutdowns and dioxin decomposes very slowly in the environment.
Conclusion:	Dioxin is unlikely to be the cause.

This stimulus begins with the presentation of one hypothetical cause of fish abnormalities: dioxin, a chemical which can alter the concentration of hormones in fish. The author concludes that *dioxin is unlikely to be the cause*, based on the fact that fish recover normal hormone levels quickly during mill shutdowns, even though dioxin remains present in the environment ("it decomposes slowly"). The conclusion is notable in that it concludes that dioxin is *not* a likely cause, and thus it asserts that a causal relationship does not exist.

This is a very controversial LSAT problem, with a number of test takers suggesting that the credited may strengthen the argument and that (D) is a better weakening answer even if (C) does weaken the argument. Test takers were clearly confused by the problem, selecting the first four answers in roughly equal proportions. In the responses to (C) and (D) we will address some of the issues underpinning the controversy as it was the answer choices that were trickier than the stimulus itself.

Answer choice (A): This answer attempts to weaken the argument by presenting a source attack. A source attack is logically invalid, and does not undermine the argument.

Answer choice (B): The problem with this answer is that it does not give you any concrete evidence with which to attack the argument. Yes, the dioxin decomposition rate varies, but how much does it vary in the environment where the fish are?

Using an analogy, selecting this answer is like saying that the statement "the temperature in the environment changes depending on the season" weakens the argument that "it is not usually hot in Norway." Sure, the seasons may have an effect, but how much of one, and perhaps that effect is to simply make it mildly warm during the summer and bitterly cold during the winter. Without concrete information, there can be no way to know that this answer weakens the stimulus.

Answer choice (C): This is the correct answer choice. The argument is that dioxin is not the likely culprit, based on the fact that the fish recover quickly during shutdowns despite their continued access to the chemical (based on its slow decomposition). If, as this answer choice provides, dioxin gets washed quickly downstream, it seems more likely that the fish benefit from these occasional shutdowns because their environment is temporarily free of this chemical. This makes dioxin a *more likely culprit*, thus weakening the argument in the stimulus.

In Law Services' view, "The conclusion of the argument is that dioxin is unlikely to be the cause of reproductive abnormalities in fish that are immediately downstream of paper mills. The reasons given are that those fish recover normal hormone concentrations relatively quickly when the paper mills are shut down even though dioxin decomposes very slowly in the environment. Thus, if dioxin is the cause of the abnormal hormone concentrations that may be causing the reproductive abnormalities, those fish should not recover normal hormone concentrations relatively quickly when the paper mills are shut down, since dioxin would remain in the waters immediately below the mills even though it is not being released by the mills. So, this suggests that it is not dioxin, but, perhaps, something that decomposes rapidly in the environment, that is the cause of the abnormal hormone concentrations that may be causing reproductive abnormalities in the fish immediately downstream from the paper mills.

The credited response weakens the argument by indicating a mechanism by means of which dioxin does not continue to be in the area immediately downstream of the paper mills when they are shut down in spite of the fact that it decomposes very slowly in the environment. Thus, recovery of normal hormone concentrations in the fish when the paper mills shut down could be due to their not being exposed to dioxin during the period, even though dioxin decomposes slowly. In that case, dioxin could be the cause of the alteration of hormone concentrations and of resultant reproductive abnormalities despite the evidence offered in the stimulus."

Part of the controversy arises because some students interpret this answer as seeming to support the conclusion rather than weaken it, as it states that dioxin is quickly removed from the fish's habitat (i.e. those fish that are "immediately downstream of paper mills") and would therefore be an *unlikely* cause for the observed reproductive abnormalities. Answer choice (C) certainly does not seem to promote the idea that dioxin *could* be the cause for these abnormalities, as it is carried far downstream too quickly to have any significant effect on the fish in question.

By way of addressing the controversy, Law Services has stated that "the stimulus indicates that the paper mills release dioxin daily. Thus, even if normal river currents carry the dioxin far downstream in a few hours, while the paper mills are operating the dioxin in the water immediately downstream of the paper mills is being regularly replenished and the fish in those waters are being exposed to dioxin on a daily basis. This is consistent with dioxin being the cause of the reproductive abnormalities in the fish immediately downstream of the paper mills. And the fact that the release of dioxin stop when the mills are shut down, allowing the currents immediately below the mills to flush away the dioxin for a significant period of time, would explain why the fish recover normal hormone concentrations during occasional mill shutdowns. Thus, (C) weakens the argument by describing conditions that would allow the fish to recover normal hormone concentrations if dioxin were the cause of the hormone changes, even though dioxin decomposes slowly in the environment."

Answer choice (D): If you selected this answer, do not feel bad. Many good test takers selected this response, and there is serious debate about whether this answer is incorrect.

On one hand, this choice states that, despite the fish recovering relatively rapidly from the abnormal hormone concentrations, the physiological effects are more long-lasting. This would appear to weaken the conclusion, as it shows that reproductive abnormalities could still be present in the dioxin-exposed fish (due to the more permanent physical effects induced by the dioxin), regardless of the hormonal adjustment.

On the other hand, Law Services claims that "(D) does not weaken the argument because it does not address the argument that is made. The argument made would cast doubt on dioxin as the cause of the abnormalities even if (D) were true. As noted above, the conclusion of the argument is that dioxin is unlikely to be the cause of the abnormalities, and the reason given for the conclusion is that abnormal hormone concentrations that might cause the abnormalities return to normal during the mill shutdowns even though dioxin decomposes very slowly in the environment and, thus, fish immediately downstream of the paper mills would still be exposed to dioxin even during the mill shutdowns. If (D) is true, this does nothing to undermine the focus of this argument. The argument does not call into question dioxin as the cause of the abnormalities by casting doubt on the link between dioxin and the hormone changes. While (D) might explain how the abnormalities could persist even if the hormone levels returned to normal, this does not address the reason given in the argument why dioxin is unlikely to be the cause, and, hence, does not weaken the argument. The credited response (C) does, however, provide an explanation of how dioxin can cause the changes in hormone levels that could be the cause of the abnormalities even given the facts about the return to normal of hormone levels when the plants are shut down and dioxin decomposing very slowly in the environment. Thus, it addresses the reason given in the argument why it is unlikely that dioxin is the cause of the abnormalities."

Answer choice (E): This was, by far, the least frequently chosen answer choice. The fact that the interaction between hormone concentrations and reproductive abnormalities is not fully understood does not weaken the assertion that hormone concentrations cause those abnormalities. The lack of understanding does not suggest that the hormone/abnormality connection is either stronger or weaker than previously believed, and without concrete information, there is no way this answer choice can attack the argument (again, like answer choice (B), a gray area or uncertainty does not serve to strengthen or weaken an argument).

Question #13: Flaw in the Reasoning—SN. The correct answer choice is (E)

The stimulus consists of a Mistaken Negation:

First sentence:

Play successful $\longrightarrow$ Adapted as a movie
or
Revived at the Festival

Second and third sentences:

Play s~u~ccessful $\longrightarrow$ Adapted a~s~ a movie
and
Revived a~t~ the Festival

Since you are asked to identify the flaw in the reasoning, you must select a response that discusses the Mistaken Negation. Remember, as discussed in the *PowerScore LSAT Logical Reasoning Bible*, Flaw in the Reasoning questions that contain conditional reasoning almost always use the terms *sufficient* or *necessary*, or a synonym. You should attempt to accelerate through this question by seeking an answer that features one or more of those terms.

Answer choice (A): This answer is wrong for two reasons. First, the two premises in the stimulus do not allow for *any* conditionally-related conclusion to be validly drawn, so stating that the flaw is that the argument "fails to draw a conclusion" cannot be correct (in one sense, the flaw is that the author *does* draw a conclusion when none is justified).

Second, if a conclusion like the one in the stimulus could be drawn, then the conclusion would be correct as given, and it would not be that "the play will not both be adapted as a movie and revived at the Decade Festival" (remember, any compound condition featuring "or" is properly negated by negating both terms and turning the "or" into "and," and the argument does just this; one the other hand, the answer attempts to imply that the correct negation would be "not both but possibly one").

Answer choice (B): The fact that the play is not successful is presented as a premise, and the flaw in the argument does not trade on a premise, but rather on the unsupported conclusion.

Answer choice (C): The argument does not discuss aesthetics, or equate aesthetics with economics.

Answer choice (D): The argument does not assume that there are no other avenues for the play; it merely discusses two avenues following a sufficient condition about the play's success. That is not a flaw, and this choice is wrong.

Answer choice (E): This is the correct answer choice. The error behind a Mistaken Negation is believing that failing to meet a sufficient condition indicates that the necessary condition will also not be met. This answer describes that exact error. Note how easy this answer appears once you recognize that a

Mistaken Negation is present in the stimulus, and once you know the error behind a Mistaken Negation. Taking the time to learn the reasoning forms used by the test makers prior to taking the LSAT gives you the opportunity to simply annihilate certain questions, leaving you more time to attack the truly difficult problems.

Question #14: Strengthen—SN. The correct answer choice is (E)

The physician's conclusion is that the proposed study should not be permitted. But this conclusion is based on a conditional premise that, by itself, does not prove the conclusion (everything before the last two sentences of the stimulus is background information and does not affect the physician's argument):

Conditional premise:

Likely to reveal important information about a medical condition

Research Permitted $\longrightarrow$ and

Known to pose minimal risk to subjects

The conclusion:

Research ~~Permitted~~

As you can see, a leap occurs between the conditional premise and the conclusion. In drawing the conclusion, the physician relies upon a contrapositive of the conditional premise:

Likely to reveal ~~important~~ information about a ~~medical~~ condition

or $\longrightarrow$ Research ~~permitted~~

Known to pose ~~minimal~~ risk to subjects

Enacting this contrapositive would justify the conclusion in the argument, but the physician did not offer any information indicating that the research is not likely to yield important information or that there is significant risk. Consequently, there is a hole in the argument, and the author's conclusion, as given, is unwarranted. To strengthen this argument, you should look for an answer choice that fills the hole by indicating that one of the two necessary conditions in the premise does not occur (knowing that one or both of the conditions does not occur would enact the contrapositive and validate the argument). As a specific prephrase, locate a choice that either shows significant risk or that the study is likely to be pointless.

Answer choice (A): This answer, while it might appeal to public interest sensibilities, is irrelevant. Moral considerations are not raised as an issue in the stimulus, and the fact that the money could be spent on more serious diseases cannot be used to strengthen the physician's argument.

Answer choice (B): This answer choice would only serve to weaken any certainty in the physician's position by showing that the necessary condition of minimal risk has quite possibly been met, so this choice is incorrect.

Answer choice (C): Informed consent is not a relevant issue, and you must eliminate this choice. Barring that the stimulus mentions public interest or morals, an answer such as this one would always be incorrect because the LSAT focuses on logic, not ethics.

Answer choice (D): This was the most frequently chosen incorrect answer. Many test takers felt that this choice provided proof that the study would not yield important information about a medical condition because a hormonal imbalance is not a medical condition. However, both the stimulus and the answer choice state that hormonal imbalances can cause diseases, and the condition in the stimulus refers to information about "*a* medical condition," not a "hormonal imbalance medical condition," and so this answer does not provide proof that the study is not likely to reveal important information about a medical condition

Answer choice (E): This is the correct answer choice. If the long-term effects are unknown, then the study is not known to pose minimal risk to the subjects, and the study should be prohibited.

Question #15: Flaw in the Reasoning. The correct answer choice is (E)

The stimulus argues that it was unfair to install speed bumps in Grove Park, since all drivers have the right to use the public roads in Grove Park whenever they wish.

You probably had the strong commonsense reaction that speed bumps prevent *speeding* through a neighborhood but do not prevent *driving* through it. That reaction is very helpful because it identifies a key flaw in the argument, and the question stem asks you to find this flaw. The challenge then becomes to find the answer choice that best reflects the author's erroneous assumption that speed bumps prevent the use of a road.

Answer choice (A): Although the argument ignores the possibility that speed bumps may not reduce the speed at which drivers drive through the neighborhood, this is not a flaw in the argument and so this answer is incorrect. Rather, this answer describes a flaw in the neighborhood's traffic control plan (and again, not a flaw in the author's argument).

Answer choice (B): Ignoring that drivers speed through the neighborhood is not the error reflected in the stimulus. In fact, the reason for putting up the bumps is actually extraneous to the reasoning in the argument since the argument takes the position that the speed bumps—whatever their intended purpose—are unfair since they deprive drivers of the *right* to use the roads.

Answer choice (C): The issue in the stimulus is one of rights and road use, not whether drivers have actually complained. So, although the stimulus does not present any information about complaints, there is no need to do so.

Whether or not those who still drive through the neighborhood complain about the speed bumps, the speed bumps could still be unfair, especially to those who quit using the road, so this response does not express a flaw in the argument.

Answer choice (D): Actually, the stimulus assumes that the residents of communities do *not* have any such right, so this response is an Opposite answer, and is incorrect.

Answer choice (E): This is the correct answer choice. The argument does not prove that the speed bumps prevent usage of the neighborhood's roads, but the argument depends on the assumption that they do.

Question #16: Weaken. The correct answer choice is (C)

The literary critic points out that often the heirs of a writer will publish much of that writer's remaining work, regardless of merit. Because many writers possess manuscripts they consider unworthy and would not want published, the critic concludes that a successful writer who decides not to publish a recently completed manuscript should destroy it immediately.

Note that the last word of the stimulus—immediately—is rather extreme (remember, always look for words that seems absolute or overly strong for the situation). You may have had a strong reaction to the critic's recommendation because of that extremity, and that reaction is relevant to the flaw in the critic's reasoning. Destroying a manuscript immediately seems like a severe step, and one that does not allow for any reassessment of the work. Over time, there might be many benefits to be derived from keeping an initially dissatisfactory manuscript (especially if the probability of immediate death is low, as would be the case for most authors).

Since you are asked to undermine the critic's reasoning, you should seek an answer choice that suggests that writers might not want to destroy their completed manuscripts immediately.

Answer choice (A): The argument is about *successful* writers, and the suggestion that successful living writers should immediately destroy works that they decide not to publish. This answer choice is about writers who become successful *after* they die, so even when this answer is taken as true it does not impact the argument made by the critic (once you are dead, you can't go back and destroy your manuscripts, obviously).

Answer choice (B): This is a classic Shell Game answer. The stimulus specifically discusses *manuscripts* and whether they should be destroyed. This answer, on the other hand, discusses *personal correspondence*, and the two are not the same.

Answer choice (C): This is the correct answer choice. If many successful writers will change their views of their recently completed works, then those writers might come to see their initial assessments as overly critical and then choose to publish a manuscript. That eventuality could not occur if they had immediately destroyed the manuscript upon completion, so this choice represents an effective attack on the critic's argument.

Answer choice (D): This is the most frequently selected incorrect answer. The key to avoiding this answer is to understand that many of the posthumously published books were judged worthy by the author prior to his or her death. For example, say that an author completed a manuscript and determined it was worthy of publication, but then died before the book was published. Does the existence of this scenario undermine the critic's argument? No, because the critic argues that manuscripts that are *not* going to be published should be destroyed, and the manuscripts in the answer choice do not fall into that category.

Answer choice (E): If anything, this answer agrees with the critic since it suggests that the heirs of a successful writer will not be able to discern a quality work from an inferior work. According to the argument, the heirs publish the works regardless of merit, so whether they deem themselves qualified to judge the works is not relevant.

Question #17: Main Point. The correct answer choice is (B)

The stimulus begins with a statement about the practical effect of government on individual rights. The next sentence contrasts the first sentence, and presents the author's conclusion: the government's view on moral rights is not necessarily the correct view. This conclusion is supported by the assertion that if the government's view is necessarily correct, individuals have only the moral rights that the government grants, meaning that individuals have no moral rights at all (because a moral "right" granted by government that could easily take that "right" away or interpret it in an arbitrary fashion is not truly a "right" in the traditional sense).

As with any Main Point question, you should be sure to isolate the conclusion of the argument before proceeding to the answer choices. By having a strong prephrase, you can do just about any Main Point question quickly. For this question, you must find an answer that paraphrases the conclusion that the government's view on moral rights is not necessarily the correct view.

Answer choice (A): This answer choice is in the form of a conditional statement (note the *unless*):

Individual has rights $\longrightarrow$ Government says that individuals have rights

However, the argument opposes the notion that individual rights rely on the government's interpretation of rights, so this choice is wrong.

Answer choice (B): This is the correct answer choice. The conclusion of the argument is that the government's view of rights is not necessarily correct, and this answer is a perfect paraphrase of that idea. Note also that the reference to "government officials and courts" is acceptable because officials and courts are mentioned in the first sentence as controlling entities within the government.

Answer choice (C): This answer choice is also in the form of a conditional statement (note the *unless*):

I̶n̶d̶i̶v̶i̶d̶u̶a̶l̶s̶ ̶h̶a̶v̶e̶ rights $\longrightarrow$ Government says that i̶n̶d̶i̶v̶i̶d̶u̶a̶l̶s̶ have rights

Or, in the form of the contrapositive:

Government says that individuals have rights $\longrightarrow$ Individuals have rights

Aside from this relationship not reflecting the conclusion, this choice is wrong because it indicates that the government dictates rights, which is contrary to the argument.

Answer choice (D): The main point of the argument concerns the conflict between the individual and the state, not between different elements of the state.

Answer choice (E): The conclusion is that the government's view is not always correct, but this choice attempts to take the argument to a whole new level by recommending a course of action for individuals. The conclusion of an argument is always what the author stated or what reasonably follows from the premises, not something that a reader might believe because of the argument. Do not go beyond the stimulus when selecting a Main Point answer!

Question #18: Weaken—CE. The correct answer choice is (D)

The argument in this stimulus indicates that there is evidence that our cave-dwelling ancestors polished their flint tools to a higher degree than necessary for hunting purposes. The author then draws the flawed conclusion that the *cause* of this extra polishing must have been an aesthetic sensibility on the part of early humans. The implied conclusion is:

Cause	Effect
Aesthetic sense ⟶	Many flints polished to a high degree

The problem is that early humans could have used the flints for activities other than hunting, so there are explanations for the polishing aside from the notion that cavemen liked the way the flints looked.

You are asked to weaken the argument, and since this is a causal stimulus, you should look for one of the five classic ways to weaken a causal argument:

1. Find an alternate cause for the stated effect.

2. Show that even when the cause occurs, the effect does not occur.

3. Show that although the effect occurs, the cause did not occur.

4. Show that the stated relationship is reversed.

5. Show that a statistical problem exists with the data used to make the causal statement.

Answer choice (A): This choice seems attractive, but it actually has no effect on the argument. First, remember that the test makers rarely attack an argument by directly undermining a premise, so you should be suspicious of any answer choice that appears to do just that. Make sure to read carefully in order to avoid a trap. In this case, the trap resides in the use of *many* in the stimulus and *most* in this answer.

Most simply means more than half, so this choice leaves open the possibility that just less than half of the flints are highly polished. Yet, imagine that there were one million flints used by our cave-dwelling ancestors. Under this scenario, just less than half a million could be highly polished, and that would certainly qualify as *many*. Consequently, even when this answer is taken as true, it does not undermine or contradict the information in the argument (in other words, this answer is consistent with the stimulus, and an answer that is consistent with the stimulus cannot be correct in a Weaken question).

Answer choice (B): The cave-dweller's seeming neglect of one form of artistic self-expression is not relevant to the possibility that the high polishing of tools was a form of aesthetic expression. You may have found this response attractive, but the absence of cave paintings speaks no more to the general aesthetic sensibilities of early humans than does the absence of writing or musical expression. And, of course, it may be that early humans used different caves for their painting than for their flint polishing.

Answer choice (C): Some test takers assume that the use of flints in a religious ceremony shows an alternate cause for the polishing of the flints. However, the answer choice specifically states that the flints were used for *display* in the ceremonies, and so this answer choice could actually serve to strengthen the conclusion by showing that cave-dwellers had an aesthetic sense. In any event, there is no proof of an alternate cause, so this choice must be eliminated.

Answer choice (D): This is the correct answer choice. If the flints were used for chores besides hunting, then there is a possible explanation for the polishing other than aesthetics. Therefore, this answer choice weakens the argument by suggesting an alternate cause (or causes) for why the flints were highly polished.

Answer choice (E): The fact that the benefits of an aesthetic sense are not fully understood is not relevant to whether the aesthetic sense exists, so this choice is wrong.

Question #19: Strengthen. The correct answer choice is (A)

The columnist points out that much of Northern America and Western Europe is more heavily forested, has less acid rain, and has better air quality now than 50 years ago, and grants that the improvement may be largely due to policies advocated by environmentalists. The columnist then concludes that the improvement lends support to people who argue that excessive restriction of the exploitation of resources may make it economically difficult to pay for the future protection of the environment. In layman's terms, the environment is better, but even though that may be because of pro-environment policies, if we don't use our natural resources then we may not have enough money in the future to continue to apply pro-environment policies.

Remember that in any argument your primary task is to identify the conclusion and supporting premises, and assess the validity of the argument. If you sensed any holes in the argument (and there are holes, such as that 50 years over a limited area is not necessarily enough of a sample to prove the claims, or that the improvement may not have necessarily have come from the policies) remember that in a Strengthen question you can look for an answer that eliminates such a gap in logic.

Answer choice (A): This is the correct answer choice. If nations did not sustain their wealth by using their natural resources, then the idea that overly protecting their resources would lead to a lack of wealth would be false. Thus, this answer supports the claim that restricting the use of natural resources may diminish the wealth necessary to sustain the pro-environment policies.

Answer choice (B): Technology is extraneous to the issues dealt with in the stimulus, so this choice is irrelevant and incorrect.

Answer choice (C): Regardless of the cause of the *majority* of ecological disasters, humans can still be the cause of *this particular* disaster. Thus, this answer choice does not affect the issue of environmental policy.

Answer choice (D): This was the most popular incorrect answer. This answer dwells on what would have occurred in the past had a different approach been used whereas the argument indicates that finances may dictate a certain course of action in the future. Aside from the fact that what would have occurred in the past does not mean the same would occur in the future, this answer does not strengthen the reasoning because it is not relevant to the argument that excessively strict policies may result in insufficient funds to sustain those policies.

Some students see this answer as strengthening the idea that the policies of the environmentalists have resulted in the environmental improvement, but the author already conceded that point in the argument so it needed no further support.

Answer choice (E): This choice suggests that a concern for the environment causes an increase in wealth. If this is the case, then the restrictive environmental policies are beneficial, and it may be that they do not diminish the nation's wealth. Thus, this answer choice weakens the reasoning in the stimulus.

Question #20: Flaw in the Reasoning. The correct answer choice is (D)

The stimulus begins with the classic argument introduction device, "Many historians claim…" As is often the case when this construction is used, the author's argument is that the historians' claims are incorrect. Specifically, the reviewer explains that many historians claim to be basically objective, but that we cannot accept their claims because it is easy to find instances of false, non-objective historical explanations.

The reviewer's reasoning is weak, particularly because *anyone*, not merely historians, can offer historical explanations, and it might be the historical explanations of non-historians which contain instances of bias. In addition, the existence of false explanations only proves that *some* historians are not objective, and it does not prove that *many* historians are not objective. The reviewer specifically notes that *many* historians claim objectivity, and that just indicates that a substantial number claim objectivity. So, when the reviewer concludes that the claims of these many historians are false, the reviewer draws an exaggerated conclusion.

Answer choice (A): The stimulus does not take this for granted. The reviewer simply rejects the claims that the historians made about their objectivity; the reviewer then makes statements about historical explanations, and does not offer a view about *other fields*.

Answer choice (B): While the evidence does not establish the conclusion, it does not undermine the conclusion, either. The evidence is consistent with either accepting or denying the conclusion, which means that the evidence is simply not compelling.

Answer choice (C): This choice is irrelevant because the reviewer does not need to take the historian's methodologies into account. Whether historians employ these methods or not, their output can still be prejudiced. If their output is flawed, then the reviewer's premise regarding the existence of instances of false explanations is not undermined. Consequently, although this is an attractive answer choice, it does not reveal a flaw in the reviewer's reasoning.

Answer choice (D): This is the correct answer choice. The reviewer argues that instances of false historical explanations show that the objectivity claims of many *historians* are false. Thus, since the explanations are not clearly stated to have come from the historians, the reviewer must assume, or take for granted, that at least some of the prejudicial works come from those historians who claim to be objective.

Answer choice (E): This answer choice, along with answer choice (C), was one of the two most popular incorrect answers. However, like (C), this answer choice misses the mark by addressing an issue that appears to involve one of the reviewer's premises, but actually leaves that premise intact and the argument unscathed.

Just because not all historical explanations embodying ideologies are false does not prove that there are not instances of false historical explanations that do embody ideological prejudices. Because the reviewer's argument is not built on the premise that *all* historical explanations embodying ideological prejudices are false (just that *some* are), this answer does not point out a flaw in the reviewer's argument.

Question #21: Justify the Conclusion. The correct answer choice is (A)

The argument can be broken down as follows:

Premise:	Although the geological record contains some hints of major meteor impacts preceding mass extinctions, there were many extinctions that did not follow any known major meteor impacts.
Premise:	Likewise, there are many records of major meteor impacts that do not seem to have been followed by mass extinctions.
Conclusion:	Thus the geological record suggests that there is no consistent causal link between major meteor impacts and mass extinctions.

The conclusion is a bit unusual in that it indicates that *no* consistent causal relationship is suggested (normally, causal conclusions indicate that a relationship *can* be drawn).

The argument as given seems reasonable, but you are asked to justify the conclusion, and so there must be an element missing. Perhaps one thing should jump out at you in retrospect: the use of the word "consistent" in the conclusion. The author does not deny any causal link, just a "consistent" one. Remember, always be on the lookout for any word or idea that seems unusual or out of place, or that modifies a relationship. If you do spot such a word or idea, attack the answer choices and see if that idea is present.

Remember also that in Justify questions you are looking for an answer that would make the conclusion undeniably true based on the combination of the premises and the answer choice (this is the essence of the Justify Formula). Thus, you are not looking for an assumption of the argument, but rather an answer that forces the conclusion to follow. In this case, you must find an answer that would suggest that no consistent causal link exists between major meteor impacts and mass extinctions.

Answer choice (A): This is the correct answer choice. This choice is in the form of a conditional relationship:

Consistent causal link   →   All major meteor impacts followed by mass extinctions

Because you are trying to justify a conclusion that includes the idea of "not consistent," take the contrapositive so that you can determine exactly what sufficient condition will produce such a conclusion:

All major ~~meteor~~ impacts
followed ~~by~~ mass extinctions   →   ~~Consistent~~
~~causal link~~

Because one of the premises states that not all major meteor impacts seem to be followed by mass extinctions, and that is the sufficient condition in this answer, then by adding that premise to this answer you would be forced to draw the conclusion that the geological record does not suggest a consistent causal link. Thus, this answer makes the Justify Formula work and is correct.

Answer choice (B): This was the most popular incorrect answer. The answer choice yields the following conditional relationship:

Can be consistently linked   →   *Many* mass extinctions followed impacts

Because you are trying to justify a conclusion that includes the idea of "not consistent," take the contrapositive so that you can determine exactly what sufficient condition will produce such a conclusion:

Many mass ~~extinctions~~ followed impacts   →   Can be ~~consistently~~ linked

The statement needed to satisfy the sufficient condition must be equivalent to, "Not many mass extinctions were followed major meteor impacts." The stimulus might appear to make this statement, but it does not. The stimulus never says that *not many* impacts *were* followed by mass extinctions, only that *many impacts were not* followed by mass extinctions, so this condition does not match the facts described in the stimulus, and this choice is wrong.

As point of clarification, *not many were* and *many were not* appear very similar but they mean different things. For example, consider the following statements:

1. Not many people were at the game
2. Many people were not at the game

The first statement means that the crowd at the game was small; the second statement means that many people (which could conceivably be the rest of the people in the world) chose not to attend the game. Note that the second statement does not say that the crowd was small. The crowd could have been huge, but still there many people not there (there are many people at the Super Bowl, but even more people are not at the Super Bowl).

Answer choice (C): An answer such as this one is easily defeated by the Justify Formula because the information in this answer, when added to the premises, does not produce a conclusion that suggests that no consistent causal link exists between major meteor impacts and mass extinctions.

Mechanistically speaking, the conclusion contained the idea of "no consistent causal link," an idea that appeared in neither of the premises. Thus, the correct answer must contain this new element. Since this answer does not, it must be incorrect.

Answer choice (D): This choice is also in the form of a conditional relationship:

Consistent~~/~~causal link $\longrightarrow$ All mass extinctions~~/~~follow meteor impacts

Immediately, this choice is wrong because it proposes the lack of a consistent causal link as a sufficient condition (remember, you cannot conclude that a sufficient condition occurred, only that a sufficient condition did *not* occur or that a necessary condition did occur). Since the argument tried to conclude that there were no consistent causal links, the best choice would claim that this circumstance is a *necessary* condition. Thus, this choice is basically a mistaken reversal of what is needed to justify the conclusion.

If the above line of explanation seems confusing, take a moment to consider the how this answer would fare using the Justify Formula. If you add this answer to the premises, would that combination yield the conclusion given in the stimulus? No.

Answer choice (E): Never forget what task the question stem asks you to perform. If this was a Flaw in the Reasoning question, this answer would be correct since it points out the exact discussed flaw in stimulus. However, you are asked to Justify the Conclusion, and this answer does not do that, so this choice is wrong.

Question #22. Must be True—CE. The correct answer choice is (E)

This stimulus is a fact set, and since there is no conclusion you should expect either a Must Be True question, or, less likely, a Cannot Be True question.

The stimulus indicates that lack of rain is a cause of crop failure, and that subsequently a number of businesses and individuals lose money. In short, uncontrollable factors such as lack of rain can cause a chain of events that lead to loss of business and decreased profits for a wide variety of groups.

The question stem asks what can be logically inferred, so you must select a response that must be true.

Answer choice (A): Just because several of the businesses that sell to farmers fail does not mean that farming itself is not prospering. For example, farming could be prospering but a business might be poorly run and consequently fail, or a business could be affected by other factors such as a lawsuit or adverse conditions in other markets they sell to. Logically, this answer choice reverses the relationship presented in the stimulus.

Answer choice (B): This choice might seem attractive, but it is wrong for several reasons. First, the stimulus does not define how much of a lack of rain causes crop failure, and *below-average* rainfall might not necessarily cause crop failure (remember, below average can still be very close to average; for example, if a locality receives an average of 100 inches of rain a year, an amount as high as 99 inches would be classified as below average, and an amount that close to the average would be very unlikely to cause crop failure).

Second, the stimulus simply noted that certain businesses are unable to make a profit when farmer's crops fail. This answer improperly expands that group to include *all* business that profit from farmers' purchases (this includes any business—personal or commercial—a farmer might buy from, including McDonald's, the grocery store, etc.), and then indicates that those businesses *tend* to lose money (which is also unknown).

Answer choice (C): The stimulus is not about who is responsible for the consequences of wheat crop failure, so this answer choice is incorrect.

Answer choice (D): The stimulus may support the idea that *wheat crop* failure can have far-reaching economic consequences, but it does not support the idea that a dependence on *agriculture* can lead to *major economic crises*. In simple terms, this answer fails the Fact Test because the ideas in this answer are not addresses in the stimulus.

Answer choice (E): This is the correct answer choice. As stated by the stimulus, a lack of rain (and a drought is an extreme form of a lack of rain), can cause crop failure, and, according to the stimulus, such failures have an impact beyond agriculture (specifically, truckers, mechanics, and fuel suppliers are all affected).

Question #23: Justify the Conclusion—SN. The correct answer choice is (C)

The argument can be viewed as follows:

Premise:	For each action we perform, we can know only some of its consequences.
Conclusion:	Thus the view that in no situation can we know what action is morally right would be true if an action's being morally right were the same as the action's having the best consequences.

This stimulus looks somewhat intimidating, but in laymen's terms, the argument really means the following:

> When you do something, there are some consequences that you cannot know about. So, if being morally right is the same as knowing the best consequences, then there is no way to know if an action is morally right.

The question asks you to Justify the Conclusion, so seek an answer that forces the conclusion to follow from the premises. In the argument, the author makes a leap between not knowing all the consequences and not knowing the best consequences, so you should look for an answer that connects those two ideas (remember, morally right requires knowing the best consequences, yet we can't know the best consequences because we can't know all the consequences).

Mechanistically speaking, the conclusion contains the new idea of "best consequences," so look for an answer that addresses that new element.

Answer choice (A): The stimulus concerns whether we can prove actions morally right, and being able to prove some of them wrong does not help decide whether some can be proven right.

Answer choice (B): The conclusion attempts to prove that we cannot know that a situation is morally right if morally right is the same as having the best consequences. This answer, which states that on occasion we can know what is morally right, does not assist us in proving that we cannot know that a situation is morally right. If anything, thus answer choice would undermine the argument.

Answer choice (C): This is the correct answer choice. Under time duress, you could use a mechanistic approach and select this answer simply because it is the only answer that includes the "best consequences" idea that appeared in the conclusion.

In the absence of that approach, consider that this answer addresses the relationship we discussed in our analysis of the stimulus ("the author makes a leap between not knowing all the consequences and not knowing the best consequences"). In order for the author to conclude that in no situation can we know what is morally right because morally right requires knowing the best consequences (and we know only some of the consequences of any action), we need to show that knowing the best consequences requires knowing *all* of the consequences.

Conditionally speaking, this answer is in the form a conditional relationship:

> Knowing whether best consequences ⟶ Knowing all consequences

The contrapositive is:

> Knowing a̶l̶l̶ consequences ⟶ Knowing whethe̶r̶ best consequences

Using this contrapositive, apply the Justify Formula by adding the following information from the stimulus:

> Some consequences of every action are unknown

In combination with this answer, that information establishes that:

> Whether an action has the best consequences is unknown

Thus, if morally right is the same as having the best consequences, and we cannot know the best consequences for an action, then it is true that in no situation can we know what action is morally right.

Answer choice (D): This choice suggests that it is *not* necessary to know all of the consequences of an action, which attacks the conditional conclusion rather than justifying it.

Answer choice (E): This answer suggests that an action could be determined to be morally right, and that sentiment does not assist in justifying a conclusion that asserts that in no situation can we know what action is morally right.

Question #24: Flaw in the Reasoning. The correct answer choice is (B)

In this stimulus, the author presents the fact that defense attorneys sometimes try to acquit suspects by comparing DNA samples from the suspect to DNA samples from the crime scene. But, even though every person has unique DNA, sometimes the DNA test does not distinguish between different people. Thus, according to the author, it is a mistake to exonerate a suspect just because the DNA of the suspect does not match the DNA from the scene.

Most students read the stimulus and think that the reasoning is valid, and so they are surprised when the question stem asks for the flaw in the reasoning. When this occurs, you should immediately glance at the stimulus again to see if you missed an important word or phrase. If you did understand the stimulus, use the answer choices to get a better sense of what flaw you might have missed.

The flaw in the reasoning is discussed in detail in the discussion of the correct answer choice.

Answer choice (A): This choice is wrong, because if the argument assumed that evidence can never be mistaken, then the argument would not have concluded that DNA evidence can be mistaken. Additionally, this answer addresses physical evidence, a broader concept than DNA.

Answer choice (B): This is the correct answer choice. This choice can be somewhat confusing to read, and many students select this answer not so much because they understand exactly what it means but because they know the other answers are incorrect (and such an approach is perfectly valid on the LSAT).

In reality, these DNA tests are imperfect because they "sometimes fail to distinguish among samples taken from distinct individuals." That is, the test sometimes "incorrectly identifies DNA samples as coming from the same person." So the test sometimes produces false positives. Based on this fact, the author mistakenly believes the test also produces false negatives; that it cannot reliably *rule out* suspects whose DNA doesn't match crime scene samples.

In other words, this is the flaw in the reasoning, and the point that the author apparently missed: Just because the test cannot distinguish every sample of DNA from every other sample, this does not necessarily mean that it is unable to recognize a clear mismatch.

Answer choice (C): This response is incorrect because the stimulus discusses only DNA evidence and does not discuss the reliability of "all methods."

Answer choice (D): There is no indication that the author has relied on data that did not hold up under non-experimental questions, and this answer choice certainly does not describe the logical flaw the author made in moving from the premises to the conclusion.

Answer choice (E): The issue of other evidence aside from DNA evidence is irrelevant because the author addresses only DNA evidence (and, if anything, the stimulus actually supports the idea that other evidence is required, not that other evidence should not be admitted).

Question #25: Parallel Reasoning—FL. The correct answer choice is (C)

There are two easy ways to attack this Parallel Reasoning question:

1. Diagram the Formal Logic relationship within the stimulus and then find the answer that contains the same relationship

2. Check the basic elements of the premises and conclusion and then quickly match those to the answers.

Approach 1. This stimulus contains formal logic, and the relationship in the two premises can be diagrammed as:

> VP = Visitors to the park
> EPSH = Engage in practices that seriously harm animals
> KSH = Know these practices seriously harm the animals

$$VP \xleftrightarrow{\ s\ } EPSH \xleftarrow{\ |\ } KSH$$

The author uses the premises above to validly conclude that:

$$VP \xleftrightarrow{\ s\ } \cancel{KSH}$$

The correct answer to this problem must have a pattern of relationships similar to those above.

Approach 2. From an Elemental Attack standpoint, the correct answer must match the fundamental relationship in each component:

> Premise: "some"
> Premise: "none"
> Conclusion: "some not"

Although the correct answer can use different words or synonymous phrases, the components of the correct answer must have the same general meaning as the components of the stimulus. Interesting, a quick glance at the answers reveals that (C), the correct answer, is the only answer to match these elements.

Note that method #2 often eliminates several answers in a Parallel Reasoning question that involves Formal Logic, and then you can use another approach (Diagramming, Validity Test, Test of Abstraction, etc) to decide between the remaining answer choices.

This problem is not hard from a logical or formal logic standpoint; it is hard because it is so long and because Parallel Reasoning questions typically take a long time to complete.

As a point of reference, each answer choice below is diagrammed. Look over each diagram to improve your knowledge of formal logic.

Answer choice (A): The relationship in the two premises can be diagrammed as:

WFP = worked on failed project
F = Fired
D = Department

D ⟶ WFP ◀—^{S}—▶ F

The author uses the premises above to *invalidly* conclude that:

D ◀—^{S}—▶ F

From the *Logical Reasoning Bible* discussion of Formal Logic, you should recognize this as a flawed inference (and so this answer is incorrect since the stimulus contained valid reasoning). The commonsense explanation for why the choice is flawed is that many departments could have worked on the project, and the fired employees could simply have come from the other departments. That commonsense explanation is related to the abstract logical observation that, without some knowledge of *group size*, you cannot connect these statements. If you assign numerical values to each group, you can see that only a few of the workers had to come from the department, and only a few (some) of workers had to be fired, so everyone from the department could be just fine.

From an elemental standpoint, the basic components are:

Premise: "some"
Premise: "all"
Conclusion: "some"

As you can see, these components are markedly different from those in the stimulus.

Answer choice (B): The relationship in the two premises can be diagrammed as:

SP = Signed the petition
MS = Mayor's supporters
MD = Mayor denounce

MD ⟶ SP ◀—^{S}—▶ MS

The author uses the premises above to *invalidly* conclude that:

MD ◀—^{S}—▶ MS

The reasoning structure is identical to answer choice (A), and is incorrect for the same reasons as (A).

Answer choice (C): This is the correct answer choice. The relationship in the two premises can be diagrammed as:

P = People polled
LOCL = Lived outside city limits
VCE = Vote in city elections

P ←——^{S}——→ LOCL ←——+——→ VCE

The author uses the premises above to *validly* conclude that:

P ←——^{S}——→ V~~C~~E

This argument is identical to the one in the stimulus.

Answer choice (D): The relationship in the two premises can be diagrammed as:

P = Planner
RP = Responsible for this problem
AR = Admit responsibility

AR ←——+——→ P ————→ RP

The author uses the premises above to *validly* conclude that:

RP ←——^{S}——→ ~~AR~~

However, even though the reasoning is valid and the language of the conclusion is the same as in the stimulus, this answer is incorrect because the basic components used to arrive at the conclusion are different from those in the stimulus:

Premise: "all"
Premise: "none"
Conclusion: "some not"

The "all" is different from the "some" in the stimulus, and this difference is sufficient to make this answer choice incorrect.

Answer choice (E): The relationship in the two premises can be diagrammed as:

LP = Member of the Liberal Party
IFPO = In favor of proposed ordinance
CC = Member of the city council

LP ←——^{S}——→ IFPO ←——+——→ CC

The author uses the premises above to *invalidly* conclude that:

$$CC \xleftarrow{\quad s \quad} \cancel{LP}$$

Although the author can validly conclude that some members of the Liberal Party are not members of the city council, this argument reverses that relationships and invalidly concludes that some members of the city council are not members of the Liberal Party.

The inference is unwarranted in commonsense terms because it is possible that all the members of the city council could be Liberals and against the proposal, and the Liberals in favor of the proposal would simply not be on the city council. Abstractly, once again you do not know the relative group sizes, so there could simply be a great many people who are Liberals but oppose the proposal, and the city council could be small enough to come entirely from that group.

Question #26: Strengthen. The correct answer choice is (E)

The argument concludes that rapid population growth can be disastrous for a small city, and supports that claim by pointing out that quick population growth overloads the city services responsible for utilities and permits, and most city budgets do not allow for the immediate hiring of new staff.

The reasoning in this argument contains a critical flaw: it fails to consider that new people bring new money. Since new people bring new money, it is possible that a small city experiencing rapid growth would be able to hire the necessary employees, regardless of what the city had budgeted. Since you are asked to strengthen the argument, you should try to address this issue.

Answer choice (A): This choice merely explains which services the city would consider to be priorities, but does not speak to whether a city would actually be overloaded by growth and thereby encounter disaster. If anything, this choice might weaken the argument because it suggests that a city might avoid disaster initially by focusing on essential services.

Answer choice (B): From a topical standpoint, the stimulus is not really concerned about ideas, and so this choice is unlikely to be correct.

If you accept that new ideas can have an immediate material affect on the city's finances (which is possible, but unlikely given the typical pace of municipal governance), then this answer is still incorrect. If new residents bring new ideas, they might actually come up with ways for the city to more effectively use its limited resources, so this response might weaken the argument. On the other hand, new ideas could create a more complicated situation and more problems, which would slightly strengthen the argument. Either way, "new ideas" can have so many effects—both positive and negative—that it is unclear what effect this choice would have on the argument, and so this choice is wrong.

Answer choice (C): Since the stimulus concerns the difficulties of *small* cities, this response, which compares small cities to large cities, is irrelevant and incorrect.

Concluding that this choice strengthens the argument is similar to making a Mistaken Negation. This choice says that if a city is large, it has an easier time than a small city absorbing rapid population growth, but the stimulus says that if a city is small, it has a more difficult time absorbing rapid population growth.

Answer choice (D): The consideration of unemployment rates neither assists nor harms the argument. A low unemployment rate could mean that wages are higher, and it is more expensive to increase city staff. On the other hand, if people move to a city because of its low unemployment rate, maybe they are unskilled people in need of work, and it might be easy to inexpensively increase city staff. The exact impact of unemployment rates is uncertain, so this choice is wrong.

Answer choice (E): This is the correct answer choice. If most new residents do not begin paying taxes for at least a year, then the city will bear the costs of providing services to those new residents but there will be no corresponding increase in funds from those residents for a year. This choice directly addresses the argument's disregard of the fact that new people bring new money by stating that, most of the time, there is a significant period in which there are new people, but *no new city tax money*.

Overall, this is not a difficult section. The first passage in particular is easy, and the second passage, while not exciting, is at most average in difficulty. Those two passages provide test takers with a solid start to the section. The third passage addresses a science-based topic, and because most LSAT test takers have trouble with that subject, the third passage is a step up in difficulty. The section closes with the most challenging passage, and that difficulty is compounded because the passage has eight questions. Test taker who got off to a fast start should have been able to fight their way through the final two passages to achieve a solid score on this section.

Passage #1: Disaster Relief

This passage concerns the issue of disaster relief, and the attendant inefficiencies in the current system. The author closes the passage by reviewing a new approach to disaster relief and possible considerations for the new approach to succeed.

The six questions are not overly difficult, and most students considered this the easiest passage of the test.

Paragraph 1 Overview

The author begins by explaining that recent disasters have caused a reevaluation of the traditional manner of handling such disasters. Lines 6-11 mention that many groups are questioning the traditional method, because they believe it is often ineffective and, in a few cases, destructive. That is a strong statement of opinion by a certain group on the topic, and you should take note of it (Whenever a passage discusses a shift in attitudes or methods, you should expect the author to either evaluate or promote the change, and you should map out the author's descriptions and arguments).

In lines 11-17, the author reviews the traditional beliefs about disaster relief:

> 1. Relief is most effective in the immediate aftermath.
> 2. Large and rapid infusions of aid are most effective—more is better.

As this section discusses a long-standing view, you should prepare for questions on these beliefs, and you should also expect that later in the passage that newer, different views will be presented.

The author does not give his opinion in this paragraph, so you will need to keep looking for it. Do not confuse the citation of the traditional view or the new view for the author's opinion.

Paragraph 2 Overview

The author proceeds to list some of the reasons that critics have cited as weaknesses of the traditional approach to disaster relief:

> 1. The influx of untargeted goods and personnel can overload local infrastructures.
> 2. Sometimes goods disappear into the market for resale, and billions in aid goes unaccounted for.

The first point is fairly straightforward. The second point is that aid that should have been free for the victims of a disaster is "stolen" amidst the confusion, and sold on the open market.

Paragraph 3 Overview

The author moves to a discussion of how the "experts" would develop a more effective approach to disaster relief. You should note that the author clearly refers to the experts' assertions as "claims," (line 34) and that implies that the author may not fully agree. Do not assume the author agrees simply because he or she refers to "experts."

The experts recommend focusing on long-term solutions that are self-generated by the community in question long before the onset of disaster. Note that the expert recommendation is in direct contrast to the traditional approach, which focuses on the immediate aftermath of a disaster. The experts believe that disaster-prone communities need to internally develop disaster preparedness, so that when disaster strikes, those communities can then effectively lead the recovery efforts. The author states that such a plan will allow a response targeted on the desires of the community, rather than an immediate but unfocused response.

Paragraph 4 Overview

The author finally supplies an evaluation, and you should note the presence of this new viewpoint. The author believes that the long-term approach proposal seems sound, but that it is somewhat dependent on how donors will respond. Historically, donors respond in the immediate aftermath of a disaster, and not at other times. Since a long-term response is actually necessary, the author concludes in lines 54-59 that donors that take the communities' desires into account could tailor better immediate responses and offer long-term aid. The author's evaluation of the situation can be taken as the main point of the passage.

Passage Summary

The strong statement of main point in lines 54-59 suggests, given the rest of the passage, that the author believes that recent events show that communities need to have internally developed goals for disaster response, and that donors could be more effective, both long-term and short-term, if they would enter into a dialogue with prepared communities.

The structure of the passage is as follows:

Paragraph 1: Introduce a situation, an old approach, and a potential change
Paragraph 2: Report critiques of the old approach
Paragraph 3: Describe a suggested new approach
Paragraph 4: Evaluate what is needed to implement the new approach

The author's attitude is impartial, but positive toward a new approach.

This passage is not overly difficult to understand, and simply noting the critiques of the old methods and the author's evaluation of the newer suggestions should be sufficient to efficiently respond to most of the questions.

Question #1: Main Point. The correct answer choice is (D)

You must select a choice that conforms, largely, to lines 54-59 of the passage.

Answer choice (A): This was the most popular incorrect answer choice. This response claims that the passage argues for a "most useful response," but the author only discussed a "more effective" response (line 31). You should not assume that the improvement is complete. Furthermore, the author discussed a "dialogue" (line 55) between donors and victims, and never suggested that the victims should "dictate" the relief response. "Dictate" actually rules out the possibility of meaningful dialogue, so in that respect this response is contrary to the passage. In addition, the author suggested that both immediate and long-term aid would be improved, so the statement that immediate aid would cease is contrary to the passage.

As with any Main Point question, the correct answer must pass the Fact Test, and thus cannot contain any details that conflict with the passage.

Answer choice (B): This statement is basically true given the passage; however, this statement is not a good expression of the main point. The author spent a significant amount of time explaining the potential of the new plan, so a response that focuses only on the traditional plan cannot express the main point.

Answer choice (C): Although the author might have intimated that long-term relief is a difficult task, the author certainly did not make that view the focus of the passage. Furthermore, there is no information in the passage that suggests that relief agencies should be responsible for constructing a dialogue among the various groups involved in the disaster relief effort. In fact, the passage implies that the communities themselves are responsible for spearheading dialogue (lines 33-36).

Answer choice (D): This is the correct answer choice. The author spends the first two paragraphs outlining the inadequacies of the traditional response to disasters, and spends the final two paragraphs explaining how the new approach might improve both immediate and long-term relief efforts.

Answer choice (E): This is a classic Half Right, Half Wrong answer choice. The first half of this answer accurately captures a statement made by the author, However, the second half of the answer is completely wrong because the passage never suggested that relief agencies had any role as mediators, this response is entirely unsupported, and incorrect.

Question #2: Parallel Reasoning. The correct answer choice is (B)

In order to parallel the recommended disaster response in the third paragraph, quickly return to that paragraph (lines 31-44) and review the recommendations of the experts. Accordingly, you must select a response that addresses long-term needs, involves consultation with local agencies, and considers of the needs of local populations (rather that decision-making purely from the "outside").

Answer choice (A): The experts' recommendations did not concern saving money. This response inappropriately assumes that saving money is the issue, when the real issue was tailoring the response to the community's desires.

Answer choice (B): This is the correct answer choice. The experts suggest developing plans in advance in order to more effectively respond to the stated needs of the community, and to address both short- and long-term needs. This response exactly describes such a situation.

Answer choice (C): This response describes the traditional response, and involves no community consultation, which the experts are attempting to improve upon. This choice is incorrect, because it represents exactly the opposite of what the experts recommend.

Answer choice (D): This choice might seem attractive, but you need to be careful to read it for exactly what it says. You might have mistakenly concluded that this response follows the expert recommendation, because it concerns targeting the specific needs of the community. However, the experts thought that the community—not some outside agency—should determine need, so this response is somewhat contrary to the passage, and incorrect. Remember, *consultation* within the community is important.

Answer choice (E): This answer neither addresses the needs of the community nor any long-term needs, and thus can be eliminated. In addition, the experts' recommendations had nothing precisely to do with donation levels.

Question #3: Author's Perspective. The correct answer choice is (D)

You must select a response that follows from the author's main point and supporting arguments. Without any specific reference present in the question stem, there is no need to attempt to prephrase prior to reviewing the answer choices. Simply make sure that the answer choice you select is supported by statements made in the passage that reflect the *author's* views (and not those of the experts or critics). Given that the fourth paragraph contained a number of statements that reflect the author's view, it is likely that at least part of the justification for the correct answer will come from the fourth paragraph.

Answer choice (A): The author suggested that disaster-prone communities need to create disaster plans, but do not take that to mean that "only" disaster-prone communities are appropriate for such plans.

Logically, this response is an illustration of a Mistaken Negation, because the author claims "Disaster Prone ⎯⎯⎯→ Disaster Plan," and this response unjustifiably concludes "D̶i̶s̶a̶s̶t̶e̶r̶ ̶Prone ⎯⎯⎯→ D̶i̶s̶a̶s̶t̶e̶r̶ ̶Plan."

Answer choice (B): In lines 47-50, the author states that "Historically, donors…have been most likely to respond only in the immediate aftermath of a crisis." This suggests that the author does not agree with this answer choice. Furthermore, since the author makes it clear that he or she is describing a new idea—something that is not even in effect at this point—there is no evidence to support this answer choice at this time.

Answer choice (C): The author points out that donors already often supply a considerable amount of immediate aid (line 26), so there is no direct support for this answer. The real issue is whether the aid is targeted, and whether it is maintained long-term. You should not confuse the idea of maintaining long-term aid with the idea of more aid, because it is quite possible that better targeting of aid could allow more effective immediate and long-term relief without actually increasing the total amount of aid.

Answer choice (D): This is the correct answer choice. One main concern of the passage is that aid is untargeted and so often does not effectively address the needs of victims. The concept of inappropriate management as expressed in this answer choice effectively captures that critique, and lines 54-59 provide the best justification for this choice.

Answer choice (E): Some test takers misinterpret the passage to suggest that short-term assistance is inappropriate and long-term assistance is more helpful, which supports this incorrect choice. However, particularly because the author explicitly states that dialogue between prepared communities and donors can improve immediate responses (lines 54-57), the idea that short-term assistance is unimportant is unsupported by, and in fact contrary to, the passage.

Furthermore, a commonsense understanding of the life-and-death nature of immediate disaster response indicates that it is simply absurd to believe that well-planned immediate disaster-relief is unhelpful. Unlike some Logical Reasoning stimuli, LSAT Reading Comprehension passages typically do not take untenable positions. If you feel that a passage is making absurd claims, re-read a bit and make sure that you are interpreting the passage correctly. The discussion in the second paragraph illustrates that immediate relief needs to be more appropriately planned, not that such relief should be eliminated.

Question #4: Specific Reference, Function. The correct answer choice is (C)

Generally, the purpose of any given section in a passage is to develop the main point in some way, either directly or indirectly. The author does not simply give the experts in the third paragraph a rubber stamp of approval; in the fourth paragraph the author suggests that the experts need to consider the actions of donors as well as relief agencies, which elaborates the situation. Select a response that captures that sense of addition.

Answer choice (A): The author states only that historically donors have had a certain behavior. That does not imply that donors *resist change*. In fact, since this passage simply concerns recommendations for a new approach, it is fairly reasonable to believe that donors have simply not had the opportunity to adapt their behavior to these new ideas.

Answer choice (B): The author does not attempt to set up a conflict between donors and victims, so this response is unjustified and incorrect. Furthermore, the author never directly discussed the "needs" of donors.

Answer choice (C): This is the correct answer choice. The experts have recommended that communities formulate plans that will allow relief agencies to better assist, but the author points out that the experts need to consider how the relief agencies will finance their response. The function of the fourth paragraph is to suggest an additional consideration, and this response adequately states that consideration.

Answer choice (D): The passage never set up any conflict between organizations, so this response is incorrect. You need to remember that the problems discussed in the passage are due to a lack of communication and planning, and not to any inherent conflicts between the goals of each group or organization (goals which, appropriately, are related to providing assistance to those in need).

Answer choice (E): The author does not "concede" that the reforms are unlikely, and does not state that donors will not respond. The author uses the last paragraph to illustrate what donors need to do, not to suggest that donors will not oblige.

Question #5: Author's Perspective. The correct answer choice is (A)

Because the author indicated that long-term issues were important, the author's attitude is positive toward a shift toward the long-term perspective. Furthermore, the author seemed to believe that a long-term view would not hurt the short-term, and might even solve some of the short-term problems, so the author's attitude is likely to be characterized as entirely positive.

Answer choice (A): This is the correct answer choice. The author states in lines 54-59 that the communities would experience an immediate short-term benefit as well as long-term benefits, and the author's discussion in the last two paragraphs centers around better management and need-fulfillment.

Even though the author does not directly discuss the needs of providers, the idea that providers would benefit is entirely consistent with the passage. In fact, the discussion in the second paragraph is very supportive of the idea that providers would benefit. Currently, mismanagement results in the destruction of infrastructure and unnecessary expenditures, which cannot help a relief agency accomplish its mission. Furthermore, such agencies currently lose billions in resources, which means that there are billions of dollars in waste. The passage strongly suggests that providers would benefit from better management, so the idea that providers with an interest in improved efforts would be aided.

You also could have kept this choice, whether or not you believed that the passage entirely proves it, and simply evaluated the other responses. Answer choices (B) and (C) contradict the passage, and answer choices (D) and (E) are based on a misreading of the passage, so you could also have confidently selected answer choice (A) by process of elimination.

Answer choice (B): The author suggests, in lines 54-59, that the shift will benefit both long-term and short-term needs, so the claim that the shift will be detrimental to short-term needs is contrary to the passage, and this response is incorrect.

Answer choice (C): The author states that the plan would have short-term benefit, but this response suggests that the plan will not resolve any short-term issues, and is incorrect.

Answer choice (D): There is no support in the passage for the conclusion that donors will not cooperate, so this response is unjustified and incorrect. This choice is based on a misreading of the last paragraph. The author mentions what donors need to do in order to expand the experts' thoughts, but does not suggest the situation is hopeless.

Answer choice (E): You should not conclude that since recipients of aid take a greater role in determining the focus of aid that donors thereby "play a minor role." In fact, the passage only suggests that the victims supply some leadership, which is not equivalent to replacing donors or relief organizations, or even to drastically changing who supplies the bulk of the effort.

Question #6: Must Be True. The correct answer choice is (E)

You should select a response that either reflects some detail of the passage or adequately mirrors the main point of the passage.

The only Contenders to answer this question are answer choices (B), (D) and (E). Answer choices (A) and (C) are somewhat contradictory to the passage, and can normally be eliminated fairly quickly. When evaluating the Contenders, it is not difficult to dispose of answer choice (D), because there is no evidence to determine for how long communities have argued for community-controlled relief. A greater difficulty, for some test takers, lies in eliminating answer choice (B). Some test takers will feel that the experts would not recommend that the communities develop plans unless the communities currently do not make such efforts, and that since the donors and relief agencies have created such debacles in certain communities, there is *de facto* evidence that they fail to recognize potential problems. Perhaps, in that case, the best reason for choosing answer choice (E) and eliminating answer choice (B) is that answer choice (E) so clearly summarizes the second paragraph, whereas answer choice (B) merely consists of conclusions that someone might draw based on the passage. You should remember that on the LSAT a choice that is "supported" can be a summary or a restatement, and that such responses are always preferred to choices that express probable conclusions.

Answer choice (A): There are two reasons to eliminate this answer. First, although the recent disasters have caused a reevaluation of how aid is distributed, there is no evidence that the recent disasters "aggravated" the inefficiencies already present. Second, there is no direct evidence that relief agencies have "limited resources" or that in recent years there has been "increased demands" on those resources.

Answer choice (B): The experts recommend that communities form plans through grassroots discussion, but that does *not* mean that communities have had "little interest" in taking responsibility. Disaster-prone communities could want to take responsibility, but simply be ill-equipped or lack proper leadership, among other factors.

This answer choice also makes an unjustified claim that donors and agencies have not been aware of "potential problems." While it may be true that their efforts are often untargeted and inefficient, that does not imply that they have no idea of potential problems. For example, it is not difficult to predict that a low-lying coastal region has a risk of flooding, and to predict the accompanying rescue and recovery problems. Just because donors and agencies might not respond in the best possible way for a community does not mean that those donors and agencies could not tell there was a potential problem.

Answer choice (C): This response is contrary to the passage, and should be eliminated immediately. The passage explicitly stated that "communities" are questioning traditional methods (lines 1-6). Even though you could argue that the passage does not specify whether those communities are the disaster-prone communities, it is fairly implausible to believe that for some reason, many communities that are never disaster-prone would be interested, but no disaster-prone communities would care.

Answer choice (D): This is a somewhat attractive choice, but since the passage does not wholly support the claim that communities have "long argued" for community control of disaster response, this response is wrong. It is reasonable to believe from the second paragraph that communities have recognized problems for some time, but that does not allow you to conclude that those communities have definitely argued for control before recent years. Remember, it is perfectly acceptable to eliminate a choice that is very likely contradictory, but you should not select a choice simply because it is possibly supported.

Answer choice (E): This is the correct answer choice. Essentially, this response expresses the point of the second paragraph. Part of the argument for community-controlled efforts is that outside agencies have frequently proven inefficient and harmful because they do not understand or account for the specific community situation. This response adequately expresses that portion of the passage, so the passage definitely supports this choice.

Passage #2: Hippocratic Oath

In the first paragraph the author discusses the function of the Hippocratic oath and then reviews criticisms of the oath. The second paragraph dismisses some of those criticisms, reaffirms some of the core principles of the oath, and finally acknowledges that some revisions of the oath are desirable.

Paragraph 1 Overview

Since this passage consists of two long paragraphs, you should realize that a reasonable map of passage development will assist you, and may possibly be necessary.

The author begins by introducing the Hippocratic oath. The author does not clearly define the oath, but does describe some of its facets in lines 1-12:

1. Physicians usually affirm the oath before entering the medical practice.
2. The oath is traditionally seen as a universal, immutable code.
3. The oath involves promises such as:
    i. A promise to act in the patient's benefit.
    ii. A promise to preserve confidence.
4. Elements of the oath have, until recently, seemed impervious to scientific and societal forces.

You should at least take note of the presence of this description, even if you do not remember every detail of it. For example, you could bracket lines 1-12, and note in the margin "oath description." That would provide an adequate cue for passage reference.

Also, remember to read aggressively and consider the direction the author will take later in the passage. Notably, given that the states that the oath has "long been" considered immutable, and uses phrases such as "until very recently," you should realize that the passage will probably discuss possible changes to the oath. In fact, in line 13, which ideally ought to begin a new paragraph, the author introduces some criticisms of the oath. You absolutely must make note of these critiques, and might want to bracket lines 13-33 and note in the margin "critics of oath," or something similar.

You should also note that the author's language does not imply total agreement with the critics of the oath. For example, the author probably would not include phrases such as "they say" in line 14, or "some critics believe" in lines 21-22 unless the author wanted some distance from those claims. In any case, you should notice the author's disagreement when you reach the second paragraph; however, the passage will probably make more sense if early on you pick up on the author's language and sense that he or she does not agree with all the claims of the critics.

The author mentions a few criticisms that others make:

1. The fixed moral code of the oath is incompatible with flexible modern ethics.
2. The code encourages an authoritarian attitude.
3. The emphasis on the individual frustrates the physician's role as gatekeeper for managed care plans, and restricts the effect of competitive market forces.
4. The oath does not cover some contemporary issues.
5. The authorship of the oath is doubtful in any case.

You should be sure to underline or note some brief portion of each of those critiques.

Paragraph 2 Overview

The author uses the second paragraph to evaluate the various complaints of the critics. You must be careful to separate the critiques one from the other.

Immediately, the author discards as entirely irrelevant point that the authorship of the oath is uncertain. The author argues that those who assess and adopt the oath are, in a practical sense, the current authors, but does not immediately explain why.

The author then points out that, more importantly, patients need assurance that physicians will pursue appropriate goals, so the core value of beneficence (acting for the benefit of the individual patient) should be retained, while adjusting other portions of the oath to reflect beneficence in modern situations. As an example, the author points out that physicians already re-interpret part of the oath. At the time of the oath's inception, surgery was probably more likely to harm the patient than to help, but today the provision against "cutting for the stone" is not interpreted to disallow surgery. Instead, the broader intent of the oath is considered—a physician who acts in accordance with beneficence will not attempt procedures outside of his or her capabilities. The author's strongly implied argument is that the provisions in the oath follow from the desire to benefit the patient, and that the provisions are not a collection of arbitrary rules, so it is reasonable to adjust the oath to modern capabilities while retaining the core value of beneficence, which supports the author's strong statement of main point from lines 47-52.

Passage Summary

The author's main point, most clearly stated in lines 47-52, is that the Hippocratic oath should be preserved at its core with some surface modification.

The structure of the passage is as follows:

> Paragraph 1: Introduce the Hippocratic oath and some criticisms of it.
> Paragraph 2: Defend the Hippocratic oath against some of those criticisms and suggest a method of modification for the oath.

Note that the two paragraph format is probably used to intentionally confuse test takers. This passage would readily lend itself to partition into more paragraphs, and a greater number of paragraphs would lend clarity to the different sub-topics.

Question #7: Main Point. The correct answer choice is (B)

Since the author states the main point most clearly in lines 47-52, you should match your response against those lines. Your response should also reference the existence of the criticisms delineated in the first paragraph.

Answer choice (A): Since the author actually concludes that the central value of the oath—beneficence—definitely applies today, and should serve as the core of medical ethics, this response is incorrect. The author does not believe that the core value of the oath needs reassessment—the critics do. That said, this answer can be attractive to test takers because it states that reevaluation is needed, and that general principle does agree with the passage. However, make sure that the details of the answer also agree with the details of the passage. In this case they do not, and therefore this answer is incorrect.

Answer choice (B): This is the correct answer choice. This answer adequately addresses the first paragraph and summarizes the author's strong statement of point in lines 47-52. The author believes that the core of the oath should be retained in order to protect patients.

Answer choice (C): The author would probably agree with this statement; however, the author does not seek to establish this extremely broad principle as the main point of the passage.

Answer choice (D): This choice is definitely supported by the passage; however, it does not reflect the author's main point. Since the author concludes that we must preserve certain central values of the oath, the correct response to a main idea question will go farther than mentioning what is essentially a premise.

Answer choice (E): This choice somewhat reflects some critics' positions and thus is not author's main point. "Obviate" means "preclude or make unnecessary," and the author clearly believes that it *is* necessary to retain a core set of values, as expressed in lines 41-52.

Question #8: Passage Organization. The correct answer choice is (E)

Since the general structure of the passage is one of introduction, followed by mention of criticism, followed by defense, you must select a response that captures that overall flow.

Answer choice (A): Even though it might be acceptable to refer to the Hippocratic oath as a "principle," the author does not clearly modify the oath. The author suggests how the periphery of the oath might change, and even gives an example; however, at the core of that change is the entirely unmodified principle of beneficence.

In short, the best reason for rejecting this somewhat attractive choice is that the author believes that the central principle of the oath must remain intact, but this choice claims that the author modifies a principle.

Answer choice (B): This choice fails to mention anything that could refer to the first 12 lines of the passage. Furthermore, this choice implies that the author accepts, or fails to counter, the criticisms in lines 13-33, but that is false. The entire second paragraph is devised to reject many of the criticisms in lines 13-33, so this response is incorrect. If you chose this response, you probably read it too quickly and thought that it stated that the author rejects criticisms of the oath; however, that is a misread because the answer states that "*replies to* those criticisms are…dismissed," not the criticisms themselves.

Answer choice (C): The author only discusses a small part of the history of the Hippocratic oath, so this response is immediately weak. Furthermore, the author largely rejects criticisms of the oath, and you should not assume that since the author fails to address certain critiques that he then accepts them. In fact, by clearly asserting the core value of beneficence (the individual patient's benefit), the author indirectly discards the notion that market forces should be given full reign and that modern issues should significantly alter the main principle of the oath. Lastly, the author discussed how the periphery of the code might be modified, but did not directly modify or construct a new code.

Answer choice (D): Since the author did not formulate the Hippocratic oath, but instead merely reported what the oath is, the passage does not justify this response. Furthermore, this response incorrectly places the defense of the oath out of the correct order in the passage.

Answer choice (E): This is the correct answer choice. This response mirrors the map of the passage that you could have prephrased. First, the author introduces the oath. Second, some criticisms are described. Third, the oath is defended. Furthermore, you will note that this response more correctly captures the fact that the author included more than a principle but less than a history in the first 12 lines ("The tradition"), and more correctly captures the *general* tone of the author's defense in the last paragraph in that the author did not reject the idea of modifying the periphery of the oath, but did believe that *on the whole* the oath should be retained.

Question #9: Specific Reference. The correct answer choice is (D)

You might need to refer back to the passage to locate the core value that most reformers would accept. Because the first paragraph primarily addressed the critics, you should expect that the views of reformers would appear in the second paragraph. Reformers are mentioned specifically in line 49, and the context of the reference is lines 47-52, which just happens to express a significant part of the author's main idea.

Answer choice (A): The author's arguments are based on the belief that the core value of beneficence was important to "most reformers." The notion of a universal community is mentioned in lines 5-6, but that is the wrong section of the passage to find the views of reformers.

Answer choice (B): Since improvements in science actually induced the need for some modification or re-interpretation of the oath (such as in the case of surgery), and the author stated that beneficence and professionalism were at the heart of the oath, not advancement, so this response is unsupported.

Note that the typical perception of modern day readers that "technology is always good." This answer appeals to that very belief, and is attractive for that reason. However, an argument can be made that you can actually infer that to some extent scientific improvement can be contrary to the oath, because a clear implication of the provision against "cutting for the stone" is that patients are not to be subjugated to dangers simply because of a physician's quest for knowledge.

Answer choice (C): The passage does not cite this value, so you should not select this response.

Even though an unwary test taker who confuses the issue on the point of market forces (lines 17-24) might select this response on the conclusion that these critics are responding specifically against a value of universal care, that test taker should still manage to eliminate this response because the question asked for a point of agreement, not one of disagreement.

Answer choice (D): This is the correct answer choice. The author plainly states this sentiment in lines 47-52.

Answer choice (E): This choice might seem attractive because the author does state that certain core values are held by most reformers. However, this choice is far too broad as it could refer to many of the moral values that the author believes can be allowed to change, while still allowing for the central values of beneficence and professionalism. Answer choice (D) is much better than this response, because that choice very clearly refers to a specific core value that the author mentioned.

Question #10: Main Point. The correct answer choice is (A)

You should remember that, in general, the primary purpose of any passage or part of the passage is to lead to establishing the author's main point (and thus these questions are classified as Main Point questions), so the correct answer will have to do with the fact that the author defends the Hippocratic oath.

Answer choice (A): This is the correct answer choice. The author generally defends the core values of the Hippocratic oath, and this response correctly refers to that defense.

Answer choice (B): The author's purpose is to defend the code, which is different from chastising the critics.

Furthermore, the test makers threw a detail error in to attract test takers who may have over-read into the text. Since the author never refers to the critics as "within the medical community," this response characterizes the author's discussion beyond what is supported by the passage.

Answer choice (C): The author does make this argument, however this is not the author's primary purpose. The correct response to a primary purpose question must refer to the author's ultimate conclusion, not merely a premise in the author's argument.

Answer choice (D): Some test takers might perceive that the author has evaluated "pros and cons." However, the author does not outline the pros and cons of *revising* a code, and so this response is incorrect.

Answer choice (E): This was the most popular incorrect answer choice. On the surface this answer is attractive, but a close reading of the answer reveals that the answer is wrong. The author does not propose a revision to the code; instead, a possible method or guideline for revision is suggested. Remember, a proposed revision would contain an actual suggestion for direct changes. The text of the passage in lines 50-52 only vaguely describes "adaptations at the oath's periphery by some combination of revision, supplementation, and modern interpretation." That vague description is insufficient to justify the language of this answer choice.

Question #11: Main Point. The correct answer choice is (E)

A question that asks you to extend the author's ideas and add a concluding sentence is best classified as a Main Point question. Of course, any added sentence must also be in agreement with the details of the final paragraph, specifically the content of the final sentence, which reads: "In fact, there is already a tradition of peripheral reinterpretation of traditional wording; for example, the oath's vaguely and archaically worded proscription against "cutting for the stone" may once have served to forbid surgery, but with today's safer and more effective surgical techniques it is understood to function as a promise to practice within the confines of one's expertise, which remains a necessary safeguard for patients' safety and well-being." Note that this final sentence involves reinterpretation, so it is quite likely that the correct answer will address interpretation as well.

Any choice that agrees with and extends the main point is possibly correct, and any choice that opposes the main point can be eliminated. Choices that bring in somewhat irrelevant lines of thought or lines of thought that occurred early in the passage can also be eliminated.

Answer choice (A): Although this answer addresses interpretation, the author's point was not that reinterpretation of the oath is "so easy." Further, the author is unlikely to close the paragraph by disagreeing with the statement that opened the paragraph, namely that the historical issue was irrelevant (lines 34-36).

Answer choice (B): This sentence undermines one of the author's main contentions, and it is unlikely that the author would add a sentence that performs that function.

Answer choice (C): This answer choice is incorrect because the author has already admitted that changes in the medical profession (line 57: "today's safer and more effective surgical techniques") have already caused a reinterpretation of some of the oath's language. Further, the motivations of the critics are not under discussion, just the criticisms they have made.

On a different track, the author's argument is very measured, and it is unlikely that the author would be willing to add a somewhat insulting attack ("a failure of imagination") on the critics of the oath.

Answer choice (D): The final sentence of the passage states that there is a "tradition of peripheral reinterpretation of traditional wording." That wording is narrower than the wording in this answer ("tradition of reinterpretation of the *Hippocratic oath*"), and thus this answer goes beyond the scope of the passage.

In addition, the focus on "modern ideas about medical ethics must be much more flexible than they have been in the past" is also somewhat at odds with the author's statements because the author believes that certain values—beneficence, for example—should not be flexible.

Finally, the fact that this response does not serve to develop the main point is cause for concern.

Answer choice (E): This is the correct answer choice. The author believes that the core values of beneficence and professionalism must be retained, and that on the whole the oath requires slight modifications and additions to reflect modern capabilities and issues. That rules out a "wholesale revision" of the oath because a wholesale revision includes more than just surface changes, and such changes would conflict with the description in lines 50-52. So, it makes sense to add a sentence that concludes that there is no need for a wholesale revision.

In addition, this response more explicitly states part of the author's point, and that improves the passage by making it easier to understand. Thus, this is not only a correct choice but also a somewhat desirable addition to the passage.

Question #12: Specific Reference, Except. The correct answer choice is (B)

Except questions can be time consuming (remember, four of the answers Must Be True and one is Not Necessarily True) because the only way to confirm the correct response is to eliminate each incorrect answer by locating direct supporting information in the passage. Because the question stem references "criticism of the Hippocratic oath," you should refer heavily to the first paragraph, specifically lines 13-33.

Answer choice (A): This criticism is mentioned in lines 15-17.

Answer choice (B): This is the correct answer choice. Whether or not the code is identical is not a specific issue raised by the critics cited in the passage.

If you eliminated this response, you may have mistakenly thought it refers to lines 28-33. Unfortunately, that selection is about the questionable authorship of the oath, and doesn't specifically imply that those critics believe the oath has been modified.

Answer choice (C): This criticism is cited in lines 24-28.

Answer choice (D): This is the very first criticism, mentioned in lines 13-15.

Answer choice (E): This is the controversial criticism made in lines 17-24.

Question #13: Author's Perspective. The correct answer choice is (C)

You must capture as precisely as possible the author's attitude toward critics of the Hippocratic oath. Of course, as with any LSAT question, you should prephrase your answer before reviewing the answer choices—how would you perceive the author's perspective on the critics? Usually, to answer a question such as this one, you can use the following three considerations: Does the author agree or disagree? Is the author rational or irrational? Is the author's tone passionate or benign?

Answer choice (A): The author's attitude was generally negative toward the critics, so you should eliminate this positive choice.

Answer choice (B): This negative response is a Contender, but you should still eliminate it. "Bemused" implies a bewildered or puzzled attitude, but the author never intimated that he or she was puzzled by the position of the critics. Furthermore, the author does not dismiss all of the criticisms. Even though the author engages in a general defense of the oath, the author concedes that some peripheral changes are desirable.

Answer choice (C): This is the correct answer choice. The author does disagree with the critics, so it is appropriate to mention "disagreement." And, the author engages in a reasoned evaluation of the criticisms, even accepting some criticisms in part, despite the generally negative evaluation of the critics.

Note that, the typical Reading Comprehension author rarely strays beyond an attitude of consideration or reason, and thus, *even without reading the passage*, this was a likely correct answer. The other possible correct answer—again, without even reading the passage—would be (E). Both (C) and (E) describe a writing style that you would expect to see in academia, and many of the passages in LSAT Reading Comprehension are drawn from academic sources. Answer choice (D) is somewhat less likely because of the "strict" reference (academics are often not strictly neutral; they tend to take a position and then provide reasonable, well-developed arguments in favor of that position).

Answer choice (D): The author is clearly negative toward the critics, and not neutral.

Answer choice (E): The author does not agree with the critics, and so this response is opposite of what is required.

Question #14: Main Point. The correct answer choice is (E)

Questions that ask you to provide a title for the passage are Main Point questions, and you must be careful to match the answer choice you select to the statements of main point in the passage.

Answer choice (A): The passage mentions that ethics are currently more flexible; however, the author actually concludes that the important ethical considerations—beneficence and professionalism—are essentially the same. This title would be more likely to describe an article written by the critics in lines 13-15, so this response is incorrect.

Answer choice (B): This response is based on an overreaction to the criticism in lines 17-24. The "Hypocritical Oafs" is a catchy, nearly homophonic pun; however, once again, the author does not take up an insulting attack on those critics.

Answer choice (C): Since the author did not discuss genetics, it does not seem likely that this should be the title of his article. This response does capture the author's point that the origins of the oath are irrelevant to its usefulness, but this response mistakenly projects that point beyond the scope of the passage.

Answer choice (D): This title would more appropriately be applied to an article written by the critics, probably those mentioned in lines 24-28, so this response is incorrect.

Answer choice (E): This is the correct answer choice. This response neatly captures the presence of both the critic's arguments ("Major Surgery") and the author's points ("Facelift"). In addition, the prescriptive choice between two courses of action that both result in some degree of change properly allows for the author's idea that some change is needed but not necessarily a major change. "Prescription for the Hippocratic Oath" correctly limits the passage to the discussion of the oath in particular.

Passage #3: Lichen-Forming Fungi DNA

This Science passage addresses the new developments in lichen-forming fungi research, and then discusses some of the implications of those developments.

Although the average student finds science-based passages intimidating, remember that they are in no way different from any other type of passage. The subject matter and terminology is designed to be daunting, so remember to keep focused on the structure of the passage, and do not get bogged down in the details; you can always return to the passage later to confirm the facts regarding a difficult concept.

Paragraph 1 Overview

The author uses the first paragraph to give definitions and introduce a discovery. The first sentence provides two definitions:

    1. Lichen: a fungus living in symbiosis with an alga.
    2. Symbiosis: a mutually beneficial relationship.

The author then informs us that even though the evolutionary origins of lichen-forming fungi have been a mystery, recent DNA evidence clears up the issue somewhat. Lichen-forming fungi are closely related to common fungi, which accounts for the visual similarity of lichens to more recognizable fungi.

Lines 6-8 state that new research has revealed the relationship of lichen-forming fungi to known portions of the fungi family tree, and you should expect that the point of the passage is to explain how that has occurred.

You should not focus too much on the examples that the passage gives. If you need to know about Dutch elm disease or the like, you can look back at the first paragraph.

Paragraph 2 Overview

The author explains why fungi are in general difficult to study, and why lichen-forming fungi are particularly difficult to study:

    1. In general, fungi are parasitic or symbiotic, which makes it difficult to separate them from their host for study purposes.
    2. Lichen-forming fungi are particularly difficult to differentiate from the host algae as they are so intertwined.

Then, the author mentions that a new technique allows researchers to separate DNA more effectively and then use the DNA testing results to understand the relationship of the lichen-forming fungi to the fungi family tree. The researchers are establishing branches of the fungi family tree to which the lichen-forming fungi belong, and further development of our understanding of these fungi is expected.

You should take note of this general increase in understanding, and consider that a precise understanding of why the testing works is probably not important.

Paragraph 3 Overview

The author proceeds to discuss an implication of the new research. The author believes that the research may help overturn the assumption that interactions lead the fungi to become more symbiotic over time. The author believes this because the new tree establishes that parasitic fungi can be found both early and late in evolutionary history.

Characteristically, the author has offered a point that is somewhat questionable.
Even though the parasitic fungi exist both early and late in evolutionary history, that does not mean that fungi do not, overall, evolve towards symbiosis. This inclusion of a highly questionable opinion is common on recent LSAT reading passages, and even though you must be careful not to overreact to it, you might expect to be questioned about this weakness.

Passage Summary

The point of the passage, as suggested in lines 6-8, is to show that new research has revealed the close relation of lichen-forming fungi to known branches of the fungi family tree.

The structure of the passage is as follows:

> Paragraph 1: Define terms, introduce a mystery, and a resolving discovery.
> Paragraph 2: Explain some difficulties involved in studying fungi, and a particular resolving method and results.
> Paragraph 3: Provide an elaboration on the results.

The important elements in this passage consist of definitions, explanations of difficulties, and results. You should have noticed that the author's elaborations in the last paragraph are questionable because not enough evidence is provided to make such a broad statement, but you should not have spent too much time critiquing the argument.

Question #15: Main Point. The correct answer choice is (D)

You should select a choice that adequately reflects lines 6-8.

Answer choice (A): The fact that fungi can have a symbiotic relationship with their hosts was not discussed as a new discovery. In fact, the first paragraph implies that scientists have known of symbiotic fungi, in lichens, for some time. The new discovery is about how those fungi are related to other fungi.

Answer choice (B): The passage never suggests that lichen-forming fungi have recently been found to be a distinct species. You can eliminate this response immediately for two reasons. First, the passage concerned the close relationship of lichen-forming fungi to other fungi. Second, the passage implied in lines 9-14 that there are at least several lichen-forming fungi ("close relatives").

Answer choice (C): The passage related lichen-forming fungi to other fungi, not to algae, so this response is incorrect. This response is based on mistaking the symbiotic relationship of fungus and alga in lichen for an evolutionary, or genetic (DNA), relationship.

Answer choice (D): This is the correct answer choice. This response accurately summarizes the strong statement in lines 6-8, and desirably references the fact that DNA evidence was the crucial factor in the discovery.

Answer choice (E): The author made a passing reference to the visual similarity between lichen-forming and more common fungi; however, that reference did not capture the main point of this passage

If you remove the only reference to visual similarity—the last sentence of the first paragraph (lines 12-14)—the passage will not be affected at all, so you should not mistake it for the main idea. The passage concerned the relationship of lichen-forming fungi and fungi in general; the fact that the relationship explains some visual similarities is just information that the author evidently thought was interesting, and the LSAT test writers thought was noticeable enough to attract test takers to an incorrect choice. Always stick to the main theme in a passage—do not let the possible intimidation factor of a science passage misdirect you.

Question #16: Specific Reference, Main Point. The correct answer choice is (B)

The main purpose of the author's last paragraph is to elaborate on implications of the new research, so you should select a response that reflects that. Furthermore, since these choices are very specific, you must be careful to eliminate any choice that misrepresents the last paragraph, even if it does, in general, capture the notion of elaboration.

Answer choice (A): The first part of this choice—"to suggest that new research overturns the assumption"—makes this answer attractive to many test takers because that is the purpose of the last paragraph. However, do not simply accept an answer because it starts off well. In this case, the remainder of the answer does not accurately describe the situation. The assumption discussed in the passage is that parasitic interactions inevitably evolve over time to symbiosis. This answer, on the other hand, states that the assumption is that lichen-forming fungi are primarily symbiotic. Because there is a difference between evolving to a state and primarily being in that state, this answer choice is incorrect.

Answer choice (B): This is the correct answer choice. If you were attracted to the first part of answer choice (A), then you should have been attracted to this answer choice as a whole.

This response refers very generally to the attack on the assumption that fungi inevitably evolve toward symbiosis. By maintaining a very abstract, uncommitted description of the observation in lines 50-53, the LSAT test-writers have created an ideal LSAT response. Some test takers will avoid this response, because they feel it does not bring out the negative nature of the implications. However, the important consideration is actually whether the response is *logically* valid. If lines 50-53 disprove an assumption, those lines definitely *imply* something about the assumption, and so it is entirely acceptable to select this generally worded, but logically strong, response. You should remember that the LSAT test writers can deliver the correct response to Must Be True questions using weaker wording than necessary, because when answering a Must Be True question, a weaker wording of information or an inference is always logically valid, but many test takers will not know that and will therefore automatically eliminate the correct choice.

As a final note, the paragraph does introduce an "implication" (line 45); however, it is best to avoid developing a tendency to word-match, because the LSAT test makers will sometimes capitalize on that behavior by using "key" words out of context in an attractive but incorrect choice, and deliver the correct choice in a completely logical fashion that avoids using *any* key words from the passage.

Answer choice (C): Since neither the last paragraph nor any part of passage made any reference to the broader field of "evolutionary science," this response is much broader than the passage and is unjustified.

Answer choice (D): Since the new research "overturns" an assumption, and this response indicates that an assumption is verified, this answer is completely contrary to the passage.

Answer choice (E): Although the paragraph mentions that symbiotic relationships can evolve into parasitic relationships, there is absolutely no description of how it could happen, and thus this answer is wrong in stating that the purpose of the paragraph is to "explain."

Question #17: Passage Organization. The correct answer choice is (C)

You should select a response that adequately reflects the flow of the passage, which is that of introduction and definition, followed by discussion of difficulties and solution, followed by discussion of results and some implications.

Answer choice (A): This answer choice fails to describe the first paragraph in any way, and that omission alone eliminates this answer. In addition, the passage does not describe the DNA sequence of lichen-forming fungi, the passage only mentions that scientists have discovered a sequence.

Answer choice (B): Perhaps the best reason for eliminating this answer choice is the reference to "application of these findings in support of an evolutionary theory." First, there term "application" may be questions, and, in lines 50-53, the author challenges a theory instead of supporting a theory. While it is possible that the contradiction implies a different hypothesis, the author never argues in favor of another proposal, so this response is unjustified.

In addition, this response can also be described as incomplete because it fails to reference the difficulties scientists had in separating lichen-forming fungi from lichens.

Answer choice (C): This is the correct answer choice. Some test takers will eliminate this response because they correctly observe that the second, not the last, paragraph discusses the resolution of difficulties, and this response appears to group the resolution and implication together. However, you are instructed to choose the best of five, which means that sometimes you will choose an imperfect response. Punctuation aside, the description in this response is very accurate. The first paragraph defines lichens, the second describes difficulties and a resolution in studying lichen-forming fungi, and the third paragraph discusses the implications of research. Even though this is an obvious case of trickery on the part of the LSAT test-writers, they would probably argue that this response does grammatically reflect the structure by separating the passage into concepts covered rather than paragraphs, and claim that the omission of the last semicolon was merely a stylistic variation, and not intended to imply that the final two items in the list appeared in the same paragraph. In a way, you could have predicted this because the exceedingly long second paragraph actually should have been broken into two paragraphs: one on difficulty, the other on resolution.

Answer choice (D): The passage did not describe the symbiotic relationship that constitutes lichens in-depth, and the passage never discussed a study distinguishing parasitic from symbiotic fungi.

Answer choice (E): Since this response does not reference the fact that scientists now can more accurately classify lichen-forming fungi from fungi, this response is incomplete. Even more convincing is that the passage did not discuss a "delineation of the implications these *problems* have" (instead, the passage discussed the implications of the new discoveries).

Question #18: Specific Reference. The correct answer choice is (A)

You are asked to identify the obstacle that was removed that allowed scientists to identify the origins of the lichen-forming fungi. Even though the passage was not particularly helpful in explaining the details, you do know that previously it was difficult to separate fungi from host DNA, and new methods allowed separation and subsequent DNA analysis. That means that the issue of separating DNA was the obstacle.

Answer choice (A): This is the correct answer choice. Lines 15-19 support the idea that, in general, it was difficult to differentiate fungal DNA from that of associated organisms, and lines 32-38 state that new procedures helped to isolate the DNA of fungi in parasitic or symbiotic relationships.

Answer choice (B): Actually, the passage specifically suggests that the fungus and the *alga* are difficult to distinguish (lines 20-30).

Answer choice (C): The passage suggests that scientists had been unsure about where to place lichen-forming fungi on the "family tree," not that an incorrect placement had led to mistaken "separate grouping."

Answer choice (D): The phrase "less common" is the problem in this answer choice because the passage never states that the rate of occurrence of lichen-forming fungi is an issue. You should not conclude that since the passage refers to "common" fungi, lichens are "less common," or are extremely rare. Do not assume that groups are in opposition unless the passage very specifically states or implies an opposition.

Answer choice (E): The phrase "more complex" is the problem in this answer choice because the passage never discussed the genetic complexity of various fungi. You should not conclude that, since varieties lichen-forming fungi belong to five branches of the "family tree" of fungi, lichen-forming fungi are genetically more complex. The passage gives no idea of the number of branches in the "family tree," so it is very possible that five branches do not represent very much variety, relatively.

Question #19: Weaken. The correct answer choice is (E)

This is the most difficult question of the passage. In reviewing the question stem, you must read carefully in order to note that you are weakening the author's *criticism* of the supposed evolutionary trend towards symbiosis. As you may recall, the author noted in lines 53-55, "Fungi both harmful and benign can now be found both early and late in fungus evolutionary history, and that consequently fungi can evolve towards symbiosis but then move just as easily back to parasitism. You need to select some evidence that helps demonstrate that the overall trend, despite the author's evidence, is toward symbiosis (and, once there, does not move easily back to parasitism).

Answer choice (A): Since this information is entirely consistent with the assumption that fungi evolve toward greater symbiosis, this response would not weaken the author's critique.

Answer choice (B): The comparison of the fungi "family tree" to that of other organisms is entirely irrelevant to the issue, and the relative complexity of the fungi evolutionary tree does not indicate anything about the development of that tree.

Answer choice (C): Whether or not the DNA of symbiotic versus parasitic fungi is more difficult to isolate is irrelevant to the correctness (or lack thereof) of the author's conclusion that fungi do not evolve towards symbiosis. You should not conclude that any relative difficulties led to imprecision and inaccuracy in research.

Answer choice (D): You should eliminate this response immediately, because its meaning is actually consistent with the author's criticism of the assumption in lines 50-55. If parasitic fungi sometimes evolved much later than symbiotic fungi, that might help criticize an assumption that evolution proceeds toward symbiosis.

Answer choice (E): This is the correct answer choice. The evolutionary assumption that parasitic fungi evolve to become symbiotic so as not to destroy the host must be based on the idea that fungi are more likely to survive in a symbiotic relationship. If it is true that fungus that return from symbiosis to parasitism usually die out, that confirms the basis of the evolutionary assumption, and that would weaken the author's critique. Furthermore, the answer states that fungi that turn back toward parasitism usually become extinct fairly soon thereafter, suggesting that there really isn't any significant evolution toward parasitism. The "regressive" branches can be seen as failed branches, and you are expected to know that evolution doesn't consist purely of promoting certain organisms—it also consists of the extinction of others. If, as this answer choice states, "regressed" fungi quickly die out, the temporary existence of regressed, parasitic fungi is irrelevant and the assumption that evolution drives toward symbiosis may be valid.

Passage #4: Canadian Aboriginal Rights

This passage concerns the rights of the aboriginal peoples of Canada, how Canadian laws and courts have attempted to protect those rights, and some of the difficulties in attempting to legally guard those rights.

Paragraph 1 Overview

The author opens by referencing a problem involving aboriginal rights (lines 1-5). The author then describes the constitutional reform that seemingly eliminated that problem (lines 5-11). However, lines 11-18 then describe why that constitutional reform did not immediately translate into complete protection of those rights. Lines 11-18 comprise the most essential portion of this paragraph, as those lines express the main point that the rest of the passage explains. The strong statement of point is that because of necessarily general constitutional language and the ensuing difficulty of interpretation, the current protection of aboriginal rights is somewhat inconsistent.

Paragraph 2 Overview

The author opens this paragraph with an enumeration of how the constitution defines aboriginal rights:

1. Ownership of land and resources.
2. Self-government.
3. Legal recognition of indigenous customs.

As always, you should notate any list of items by physically marking the passage.

In line 23, the author states that the rights as defined in the constitution are somewhat broad, and courts experience some difficulty specifying exactly what the rights are. Line 25 offers an example of this difficulty, and, as is always the case when examples are used, the example is offered to support a point that the author is arguing. In this instance, the example of interpreting the legal meaning of "indigenous" reveals that the defined legal practices in place are not favorable for indigenous peoples. Because the intent of constitutional protection is to recognize long-standing customs, not recently developed ones, the courts rely on written documentation to prove that the customs under question were practiced for a reasonably long time. However, at least until recently the aboriginal groups relied on oral tradition, and therefore it can be difficult for aboriginal groups to prove that their customs are "indigenous" or "long-standing."

Paragraph 3 Overview

This paragraph adds more support for the point that the protection of aboriginal rights is problematic.

Apparently, even when aboriginal groups are successful in protecting their rights, it is sometimes unclear exactly how to define those rights. To prove this point, another example is used. An aboriginal group in 1984 established ownership of a parcel of land, and argued that its property rights should include the right to sell the land and its resources. The court, however, used the old law to determine the definition of "ownership," and determined that the ownership granted to aboriginal groups involved only use of the land, subsequently awarding very limited land use rights to the aboriginal group. The author is clearly in disagreement (see lines 56-58), and closes the passage by mentioning that the group will not be successful unless it can move the case to the Supreme Court of Canada.

It is very important that you do not confuse this last paragraph with the goal of the passage. Even though this paragraph was very argumentative, it is primarily a discussion of an example (line 44) of the difficulties involved in applying the constitutional language. If you mistook this for a concluding paragraph, that could have caused you to miss several questions.

Passage Summary

The statement of main point in lines 11-18 indicates that the passage concerns the difficulty of interpreting the necessarily general constitutional language protecting aboriginal rights. The second and third paragraphs provide examples of that difficulty, and do not alter the author's point.

The passage structure is as follows:

> Paragraph 1: Introduce the constitutional reforms and explain that the general language presents difficulties.
> Paragraph 2: Further describe the reforms and discuss the problem of evidence.
> Paragraph 3: Discuss the problem of interpretation.

On a somewhat more abstract level, the first paragraph introduces a solution and describes a necessary problem with the solution. The second paragraph enumerates more specifically some purposes of the constitutional reforms, and gives an example. The last paragraph consists of another illustrative example.

The author's attitude is positive and sympathetic towards the aboriginal groups. Towards the courts, the author's attitude is somewhat negative, but not overly negative. The author clearly believes that the provincial courts are attempting to interpret the law correctly, and that presentation in the Canadian Supreme Court may clear some issues up. In short, there has been some success, but the protection of aboriginal rights is not quite at a satisfactory level yet (lines 60-64).

Question #20: Main Point. The correct answer choice is (C)

You should match your selection to lines 11-18, which give the main point of the passage.

Answer choice (A): This response matches elements of the third paragraph, and the passage structure indicates that the third paragraph provided an example intended to support the author's main point.

Some students view this response as reflecting the author's conclusions in the last paragraph and make the erroneous assumption that the last paragraph contains the main point of the passage. However, as has been discussed, the main point is better reflected in the first paragraph, and thus this response is incomplete.

Answer choice (B): This choice is more attractive that (A), but it incorrectly implies that the aboriginals' main goal is attaining full ownership of land. The passage presented that issue as an example of the general difficulties encountered because of the constitutional language, not as the main point.

Answer choice (C): This is the correct answer choice. The passage generally concerns the inconsistent, or uncertain, application of constitutional language to the protection of aboriginal rights.

Answer choice (D): Although the author would agree with this statement, this answer does not capture the main point of the passage. If anything, this answer seems to imply some degree of negative intent on the part of the provincial courts, and the author did not mention any political agenda behind the rulings of those courts.

Answer choice (E): The author would also agree with this answer choice, but this answer does not capture the main point of the passage. So, even though the idea in this response is discussed in the last paragraph, this answer does not describe the bulk of the passage and thus cannot describe the main point.

Question #21: Specific Reference, Function. The correct answer choice is (B)

Lines 11-14 are comprised of the following sentence: "But this decision has placed on provincial courts the enormous burden of interpreting and translating the necessarily general constitutional language into specific rulings." Because the remainder of the passage goes on to provide examples that relate to this idea, we know that this sentence helps explain why there are problems with protecting aboriginal rights.

Answer choice (A): This response goes too far in characterizing lines 11-14. Although the author implied that the rulings were inconsistent with each other, the author did not intend to imply that the decisions of courts rarely conform to the goals of reform law.

Answer choice (B): This is the correct answer choice. The vagueness of the constitutional language, and the burden that the interpretation of that language places on provincial courts is stated in lines 11-18 as the reason it is so difficult to protect aboriginal rights. That is a systemic problem, because the need to interpret and apply law is integral to the whole of the court system.

Answer choice (C): At first glance, this response seems very similar to the correct answer, especially because it refers to a "specific source," which correctly refers to constitutional language. However, this choice can be easily eliminated because it does not refer specifically to the aboriginal peoples. The passage has a very narrow scope, so this response, which can refer to *all* Canadian constitutional reform, is unsupported.

Answer choice (D): This response is once again overbroad, because it refers in general to *all* constitutional reforms in Canada. Since it is uncertain that this aspect exists in all reforms, this response is unsupported. Furthermore, the passage more specifically concerned the application, not the creation, of a constitutional reform, so this response is somewhat off-topic.

Answer choice (E): The purpose of the passage is certainly not to criticize the use of general language, because lines 11-14 refer to the "necessarily" general language. Further, this answer is far too broad in stating that the referenced lines imply a criticism of the Canadian constitution.

Question #22: Specific Reference. The correct answer choice is (C)

Since the question asks what is "explicitly stated," you must select a response that expresses something that is directly stated, not something that merely follows the passage. Also, be wary about selecting a response that simply contains keywords from the passage. Incorrect answers often use keywords from the passage but then misrepresent the ideas from the passage.

Answer choice (A): There are no statements in the passage that indicate that the constitutional protection attempted to define the *type* of property rights extended to aboriginals. In fact, the passage actually implies that there is significant confusion and inconsistency over property rights. That would tend to make it unclear whether any specific definition of property rights was a goal.

Answer choice (B): The author did argue that the specific property rights case would have to go to the Canadian Supreme Court to obtain proper interpretation; however, there is no evidence that this was an intended consequence of the constitutional protections.

Answer choice (C): This is the correct answer choice. Lines 28-31 explicitly state that the *intent* of the reforms is to grant rights based on traditional, not recent, customs.

Answer choice (D): The passage lists the aboriginal groups as "Indian, Inuit, and Métis peoples" (lines 8-11). However, although the *passage* defined those groups as aboriginal, you cannot find explicit justification that clarifying those groups would be an intended consequence of *constitutional protection* of aboriginal rights.

Answer choice (E): This response attempts to draw the reader into misinterpreting lines 19-23. The passage refers to the aboriginal right to self-government, and this response suggests that the reforms involve creating governments for the aboriginals.

Question #23: Author's Perspective. The correct answer choice is (E)

You must select an attitude that the author most likely has, remembering to match the choices against the author's points and arguments. This problem is notable because several of the answer choices are attractive, and even though the correct answer is easy to justify, a fair portion of test takers became sidetracked prior to evaluating (E).

Answer choice (A): Since in line 13 the author referred to the general language as "necessary," and it is that language that led to burdening the court, it is unlikely that the author has an extremely negative attitude toward burdening the provincial courts. The author may wish for a better scenario, but it is not logical to conclude that his or her attitude toward the burden on the court is negative.

Answer choice (B): As discussed in answer choice (A), the author does not have an overly negative attitude toward the general language and the difficulties it entails, because the author views it as necessary.

Answer choice (C): The author states that this criterion makes it difficult for aboriginals to support their claims (lines 36-39), but does not actually make a specifically negative evaluation of that difficulty. Once again, the author probably considers the difficulty somewhat necessary in the light of the constitutional intent..

Answer choice (D): Similar to answer choice (C), the author does grant that the documentation requirement creates difficulties, but that is not tantamount to a negative evaluation. Difficulty may be necessary, so this response is incorrect.

Answer choice (E): This is the correct answer choice. This answer is easily justified because the author spent a good portion of the final paragraph condemning the provincial court's "excessively conservative" interpretation, and implying that the provincial courts had done an unsatisfactory job ("Regrettably"). Based on these statements, it is clear that the author makes a negative evaluation of the provincial court's decision.

Interestingly, answer choices (A) and (B) have a high degree of similarity, and answer choices (C) and (D) have a high degree of similarity. Whether or not the answers in each pair are 100% identical, the similarity of between the answer sets should concern you. As a result, answer choice (E) should stand out somewhat.

Question #24: Author's Perspective. The correct answer choice is (B)

Once again, you must select a response that is consistent and likely given the author's main point and arguments.

Answer choice (A): This response is too strong. The author would not necessarily agree with the idea that aboriginals should not answer to Canadian federal law, even though the author mentioned "self-government" in line 22. Self-governance does not imply independence from Canadian law, and the very nature of the discussion probably commits the author to the notion that aboriginals should exist within, and obtain protection from, Canadian federal law.

Answer choice (B): This is the correct answer choice. In lines 36-39, the author states that the difficulty aboriginals have in supporting their claims is related to the fact that they often rely on oral tradition rather than written records. Since the author is clearly in favor of better, or broader, court protection of aboriginal rights, he or she would almost certainly be in favor of extending recognition of evidence to oral traditions.

As further support for this answer, note that the response says "sometimes," and thus it avoids committing the author to an absolute or overly broad position.

Answer choice (C): The author never claims that aboriginals should obtain full recognition of *all* of their customs (at most the author seems to agree with the intent that the constitutional reforms protect only long-standing traditional customs). Because the author never provides an indication that he or she thinks recent customs should be recognized, this answer can be eliminated.

Answer choice (D): The initial failures and inconsistencies of provincial courts would not lead the author to believe that provincial courts should have *no* authority in aboriginal cases. The author believes the provincial courts could do a better job, but that is not the same as thinking they should have no authority at all.

Answer choice (E): This was the most popular incorrect answer choice. Although on the surface the answer sounds reasonable, it ignores language used by the author. In line 13 the author very specifically states that the "general language" of the constitutional reforms was "necessary." If general language is necessary, then the author would not agree that the language of the reform law should be more specific.

Question #25: Specific Reference, Strengthen. The correct answer choice is (A)

Lines 56-58 contain the following statement: "Here, the provincial court's ruling was excessively conservative in its assessment of the current law." Of course, the court's ruling was that the law had previously recognized only the aboriginal right to use the land and therefore granted minimal property rights. Find an answer that shows that the right to use the land should have been more broadly interpreted.

Answer choice (A): This is the correct answer choice. If, previously, courts have found that "use" includes the right to sell land and resources, it is much more likely that the provincial court was excessively conservative when they did not extend the same definition of "use" to the aboriginal group as they would to another group.

Answer choice (B): Some students attempt to interpret this answer as meaning the provincial courts were too conservative because had the aboriginals been given the use rights, then the aboriginals could have profited in a fashion similar to the logging company. However, the argument is not about the effects of the ruling, but rather about whether the court was too conservative in how it viewed and applied a current body of law. In the context of the passage, information about post-ruling economic effects do not strengthen an argument about excessive conservatism in assessing current law. And, of course, there is no evidence that the court would have been aware of, or considered, the economic consequences of its decisions.

Answer choice (C): If the courts have previously distinguished "use" from the right to sell land and resources, there is precedent supporting the provincial court's decision, and that weakens the author's position. This response implies that it is entirely normal, and not necessarily excessively conservative, to rule that "use" does not have to include sale rights.

Answer choice (D): It is unclear why this ruling would prompt other aboriginal groups to pursue land claims, and you cannot conclude that these new claims help prove that the provincial court was excessively conservative (for example, it is possible that the case could have simply brought possible land claims to the attention of aboriginal groups, whether or not those groups are aware of the details of the case).

Furthermore, since "land claims" does not imply that these other aboriginal groups are definitely pursuing the right to sell land and resources, the analogy between these groups and the case the author discusses is extremely weak.

Answer choice (E): The fact that the court had not hear another case involving constitutional reforms does not help prove or disprove that the court was conservative in its assessment of current law.

You must once again match the correct response against the author's points and arguments. In this case the question stem references the latter part of the third paragraph, which you have fortunately just considered in responding to question #25.

Answer choice (A): To contravene means "to come in conflict with, or to oppose" and thus the phrase "directly contravene" is much too strong for the author to apply to the court's ruling. The author stated that the ruling was "excessively conservative" but that is considerably different than "directly contravene."

Answer choice (B): This answer choice is incorrect because the author indicated that the provincial court was authorized to rule on property rights, and that in their ruling they chose a conservative path as far as defining what those rights were under the current law.

Answer choice (C): This response is contrary to the passage. The aboriginal claim in the last paragraph is given as an example of difficulties groups encounter even *after* they have established their claims (lines 40-47). In the 1984 case the court has already granted the claim, and is simply defining the exact parameters of the claim.

Answer choice (D): Do not confuse the different meanings of the word "conservative." Since the author stated that the court conformed to the old interpretation of "use," the only legitimate interpretation of "conservative" as used in line 57 is in the non-political sense. This answer choice clearly explicitly refers to politics and political agendas, and there is no information whatsoever that suggests the author has any information or beliefs about political influences on the ruling.

Answer choice (E): This is the correct answer choice. The court understood that the intent was to protect aboriginal claims, and the court in fact attempted to do so. In the author's opinion, the court's failure was that it used an older definition of "use" (lines 51-56), incorrectly assuming that the court should derive the definition from precedent. The author implies that the more recent constitutional reforms might be interpreted more broadly than the old law, so precedent might not be the best decision method (lines 56-58).

Question #27: Main Point. The correct answer choice is (C)

You are asked to describe the passage, and the choices give abstract, general descriptions. Select the response that adequately reflects the topic on which the author takes his or her position—the response should be similar to the main point.

Answer choice (A): The author discusses no strategies, so this choice is wrong.

Answer choice (B): This passage cannot be classified as "comprehensive" because it only provides a few examples. Comprehensive by definition means "of extensive scope and covering much," and the typical LSAT passage is too short to adequately provide "comprehensive" coverage of any topic of significance.

Answer choice (C): This is the correct answer choice. The passage examines some difficulties in protecting aboriginal rights. This choice is similar to the main point, which is that the constitutional language creates some uncertainty in the protection of aboriginal rights.

Answer choice (D): The author does not argue for redefining certain rights. You should not conclude that the last paragraph is such an argument—the author claims that a modern, existing definition should be used, not that a new definition should be created.

Answer choice (E): The author mentions difficulties and even discusses one in detail, but does not actually explain enough to even correct the "misunderstanding" in line 56-58 of the last paragraph.

Overview: This section is slightly more challenging than the October 2004 games section, and certainly more difficult than the June 2004 LSAT games section. This section contains two Grouping games, which most students find difficult, but, like the other two exams in this book, this test begins with an easy Linear game, making the section seem a bit less intimidating. And, similar to the other tests in this book, this games section contains only 22 questions. Each game is dissected in detail below.

December 2004 Game #1: Questions 1-6

This is a basic Linear game featuring six clients for six time slots (the gym workout can, for the most part, simply be treated as another "client," so the game is balanced as six into six). As mentioned previously, this type of basic linear game is often easy and provides a perfect starting game for an LSAT section.

A diagram of just the game scenario and rules leads to the following basic setup for this game:

R S T U Y W ^{6}

$$S > \boxed{\begin{array}{c} WY \\ YW \end{array}} > T$$

$$\underline{}_1 \ \underline{}_2 \ \underline{}_3 \ \underline{}_4 \ \underline{}_5 \ \underline{}_6$$

$$U > R$$

We have presented the "skeleton" diagram above because this game requires you to make some diagramming choices before moving on to the questions. First, let's review the rules.

Rule #1. This is a basic sequential rule that can be diagrammed as follows:

$$S > W$$

Rule #2. This is another basic sequential rule that can be diagrammed as follows:

$$W > T$$

Rule #3. This is a standard linear rule that places W and Y in an unfixed block:

$$\boxed{W\,Y}$$

or

$$\boxed{Y\,W}$$

Note that we prefer to diagram unfixed blocks with both possibilities shown because that minimizes the possibility of making a mistake under the pressure of the actual LSAT.

Of course, the first three rules can be connected together to create the following super-sequence:

$$S > \boxed{\begin{array}{c} \text{WY} \\ \text{YW} \end{array}} > T$$

This sequence requires at least four spaces, and we have shown the dual-possibilities of the WY block in the middle so there is no chance of making the false assumption that one of the two is necessarily before the other.

Rule #4. This is another basic sequential rule that can be diagrammed as follows:

$$U > R$$

In a typical Linear game, we would diagram the Not Laws that follow from each of the rules above, and indeed there are plenty of Not Laws produced by the rules above. However, given the fact that we have reduced the rules to two sequences (one of which is especially powerful), and because all six variables are contained within the two sequences, the best decision would be to forgo drawing all of the Not Laws and instead to make a basic sequential analysis of which clients could be first or last, and then attack the questions with the two sequences. Using this approach, we will save the time involved in drawing the Not Laws yet not lose any knowledge or ease of attack in the game.

From the sequences, only S or U can be first in this game, and only R or T can be last in the game (more on this in question #2). These facts can be shown on the diagram as dual-options:

$$S > \boxed{\begin{array}{c} \text{WY} \\ \text{YW} \end{array}} > T$$

$$U > R$$

S/U					R/T
1	2	3	4	5	6

At this point we are ready to attack the game, and we should be somewhat confident since our setup took very little time yet the sequences are easy to use and powerful.

Question #1: Global, List. The correct answer choice is (E)

As with any List question, simply apply the rules to the answer choices. In this game, the easiest approach is to apply the rules in the order given (individually, none of the rules is more complex than any other rule, so there is no reason to apply them out of order).

Answer choice (A): This answer is eliminated by the first rule because the meeting with S is not before the workout.

Answer choice (B): This answer choice is eliminated by the second rule because the meeting with T is not after the workout.

Answer choice (C): This answer violates the third rule because W and Y are not consecutive.

Answer choice (D): This answer violates the fourth rule because the meeting with U is not ahead of the meeting with R.

Answer choice (E): This is the correct answer choice.

Question #2: Global, Must Be True. The correct answer choice is (B)

As briefly mentioned in the game setup, only two of the clients can possibly meet first, at 1:00. Let's take a moment to review this inference further.

As established in the discussion of the third rule, the first three rules can be connected together to create the following chain:

$$S > \boxed{\begin{array}{c} WY \\ \hline YW \end{array}} > T$$

From this chain we can infer that T, W, and Y can never be first since each must come after S (although, for the purposes of this question, W is irrelevant since W is not an actual client).

From the fourth rule, we can infer that R can never be first since R must always meet with Patterson after U meets with Patterson. Consequently, we have eliminated R, T, and Y from meeting with Patterson at 1:00. This leaves only S and U as clients who could possibly meet with Patterson at 1:00, and thus "two" is the correct answer.

Answer choice (A), (C), (D), and (E): As discussed above, these answer choices must be incorrect because they do not state the maximum number of clients that could meet with Patterson at 1:00.

Answer choice (B): This is the correct answer choice.

Question #3: Global, Cannot Be True. The correct answer choice is (C)

This is the most difficult question of the game, and one that is not easy to answer from a quick glance at the rules.

When you encounter a Global question with no obvious answer, remember that one approach is to refer to the hypotheticals created in other questions. For example, question #1 produced a solution that placed U at 2:00. On the strength of that answer, we can eliminate answer choice (B). The discussion in question #2 indicated that U could meet at 1:00, eliminating answer choice (A). However, none of the three remaining answer choices is obviously incorrect so you have a choice: either skip the remaining answer choices and hope that future questions provide more hypotheticals so you can come back and eliminate some answers, or make a few hypotheticals right now to solve the problem.

If you choose to wait until later to answer this question, you will find that the hypothetical from question #5 eliminates answer choice (E). At that point you could simply create a hypothetical to eliminate or confirm answer choice (C) or (D).

If you choose to make hypotheticals to work your way through the final three answer choices, you would be best served by first attacking answer choice (C) or (D), and not by starting with answer choice (E). This is because (E) would seemingly be easily eliminated by the somewhat obvious hypothetical where U and R meet at 5:00 and 6:00, and the four variables in the other sequence fill in the first four hours (as in S-W-Y-T-R-U, for example). In a moment we will create hypotheticals for both answer choices (C) and (D), but before doing so, let's discuss the logic of why U is limited at all in this game.

At first glance, U appears to be a fairly unrestricted variable, with U's only limitation coming from the rule involving R. Obviously, though, 6:00 is not one of the answers to this question, so there must be some further limitation on U that has thus far gone unnoticed. In examining the two chains, the one point of concern is the WY block. The block not only requires two consecutive spaces, but it also affects S and T. Although that may not appear to be of an much issue for U, if U is placed at 3:00, there is not enough room for all the variables:

Step 1. U is placed at 3:00; R must meet at 4:00, 5:00, or 6:00:

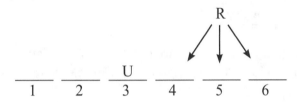

Step 2. Consider the other sequence:

Because there are three meetings after Patterson's meeting with S, normally the latest that S could meet is 3:00. But, since U already occupies the 3:00 meeting, S must be somewhere before U. Because this placement leaves only one open time slot before U, it must be that the WY block comes somewhere after U, and, of course, T is somewhere after the WY block. This chain of inferences results in a scenario where R, W, Y, and T must all come somewhere after U, but there are only three spaces for the four variables:

$$
\begin{array}{cccccc}
\text{R, W, Y, T} \\
\swarrow \quad \downarrow \quad \searrow \\
\underline{\text{S/}} \quad \underline{\text{/S}} \quad \underline{\text{U}} \quad \underline{\quad} \quad \underline{\quad} \quad \underline{\quad} \\
1 \quad\quad 2 \quad\quad 3 \quad\quad 4 \quad\quad 5 \quad\quad 6
\end{array}
$$

Thus, we cannot create a workable solution when U is placed third, and answer choice (C) is correct.

By the way, a similar type of logic holds for R: if R is placed in the fourth position, a workable solution to the game cannot be created.

Answer choice (A): This answer choice is incorrect. Patterson can meet with U at 1:00, as shown by the following hypothetical: U-R-S-W-Y-T.

Answer choice (B): This answer choice is incorrect. Patterson can meet with U at 2:00, as shown by the following hypothetical: S-U-W-Y-T-R.

Answer choice (C): This is the correct answer choice. Although it is proven by the previous discussion, this answer choice is difficult to arrive at without testing a few solutions.

Answer choice (D): This answer choice is incorrect. Patterson can meet with U at 4:00, as shown by the following hypothetical: S-W-Y-U-T-R.

Answer choice (E): This answer choice is incorrect. Patterson can meet with U at 5:00, as shown by the following hypothetical: S-W-Y-T-U-R.

Question #4: Local, Could Be True, Except. The correct answer choice is (D)

The condition in the question stem creates the following block and sequence:

$$\boxed{S\ Y\ W}\ > T$$

From this sequence, it is obvious that Patterson cannot meet with Y any later than 4:00 because Patterson must meet with W and T later than with Y. Consequently, answer choice (D) is correct.

Answer choice (A): This answer choice is incorrect. Patterson can meet with R at 2:00, as shown by the following hypothetical: U-R-S-Y-W-T.

Answer choice (B): This answer choice is incorrect. Patterson can meet with Y at 3:00, as shown by the following hypothetical: U-S-Y-W-T-R.

Answer choice (C): This answer choice is incorrect. Patterson can meet with T at 4:00, as shown by the following hypothetical: S-Y-W-T-U-R.

Answer choice (D): This is the correct answer choice.

Answer choice (E): This answer choice is incorrect. Patterson can meet with T at 6:00, as shown by the following hypothetical: U-R-S-Y-W-T.

Question #5: Local, Must Be True. The correct answer choice is (B)

When Patterson meets with T at 4:00, then from the super-sequence we know that S, W, and Y must meet with Patterson prior to 4:00, with S at 1:00, and with W and Y rotating between 2:00 and 3:00:

S	W/Y	Y/W	T		
1	2	3	4	5	6

Placing S, T, W, and Y forces U and R into the final two meetings, with U at 5:00 and R at 6:00:

S	W/Y	Y/W	T	U	R
1	2	3	4	5	6

Since this is a Must be true question, you should look for answer choices containing fixed variables (such as S, T, U, and R) and avoid answer choices that contain variables with uncertainty (W and Y).

Answer choice (A): This answer choice is incorrect because R must meet with Patterson at 6:00.

Answer choice (B): This is the correct answer choice.

Answer choice (C): This answer choice is incorrect because Patterson can meet with Y at 2:00 or 3:00.

Answer choice (D): This answer choice is incorrect because Patterson can meet with Y at 2:00 or 3:00.

Answer choice (E): This answer choice is incorrect because Patterson can workout at 2:00 or 3:00.

Question #6: Global, List. The correct answer choice is (E)

This question is identical to question #1, with the exception that W has been dropped from the ordering (but, of course, the rules involving W are still active). Thus, you should approach this question in the same fashion as any List question.

Answer choice (A): This answer specifies that Patterson meets with Y before S, but, as we know from the combination of the first and second rule, Patterson cannot meet with Y before S, and thus this answer choice is incorrect.

Answer choice (B): This answer specifies that Patterson meets with T before Y, but, as we know from the combination of the second and third rule, Patterson cannot meet with T before Y, and thus this answer choice is incorrect.

Answer choice (C): This answer violates the fourth rule because the meeting with U is not ahead of the meeting with R.

Answer choice (D): Like answer choice (B), this answer specifies that Patterson meets with T before Y, but since Patterson cannot meet with T before Y, this answer choice is incorrect.

Answer choice (E): This is the correct answer choice.

This Grouping and Linear combination game features six players who must form four groups of two players each. The Linear aspect of this game is that the four games are played consecutively. However, one benefit for test takers is that no individual seat assignments are made within each game, and this limits the complexity of the game. The Grouping element results from the rules governing the formation of acceptable two-person games. From the game scenario it is immediately evident that some players will play multiple times, and you should actively seek a Numerical Distribution while working with the rules.

Our initial diagram references the six people, and represents the four games:

L N O P S T [6]

___	___	___	___
___	___	___	___
1	2	3	4

Rules #1 and #2. The first two rules can be added to the diagram easily. The first rule is reflected by T split-option on the second and fourth games (plus the Not Laws on the first and third games), and the second rule is represented by placing L in one of the spaces of the fourth game (it does not matter which space L occupies since the game does not assign seat positions):

___	T/ ___	___	T/ ___
___	___	___	L ___
1	2	3	4
T̶		T̶	

Note that T could play in *both* the second and fourth games.

Rule #3. This rule establishes that N and P do not play in the same game, and it additionally establishes that N plays in one and only one game. The Grouping aspect of this rule can be diagrammed as:

We will discuss the numerical aspect of this rule during the discussion of rule #4.

Rule #4. With six players for eight spots, and with each player playing in at least one game, there are initially only two Numerical Distributions of the eight positions to the six players: 3-1-1-1-1- or 2-2-1-1-1-1. The first three rules do not provide us with any numerically useful information aside from the fact that T cannot be a player who plays in three games and that N must be a player who plays exactly one game, but the fourth rule is more useful because it eliminates one of the distributions. By establishing that S plays in exactly two games, this rule eliminates the possibility that a 3-1-1-1-1 distribution could exist. Hence, the eight positions must be distributed to the six players in a 2-2-1-1-1-1 relationship:

2: S   (from the fourth rule, S plays in two games)

2:

1:

1:

1: O   (from the third rule, O plays in one game)

1: N   (from the fourth rule, N plays in one game)

Consequently, the three players not assigned above—L, P, and T—must be distributed in a 2-1-1 relationship, where one of the three must play twice and the other two play just once.

The fourth rule also creates a powerful horizontal block:

$$\boxed{\text{S O S}}$$

Because this SOS block requires so much space, it can only be placed in two positions: games 1-2-3 or games 2-3-4. Because this block is limited, and because there are several other powerful rules, you should make the decision to diagram both of the templates created by the SOS block:

Template #1: SOS in games 1-2-3.

With the assignment of the SOS block to games 1-2-3, and with the placement of L in game 4 (from the second rule), we now have one player assigned to each game:

N, P, L/P/T ⟶ _____   _T/_   _____   _T/_

           __S__   __O__   __S__   __L__
             1   2   3   4
            ꭗ   ꭗ

Because each player must play in at least one game, we must still assign N, P, and T to games. However, assigning N, P, and T would only fill three of the remaining four spaces, and so, from the distribution discussed previously, we know that the remaining space must be filled by one of L, P, or T (that is, one of those three plays in two games).

At this point in the template, we have placed the SOS block and determined which players must still be assigned. Since there is only one open space in each game, we can ignore the NP not-block rule since N and P cannot now be placed together. We have also fully addressed the second and fourth rules, and so the only concerns still present in this template is which game(s) T will play in and who, aside from S, will be assigned to play twice (L, P, or T).

<u>Template #2</u>: SOS in games 2-3-4.

When the SOS block is assigned to games 2-3-4, the fourth game is now fully assigned to L and S. This placement affects T, who can only play in the second and fourth games. Thus, T must play in the second game:

	T		L
	S	O	S
1	2	3	4
X		X	

The remaining three spaces must be occupied by N and P (who have thus far not been assigned to a game), and the apparent choice L, P, or T to play in a second game (someone must play twice and fill the final space). But, look closely at L, P, and T as possible two-game players: T can be eliminated because the remaining spaces are in the first and third games; P can be eliminated because selecting P would create the group of N, P, and P to fill in the final three spaces, and since two of the spaces are in the same game, the result would be that either N and P would play together (a violation of the third rule) or P would play both positions in one game (a violation of the stipulations in the game scenario). Consequently, we can conclude that L must be the player that plays two games, and that the group that fills the final three open spaces in this template is L, N, and P.

As if the determining the remaining players were not powerful enough, because two of the spaces are in the same game, we can also use the third rule to infer that one of N or P must play in the first game, and the other must play in the third game (if one of N and P does not play in the third game, then both play in the first game, a violation of the third rule). This forces L into the first game, resulting in a template with only two solutions:

L	T	P/N	L
N/P	S	O	S
1	2	3	4

The two templates give us an excellent overview of the general formations within this game, but because the first template has so many solutions, they do not give us complete information.

Question #7: Global, List. The correct answer choice is (A)

As with any List question, simply apply the rules to the answer choices. Given the presentation of the answer choices in this problem (the test makers have made them somewhat difficult to read), the easiest order of attack is to apply the second rule, then the first rule, then the third rule, and finally the last rule.

Answer choice (A): This is the correct answer choice.

Answer choice (B): This answer choice is incorrect because the first rule specifies that T cannot play in the third game.

Answer choice (C): This answer choice is incorrect because it violates both the third and fourth rules. The third rule is violated because N appears in two games; the fourth rule is violated because there is no SOS block.

Answer choice (D): This answer choice is incorrect because N can only play in one game, yet the answer features N in two games.

Answer choice (E): This answer choice is incorrect because L must play in the fourth game.

Question #8: Global, Could Be True. The correct answer choice is (A)

There are two ways to answer this question. The first way is to use the rules to eliminate each of the incorrect answer choices. The second is to use the templates to see which player could possibly play in two consecutive games. Let's examine both approaches:

Use the Rules

This is the easiest and fastest approach. The third and fourth rules tell us that N and O play in exactly one game, and so answer choices (B) and (C) can be eliminated. The fourth rule also indicates that while S plays in two games, those two games cannot be consecutive, so answer choice (D) can be eliminated. The first rule states that T cannot play in the first or third games, and so T could not play in consecutive games, and answer choice (E) can be eliminated. Thus, answer choice (A) is proven correct by process of elimination.

Use the Templates

When examining the templates, always look at Template #2 first because it contains more specific information. In Template #2, none of the variables could play in consecutive games, so we automatically know that the variable that plays consecutively does so under the parameters of Template #1.

Template #1 immediately eliminates all players except L, P, or T, because only L, P, or T could play twice and could conceivably be consecutive (although S plays twice, the template shows that S is not consecutive and is thus eliminated). However, P is not one of the answer choices, so the answer must be L or T. Of course, as shown on the template, T cannot be consecutive, and so L is the player who could play consecutively and answer choice (A) is the correct answer.

Answer choice (A): This is the correct answer choice.

Answer choices (B), (C), (D), and (E): The players in each of these answer cannot play in consecutive games, and thus each one of these answers is incorrect.

Question #9: Local, Could Be True. The correct answer choice is (A)

If T plays in the fourth game, then only Template #1 can apply to this question. Let's revisit template #1 with the addition of T in the fourth game:

N, P, L/P/T ⟶ _____   _____   _____   T

$$\underline{\quad S \quad}_{1} \qquad \underline{\quad O \quad}_{2} \qquad \underline{\quad S \quad}_{3} \qquad \underline{\quad L \quad}_{4}$$

The variables yet to be placed include N, P, and the choice of L, P, or T, but there is no way to place those remaining variables exactly. So, although you might wish you could derive more information as a consequence of the placement of T, there are still a number of possibilities and you must move forward and attack the answer choices without getting bogged down trying to assign every player.

Answer choice (A): This is the correct answer choice. N could play in the second game as proven in the following hypothetical:

$$\underline{\quad P \quad} \qquad \underline{\quad N \quad} \qquad \underline{\quad L \quad} \qquad \underline{\quad T \quad}$$

$$\underline{\quad S \quad}_{1} \qquad \underline{\quad O \quad}_{2} \qquad \underline{\quad S \quad}_{3} \qquad \underline{\quad L \quad}_{4}$$

Answer choice (B): This answer choice cannot be true because O plays only once, in the second game.

Answer choice (C): This answer choice is incorrect because S must play in the first and third games, not the second game.

Answer choice (D): This answer choice is incorrect. N can only play in one game, and N's choices for playing partners are S or O (that is, the only open spaces in the diagram are paired with S or O). Thus, N cannot play with L.

Answer choice (E): This answer choice is similar to answer choice (D). Although P can play in more than one game, there is no possibility of P playing with L. As with (D), the only open spaces in the diagram are paired with S or O. Thus, P cannot play with L, and this answer is incorrect.

Question #10: Global, Could Be True. The correct answer choice is (A)

A Global question is made for the templates, and so you should immediately refer to the templates as you attack each answer choice.

Answer choice (A): This is the correct answer choice. P could play L in the first game as proven by the following hypothetical from Template #1:

L	T	N	L
P	S	O	S
1	2	3	4

Answer choice (B): As shown by the two templates, either O or S always plays in the second game. Thus, P cannot play N in the second game, and this answer choice is incorrect.

Answer choice (C): The fourth rule specifies that O plays exactly one game, and that S plays two games, one just before O and one just after O. Hence, O and S can never play in a game together.

Answer choice (D): As shown by the two templates, either O or S always plays in the third game. Thus, P cannot play L in the third game, and this answer choice is incorrect.

Answer choice (E): The second rule indicates that L must play in the fourth game, and hence N cannot play S in the fourth game.

Question #11: Global, List. The correct answer choice is (C)

This Global question asks for who cannot be paired with T. As with question #8, there are two ways to answer this question. The first way is to use previously created hypotheticals to eliminate each of the incorrect answer choices. The second is to use the templates to see who cannot play against T. Let's examine both approaches:

<u>Use Hypotheticals</u>

This approach has the benefit of eliminating several answer choices quickly. From question #7, answer choice (A), we know that T can play against O. Hence, any answer choice that contains O can be eliminated, and answer choices (B) and (E) can be removed from consideration.

The question stem of #9 places T in the last game. From the second rule, we know L plays in the last game, and thus T can play against L. Answer choice (A), which contains L, can therefore be eliminated.
At this juncture, answer choices (C) and (D) remain in contention, and both contain N. Thus, we need not concern ourselves with N and we can focus on the other variables in each answer: P and S, respectively. There are two different paths to the correct answer from this point:

1. Analyze the possibilities without writing them down. From a logical point of view, it is likely that T can play against S since S plays twice, and S can be placed in such a way as to conform to T's requirements (T must play in the second or fourth game). T and P, on the other hand, present a problem since they form a vertical block, and in order to make room for the horizontal SOS block, the TP vertical block would have to be placed in the fourth game. However, since L already plays in the fourth game, this cannot occur, and thus there is no way to reach a viable solution when T plays with P. Hence, answer choice (C) is correct.

2. Create a new hypothetical. Once you are down to two answer choices, you can simply power through the problem by creating a hypothetical to match one of the remaining answer choices. This hypothetical, for instance, shows that S can play against T, and that therefore answer choice (D) is incorrect:

L	T	N	L
P	S	O	S
1	2	3	4

The Hypothetical approach has the advantage of eliminating several answers quickly, and then it is not too difficult to eliminate the final answer choice.

Use the Templates

This approach is somewhat more logically attractive because it relies completely on work you did during the setup. In creating the templates, Template #2 paired T and S. Thus, we can eliminate any answer choice that contains S, and answer choice (D) can be removed from consideration.

Template #1 allows T to play against L or O, the players in the second and fourth games, respectively. Since there no limitations on variable placement in that template, both L and O can play against T, and any answer choice containing L or O is incorrect. That inference eliminates answer choices (A), (B), and (E), and thus answer choice (C) is correct.

Regardless of which method you use to arrive at the correct answer, the reasoning that underlies the answer is the same: placing T with either N or P creates a placement issue with the SOS block. The only way to successfully place the SOS block and a TN or TP vertical block forces the T block into the fourth game, which cannot occur since L already is there.

Answer choice (A): T can play against L, and so this answer choice is incorrect.

Answer choice (B): T can play against O, and so this answer choice is incorrect.

Answer choice (C): This is the correct answer choice.

Answer choice (D): T can play against S, and so this answer choice is incorrect.

Answer choice (E): T can play against O, and so this answer choice is incorrect.

Question #12: Local, Must Be True. The correct answer choice is (E)

If O plays in the third game, this enacts the scenario in Template #2:

L	T	P/N	L
N/P	S	O	S
1	2	3	4

Consequently, T must play in the second game, and answer choice (E) is correct.

Answer choice (A): This answer choice is incorrect because L plays in the first and last games.

Answer choice (B): This answer choice is incorrect because although N could play in the third game, N does not have to play in the third game.

Answer choice (C): This answer choice is incorrect because although P could play in the first game, P does not have to play in the first game.

Answer choice (D): This answer choice is incorrect because although P could play in the third game, P does not have to play in the third game.

Answer choice (E): This is the correct answer choice. If you are looking for the reasoning of how we arrived at the diagram above, please go back to the discussion of Template #2 in the setup analysis.

This is an undefined Grouping game. The game is undefined because we do not know how many photographs are displayed in the album, nor do we know exactly how many people are in a photograph. With these elements unspecified, we cannot create a diagram in the traditional sense; that is, we cannot create a group of say, five spaces and then place variables in those spaces. Instead, we must diagram the rules and make inferences, and then proceed to the questions without a defined group in place. Although this task sounds difficult, it is not, and games of this nature are not unusual on the LSAT. Some similar games are: December 2000 game #2 (Birds in the Forest), December 2001 game #1 (Fruit Stand), and December 2002 game #4 (Aquarium Fish).

Instead of showing an initial diagram, we will begin by examining each rule and then at the end of the rule analysis and inference we will present the completed setup.

The Rules

Rule #1. One of the easiest mistakes to make in this game is to misinterpret the wording in each of the rules. This rule indicates that whenever S appears in a photograph, then W appears in that same photograph. The correct diagram for that relationship is:

$$S \longrightarrow W$$

Many students mistakenly reverse the above diagram. To avoid doing so, consider the rule for a moment: does the rule say that every time W appears in a photograph that S also appears? No. Although the difference is subtle, the wording in the rule is that W appears in every photograph *that S appears in*. Thus, S is the sufficient condition, and the appearance of S indicates that W will appear in that same photograph.

Rule #2. The wording in this rule is identical to the wording in rule #1, and so it is just as easy to make an error when diagramming this rule. The correct diagram is:

$$U \longrightarrow S$$

When we get to the "Inference" section we will discuss how the first and second rules can be linked. Also, note that since both of the first two rules are "positive" (no negative terms involved) we are not diagramming contrapositives since you should know those as an automatic result of seeing any conditional statement.

Rule #3. This is also a tricky rule, not only because of the wording, but also because the conditional relationship between R and Y is easy to misunderstand. First, let's diagram the rule:

$$\cancel{Y} \longrightarrow R$$

Since this rule contains a negative, let's also diagram the contrapositive:

$$\cancel{R} \longrightarrow Y$$

Many students will interpret these two diagrams as reducing to a simple double-not arrow relationship:

Y ←—|—→ R. This is *not* the meaning of the rule! Instead, consider the exact relationship between Y and R: when Y is not in the photograph, then R must be in the photograph; and, via the contrapositive, when R is not in the photograph, then Y must be in the photograph. Thus, when one of the two is *not* in the photograph, the other *must* be in the photograph, and that relationship can best be expressed by stating that both cannot be absent from the photograph. The correct double-not arrow diagram, then, is:

$$\cancel{R} \longleftarrow\!\!|\!\!\longrightarrow \cancel{Y}$$

The operating result of this rule is that *either Y or R, or both, must appear in each photograph* (note that R and Y *can* appear in a photograph together; the rule does not prohibit this occurrence).

Rule #4. This rule is actually two rules in one: one rule states that T and W do not appear in the same photograph, and the other states that R and W do not appear in the same photograph. Let's consider each part separately.

As stated directly, when W is in a photograph, T is not in that same photograph:

$$W \longrightarrow T$$

This rule can be turned into the a double-not arrow indicating that T and W are never in the same photograph:

$$W \longleftarrow\!\!|\!\!\longrightarrow T$$

The other part of the rule states that when W is in a photograph, R is not in that same photograph:

$$W \longrightarrow \cancel{R}$$

This rule can be turned into the a double-not arrow indicating that R and W are never in the same photograph:

$$W \longleftarrow\!\!|\!\!\longrightarrow R$$

One note about the rules: every variable is mentioned in the rules except Z. Thus, Z is a random in this game, and since there is not a specified number of spaces, Z is largely powerless in this game. If a question stem includes Z as part of a local condition, there *must* be other information included in the question stem, and you should focus on the other information first.

In review, the four rules contain five basic grouping relationships that create many different inferences. When you consider the four rules, you can see that the test makers placed a trap for the unwary student. A student who quickly reads through the rules and does not read for meaning can easily misdiagram one or more of the rules, and of course misdiagramming during the setup is almost always very costly.

After correctly negotiating each of the rule diagrams, the next step is to make inferences by connecting the rules. In this game, there are many inferences, and so the challenge becomes managing the information.

The Inferences

Inference #1. By connecting the first and second rules, we can create the following chain:

$$U \longrightarrow S \longrightarrow W$$

This connection is important because it shows that if U appears in a photograph then two other friends must also appear in that same photograph. Via the contrapositive, the relationship also indicates that if W does not appear in a photograph, then neither S nor U can appear in that photograph.

Inferences #2 and #3. The first and fourth rules can be connected through W:

$$S \longrightarrow W \longleftarrow\!\!\!|\!\!\!\longrightarrow T$$

and

$$S \longrightarrow W \longleftarrow\!\!\!|\!\!\!\longrightarrow R$$

These two relationships yield the following inferences:

$$S \longleftarrow\!\!\!|\!\!\!\longrightarrow T$$

and

$$S \longleftarrow\!\!\!|\!\!\!\longrightarrow R$$

Inferences #4 and #5. The two previous inferences connected S to T and R through S's relationship with W. Since U also has a relationship with S from the second rule, we can connect the second rule to inferences we just made:

$$U \longrightarrow S \longleftarrow\!\!\!|\!\!\!\longrightarrow T$$

and

$$U \longrightarrow S \longleftarrow\!\!\!|\!\!\!\longrightarrow R$$

These two relationships yield the following inferences:

$$U \longleftarrow\!\!\!|\!\!\!\longrightarrow T$$

and

$$U \longleftarrow\!\!\!|\!\!\!\longrightarrow R$$

Inference #6. Because R appears in the third and fourth rules, we can make a connection using R:

$$\cancel{Y} \longrightarrow R \longrightarrow \cancel{W}$$

This relationship results in the unique inference that:

$$\cancel{Y} \longrightarrow \cancel{W}$$

Because both conditions are negative, take the contrapositive:

$$W \longrightarrow Y$$

Thus, if W appears in a photograph, then Y must appear in that photograph as well.

Inferences #7 and #8. From the inference we just made we know that when W is in a photograph, then Y must also be in that photograph. We can add this to the chain that appeared in inference #1 (which was the combination of the first two rules):

$$U \longrightarrow S \longrightarrow W \longrightarrow Y$$

These relationships yield the following two inferences:

$$S \longrightarrow Y$$

and

$$U \longrightarrow Y$$

Thus, the appearance of either S or U will ultimately force Y to appear. This makes U a powerful variable: when U appears in a photograph, then S, W, and Y must also appear, and R and T cannot appear. Thus, the appearance of U allows for only two solutions, depending on whether Z is in the photograph.

There are other ways to arrive at some of these inferences (for example, when S has a relationship with a variable, U has the same relationship because of the second rule), but each inference above is a product of combining the rules or of combining the rules and inferences (do not forget to recycle your inferences!).

Compiling all of the information above, we arrive at the final setup for this game:

R S T U W Y Z [7]
*

R or Y must appear in each picture: R/Y

Rules	Inferences
S ———▶ W	U ———▶ S ———▶ W ———▶ Y
U ———▶ S	S ◀——|——▶ T
~~S~~ ———▶ R	S ◀——|——▶ R
~~R~~ ———▶ Y	U ◀——|——▶ T
W ◀——|——▶ T	U ◀——|——▶ R
W ◀——|——▶ R	~~S~~ ———▶ ~~W~~
	W ———▶ Y
	S ———▶ Y
	U ———▶ Y

As long as you focus on connecting the variables in the rules and inferences, you can attack the questions and complete each problem with relative ease. Remember, this game is not logically difficult; it is simply an information management game, so do not be intimidated!

Question #13: Global, List. The correct answer choice is (B)

Because there is no lack of rules or inferences to apply to this List question, this should be a relatively easy question.

Answer choice (A): This answer choice is incorrect because W cannot appear in a photograph with R, T, or W. Alternately, this answer could be eliminated because when W is in a photograph then Y must be in that photograph.

Answer choice (B): This is the correct answer choice.

Answer choice (C): This answer choice is incorrect because W cannot appear in a photograph with R.

Answer choice (D): This answer choice can be eliminated because when S appears in a photograph, W must also appear in that photograph. Alternately, this answer can be eliminated because T cannot appear in a photograph with S or U.

Answer choice (E): This answer choice can be eliminated because when S appears in a photograph, W must also appear in that photograph. Alternately, this answer can be eliminated because either Y or R must appear in the photograph, or because T cannot appear in a photograph with S or U.

Question #14: Local, Must Be True. The correct answer choice is (E)

The question stem indicates that T and Z appear in a photograph. As discussed before, because Z is a random you should ignore Z in your consideration of who can and cannot appear together in a photograph. Consequently, let's revisit what we know about T:

From the fourth rule:	W ←——	——→ T
From the second inference:	S ←——	——→ T
From the fourth inference:	U ←——	——→ T

Thus, when T is in a photograph, then W, S, and U cannot appear in that photograph. Consequently, answer choice (E) must be correct.

Another way of thinking about this question would be to apply the fourth rule and conclude that when T is in a photograph then W is not in that photograph. Then, using the contrapositive of the first two rules, we can conclude that when W is not in a photograph, then S is not in that photograph, and U is not in that photograph.

Answer choice (A): This answer is incorrect because S cannot appear in any photograph that T appears in.

Answer choice (B): This answer choice is incorrect because although Y could appear in a photograph with T, Y does not have to appear in a photograph when T is in that photograph.

Answer choice (C): This answer is incorrect because S cannot appear in any photograph that W appears in.

Answer choice (D): This answer choice is incorrect because although R does not have to appear in a photograph with T, R could appear in a photograph when T is in that photograph.

Answer choice (E): This is the correct answer choice.

Note how the first three answer choices specify variables that must appear with T, whereas the last two answers specify variables that *cannot* appear with T. Always make sure to read each answer choice closely!

Question #15: Local, Maximum. The correct answer choice is (D)

In this question you are asked to find the maximum number of friends that can appear in a photograph when Y does not appear in the photograph. This requires two steps: first you must establish what must be true and what cannot be true when Y does not appear, and second you must then arrange the other variables in a way that allows for the most number of friends to appear in the picture. Let's examine both steps:

Step 1: From the third rule, when Y does not appear in a photograph, then R must appear in that photograph:

$$\cancel{Y} \longrightarrow R$$

From the fourth rule, when R appears in a photograph, then W cannot appear in that photograph:

$$R \longrightarrow \cancel{W}$$

Via the contrapositive of the first and second rules, when W does not appear in a photograph, then S and U cannot appear in that photograph:

$$\cancel{W} \longrightarrow \cancel{S} \longrightarrow \cancel{U}$$

Thus, when Y does not appear in a photograph, then R must appear in the photograph, and W, S, and U cannot appear in the photograph.

Step 2: The remaining two variables that have not yet been addressed are T and Z. Because Z is a random, Z can automatically be included in the photograph. So, the final question is whether T is compatible with R, and the answer is yes. Although R and T both figure in the fourth rule, that rule individually relates R and T to W, and it does not make a direct connection between R and T. Thus, R and T can appear in a photograph together, and the maximum number of friends that can appear is three—R, T, and Z. Answer choice (D) is correct.

Answer choices (A), (B), (C): Each of these answer choice is incorrect because more than three friends cannot appear in the photograph when Y does not appear.

Answer choice (D): This is the correct answer choice.

Answer choice (E): This answer choice is incorrect because the question asks for the *maximum* number friends who can appear in the photograph when Y does not appear, and this answer is not the maximum.

Question #16: Local, Must Be True. The correct answer choice is (B)

The question stem asks for the number of *other* friends who must appear when U and Z appear together in a photograph.

As we have already established, Z is irrelevant in this type of question because Z is a random. Thus, the question revolves around U. From the first two rules, we know that when U appears in a photograph then S and W must also appear in that photograph. The appearance of W in the photograph (and S and U), forces Y to appear in the photograph. None of the other friends must appear, and thus the correct answer is three: S, W, and Y.

Answer choices (A), (C), (D), and (E): These answer choices are incorrect because they do not contain a number that equals the number of other friends who *must* appear in the photograph.

Answer choice (B): This is the correct answer choice.

Question #17: Local, Could Be True Except. The correct answer choice is (A)

This is the only question of the game to define the number of friends who can appear in a photograph, in this case, three. With only three spaces in the photograph, every variable becomes important, especially those that bring along other variables.

Because this is a Could be true Except question, the correct answer choice Cannot be true, and is one that provides a pair of friends that together result in four or more friends appearing in the photograph. Thus, you should immediately scan the answers for a variable such as U, who by itself brings S, W, and Y. Unfortunately, U does not appear in the answers (but it is worth taking the time to see if the question could be solved that easily).

Answer choice (A): This is the correct answer choice. When S appears in a photograph, then W and Y must also appear in that photograph. Since the answer choice also establishes that Z is in this photograph, that totals four friends (S, W, Y, and Z), and thus this answer cannot be true and is correct.

Answer choice (B): This answer choice is incorrect. T and Y could appear in a photograph of exactly three friends, as proven by the following hypothetical: T-Y-Z.

Answer choice (C): This answer choice is incorrect. W and S could appear in a photograph of exactly three friends, as proven by the following hypothetical: W-S-Y.

Answer choice (D): This answer choice is incorrect. Y and Z could appear in a photograph of exactly three friends, as proven by the following hypothetical: T-Y-Z.

Answer choice (E): This answer choice is incorrect. Z and R could appear in a photograph of exactly three friends, as proven by the following hypothetical: R-T-Z.

Remember, if you do not see a quick solution to a problem such as this one, you should immediately make hypotheticals from the answer choices to see what is possible. Never waste time on the LSAT simply staring at a problem!

This is the most difficult game of the section. At first, this appears to be a standard Grouping game, but the test makers use the Numerical Distribution to raise the level of difficulty.

The game scenario establishes that three nations—X, Y, and Z—each export exactly two crops from a group of five:

O R S T W [5]

Since there are only five crops (and each crop must be exported by at least one nation), but there are six exporting slots to be filled, exactly one of the crops must exported twice, and there is a 2-1-1-1-1 Numerical Distribution present. This distribution is critical, because any time one of the crops is known to be exported twice, then no other crop can be exported twice. Since some of the rules result in a crop being exported twice, this distribution comes up in many of the questions. As we analyze the rules, we will discuss how each rule affects the distribution, where applicable.

Note that we have chosen the nations as the base because they establish a fixed 2-2-2 spread; if we chose the crops as the base, then we would have to deal with the uncertainty of which crop is doubled in our diagram.

Rule #1. This is the least complex of the four rules, and the correct diagram is:

This rule does not allow us to make any powerful inferences, but can infer that if O is the crop exported twice, then W would have to be exported by the country that does not export O; if W is the crop exported twice, then O would have to be exported by the country that does not export W.

Rule #2. This can be a tricky rule to diagram if you are not familiar with the phrasing used by the test makers. The phrase "if but only if" is identical to the phrase "if and only," which produces a double-arrow diagram. The proper diagram for "if but only if" is also a double arrow:

$$X_S \longleftrightarrow Y_S$$

Functionally, this rule means that if X exports S, then Y exports S; and if Y exports S, then X exports S.

A horizontal block could be used to show this relationship, but a block would not show the conditional aspect of this rule, which is that if one of the two countries exports S, then the other must do so as well (a block might imply to someone that both countries must always export S, which is not true).

From a numerical standpoint, this is a powerful rule because if either X or Y exports S, then the other country must do so as well, and that means that S would be the one and only crop that is exported twice. The other four crops would then be exported a single time.

We can also infer that if either X or Y exports S, then Z cannot export S:

$$X_S \longleftarrow\!\!\!+\!\!\!\longrightarrow Z_S$$

and

$$Y_S \longleftarrow\!\!\!+\!\!\!\longrightarrow Z_S$$

This occurs because if once X or Y exports S, then the other must also export S, and if Z also attempts to export S, then each nation would export S. With all three nations exporting S, the Numerical Distribution is violated (S would occupy three of the six available exportation slots, leaving an insufficient number of spaces to export each of O, R, T, and W).

Rule #3. This is a conditional rule with two necessary conditions:

$$X_T$$

$$X_R \longrightarrow \text{and}$$

$$Z_T$$

Like the previous rule, this rule also results in one of the crops being exported twice, in this case T. So, the immediate inference we can draw is that the second and third rules pose a conflict because both result in different crops being exported twice, and if one rule is enacted, then the other one cannot be enacted:

$$X_S$$

$$\text{or} \longrightarrow \cancel{Y}_R$$

$$Y_S$$

and

$$\cancel{X}_S$$

$$Y_R \longrightarrow \text{and}$$

$$\cancel{Y}_S$$

The two diagrams above, although perfectly accurate, are a bit unwieldy. A simplified representation would be these two double-not arrow diagrams:

$$Y_R \longleftarrow\!\mid\!\longrightarrow X_S$$

and

$$Y_R \longleftarrow\!\mid\!\longrightarrow Y_S$$

The inferences above are easily missed, so let's cover the reasoning behind them again:

> The game scenario establishes that the five exported crops must fill a total of six exportation slots (two per nation). Thus, exactly one of the crops must be exported twice (this balances the crops to export slots at six to six, eliminating the underfunded aspect of the game). Because only one crop can be exported twice, any rule that results in a crop being exported twice automatically prohibits any other rule from being enacted that results in a crop being exported twice. Since both the second and third rules result in different crops being exported twice, those two rules cannot both occur in a viable solution to the game. Therefore, if one of those two rules occurs, the other will not occur. This can be directly stated as if X or Y exports S (the second rule), then Y cannot export R (the sufficient condition of the third rule), and if Y exports R (the sufficient condition of the third rule), then neither X nor Y cannot export S.

Rule #4. This rule can be diagrammed as:

$$Z \longrightarrow \cancel{Y}$$

The contrapositive is:

$$Y \longrightarrow \cancel{Z}$$

The combination of those two diagrams creates a double-not arrow relationship, where Y and Z cannot have any exports in common:

$$Y \longleftarrow\!\mid\!\longrightarrow Z$$

However, if you diagram this relationship off to the side, you might forget the rule, so a better approach is to diagram the rule internally by placing it right into the main diagram:

O R S T W [5]

$$\underline{\quad\quad} \qquad \underline{\quad\quad} \qquad \underline{\quad\quad}$$

$$\underline{\quad X \quad} \qquad \underline{\quad Y \longleftarrow\!\mid\!\longrightarrow Z \quad}$$

The other rules and inferences can be diagrammed on the side, creating the following master setup:

ORSTW⁵

2-1-1-1-1

$$X \quad Y \longleftrightarrow\!\!\!| \longrightarrow Z$$

$$X_S \longleftrightarrow Y_S$$

$$X_S \longleftrightarrow\!\!\!| \longrightarrow Z_S$$

$$Y_S \longleftrightarrow\!\!\!| \longrightarrow Z_S$$

$$X_R \longrightarrow \begin{array}{c} X_T \\ \text{and} \\ Z_T \end{array}$$

$$Y_R \longleftrightarrow\!\!\!| \longrightarrow X_S$$

$$Y_R \longleftrightarrow\!\!\!| \longrightarrow Y_S$$

Using the setup above and keeping the Numerical Distribution firmly in mind, we are ready to attack the questions.

Question #18: Global, List. The correct answer choice is (A)

To attack this List question apply the rules in the following order: Rule #1, Rule #4, Rule #2, Rule #3.

Answer choice (A): This is the correct answer choice.

Answer choice (B): This answer choice violates the third rule because Y exports R, but Z does not export T.

Answer choice (C): This answer choice violates the first rule because X exports both O and W.

Answer choice (D): This answer choice violates the fourth rule because Y and Z both export O.

Answer choice (E): This answer choice violates the second rule because X exports S, but Y does not export S.

Question #19: Local, Could Be True. The correct answer choice is (A)

The question stem indicates that X exports S and T, so from the second rule since X exports S then Y must also export S as well (and Z cannot export S):

```
    T        ___       ___

    S         S
   ───       ───
    X         Y ◄──┼──► Z
                        S̸
```

Because S is now exported by two countries, we know that every other crop is exported just once. This means that Y cannot export R, as discussed in the analysis of rule #3:

```
    T        ___       ___

    S         S
   ───       ───
    X         Y ◄──┼──► Z
              R̸        S̸
```

Answer choice (A): This is the correct answer choice. It is proven by the following hypothetical:

```
    T         O         R

    S         S         W
   ───       ───       ───
    X         Y ◄──┼──► Z
```

Answer choice (B): This answer choice cannot be true, and is therefore incorrect. If Y exports R, then X and Z would have to export T. This results in a scenario where S is exported twice, T is exported twice, R is exported once, and then there is not sufficient space to export both O and W.

Answer choice (C): If Y exports T, then in this question both X and Y export S and T. In somewhat of a similar manner as answer choice (B), this results in a scenario where S is exported twice and T is exported twice, and then there is not sufficient space to export all three of O, R and W. Thus, this answer is incorrect.

Answer choice (D): This answer choice is incorrect for two reasons. First, if Z exports S, then both Y and Z would export S, a violation of the last rule. Second, if Z exports S, then X, Y, and Z each export S, a violation of the numerical possibilities within the game.

Answer choice (E): If Z exports T, then in this question X and Y both export S, and X and Z both export T. Similar to answer choices (C), this results in a scenario where S is exported twice and T is exported twice, and then there is not sufficient space to export all three of O, R and W. Thus, this answer is incorrect.

Note that every single wrong answer choice plays upon the limitations created by the Numerical Distribution.

Question #20: Local, Must Be True. The correct answer choice is (E)

This is the most difficult question of the game. The question stem indicates that Z exports T and W, and as a consequence of the fourth rule, we can immediately infer that Y does not export T and W:

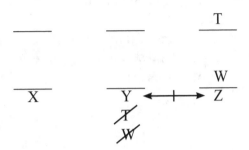

With nation Z's exports fully assigned, crops O, R, and S must be exported by X and Y. Of course, from the second rule we know that when X or Y exports S, then the other must also export S, and we can then infer that S is exported by both:

$$\underline{\hspace{2cm}} \qquad \underline{\hspace{2cm}} \qquad \underline{T}$$

$$\frac{\underline{S}}{X} \qquad \frac{\underline{S}}{Y} \xleftarrow{\hspace{0.3cm}\mid\hspace{0.3cm}}\xrightarrow{} \frac{\underline{W}}{Z}$$

O and R are the two remaining crops to be assigned. Because of the third rule, however, we can infer that R cannot be exported by Y because if R was exported by Y, we could not meet the condition of nations X and Z both exporting T. Thus, X must export R, and Y must export O:

$$\underline{R} \qquad \underline{O} \qquad \underline{T}$$

$$\frac{\underline{S}}{X} \qquad \frac{\underline{S}}{Y} \xleftarrow{\hspace{0.3cm}\mid\hspace{0.3cm}}\xrightarrow{} \frac{\underline{W}}{Z}$$

This is the only solution to this question, and thus answer choice (E) is the correct answer.

The inference above that X and Y must export S is not easy to see, especially under the time pressure of the test. If you did not see the inferences above, you can still solve this problem effectively by using hypotheticals. The best approach for creating hypotheticals in this question would be to attack Y because we already have two Not Laws on Y. Because Y cannot export T or W, there are only three crops—O, R, and S—available for Y to export. Making hypotheticals that use two of these three crops for Y will quickly and effectively help you see why crop S must be exported by Y.

Answer choices (A), (B), (C), and (D): As shown in the diagram above, none of the statements in these answer choices can be true.

Answer choice (E): This is the correct answer choice.

Question #21: Global, Cannot Be True. The correct answer choice is (C)

As mentioned in the discussion of Rule #2, when X or Y exports S, then Z cannot export S. Let's revisit the reasoning behind this inference, as it applies to this question stem:

> If both X and Z export S, then from the second rule we know Y will also export S. Thus, each nation would export S. This assignment would occupy three of the six available exportation slots, leaving an insufficient number of spaces available to export each of O, R, T, and W.

Answer choices (A), (B), (D), and (E): These answer choices are incorrect because X and Z can both export each listed crop.

Answer choice (C): This is the correct answer choice.

Question #22: Global, Cannot Be True. The correct answer choice is (C)

Given that three of the rules directly reference Y, it is not surprising that there is a pair of crops that Y cannot export. And, as you might expect, the reasoning behind the inference centers on the way these rules interact with the Numerical Distribution.

To initially attack this question, most students link the second and third rules together and immediately look for R and S as the answer. This is exactly the right approach, because if Y exports R and S, then the Numerical Distribution would be violated since S would be exported twice (from the second rule) and T would be exported twice (from the third rule). However, the test makers choose not to use R and S as the answer to this problem.

Focusing on R and S is not a mistake, and the role played by R ultimately leads to the correct answer. When Y exports R we know from the third rule that both X and Z must export T. Thus, if Y tried to export T in addition to R, the result would be a violation of the Numerical Distribution because all three nations would export T. Thus, Y cannot export both R and T, and answer choice (C) is correct. Note that the reasoning behind this question is very similar to that in question #21, another Global, Cannot be true question.

If you did not see the reasoning path behind the correct answer, remember that you can always rely on hypotheticals to attack and eliminate answers. This approach works perfectly on a question such as this one, where you will immediately see why a certain pair of answer would or would not work.

If you have very little time to solve this problem, one way to make an informed guess would be to consider each of the five answers by their similarities to other answer choices. For example, O and W are functionally interchangeable variables in this game. Answer choices (A) and (D), which pair R with O and W, respectively, are therefore very similar in the results they produce and are less likely to be correct. The same reasoning holds for answer choices (B) and (E), which pair S with O and W, respectively. Remember, the correct answer to any LSAT problem must be wholly unique, and if two answer choices are functionally identical, then both answers are incorrect. Using this reasoning, we can eliminate the four incorrect answer choices in this problem, leaving only answer choice (C).

Answer choices (A) and (D): These two answers can be eliminated by the following hypothetical, which uses a dual-option to show how R and either O or W can be exported by Y without causing a problem. To eliminate (A), simply consider the scenario as if Y exported O and R; to eliminate (D), consider the scenario in reverse, as if Y exported W and R.

W/O	O/W	S
T	R	T
X	Y ←—→ Z

Answer choices (B) and (E): These two answers can be eliminated by the following hypothetical, which uses a dual-option to show how S and either O or W can be exported by Y without causing a problem. To eliminate (B), simply consider the scenario as if Y exported S and O; to eliminate (E), consider the scenario in reverse, as if Y exported S and W.

W/O	O/W	T
S	S	R
X	Y ←—→ Z

Answer choice (C): This is the correct answer choice. If Y exports both R and T, then all three nations would export T, violating the Numerical Distribution and not leaving sufficient room to export the other three crops.

Many students feel this is the easier of the two Logical Reasoning sections, in part because four of the first seven questions are extremely easy, and the first seventeen questions do not contain any truly difficult problems. After question #17 there are a few very challenging problems, but most students feel fairly confident by the time they reach that point in the section.

Compared to the first section, this section has a wider variety of question types (12 different question types in this section versus 10 in the first section). In addition, this section puts more variation on those questions: 4 are principle questions, two are Except questions. This wider selection of question types is designed to keep test takers a bit more off-balance in the hopes they will simply make an error.

Question #1: Main Point. The correct answer choice is (D)

The stimulus opens with a presentation of competing viewpoints on Mayor McKinney. The Mayor's policies have been criticized as benefiting *only* the wealthy residents of the city, but the author states that this criticism is unfair, and this is the conclusion of the argument. In the remaining sentences the author offers supporting evidence for that conclusion, namely that McKinney's policies benefit all by keeping housing costs in check.

Remember that in Main Point questions you may encounter one or more answer choices that express statements supported by the stimulus, but you are required to select the statement that is the conclusion.

Answer choice (A): The stimulus did not attempt to decide which group McKinney favors. We know that the critics believe that McKinney favors the wealthy, but the author's exact position is unknown (only that some of McKinney's policies favor the less affluent), and certainly the main point is not that it is impossible to tell which group McKinney favors.

Answer choice (B): This answer choice refers to the position of McKinney's critics, and that is a position that the author rebuts. This response is exactly opposite of what is required.

Answer choice (C): This is a premise of the argument, not the conclusion. The premise of an argument is never the correct answer in a Main Point question.

Answer choice (D): This is the correct answer choice. This answer paraphrases the author's stance in the first sentence. According to the argument, the criticisms are unfair, and incorrect, so they are in fact unjustified.

Answer choice (E): This is a premise in the argument, and supports the idea that McKinney's policies have benefited the less affluent. This response is incorrect because the correct answer should reflect the conclusion of the argument.

Question #2: Must Be True—Principle. The correct answer choice is (B)

The factory spokesperson argues that the factory should not be required to clean up the pollution caused by its wastewater because the real offender is the contractor who disposes of the factory's wastewater.

Although the argument contains flaws (for example, couldn't the factory have selected a more environmentally conscious contractor?), the question asks you to select a response based on the *same principle*, so you must seek the answer choice that best reflects the reasoning in the stimulus.

A principle is a broad rule that specifies what actions or judgments are correct in a certain situation, but a principle does not have to be stated in logical terms, just terms that make sense to you. One way to state the principle in this problem would be, "we are not to blame since we didn't actually do it," or, perhaps more succinctly, as "let's pass the buck."

Answer choice (A): This response implies that parents have a responsibility or interest, which is an idea contrary to the reasoning in the stimulus.

Answer choice (B): This is the correct answer choice. Similar to the stimulus, this response is broadly based on the principle that people should not be held responsible for the independent actions of others. This response also contains a similar type of flaw as the stimulus: just as the factory could have selected a more responsible contractor or taken action to insist on proper disposal, a parent of an adolescent has had influence over the formation of that individual and can take action to insist on proper behavior.

Answer choice (C): This response attempts to absolve students of a responsibility; however, it contains no separation between a responsible party and the students. The process of blaming someone else was a critical part of the principle, so this response is unsatisfactory.

Answer choice (D): Does this answer choice fit the principle of, "we are not to blame since we didn't actually do it?" No, this response merely limits someone's activity.

Answer choice (E): This response is not at all related to the principle that one not be blamed for another's actions. Instead, this answer seems to better characterize a principle such as, "when there is evidence to the contrary, I will be skeptical."

Question #3: Strengthen—Principle. The correct answer choice is (E)

Statistically, this was one of the easiest questions on the test. The nylon industry spokesperson argues that since nylon is made mainly from petroleum and nitrogen—both of which are derived from natural resources—nylon is in fact natural (the conclusion of the argument is stated in the phrase "some people have the mistaken notion that cotton is natural and nylon is not.").

The argument seems weak to most readers. The spokesperson's reasoning plays fast and loose with the common sense meaning of "natural" because the author admits that it is the "main" components that come from natural products, and no mention is made of the processes to which these substances are subjected. However, the question asks you to strengthen that position, so you must find a response that helps proves that anything made mainly from "natural" sources can be called "natural." And remember, because this is a principle question the correct answer need not mention "nylon" or cotton" but can instead just generally encompass ideas that will assist the author's position.

Answer choice (A): The stimulus did not discuss the *function* a substance serves, only its components. Thus this answer cannot assist in strengthening the argument.

In addition, note that this answer is in the form of a conditional statement:

Substance unnatural ⟶ Function it serves unnatural

Contrapositive:

Function it serves natural ⟶ Substance natural

However, you cannot reasonably conclude or know that every use of nylon is natural (and thus you cannot enact the sufficient condition), so this response does not strengthen the stimulus.

Answer choice (B): This choice might actually weaken the stimulus because this choice suggests that we might focus on how nylon is manufactured, and there may be processes applied to create nylon that are not natural.

Answer choice (C): This response could either strengthen or weaken the argument, so it is incorrect. On the weaken side, the stimulus allowed for the possibility that nylon might have non-natural ingredients ("main components"). If the substance can be considered no more natural than its least natural ingredients, that could make nylon non-natural.

Answer choice (D): The stimulus never concerned which substance was "more natural," only whether nylon was "natural." Thus, this response addresses a different issue than the one in the stimulus, and it cannot strengthen the reasoning.

Answer choice (E): This is the correct answer choice. The answer is in the form of the following conditional relationship:

Origins of main components natural ⟶ Substance natural

Since the main components of nylon are of natural origins, according this relationship we can then conclude that nylon is natural. Thus, if this principle is valid (and we are told it is by the question stem), then the argument is strengthened.

By the way, it does not matter no reasonable person will accept the confusion of the sense of natural, no such person will accept this premise. The question asks you which principle, if valid, justifies the response—not whether the principle could actually be valid.

Question #4: Weaken—CE. The correct answer choice is (D)

The stimulus uses a variation of the classic "Some people claim" argument structure. In this case, computer manufacturers and retailers claim that the complexity involved in connecting the components of personal computers is not a barrier to their use. As is usual with this structure, the author denies that claim, concluding that "this is wrong." The remainder of the stimulus is comprised of two premises that provide support for the author's conclusion and show the causes of the complexity.

You are asked to weaken the argument, which is beneficial since most students feel the argument has several holes. If you felt that way, use your gut reaction to prephrase possible answers. If you did not feel the argument had a hole before seeing the Weaken question, ask yourself if the premises truly prove the author's conclusion, and what might counter the author's argument.

Answer choice (A): This response attracted many test takers, since they assumed that it would make it less likely that the addition of accessories was difficult. However, explaining the *purpose* of a switch or jumper does not necessarily clarify the proper settings, and this response does not address the problems with accompanying software. Most importantly, this answer does not attack the idea in the stimulus that customers "have to take full responsibility for the settings of jumpers and switches." This answer does not change the fact that customers still have to deal with the settings.

Overall, this was by far the most popular incorrect answer.

Answer choice (B): The cost of the software for accessories has nothing to do with the issue of difficulty of proper installation, so this response is incorrect.

Answer choice (C): Since the argument concerns the present, this response, which concerns the future, is off-topic and incorrect.

Answer choice (D): This is the correct answer choice. If personal computers are sold as a package including accessories and free installation, the difficulties described in the stimulus become irrelevant as an expert, not the consumer, will resolve the problems. In the case of installation, cost is relevant, because a costly installation might inspire many consumers to do it themselves, thus making the claims about difficulty more compelling. In this response, the suggestion that installation is free counters the idea that consumers would need, or want, to install components on their own.

Answer choice (E): This response serves to strengthen the argument by showing that manufacturers do not knowingly or intentionally try to make it easier to install accessories.

If you selected this choice, you may have misread the stimulus and incorrectly identified the manufacturer's position as the conclusion, or misunderstood the question as asking you to help the author attack the manufacturers.

Question #5: Resolve. The correct answer choice is (A)

This stimulus contains a fact set that presents a paradox, so you should have expected a Resolve question. To do resolve the discrepancy, you must understand the contrast:

1. Rats fed high doses of saccharine get bladder cancer.
2. Mice fed high doses of saccharine don't.

Even though it is difficult to predict the exact solution to most Resolve questions, it is safe to say that the rats and mice must be different from each other in some important way (other than species).

Answer choice (A): This is the correct answer choice. This answer resolves the paradox by offering an explanation that accounts for the differing outcomes. Since the toxic crystals seem to be part of the process that leads to cancer in rats, their absence in mice might explain why mice do not get bladder cancer from saccharine.

Answer choice (B): This response mentions an important difference between rats and mice, but does not resolve the paradox. First of all, it is unclear what the effect of the different regeneration rates would be. It is entirely possible that a faster regeneration rate would make an animal more prone to cancer, and that would actually make the paradox worse.

Second, on a more esoteric note, some test takers who chose this response carelessly assumed that it implied the cancer could come about because certain areas of the bladder are damaged for too long in rats, or at least for much longer than in mice. Unfortunately, this response neither suggests that the rat's regeneration rates are insufficient nor suggests that the mice have a much greater regeneration rate.

Answer choice (C): This attempted explanation might be consistent with the information we have regarding rats, but we have no information on crystal formation in mice. Thus, this answer cannot explain the differing cancer rates.

Answer choice (D): This information might explain that the silicate crystals have a limited possible effect; however, it does not explain why mice wouldn't experience an effect from the crystals, similar to rats.

Answer choice (E): This answer points out a difference between rats and mice, and it suggests that certain sweeteners have different effects on the two animals. However, you are trying to explain why the high doses of saccharin have one effect in rats and a different effect in mice. This answer does nothing to help explain that difference because it does not mention saccharin, and nothing can be inferred form the actions of the other sweeteners.

Question #6: Assumption. The correct answer choice is (E)

The argument in the stimulus appears as follows:

Premise: Although we could replace the beautiful—but dilapidated—old bridge across Black River with a concrete skyway,

Conclusion: we should instead replace it with a cable bridge

Premise: even though this would be more expensive than building a concrete skyway.

Premise: The extra cost is clearly justified by the importance of maintaining the beauty of our river crossing.

Since you are asked to identify an assumption on which the argument depends, you must look for any leaps in the reasoning (Supporters), or any ideas that threaten the stimulus that must be rejected (Defenders).

As in any Assumption question, consider the conclusion: we should replace the old bridge with a cable bridge. Why is that the case? The author states that we must do so despite the expense in order to maintain the beauty of the river crossing (this reasoning is extremely questionable because it fails to consider that a properly designed concrete skyway might be just as beautiful as a cable bridge). Most students, when examining this stimulus, see that connection and realize that the author has assumed that the cable bridge will be more attractive. Using that prephrase, they are then able to effectively dispose of this question by accelerating through this problem and selecting (E).

If you did not see that connection after reading the stimulus, do not forget to use the Assumption Negation Technique, which can help confirm that you have selected the correct answer.

Answer choice (A): The author does not see cost as a major issue, so the author is not committed to the idea that the cable bridge is not more costly to maintain.

If you are unconvinced, negate the answer, and consider how the author would respond to the negation. Even if the cable bridge were more expensive to maintain, the author of this argument might still insist that the beauty is worth the cost, so this response is not critical to the argument.

Answer choice (B): The argument cannot depend on an assumption that is contradictory to the argument's premises (cost advantage is most certainly a practical advantage), so this response is definitely wrong. Furthermore, even allowing for some leeway with this response, the author might not care about practical concerns.

Answer choice (C): This is the most attractive incorrect answer. However, "beauty" in this stimulus is only tied to a concept the author wishes to maintain, and the author is not tied to a specific level of beauty. For example, preservation implies a reasonably equal level of beauty, and technically the author's argument allows for the possibility that preservation of the site's current level of beauty is not essential. The author could accept some lower standard of beauty, and therefore still choose to advocate a more beautiful bridge.

From an Assumption Negation Technique standpoint, the correct negation of this answer is: "The beauty of the river crossing does not necessarily need to be preserved." In response to this negation, the author could note that while it doesn't need to be preserved, there are still benefits to having some level of beauty present, and that therefore the cable bridge is still the preferred choice.

Answer choice (D): This answer choice trades on how people would react to the cable bridge, but popular opinion is not a good method of proof or disproof on the LSAT. Even if most people believed the money poorly spent, the money could still be well spent. Also, people could simply have no particular opinion at all, and that would not damage the argument. In the realm of argumentation, opinions mean little and prove less. Search for an answer with a basis in fact.

Answer choice (E): This is the correct answer choice. If you are uncertain as to whether this answer is correct, use the Assumption Negation Technique. If the cable bridge is *not* more beautiful than the concrete bridge, how is the author's argument affected? Because beauty was a driving factor in advocating a cable bridge, the negation of this answer choice would severely weaken the author's argument, and hence this answer is correct.

Mechanistically, notice that "beauty" appears in one of the premises and nowhere else, and "cable bridge" appears in the conclusion but nowhere else. Not surprisingly, these ideas are linked in this assumption of the argument.

Question #7: Strengthen. The correct answer choice is (C)

The argument can be summarized as follows: because electric mowers produce no air pollution, but gas-powered mowers produce significant air pollution, people can help reduce air pollution by using electric instead of gas-powered mowers.

As always, try to personalize the argument. If someone were to make this argument to you, would you just accept it? Or would you have further questions about electric mowers, such as how much pollution does the production of electricity produce? An electric mower might not produce immediate pollution, but this is of course a case of ignoring the actual initial power source of the electric mower.

Because you are asked to strengthen the argument, you should look for a choice that supports the idea that adopting a gas-powered mower is a good idea.

Answer choice (A): This response is irrelevant because the stimulus is about lawn mowers, not lawns. And, of course, we cannot assume that cutting the lawn with one mower rather than another would change the effect of mowing on the grasses' ability to clean the air.

Answer choice (B): The cost of the product does not affect whether people *should* adopt it, only whether they ultimately will. Thus, this answer choice cannot help the argument prove that "people can help reduce air pollution by choosing electric mowers."

Answer choice (C): This is the correct answer choice. The power for an electric mower has to come from somewhere, and this choice establishes that producing the power for an electric mower causes less pollution than producing the power for a gas-powered mower. This information makes the argument much more believable since it establishes that there is not a "hidden" pollution cost somewhere along the line of electrical power production.

Answer choice (D): This response only serves to suggest that using electric-powered mowers might not have much effect, since the gas-powered mowers are improving. If anything, this answer may weaken the argument by suggesting that in the future gas-powered mowers may be more emission efficient.

Answer choice (E): The stimulus compared gas mowers to electric mowers, and the reference to automobiles is only intended to imply that gas mowers produce pollution at a significant rate. In short, whether or not lawn mowers produce as much pollution as automobiles is irrelevant, because the issue is whether gas mowers produce more than electric mowers.

Question #8: Point at Issue—CE. The correct answer choice is (D)

Ariel's conclusion is that government subsidies never benefit art. Sasha's conclusion is that democratic government subsidies can benefit art by allowing artists to be fully devoted and artistically free.

Since this two-speaker stimulus is followed by a Point at Issue question, you must make sure you understand the general nature of the disagreement before heading to the answer choices. Do not worry too much about the details of the premises because you will likely need to refer back to the stimulus during the problem to confirm the particulars of the statements made by each speaker. If you understand the basic disagreement, that may be sufficient, so simply move forward.

Remember, all answer choices in a Point at Issue question must pass the Agree/Disagree Test.

Answer choice (A): Both Ariel and Sasha agree that the role of art is to challenge values, so this response is incorrect.

Answer choice (B): Ariel would agree with this answer choice. Sasha's exact position on this statement is unknown, and you cannot infer from her statement that "a democratic government…encourages challenges to its own values" that those values are not the same as society's values.

Answer choice (C): One easy way to eliminate this answer is to realize that Sasha never commented on nondemocractic societies, just on a democratic one. Thus, since her position on this statement would be unknown, this answer choice is immediately incorrect.

Answer choice (D): This is the correct answer choice. Ariel would disagree with this statement, because she states that government subsidy never benefits art. Sasha would agree with this statement, because her entire argument is structured to support the idea that democratic governments are able to benefit art through subsidy.

Answer choice (E): The issue of fair distribution is never mentioned by either speaker, so this answer can be eliminated immediately.

In addition, this answer is quasi-Mistaken Reversal of Sasha's argument, because this response states:

Art subsidies fairly distributed ———→ Government respects dissent

However, Sasha's argument implies that a respect of dissent is a sufficient condition, not necessary, for art subsidy distribution. Thus, Sasha's stance on this choice is again unknown.

Question #9: Main Point. The correct answer choice is (C)

The structure of this argument requires you to follow the indicator words used by the public health expert. The first sentence is a premise that sets up a point of view. The second sentence offers a counter-premise ("however") that provides new information suggesting that the beliefs are unlikely to be achieved. The final sentence is the conclusion ("therefore") of the argument, wherein the expert suggests that a new health policy is required.

Your task in this problem is to find the answer choice that best matches the conclusion.

Answer choice (A): This is a premise of the argument, not the conclusion. In Main Point questions a premise is never the correct answer.

Answer choice (B): This is unsupported by the argument. Microorganisms are evolving, and cannot, in general, be eradicated, but that does not mean that a specific patient cannot be cured of a specific disease.

Answer choice (C): This is the correct answer choice. In the last sentence the expert believes that there should be a change of strategy regarding microorganisms, and that idea matches the idea in this answer choice. It does not matter that this choice abstractly, rather than specifically, describes the conclusion; this answer provides a general description of the main point of the argument, and that is sufficient to be correct.

Answer choice (D): The expert referred specifically to "*minimizing* the incidence of such diseases," so there is no reason to believe that he or she concludes that educating people about transmission will *eliminate* the diseases.

Answer choice (E): Some test takers select this choice because it sounds more specific than answer choice (C). However, there are two reasons this answer is incorrect. First, the conclusion of the argument goes beyond the possible flaws of previous approaches to advocate a new approach. So, even if this statement were true, it is not the main point. Second, when current medical research reveals new information about a situation, it would be improper to say that previous beliefs "ignored" that evidence. A better phrasing would have been that previous approaches were unaware of that information.

Question #10: Flaw in the Reasoning. The correct answer choice is (B)

The conclusion of the argument is that medieval societies were much less concerned about money than are today's Western cultures. The premise that is given to support that conclusion is that the writings of medieval monks showed that they enthusiastically embraced an austere lifestyle. Remember, always try to personalize arguments when you read them. Does this premise convince you that the conclusion is true? To get a true sense of our society today would we refer solely to the writings of the clergy? Of course not, so this argument is flawed.

Since the question stem asks you to identify the flaw, simply accelerate through the answers and find the choice that best captures a weakness in the author's argument.

Answer choice (A): This answer falls under the category of flaw known as the Uncertain use of a Term. Ascetic, which Webster's defines as "a person who dedicates his or her life to a pursuit of contemplative ideals and practices extreme self-denial or self-mortification for religious reasons," is not an imprecise term as it is used here, and you should never assume a term on the LSAT is flawed simply because you lack familiarity.

Furthermore, every time the LSAT has contained a flaw based on usage, the term has been a very common one with which most reasonably aware persons would be acquainted (which is not to say it is always easy to pick out). This is because the LSAT is supposed to test your reasoning skills, and knowledge of abstruse vocabulary is *not* a reasoning skill. Ascetic, as you know, is *not* a common term and plenty of people may have no idea what it means.

Answer choice (B): This is the correct answer choice. Medieval monks present a certain view of life in medieval society, but their writings would certainly not capture all aspects of life. So, to claim that on the basis of their writings that there was an enthusiastic acceptance of ascetic lifestyles is to generalize from a sample that does not represent the views of all of society.

Notice that understanding the meaning of "ascetic" is entirely irrelevant to recognizing that monks probably do not represent common attitudes. The LSAT test-writers do in fact hope that some students get hung up on "ascetic," but you should focus on the broad method of reasoning.

Answer choice (C): Be careful when reading this answer choice. Some students think this answer says, "*Compares* contemporary standards…" and since there was a discussion of the medieval and contemporary societies, they incorrectly select this answer. Remember, any correct Flaw in the Reasoning answer choice must pass the Fact Test, so test each part of the answer to see whether it occurred. First, were contemporary standards applied? No. A comparison was made, but no standard from contemporary society was applied. Thus, this answer cannot be correct.

Answer choice (D): The stimulus makes no reference to personal opinion.

Answer choice (E): The premise is not inconsistent with itself, and the premise and conclusion are not inconsistent because they concern different time periods. This answer would fall into the category of flaw known as the Internal Contradiction.

Question #11: Evaluate the Argument Except—CE. The correct answer choice is (C)

The argument opens by presenting two premises: in the past chemical wastes were dumped into Cod Bay, and today 3 percent of the bluefin cod have deformed fins, which has caused consumers to stop buying the cod. The Cod Bay fishing representatives claim that since the chemicals that were dumped are known to cause genetic mutations, those chemicals must have then caused the deformities in the bluefin cod. Accordingly, they believe the companies that dumped the chemicals should be financially liable for, presumptively, the fishing industry's loss in sales of bluefin cod

The argument on the surface does not seem entirely unreasonable, although there are so many unknown factors that could affect this situation that considerably more information is required before the argument can be assessed.

The question stem is an unusual Evaluate the Argument Except question, where the four incorrect answers help evaluate the validity of the argument and the one correct answer does not help evaluate the validity of the argument. Remember to use the Variance Test when trying to confirm the correct answer or eliminate wrong answers.

Answer choice (A): This answer helps in evaluating the argument because it would help determine if the 3 percent deformity rate is normal or unusual. If the incidence of fin-deformity in non-exposed cod is always about 3%, or is close, there is no reason to believe that the chemicals cause the deformity. Therefore, even if consumers are wary of the fish because of its deformities, the chemical companies are not necessarily responsible. On the other hand, if the incidence of fin-deformity is normally zero, the assertion that chemical dumping caused the problem is more plausible.

Remember that with answers requiring percentages, the Variance Test suggests that you use 0 and 100. If the answer to the question in this answer is 0, the representatives' claim is strengthened; if the answer to the question in this answer is 100, the representatives' claim is severely weakened. Thus, this answer passes the Variance Test, and in an Except question we know the answer is incorrect.

Answer choice (B): This response is in the same vein as answer choice (A). Using the Variance Test, if the answer to the question in this answer is 0, the representatives' claim is strengthened; if the answer to the question in this answer is 100, the representatives' claim is severely weakened. Thus, this answer passes the Variance Test, and in an Except question the answer is incorrect.

Answer choice (C): This is the correct answer choice. Remember, this is an Except question, so this answer does not help in evaluating the representatives' claim.

In short, the argument is about what caused the deformed fins and who is liable for the losses incurred from lost sales. This answer deals with an after-the-issue fact, and so it does not bear on the representatives' claim.

Using the Variance Test, try "yes" and "no" responses to the question posed in this answer choice. If the answer to the question in this answer is Yes, the representatives' claim is unaffected; if the answer to the question in this answer is No, the representatives' claim is unaffected. Thus, this answer fails the Variance Test, and in an Except question we know the answer is correct.

Answer choice (D): If bluefin cod in general are susceptible to deformity-causing illnesses, it is possible that disease, rather than the chemicals, is the cause of the deformities in the Cod Bay bluefin. This response raises the possibility of an alternate cause, which is critical, so this response is incorrect.

Using the Variance Test, if the answer to the question in this answer is No, the representatives' claim is strengthened; if the answer to the question in this answer is Yes, the representatives' claim is weakened. Thus, this answer passes the Variance Test, and in an Except question the answer is incorrect.

Answer choice (E): Read this answer closely: "Are there gene-altering pollutants present...*other than* the chemical wastes that were dumped?" This answer is asking whether there could be some other type of pollutant besides the dumped chemicals. If so, that would call into question whether the dumped chemicals really did cause the deformities. Thus, this choice, like answer choice (D) raises the possibility that there is an alternate cause for the deformities.

Using the Variance Test, if the answer to the question in this answer is No, the representatives' claim is strengthened; if the answer to the question in this answer is Yes, the representatives' claim is weakened. Thus, this answer passes the Variance Test, and in an Except question the answer is incorrect.

Question #12: Method of Reasoning. The correct answer choice is (A)

The columnist notes that although both unsigned letters and certain news sources are anonymous, the news sources are usually accepted without question. However, because in both cases a person may be able to make incorrect statements with impunity, the columnist concludes that it makes sense to be skeptical of anonymous news sources.

Because the author is making a comparison, ask yourself if the two items are in fact comparable. Is an unsigned letter the same as an anonymous news source? Not really. The columnist confuses the news story sense of "anonymous," which is generally a source that a journalist is aware of, but protects from exposure.

The question stem asks you to identify the method of reasoning, and you should seek an answer that describes the comparison made by the author.

Answer choice (A): This is the correct answer choice. A comparison between two like things is an analogy, so any answer using the word "analogy" would be an initial Contender. Let's break down this answer choice and make sure it passes the Fact Test:

> "pointing out that a certain attitude would presumably be adopted in one situation..."

The "certain attitude" is skepticism, and the "one situation" is skepticism toward an unsigned letter.

> "...in order to support the claim that a similar attitude would be justified in an analogous situation"

The "similar attitude" is again skepticism, and the "analogous situation" is anonymous news sources.

Thus, each element of the answer does occur, and this does correctly describe the reasoning used by the author.

Note that the validity of the analogy is irrelevant, because you are not asked to describe the flaw in the reasoning.

Answer choice (B): This response may seem attractive because it also references an "analogy." However, the answer is wrong for two reasons. Perhaps the easiest flaw to focus on is the fact that this choice claims that the "latter attitude is more justified than the former," but the argument claimed that the skepticism toward the letter—the former attitude presented—was the more justified. Thus, this answer has the relationship backward, and that alone is enough to eliminate this choice.

Furthermore, the analogy was between the sources, not the attitudes.

Answer choice (C): This argument involved an analogy between different things that actually occur, and not a generalization from a hypothetical situation, so this choice is incorrect.

There is also a problem with the phrase "all situations of a given type," because the "given type" would refer to anonymous items, yet there has only been a discussion of two types of anonymous items (and therefore not "all situations").

Answer choice (D): This response may also seem attractive because it references an "analogy." But, the argument does not show that any evidence is "usually false," only that a person would likely have some doubts and should be skeptical.

Answer choice (E): The argument does not conclude that the evidence is "likely to be false," only that a person would likely have some doubts and should be skeptical.

Question #13: Assumption. The correct answer choice is (B)

The stimulus points out that art theft is on the rise, and that most stolen art is sold to wealthy collectors. The author then argues that since thieves steal what their customers are most interested in buying, security should focus on protecting museums' most valuable pieces.

If you are having trouble identifying the conclusion, note the use of the conclusion/premise indicator form "Consequently, since…" The conclusion is "museums ought to focus more of their security on their most valuable pieces."

The conclusion of the argument introduces a new idea: "most valuable pieces." Where does the basis for this new idea come from? There is no concrete statement about the value of the pieces, so obviously the author makes a leap to arrive at this concept, and in an Assumption question it is highly likely that the correct answer will address this new idea (notably, only answer choices (A), (B), and (D) address the value of art, and this means that answer choices (C) and (E) are unlikely to be correct). The premise just prior to the conclusion also includes a new idea: "what their customers are most interested in buying." This new idea will also likely be addressed in the correct answer, and notably only answer choice (B) addresses this idea. Thus, just based on an analysis of the pieces of this argument, answer choice (B) jumps out as the most likely correct answer because it connect the "new ideas" in the premise and conclusion. Remember, to excel on the LSAT you must understand how the test makers operate and take advantage of the patterns they use.

Answer choice (A): This response would serve to undermine the argument, so this choice is wrong.

Answer choice (B): This is the correct answer choice. This Supporter answer establishes a connection between value of the art and what the collectors want, and that fills the gap in the author's argument.

Note the proper negation of this answer: "Art pieces that are not very valuable *are* very much in demand by wealthy private collectors." As this negation would undermine the author's argument, we know from the Assumption Negation Technique that this is the correct answer.

Answer choice (C): This response is irrelevant because the stimulus does not concern adding security, but refocusing it. In any case, the general need for security is neither essential nor helpful in establishing that a refocusing of security is a good plan.

Answer choice (D): This was the most popular incorrect answer. The author's argument does not depend on the idea that most museums equally protect all their art, just that the most valuable art in some museums is not maximally protected.

Consider the negation of this answer: "Most museums provide *different* amounts of security for valuable and not-so-valuable art." Does this statement undermine the argument? No, because even if the security currently focuses more on valuable items than on non-valuable items, the author could claim it is a good idea to focus *even more* on those items. Since the negation of this answer choice does not undermine the author's argument, we know from the Assumption Negation Technique that this is an incorrect answer.

Answer choice (E): What wealthy private collectors do with their art after they buy it is beyond the scope of this argument, and so this choice is wrong.

Question #14: Flaw in the Reasoning—CE. The correct answer choice is (D)

The stimulus begins by presenting a statement indicating that insufficient rain *can* cause crops to falter and prices to rise. Then the author proceeds to state that in a recent crisis a nation experienced rising prices and faltering crops (which led to government intervention). Finally, the author draws a causal conclusion indicating that weather *must* have played a role in causing the crisis.

The abstract form of this argument is, "A can cause B. B occurred, so A must have caused B."

As with all causal conclusions, this one is suspect because there is the possibility that other causes created the effect, or that there is no causal relationship at all. There is also another error in the argument because the stimulus only states that insufficient rain is *possibly* a cause for faltering crops and rising prices. The conclusion is that, in this case, weather *must* have played a role, or was the cause, even though the premises neither state that weather has to be the cause, nor give any reason to believe that some other factor (insects, perhaps) could not cause crop failure as well.

Since you are asked to identify a flaw, and the stimulus features causal reasoning, remember to look for answer choices that use the word *cause* or *effect*, as those answers are much more likely to be correct. In this case, only answer choices (A) and (D) contain those words, and you should seek and attack those answer choices.

Answer choice (A): The stimulus seeks to *conclude* that insufficient rain occurred, and does not start from the *premise* that insufficient rain occurs. This response, which confuses the conclusion with a premise, is incorrect.

Answer choice (B): Since the argument is not about whether the government was justified in its efforts to prevent starvation, this answer choice is off-topic. Furthermore, the severity of the crisis is not clearly related to the cause of the crisis.

Answer choice (C): This answer describes a flaw known as the Uncertain Use of a Term. However, "crisis" is not used differently in two separate contexts. Each use of the term refers very clearly to the crisis involving faltering crops and rising prices. This response attempts to respond to a political dimension that may exist in the test taker's mind, but certainly does not exist in the stimulus, and this choice is wrong.

Answer choice (D): This is the correct answer choice. The argument infers that because insufficient rain is a possible cause, it is in this case the definite cause, and that unsupported shift from possibility to certainty is a flaw.

Answer choice (E): This answer describes an error of conditional reasoning, not an error of causal reasoning.

Question #15: Resolve the Paradox Except. The correct answer choice is (A)

The stimulus presents an apparent paradox, so you must be aware of the contrasting elements:

1. Tuition per class has not risen over a four-year period.
2. Within that period, many students who once could afford tuition cannot now.

There are many ways to resolve this paradox. First of all, the stimulus leaves you a clue when it refers to tuition per class. Perhaps the students are taking more classes now, which would make their tuition rise even though tuition per class is constant. Second, there are many other factors—including income, scholarships, and living costs—that play into whether a student can afford even a constant tuition.

Since the question is a Resolve EXCEPT question, you should eliminate the four choices that resolve the paradox, and select the choice that does not resolve the paradox.

Answer choice (A): This is the correct answer choice. This answer addresses teacher salaries, and teacher salaries do not affect the ability of students to afford tuition when the tuition per class is constant.

Answer choice (B): This choice resolves the paradox by pointing out that full-time students are required to enroll in more classes, and thus they pay more money this year (remember, the stimulus referenced *per-class* tuition as being constant).

Answer choice (C): This choice resolves the paradox by establishing that living costs are rising, which would mean that the students have less money to spend on tuition.

Answer choice (D): This response resolves the paradox in very sly fashion. Even though it definitely does not establish that a significant number of students fail to keep their scholarships, it does suggest that a great number of the students would initially be able to afford tuition because of the scholarships, and establish that it is possible to lose that scholarship, somewhat reducing one's ability to afford tuition.

Answer choice (E): This choice resolves the paradox by suggesting that many students no longer have work-study jobs available. Those students who needed the part-time office jobs might find employment elsewhere, but cutting the students out of the university jobs would have some effect on student income, and therefore their ability to afford tuition. For instance, the university town could be small and unable to support the students as part-time employees, working in-town could present conflicts with classes, or non-university jobs might tend to pay much less.

Question #16: Must be True—FL. The correct answer choice is (E)

The stimulus is a fact set that does not contain a paradox, so you should expect a Must Be True question, or, less likely, a Cannot Be True question. In this instance, you are presented with a Must Be True question. In such a situation, it is important to be acquainted with the facts and any immediate conclusions that you can legitimately draw.

The first premise is that people are not happy unless they feel needed by others, and the second premise is that most people can feel needed only within the sphere family and friends. Given the presence of the formal logic terms "unless" and "most," you should realize that this stimulus contains a formal logic relationship:

$$\text{Happy} \longrightarrow \text{Feel Needed} \overset{M}{\longrightarrow} \text{Within Sphere of Friends and Family}$$

However, this relationship does not yield a traditional inference, leaving some test takers at a loss. In a situation like this, move on to the answer choices and use them to help gain perspective on the problem.

Answer choice (A): This choice tries to trade on the last phrase of the stimulus, which suggests that almost everyone knows they can be replaced. However, this answer ignores the possibility of obtaining happiness within the sphere of family and friends, and so it is incorrect.

Answer choice (B): If anything, the stimulus implies that family life is very important to an individual's happiness, and so this answer choice moves in the opposite direction of what is needed.

Answer choice (C): There is no reason in the stimulus to suppose that most people actually find happiness. The stimulus concerned only how people might achieve happiness, not whether they have actually found it.

Answer choice (D): There was no indication that people do not appreciate having their jobs. It is illogical to conclude that the fact that others could do the job would cause people to appreciate their jobs less. In fact, the knowledge that someone else could do your job might actually cause you to value your job more.

Answer choice (E): This is the correct answer choice. Based on the weakness of the previous four answers (with the possible exception of (C)), this may have been an easy answer to select, especially since this answer seems to link several of the key ideas from the stimulus. Regardless, let's examine the logic of this answer and find the support in the stimulus. We know the following:

1. Everyone who is Happy is in the Feel Needed group
2. More than half of the Feel Needed group is in the Within Sphere of Friends and Family group

Thus, looking solely at the Feel Needed group, since most of them are in the Sphere group, we know that less than half of the Feel Needed group could be Happy but at the same time not in the Sphere group. Thus, we can conclude that less than a majority of people can be Happy but at the same time not be Within Sphere of Friends and Family group.

Since this is a tricky concept, here is a numerical illustration based on a group of 100 people:

1. Suppose that 51 people are Happy. Accordingly, all 51 Happy people also Feel Needed.

2. Using the maximally beneficial circumstance for this answer, then, of the Feel Needed group we could say that 51 are Happy, and 49 are not Happy.

3. Using the maximally beneficial circumstance for this answer, at least 51 people in the Feel Needed group are in the Sphere group and at most 49 people are not in the Sphere group.

Conclusion 1: At least 2 of the people in the Sphere group are Happy, so a majority of the people cannot be Happy without some of them also being in the Sphere group.

So, a majority of people cannot be Happy without some of them being in the Sphere group, and less than a majority of people are Happy without being in the Sphere group (Even if you play with the numbers, you will find that the statement in this answer choice is supported).

Notice also, this is a conclusion about the *majority of all people*, which is warranted, rather than about the *majority of happy people*, which would be unwarranted.

Question #17: Flaw in the Reasoning. The correct answer choice is (C)

When you read through this stimulus, hopefully you realized that in the last sentence the author assumes that judgments about extrinsic value must be a matter of taste and cannot be objective. If you recognize the presence of that assumption, this question is easy.

However, if you do not see that leap, this stimulus is best addressed by understanding the conditions in the critic's argument. The critic claims that the issues of value and judgment are related, and offers a conditional statement in the first part of the last sentence:

Value Not Intrinsic $\longrightarrow$ Value Extrinsic

The critic then concludes that if an artwork's value is extrinsic, then judgments about the quality of the work can only be a matter of taste. The critic is incorrectly confusing objectivity with intrinsic qualities, and assuming that any extrinsic value cannot be objective.

Answer choice (A): The critic attempts to say that judgments are merely taste in a certain instance, so critic does not take for granted that the judgments are *always* a matter of taste.

Answer choice (B): The critic only believes that in certain situations judgments can only be a matter of taste, not that people sometimes *agree about judgments* that are only matters of taste.

Answer choice (C): This is the correct answer choice. As discussed, this is exactly the premise that the critic assumes to draw his conclusion.

Answer choice (D): This answer is attractive because it connects judgments to objectivity. However, despite having some of the terms we expect to see in the correct answer, this is actually a Mistaken Negation of the correct answer (and thus a Mistaken Negation of the actual assumption in the argument). The correct answer can be diagrammed as:

Judgment about extrinsic value ⟶ Obj~~e~~ctive

This answer can be diagrammed as:

Judgment ab~~ou~~t extrinsic value ⟶ Objective

Although it is easy to see why this was an attractive answer choice, the critic did not take this relationship for granted in the argument.

Answer choice (E): The author does seem to take this statement for granted, but that is not a flaw in the argument because the argument concerns linking extrinsic value to judgment based on taste.

Question #18: Must be True—SN. The correct answer choice is (A)

By the percentages of people answering this problem correctly, this is the first truly killer question of the section. Interestingly, the stimulus is fairly easy to understand. The stimulus consists of information describing the various benefits of decentralization to large organizations:

> Decentralization allows for autonomy, which *always* permits more realistic planning and encourages innovation.

> Decentralization allows the central administration to focus on the big picture rather than details.

Since you are asked to find the most strongly supported statement, you should simply look for a response that follows from the information in the stimulus.

Answer choice (A): This is the correct answer choice. Most students are probably turned off by the certainty of this answer choice, but such language is supported by the stimulus. Since, in large organizations, autonomy *always* allows more realistic planning, planning in a large organization without autonomous divisions *cannot* be as realistic as possible.

Remember, extreme answers are not necessarily wrong in Must Be True questions. They are only incorrect if the language of the stimulus is not extreme.

Answer choice (B): This response may be attractive, but is incorrect. The autonomy involved in decentralization encourages innovation, but that does not mean that centralized organizations discourage innovation. This answer choice is similar to a Mistaken Negation, and must be eliminated.

Answer choice (C): The stimulus listed some benefits of decentralization, but never weighed them against any drawbacks, so you cannot conclude from the stimulus anything certain about the value of decentralization relative to centralization, so this choice is wrong.

Answer choice (D): This was the most popular incorrect answer choice. Although the stimulus indicates that the central administrations of large institutions are partially responsible for *some* of the details of daily operations, we do not know that the central administrations of large institutions are partially responsible for *most* of the details of daily operations.

Answer choice (E): The stimulus stated that autonomy always *permits* more realistic planning, and *strongly encourages* innovation, but those statements do not mean that the people implementing the policies are *always* able to achieve those ends. This difference in certainty makes this answer choice incorrect.

Furthermore, the stimulus discussed people who make decisions and are involved in implementation, but this choice only mentions people who are involved in implementation. Implementation was an *essential* part of improving decision making, but you should not make the mistake of assuming that anyone involved in implementation is also involved in decision-making, because that would be a Mistaken Reversal.

Question #19: Flaw in the Reasoning—#%. The correct answer choice is (C)

The argument has a complex structure, featuring two premises and a sub-conclusion that is then used to support the main conclusion of the argument:

Premise:	According to some astronomers, Earth is struck by a meteorite large enough to cause an ice age on an average of once every 100 million years.
Premise:	The last such incident occurred nearly 100 million years ago,
Sub-conclusion:	so we can expect that Earth will be struck by such a meteorite in the near future.
Main Conclusion:	This clearly warrants funding to determine whether there is a means to protect our planet from such meteorite strikes.

Do the supporting statements prove the main conclusion? Again, personalize the argument—does it make sense that if the earth has been struck "on an average of once every 100 million years" that suddenly we are in imminent danger? Of course not. The problem is that historical averages are only averages, and you cannot predict that a meteorite strike is overdue or likely based on such averages. The reasoning in the argument is made even weaker when you consider the scale of time involved. Even if the historical pattern holds on average, a million or two million year variation would be a very small deviation compared to 100 million years, so it makes absolutely no sense to conclude that there will definitely be a meteorite strike in the "near future." And, of course, if there is no certainty that earth will be struck in the near future, how can funding be "clearly warranted?"

Answer choice (A): This choice was commonly selected, but there is no justification for this answer. The first section of the answer—"makes a bold prescription"—does occur in the reasoning. However, the second part—"on the basis of evidence that establishes only a high probability for a disastrous event"—does not occur because the stimulus does not establish a high probability for a disastrous event.

Of course, even if you saw the stimulus as establishing a high probability for disaster, wouldn't that high probability of disaster actually be a good justification for a "bold prescription?" Probably so, and thus it is hard to see how this choice would actually describes a flaw even if everything described within it had occurred.

Answer choice (B): The argument presumes precisely the opposite of this choice because the author believes that the probability of a chance event—the meteorite—is affected by whether or not it has happened recently. In the stimulus, the author makes clear that she believes that there is a greater likelihood of a meteorite strike today because there has not been a meteorite strike recently.

Furthermore, this choice describes reasoning that is often sound, as opposed to unsound, reasoning. Typically, a chance event is not affected by preceding events or whether there has been a recent occurrence of that event, and that is what is described in this answer. The reasoning in the stimulus, on the other hand, implies that for chance events, the past affects the future. Believing the stimulus is similar to a gambler believing that since he has thrown snake-eyes on average every third roll, it will keep happening every third roll. Historical averages, without some other supporting data, are prone to misrepresentation and misinterpretation, and should not be assumed to repeat.

Answer choice (C): This is the correct answer choice. Both parts of the answer occur, and what is described is a flaw:

> "moves from evidence about the average frequency of an event"—this section describes the fact that a large meteorite strikes earth on an average of once every 100 million years.

> "to a specific prediction about when the next such event will occur"—this section describes the sub-conclusion that "we can expect that Earth will be struck by such a meteorite in the near future."

An average cannot be used to make a specific prediction, and therein lies the flaw.

Answer choice (D): This choice could be relevant to whether investing in preventing a strike makes good public policy; however, it does not address the main flaw in the argument. Furthermore, even if the likelihood of an ice age resulting from a strike is very low, there could be other effects such as the destruction of cities that would suggest meteorite strike prevention as valuable, so the issue of ice ages is not critical.

Answer choice (E): The argument does not make any presumption that preventing large strikes is feasible, it only suggests that we begin investigations into protecting Earth.

CHAPTER SEVEN: THE DECEMBER 2004 LSAT Deconstructed

Question #20: Parallel Flaw—CE. The correct answer choice is (A)

This is the hardest question in this section, primarily because one of the wrong answer choices is quite attractive. The argument claims that because most nine-year-olds correctly identify the logos of major cigarette brands but very few nine-year-olds smoke, there is little connection between logo recognition and smoking. Abstractly, the argument attempts to show that a possible cause (logo recognition) does not have an expected effect (smoking).

The question stem asks you to identify the answer choice with the most similar flawed reasoning. Keeping in mind the different tests for Parallel Reasoning questions, consider the following when selecting an answer:

> Match the Method of Reasoning: The argument asserts that a cause and effect relationship does not exist, so the correct answer choice must feature a similar type of relationship.

> Match the Conclusion: The conclusion is fairly strong—"there is little or no connection between two items." The correct answer must feature a similar idea.

> Match the Premises: There are two premises, one of which addresses a poll (a survey or a study would be similar ideas) and the other about results from that poll which indicate that a possible cause is not having an effect.

> Match the Validity of the Reasoning: In this case the question stem tells you that the correct answer must contain flawed reasoning.

Obviously, the poll proves little, because it refers to juveniles who cannot purchase their own cigarettes, and ignores the potential effect that may occur by the time the child is old enough to plausibly pursue obtaining cigarettes. Since you are asked to identify the choice that contains similar reasoning, you should look for a response that refers to a group that has not yet had ample opportunity to develop a response to a particular cause.

Answer choice (A): This is the correct answer choice. Similar to the stimulus, a causal relationship is denied on the basis of a study. The conclusion, although worded differently, has the same meaning as that in the stimulus.

Specifically, three months is definitely not enough time to infer anything about the long-term effect of mercury poisoning, so this answer choice similarly does not cover enough time to rule out a cause-effect relationship.

Answer choice (B): This choice introduces two potential causes—dreams and parental influence—and asserts that one is more important to establishing an effect. The stimulus only involves ruling out a single cause and does not posit another, so this response is incorrect. The intent of this conclusion also differs from that in the stimulus.

Answer choice (C): This choice involves deciding which strategy—using fluoride or avoiding sweets—would have the greatest effect. However, the stimulus does not evaluate strategies or the importance of multiple causal factors, so this choice is wrong.

Answer choice (D): This answer choice was, by far, the most popular wrong answer choice *on this LSAT*. Most likely the cause of this popularity is that the wording of the conclusion is virtually identical to that in the stimulus. So, the problem with this answer lies elsewhere.

One serious problem is that this answer switches terms from the premise to the conclusion. One of the premises is about "average life span," but the conclusion is about "good health," and those two concepts are not the same. The stimulus, on the other hand, used the same terms from premise to conclusion.

Another problem is that this answer relates the group to an average ("average life span") whereas the stimulus related the group to a specific, definable result ("smoking"). This difference, while minor, helps indicate that this answer is problematic.

Answer choice (E): This quite possibly reasonable argument assumes that command of the issues, not knowledge of representatives' names, is a more important factor. Since the assumption is not entirely unwarranted, it is difficult to say that this choice is fatally flawed, though it certainly would be somewhat more strongly reasoned with the addition of another premise. In any case, the stimulus did not involve a comparison of factors, so this choice is dissimilar and incorrect.

Question #21: Must be True—Principle. The correct answer choice is (E)

In a nutshell, the stimulus engages in an explanation of etiquette's relation to offensive speech. The argument states that etiquette need not involve the restriction of speech by law, but that it does demand that the expression of potentially offensive ideas be done in appropriate forums in a civil manner.

Since you are asked to apply the principle in the stimulus, you should search for an answer that conforms to these restrictions:

1.   Etiquette opposes obscene and malicious speech.

2.   Etiquette allows for civil discussion of possibly offensive ideas in the proper forum.

Answer choice (A): This answer choice very likely reflects some aspect of etiquette, but this particular aspect is not discussed in the stimulus. The correct response will involve potentially offensive ideas or language.

Answer choice (B): There is no reason to suppose that the stimulus refers to this sort of etiquette. The ideas expressed in a court room are not necessarily offensive. This choice is incorrect.

Answer choice (C): The stimulus does not give reason to believe there should be any legal restrictions on free speech, and you should not conclude that etiquette is governed by "majority rule." In fact, considering what etiquette is, and what common opinion is, you should realize that it is unwarranted to equate etiquette to popular opinion.

Answer choice (D): A news conference is precisely the forum in which a politician ought be asked relevant questions of any sort, as long as the questioning is civil, so this choice contains a recommendation that is possibly contrary to the principles in the stimulus. Further, assuming the questions are posed in a civil manner, a question by itself is not necessarily offensive or embarrassing even though the underlying topic may be offensive, and thus this answer does not necessarily correspond to the principles discussed.

Answer choice (E): This is the correct answer choice. The principle of etiquette in the stimulus allows us to oppose obscene, malicious, or uncivil speech. Name-calling is probably malicious, and certainly uncivil. Since this response establishes the context as a panel on a "divisive moral issue," the ideas expressed may be potentially offensive and definitely controversial, bringing in the criteria of civil expression in that proper forum, so the moderator would be correct in disallowing name-calling under the principles in the stimulus.

Question #22: Justify the Conclusion—FL. The correct answer choice is (E)

The stimulus states that only recordings projected to sell profitably will be transferred to compact disc, and concludes that most classic jazz recordings will not be transferred, because few such recordings are played on the radio.

Mechanistically speaking, there are two elements in the stimulus that are not duplicated elsewhere. The first is the idea of profitability, and the second is the idea of being played on the radio. As the mechanistic approach to Justify questions dictates that new or rogue elements typically appear in the correct answer, you should seek an answer that contains *both* of these elements. A scan of the answers indicates that answer choices (A), (B), and (D) include, in each case, just one of the two elements. These answers are thus less likely to be correct. Answer choices (C) and (E) contain both elements, and are much more likely to be correct. Not surprisingly, one is the right answer, and below we discuss why (C) is incorrect and (E) is correct. Note that, if you are pressed for time, you could simply guess between (C) and (E) since working through the formal logic aspect of this problem is time-consuming for most students.

In the interests of thoroughness, to separate answer choices (C) and (E) we must analyze the formal logic relationship present in the stimulus, so let's take a moment to deconstruct the structure of the author's argument:

> Remember that in a Justify question the premises do not, by themselves, prove the conclusion. So, you must first isolate the premises and then analyze the conclusion separately. In this problem, the first sentence is a premise and the last clause is a premise; the conclusion is in the middle, prefaced by "So."

To designate the terms in the stimulus, we will use the following notation:

> TCD = Transferred onto Compact Disc
> P = Profitably sell on compact disc
> CJ = Classic Jazz
> PR = Played on Radio

Using these symbols, reduce the stimulus to its diagrammatic components:

First premise:

$$TCD \longrightarrow P$$

Contrapositive of the first premise:

$$\cancel{P} \longrightarrow T\cancel{CD}$$

Second premise:

$$CJ \xrightarrow{\text{ M }} \cancel{PR}$$

Conclusion:

$$CJ \xrightarrow{\text{ M }} T\cancel{CD}$$

The justifying statement, $\cancel{PR} \longrightarrow \cancel{P}$, would link the second statement to the first contrapositive to create the following chain:

$$CJ \xrightarrow{\text{ M }} \cancel{PR} \longrightarrow \cancel{P} \longrightarrow T\cancel{CD}$$

Resulting in the following conclusion, which is identical to the one in the stimulus:

$$CJ \xrightarrow{\text{ M }} T\cancel{CD}$$

Since you are asked to justify the conclusion by making it follow logically, you will need to supply the sufficient assumption, $\cancel{PR} \longrightarrow \cancel{P}$, or its contrapositive.

Answer choice (A): From a mechanistic perspective we already know this answer is insufficient to produce the conclusion in the argument.

Specifically, even if very few of the profitably transferable recordings are jazz recordings, all the jazz recordings could be included, since *all recordings* is a much larger group than *all jazz recordings*. Thus, there would be no justification for the conclusion that most classic jazz recordings will not be transferred onto compact disc.

Answer choice (B): Again, mechanistically, we know this answer does not have the correct components to produce the conclusion in the argument.

This choice somewhat reiterates the notion that few classic jazz recordings are played on the radio. Since compact disc transferals of jazz recordings will not in a sense outnumber originals, this statement tells us nothing that was not already inferred from the premises, and cannot justify the stimulus.

Answer choice (C): From our mechanistic analysis, we know this is one of the two leading Contenders. From a formal logic standpoint, this answer is close, but it is actually a Mistaken Negation of what is required to justify the conclusion.

This answer choice associates PR with P, and can be diagrammed as follows:

$$PR \longrightarrow P$$

This choice is a Mistaken Negation of the statement sufficient to justify the conclusion, which is:

$$\cancel{PR} \longrightarrow \cancel{P}$$

In this answer choice, the word "only" has a dramatic effect on the conditional relationship presented, and ultimately causes this answer to be incorrect. In addition, you should be aware that the test makers know that some students have learned to look just for modifiers, so the test makers have used a confusing grammatical structure that places "only" and its modified phrase "profit" on opposite ends of the sentence. Always remember that LSAT problems require careful, detailed reading.

Answer choice (D): Mechanistically, we know this answer is insufficient to produce the conclusion in the argument. This choice might offer an explanation for the companies' behaviors; however, it is neither a useful nor a sufficient assumption. The stimulus has already stated that only expectably profitable recordings are transferred, and the companies' motives do not matter.

Answer choice (E): This is the correct answer choice. The wording, however, is challenging and intentionally designed to confuse. Let's look at the language in the answer choice closely:

> "No recording that is not played on the radio is one that record companies believe would be profitable if transferred to compact disc."

The "No recording" refers to "one that record companies believe would be profitable if transferred to compact disc." The remaining section—"that is not played on the radio"—is the sufficient condition. Had the test makers been more benevolent, they could have rewritten this answer in the following simplified manner:

> "If a recording is not played on the radio, then record companies do not believe that recording would be profitable in compact disc format."

The correct diagram for this answer choice is:

$$\cancel{PR} \longrightarrow \cancel{P}$$

As explained in the discussion of the stimulus, this is the statement that justifies the conclusion.

Question #23: Method of Reasoning—AP. The correct answer choice is (E)

As with all Method-Argument Part questions, you must be able to identify the logical components of the argument:

Premise:	Over the past several years, increases in worldwide grain production have virtually ceased.
Sub-conclusion:	Further increases will be extremely difficult to achieve;
Premise:	most usable farmland is already being farmed with near-maximal efficiency.
Premise:	But worldwide demand for grain has been increasing steadily, due largely to continuing population growth.
Main Conclusion:	Hence, a severe worldwide grain shortage is likely.

The agricultural economist concludes that a worldwide grain-shortage is likely, and supports that by claiming that, while demand for grain is increasing, it will be difficult to significantly increase production of grain.

Note that in a question of this type you do not need to spend a long time thinking about the validity of the argument. Yes, the stimulus is flawed in that it does not consider the likelihood of advanced technologies or the like, but since the question simply asks you to identify the role played by one of the statements, you only need to know the structure of the argument. In this case, the role is that of sub-conclusion; that is, the claim follows from a premise and is then used to support the main conclusion.

Answer choice (A): This is a classic Half Right, Half Wrong answer. The first part of this answer—"It is one of the two conclusions drawn by the agricultural economist"—is an accurate description of the statement in question. However, since the claim is then used to support the main conclusion, the remainder of this answer incorrectly describes the statement.

Answer choice (B): This choice might have been attractive, but fails to grasp the correct causal flow, so this choice is wrong. The argument does attempt to justify the claim that future increases would be difficult by mentioning that farmland is almost maximally used already; however, the difficulty is offered as a cause of shortage, so the *main conclusion* uses difficulty as a cause instead of trying to explain what causes difficulty.

Answer choice (C): The claim is a premise, but it is certainly not the only premise.

Answer choice (D): The claim that future increases will be difficult to achieve is actually unsupported by the first sentence, so this response is incorrect. The economist's intent was to show that the situation has been present for some time, not to justify the idea that the situation would continue into the future. In any case, this response totally fails to identify the claim as a premise supporting the main conclusion.

Answer choice (E): This is the correct answer choice. In the second sentence, the claim is supported by the information that most available farmland is already being farmed with near-maximal efficiency, so the claim is a conclusion. The claim is also used to support the main conclusion, so all parts of this answer choice are verified.

Question #24: Flaw in the Reasoning—CE. The correct answer choice is (D)

Bardis presents evidence concerning the effects of television imagery on viewers. Apparently, research has proven that television advertisements affect consumers. On the basis of this evidence, some people have further concluded that violent television imagery sometimes causes violent behavior. Bardis disputes this notion by pointing out that the television ads might be effective because they are designed for that purpose whereas the violent imagery is not designed to cause violence. On the strength of this premise, Bardis concludes that television violence does not cause actual violence.

When examining the conclusion, note the absolute nature of the language. Does the premise prove beyond a shadow of a doubt that violent television imagery does not cause violence? Considering this issue will assist you in identifying the flaw in the reasoning.

Answer choice (A): Bardis never claims that advertisements can cause violent behavior, so this choice fails the Fact Test.

Answer choice (B): This was the most popular incorrect answer choice, primarily because it addresses cause and effect and it is clear that the stimulus contains causal reasoning. However, the flaw described in this answer choice is not the same as the flaw in the argument.

This response claims that Bardis confuses a "behavior" with a "stimulus," which is equivalent to confusing an effect with a cause. Since Bardis actually clearly defines his posited cause and effect, and there is no confusion between the two, this answer is incorrect.

Answer choice (C): The argument does not undermine itself, and does not question the persuasive power of advertising. It merely presumes that images have to be intended for a purpose to accomplish that purpose (this is illogical but it does call into not question the power of advertising).

Answer choice (D): This is the correct answer choice. The choice describes a classic error in the use of evidence, specifically one where some evidence against a position is taken to prove that the position is false. Bardis has raised a valid point against the people concluding that television violence causes violent behavior, namely that television violence is not designed to achieve this end where as television advertising is designed to achieve a specific end. However, that one point does not justify a concluding that violent television imagery *never* causes violence.

For the record, the claim in "concluding that a claim is false" refers to the belief that television violence sometimes causes violent behavior. The "one purported fault" refers to the evidence that television violence is not designed to produce violence.

Answer choice (E): It is difficult to see how "causing violence" could be a separate issue from "causing violence." There is no key term that is confused, and the argument, while somewhat weak, does not get off-target, and the aim is always to define whether television violence causes actual violence.

Question #25: Strengthen—Principle. The correct answer choice is (B)

Sarah points out that the regulations for staff review are vague and difficult to interpret. She offers the example of regulations that state that unsatisfactory performance will be met with dismissal, but those same regulations do not define unsatisfactory performance. She concludes that some staffers may be dismissed simply because their personal views are different from their supervisors' views.

Sarah's reasoning is flawed because she ignores the likelihood that other employee contracts and guidelines define required performance quite well, and that the regulations are merely broad so as to avoid restatements or possible conflicts when future policy changes are made. Furthermore, she cynically assumes that supervisors will equate personal views with job performance and use their positions of power to blatantly exceed the review guidelines.

Regardless of the flaws in Sarah's argument, you are asked to find a principle that will strengthen Sarah's conclusion, which is that "some staff may be dismissed merely because their personal views conflict with those of their supervisors."

Answer choice (A): This principle does not serve to strengthen the claim that supervisors will or can act in a capricious manner, so this answer does not strengthen the conclusion.

If anything, this choice might actually serve to weaken the stimulus. If performance that falls slightly below standards is not met with dismissal, that might establish that supervisors have some leeway. But, it also establishes that supervisors have some tendency toward leniency. If supervisors are lenient, how does that help establish that they will terminate employees for personal differences?

Answer choice (B): This is the correct answer choice. If supervisors have the sole prerogative to interpret the regulations, that means that there are no other documents or guidelines that could restrict the supervisors from making the interpretation they wish to make. Accordingly, the supervisors would then have the power to dismiss employees for whatever reason they saw fit, and that fact helps strengthen the stimulus.

Answer choice (C): Sarah suggests that the regulations could be used to inappropriately punish people for having certain personal views, but she does not establish that supervisors could take that kind of action. This response helps support the idea that employees are accountable for their performance, and that is contrary to the idea (or at worst, neutral) that they would be punished for their personal views.

Answer choice (D): The argument attempted to show that some staff could be *dismissed* for their personal views. This answer only shows that employees can be kept in control or withheld from promotion. As those two issues are not the same, this answer does not assist in establishing Sarah's reasoning.

An answer such as this one can be attractive because it paints the company in a negative light. However, the task in this question is not to simply show that the company has poor policies, but rather that the policy in place can lead to the termination of an employee over their personal views. Always keep in mind precisely what you are supposed to strengthen in a question like this one.

Answer choice (E): Whether or not *employees* consider specific regulations to be fairer is not central to the issue at hand, which concerns how *supervisors* act.

CHAPTER EIGHT: GLOSSARY

Introduction

This section contains a brief definition of the terms used in this book. The terms are given in alphabetical order. For more comprehensive explanations of each term or concept, refer to either the *Logic Games Bible* or the *Logical Reasoning Bible*.

Alphabetical Glossary

#%:   See Numbers and Percentages.

Additional Premise: Additional premises are premises that may be central to the argument or they may be secondary. To determine the importance of the premise, examine the remainder of the argument.

Agree/Disagree Test™: This test is used to solve Point at Issue questions. The correct answer must produce responses where one speaker would say "I agree, the statement is correct" and the other speaker would say, "I disagree, the statement is incorrect." If those two responses are not produced, then the answer is incorrect. The Agree/Disagree Test crystallizes the essence of Point at Issue questions by forcing you to concretely identify the elements that determine the correct answer.

AP: See Author's Perspective and Tone.

Appeal Fallacies: A common error of reasoning that attempts to "appeal" to various insubstantial viewpoints of the reader (emotion, popular opinion, tradition, authority, etc.). However the appeal is not valid, and concrete evidence is needed to support the argument.

Argument: A set of statements wherein one statement is claimed to follow from or be derived from the others. An argument requires a conclusion.

Argument Part Question: A subset of Method of Reasoning questions. In Argument Part questions, the question stem cites a specific portion of the stimulus and then asks you to identify the role the cited portion plays in the structure of the argument.

Assumption: An assumption is an unstated premise of the argument. Assumptions are an integral component of the argument that the author takes for granted and leaves unsaid.

Assumption Question: These questions ask you to identify an assumption of the author's argument. Question stem example:
> "Which one of the following is an assumption required by the argument above?"

Assumption Negation Technique™: This technique requires you to logically negate the answer choice under consideration, which results in a negated answer choice that attacks the argument. If the negated answer does not attack the argument, then it is incorrect. The purpose of this technique is to take an Assumption question, which is generally difficult for most students, and turn it into a Weaken question, which is easier for most students. This technique can only be used on Assumption questions.

Author's Perspective and Tone (AP): These Reading Comprehension questions ask you to select the answer choice that best reflects the author's views, such as "The author of the passage would most likely agree with which one of the following statements?" Tone questions ask you to identify the author's attitude toward the subject.

Balanced (see also Grouping, Linearity, Unbalanced, Defined, Undefined, etc.): In a Defined game, when the number of variables to be selected is equal to the overall number of available spaces.

Block (See also Linearity): In Linear games, blocks reflect the idea of a fixed spatial relationship between variables. Blocks represent variables that are next to one another, not next to one another, or separated by a fixed number of spaces. Basic blocks indicate adjacency.

C: In diagramming Logical Reasoning questions, "C" indicates Cause. Also see Cause.

Cannot Be True Questions: Ask you to identify the answer choice that cannot be true or is most weakened based on the information in the stimulus.
Question stem example:
    "If the statements above are true, which one of the following CANNOT be true?"

Causal Reasoning: Asserts or denies that one thing causes another, or that one thing is caused by another. On the LSAT, cause and effect reasoning appears in many Logical Reasoning problems, often in the conclusion where the author mistakenly claims that one event causes another.

Cause (C): The event that makes another occur.

Cause and Effect (CE): When one event is said to make another occur. The cause is the event that makes the other occur; the effect is the event that follows from the cause. By definition, the cause must occur before the effect, and the cause is the "activator" or "ignitor" in the relationship. The effect always happens at some point in time after the cause.

CE: See Cause and Effect.

Circular Reasoning: A flaw where the author assumes as true what is supposed to be proved. The premise supports the conclusion, but the conclusion equally supports the premise, creating a "circular" situation where you can move from premise to conclusion, and then back again to the premise, and so on.

Circular Sequencing: Games that consist of a fixed number of variables assigned to spaces distributed around a circle (usually a table). Essentially these games are Linear games wrapped around a circular diagram.

Complex Argument: Arguments that contain more than one conclusion. In these instances, one of the conclusions is the main conclusion, and the other conclusions are subsidiary conclusions (also known as sub-conclusions). In basic terms, a complex argument makes an initial conclusion based on a premise. The author then uses that conclusion as the foundation (or premise) for another conclusion, thus building a chain with several levels.

Conclusion: A statement or judgment that follows from one or more reasons. Conclusions, as summary statements, are supposed to be drawn from and rest on the premises.

Conclusion/Premise Indicator Form: The test makers will sometimes arrange premise and conclusion indicators in a way that is designed to be confusing. One of their favorite forms places a conclusion indicator and premise indicator back-to-back, separated by a comma, as in the following examples:

> "Therefore, since..."
> "Thus, because..."
> "Hence, due to..."

Conditional Reasoning: The broad name given to logical relationships composed of sufficient and necessary conditions. Any conditional statement consists of at least one sufficient condition and at least one necessary condition. In everyday use, conditional statements are often brought up using the "if...then" construction. Conditional reasoning can occur in any question type.

Contender: An answer choice that appears somewhat attractive, interesting, or even confusing. Basically, any answer choice that you cannot immediately identify as incorrect.

Contrapositive: Denies the necessary condition, thereby making it impossible for the sufficient condition to occur. Contrapositives can often yield important insights in Logic Games.

Counter-premise: A premise that actually contains an idea that is counter to the argument. Counter-premises, also called adversatives, bring up points of opposition or comparison.

Defender: In the Supporter/Defender Assumption Model™, the Defender assumptions contain statements that eliminate ideas or assertions that would undermine the conclusion. In this sense, they "defend" the argument by showing that a possible source of attack has been eliminated.

Defined: In these Logic Games, the exact number of variables to be selected is fixed in the rules.

Double Arrow: Indicates that the two terms must always occur together. The double arrow is typically introduced in any of the following three ways:
> 1. Use of the phrase "if and only if"
> 2. Use of the phrase "vice versa" (as in "If A attends then B attends, and vice versa")
> 3. By repeating and reversing the terms (as in "If A attends then B attends, and if B attends then A attends")

Double-not Arrow: Indicates that two terms cannot occur together. The double not-arrow only prohibits one scenario—one where the two terms occur together.

Dual Option: When only one of two variables can occupy a single slot. Represented with a slash, as in "A/B."

E: In diagramming, indicates Effect. See also Effect.

Effect: The event that follows from the cause.

Either/Or: For the purposes of the LSAT, the definition of "either/or" is "at least one of the two." Note that this definition implicitly allows for the possibility that both elements occur, and the existence of this possibility makes diagramming sentences containing the "either/or" term confusing. A careful examination of the definition of "either/or" reveals that a conditional relationship is at the heart of the construction: since at least one of the terms must occur, if one fails to occur then the other must occur.

Elemental Attack™: When attacking Parallel Reasoning questions, compare the big-picture elements of the argument: intent of the conclusion, force and use of the premises, the relationship of the premises and the conclusion, and the soundness of the argument. The four tests you can use to evaluate answers are Match the Method of Reasoning, Match the Conclusion, Match the Premises, and Match the Validity of the Argument.

Errors in the Use of Evidence: A common error of reasoning that involves the misuse of evidence in one of these ways:
1. Lack of evidence for a position is taken to prove that position is false.
2. Lack of evidence against a position is taken to prove that position is true.
3. Some evidence against a position is taken to prove that position is false.
4. Some evidence for a position is taken to prove that position is true.

Errors of Composition and Division: A common error of reasoning that involves judgments made about groups and parts of a group. An error of composition occurs when the author attributes a characteristic of part of the group to the group as a whole or to each member of the group. An error of division occurs when the author attributes a characteristic of the whole (or each member of the whole) to a part of the group.

Errors of Conditional Reasoning: A common error of reasoning that involves confusing the sufficient condition with the necessary condition. Note that the authors can either mistake a necessary condition for a sufficient condition, or mistake a sufficient condition for a necessary condition.

Evaluate the Argument Questions: With Evaluate the Argument questions you must decide which answer choice will allow you to determine the logical validity of the argument. Use the Variance Test™ to prove or disprove answers as needed.
Question stem example:
"The answer to which one of the following questions would contribute most to an evaluation of the argument?"

Except: When "except" is placed in a question it negates the logical quality of the answer choice you seek. Literally, it turns the intent of the question stem upside down.

Exceptional Case/Overgeneralization: A common error of reasoning that involves taking a small number of instances and treating those instances as if they support a broad, sweeping conclusion.

F: See also Function.

Fact Set: A collection of statements without a conclusion. Fact sets make a series of assertions without making a judgment.

Fact Test™: The correct answer to a Must Be True question (and other First Family questions) can always be proven by referring to the facts stated in the stimulus. An answer choice that cannot be substantiated by proof in the stimulus is incorrect.

False Analogy: A common error of reasoning that involves an author using an analogy that is too dissimilar to the original situation to be applicable.

False Dilemma: A common error of reasoning that involves assuming that only two courses of action are available when there may be others (for example, "You are either rich or impoverished"). Do not confuse a False Dilemma with a situation where the author legitimately establishes that only two possibilities exist. Phrases such as "either A or B will occur, but not both" can establish a limited set of possibilities, and certain real-world situations yield only two possibilities, such as "you are either dead or alive."

First Family: Consists of question types that use the stimulus to prove that one of the answer choices must be true. No information outside the sphere of the stimulus is allowed in the correct answer choice. Includes the following question types: Must Be True, Main Point, Point at Issue, Method of Reasoning, Flaw in the Reasoning, and Parallel Reasoning.

FL: See Formal Logic.

Flaw in the Reasoning Questions: Flaw in the Reasoning questions ask you to describe, in abstract terms, the error of reasoning committed by the author.
Question stem example:
"The reasoning in the argument is flawed because this argument"

Formal Logic (FL): A standard system of translating relationships into symbols and then making inferences from those symbolized relationships.

Fourth Family: Consists of question types that use the stimulus to prove that one of the answer choices cannot occur. No information outside the sphere of the stimulus is allowed in the answer choices. Includes the following question type: Cannot Be True.

Function (F): These Reading Comprehension questions ask why the author referred to a particular word, phrase, or idea. This is essentially an extended Method of Reasoning question, requiring you to go beyond simply identifying the argument structure, and asking you the reasons behind the author's use of words or ideas.

Game Scenario: In Logic Games, introduces sets of variables, people, places, things, or events, involved in an easy to understand activity such as sitting in seats or singing songs.

General Lack of Relevant Evidence for the Conclusion: A common error of reasoning that involves authors misusing information to such a degree that they fail to provide any information to support their conclusion or they provide information that is irrelevant to their conclusion.

Global: These Logic Games questions ask about information derived only from the initial rules, such as "Who can finish first?" or "Which one of the following must be true?"

Grouping: These Logic Games require you to analyze the variables in terms of which ones can and cannot be together.

Horizontality: When a game is diagrammed in a horizontal line (or setup), the relationship between variables arranged horizontally indicates adjacency, while the relationship of variables arranged vertically indicates similarity. This is also true of horizontality in blocks.

Hurdle the Uncertainity™: In Logic Games, during the placement of variables, situations occur where even though you cannot determine the exact variables being selected, you can "leap" that uncertainty to determine that other variables that must be selected. This powerful technique can be used in many different games, and it attacks a concept frequently used by the test makers an appears in virtually every Grouping game.

Hypothetical: A possible solution to a question that you quickly create to gain insight into Logic Game answers. Hypotheticals can be the fastest way to solve a question, and sometimes they give you information that can be used to solve other problems.

Inference: In logic, an inference can be defined as something that must be true. If you are asked to identify an inference of the argument, you must find an item that must be true based on the information presented in the argument.

Internal Contradiction: A common error of reasoning (also known as a self-contradiction) that occurs when an author makes conflicting statements.

Justify Formula™: Premises + Answer choice = Conclusion
The Justify Formula is a useful tool for understanding how Justify the Conclusion questions work. If the answer choice is correct, the application of the Justify Formula will produce the given conclusion. If the answer choice is incorrect, the application of the Justify Formula will fail to produce the given conclusion.

Justify the Conclusion Questions: Justify the Conclusion questions ask you to supply a piece of information that, when added to the premises, proves the conclusion.
Question stem example:
"Which one of the following, if assumed, allows the conclusion above to be properly drawn?"

Least: When "least" appears in a question stem you should treat it exactly the same as "except." Note: this advice holds true only when this word appears in the question stem! If you see the word "least" elsewhere on the LSAT, consider it to have its usual meaning of "in the lowest or smallest degree."

Linearity: Involves the fixed positioning and ordering of variables. In every Linear game, one of the variable sets is chosen as the "base" and is diagrammed in a straight line, either horizontally or vertically, and the remaining variable sets are placed into slots above or next to the base.

Linkage: Linkage involves finding a variable that appears in at least two rules and then combining those two rules. Often that combination will produce an inference of value. Linkage is the easiest and most basic way to make inferences.

List Question: In Logic Games, list questions present a list of variables that can either fill a slot or possibly solve the game. The best technique for attacking List questions is to take a single rule and apply it to each of the five answer choices, one at a time. The first question in a game is often a List Question.

Local: These games questions occur when the question imposes a new condition in addition to the initial rules, such as "If Laura sits in the third chair, which one of the following must be true?" Local questions almost always require you to produce a "mini-setup" next to the question.

Loser: An answer choice which immediately strikes you as incorrect.

Main Point (MP): Main Point questions are a variant of Must Be True questions. As you might expect, a Main Point question asks you to find the primary conclusion made by the author.
Question stem example:
"The main point of the argument is that"

Mapping: These games either do not fix the physical relationships among the variables (Spatial Relations), involve a fixed point and all other variables are placed North, East, South, and West of that point (Directional), or the makers of the test supply a diagram intended to represent the relationship of the variables (Supplied Diagram). There are no numerical elements in a Mapping game.

Mechanistic Approach: This approach requires you to reduce the stimulus to its component parts (a process that occurs naturally as you identify premises and conclusions), and then identify which elements appear in the conclusion but not in the premises. In a nutshell, the rules for this approach condense to: link new elements in the premises and conclusion and ignore elements common to both. The mechanistic approach works for the vast majority of Justify the Conclusion questions.

Method of Reasoning: Method of Reasoning questions ask you to describe, in abstract terms, the way in which the author made his or her argument.
Question stem example:
"Which one of the following describes the technique of reasoning used above?"

Mistaken Cause and Effect: A common error of reasoning that occurs because arguments that draw causal conclusions are inherently flawed because there may be another explanation for the stated relationship. This can occur by assuming a causal relationship on the basis of the sequence of events or when only a correlation exists. This can also occur due to failure to consider an alternate cause for the effect, an alternate cause for both the cause and the effect, or that the events may be reversed.

Mistaken Negation™: Negates both sufficient and necessary conditions, creating a statement that does not have to be true.

Mistaken Reversal™: Switches the elements in the sufficient and necessary conditions, creating a statement that does not have to be true.

Most (in Question Stems): In order to maintain test integrity the test makers need to make sure their credited answer choice is as airtight and defensible as possible. Imagine what would occur if a question stem, let us say a Weaken question, did not include a "most" qualifier: any answer choice that weakened the argument, even if only very slightly, could then be argued to meet the criteria of the question stem. A situation like this would make constructing the test exceedingly difficult because any given problem might have multiple correct answer choices. To eliminate this predicament, the test makers insert "most" into the question stem, and then they can always claim there is one and only one correct answer choice.

Most (in Formal Logic): A majority, and possibly all.

MP: See Main Point.

Must Be True: Must Be True questions ask you to identify the answer choice that is best proven by the information in the stimulus.
Question stem examples:
"If the statements above are true, which one of the following must also be true?"
"Which one of the following can be properly inferred from the passage?"

N: See Necessary Condition.

Necessary Condition (N): An event or circumstance whose occurrence is required in order for a sufficient condition to occur.

Negation: Negating a statement consists of creating the logical opposite of the statement. The logical opposite is the statement that denies the truth of the original statement, and a logical opposite is different than the polar opposite.

New Information: Information not mentioned explicitly in the stimulus of a Logical Reasoning question.

Not All: At least one is not, possibly all are not. Functionally equivalent to "some are not."

Not Block: Indicate that variables cannot be next to one another. Not-blocks only come into play once one of the variables has been placed.

Not Law™: Physically notate where a variable cannot be placed. Not Laws are very useful since it is essential that you establish the events that cannot be true in a game.

Not Necessarily True: The logical opposite of "Must be true." When an answer choice is not proven by the information in the stimulus.

NP: See Numbers and Percentages.

Numbers and Percentages (NP or #%): Numerical situations normally hinge on three elements: an overall total, a number within that total, and a percentage within the total. LSAT problems will often give you one of the elements, but without at least two elements present, you cannot make a definitive judgment about what is occurring with another element. When you are given just percentage information, you cannot make a judgment about numbers. Likewise, when you are given just numerical information you cannot make a judgment about percentages.

Numbers and Percentages Errors: A common error of reasoning that is committed when an author improperly equates a percentage with a definite quantity, or when an author uses quantity information to make a judgment about the percentage represented by that quantity.

Numerical Distribution: Allocates one set of variables among another set of variables. Numerical Distributions occur in every game except Mapping games.

Opposite Answer: Provides an answer that is completely opposite of the stated facts of the stimulus. Opposite Answers are very attractive to students who are reading too quickly or carelessly and quite frequently appear in Strengthen and Weaken questions.

Overloaded: Description of an Unbalanced game in which there are extra candidates for the available spaces.

Parallel Reasoning (in Logical Reasoning): Parallel Reasoning questions ask you to identify the answer choice that contains reasoning most similar in structure to the reasoning presented in the stimulus.
Question stem example:
"Which one of the following arguments is most similar in its pattern of reasoning to the argument above?"

Parallel Reasoning (in Reading Comprehension): These questions are usually broader in scope, asking you to find the scenario most analogous to an action in the passage. There is less of a focus on identifying premises and conclusions than in the Logical Reasoning section.

Partially Defined: There is a minimum and/or maximum number of variables to be selected, but the exact number of variables selected in the game cannot be determined.

Passage Organization (PO): These Reading Comprehension questions ask you to describe a characteristic of the overall structure of the passage. For example, "The second paragraph serves primarily to...," or "Which one of the following best describes the organization of the passage." These questions are similar to the Method of Reasoning questions in the Logical Reasoning section, but are generally broader.

Pattern: A variation on Linear games where the rules equally govern the general action of all variables, as opposed to the specific variable governance found in standard Linear games.

PO: See Passage Organization.

Point at Issue Questions: Point at Issue questions require you to identify a point of contention between two speakers, and thus these questions appear almost exclusively with two-speaker stimuli. Question stem example:

> "Larew and Mendota disagree about whether"

Polar Opposite: A statement that is the extreme opposite of another. "Hot" and "cold" are polar opposites.

Premise: A fact, proposition, or statement from which a conclusion is made. Literally, the premises give the reasons why the conclusion should be accepted.

Primary Objectives™: A cohesive strategy for attacking any Logical Reasoning question. By consistently applying the objectives, you give yourself the best opportunity to succeed on each question.

Principle (PR): A broad rule that specifies what actions or judgments are correct in certain situations. These are not a separate question type but are instead an "overlay" that appears in a variety of question types and the presence of the Principle indicator serves to broaden the scope of the question.

Question Stem: Follows the stimulus and poses a question directed at the stimulus. Make sure to read the question stem very carefully. Some stems direct you to focus on certain aspects of the stimulus and if you miss these clues you make the problem much more difficult.

Random: A variable in a Logic Game that does not appear in any of the rules. Because randoms are not referenced in a rule, they are typically weaker players in the game.

Repeat Form: Simply restates the elements of a conditional statement in the original order they appeared. This creates a valid argument.

Resolve the Paradox Questions: Every Resolve the Paradox stimulus contains a discrepancy or seeming contradiction. You must find the answer choice that best explains the situation. Question stem example:

> "Which one of the following, if true, would most effectively resolve the apparent paradox above?"

Reverse Answer: Occurs when an answer choice contains familiar elements from the stimulus, but rearranges those elements to create a new, unsupported statement.

Rules: In Logic Games, a set of statements that describe the relationships between the variables.

S: See Sufficient Condition

Scope: The range to which the premises and conclusion encompass certain ideas. An argument with a narrow scope is definite in its statements, whereas a wide scope argument is less definite and allows for a greater range of possibility.

Second Family: Consists of question types that take the answer choices as true and uses them to help the stimulus. Information outside the sphere of the stimulus is allowed in the correct answer choice. Includes the following question types: Assumption, Justify the Conclusion, Strengthen/ Support, and Resolve the Paradox.

Sequencing Game: A game type where the rules do not fix the variables in exact positions but instead provide information about the relative order of the variables, as in "J was hired earlier than K."

Sequencing Rule: Establishes the relative ordering of variables. The key to differentiating a sequencing rule from a block rule is that block rules precisely fix the variables in relationship to each other (for example, one space ahead or two spaces in between) and sequencing rules do not.

Shell Game: An idea or concept is raised in the stimulus, and then a very similar idea appears in the answer choice, but the idea is changed just enough to be incorrect but still attractive. This trick is called the Shell Game because it abstractly resembles those street corner gambling games where a person hides a small object underneath one of three shells, and then scrambles them on a flat surface while a bettor tries to guess which shell the object is under.

SN: Abbreviation for Sufficient and Necessary Conditions. Maybe be seen separately in diagramming as "S" and "N." See also Sufficient Condition and Necessary Condition.

Source Argument: A common error of reasoning that attacks the person (or source) instead of the argument they advance. Because the LSAT is concerned solely with argument forms, a speaker can never validly attack the character or motives of a person; instead, a speaker must always attack the argument advanced by a person.

Some: At least one, possibly all.

Some Are Not: At least one is not, possibly all are not. Functionally equivalent to "not all."

Specific Reference (SR): These Reading Comprehension questions provide you with a specific line reference or a reference to an easily found word or phrase within the passage. To attack the questions, refer to the line reference in the question and then begin reading about 5 lines above the reference.

Split-blocks: Indicates that there is a fixed number of spaces between two or more variables.

SR: See Specific Reference.

Stacks: In Logic Games, when two variable sets occur in the same position, one set of variables is diagrammed normally (identified as the base), while the other variable set is placed in slots above the initial slots, essentially "stacking" the variable sets and allowing for the appropriate relationship between variable sets.

Straw Man: A common error of reasoning that occurs when an author attempts to attack an opponent's position by ignoring the actual statements made by the opposing speaker and instead distorts and refashions the argument, making it weaker in the process.

Stimulus: A short passage containing arguments taken from a variety of topics reflecting a broad range of academic disciplines (including letters to the editor, speeches, advertisements, newspaper articles and editorials, informal discussions and conversations, as well as articles in the humanities, the social sciences, and the natural sciences) that presents all of the necessary information to answer the subsequent question stem.

Strengthen/Support Questions: These questions ask you to select the answer choice that provides support for the author's argument or strengthens it in some way.
Question stem examples:
"Which one of the following, if true, most strengthens the argument?"
"Which one of the following, if true, most strongly supports the statement above?"

Sub-conclusion: A conclusion that is then used as a premise to support another conclusion. This is also known as a secondary or subsidiary conclusion.

Sufficient Condition (S): An event or circumstance whose occurrence indicates that a necessary condition must also occur. The sufficient condition does not make the necessary condition occur, it is simply an indicator.

Super-block: In Logic Games, when two or more block rules can be combined to produce a single diagram. Super-blocks tend to be quite powerful and often control the game.

Supporter: In the Supporter/Defender Assumption Model™, the Supporter Assumptions link together new or rogue elements in the stimulus or fill logical gaps in the argument.

Survey Errors: A common error of reasoning that occurs when a survey uses a biased sample, the survey questions are improperly constructed or the respondents to the survey give inaccurate responses. Surveys, when conducted properly, produce reliable results. However, surveys can be invalidated when any of these errors occur.

Templates: In Logic Games, when certain variables or blocks have a limited number of placement options the best strategy is often to show the basic possibilities for each option. This powerful technique can sometimes quickly solve the game, and at the least it tends to reveal important information about the relationship between certain variables.

Third Family: Consists of question types that take the answer choices as true and uses them to hurt the stimulus. Information outside the sphere of the stimulus is allowed in the correct answer choice. Includes the following question type: Weaken.

Time Shift Errors: A common error of reasoning that involves assuming that conditions will remain constant over time, and that what was the case in the past will be the case in the present or future.

2-Value System: In Logic Games, a section where all variables must be used and each variable must be placed in exactly one of two groups. Powerful inferences can be drawn from the fact that when a variable is not in one group it must be in the other group (these inferences often involve the contrapositive).

Unbalanced: In a Defined game, when the number of variables to be selected is not equal to the overall number of available spaces. Unbalanced games are either Overloaded or Underfunded.

Uncertain Use of a Term or Concept: A common error of reasoning that occurs when the author uses a term or concept in different ways instead of using each term or concept in a constant, coherent fashion. This error is inherently confusing and undermines the integrity of the argument.

Undefined: When the number of variables to be selected for the game is not fixed, and is only limited by the total number of variables. Undefined games are generally the most difficult type of Grouping game.

Underfunded: Description of an Unbalanced game in which there are not enough candidates for the available spaces. This lack is almost always solved by reusing one or more of the candidates.

Variable Set: The set of people, places, things, or events that are involved in each game. The variables will be involved in an easy to understand activity such as sitting in seats or singing songs. It is very important to always write down and keep track of each variable set.

Variance Test™: Consists of supplying two polar opposite responses to the question posed in the answer choice and then analyzing how the varying responses affect the conclusion in the stimulus. If different responses produce different effects on the conclusion, then the answer choice is correct. If different responses do not produce different effects, then the answer choice is incorrect. The Variance Test can only be used with Evaluate the Argument questions.

Verticality: When a game is diagrammed in a vertical line (or setup), the relationship between the variables arranged vertically indicates adjacency, while the relationship of variables arranged horizontally indicates similarity. This is also true of verticality in blocks.

Weaken Questions: Weaken questions ask you to attack or undermine the author's argument. Question stem example:
"Which one of the following, if true, most seriously weakens the argument?"

CONTACTING POWERSCORE

Contact Information

PowerScore International Headquarters:

> PowerScore Incorporated
> 37V New Orleans Road
> Hilton Head Island, SC 29928
>
> Toll-free information: (800) 545-1750
> Fax: (843) 785-8203
> Website: www.powerscore.com
> Email: lsat@powerscore.com

PowerScore LSAT Publications Information:
For information on the *LSAT Logic Games Bible*, *LSAT Logical Reasoning Bible*, or *LSAT Logic Games Ultimate Setups Guide*.

> Website: www.powerscore.com/pubs.htm

PowerScore Full-length LSAT Course Information:
Complete preparation for the LSAT. Classes available nationwide.

> Website: www.powerscore.com/lsat/lsat.htm
> Request Information: www.powerscore.com/contact.htm

PowerScore Weekend LSAT Course Information:
Fast and effective LSAT preparation: 16 hour courses, 99th percentile instructors, and real LSAT questions.

> Website: www.powerscore.com/lsat/weekend.htm
> Request Information: www.powerscore.com/contact.htm

PowerScore LSAT Tutoring Information:
One-on-one meetings with a PowerScore LSAT expert.

> Website: www.powerscore.com/lsat/tutoring.htm
> Request Information: www.powerscore.com/contact.htm

PowerScore Law School Admissions Counseling Information:
Personalized application and admission assistance.

> Website: www.powerscore.com/lsat/admissions.htm
> Request Information: www.powerscore.com/contact.htm